D1564215

FRANCIS OF ASSISI

Arnaldo Fortini

FRANCIS
OF
ASSISI

❖ ❖ ❖

A Translation of
Nova Vita di San Francesco
by Helen Moak

Crossroad • New York

TO LENNOX
WITHOUT WHOM THIS TRANSLATION
COULD NOT HAVE BEEN MADE

1981
The Crossroad Publishing Company
575 Lexington Avenue, New York, NY 10022

Original edition: *Nova Vita di San Francesco* published in 1959
by Tipografia Porziuncola at Santa Maria degli Angeli
Assisi Edition

English translation copyright © 1980 by Helen Moak

Library of Congress Cataloging in Publication Data

Fortini, Arnaldo.   Francis of Assisi.
A translation of 2 books of v. 1, together with the bibliography and index which make up v. 4
from the 4 v. ed. originally published in 1959 by Porziuncola Assisi.
"A Crossroad book."
Bibliography: p. 671
1. Francesco d'Assisi, Saint, 1182-1226.
2. Christian saints—Italy—Assisi—Biography.
3. Assisi—Biography.
BX4700.F6F655213   271'.3'024 [B]   80-12359
ISBN 0-8245-0003-2 Previously ISBN 0-8164-0116-0

Contents

Foreword

There ought to be a reason for the writing of any book, particularly a big book. An author ought to do it because he has something new to say or a new way of saying something over again.

One cannot say this has always been true in the world of Franciscan studies. Very few authors, in fact, have had a valuable, new, or original contribution to make.

Arnaldo Fortini is not among these. He must be counted among the most authoritative of Franciscan historians, especially in the light of four monumental works: *Assisi nel medioevo,* a comprehensive political and historical study of Assisi during the whole of the Middle Ages; *Francesco d'Assisi e l'Italia del suo tempo,* a portrayal of the historical, military, and social setting in which the vocation of the Poverello was born; *La lauda in Assisi e le origini del teatro italiano,* the history of the flowering of poetry in the new religious movements of the time of Saint Francis and the years thereafter; and *Nova Vita di San Francesco,* the book that concerns us here. It is the greatest of his contributions—a fundamental and irreplaceable work, necessary for realistically placing the Franciscan movement in its historical context.

It is high time that we examine the Franciscan phenomenon closely and critically. First, we must recognize that it contains a great number of popular legends and traditions that have grown out of sentimentality and the trusting faith of our forebears.

We also must not ignore the fact that there are many blanks in the narrations of the ancient biographers as well as in the writings of modern historians. Everyone familiar with Franciscan studies and the many questions inherent in them is well aware of these.

Arnaldo Fortini's work fills some of these major gaps. It is the first critical reconstruction of the social, economic, political, and religious milieux in the time of Saint Francis and the first account of the events in his city that has all the immediacy of an eyewitness report, both intimately tied to Saint Francis's conversion and mission. Without knowing them, it has been impossible to understand his personality or explain the emergence and original character of the Franciscan movement, easy to fill the gaps with sentimental legends.

The ancient biographers were intent only upon giving us a spiritual portrait of Saint Francis. As for the rest of his life, they limited themselves to sketches that are all but evanescent. Later historians found they had no specific information that would permit them to bring to life again a world that had become far away and alien. None at any time has had the background that enables Professor Fortini to bring a special perception to his work: he was a native son who lived his entire life in Francis's city and there was the principal actor in every event that took place for more than fifty years. He, in fact, played the leading role in delivering Assisi from centuries of economic stagnation, and stimulating the physical restoration and cultural revival of the city that have made it a center of pilgrimage, both for those drawn by its saints and by its treasures of art and architecture.

Questions plague us in reading the life of Saint Francis. Why did he have such a complete and dramatic religious conversion? Why his passionate desire to embrace poverty? What drove him to go about preaching *pace e bene*—peace and everything good? Whence his insistence on making himself humble with the humblest? His missionary zeal? His love for penitence and prayer, his dedication to the Gospel and to love?

The answers are in his response to the society of his times—the society depicted and documented so carefully by Arnaldo Fortini. They lie in its complex story of merchant *nouveaux riches,* bands of pleasure-loving troubadour knights who loved parties and dreamed of high adventure, an encastled feudal society clinging to tradition as to an anchor of salvation, the fierce quarrels between civil and religious authorities at all levels, the shortcomings of the clergy and church arising from being too closely tied to the feudal structure, the war between Assisi and Perugia and all its complex causes and circumstances, the tragedy of incurable leprosy, the misery and ignorance of abandoned and enslaved victims of feudal society, the intricate mentality of the time, the personalities of the numerous and unforgettable persons who were a part of the Franciscan drama. Not to understand these things is to fail to understand Saint Francis and Franciscanism. The roots and nature of the Franciscan movement, which has played such a great constructive role in Western life for nearly eight centuries, are in all these things.

This work indeed marks a decisive moment in Franciscan historiography. It is due to Arnaldo Fortini that we now see clearly how in Francis's time an increase in trade led to a scramble for more riches, how political antagonisms fomented envy and fraternal hatred, and how the emergence of the middle class was linked to an ambition and a cutthroat competition that had in them no conscience or pity for the less fortunate. Material from Assisi archives shows us priests and clerics ensnared in politics and greedy and jealous of their great possessions; they neglected the people and did not exactly quiver with enthusiasm for spreading Christ's message. From documentation in this biography we learn that the new economic avenues open to Assisi merchants created a comfortable and pagan life in which the poor, the lepers, and the oppressed were forgotten.

Much new and, to the Franciscan historian, sometimes disconcerting material is also set forth on many topics. Among them are the genealogy of Saint Clare, her paternal house and the paternal house of Saint Francis, events in the youth of Saint Francis, the proper identification of the "Company of the Sceptre (or Wand)" about which his earliest biographers wrote, the author's identification of many places and persons of the Assisi and Franciscan world. There will no doubt be arguments about some of these for some time to come. In the past some of the conclusions reached by Fortini through his research have led to attacks on the book which have had in them very little of a passion for the discovery of the truth. Sometimes there has even seemed to have been more effort to seek out and call attention to small faults than to recognize Professor Fortini's enormous accomplishment in bringing to life the world of Saint Francis as no one has ever done before. Despite both honest disagreement and attacks by the pseudo-scholarly, since this book appeared no one who has been interested in doing a serious study of Saint Francis or Assisi has gotten—or will get—far without relying on it.

The real limitations of the work lie with the subject, with Saint Francis. He cannot be shut inside any volume. No biography has ever completely contained him, neither old nor new, and none ever will. He is too rich and many-sided a person for that, and his intense interior life makes it difficult to depict his psychological, spiritual, and charismatic reality. There will always be something more to say about Saint Francis.

P. Lino Temperini, T.O.R.
Commissione Storica Internazionale
Terz'Ordine Regolare
Rome, Italy

(Father Lino Temperini was a close associate and friend of Arnaldo Fortini and his family for many years. He has written a number of articles about his life and work.)

Translator's Preface

Rarely is there a worldwide celebration of someone's 800th birthday. But in 1982, there will be such a celebration for Saint Francis of Assisi. Even more rarely does it happen that someone admired in his own time becomes more admired, more popular, and more relevant in the twentieth century than in his own. But that's the way it is with Saint Francis.

In the fascinating, endearing, and puzzling phenomenon that is Saint Francis of Assisi lies the reason for translating still another biography of him. We itch to know what it is about him that makes him the idol of people of all classes, all nationalities, all faiths, all walks of life, how it is that what he said and did seem to hold so many solutions to our own problems today, from those of environment (he was named Patron of Ecology by Pope John Paul II in 1980) to peace, from patterns for the future of the church and of religious orders to the improvement of human relationships, from economic inequities to compassionate care of the suffering.

While he was living, people turned to him, too. There is a story that at the peak of the political power of the papacy, Innocent III had a dream that the pope's own church, Saint John Lateran of Rome, with all its infinite number of treasures from civilizations of all ages, was falling down. In his dream a single barefoot beggar—Saint Francis—rushed forward and supported the entire weight of it on his own shoulders. So it was that the pope, against the advice of the Curia and in contrast to his own military campaigns against other groups preaching poverty and penance, granted to the ragged beggar, who was being called a crazy fool from Assisi, a madman, an impractical dreamer, a disobedient son who had shamed his nice parents, permission to form an entirely new kind of religious order. Within the short space of a few years, the group he led had grown from the twelve shabby companions who had been with Francis before the pope in Rome into many thousands of men and women enrolled in three religious orders, the Friars Minor, the Poor Clares, and the Secular Order of Saint Francis.

People of Francis's own time were puzzled by it and asked how and why it had all come about. The question has occupied theologians, biographers, and historians through the centuries. One aspect of it that was not touched upon until the publication of Fortini's book, because the facts were unknown, is the history of life and events in his own city and how they affected the making of a Francis and the course of his life. In a study of Assisi records and libraries that extended over more than thirty years, Signore Fortini has supplied these missing pieces.

There are translations of this work in French and Japanese, and historians and biographers who have studied and written of it in the years after it first appeared have made extensive use of all editions of it.

Readers who are familiar with the original Italian edition of *Nova Vita di San Francesco* may notice some changes in this book, though in no way is either the material presented by the author or the order in which he presented it altered. There are, for example, a few changes in citations. Some were made to eliminate references to more than one edition of the same book, unless there were a special reason for them. I have also edited others (in all cases where I could locate the work cited) in order to complete them or correct minor errors caused by the fact that the author became ill and could not finish the editing himself. I have also translated freely rather than literally and abbreviated some passages, in the simple recognition that Italian and English demand different forms of expression for clarity. It should be said, however, that the author's style is not the sober one most English-speaking readers expect of serious historical works. It is written in emotional and poetic language that perhaps is a conscious recall of Francis's first biographer, Thomas of Celano, perhaps reflects his admiration for Gabriele D'Annunzio, who was his close personal friend. Enough of his style surely remains to convey the warm personality of the writer, but it has been adapted somewhat for English-speaking readers.

Special thanks for the help given me in doing this book is due to many persons, especially to my husband, without whose patient and generous support it would not have been possible to do it at all. To **Silvia and Frederic Mann and to Arthur Solmssen, for their encouragement and interest in this project. To many Assisi and Italian** friends who enabled me to know Francis's city and the places associated with him, especially the author's daughter, Gemma Fortini, and Fathers Raffaele Pazzelli and Lino Temperini, of the Commissione Storica Internazionale, Terz'Ordine Regolare, in Rome, who were patient and tireless in doing on-the-spot research to clarify obscure terms and references. To the staffs of the Franciscan Institute, the Library of Saint Bonaventure University, and the Library of the University of Pennsylvania, who generously made all their rich collections of material available to me. To the Sisters of Saint Joseph in Philadelphia, who provided me a place to work, especially to those of Saint Michael's Hall, who endured late night typing without complaint, and Sister Amata Wardle, who generously shared her knowledge of Latin and her time. To my editors, Frank Oveis and Howard Galley. To my family, among whom I include Dorothy Whitaker and Barbara Noska, for unfailing support and assistance. To a host of others, but especially two persons who are no longer with us—Franz Liszt, a lay Franciscan whose devotion to Saint Francis made, in a very special way, this book possible, and Saint Francis himself, whom Ernst Renan accurately described as always smiling on his historians.

HELEN MOAK

Acknowledgements

Grateful acknowledgement for permission to use quotations from the works listed below is hereby made to these publishers and copyright owners:

Chatto and Windus, Ltd., London: Excerpt from *Can vei la leuzeta mover* by Bernart of Ventadorn, translated by Barbara Smythe, in *Trobador Poets*, 1929. All rights reserved.

Estate of Hubert Creekmore: Excerpts from *The Monk of Montaudon*, translated by Hubert Creekmore, in *Lyrics of the Middle Ages*. Copyright © 1959 by Grove Press.

Doubleday, New York: Selections and excerpts from *The Little Flowers of St. Francis*, translated by Raphael Brown. Copyright © by Beverly H. Brown, 1958.

Franciscan Herald Press, Chicago: Selections from *St. Francis of Assisi, Omnibus of Sources*, edited by Marion A. Habig. These include *The Canticle of Brother Sun*, excerpts from *The Writings of St. Francis*, and from *Major Life* by Saint Bonaventure, all translated by Benen Fahy; excerpts from *First Life, Second Life*, and *Treatise on Miracles* by Thomas of Celano, and from *Sacrum Commercium*, all translated by Placid Hermann; from *Legend of Three Companions*, translated by Nesta de Robeck; from *Legend of Perugia*, translated by Paul Oligny; from *Mirror of Perfection*, translated by Leo Sherley-Price; from *Little Flowers of St. Francis*, translated by Raphael Brown; from letters and *History of the Orient* by Jacques de Vitry, translated by Damien Vorreux. Copyright © by Franciscan Herald Press, 1973.

———: "Message of St. Francis to the Poor Clares of San Damiano," translated by Raphael Brown, in *The Rule and Testament of St. Francis* by Cajetan Esser. Copyright © by Franciscan Herald Press, 1977.

Franciscan Institute, St. Bonaventure, N. Y.: Excerpts from *The Legend and Writings of Saint Clare of Assisi*, translated by Ignatius Brady. Copyright © by The Franciscan Institute, 1953.

Franciscan Liturgical Projects, Washington, D.C.: Excerpts from *Lo, new signs of sanctity*, in *The Roman-Franciscan Lectionary*. Copyright © by Franciscan Liturgical Projects, 1975. International copyright secured.

Estate of Gilbert Highet: Excerpt from *Elegiarum* by Propertius, translated by Gilbert Highet, in *Poets in a Landscape*. Copyright © by Gilbert Highet, 1957.

The New American Library, New York: Excerpts from *The Inferno* by Dante Alighieri, translated by John Ciardi. Copyright © by John Ciardi, 1954. Reprinted by arrangement with The New American Library, Inc., New York, New York.

———: Excerpt from *The Purgatorio* by Dante Alighieri, translated by John Ciardi. Copyright © 1957, 1959, 1960, 1961 by John Ciardi. Reprinted by arrangement with The New American Library, Inc., New York, New York.

———: Excerpts from *The Paradiso* by Dante Alighieri, translated by John Ciardi. Copyright © 1961, 1965, 1967, 1970 by John Ciardi. Reprinted by arrangement with The New American Library, Inc., New York, New York.

New Directions Publishing Corporation, New York: Excerpt from *Alba Innominata*, translated by Ezra Pound, in *The Collected Early Poems of Ezra Pound*. Copyright © 1976 by The Trustees of the Ezra Pound Literary Property Trust. Reprinted by permission of New Directions Publishing Corporation. All rights reserved.

———: Excerpt from *Ballata XI* by Guido Calvacanti, translated by Ezra Pound, in *Translations*, edited by Hugh Kenner. Copyright © 1926, 1954, 1957, 1960, 1962, 1963 by Ezra Pound. Reprinted by permission of New Directions Publishing Corporation. All rights reserved.

———: Excerpt from *Langue d'Oc II*, translated by Ezra Pound, in *Personae*. Copyright © 1926 by Ezra Pound. Reprinted by permission of New Directions Publishing Corporation. All rights reserved.

Penn State Press, University Park, Pennsylvania: Excerpt from a farewell song by William, duke of Aquitaine, translated by James J. Wilhelm, in *Seven Troubadours;* Copyright © 1970 by The Pennsylvania State University.

Estate of Dorothy L. Sayers: Excerpt from *Song of Roland*, translated by Dorothy Sayers. Copyright © 1957 by Executors of Dorothy L. Sayers.

Wayne State University Press: Excerpt from *Veris dulcis in tempore*, translated by Edwin Zeydel, in *Vagabond Verse, Secular Latin Poems of the Middle Ages*. Copyright © 1966 by Wayne State University Press.

List of Abbreviations

AA. SS.	*Acta Sanctorum*
Actus	*Actus Beati Francisci et sociorum eius.* Numbers in citations refer to chapters of the work.
AF	*Analecta Franciscana*
AFH	*Archivum Franciscanum Historicum*
Anal. Boll.	*Analecta Bollandiana*
An. Min.	Luke Wadding, *Annales Minorum*
Ann. d'Ital.	L.A. Muratori, *Annali d'Italia*
Anon. Per.	*Anonymus Perusinus.* Numbers in citations refer to numbered sections of the work.
Arch. Cath.	Archivio della Cattedrale di San Rufino
Arch. Com.	Archivio del Comune di Assisi
Arch. Com. Perugia	Archivio del Comune di Perugia
Arch. S. Conv.	Archivio del Sacro Convento
Arch. Stor. Ital.	*Archivio Storico Italiano*
CED	Collection d'études et de documents sur l'histoire religieuse et littéraire du moyen âge. Edited by Paul Sabatier. 8 vols. 1893–1909.
1 Cel.	Thomas of Celano, *Vita Prima.* Numbers refer to numbered sections.
2 Cel.	Thomas of Celano, *Vita Secunda.* See above.
3 Cel.	Thomas of Celano, *Tractatus de Miraculis.* See above.
Cod. Sott.	I codici delle Sommissioni (or Sottomissioni) al Comune di Perugia. See V. Ansidei and L. Giannantoni, also M. Faloci-Pulignano articles listed in bibliography.

DPSU	*Bollettino di Deputazione di Storia Patria per l'Umbria*
Eccleston	Thomas of Eccleston, *De Adventu Fratrum Minorum in Angliam.* Numbers refer to numbered sections.
Fioretti	*I Fioretti di San Francesco* (*Little Flowers of Saint Francis*). Numbers refer to chapters.
Leg. Maior	Saint Bonaventure (Giovanni di Fidanza), *Legenda Maior.* Numbers refer to chapters and numbered sections.
Leg. Min.	Idem., *Legenda Minor.* See above.
Leg. S. Clarae	*Legenda Sanctae Clarae Virginis.* Numbers refer to numbered sections.
Leg. Vers.	Henri d'Avranches, *Legenda versificata S. Francisci*
MGH	*Monumenta Germaniae Historica*
Misc. Fran.	*Miscellanea Franciscana*
NV	Arnaldo Fortini, *Nova Vita di San Francesco*
ODCC	*Oxford Dictionary of the Christian Church*
Omnibus	*St. Francis of Assisi, Omnibus of Sources*
Per.	*Legenda Antiqua S. Francisci de Pérouse* (*Legend of Perugia*). Numbers refer to numbered sections.
PG	*Patrologia Graeca,* ed. J.P. Migne
PL	*Patrologia Latina,* ed. J.P. Migne
Processo	Z. Lazzeri, ed., *Il processo di canonizzazione di S. Chiara di Assisi*
RIS	*Rerum Italicarum Scriptores*
Spec. Perf.	*Speculum Perfectionis* (*Mirror of Perfection*). Numbers refer to numbered sections.
Spec. Vitae	*Speculum Vitae beati Francisci et sociorum eius*
3 Soc.	*Legenda Trium Sociorum* (*Legend of the Three*

Companions). Numbers refer to numbered sections.

24 Gen.   *Chronica XXIV Generalium Ordinis Minorum*

Treccani   *Enciclopedia Italiana* (pubblicata dall'Instituto Treccani)

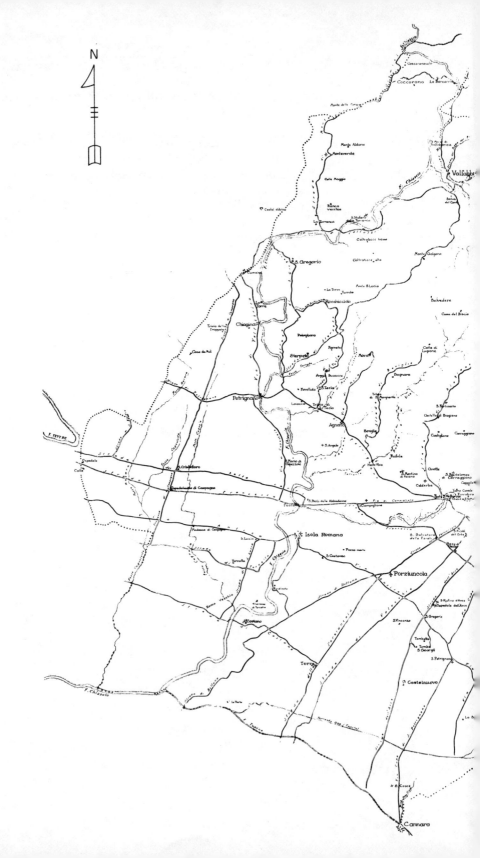

The Commune of Assisi in the time of Saint Francis

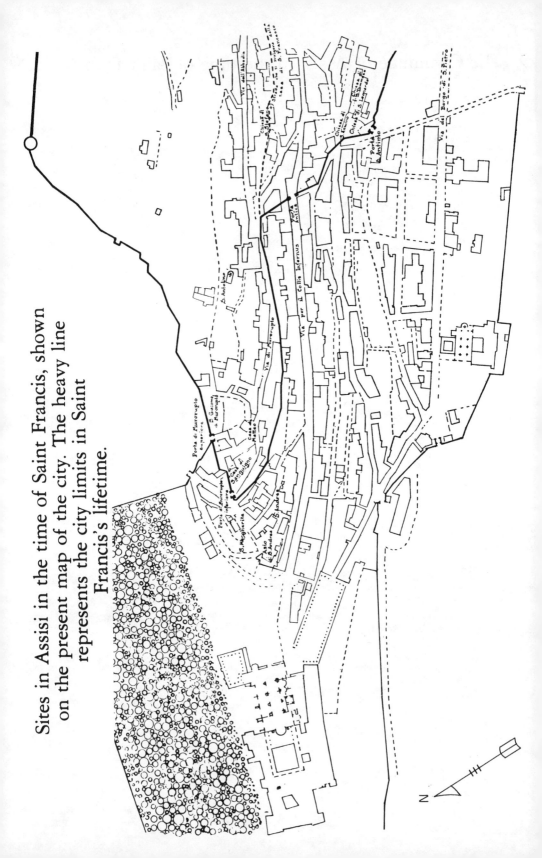

Sites in Assisi in the time of Saint Francis, shown on the present map of the city. The heavy line represents the city limits in Saint Francis's lifetime.

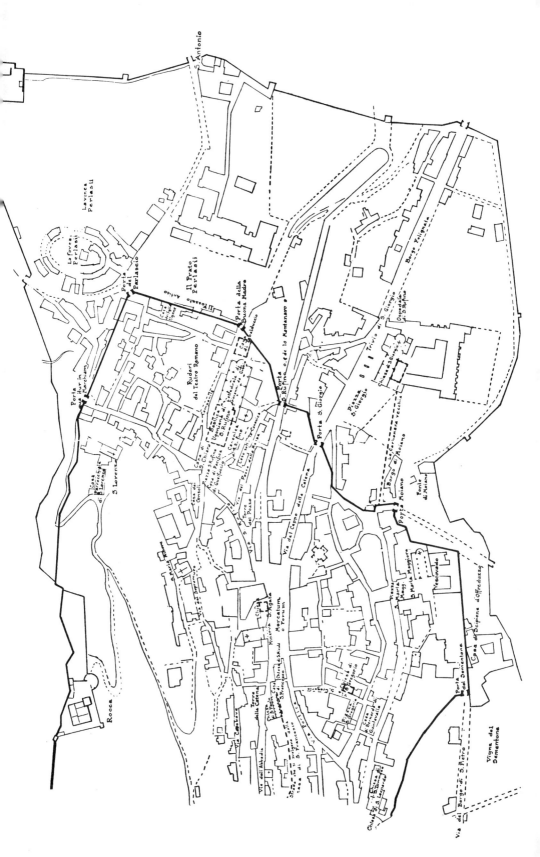

FRANCIS OF ASSISI

·1·

THE WORLD OF SAINT FRANCIS: LORDS AND SERFS

It has often been said that Francis makes Assisi. Indeed, it would be hard to find a town whose reputation, economy, way of life, even existence, are so dependent on one native son.

What is not so often said is that Assisi also made Saint Francis. This is the thesis of this book. From his cradle, Assisi's legends, beliefs, traditions, and customs shaped the thinking of this unique young man. Assisi schools, churches, and social institutions taught him. Assisi laws set a standard for his conduct. The day to day happenings in Assisi—both small and large—in a turbulent period in its long history demanded his participation and inevitably left their mark upon him. Assisi social structure and economy defined him to himself and determined the channels in which his life as a youth moved, even the channels into which his life was directed once he rebelled against them. His Assisi friends and neighbours, along with his heroes and enemies, touched him and played their role in the view of life that in time he worked out as his own.

It should come as no surprise, then, that we meet Assisi before we meet Francis. The author forces us to become ourselves Assisani, *citizens of Francis's small city, in the dying years of feudalism. To do so, he tells us, is the best way to know Francis, who somehow transformed local circumstances and individual experiences into a life that seemingly touches everyone who comes to know him, in every age, everywhere.*

Assisi's earliest surviving records date from about the year 1000 A.D. *The way of life they reveal is essentially the one into which Francis was born more than a century and a half later. So it is with them that the author begins his account.*

This feudal era was even then but one of a succession of ages and periods in Assisi, which is very likely older than Rome. Strands of all of them remained in the life of the city—many are there still. One cannot know Assisi well, and therefore one cannot know Francis well, without some understanding of them.

—Translator

The capitulary parchments of Assisi and the ancient chronicles drawn from the archives of the Sacro Convento[a] show us a convulsed world at the approach of the year A.D. 1000. Kingdoms and empires dissolve, mighty fires blaze, the lamentations of a ravaged people rise, at this time of the first millenium. To read them is to feel in one's very bones this tragedy, one that determined the way of life Saint Francis knew and that still affects the life of all Italian cities.

In Assisi the barbarian invasions came like thunderbolts during the dark centuries.

The Byzantines occupied it.[b] No record remains of this great battle except the name of a *condottiero*, Sisifrido,[c] shouted on Assisi's Roman walls as they fall under the overwhelming rush of the Goths, led by their fearless king, Totila. The duke, Sisifrido, who holds Assisi for

---

a. The Franciscan friary of the Basilica di San Francesco in Assisi.—Trans.

b. A few historical notes may help to clarify references here and elsewhere to events of Assisi history, likely to be unfamiliar to most of us. Assisi, one of the oldest towns in Italy and very likely considerably older than Rome, enters history as a city-state of the Umbrians, its government headed by a priestly college and its civil affairs under the authority of *marones*, the Umbrian magistrates. It was then allied, though in a subordinate role, with its neighbouring Etruscan town (which had undoubtedly once conquered it), Perugia. Both cities fell to the Romans in 295 B.C. (Battle of Sentino). In time, Assisi became a flourishing Roman municipality of the Sergia tribe. Like the rest of Italy, it came under the rule of the Byzantine Empire after the so-called fall of Rome in 476 A.D. A few years later it became a part of the kingdom of the Ostrogoths, when they, first in league with and then in opposition to the Eastern empire, took over the rule of most of Italy. The emperor Justinian sent armies under the command of Belisarius to reconquer Italy from the Goths; the Byzantines referred to in the text occupied Assisi, along with several other cities in Umbria. In 541 A.D. the Ostrogoth king, Totila, began a campaign in Umbria to retake these cities. Fabbi, *Antichità Umbre*, pp. 74, 88–89, 120–21, 128–29, 328–29; Cristofani, *Storie di Assisi*, pp. 9–38.—Trans.

c. Sisifrido was an Ostrogoth who had entered Justinian's service. He was named duke of Assisi and the city placed under his rule. He held Assisi through a prolonged siege by Totila's armies; when he rashly left the protection of the walls to take the field, he was killed and the city fell to the Goths. This occupation of Assisi took place in 545 A.D. Seven years later, in 552, Totila fell in the defeat inflicted on his army by the Eastern general Narsete in a battle a few kilometres from Assisi, near Gualdo Tadino. Fabbi, *Antichità Umbre*, p. 129; Cristofani, *Storie di Assisi*, p. 36; Procopius, *De bello Gothico*, bk. 3, chap. 12 (*Biblioteca Teubneriana*); Pratesi, *Sul vero luogo*.—Trans.

the Byzantine emperor, fights strenuously, spurns the invitation to surrender, but falls at last, overcome by the number of the enemy. The episode stands out like a vivid patch of epic poetry in the chronicle of Procopius in which the martyrdom of the Italian people is described in somber detail—the sieges, the slaughters, the plagues. On the evidence offered by this writer, a good sixteen million Italians perished by the time of the last war fought by Belisarius.

The Lombards took it.[d] Of the events of that conquest, nothing survives other than a certain shudder in the chronicle of a friar living at the end of the thirteenth century, Brother Elemosina: "We found in the ancient writings that the city of Assisi, which was surrounded by the strongest walls and towers, adorned with palaces and strong structures, well populated with many gallant, high-spirited people, defended by numerous brave warriors, was occupied by a terrible and ferocious people, who inflicted havoc on all the surrounding land, and who remained rebellious against the church of Rome . . . "[1]

Gens terribilis et ferox. Brother Elemosina's voice is one among many lifted up in the same sad lament that in this period breaks from the heart of Pope Gregory I: "What can be a pleasure in this world? Everywhere we see mourning, everywhere we hear weeping. Cities are destroyed, villages leveled, countrysides sacked; almost no one is left in the city; and the remnants of the human race still alive are being struck down without respite. Some are taken into slavery, some killed, some cruelly maimed."[2]

The Franks destroyed it.[e] They arrive, according to the same Brother Elemosina, in the year 810, with a strong army led by Char-

---

d. This occupation took place in 568 A.D. Assisi became, possibly from this early date, a part of the powerful Lombardian duchy of Spoleto. See Cristofani, *Storie di Assisi,* p. 39.—Trans.

e. Charlemagne's destruction of Assisi is known to us only through Fra Elemosina's history; he gives no reason. Most historians place this event no later than 774 A.D. In the fall of 773, Charlemagne marched to Rome and stayed through Easter, 774. The most likely date for Assisi's destruction was during this time. This translator was not permitted to examine the manuscript, reported to be in too bad condition to decipher.

On April 6, 774, Charlemagne renewed an earlier donation of lands to the pope; this gift included the duchy of Spoleto, and Assisi was within its boundaries. (Not until many centuries later, however, was the authority of the pope over the duchy established—see chap. 4.)

In June of 774, Charlemagne captured Pavia, and this was the end for the Lombards. He deposed the last Lombardian king, Desiderius, and took the title of King of the Lombards; he also took over the whole Lombardian administrative structure with few major changes, though he kept everything under closer control of the monarchy. On Christmas Day of 800 he was crowned emperor by Pope Leo III. He did not return to Italy with an army after that year.

If his destruction of Assisi came later than that, it must have been ordered because of rebellions by those loyal to the Lombards or by some threat to the safety of the pope or to the new Papal State (see below). Fra Elemosina tells us that after the city was destroyed and many of its inhabitants killed, Charlemagne ordered it rebuilt.

The two centuries between Assisi's fall to the Lombards and Charlemagne's coming to power were turbulent, marked by a horrendous series of barbaric events in the never-ending clashes of

lemagne and his paladins and lay siege to the city from the mountain and from the plain. They enter by stealth, passing through an old abandoned Roman aqueduct, the Sanguinone; they surprise the guards, kill the citizens, and in unrestrained sacking topple the towers and walls.[3]

Centuries of devastation upon devastation, ruin atop ruin. The ancient temples, the arches, the baths, the villas, collapse. The city falls into squalor and sepulchral silence. It seems that the future can hold nothing but death; and in the sleepless nights of the frightened survivors, the words of the Evangelist flame amid monstrous comets and ominous apocalyptic signs: "When the thousand years are over, Satan will be released from his prison . . . " As the year 1000 approaches, terror of the forthcoming dissolution of the world echoes in assemblies, in sermons, even in the formulae of notarial acts— *Appropinquante fine mundi* ("At the approach of the end of the world").[4]

But at the very moment that the lost soul gives up hope of refinding the straight road,[f] a first quiver of new life, a first proclamation of a new day, rises from a battered, shrivelled, musty parchment. It is a legal record in the Assisi cathedral, its hint of renewed hope making it unique among the records consulted by students of this agonizing period. It was drawn in January of the year 1000.[5]

The New Millenium

It does not deal with buying and selling or with exchanges of goods and properties or with decrees of dukes and counts; it is a light and distant sigh of love, a *morincaput,* which in the ancient Lombardian language means "morning gift."

In solemn acknowledgement of her virginal purity, a noble of the

---

the Lombards (who controlled most of Italy by the end of the seventh century), the Byzantine emperors and their representatives in Ravenna (who held some parts of Italy, and, of most importance, Rome), and the popes (who were subjects of emperors too weak to protect them and were in any case locked in bitter theological battles with them).

The Franks, led by Charlemagne's father, Pippin III, joined this cast in the eighth century, when Pope Stephen II appealed to them for protection against the Lombards. The most important result of this new alliance was the creation of the independent nation of the Papal States, formed primarily from territories conquered by the Franks and given to the pope but also from territories given to the pope at an earlier time, especially by the Lombardian king Liutprando. See Cristofani, *Storie di Assisi,* as above; Hughes, *History of the Church,* 2:132–52; *Encyclopaedia Britannica,* s.v. "Italy."—Trans.

f. From the opening lines of Dante's *La Divina Commedia* (Canto 1, lines 1–3). As translated by Ciardi:

> . . . I went astray
> from the straight road and woke to find myself
> alone in a dark wood . . .

Lombardian race gives to his bride the morning after their wedding the fourth part of his goods, according to the custom of his fathers.

From the parchment rises the warmth of an infinitely tender love: "And this is the gift that, through the grace of God, I, Adalberto, son of Maria, bring to you, Itta, daughter of Gunberto, my sweet and beloved bride . . . " A noble poetry beats in each word of the corrupt and legalistic Latin.

This new dawn that is now breaking over the anguish of an age-long night reveals fortified castles on tops of hills, battlemented enclosures, courtyards, drawbridges, and towers. Surrounding them are green meadows, vineyards, olive trees, and forests. Paying homage to the young Lombardian wife are enslaved descendants of the old Italian people: *aldi*[g] and serfs, both men and women.

In such a scene—a new landscape after a thousand years of oblivion—we have a picturesque image of the feudal world that will play so large a part in the emergence and assertion of the Franciscan concept.

Here in Assisi, five centuries after the Lombardian conquest, all is still as it was in the time of the first Lombardian kings: the customs, the measures, the territorial ordinances. Even the names of the girls, who dress in white and have long heavy hair, have not changed: Itta, Adelberga.[6]

Secundum lex nostra Longobardorum. How much fierce pride, how much tenacious nostalgia, is there in this appeal to the ancient law of the conquerors! It endures to rule the life of the survivors, hard-pressed in the bluster and brawls of the new lords, now so well-rooted to the stones of their solitary castles in the *contado*[h] of Assisi.

It is not possible to understand in depth the great dream of Saint Francis, its emergence, its development, its fundamental rule, without reconstructing patiently, piece by piece, this atmosphere in which he grew up and in which he fought his hardest battles. But this simple local story would have no significance except that the life of Assisi and the life of Francis were joined for more than a quarter of a century—and the drama of Assisi in this time is the drama of all

---

g. *Aldi,* in the period of Lombardian domination, were semi-free serfs, often prisoners of war, who usually became peasants attached to the land. (See p. 31.)—Trans.

h. The *contado* is the countryside that immediately surrounds a town, together with all the villages and populated centers in it. It was the second territorial band of a commune or *comune* (a self-governing, virtually independent town). The first band was the *terra,* the urban center enclosed by walls, and the third, the *districtus,* all outlying lands subject to the city, including *castelli* at a considerable distance. Fabbi, *Antichità Umbre,* pp. 147, 373. It should be noted that the word *castello* refers to a fortified village—a large fortified dwelling plus all the houses and subsidiary buildings surrounding it, all enclosed within walls.—Trans.

Italian cities, and, more than that, of other cities and other nations beyond the Alps and the sea. In fact, this story, with the change of a few exterior details, is in its essence the age-old drama of a society's arriving at an hour of definitive change.

The New Masters: Feudal Lords

In this new millenium, feudalism is in full flower. On the bank of every river, on the plain, on the top of every hill, there is a *castello;* every road leads to one. Some of the heroes of Franciscan history will come from the castles of Assisi's Mount Subasio.

Among the many *castelli* in the immediate vicinity of Assisi are Mosale, Petrata, San Donato, Pian della Pieve, Rocca del Tescio, Torre di Bili, Torre di Cencio, Torre dello Zampa, Torre Tonda, Torre Spaccata, Colle del Lupo, Monte Moro, Porziano, Castellaccio, Bandita, Armezzano, Rocca Pàida, Torre di Levanto, Torre di Gioacchino, Torricelle, Torre di Zampitto, Colle di San Martino, Poggio Morico, and Monte Sabatino.[7] The remains of many of them may be seen even today, ruins that rise fiercely as if still demanding homage and toll, crumbling bartizans darkening in the evening when the sun has set, festooned with ivy that seems to wreathe romantic legends of arms and love.

Mount Subasio is completely covered with castles. The rapacious lords, like ferocious young eagles, seem to have searched out aeries on the jumbles of bare rocks that encircle the mountain, the inaccessible and solitary cliffs, the rocky precipices with sheer, homicidal drops to the land below. These sites are the visual evidence of our ancestors' barbarian wildness, their untamed spirit that they transmitted into the very soul of the new generations.

Even the top of the mountain has its own fortress, and its name remains in the local traditions to recall the homage once paid to an unknown powerful feudal lord: Torre del Messere. It is then the tallest and strongest of all; it overlooks the green pastures on top of the mountain, the distant ridges of the Apennines, the wandering clouds. At grazing time it keeps watch over the flocks brought there—flocks on which the feudal tax of the *dativa* has to be paid. They spread over the abundant grasslands, wide valleys, and vast grassy hollows on the top of the mountain: Stazzi, Monte di Civitella, Prato Pistello, Fossa Rotonda, Mortaro Vecchio, Mortaro delle Trosce.

Also on the mountain is a fortress guarding the pass on the boundaries of the commune towards Spello that will be very famous in Saint Francis's time, Sasso Rosso, Red Rock or Cliff.[8]

The shadows of other fortresses stretch over the area in the valley where Saint Francis will take up a new life: Arce, the fortress that keeps watch over the lepers enclosed in the hospital of San Lazzaro; Bassiano (sometimes spelled Bassano, Basiano or Basciano), the castle in the fever-ridden swamp of Rivo Torto, the crooked stream that flows alongside land to be acquired by Pietro Bernardone; San Savino, the tower *par excellence,* night and day under the vigilance of the consortium of knights that guards the trivium of the Strada Francesca.[9]

The same sort of description could be made of all the regions of Italy.

These were the outward signs that the city, which had been the center of life in the classical world, had decayed after the coming of feudalism (which had its beginning around the seventh century) and particularly after the fall of the Carolingians (in the tenth century). The dominant role had then shifted to the rural areas, with their fortified castles and abbeys. All society had become divided into two parts: on the one hand, the feudal nobility, the *milites* or warrior class, who looked upon the emperor as their head; on the other, the subject peoples.

This is reflected in the archives of Assisi's cathedral, where we see a procession of counts, the violent tyrants who were the local rulers: Ermenaldo,[10] Inrizzo, Offredo, il Guitto, Ottone, Lupo, Anastasio, Ingino, Signoritto, Leto, Adenolfo, Pezzitto, Lupone, Berardo, Bucaione, Sanguigno. They are thugs, these ancestors of equally violent men whose way of life will be challenged by the son of the merchant Pietro Bernardone.

The nature of life in the castles is brought to mind by these names, which are repeated with jealous care each alternate generation. To the castellans war is the normal thing; strength, the law; revenge, a duty of honour.

The church, with difficulty, at last succeeds in putting limits on their constant fighting.

We find the evidence in a legal paper of 1103, in which a serf and land are handed over to the church of San Rufino. The concerned parties take their oaths "on a white stole and a truce of God," *per stolam candidam et treguam Dei.*[11] The "truce of God" means that hostilities were forbidden from sunset on Wednesday to dawn on Sunday, since these were days dedicated to the Passion and Resurrection of Jesus. On Wednesday evening all the bells gave the signal for the little peace that interrupted this perpetual madness.[i]

We also find in the old papers names that prove that already in the twelfth century there was a well-developed taste in Assisi territory for the poems of chivalry: Viviano, Marco, Ginevra, for example [in their English forms, Vivian, Mark, Guinevere]. One of those that recurs most frequently is Abbrunamonte—Brunamont, the hero of the story of Ogier the Dane.

Two records[12] attest that the Carolingian cycle of epic poetry was well known in Assisi even before the twelfth century; they indicate that the *chansons de geste* had spread into Italy even earlier than most scholars have thought.[j] One, dated 1121, lists an "Oliviero (Oliver) di Mascarello" living in one of the houses below the residence of the San Rufino priests; the other, of 1122, is a record of the sale of land in the *vocabolo*[k] San Pietro della Spina to a "Rollando (Roland) di Gualfredo." (Keep this locality in mind from now on; in it the new life of Saint Francis will begin.) These names bring back to us the medieval stories of chivalry, of prodigious feats and faith [stories that will be important to Francis], the *Chanson de Roland,* for example, telling of the war waged by Charlemagne against King Marsilius of Spain. There are names, too, that tell us that knights from Assisi must have participated in the Crusades and in the general zeal for liberation of the holy places: Baldovino [Baldwin], Tancredi.[13]

Linked to the feudal order is the system of *signoria fondiaria,* the grouping of people about great estates ruled by lords [in English, the manor system]. In the eleventh century these estates form the predominant element of the national economy. The feudal lord owns the estate, which was cultivated through the obligatory service of his

---

i. The attempt of the church to curb the evils of private warfare apparently developed first in France during the tenth century with the *pax ecclesiae* or *Dei,* prohibitions enacted by various synods against violence or acts of private warfare against certain classes of persons or things (clerics, women, peasants, and pilgrims, for example, also ecclesiastical buildings, agricultural implements, animals). From these rules developed the *treuga* (or *treguam*) *Dei,* which suspended all warfare on certain days. These local "truces of God" spread throughout France, Germany, and Italy during the tenth and eleventh centuries; and in 1082 a synod held in Mainz in the presence of the emperor Henry IV extended the truce to the whole empire. It was most effective during the twelfth century but declined in the thirteenth as kings gained in power and substituted the king's peace for the Truce of God. *Encyclopaedia Britannica,* s.v. "Truce of God."—Trans.

j. It has been generally believed that the *chansons de geste,* cycles of poems woven about historical events, did not spread into Italy until the thirteenth century. The Carolingian cycle referred to here is one of the three major ones, undoubtedly all known to Saint Francis; the other two are the Breton about King Arthur and his knights, and the classical, about the siege of Troy and the conquests of Alexander.—Trans.

k. The scholarly word *vocabolo* (and its rare English equivalent, "vocable") means the name or designation of a specific place.—Trans.

subjects—serfs, free and semi-free. Several properties belonging to the same proprietor, on which crops are produced, animals bred, and various products manufactured in the home, constitute the economic and juridical unit of the *curtis* or manor [the *corte, cour,* or *court* in words of Romance derivation], an establishment that probably had its origins in the latifundium, a great rural estate of ancient Rome.[14]

In a document in the Assisi cathedral dated 1104 is a record of the "curte de la Spina," located between Rivo Torto and the leper hospital; in another of 1119, the "curte de lu villano," "the countryman's *curtis,*" is mentioned.[15]

The *curtis* is supervised by a *gastaldo,* a steward who represents the proprietor and to whom the other subordinates are subject. The establishment includes a great house (a palazzo or palagio) in the city or country, stables and pens for the animals, granaries, storehouses, workshops for artisans, women's quarters for the spinning of wool, and often also a chapel.

By the end of the tenth century, the manor system begins to decline, both because of the drive of the subject people to win their freedom and because of the gradual assertion of an economy based on money. In Assisi this social movement is to culminate in the revolution of the people against the feudal lords between 1198 and 1210, in which Saint Francis is to participate in the ranks of the army of the commune—that is, of the people.

Nevertheless, it is in the poetry of feudalism—the virtues associated with chivalry and knights in shining armour—that we find the seeds of Francis's outlook on life.[16]

Francis was, above everything, brave. He scorned cowardice and he accomplished with boldness the difficult deed of total renunciation.

He served his lady with such fervour that Giotto and Dante, taking their image of him from the ancient biographers, found they could depict him only as the perfect lover, faithful until his final breath to the lady of his heart.

His faithfulness to God, bright and pure, was so shining that he was saluted as *alter Christus.*

He extended the obligation to defend the oppressed to the lowest creatures, those most damaged by human brutality and injustice.

He liked to write poetry and to sing in the manner of the troubadours, and his songs were more eloquent than those to be found in any court of love.

He was a light in his own country and is saluted as the most Italian of all the saints.

He was contemptuous of material values, even to making that contempt the fundamental rule of his order.

He delighted in the wandering life and in adventures in far-off lands. He fought in the Crusades; and he, and he alone, emerged as victor.

He exalted courtesy, the first virtue of knighthood, and counted it a divine grace: "Courtesy is one of the qualities of God, who courteously gives his sun and his rain and everything to the just and the unjust. And courtesy is a sister of charity. It extinguishes hatred and keeps love alive."[17]

Often he even liked to speak in figurative language that recalled to the minds of his listeners the heroic spirit of the Carolingian legend: "The Emperor Charles, and Oliver, and all the paladins and valiant knights who were mighty in battle, pursued the infidels even to death, sparing neither toil nor fatigue, and gained a memorable victory . . ."[18]

Moreover, when he praised the brothers who followed him on the harsh road he had marked out, he compared them to the knights of the Breton cycle of the songs of chivalry: "These friars are my Knights of the Round Table, who remain hidden in deserts and lonely places in order to devote themselves more completely to prayer and meditation . . ."[19]

His disciples—Brother Giles comes to mind—understood all this completely and tried to be worthy of such an investiture.

The link between the stories of chivalry and Francis is reflected in the chronicles of Assisi in the Sacro Convento, compiled less than a century after Francis's death. Among them is a legend current among the people, told by Brother Elemosina. Roland and Oliver, according to the story, were in the armies of Charlemagne that conquered Assisi. The figure of Charlemagne is embellished by elements drawn from the *chansons de geste*. He is gigantic; with a blow of his sword he cuts horse and rider in two; with the vise of his fingers he squeezes and crumples four horseshoes joined together; with one hand alone he raises a warrior dressed in all his armour. Other traditional legends are repeated, such as the story of Amis and Amile, the two French knights who are killed in battle and buried in separate tombs, only to be miraculously reunited because of the love that united them in life.[20]

The deeds of the Friars Minor are related in the same vein and to this local history new legends are added—stories of wicked giants who infest the land. Like Roland, the Friars take up arms and go out to battle against great evils.

It is known that chivalry never developed in Italy as it did in other nations. Far better known in Italy was the rule of chivalry of Saint Francis of Assisi.

Warrior Monks, Worldly Nuns

Monasteries (in this new millenium) are also organized very much on the feudal pattern. The abbots are more often warriors than men of the church. Great patrimonies are accumulated through donations, legacies, and personal contributions of the monks. The Benedictine abbeys are true castles with vast jurisdictions, serfs, men-at-arms.

But the monks are also devoted to the solitude so propitious for the study of old manuscripts and the delicate illumination of sacred books. They also, faithful to their principle of diligent work, plough the fields, drain the swampy land, establish farmhouses, workshops, and hospitals.

In Assisi monks drain the swamps of the Chiagio River and thin the forest between Valfabbrica and Chiagio. Their greatest deed is the reclamation of the plain below Assisi, where Francis is to live out his great dream.[21]

But even monastery life is not a peaceful one. Often enough even the high towers of monasteries are shaken by the storms of these turbulent times; and the monks do not hesitate to put on a cuirass, buckle on a sword, and ride out on horseback, like other fighting men.

Records show the Benedictine monasteries for women,[1] governed by abbesses, are also not oases of peace. They engage in quarrels with the bishop and neighbouring feudal lords.[22] Sometimes they are not even places of sanctity. The capitulary of Arechi (or Arichi) of Benevento accused nuns of being too interested in such things as a good complexion and soft white hands, of seeking ways to meet men, and of worse things yet.[m]

There were many Benedictine monasteries in and about Assisi. Many of the structures still survive, and numerous documents in the various archives testify to their rapid spread. Some of the same monas-

---

1. The word "monastery" historically applies to the residence of members of a religious order, either men or women, who take vows and live apart from the world, not to the houses of men religious alone.—Trans.

m. The capitulary of Arechi (*MGH, Leges,* vol. 4) dates from the year 774 A.D. Duke of the powerful and independent Lombardian duchy of Benevento, he was the son-in-law of the last Lombardian king, Desiderius, who was deposed by Charlemagne. After the king's death, he assumed the title of king, but Charlemagne soon convinced him of his error.—Trans.

teries, so old that their origins are lost in the years before the millenium, are still flourishing inside the city walls.

Such is the monastery (and church) of San Pietro, which we find mentioned for the first time in a cathedral document of 1029: *terra sancti Petrus, qui est monasterio de Asisie.*[23] In another we find an abbot of San Pietro present in 1072 at an assembly on the borders of Assisi territory called by the Countess Beatrice and her daughter, Countess Matilda of Canossa.[24]

This church has often been identified as the San Pietro that Francis restored with his own hands after his conversion, along with San Damiano and the Porziuncola chapel. It is difficult to understand such a supposition. From evidence in the earliest documents, this monastery appears to have been endowed with great possessions. It is impossible to think that it lacked the means to repair its church. Given the size of the building, it is equally impossible to think that it was ever regarded as a small and unimportant structure.[25] Its possessions used to extend beyond the bridge of San Vittorino on the Tescio River, the point of land on which the great Franciscan convent and basilica now stand; they included properties in Colderba, Rufole, Vaiano, Macerata, Pallareto. It also had a mill on the Tescio River, *molendinum sancti Petri positum iuxta Tessium.*

An extraordinary spirit of immutability rests over the estates of this ancient abbey. Its mill, which up until a few years ago remained the property of the monastery, continues to grind the grain of the peasants who come down from the surrounding hills. The monks supervise, as at an earlier day, the cultivation of the farmlands, a part of which they still own. Ten centuries of history have touched very lightly this world on which Saint Francis looked and in which his heart lay.

An ancient tradition places here on the river the martyrdom of the second bishop of Assisi, Saint Victorinus, who, along with Saint Rufinus, is patron of the ancient commune.[26]

On the bank of the river where Saint Victorinus was beheaded, sons of Saint Benedict built an earlier monastery with a cloister and a church. There the body of the martyr was preserved until about the year 1000, when it was taken to the church of San Pietro inside the city walls.[27]

The story of the holiness and immolation of Saint Victorinus was a familiar one to Saint Francis, who with eager heart led in his youth the boisterous rites that took place on the feast of the martyr, a show for the edification and entertainment of the whole city.[28] The old monastery was a part of his life. Many times, when going along the road that leads to Perugia, he must have stopped at the bridge of San Vittorino to consider the austere structure that once stood there, its walls looking out over the broad pebble-choked stream that exactly at this point issues from its constricted course through the mountains to snake in rough coils towards its outlet in the middle of the wide plain. That building is now gone. Its stones were used at the end of the sixteenth century to build the new Basilica di Santa Maria degli Angeli, erected over the Porziuncola chapel.

However, in the Basilica di San Francesco in Assisi, one may see a chalice that must have come from there. Pietro, one of the San Pietro abbots, gave it to Francis in token of his friendship. It is of smooth, polished silver, small and plain. Francis, according to an inventory made by the Franciscans in the fourteenth century, used it for purification after communion.

The church of San Pietro, however, is where it has always been, on the broad meadow lying just inside the medieval city gate of the same name. Except for a splendid rose window added in the thirteenth century, it remains just as it was when built, tall and imposing, with a tripartite façade, an elegant line of arches (under which runs an inscription added by the abbot Rustico, who was responsible for some thirteenth-century additions), a portal ornate with birds and beasts and guarded by two granite lions, a quadrangular campanile. The structure itself rebuts completely the idea that Saint Francis was responsible for its restoration.

On the inside its three aisles are as plain as those of the primitive Christian churches. Here and there are tombs. The altar, raised from the nave by several steps, is the focal point in front of the apse. Under it is the sarcophagus that encloses the precious bones of Saint Victorinus. Frescoes, dating from several epochs (the earliest are some twelfth-century figures in the chapel at the left of the choir), testify to the loyalty of generations to Bishop Victorinus. He is portrayed in white camice and red mantle, wearing a mitre and carrying his pastoral staff.

The same continuity of life is seen in three Benedictine monasteries for women that existed in the time of Saint Francis and are continuing their life today—San Donato, Sant'Apollinare, and San Paolo.

The first was then beyond the Tescio, on the hill at the edge of the woods now belonging to the Sacro Convento; it was transferred into Assisi in the early part of the fourteenth century, into the church of San Giacomo, where it stayed for more than four centuries. Then it was moved to the building once occupied by the ancient monasteries of San Paolo and Sant'Apollinare and is still there today. The original old church on the hill, its lovely apse still recognizable among a thick stand of cypress, has been transformed into a farmhouse.

Sant'Apollinare and San Paolo, before their transfer into the city, stood where the river Tescio meets the Chiagio, one on each side of the river. Of San Paolo (the monastery that offered the first asylum to Saint Clare when she ran away from her parents' house), only the church remains; it is today the mortuary chapel of the Bastia cemetery. There is not a trace of the primitive Sant'Apollinare. The monastery itself, united to that of San Paolo toward the end of the fifteenth century, continues its thousand year life within the walls of Assisi in the ancient consular palace, on the road that goes from the cathedral to the old church of Santa Maria delle Rose.

Other monasteries for women with origins going back to the eleventh century stood on the hills rising from the wooded valley of the Tescio. Santa Maria degli Episcopi, outside Porta San Giacomo, was on the reddish cliff that plunges amid stretches of fallen rock to the river. Its church is still intact and is now the chapel of the Assisi cemetery. Sant'Annessa was outside the Perlici gate, where there is now a small open space with ruins encroaching on it. There is a skeleton of a wall in steep wooded land, a Gothic window reflecting the rays of the moon in the countless nights when the monotonous plaint of the river is like the prayers of the forgotten virgins.

Along the same stream, under the cemetery hill, are the remains of still another monastery for women, Santa Croce del Ponte dei Galli (according to an ancient legend, the army of Charlemagne passed over this bridge). It was later transferred inside the city: that structure is in fine condition and now houses an order of Bavarian Franciscan nuns.

The richest and most influential among all these monasteries for women in the Assisi area was Panzo, situated along the side of Mount Subasio, below the Carceri. Clare and her sister Agnes stayed at Panzo before they moved to San Damiano and it is rightly considered the first home of the Poor Clares.

There are still other Benedictine churches on the line of hills that rise beyond the bridge of San Vittorino, the priory of San Bartolomeo, the chapel of San Giovanni di Beviglie.[29] The documents of the monastery of Farfa before and after the year 1000 refer to them as two of its direct dependencies.

This celebrated monastery of Farfa, which must have owed its foundation and growth to the dukes of Spoleto, served as a model of life to the Assisi monasteries; they, according to their means, mirrored its political, economic, and cultural character. Farfa's *regesto,* its register, is entirely a list of sales, donations, transactions, revenues, commendations.[30] Reading it takes us into the presence of one of the most complex and formidable of all the feudal organisms, one with a patrimony that has never been equaled on either side of the Alps. Enumerated are bushels of grain, amphorae of wine, cartloads of hay, *some*[n] of oil, millstones, pastures, forests, householders, farmers, slaves. The hierarchy is set forth: the dean, the cellarer, the bread custodian, the fruit custodian, the infirmarian, the chamberlain. The prebendaries who are entitled to the *curtis* provisions are listed: they are the caretakers of horses, cattle, sheep, goats. It brings to mind the Edict of Rotari:[o] *Porcarius magister, qui sub se discipulos habet duos aut tres amplius* ("The master swineherd, who has two or three or more disciples under him"). The tributes are fixed: wool, linen, silver, homespun cloth, hatchets, scythes, farming tools.

To offer riches in return for assured salvation of one's soul was then the process through which the goods of many a wealthy donor passed to the monasteries.

An eleventh-century document in the cathedral archives[31] tells us that donations to this monastery of Farfa served as the foundation of the Assisi church of San Giacomo. It plays a part in Franciscan history: after the death of Saint Clare, it was assigned in the bull of Alexander IV to the cathedral chapter of San Rufino in exchange for the church and hospital of San Giorgio. The San Giorgio structures were used (by the Poor Clares) for the construction of the new basilica honouring Saint Clare.

In the eleventh century there lived in Assisi one Ubertino, son of Guittone di Leto, who had committed a number of unjustifiable murders. He was persuaded to a state of penitence and entered San Bartolomeo; one of the most common means of atoning for one's sins at that time was confinement in a Benedictine monastery. San Bartolomeo may still be seen; it stands in its old place overlooking the hills through which the Tescio winds. Its apse of rough cut stones is intact, but it has become only a shed.

In its days of prosperity, the prior, Letone, received on an October day of 1088 the abbot of Farfa, Berardo, along with the bishop of

---

n. A *soma* (pl. *some*) is a unit of measure, liquid or dry, set according to the weight or volume that can be carried by a beast of burden. A unit in use before the adoption of the metric system, its value varied from place to place. Even today in Umbrian territory, the term may be used; it denotes about 100 litres.

o. The Edict of Rotari or *Edictus Langobardorum* (*MGH, Leges,* vol. 4) is the earliest existing collection of the laws of the Lombards. It was promulgated by King Rotari at a diet held in Pavia November 22, 643 A.D.—Trans.

Gubbio, the notary Ungaro, and many others. We have the names of Diluvio, Arciardo di Avultrino, Britto, Rosso, Paganuccio di Gerarduccio, Bernardo di Avultrino, and Letulo di Baroncello. They all went to the cell where the sinner was to be found, and there he made his declaration. But let us allow him to speak for himself, in this faithful transcription of his words from the document:

"In the name of the Eternal Lord Our Saviour Jesus Christ; in the one thousand and eighty-eighth year of his Incarnation; in the month of October; in the reign of Corrado, emperor of the Romans and always Augustus; I, Ubertino, son of Guittone di Leto, declare for the salvation and illumination of my soul and those of my parents that I have given and consigned and truly invested you, Berardo, abbot of the Monastery of Santa Maria of Farfa, which is built near Mount Acuziano, twelve *modioli*[p] of land and of vineyards, through the hand of domino Letone, prior of the church of San Bartolomeo, in the *vocabolo* Orsano, and through the hand of the Bishop of the city of Gubbio, who gave me three hundred years of penitence because I killed my *compare*[q] and his son whom I held at the holy font, and many others. Thus I have given the aforesaid land to the end that a church shall be constructed there in honour of Saint James; and the aforesaid abbot, and whoever shall succeed him, shall order the priests there to sing psalms, hymns, and prayers, for my sins and for those of my parents. And the sacrifices, and the fasts, and the offerings, and all other good works that God has authorized, be *pro remedio et illuminatione anime mee.*"

At this point the abbot, Berardo, joins in and pronounces the formula of absolution. "And the aforesaid abbot has absolved Ubertino of the penitence of three hundred years laid upon him for his sins, and has taken upon himself and his congregation that penitence, in honour of the Most Blessed Mary, Mother of God, and of the Most Holy James, brother apostle of the Lord."

That done, Ubertino enumerates the lands he had given to the abbot of Farfa as endowments for the future church of San Giacomo: a vineyard and an orchard in Clesia, all his properties in Bassiano, Tegolai, Fraticciola, Torcella, Campagna.

This dedication to Saint James (San Giacomo) leads us to believe

---

p. *Modioli* were measurements of land based on the amount needed to sow one *moggio* (a cylindrical wooden container) of grain. Measurements varied from place to place; in Umbria, the amount would have been about one-fourth hectare or .618 acres—roughly twice the size of an American football field or a little less than two and one-half times the size of a standard soccer field. Fabbi, *Antichità Umbre*, p. 377.—Trans.

q. *Compare* means "godfather," but it is also the term used by the parents of a baptized child to define their own relationship to that child's godparent ("my *compare*").—Trans.

that Ubertino had gone for the expiation of his sins to Saint James of Compostella, the sanctuary to which those other pilgrims, Francis and two companions, Bernardo and Giles, will subsequently go.[32]

Another devout founder was Lupo di Monaldo, who in 1091 built the church of San Masseo a short distance from San Damiano. The extensive remains of it convey a sense of primitive barbarian splendour. Still beautiful are its semicircular apse, a crypt divided into three aisles with two orders of rough columns, an altar consisting of a simple stone table supported by a truncated column.[33]

Still other monasteries played a part in the life of Saint Francis: San Nicolò di Campolungo, San Benedetto of Satriano.[34]

But of all of them, the most important was the monastery of San Benedetto (Saint Benedict) of Mount Subasio, which from the first opened its doors to Francis and welcomed his yearning for meditation and prayer.

The Benedictine Monks of Mount Subasio

This monastery is first mentioned in a cathedral document of the year 1041, *Sancte Benedictum quod est monasterium;* but certainly it must go back to a more ancient era.[r] Some eighteenth-century writers attributed its foundation to Saint Benedict himself. We need not pay any attention to such a fantastic assertion; but it is certain that in the 1041 document and in another of 1043, the monastery already seemed to be in possession of lands on Mount Subasio between Maddalena and the Carceri, which include Calcinaro and Fontemaggio. Therefore, we can believe that from this zone, located above the Perlici gate, its property extended along the side of the mountain all the way to the boundaries of the city of Spello. An opinion handed down by arbiters in 1298 confirms such a hypothesis, for it lists a part of the properties of the monastery on the mountain: Mortaro Vecchio, the valley of Panicasolo (which extends from the Mortaro meadows to the monastery), Sassopiano, the narrow stream of Rosceto, then across the plain to Topino where the abbots and the commune jointly owned mills and fulling mills.

In 1050 the abbot of Farfa, Berardo, acquired the monastery, but this subjugation was annulled between 1065 and 1084, when the

---

r. The remains of this monastery are still impressively visible on Mount Subasio. It was ruined in 1399 as a result of one of the numerous factional wars in Assisi. One of the groups (led by Ceccolino Michelotti) seized the monastery and took refuge in it; the commune, which was under the control of his rival (Broglia di Trino), captured it and had it torn down so that it would no longer be available as a refuge. For its complete history: *NV* 3:163–69.

monks of Mount Subasio were able to recover their independence. Other documents of 1083 and 1088 demonstrate that they also owned land in Sant'Angelo di Caula, a little below the Galletta spring. A record of 1110 attributes to them other lands in the Panzo district.

The abbots were concerned with purchases and sales, sowing and harvesting, hay and flocks, the duties of serfs, and tithes. A document of January, 1160, from the San Paolo archives, for example, shows us one of them, the abbot Nicolò, intent on acquiring a mill on the Tescio at Ponte dei Galli. Even here, from the text of the document, we can know the spirit that animated all of them: "I, Ugolino, son of Suppolino, of good and sane mind and of my own free will, and I Sidelgaita, his mother, with the consent of this by my son Ugolino, together have consigned and sold and corporeally invested you, Nicolò, abbot of San Benedetto, who shall possess it in perpetuity, a piece of land with a mill constructed on it, situated in the *Comitato* of Assisi, *vocabolo* Ponte dei Galli, the first side being bound by the river Tescio; the second by the land of Letone di Tignoso and the sons of Rigolo; the third, by the land of the Ospedale di San Rufino; the fourth, by the sons of Fuscolo di Bernardo and the land of the sons of Pizzocco. We have thus brought you into the possession of all the aforesaid land *in integrum et ad finitum,* with all our part of the mill, the form, and the dam, and the millstones, and the ironware . . . "

This mill served the houses in the part of the city where Saint Francis is to live.

Here, too, the centuries have passed without effect. The decrepit bridge is still in its place, millstones still turn in the mill, the water continues to race in the millstream.

Among these monks, commercial affairs did not impede prayer and meditation. We have an inventory of the ancient library of San Benedetto: great antiphonaries *de die et de nocte* bound in white, red, and black leather, martyrologies with covers of handsomely decorated woods, Bibles, Gospels, missals, psalters, collections of sermons, the Dialogues of Saint Gregory, the Rule of Saint Benedict, the Office of the Dead, a treatise on the death of a sinner, a book of laws.

Likewise in the inventory many papal and imperial privileges are listed: a bull of Honorius III, two bulls of Innocent IV, one of Pope Martin, and still others, all with the papal leaden seals with red and yellow silk cords. Before Saint Francis was born, a violent quarrel between the monastery and the bishop over exemptions and tithes had begun; it continued through his life. A bull of Eugenius III, confirmed later by Alexander IV, exempted the abbots from every jurisdiction, secular and ecclesiastical, and set forth long lists of dependent churches: Santo Stefano of Foligno, San Paolo of Spello, Santa Croce on the Timia, San Biagio of Cannara, Sant'Orfito outside Perugia, Sant'Angelo of Gabbiano, San Giovanni of Beviglie, San Paolo of Satriano, San Pietro of Lucellano, San Giovanni of Grellano, Santa Maria of Porziuncola, and many others. "We wish these churches to remain in your possession, free for you and your successors, together with the land and the other properties, pastures, vineyards, woodlands on the mountain and on the plain, mills, roads, and everything cultivated by your hand or by the work of serfs."[s]

The monastery, fortified and turreted like a castle, stood below the pasture land on top of the mountain, between thick woods and a steep precipice. It had a martial life, and monastic solitude alternated with the clash of arms. It was continually under siege in political battles or by mercenary troops until 1399, when, after a furious battle, it was torn down by order of the commune. Several years ago, excavations in the small enclosed area in front of the church brought to light the dead of that last battle.

Enough remains of the church, closed in to the north by a crown of stone blocks, to allow us to make an exact reconstruction of it.

In front was a cloister, today gone, and a fountain fed by a fresh spring. The spring still flows into a drinking pool at the edge of a clearing. The church had a Romanesque façade built of squared white stones, which now appears to be lopped off at a third of its original height. It had a triple arched door, surviving today almost unchanged, as may be seen from the fresco by Giotto in the upper church of the Basilica di San Francesco. He depicted the monastery surmounted by a tall campanile with a spire. It dominated the mountain slope.

The nave is now unroofed all the way to the choir. The apse, facing east, rises from a heap of ruins covered with ivy. A narrow stairway leads down to the beautiful crypt, miraculously intact. The old campanile disappeared in the cold destruction—that campanile that until its last days announced the Ave Maria at dawn and at sunset to the shepherds bivouacked alongside the sheepfolds. They came in June and left in November, when the mists begin to smoke along the summit of the high meadows. The flocks would amble along, led by their guardians wrapped in goat skins. They would pause to quench

---

s. The inventory was compiled in 1401, after the destruction of the monastery made it necessary to take the books to the church of San Paolo. See Arch. Not. (Atti di Gerardo di Giovanni, 1400–02, no. 3, c. 23–24); *NV* 3:169.

their thirst, then depart in a hurry, urged along by enormous dogs. From the heights would come the sweet faint sound of goat bells.

Afterwards, winter, with its interminable nights. The trees became bare. Snow fell and mantled the towers, the bastions, the rocks, the deserted pastures. When the sky was clear, other peaks, shining white, could be seen far away.

A great clangour of bells would arouse the flocks. It came on the first day of spring, the special festival of the monastery, a day dedicated to Saint Benedict. The wave of sound found every gorge, every rock, every remote peak. The monks, two by two, carrying burning candles, formed a procession that coiled behind the high Byzantine cross, their white surplices shining against the background of solemn oaks. The ancient songs would rise up, to tell again in stately Gregorian chant of the eternal glory of the founder.

We can think that Saint Francis, who from the time of his infancy had especially intimate ties to these monks of Mount Subasio, often climbed all the way up here to enjoy the life of the solitary monastery on the mountain that was so dear to him. And we can wonder: under what pile of debris is buried the ruin of the room in which he discussed with the abbot the transfer of the chapel of Porziuncola to the Franciscans?

Recent excavations permit us to reconstruct the arrangement of the buildings that extended to the right of the church, in the area today occupied by a country house, its windows looking out over the valley, and by an open space thick with vines.

A passageway extended alongside the church, crowned at the presbytery end by an open gallery that faced the plain. On the near side of it there was the cloister, around which stood the various other buildings: the dormitory, the chapter house, the refectory, the kitchen, the larder, the warehouses, the animal pens, the workshops of the artisans.

Given the nearness of pastures and the abundance of sheep, the *curtis* of the monastery was organized for the production and working of wool. The gallery must have been used for this purpose; one can see today arches where the washed wool was placed in the sun to dry. (We know that the industry was at its most flourishing in the *curtes* of Benedictine monasteries; the art of wool production had its place with work done on the land and stockbreeding. Even before Saint Benedict, Saint Jerome sent a *lanam fecit,* a Roman matron's directions for weaving wool, to a medieval nun. His letter to Demedriade, superior of a Roman monastery, is well known: "When you have finished the prayer of the choir, do not put the wool from your hands;

move your fingers continually on the thread of the distaff or on the little bridge of the loom. Gather the products of the diligence of the sisters in order to instruct the weavers, and examine the cloth with care; if it is bad, reject it, and dispose of it as ought to be done.")

A strong wall crowned by towers (some ruins of it remain) and a palisade built along the narrow ledge of space on the edge of the mountain defended the monastery from the plain.

From this falcons' nest, perched on the steepness of the "high mountain," the spirit is launched into a dizzy expanse of space lying between the sky, curving to a far-off horizon, and the lightly veiled great plain, on which there is now a tangle of innumerable white roads. But up on the heights of Mount Subasio, every anxiety is relieved, every fever diminished, every frenzy stilled in peace. *Ascesi*—mystical exaltations, spiritual ascensions—are the secret of this land.[t]

A few steps lead to the crypt. It is dark, cold, cruciform, with sepulchral light falling from openings cut into the apse. In the walls, roughly cut stones alternate with the bare rock of the mountain. Eight Romanesque columns, short and stumpy, with leafy capitals, support heavy arcades. A stone bench runs along the walls just above the floor.

On the ground lies a great split slab tomb. On it is depicted an abbot of the monastery in the pontifical vestments he wore in the days when he went to the altar amid dazzling lights and songs that awakened echoes in the solitude of the mountain. Under the mitre is a solemn priestly face, rather like a stone sphinx. A gloved hand holds the pastoral staff of the abbot; the other, against his chest, gathers up the ample folds of the cope. The figure does not stand out in relief; its outlines are chiselled into the rock. The lines are somewhat evanescent; the figure is almost a shadow, a phantom. All the other monks are gone. He alone remains, custodian of the world that has dissolved into dust.

My Lord Bishop

There was a bishop's house in Assisi even in very remote times. The martyr Saint Sabinus, who lived in the fourth century, is said to have

---

t. In these paragraphs Fortini forcibly recalls to the reader Canto 11 of Dante's *Paradiso;* unfortunately there is no way to do the same thing in English—an example of the frustrations of translation. Fortini does it by putting Dante's words *alto monte* ("high mountain") in quotations, using Dante's literary word *rattezza* for "steepness," and playing on the word "Ascesi," which was also the variant form of "Assisi" used by Dante. "Ascesi" for Assisi is indeed found in many medieval writings, but the word itself also means spiritual ascensions and mystical exaltations. Dante writes, *Non dica Ascesi . . . ma Oriente,* by which he means, "Do not call this city Ascesi (Assisi) but the East, because from here a sun (Saint Francis) rose to the world."—Trans.

established it on the site of the temple of Janus. The tradition is supported by the fact that in the city museum is a memorial stone found in the area on which it is recorded that two slaves, Pannico, servant of Fosforo, and Primogenio, servant of Primo, had offered an altar to the god *Iano patri*, "our father Janus." This part of the city was called *mons Iani*, Mount or Hill of Janus, from which was derived the name that came into use in the high Middle Ages and is still used, Moiano.[35]

Janus was venerated as the first indigenous god of the Romans, hence that designation of *pater*. His name comes from the word *ianus*, a door or passageway, in that he was the god of each beginning in space and in time: the beginning of the year, of religion, of life. For this reason he is depicted with two faces, one that looks to the east, the other to the west. Janus: a door that opens, an era that begins, a hope that is rekindled, a renewal beyond each time of sorrow.

There is also an extremely ancient little door in the Roman wall of the bishop's garden in Assisi on which are the mysterious words *post quartam precationem*. They mean that the door, which perhaps led to the temple, was opened after the god was invoked four times.

The house of the bishop has undergone many alterations but it still stands on the footings on which the first builders rested it, the mighty Roman wall of the *cinta urbica*, the encircling city wall.

This is not without profound symbolic significance. During the invasions of the high Middle Ages the bishop represented in Italian cities the last glimmer of the light of the Roman world. He was the numen of the city against the barbarians, serving literally as the governor, *condottiero*, and defender. At first he was harassed by the new masters, in part because of a difference in religious beliefs, since most of the conquerors were Arians, and in part because of the national and Latin origins of his office. Very quickly, however (especially after the conversion of the Goths and Lombards to Catholic Christianity), he assumed such political importance that the new peoples coming into Italy did not hesitate to recognize his powers and to commit high and honourable responsibilities to him.

Thus, a bishop of Assisi, Avenzio, was entrusted with an ambassadorial mission to the emperor by the Ostrogoth king Totila about the year 547, as is recorded by Marcellino, *comite*.[36]

Avenzio is the first bishop of the city, after those martyred in Roman times, of whom the documents speak. Afterwards, some names become fleetingly visible in the somewhat uncertain lists; they are bishops who participated in church councils, Aquilino in 649, Magione in 821 and 826.[37]

Then we find references that give us a glimpse of the bishop's powers—bishops involved in struggles with dukes and counts, bishops concerning themselves with exchanges and barters and emphyteutic leases,[u] bishops seated with other judges in judicial proceedings.

In a 963 document there is an agreement about an emphyteusis of a property on the Tescio, between Eremedio, bishop of Assisi, *vir venerabilis,* and Giovanni Filiberto. The cross over the bishop's signature looks like the hilt of a sword; and the signature itself (*ego Eremedius episcopus*) is straight, strong, sure, written by a hand accustomed not only to blessing but also to raising a sword in battle.[38]

In this legal paper the bishop's church, consecrated to Saint Mary of the Assumption, Assisi's first cathedral, emerges from the mist of the centuries. On the feast of the Assumption in August, *coloni* [farmers permanently attached to the land] and *fittavoli* [tenant farmers] went there to pay the canon, a quit rent for land. We see the bishop surrounded by his priests; transactions are made "by the will and consent of the major cleric and of the priests who received their ordination in my holy Episcopate."

The territory over which by this time the bishop exercised lordship was no less extensive than that of the Benedictine monasteries. The awakening of the religious spirit, the need to obtain pardon for monstrous crimes through gifts of lands, the need to find a protector from the oppression of the counts—all are factors that influenced many to cede their material possessions to the church and become vassals of the bishop.

Eremedio is succeeded by Ingizo, *Episcopus sanctae Asisinatae Ecclesiae* ("Bishop of the Holy Church of Assisi").[39]

The phrase reminds us that we should keep in mind, for the better understanding of some episodes in Saint Francis's life, that the churches of cities were by and large autonomous, their perfect orthodoxy and obedience to Rome notwithstanding. The autonomy extended even to special rites, so that the liturgy of the church of Assisi was, for example, notably different from those of Perugia and Spoleto.

And after Ingizo comes Leo, *Leo umilis Episcopus sanctae Asisinate ecclesie,* ("the humble Bishop of the Holy Church of Assisi"). In October 985 he barters with Stavile, son of Raimperto, a property located just outside the city; it is described according to the Lombar-

---

u. The holder of an emphyteutic lease (or emphyteusis) has a perpetual or very long term right to a piece of another's land at a permanently fixed rent.—Trans.

dian measurement, King Liutprand's *gubitale* foot.ᵛ The bishop, honoured with the title of pontiff (*de pars tua Pontifici,* the document notes, "with respect to the part of you, the Pontiff"), is on his throne, *intus tuo Episcopio,* for the proceedings. In addition to the notary, a judge representing the royal authority, *de pars regi,* participates.[40]

With the coming of the princes of the house of Saxony, the Italian bishops, already rich in lands, vassals, and privileges, begin also to stand up to the lay counts, especially in the matter of their right to jurisdiction over the clergy and over persons living on lands belonging to the church.ʷ This strength, which in some cities carried the bishop to power with the title of "count" and made a clash with feudal lords inevitable, reached its peak after the defeat of Arduino of Ivrea, whom the lords considered their leader, by Henry II of Saxony.[41]

Thus we find a very important document of 1018 in the Assisi cathedral in which the bishop, Giorgio, and his lawyer, Pietro, uphold this jurisdiction of the church against every abuse of the feudal lords and counts. The bishop, *Georgeus vir venerabilis Episcopus Sancte Asisinate Eglesia,* takes a commanding posture: "I affirm my authority in the Episcopacy of Assisi and on all ecclesiastical things that relate to it, as for the love of God and for the health of his soul, Henry, Emperor, invested me . . . "[42]

We are not dealing here with the simple affirmation of rights of a

---

v. This *gubitale* foot, which is mentioned in a number of Assisi records, is an antique measure of length, presumably established during the reign of the Lombardian king Liutprand (712–744 A.D.). It varied from 30 to 50 centimetres (about 12 to 20 inches), according to locality. This is probably the *piede Liutprando,* known also as the *piede cubitale, giusto, legittimo,* and *grosso,* used in that early period along with the *piede romano,* which was smaller: one *pertica* (a rod or perch, which varied locally; the present standard is 5½ yards) had in it twelve Liutprandian feet, twenty Roman feet.—Trans.

w. As indicated in this passage, the office of bishop had gone through many alterations in these tumultuous centuries. The secular powers the bishops had assumed during the disorders of the invasions, and that had been declared legal by Justinian, were eroded or lost in the growth of feudalism and the tightening controls of kings and emperors—Charlemagne, for example, not only insisted on his right to appoint all bishops (and to use the office as a reward for favours) but also required that all bishops maintain and lead armed companies in his service, like any other vassal. The rights of bishops vis-a-vis their lords varied according to circumstances after the break-up of the Carolingian empire, but it is safe to say that virtually no one questioned either the matter of the sees being bestowed by secular lords or the right of those lords to interfere mightily in ecclesiastical affairs.

In 962, Otto I, king of Germany, having defeated the king of Italy (Berengar of Ivrea), was crowned emperor of the two unified kingdoms, thus becoming the founder of the Holy Roman Empire. He and his successors were opposed by the feudal lords in Italy, and in 1002 they elected a king of Italy: Arduino of Ivrea. Bishops strongly opposed him during his brief reign, which was ended by the superior strength of the German king, Henry II, who was crowned emperor in 1014. Though prone to interfere high-handedly in church affairs, Henry (canonized in 1146) was a pious and moral man, allied with the pope in the work of reforming the church. *ODCC,* s.v. "Henry II"; Hughes, *History of the Church,* 2:197–98, 212–13; *Encyclopaedia Britannica,* s.v. "Henry II" and "Italy."—Trans.

patrimonial nature but of real jurisdiction. *Praeceptum habeo,* says Bishop Giorgio, "I have authority." And the duke of Spoleto, Rodolfo, who declares that he has the right to make the decision by order of the emperor, *per iussionem Imperatoris,* confirms those rights and specifies the churches and material possessions recognized as under the episcopal authority: the *pieve*[x] of the city, that is, the territory in which the bishop is the pastor, an area that takes in both city and suburbs. Included are the city churches both within and without the walls, together with their lands, their vineyards, their fixed donations from the living and the dead; the rural churches— Sant'Apollinare del Sambro beyond Cannara, Santa Maria di Orvinio near Collemancio, Santa Maria of Bettona, San Giovanni of Pomonte, San Costanzo, Santa Tecla, San Venanzo on the mountain; the monastery of San Crispolto on the border between Assisi and Bettona. Manors subject to the bishop are also listed: the *curtis* of Morano on the hill between Assisi and Nocera, the *curtis* of Arondineto on the Chiagio toward Costano.

Lands that have been usurped are to be restored to the bishop: those in Costano and in Campo Colonio that Stephen di Gislerio and his sons are occupying; those in the Nocera area that the sons of Rambaldo have taken away from him.

"And thus," concludes Duke Rodolfo's decision, "I invest Giorgio, bishop, and Pietro, his lawyer, with the episcopacy, the parishes, the churches, the lands, the vineyards, the serfs, the female servants, and with all things belonging to and being the concern of the church, and with the tithes."

And after Giorgio, there is another resolute and pugnacious bishop, Guglielmo. He passionately takes the field before an assembly of *buoni uomini* (magnates) in Costano in October, 1019, against Pietro, son of Romano, to claim a piece of land for his church, *Ecclesie Sancte Marie.* Despite the numerous lacunae due to the bad state of the parchment, the document is very important because in it is described the legal procedure of a "judgement of God," that is, a trial by combat.[43]

In the field facing the river are the count, the royal ambassador, the *buoni uomini* (judges, notaries, lords of manors), the people. The bishop, *Guillelmo episcopo vir venerabilis,* comes forward, followed

---

x. The *pieve* (or *plebs*) in this early time was the baptismal church of a given area, with all other churches in the area subordinate to it. As Fortini's usage indicates, it was in an urban area the same as a cathedral—the bishop's church; like the rural *pievi,* with the sole right in the area to baptize, conduct burials, and collect the obligatory tithes. Cf. Boyd, *Tithes and Parishes,* pp. 47–74, 154–64; Brentano, *Two Churches,* pp. 68–76.—Trans.

even here by his legal counsellor, Giovanni, *Iohannes, adbocato, de donum Episcopo.* The bishop's legal counsellor is the administrator of the material possessions, the defender, the champion who protects the causes of the church in legal proceedings. He takes an oath to do this; when the need arises, he even undertakes a judicial duel.

Guglielmo states his claim. If it is contested, he will invoke divine justice. The blade will decide on which side right lies. Inzitto, the count, and Elfito, the royal legate, grant *la wadia,* the official protection from prosecution for the victor of the duel: *Et Guadia dedi de pugna.*

Nerves tense over the bloody event about to take place, those present press around. But their expectation is a delusion. Pietro will not fight. He recognizes the justice of the bishop's position and declares that he has no claim on the land. And so the count, taking up his baton and laying his hand on the head of the bishop, pronounces the usual formula of investiture.

From the time of such early episodes as these to the end of the twelfth century, the bishop of Assisi, shrewdly steering a course between popes and emperors, comes to acquire an enormous holding. By the time of Saint Francis he was apparently the owner of half the property in the commune.

A bull of Innocent III of May 12, 1198,[44] lists the churches, the monasteries, the lands, the *castelli* that are under his jurisdiction. In the long list are almost all the churches of the city and the *contado,* also the principal monasteries, including San Benedetto of Mount Subasio. It also lists a court in Moiano that must have been around the bishop's palace itself.

The lands extend over mountain and plain, from one end to another of Assisi territory. They touch the walls and spread into the city. A vineyard in Sementone "close to the walls of the city," *iuxta murum civitatis;* the area surrounding the bishop's palace, *area Episcopii cum omnibus appenditiis eius partis civitatis;* the Caprile hill. There are names of localities that will become famous in the life of Francis—the Carceri, the woods of Porziuncola, the *cerqueto grosso* or thick oak woods, Ospedale delle Pareti. Some of the most noteworthy donations are listed, such as those of Ildebrando, son of Guidone, and of his daughter, Leta, and her husband, Corvo, who ceded to the bishop the castle of Campolungo, the castle of Vallesorda, and all the surrounding lands.

There is still more. All one part of the city appears to be directly subject to the bishop, the section "that goes from the Moiano gate to the house of Accursale, son of Rainone, to the house of Pietro de

Peppone, and down to San Gregorio, and out the Sant'Antimo gate."
We know that Peppone's house was on Via Portica. The Sant'Antimo
gate is the old Roman gate; the houses of the Fiumi family were built
against it at a later time. When Saint Francis lived, it was the principal
gate of the city, the one facing the plain. The inner side may still be
seen, beautiful, majestic, tall as a palazzo. It was square in form and
had an arch with marble posts on the valley side. From this much
information we can reconstruct very well the boundaries of the city
under the jurisdiction of the bishop: from the houses on the left of the
gate to the middle of Via Portica, then to Via San Gregorio, down
along Via San Gregorio, and thence back to the gate. We are dealing
here with a large parallelogram, a citadel with its own walls, gates,
fortifications, its own special emblems.

The bull of Innocent III speaks of "confirming" ancient privileges,
some of which go back to the pontificate of Pascal II (1099–1118). In
fact, a document of 1104 in the cathedral archives mentions "the
bishop's hill in the city of Assisi" and places on it the church of
Sant'Ansuino. This means that the bishop's church (*chiesa par-
rochiale*)[y] was at one time nearby the present Confraternity of the
Stigmata. The term "bishop's hill" calls to mind the ancient name for
the site, "the hill of Janus."[45]

This bull of 1198 reconfirms the exclusive jurisdiction of the
bishop on everything and everyone subject to him. "We forbid any
authority or representative of such authority to exact undue levies or
to bring to trial the clergymen of your churches or the men who live
on the lands of the episcopacy, without the consent of the Bishop."

This is the diploma that will establish the legal competence of the
bishop to judge Francis on the day of his mystic wedding. By then the
bishop of Assisi will have reached the highest point of his power and
wealth; he seems to have been the strongest and richest feudal lord of
all the area. Avid for material goods and thirsty for power, this bishop
will not hesitate, as we shall see, to fight incessantly for his power or
for his riches against the magistrates of the commune who do not wish
to bend to his will and against the monasteries that rebel against his
authority. And yet this same bishop, without hesitation, will put his
own mantle on the man who strips naked in front of him to make

---

y. The *parochia* or parish also meant in early centuries the bishop's territory; it was used
interchangeably with *diocesis*. The word did not begin to gain its modern meaning until about
the twelfth century, when some subordinate churches gained the right to baptize and perform
other functions previously reserved to the cathedral and *pieve*. See references cited in n. x.
—Trans.

Poverty the rule of his own life, to show Poverty as the salvation of all those driven from the good by power or greed.

In that hour of great decisions even the fiery Bishop Guido was touched by this ardent appeal and answered it with a magnificent gesture, one that will remain alive through the centuries as a symbol of the authenticity of his priestly calling, while all other aspects of his unsavoury life, shot through with worldly preoccupations, will disappear like withered leaves at the first blast of the winter wind.

The greatest glory in the varied and stormy lives of the bishops of Assisi will be the act of this one, who, called to judge the sublime folly of the man called the *alter Christus,* knew (unlike another judge more than eleven hundred years earlier) how to recognize the truth.

Serfs and Servitude

The formation of the great manors meant that most of the people became enslaved to the land. The historical milieu in which the Franciscan concept was formed can only be understood in the light of this unique aspect of the society of the times.

Most of the free farmers were sorely tried in the disorders of frequent invasions, and eventually had to seek the protection of a lord, a *signore,* upon whom they became, to a greater or lesser degree, dependent. The name given to the relationship between the dependent and the lord varied from city to city and from region to region; in the territory of Assisi it was called *hominicium,* from the fact that the dependents became the men, *homines,* of those to whom they were subject.

Numerous documents from the tenth and eleventh centuries in the cathedral archives speak to us of those whose lives, properties, and families were completely subject to the arbitrary will of the signori: *servi* and *ancillae*—serfs, both men and women.

We see them handed over to new owners, used as gifts, given in usufruct, used as pledges or pawns.

In a deed of 1118, for example, a family of peasants is sold for a small price to a prior of San Rufino, Vidone.[46] Here, in this transaction promoted by a leading citizen whose name, Sarraceno, virtually exhales heroic associations with the recent Crusade, the old and the new generations are delivered to the glebe, without hope of escape, like oxen to the plow. Pietro and Bonizzo, veterans exhausted from a whole lifetime of hard labour, are the victims; and so are their sons and grandsons, surely already brooding over plans for early rebellion.

The lord, proprietor of land on Lupone's Hill, makes note of his power to nail down the fate of these outcasts, to whom is denied every dignity and every right: *omne usum omneque ius ac potestatem que in eos habebat in perpetuum* ("every usage, every right and power over them, belonging to him in perpetuity").

We recognize in him an ancestor of Saint Clare;[z] he has the same name and patronym as the uncle whose arrogance and pride eventually erupted into a sacrilegious act in front of the altar of a monastery for women, Monaldo di Offredo. This earlier Monaldo, also a haughty noble, parades his feudal ancestry before Rodolfo, justice and doctor of law: *Ego, comes Monaldus* ("I, Count Monaldo . . . ").

It was possible for serfs to rise to a less burdensome state in life. Manumission was the most important means. It was bestowed upon the serf in one of several solemn and ceremonious forms, all of which were poignant demonstrations of the universal aspiration for freedom.[47] In manumission *per sagittam,* for example, the rite included the shooting of an arrow. Thus was the life of the serf—an arrow fitted to the string of the crossbow stretched by the archer. If Fate were propitious, the sharp iron-tipped arrow that could flatten one forever is instead propelled skyward to search for light and sun.

A fine example of another form of manumission, *in ecclesia circa sacrosanto altare,* is found in a document of March, 1030.[48] For the first time in the records, the name of the small church at the foot of the hill on which Assisi stands appears. It is a church destined to become famous in the Franciscan story—San Damiano.

It stood between a sea of olive trees and the ruins of a nearby Roman sepulcher, just as, after a thousand years, it does today. A little church, with a low vault, a narrow window like a slit in a fortress wall, a semicircular apse painted blue and richly adorned with stars, traces of which may still be seen.

Here, one Anastasio, son of the *quondam* Domenico, lifts up a prayer as anguished as the one that will come from the heart of Saint Francis in the same church some two centuries later. Human life is fragile. One must fear at each moment that he will find himself before the Supreme Judge. Who will be saved? Who will be lost? Prayer is vain if it is not accompanied by good works. And the work of greatest merit is that of restoring liberty to one deprived of it. Merciful God, accept the offering of giving freedom to a serf bound to the land of his lord. "For the love of God, for the salvation of the soul of our relatives and of Domenico, our father, for the remission of all our sins,

---

z. Monaldo was probably the uncle of Saint Clare's grandfather, Offreduccio. *NV* 2:328 and 3:499.

for that blessed life where our Lord Jesus Christ, compassionate and merciful, will deign to pardon all our sins . . . "

Thus does Anastasio give freedom to his serf Petruzzolo, son of his servant Marziola.

The formula of manumission is proclaimed on the following day. It is spoken by this devout lord to the slave, who kneels in the dust before him, his head shaved and his body clad in coarse grey garments: "On this day be free, and remain free until death and be free with you in perpetuity your children, those already born, those who will come."

The priest then takes charge of Petruzzolo and walks around the altar with him four times.

(This ceremony could be a symbol of things to happen in the future. The priest, whose name is Runto, is the distant predecessor of the one who will receive the young Francis into his own quarters. This altar around which the minister of God and the freed serf walk—this "most holy altar," according to the document, *sacrosanto altare beatum Sancti Damiani qui est in comitatum Asisinatum*—is the same altar from which the young Francis will hear an anguished cry from the crucifix.)

At last the priest Runto turns to Petruzzolo with the words for which he has been waiting: "I give you permission to walk the four roads and to take with you your children and your goods, wheresoever God will wish to lead you. From this day you are free, with all your children, world without end."

The "four roads" of the ceremonial formula recall the original rite of the Lombardian people, in which the serf was taken literally to a cross-roads at the moment of liberation. No longer must he follow a single road, that of his lord. Now he has four roads from which to choose, four roads to follow, as he pleased. These, too, signified other roads: the roads of good and of evil, of life and of death. The man was now his own master and master of his destiny.

(Again we can find a prophetic quality in these events. Francis, too, will find freedom in this church, an even greater freedom, one that will leave him free to walk on an infinite number of roads in his task of winning the whole world.)

The manumitted serf still had certain obligations to his former master, who had now become his protector.[aa] These usually consisted

---

aa. Herr writes: "In the twelfth century, apart from some tiny and much debated areas . . . there were no longer any completely free peasants. The peasants described as 'free' were nevertheless bound to a lord in a protective relationship of some kind, just like the rest. . . . Bound to the service of one or more lords, the rural population of Europe lived in varying

of a prescribed number of days of work without pay and of set tributes or payments. Such things were required of other semi-free classes, the *aldi* and the *coloni.*

The *aldi* were for the most part prisoners of war who had given themselves up. They had a juridical personality but were tied to the land and held to the payment of tribute and duties stabilized by custom. There is no trace of them in the records after the year 1000. The *coloni* cultivated the land assigned to them; their rights and obligations were the same as those of the *aldi.*

We find in the documents of San Rufino a variety of contractual forms through which the various systems of bondage were established. Among them is the *livello,* an agreement made through the written document called the libellus, and the *prestaria* or precarium, the accommodation made by a *signore* for one who has asked to work on the land.

Both these forms could be drawn up for a specific number of years or for life. There was also a form known as commendation, in which the farmer took upon himself the payment of tribute and services but preserved his liberty.

During the eleventh and twelfth centuries, these categories were combined into the single one of *hominicium.* Those who have a need to examine in detail the forms of servitude should undertake a study of the three forms: the commendation, *pro feudo;* the *colonato, pro laboritio;* the precarium, *pro tenimento.* But a general discussion of them is in itself of scant interest, and the obligations deriving from all of them do not differ materially one from the other.

From various documents of the early thirteenth century, including those in the archives of the cathedral, we find that obligations of the *hominicium* consisted of hoeing the vineyard, ploughing the fields with oxen, harvesting and grinding the grain, cutting hay, gathering grapes, running the mill, and drawing the *treggia,* a sledge used for transporting materials over rocky and difficult areas.[49]

Periodic required gifts or tributes called *amiscere* constituted the outward sign of the *hominicium;* they symbolized the authority of the proprietor over the estate. The principal ones were made at Christmas and on the feast of the Assumption. At Christmas they consisted

degrees of dependence, unfreedom or serfdom, and the distinctions of grade were in practice as great as that between highly born vassals of the crown and 'knights and noble squires' who had virtually nothing to call their own, or between highly educated wealthy prelates and village priests bound to the soil. Our vocabulary does not even possess the words necessary to distinguish clearly between the different groups, classes, and ranks of 'free,' 'half-free,' 'unfree,' and 'dependent' peasants." *Medieval World,* p. 24.—Trans.

of bread, pork, *spalletta* (a shoulder of ham), and lard. On the feast of the Assumption, bread and chickens constituted the *amiscere*. In May the tenant took ricotta to his signore, buns on Saint Stephen's day, and at other times, eggs, cheese, and fish.[50]

When Francis received the Porziuncola chapel from the monastery of San Benedetto, he wished to acknowledge the authority of the monastery over the property with *amiscere* of fish.

If the serf did not live up to his obligations, the lord had the legal right of depredation, the confiscation of the rebellious farmer's goods. Documents in the archives give us ample evidence that the proprietors made use of this right, being especially ready to help themselves to oxen. The signore also had the legal right in such cases to impose additional duties and harsher terms of service.[51]

Saint Pier Damiani tells in his *Sermons* of an episode in Assisi about the middle of the twelfth century that illustrates how the lord exercised his privileges.[52] A particular lord had made a certain "writing" in favour of a woman who cultivated his land, perhaps a written agreement that would allow her to become semi-free. Whatever it was, he immediately regretted having done it. Since he was aggressive and cruel, he went to her and asked for the paper. She refused to give it back, and he went out in a great rage and exercised his right of depredation, taking away an ox and an axe. The woman was extremely poor, so much so that these things were her only means of providing for herself and her family, all of whom she supported. Overcome with grief, she could think of nothing to do but to go to the church of San Rufino, where she knelt in front of the altar to invoke the help of the Patron Saint. As she got up, she saw her axe lying on the ground in front of her. Others in the church certified the miracle and all together they thanked God for it. At that moment the arrogant lord came into the church, still beside himself with rage. He began to shout at the woman that unless she gave him his paper, he would have her tortured. Then he saw the axe. He shut up and began to tremble, fearing that Saint Rufinus would inflict just punishment on him. He returned the ox and the axe to his servant, submitted himself to penance, changed his ferocious nature, and never again engaged in quarrels or disputations.

No small number of serfs sought to escape such bondage by denying the existence of a relationship of subjugation to the lords. And also unethical lords often swore falsely that such a bond existed with those who had always been free and exempt from it. There was a constant succession of legal assemblies to hear such cases and render decisions on them.

A cathedral record gives the details of one of these *placita*, the assemblies called to pass such judgements. It was held in the year 1072, and Matilda, the countess of Canossa, and her mother, Beatrice, participated in it.[53]

We are in the *villa*[bb] of Collestrada, another locality to be important in the life and apostolate of Saint Francis. The month is July, the year 1072. On the summit of the little hill, where vineyards march up the slopes, the young countess of Canossa is seated, surrounded by many people. Among them are Bishop Agino, the abbot of San Pietro, a judge named Arderico, another judge called Uberto, and a judge of the Holy Roman Empire, Gerardo.

A large family comes forward, men and women, old and young: Vidone, son of Maria; his brother, Berardo; his sister, Burga; Azzo; Vido; Pagano; the children; the grandchildren. All the hill rings with their plea " . . . that their persons be free, and their sons and their daughters, and all their movable and immovable things remain in their possession with the title of ownership." The ritual challenge follows: "And if anyone wishes to interfere in any way with our things and our persons, we are ready to go with him to judgement and to settle each controversy according to the law."

No one comes forward; and the two women conclude the assembly by declaring for the plaintiffs: "No one dare claim them as serfs and dishonour their state or make claims over their things; and anyone who presumes to do so must pay two thousand *bisanti* of gold, half of which will go to the king's treasury and the other half to the aforesaid plaintiffs."

With this *bannum* the one claimed as a serf is safe. No one would dare bother him for fear of having to pay the penalty threatened by the magistrate who had ruled them to be free.

The Cathedral: House of the People

There is no trace in the documents of the life of the city between the end of the Roman period and the middle of the tenth century except for the name of a notary that survives in a legal document of the monastery Farfa from the year 763, *Aurimo notarius civitatis Asisinatae* ("Aurimo, notary of the city of Assisi").[cc] From this we

---

bb. A *villa*, in the period being discussed, was a specific territorial division of the ancient *comitato* of Assisi. It was originally a dependency of the inhabited rural center called the *locus*. NV 3:67.

cc. During that same year of 763 A.D., another trace of city life is noted. An *Insualdus de Asisio* is among the envoys who meet in Todi to determine the borders of the city and *comitato* of Todi and also of Spoleto, Bevagna, Assisi (*Asisinatum*), and Perugia. Amaduzzi, *Anecdota*, 1:449.

may deduce that the city continued its corporate existence, since it had not only the count and the bishop but also its court and its notary.

But the name of an old *contrada* of Assisi, a name that has survived all the events of fourteen centuries, demonstrates more than anything else that even in the dark ages of Lombard domination, people in the city lived, were stirred, had their troubles, deliberated—in short, participated in a common life. The *contrada* or district is Perlici. It is on the mountain side of the city in a sort of hollow that from the most remote times was called the "fossa di Perlasio" or "fossa di Parlascio," *fovea Perlasii,* the Perlascio hollow. The ruins of Assisi's Roman amphitheatre remain here, as elsewhere, immediately outside the city walls.[dd]

Perlasium, parlasium, parlascium: these were the names given in the high Middle Ages to the Roman amphitheatre, in which the citizen assembly was convoked.[54] *Parlagio,* the place where one talked, where public affairs were discussed. Here, amid the falling arcades of the amphitheatre, where once the cry of Christian martyrs had been raised, the people of the city continued to seat themselves in the tradition of their thousand-year-old civilization.

Later the people of Assisi assembled in front of the church they considered their own, built over the relics of their first bishop, Saint Rufinus. No record of Bishop Rufinus is known to survive earlier than the eleventh century other than the story of his martyrdom in the territory of Costano, on the Chiagio River, where, having refused to sacrifice to the pagan gods, he was drowned. There used to be a church in Costano dedicated to him. In front of it, early in the eleventh century, the "judgements of God," the trials by combat, were held in the certainty that this champion of Christ would himself take the field to uphold the cause of truth.[55]

According to Saint Pier Damiani, the sacred body of the bishop was taken from the water near Assisi and placed in a sarcophagus, where it remained for some time. Then, in fear that it would be seized and desecrated by pagans, it was carried inside the walls of the city. Still later, perhaps in the eighth century, to judge by some of the construction of the crypt (which was rebuilt in the eleventh century),[56] a church, a "small basilica" in the words of the Holy Doctor, was erected in his honour. It was built on the site of an ancient

---

dd. Until a century ago the arcades of the amphitheatre in Assisi could still be seen; even today, in the foundations of the adjacent houses, the remains of the corridors that supported the tiers can be made out. The area is today a garden surrounded by houses, the whole enclosed by a wall that preserves the elliptical form of the ancient amphitheatre. For a full description of the amphitheatre and the documents relating to it, *NV* 3:47–48.

Roman temple dedicated to the Good Mother, adjacent to the city walls.

To this "small basilica" must have belonged the bas-relief that we see today mounted on the lunette of today's beautiful cathedral portal. Here the Martyr Bishop appears for the first time, together with God the Father amid the moon and the stars, and the Virgin, who is suckling the Baby.[57] His head is bare, his beard shaved, his hair cut short over the ears; he wears a pontifical chasuble and presses the Gospels against his chest, that Book for which he knew how to fight and die so bravely. An indescribable mixture of emotions seems to emanate from the rough sculptured black stone figure—horror and love, crude ferocity and simple faith. It speaks to us of the devotion of the people, who never ceased to suffer from terror of divine punishment, who were obsessed by the idea of achieving greatness for their city through the power of their saint, a people equally ready to cry out in entreaty at the altar and in ferocity in battle.[ee]

The people of the city had their martyrs as the feudal lords had their paladins. Francis himself did not hesitate to rank as equal brave feats consecrated with blood for either the triumph of the Faith or the triumph of justice. In the same way, the dream of being a knight, which was greater than anything else to him in his youth, was changed after his conversion into a dream of being a martyr. He was "burning intensely with the desire for holy martyrdom," Thomas of Celano wrote of him.[58]

After the erection of San Rufino, attendance there steadily increases. The bishop is first obliged to appoint some priests of the cathedral (then Santa Maria Maggiore) to serve at San Rufino; later,

---

ee. Fortini gives the generally accepted (and most likely) interpretation of the crude but strong figures over the main doorway. Over the centuries a variety of other symbolic meanings have been read into them, each arousing strong local passions. A recent one is by a present canon of the cathedral, Don Mario Pierluca, who sees in the central figure Christ surrounded by symbols signifying the Light of the World and the Supreme High Priest. Holding the Gospels in his left hand and raising his right in blessing, the figure represents the Gospel passage, "Full authority has been given to me both in heaven and on earth . . . know that I am with you always, until the end of the world!" The mother nursing a baby he believes to be a symbol of the church, spouse of Christ, who nurtures the human race; the bishop, a symbol of the hierarchy; and the three small heads, representations of the architect, a patron, and Rainerio, the eleventh century prior who built the church (rather than Bishop Rufino's son and two deacons, all martyred—the usual interpretation).

The intriguing carvings that surround these central figures have been equally the subject of speculation and argument. As Stanislao da Campagnola relates in *L'Angelo del Sesto Sigillo* (pp. 42–45), among the interpretations are that they are scenes inspired by the Old Testament Genesis, the New Testament Revelation, and the teachings of both the Catholic faith and of history (Elisei, *Studio sulla chiesa cattedrale di S. Rufino* pp. 33–62). Another is that they are complex symbols representing the equally complex theories of Joachim of Fiore (Prosperi, *La facciata della cattedrale di Assisi*). The intensity of the interest in these matters and of the arguments about them tell a great deal about life in Assisi!—Trans.

to establish a presbytery or priests' house. We find the name of the prior in 1029, Leto, and those of some of the canons, Adamo, Martino, Franco.[59]

At this same time the first communal government is being organized around the prior of San Rufino. Originally, he was considered a representative of the bishop, but little by little he separated himself from the bishop and finally became autonomous.

These same years saw the rising of the class of *buoni uomini* (or *boni homines*), the important men of the city: feudal lords who had moved into the city from the country, judges, notaries.[ff] In legal proceedings we find them beside the bishop, the dukes of Spoleto, and the royal legates; from the early part of the eleventh century, we know their names.

The first independent city government was none other than the free organization of these *boni homines,* who joined together to assert their right to judge in civil and criminal trials, to administer the communal patrimony, and to provide everything necessary for the needs of the city. For some time they and the bishop acted together; but then, desiring greater independence, they allied themselves with the prior of San Rufino.

Naturally this did not happen without fierce quarrels. The bishop did not resign himself to the loss of supremacy. From the situation came a bitter conflict between the bishops and the city people, lasting through a number of more or less acute crises and terminating only with the miracle of reconciliation effected by Saint Francis on the eve of his death. It is probable that the establishment of the episcopal citadel in Assisi took place in the early years of the eleventh century.

Santa Maria, the cathedral, began to decline rapidly. It had no relics to venerate, no holy bodies of which to boast, no miracles to excite the people. In the minds of the people there now was but one church: San Rufino, the *domus,* the house of the people of Assisi.

Thus the first prayer to be found in the records, amid the monotonous succession of notarial records and tiresome legalistic jargon,[gg] is a plea to Saint Rufinus for protection against the evils that constantly hover over all persons and all things:

---

ff. The *buoni uomini* appear in the history of all Italian cities, always indicating the class invested with command and public power, made up of nobles, judges, notaries—the magnates of the city. In Assisi the records make it clear that this class was predominantly made up of the feudal lords of city and country. *NV* 2:131–32.

gg. This elegiac poem, preserved for us by Di Costanza (*Disamina*, p. 424), was in a codex of the Chiesa Collegiata di Santa Maria of Spello. It is now lost. The poem is of a form

Sancte Ruphine, tuos jugiter defende famulos,
Exaudi populos, Sancte Ruphine, tuos.

O Saint Rufinus, always protect your servants;
Hear the prayer of your people, O Holy Saint.

Grando nec ignis edax perimat hos nec mala pestis . . .
Tristia bella tere . . . . . Et lites remove . . .

Protect us against devastating hail, devouring fire,
Against hunger and pestilence, war and futile strifes.

Nec segetes pereant campo, nec vitibus uve;
Omnia salvifica. Nec segetes pereant.

Grant that the harvests will be good,
That the grapes will be safe.

Tu pius atque bonus, iustus, insonsque benignus
Et nostra salus. Tu pius atque bonus.

You who are pious and good, just, innocent, and kind;
You, our salvation.

A new era has begun in the city. A heady youthfulness seems to be
breaking out of the worn stones like an unexpected flowering in an
ancient wall. But unchanged is the structure that is presiding over it
in the piazza still cluttered with ruins, the Roman temple dedicated to
Minerva.

The Threat of the Merchants

This central piazza still has the same name that it did in Roman days,
Piazza della Minerva. In Saint Francis's lifetime it was also called—as
it had been in the Roman period—the forum. It was the first nucleus

widespread during the eleventh century. It surely is of a time when the new people of the
commune were looking at their patron saint as both a help and a symbol in the beginning
struggle against their oppressor lords. Fortini, *Assisi nel medioevo*, pp. 51 and 75.—Trans.

of commercial activity in the city, in a pattern that was characteristic of the fully developed commune.[hh]

From the time of the Frankish kings, as a matter of fact, the dependents of the manors had gathered here to sell their crops and small necessities. Later, a permanent market was established with shops, warehouses, commercial displays, and the offices of notaries. Because of that the piazza in this medieval period was also called the Mercato or Market. The name *Mercatum* appears for the first time in a 1093 document, evidence that a century before the time of Saint Francis, the city had both embarked on and consolidated its mercantile and commercial activity.

In this new millenium all Italian cities have been seized by a mania for trade, by land and by sea, with the east and the west. The seigniorial estates decay as the merchants assert their supremacy, a supremacy based on money. They constitute a new and heterogeneous class, turbulent, very much occupied with buying and selling, jealous, vain, fractious. In importance it is a class rivalling that of the feudal lords.

The two classes, merchants and lords, are locked in a struggle. Both are powerful, both are proud. The feudal lords envy the riches of the parvenus, who in turn yearn to emulate the lords—in responsibilities, honours, arms, even in knightly rank. A 1203 document in the communal archives of Assisi defining the responsibilities of the commune for offences committed against the privileged classes ranks the *milites* (warriors) and *mercatores* (merchants) at the same level.[60] By then the merchants are taking part in the government of the city and the administration of the common goods.

By the end of the eleventh century Assisi merchants have already established important connections with France. In the cathedral archives is a paper of March, 1065,[61] previously unknown, that is important to the Franciscan story: in the text, which deals with the sale of a piece of ground, there is a reference to a "Guido *francisco*" ("Guido, 'the Frenchy' or 'the Frenchman'"). Anticipated here by more than a century is the thinking through which Saint Francis, son

---

hh. Since Roman days the life of the city has been—and still is—concentrated on this central piazza, now known as the Piazza del Comune or the Piazza della Minerva. Its location reflects the usual Roman pattern for cities: a central point where the main streets meet and flow into one another. Some idea of the Roman look of the city may be obtained by visiting the excavation under the present piazza, where the remains of the forum may still be seen: the Roman wall, the names of the *quatuorviri* and *quinqueviri* (four man and five man council) who supervised the construction, the tetrastyle on which once stood statues of Castor and Pollux. As in most Italian cities, the forum was transformed into the official marketplace. *NV* 3:11–12. (See also chap. 3, n.u.)

of a merchant who spent much of his life in France, will become known by the name of Francesco (Francis) rather than by his baptismal name of Giovanni (John). In the same way Assisi records show that those who participated in the Crusades or lived in the lands of the "infidels" were often called "Saracino" ("Saracen").

By the twelfth century the activity of the merchants assumes enormous importance. The great fair of Champagne, the most famous of all fairs from 1150 to 1300, was the international market for the exchange of goods between the peoples of the Mediterranean and the North Sea. There merchants from France and from Flanders, Germans and Englishmen, Catalans and Arabs of Spain, men of Languedoc and of Provence, Jews and Samaritans, Levantines and Westerners assembled.

The influx of Italians was impressive. These were Lombards of Piacenza, Parma, Vercelli, and Pavia; Piemontese of Asti, Alba and Chieri, come through the mountain passes of Mont Cenis, Great Saint Bernard, Simplon; Genovese come by the Marseilles road; Bolognese and Romans.

The Tuscans were among the first, with a movement of merchandise and money that even today is astonishing. In Paris an entire quarter was inhabited by Florentine merchants. The Sienese lent money to the French court and also to the king of France. Merchants of Lucca and Pistoia dominated the wool and silk markets. Each had his own jurisdiction. They all enjoyed fiscal exemptions, immunity from execution and reprisals, safe conduct for their trips.[62]

All these multitudes who practiced the most diverse customs, spoke the most diverse languages, came from every port, descended from every mountain, had a common goal: profit. It drove them to leave their houses, venture forth on unsafe roads, travel for weeks and months, fight against armed gangs holding mountain passes, deal with tolls and ransoms, clamber up vertiginous mountain peaks, skirt the edges of glaciers, sail on frail boats on which they braved tempests and attacks by pirates. Each of their trips was like going into battle; each return something akin to a miracle.

Saint Francis's father, Pietro Bernardone, an exceedingly rich cloth merchant, will be one of these, drawn to the fair in Champagne to buy *panni franceschi* (the finest French and Flemish fabrics), and other textiles woven in Flanders, Holland, England, Brabant. He will become, according to the term used in the statutes of the time, a *franciarolo,* a merchant specializing in the sale of *panni franceschi,* as distinguished from a *tagliarolo,* who sold all kinds.[63] It is probable that he, following the usual custom of joining other merchants to make the trips under the command of an appointed leader, went with the Tuscan caravans, particularly those from Florence. The fact that he is named in a sixteenth-century source as one of the most prominent merchants of the Tuscan region would seem to confirm this supposition.[64]

The two most important fairs of Champagne were those held in Provins during May and in Troyes from the middle of July to the fourteenth of September. The latter, called the "warm fair of Champagne," was the most propitious for the Italian merchants, who had to go by sea (as the Florentines and the Sienese, who usually went by ship to the ports of Provence, had to do) or to cross over the Alps. In many contracts preserved in the archives of Italian cities is the notation that a required payment will be made "at the next fair of Troyes."[65]

Assisi was especially well situated for this commercial traffic, being on a road that would today be called a main artery of communication. It linked Rome and France, and therefore was called Strada (or Via) Francesca (or Francigena). There is a reference to it in an eleventh-century document of the cathedral. This road went along the foot of the hill and so was also called "the road at the base of the mountain." Where the Ospedale delle Pareti once stood, it joined another road coming down from Assisi, one that, passing by the monastery of San Nicolò dell'Orto, went directly to Porziuncola.[ii]

The people of the city listened open-mouthed to the talk of the merchants who came back from France. All the goods of the earth, the delights of both East and West, the most splendid riches, the rarest treasures, the most exquisite articles, were to be found for a short time, they said, in the fabulous fair.

Entire roads shone with embossed golds, silvers, ivories, piled up in open coffers, caskets, cases. There were such heaps of fine pearls and jewels that they could be measured out in grain ladles. Counters disappeared under the accumulations of tapestries, rugs, and furs. There were warehouses where one walked on silk and velvet.

In one district the acrid odor of spices and drugs, redolent in the great heat of summer, cut off the breath as in a market of Aleppo or

---

ii. The Via (or Strada) Francesca was of special importance in the Middle Ages since it linked Rome and France. It went up along the Tiber, through Orvieto and then toward Assisi, and from there to the border of Lake Trasimeno. It continued through Arezzo, Bologna, Modena, and along the ancient Via Emilia; from there, after crossing the Po Valley, it went over the Gran San Bernardo, Mont Cenis, and the hill of Tena. It followed the route of old Roman roads. Appropriate maps were in use, and they showed the cities or *stationes* where the traveller could stop for rest. It was used not only by merchants but also by pilgrims, ambassadors, *condottieri* and their armies. For further details and a description of the records concerning it in the Assisi archives: *NV* 3:70–71.

Damascus. There were sacks of cinnamon and cardamon, cloves and cinnamon sticks and ginger, indigo and spiced gum, pepper, and saffron.

In another, perfumes and incense on fires atop tripods raised sweet smelling clouds. In still another, slaves were ranged in long files, like beasts of burden on the open square. Young women, both black and white, some marvellously beautiful, were among them. Upon request they were shown almost nude. And there was an emporium for grain, and one for wine, and one for oil, and another for iron, and another for steel, and others for leather, salt, coal.

But the greatest of all the attractions was the display of fabrics, so famous that this fair in its last period was called the *foire de draps.*

No fabric that the skill and industry of the various peoples could produce was lacking. Among them were changeable silks, sendals so thin that they made only a tenuous veil to cover the flesh, brocades heavy with raised embroidery, bedcovers decorated with arabasques, worsteds, camel's hair, embossed velvets—black and vermilion, with arabasques and flowers, white satins—some shining with double twists of gold and silver, some twilled, some plain, half-satins, cloths of Normandy, Flanders, Cornwall.

The fair was jammed. A huge crowd milled about through the covered streets, along the vaulted passageways, under the loggias of the privileged nations. Here were notaries busy drawing up legal documents, employers, brokers, clerks, appraisers, connoisseurs, sergeants of the count of Champagne, consuls of the cities, captains of the caravans.

The last two weeks of September were allotted to settle the accounts, the work of moneychangers and bankers. Great rivers of coins flooded the counters, inundated the warehouses, overflowed along the wooden arcades, money of every denomination and of every nation: Saracen *bisanti,* Florentine florins stamped with the figure of Saint John the Baptist, Parisian *lire, lire* of Lucca, Apostolic ducats, Venetian ducats, *genovini* of Genoa. All that money created a certain delirium. Tempers blazed up, quarrels broke out, and shouts and threats. The hate and jealousy between the cities, between the partisans of the various nations, between the different sects and opposing religious groups, overtook and added fuel to the greed of buyers and sellers.[jj]

The description of Pietro Bernardone contained in the *Legenda*

---

jj. This description of the fairs covers all the medieval period, as is obvious from the coins mentioned, some in use during the lifetime of Saint Francis and even earlier, some appearing a bit later.—Trans.

Versificata of Henri d'Avranches can well be employed to describe the international merchant of that time: "Dominated solely by the instinct of lucre, master of swindles, interested always in increasing his business and in laying snares, haughty and wheedling all at the same time, now treacherous, now violent."[66]

Assisi's Patron Saint

It must have been Assisi merchants who went to the fair in Troyes who toward the middle of the eleventh century brought back an account of the events in that city that made a deep impression on those devoted to Saint Rufinus.

Troyes also had its martyr, Saint Patroclus, but no one had paid much attention to him until the story of his martyrdom was rediscovered. From that moment he became a famous saint, as was fitting for a city to which all the people of the world came. The citizens built a large basilica over his relics, where every year they solemnly celebrated the day of his death.[67]

On learning of this, the people of Assisi nursed a rival aspiration: to discover the story of the martyrdom of *their* patron saint.

In two codices, one of Perugia and the other of Spello,[68] a certain Maurino tells how he accomplished the difficult task. He was already an old man, and he felt that he could not close his eyes without first learning, in all its details, the story of that glorious martyrdom.

The stories of the martyrs, he wrote, are for troubled men what medicine is for the sick. These valiant soldiers of Christ had not feared the threats of judges; and they had received the palm of martyrdom in the midst of tortures, and thus entered into glory. But we, he said, do not have the strength unaided to follow their wonderful example. The old man needed comfort, for it seems that the abuse of a cruel lord had ruined his life. So he left Assisi on his anxious quest to discover the deeds of Blessed Rufinus, Bishop, and of Cesidius, his son. He wandered all over Campania in search of information, but without success, so that his heart filled with pain and bitterness.

Nevertheless [he said], God, who created the world and strengthened it with the blood of martyrs, cannot permit the memory of their deeds to be lost. His faith was justified, for when he reached Anagni, he made the acquaintance of a monk by the name of Giorgio, who knew how to read. He followed him to the monastery, gave him some money, and after many entreaties, persuaded him, after he had consulted the proper ancient documents, to write down the desired history.

Incipit Passio Sancti Ruphini Episcopi. It was the poem of which the citizens had dreamed, the legend of heroism and of sanctity destined to become a living thing to all succeeding generations. It was the wonderful story told to lull Saint Francis when he was an infant.

Bishop Rufinus was preaching the Gospel in the city of Amasia, in Ponto, when by order of the proconsul, he was arrested, along with his son Cesidius. To convert him to the pagan religion, the proconsul sent two women to the jail who were skilled in the art of magic, Nicea and Aquilina. No sooner had they entered than a great light struck them and made them fall to the ground. Thus they came to know the true faith, and they received baptism from the hands of Bishop Rufinus himself. By order of the proconsul, they were cruelly beaten with iron rods and then decapitated.

According to the legend, soldiers who had assisted in the torture were also converted, and finally, so was the proconsul himself. After having liberated Rufinus and his son, he was murdered by his own pagan soldiers. But Rufinus and Cesidius continued to spread the Gospel and at last they came to Assisi.

Here the proconsul, Aspasio by name, ordered that they be brought before him. For the people of Assisi, the story now reaches its crucial part in a dialogue between the proconsul, the *comes* or count, the lord who governs for the Roman emperor, and Rufinus, the servant of the Lord Jesus Christ, and in the events that follow.

Rufinus resists all threats and bravely declares, "I fear neither you nor your emperors."

They beat him with whips with pieces of lead tied at the ends. They strike him on the mouth with stones. They throw him into a fiery furnace. While the flames are blazing up, the proconsul says, "Let us see if your god knows how to liberate you from my hands." This is exactly what happens, for the Angel of God comes, walks into the flames, and brings him out to safety.

At last the emperor himself sentences him: "Tie a great rock about his neck and throw him into water so deep that the Christians cannot retrieve him."

It is done. They tie a millstone around his neck and throw him into the river. "On the eleventh day of August he completed his martyrdom, *glorificans Patrem et Filium et Spiritum Sanctum, et cum eo regnat et permanet in saecula saeculorum.*"[69]

The people of Assisi were exultant. They had found what they had been searching for so long, a noble claim to fame for both the old and the new city, a story of valour before which all the French and Lombardian legends of heroism and chivalry grew pale. The fame of the saint swept through the neighbouring areas and spread to other regions. Many came to Assisi seeking miracles. It was enough to kneel outside the crypt where the saint's body was buried that the blind should receive their sight, the crippled walk, the insane return to peace.

Saint Pier Damiani wrote of one of these miracles.

Twelve robbers entered a peasant's house, tied him up, and made off with his cows and sheep. The victim wept and invoked the aid of Saint Rufinus. And suddenly, despite the fact that the robbers were by then a good dozen miles away with their loot, the man's beasts came running in great haste and, mooing and bleating, went back into the barn.

Places blessed by the possession of relics of the saints are bits of heaven on earth. "Divine Providence," the Holy Doctor concludes, "elects them to preserve, almost as if in interim deposit, those blessed bodies that one day will be reunited to their spirits in the reign of eternal light."

·2·

THE WORLD OF SAINT FRANCIS: WARRIORS AND MERCHANTS

The eleventh century search for the story of Saint Rufinus and the development of Assisi as a place of pilgrimage had a great deal to do with shaping both the spirit of the city and events in it. In a curious way, this chapter of city history is a drama that would be re-enacted on a greater scale in the future. It also gives us great insight into the society that already had in it seeds that would mature a century and a half later in the lives of Saint Francis and "the Men of Penitence of the city of Assisi."

Bishop Ugone, who, according to cathedral records,[a] governed the church in Assisi from 1036 to 1052, was fired with great zeal to bring about a renewal of devotion to Saint Rufinus. He loved to sign himself the successor and vicar of that martyr bishop, *Ugo episcopus vicarius Sancti Rufini,* in the same way that the pope is called "the Vicar of Our Lord Jesus Christ."[1] But at the same time he grieved over the decline of his own church, the cathedral of Santa Maria Maggiore, where the ranks of the faithful were constantly growing thinner.

By his time, the canons of the church of San Rufino were vaunting the title of *maggiori,* in contrast to those of Santa Maria Maggiore, who had become *minori.*[b] The two Latin adjectives *maiores* and *mi-*

---

a. Records in cathedral archives are used as the basis for the dates of Bishop Ugone's episcopacy, although there is some disagreement about whether fasc. 1, no. 30, is of the year 1036 or 1042. The last record in which he appears is dated 1052; however, the name of no other bishop appears in the surviving records until 1059 (fasc. 1, no. 63), when Agino is named.—Trans.

b. Records in the cathedral archives reflect a growing rivalry between the bishop and the canons of San Rufino during the eleventh century, a struggle very plain in fasc. 2, no. 44, of the

45

nores were used by the medieval Italian to measure and classify power, virtue, nobility, authority. There were *maggiori militi,* greater fighting men, and *minori militi,* lesser warriors, *maggiori* and *minori* townsmen. Even the merchants are by now divided into three grades: *maiores, sequentes, et minores,* according to their wealth. In battle, the *mercanti maggiori* fight on horseback with cuirass, lance, and sword, the *sequentes* also fight on horseback with lance and sword but without the cuirass, the *minori,* on foot with bows and arrows.[2]

Ugone had been willing enough to receive his consecration at San Rufino, which constituted official recognition of this church as the new cathedral, where the people would assemble on the high solemn feasts of Christmas, Easter, Ascension, and Pentecost. On the altar of the Martyr Saint Rufinus, Ugone unfurls his gonfalon and lays down a naked sword, symbol of his jurisdiction.[c]

Nevertheless, he continues to mourn over the old cathedral dedicated to Our Lady of the Assumption, with its heavy arches and powerful Byzantine columns, its episcopal chair of carved stone, its altar adorned with mosaics. For some time he prudently seeks to keep the two churches on the same level, in prerogatives, honours, tithes, and revenues. We can see this in the records, in which the *Casa de Sancte Maria* is listed first, then the *Casa de Santo Rufino qui est Episcopium.*

This works for some time, for Ugone is imperious, like his predecessors. He sits with the *buoni uomini* in the judgements of God, the trials by combat, which are held on the banks of the river where Saint Rufinus was martyred. He challenges those who refuse to pay him his due revenues or recognize the rights of the bishop, receives fields and vineyards as donations, gives emphyteutic leases to tenants.

In authority and constructive tenacity he surpasses all his predecessors. In 1048 he is head of a legation of Roman prelates who go to Worms to come to an agreement about the election of the new pope,

---

year 1117, in which the bishop transfers lands that had belonged to Santa Maria Maggiore, the first cathedral, to the canons and prior of San Rufino, who are clearly dealing with the bishop on the same level of authority. Fortini, *Assisi nel medioevo,* p. 76, n. 68.—Trans.

c. The church of San Rufino was obviously already considered the cathedral before Bishop Ugone assumed his office; not only is it termed the cathedral in some earlier records but also Ugone was consecrated there. The consecration of the bishop always took place in the cathedral; he went there ceremoniously on horseback and was solemnly seated on the episcopal throne by the advocate of the church.

The stories and legends surrounding the denomination of San Rufino as the Assisi cathedral and the building of the new church surely come from the beginning of the struggle of the "new people" of the commune against feudal lords—among whom was numbered the bishop. Even the site of San Rufino, the same today as of the first small church built to house the remains of the saint, indicates that it was both a symbol and a source of strength to the emerging new classes, for it was placed on the ancient place of public assembly called Parlascio. Fortini, *Assisi nel medioevo,* pp. 49, 51.

Leo IX.[3] To his participation in this election is due the tradition, still alive up to a few years ago, that the church of Assisi has the right to vote in the election of popes.

Eventually, though, the rivalry between the two churches, the older one favoured by the bishop and the other by the people, breaks into rowdy conflict. We find the details in another page of the *Sermons* of Saint Pier Damiani. His story about Assisi's church of San Rufino merits being told in detail. From this author, it is impossible to discount that it rests on historical foundations.

Saint Pier Damiani's Story

After the body of Saint Rufinus had been taken out of the river, it was placed in a stone coffin (in Costano) that had earlier served as the container for the mixed ashes of two young lovers. Paradoxically, it was an old Roman sarcophagus encircled by the very gods that Rufinus had contemptuously smashed, depicted in open exaltation of pagan sensuality.

It is not easy to explain precisely what the unknown sculptor had intended to signify by his complex elegy in marble, which still exists in the deserted crypt of the Assisi cathedral. The passionate love story of Selene and Endymion is depicted in voluptuous figures: the goddess and her sleeping shepherd, surrounded by Aurora and Terra and Somnus, a host of naked cupids, and lovely nymphs, slender and supple, their breasts uncorrupted by the centuries.[4]

But this creation to lull the dead in their darkness was only of brief comfort to the lovers. Their ashes were scattered in some ancient time, and their sarcophagus was consecrated to the worship of the true God and used to shelter the body of Rufinus, the Confessor of Christ. But that, too, lasted only a brief period. According to Saint Pier Damiani, the relics were soon removed and placed in the small church dedicated to him.

No one paid further attention to the old abandoned sarcophagus on the shingle bed of the river. But at last, when in a season of flood the river burst forth and threatened the sarcophagus, the people, aroused by the newly discovered story of their first bishop's martyrdom, swarmed onto the bank to take it inside the city walls.

The revered sarcophagus was lifted onto a cart drawn by white oxen, and the procession got underway. Trumpets sounded and responsories rang out. But suddenly an uproar arose stronger than any trumpet call or song. Bishop Ugone had announced his intention. Since the church of Santa Maria Maggiore did not have the good fortune of having the relics of the first bishop, it would have the consolation of the empty sarcophagus.

The people retorted that the fate of the body had been ordained by divine will and could not be changed. Who was impertinent enough to separate the body from its safeguard, the Martyr from his sepulchre? And who was presuming to issue orders in the house of the people?

Tempers rise; the furor increases; violent proposals boil up. We see in the surviving records and in a painting in the cathedral the names and fiery faces of the factions: Bishop Ugone. The priest Raino. The canons of San Rufino, inciting the people to rebel against the bishop's decision. The canons of Santa Maria Maggiore. The company of *buoni uomini*—Albello d'Alberico, Aldo's sons Immo and Anastasio, Eldibrando, Maginardo, Guglielmo, Madio, Rodolfo, Grimaldo, Baroncello, Bonizo, Grifo, Stefano d'Aguso, Giovanni di Gizo, Leo di Immo, Orso di Vitale. All the heterogenous men of the people—merchants, wool workers, master carpenters, stonecutters, tavern keepers, potters, millers.

The procession reaches the bridge of San Vittorino. The setting sun makes a bonfire of dancing flames around the crosses, the burning candles, the red chasubles, and the coarse blue garments of the artisans, all on the silent plain slashed by the furrows of dry stream beds.

The line comes to a halt after it passes the old Roman gate, from which two roads lead into the city, one going through the piazza to San Rufino, the other through the bishop's territory to Santa Maria Maggiore.

The white sarcophagus with its tantalizing nymphs stands above the sea of faces. By now everyone is shouting insults, imprecations, derisive remarks, challenges, threats. Then the first sword gleams, and instantly everyone noisily gets out a weapon. A forest of swords, daggers, axes, and knives is raised above the mob. Men strike out in cleaving blows and blind slashing strokes.

Then, says Saint Pier Damiani, a miracle happens. No one falls down wounded; no blood flows. The swords do not strike human bodies. The Patron Saint sees to it that there is no bloodshed among his people.

Sixty men of the bishop's party come forward to take the sarcophagus to Santa Maria Maggiore. They are not able to raise it so much as an inch. Seven men of the people's faction pick up the marble as if it were a bit of straw and carry it to the new cathedral.[d]

---

d. There is a painting of this stormy procession at the base of a triptych by Nicolò Alunno in the museum of the cathedral. Also, in the lectionary of the cathedral there is an even more

Thus Saint Rufinus makes known his sympathies. In the conflict between the bishop and the people, he takes the side of the people.[5]

The People's Saint

Ugone was not a man to give up easily. In the rest of his sermon, Saint Pier Damiani tells us that he refused absolutely to yield to the people's triumph and flew into a rage. He prepared to take revenge on those who had dared to oppose him. They, for good enough reason fearing his anger, declared that they were ready to submit to his wishes. But once again the Martyr intervened.

He appeared one night to the priest Raino, prior of San Rufino, and ordered him to go to Bishop Ugone and ask him to take no reprisals against the people, but to restore to them the grace of his blessing and love. "What happened," the Blessed Rufinus told him, "was my doing. It was my will that the sarcophagus should be carried into my church and that in it what remains of my body should find peace. This Raino should know: if I had not thrown myself into the thick of the fighting and made myself the target of all the blows, there would have been a great number of dead lying all over the city."

The bishop, who had refused to accept the events as miracles, did not believe what the priest told him. It was necessary for Saint Rufinus to send a second messenger, a poor witless creature whom he miraculously restored to health. He repeated word for word what the priest Raino had said. So Ugone could only resign himself to defeat.

He now seconded the proposal to build a new cathedral, and he decided that it should be no longer a "small basilica" but a great church. He also ordered that a second great new feast day for Saint Rufinus be held on August 11, the anniversary of his martyrdom, and said that everyone in the diocese was obligated to observe it, along with the older feast day of August 3, the anniversary of the dedication of the first church.

The struggle between the city, with its new claim to power, and the men of the *castelli* of the countryside, who were refusing to submit to its rule, had already begun. This conflict, a long and stormy one that is to reach its climax during Saint Francis's youth, is surely the background for Saint Pier Damiani's description of this new feast day.

Some of the people (especially in the rural areas), moved by envy

---

popular version of the story, considerably more embellished with miraculous events; see Fortini, *Assisi nel medioevo,* pp. 48–49.—Trans.

We owe to Saint Pier Damiani this version of the story of the sarcophagus. He attributes it to Bishop Ugone, from whom he says he learned the details when the bishop stayed for a time at the monastery of Fonte Avellana. Cajetan, ed., *Petri Damiani,* 2:178–84.

or old grudges, rebel against the new episcopal edict. They say that two feasts are too much for one saint and that they, who have to work, cannot afford to pay attention to the fantastic notions of prelates, always in search of pretexts to make money. The men of Isola (Bastìa) arrogantly complain more bitterly than anyone else. When the new feast day comes around, they ostentatiously go to work as usual—the women to their looms, the men to the fields.

But fires blaze up in their houses. The beds are burned, the tables, the benches, the cupboards, the shuttles, the carding combs, the spindles, the looms. The tools of those who have been hoeing, digging, and driving the animals are burned. The *villa* catches on fire; the fields themselves go up in flames; and soon the people, too, are wrapped in flames. They run shrieking to the river and throw themselves into the water. They immerse their half-consumed belongings. The fire burns on. At last they realize that the fire is a punishment for their arrogance. Singed, smelling like smoking coals, they rush to the church of the Martyr and throw themselves in front of the altar, crying aloud for mercy. Immediately the fires go out and they return to Isola, safe and sound.

All this is a stimulus to work on the new cathedral. The people, passionate, fanatic, pugnacious, set about building their church and their life, using the wood of the forests and stones from the ruins that surround them.

The master carpenters go out to the surrounding forest to cut down trees, split planks, and prepare cross beams. There all this activity attracts the attention and arouses the jealousy of their bitter rivals, the men of the neighbouring city of Perugia.

One day (it is still Saint Pier Damiani who speaks) as they make ready to carry to the church a beam of oak, already finished, squared and smoothed, some Perugini waiting in ambush burst out, seize the beam, and drag it away, determined to take it to their own city. When they are only a mile from Perugia, the beam suddenly seems to be made of lead, and they can no longer lift it. They put in on the ground and take counsel. The beam resists every effort to move it, as if it had grown roots. Other men come in to help. They attach teams of oxen to it and make arrangements with great care. At a signal, all pull together, urging on the oxen, digging in their toes, shouting encouragement to each other. The beam remains fixed. Then the scales fall from their eyes. They understand they have committed a sacrilege. Turning their oxen toward Assisi, they in great humility restore the beam to the Martyr.

Thus, the people of the city say, Saint Rufinus fights in their ranks,

using the weapons at his disposal—the instruments of his martyrdom:
the fire that he passed through uninjured and the weight of the
millstone that took him to the bottom of the river.

At last the church is finished. Amid the flames of candles and
clouds of incense, the new hymn that Saint Pier Damiani has written
for the people rises.[e] It is no longer the ancient plea from supplicants.
It is a battle cry. The Patron is saluted as *bellator invictissimus,* most
invincible warrior.

> *Magnum Rufini meritum*
> *Turba canat fidelium;*
> *Quo mundi victor extitit*
> *Et liber astra petit;*
>
> *Bellator invictissimus*
> *Praebet ora lapidibus:*
> *Sed verbis grando lapidum*
> *Non indidit silentium;*
>
> *Plumbatis inde caeditur*
> *Iam iam obiisse creditur,*
> *Sed qui putatur mortuus*
> *Surgit in arma promptius.*

Sing, ye throng of the devout, of the great merit of Rufinus, who was a
victor in this world and who then free rose to the stars. Most invincible
warrior, his mouth has been smashed with stones, but the storm of
blows cannot smother his words. They beat him with leaded whips;
they believe him to be finished; but he who is believed to be dead rises
to his feet, more ready then ever to take up arms.

It was not now a hymn about a martyr; it was the story of miraculous deeds, new and old:

> *Certat martyr egregius,*
> *Ut leo vinci nescius . . .*

"The martyr fights valiantly, like the lion; he does not know the
meaning of defeat." This could be the motto of these new champions

---

e. This hymn to Saint Rufinus, which was certainly sung in Saint Francis's time, is still sung
on his feast day today.—Trans.

of the city, determined to make it supreme. To their protection Saint Rufinus has come, dressed in red and crowned with jewels—almost a new king.

Today nothing remains of the old Ugonian church, where once Saint Francis's own words echoed, but a part of the crypt, built of materials from the earlier structure.[f] Its presbytery [sanctuary] was where the bay just inside the entrance to the present church now is, so its apse must have been about where the first two interior columns now stand. The bell tower (the same one as now, minus the section over the second cornice, added later) was at the left of the apse. At the right of the apse was the baptismal font. It is still in place, now at the entrance to the church. The structure extended forward from about the façade of the present church to about the middle of the present piazza.[g] Beside it was the chapter house.

Inside the church there were three naves divided by stone columns; some of the Romanesque capitals from them have been preserved. One of them is now used for the holy water stoup; others are in the atrium of the sacristy. This stoup has known the touch of many hands over the centuries . . . among them, the hands of Saint Francis.

Once there were two small stairways leading to the crypt at each side of the altar. Both are now closed. The crypt (which would have been under the presbytery of the Ugonian church) is now a subterranean chamber with low vaults supported by six Roman columns, probably taken from the ruins of the ancient temple. The rough apse has a low bench projecting from the wall all the way around. The last vestiges of the Ugonian paintings are still visible: symbols of the Evangelists and the martyr Saint Constantius, the first bishop of Perugia, dressed in episcopal vestments and holding the New Testament.

There was no need in Ugone's day to discard the already existing foundation, and his people built the great church on it. A square cistern surviving from the ruins of the Roman city, built of enormous blocks of squared travertine, is on the site. On it are engraved in large characters the names of the Umbrian magistrates (among whom was a Rufinus) who had charge of the water supply in an extremely remote time, prior to the invasion by Rome. Not only did these *marones*,[h]

---

f. This crypt is a part of the first bay of the present church, which is formed from a part of the Ugonian church. The campanile, now near the façade of the cathedral, was also, as noted in the text, a part of the Ugonian church. For full description of the Ugonian church: *NV* 3:35–37.

g. The exact position of the church on the piazza will be seen in chap. 9 to be of considerable importance in locating the house of Saint Clare.—Trans.

h. *Marones:* see n. b, chap. 1.—Trans.

who were in charge of city building projects, construct the cistern, they also built the wall that enclosed the piazza and extended toward the amphitheatre. In it they put a fornix, an arched opening: *Murum ab fornice ad circum et fornicem cisternamque D.S.S. faciundum coiravere* ("They took care to build a wall from the public square to the amphitheatre and the arch").[6]

On this cistern the workmen placed the campanile, making it conform perfectly to the older structure, so that it constituted almost a natural continuation of it. One reason for their doing so must have been that the campanile could be used in decisive hours as a war arsenal; the *domus* was transformed often enough into a fortified house in the struggles against enemies, those both inside and outside the city. One of the requisites for a truly efficient strong tower was an underground cistern so that during a prolonged siege there would be an adequate supply of water.

It is an appeal to the city's ancient past and a marvellous symbol of a perfect continuity, this tower, a continuity not only in the stones but also in the love for their city in the hearts of the builders. These Ugonian builders had already placed the eastern wall of the church on the wall of the Umbrian *marones* when they adopted both the idea and the design born of the people's love for their city a thousand years earlier. In conformity to it, they fashioned a tower that is both sacred and warlike, from which the bell would ring out for prayer and for assembly, for peace and for war, for life and for death. They built it of stones from the quarry on the mountain, scarcely shaped, together with steps and cornices excavated from the ruins of the amphitheatre and the wedge-shaped pieces of the old fornix, which went down in the barbarian invasions.

Since then another millenium has gone by. This same tower, this old campanile, is still there, still living the life of its people.

The Heady Privilege of War

The new and youthful beat of life that had arisen within Assisi's ancient walls is suddenly revealed by the city's claim to a right that up until then had been the exclusive prerogative of the feudal lords: the right to make war.

War was a condition of life for every city. It was the sign of liberty, a joy of living. It was also the way to wealth and commercial expansion. Any means were acceptable to subjugate other cities, even an alliance with feudal lords and with the German emperor himself.

In the year 1054 there is a record of a war fought by Assisi against

Perugia.[7] Assisi, along with Foligno and Todi, was an imperial city; Perugia, a papal city.

It was the beginning of the long period of wars of city against city: Venice against Genoa, Genoa against Pisa, Pisa against Lucca, Lodi against Milan, Faenza against Ravenna, Verona against Modena, Florence against Siena and Arezzo, Rome against Velletri. Otto of Freising, the imperial jurist, held that these wars of the cities were acts of rebellion against the emperor, but the Peace of Constance in the end had to recognize this freedom. The cities, even when conquered, preferred war; it made them feel, with their very wounds, the happiness of existence, preferable to the sepulchral peace of the old feudal reign.

All the municipal chronicles abound with accounts of cruel and vulgar crowing and jeering over the humiliations inflicted on enemy cities. Here, an ass is hurled with the trabuch over walls under siege. There, horses are led to drink in the moats around city walls. Annual festivals are held in which pigs and asses represent people of the conquered cities.

There was no pity for prisoners, enemies from birth, killers of one's own people. Forlì shoed them like mules. Milan tied their hands behind their backs, wrapped them in straw, and ignited the straw.

The most monstrous expedients were used to collect ransom. Tortures were multiplied. Day by day mutilations and abuses were ladled out. The unfortunate victims were hung up by hands and by feet. Their teeth were wrenched out. Toads were stuffed in their mouths, "which," said a contemporary historian, "was the most dreaded of every kind of torture." Cremona interred its prisoners. It reduced them to quenching their thirst with oil for the lamps and eating the cadavers of their companions, which are not removed from the prison until the survivors paid the death tax. Aggressive Mantua prepared to attack Verona. It was instead invaded, sacked, its women violated, and the noses cut off three thousand of its inhabitants so that it would remember its bloody defeat. Florence destroyed Semifonti because its people went about singing:

> *Fiorenza, fatti in là,*
> *Che Semifonti si fa città.*

It may be freely translated as:

> Florence, go away!
> Semifonti's the city today!

Lucca put mirrors on the tower of Asciano so that the women of Pisa could look at themselves in them. Immediately all the Pisa people marched against Lucca and put mirrors below the walls of that city so that in turn the inhabitants could see on their own faces the fear that was killing them.[i]

Derisive songs were sung. Colossal inscriptions were raised, such as this one placed by the people of Pisa on the fort of Alice:

> *Scopa bocca al Zenvese,*
> *Crepe cuor al Portovenerese,*
> *Strappa borsello al Lucchese.*

It is a series of curses upon people of the nearby towns of San Zeno, Porto Venere, and Lucca:

> A mouth-battering to the Zenvese!
> A heart torn apart to the Portovenerese!
> The purse ripped off the Lucchese!

Renowned cities disappeared forever in this fury. In 1191 the people of Rome destroyed Tusculum and triumphantly crushed some of its most venerable monuments and put them on the Campidoglio.

In the time of Saint Francis, the people laughed at the agonies of enemies who were tortured and killed. They bragged with crude vulgarity about the things they had done to the women of the conquered cities. They made games of inflicting slow tormenting agonies. They shed blood now in arrogant wholesale slaughter, now with delicacy. Revenge—the vendetta—became a fixed idea.

Dante himself rode out in his commune's cavalcade against Caprona; he also fought against Arezzo. He was in the ranks of the select military group on the field of Campaldino. From this experience comes his description of Buonconte of Montefeltro, who flees with his throat pierced through, "staining all (his) course with (his) life's blood," and then falls, feeling life and speech ebbing away.[8]

And it is also Dante, the scornful poet, who in his *Inferno* opens with this cry the Florentine curses at the city that had become the chief Ghibelline center of Tuscany:

---

i. This strange exchange took place in the late thirteenth and early fourteenth centuries when the Lucchese took and held Pisa's tower of Asciano, and in the various exchanges between the cities, made the insulting and mocking remark about Pisa's women. See *Cronica di Pisa* (*RIS,* vol. 15); Carducci, *Cantilene e ballate,* p. 31.—Trans.

Ahi, Pisa, vituperio delle genti!

Oh, Pisa, foulest blemish to your land![9]

Marco Polo, the audacious Venetian who travelled to the fabulous empires of the Orient, participated after his return to Venice in the city's war against Genoa. He was captured and confined to a prison cell. It was there that he lived on his marvellous memories and dictated to a fellow prisoner the story of his travels, his *Milione.*

The Deadly Enmity of Assisi and Perugia

Saint Francis's gift for love would be revealed only after he himself took part in this incredible violence. It destroyed his youth.

In order to understand this essential point about his life, we must recall the implacable rivalry during the Middle Ages that divided Assisi and Perugia, the two cities on opposite sides of the Tiber, facing each other from the hills enclosing the sweet valley of the Porziuncola. Probably in the history of the wars of Italian communes there was no hatred so tenacious as this one. It began at the dawn of communal life and was extinguished only with the diminution of city autonomy at the time of the harsh papal restoration.[j]

At the end of the thirteenth century, Perugia, strong, powerful, heady from its rise to power, commissioned the carving of its superb poem of a fountain, the marble Fontana Maggiore, which glorifies the seasons, the arts, the saints, the heroes, the Guelph lion, the Perugia gryphon—a fountain with carvings of dream and reality, history and legend. At the same time Perugia also commissioned a poem to proclaim its enormous pride in itself, to celebrate the commune's wars, its armies, its victories, its conquests. The task of writing it was entrusted to Bonifazio da Verona, a poet who had been forced to flee from his own city by rabid Ghibelline feeling. He was also a master of astrology and a fortune teller good at reading destiny in the stars and making predictions in time of battle. His poem is the *Eulistea,* comprising nine books of Latin hexameters,[10] an ode about the descendants of Ulysses, the legendary founder of Perugia. The city introduces itself in these words: "The most noble Odysseus, founder of Perugia, led many wars against the Trojans. Who would wish to know me, know that I am the city of Perugia, risen in the shadow of the

---

j. The "harsh papal restoration" came in 1540, when after a long period of independent government, Perugia fell to the forces of Pope Paul III and came under a repressive government of the Papal States.—Trans.

strength of Rome. Fruitful and strong am I, free, ready to grant to all my protection."

> *Nobilis Eulistes, Perusine conditor urbis,*
> *Contra Troianos bella multa tulit.*
> *Urbs Perusina vocor, Rome reparata vigore;*
> *Fertilis et fortis sum, libera, prompta favore.*

This is the book that gives us an account of the war with Assisi in which Saint Francis participated, boastfully written *pro honore Communis Perusii,* as we read in *Annali decemvirali,* the annals of the ten councillors of Perugia.[k] Students of Franciscanism should study it well, if they would understand the full dimensions of the violence from which emerged Saint Francis's great dream.

The verse is rude, dry, laced with improper usages and barbarisms; but it has the same fierce power, the same vigour and impact, as does the façade of the commune's palace, which was, as a matter of fact, erected in the major piazza of Perugia at the same time.

There are many themes and emotions in this "heroic ode celebrating the deeds of the Perugini people." It is a poem about tyrants against their victims, conquerors against those they conquered, masters against servants. The Perugia gryphons scream in it.

In it the defeated citizens of Todi, conquered by Perugia, cry out, *O lux regionis!* "O light and mirror of this region; O you, who bow down the neck of the strong! O you, who reduce to nothing the pride of the powerful and the cunning of your shattered and oppressed enemies!"

In it the inhabitants of Foligno appear before us as they did in that terrible year of 1253 when, worn down by a cruel siege, they were forced to put themselves in the hands of their Perugini victors. The people, carrying their ensigns and accompanied by their magistrates, came out of their city gates and went to the field of their merciless enemy. They were all on foot; they all had ropes around their necks; they wore, to show their abject misery, only a minimum of clothing. In their hands they carried their unsheathed swords and their daggers, with the points turned against their own breasts. They fell on

---

k. Bonaini, Fabretti, and Polidori, *Bonifacii Veronensis* (*Arch. Stor. Ital.* 16:1–52). According to this poem, the magistrates of Perugia gave Bonifazio all possible help in the preparation of his work, including appointing men learned in the history of the city to help him and giving him free access to the original records of the commune. In confirmation of this is the fact that all the names mentioned in the poem are also to be found in the records of the time. Leaving aside the poetic images and lyrical flights, the work is, therefore, of tremendous historical importance. For a more detailed discussion of it: *NV* 2:166–67.

their knees and implored pardon for damages and offences. They were ordered to tear down their walls and fill up their moats. The gates and the keys of the conquered city were carried triumphantly to Perugia on a cart bright with scarlet, drawn by oxen also covered in scarlet, as were the men leading them.[11]

We see the humiliating scene repeated in 1289, in a new war fought despite the express prohibition of the pope. The leaders of the Foligno guilds again had to prostrate themselves at the feet of the consuls of Perugia, swearing that they would "adore and honour them after God." The Perugini were excommunicated, but that did nothing but increase their contemptuous behavior. Fra Salimbene wrote that "they made a pope and cardinals of straw and disgracefully dragged them through all the city of Perugia and then pulled them to a hill; and on the top of this hill they burned the pope that they had dressed in red. And so likewise they burned the cardinals, saying 'This is such-and-such a cardinal, and this is so-and-so.'"

Bonifazio continues his narration of the defeat of Foligno with a joke told by those who had returned laden with the spoils of the prostrate city: one must no longer say *Fulgineum* (the ancient name of the city, meaning light and shining) but *fulligo* (spot or grime)—it was a miserable heap of ashes whose survivors will have to live in constant awareness of their servitude:

> *Nil nobis aliud restat nisi iussa subire:*
> *Quae Perusinus agit, iubet, vult, integra fiant.*

To us nothing is left but to obey commands; therefore, whatever the Perugino does, orders, wishes, is to be completely fulfilled.

It was fatal to rebel. Here is the poet's apotheosis of the destruction of rebellious Castiglione, which took place during Saint Francis's youth: "Here the Perugino showed no pity. He demolished the walls, destroyed the palaces, burned the houses, murdered, and sacked. Nothing was respected, neither the innocence of babes nor the tender age of children nor the youth of adolescents. And not even the feebleness of the old saved them from the arrow. Here it was the will of the Perugino to repudiate every charity, forget every compassion, trample down every justice. War alone was his intention: to put down everything by the weight of his arms, to shatter his enemies. Crushed is the arrogance of Castiglione; destroyed is the presumption of Castiglione; the daring of Castiglione has had its reward."

There is a similar exaltation of Perugia's defeat of Gubbio in the same period. The Chiagio, which Dante describes as flowing down from the hill carrying the prayer of the holy bishop rapt in God,[12] in this work boils up with the blood of the massacred people of Gubbio: *Immatatus est Clasius a sanguine uccisorum.*

Even without recourse to the book of the astrologer-poet, one learns what the age was like by looking at the sinister façade of the Palace of the Priors. It still preserves intact the colours made by slaughter and fire, still flaunts its clawing gryphon and Guelph lion, still conjures the ghosts of murdered men in every window.

One thinks of those Bettona peasants who were led here in bonds, followed by their desperate women. "And all the women set out at the rear, so that the road seemed black, only to hear in Perugia the cry, 'Hang the dirty thieves!' "[13]

One thinks also of prisoners encaged in the tower prison, thrown from the windows of the palace, hanged on the chandeliers, murdered and dragged to the fountain, encircled by torturers who competed for the pleasure of the first blow. They were made to die slowly, for the entertainment of guests at lavish suppers to which women were invited to make the occasion more exciting. They were forced to march in a parade holding reeds from the swamp in their hands as a symbol of their impotence. They were ordered to ride backward on an ass, grasping the tail instead of the reins; made to walk between rows of people, dragging their humiliated flags in the dust behind them.

The same story continues throughout the medieval period. In August of 1335 the people of Arezzo almost reached the walls of Perugia; they arrived at the site of the public gallows; there they hanged their Perugini prisoners. For mockery they put lines of *lasche,* the small fish of Lake Trasimeno, inside their trousers; consequently, the Perugini were known derisively by the name of *"lasca*-eaters." At the side of the gallows they put a female cat as a caricature of the gryphon.

Three months later the Perugini were outside Arezzo. There they made prostitutes, their dresses held high, run the palio, the traditional race for a highly prized banner. They planted the Perugian flag on top of the cathedral, and in the cathedral they stamped money with the Perugian mint-mark. They chose a bishop of Arezzo and made him sing the Mass. "And besides all this," adds the chronicler, "many other shameful things were done that are not written here."

Five days later the avenging army returned home to Perugia, led by its gonfalonier. A triumphal procession was formed. First came the prostitutes dressed in red, riding red-caparisoned horses; next were carts drawn by oxen covered with red velvet, bearing columns and statues from the conquered Arezzo cathedral; and then the army, shouting and bawling. The statues of the saints, the sacred columns, the race of the prostitutes, are all depicted in the murals on the façade of San Lorenzo, the Perugia cathedral, on the side toward the piazza, a commemoration of the insult and its revenge.[14]

In this war Assisi fought with Perugia. It seems that it was the Assisani who destroyed the Arezzo cathedral, judging by a memorial plaque still existing, under the arch of the Santa Chiara gate in Assisi. It is set into the arch, along with two small columns; the Latin inscription reads: "These are the stones, or columns, taken as a memento from the Duomo of Arezzo, at the time that it was captured by the people of Assisi, who fought in the victorious Perugia army against the Aretini, in 1335, in the month of September." Because of it, the street that extends beyond this gate is still called the "Borgo Aretino."[15]

The truculent Gryphon crushed all its adversaries. Among them was a William dei Buonguglielmi, who died in 1335, at the age of ninety still in exile; he is buried in the atrium of the lower church of the Basilica di San Francesco in Assisi. An inscription there records that "a great iniquitous stroke of gryphon's wings" felled him: *alabus perusinis pulsus inique.*[16]

Dante, preparing to praise the infinite love of Saint Francis in the eleventh canto of *Il Paradiso,* contrasts it with the oppression that lurked in the shadows on the other side of the "high mountain":

> *onde Perugia sente freddo e caldo*
> *da Porta Sole e di rieto le piange*
> *per grave giogo Nocera can Gualdo.*

> Perugia breathes its heat and cold from there
> through Porta Sole, and Nocera and Gualdo
> behind it mourn the heavy yoke they bear.[17]

The heavy Perugian yoke, *grave iugum intolerabilis servitutis,* as it is described in certain Assisi documents of the early part of the fourteenth century, is a sober description of the tyrannous rule of Perugia.[18]

This threat hung over the city of the Subasio for more than five centuries.

"Assisani, pertinaceous enemies," a Perugian chronicler writes, in an account of the war that broke out in 1291 for rule over Cannara.

"And yet," he continues, "they must resign themselves to being under Perugia as chicks are under the mother hen."[19]

In 1321 the decisive war for the control of Umbria was fought. Perugia was, as always, the fiercely proud Guelph fortress; Assisi was at the center of the Ghibelline movement. Perugia's forces marched against Assisi, led by Cante Gabrielli of Gubbio, the man who passed sentence on Dante Alighieri, calling him a swindler and condemning him to be burned. After a year of siege, Assisi surrendered. One hundred Assisi people were killed amid the horrors of the sack. The walls were torn down and the city was reduced to an open, undefended area. The commune's statutes that had to do with the free government were butchered and revised to be suitable for the government of a subject city.[20]

But a few years later, the city was on its feet, brought to life again by its longing for revenge.

After the second half of the fourteenth century, the wars between Assisi and Perugia became countless. The famous Perugini captains, who fought as mercenaries in the service of the principal Italian seigniories, never forgot, even in the midst of their most ambitious schemes, their hatred of Assisi. This was the spirit in which Niccolò Piccinino laid siege to Assisi in 1442 at the head of an army of 20,000 adventurers. Lorenzo Spirito Gualtieri, who as a young man participated in this enterprise, along with his father, the notary of Porta San Pietro (of Perugia), wrote a poem about it:

> . . . *E venne a poner campo al forte Asese,*
> *popul crudele e malvicino, iniquo,*
> *che tanto fece danno al mio paese.*

> *Sempre era stato assai crudel nemico;*
> *il Capitano allor, volenteroso,*
> *venne per gastigar quell'odio antico.*

The siege was laid to strong Assisi, a cruel and wicked people, mean neighbours, who had greatly harmed my city. It had always been a merciless enemy; the Captain willingly came to chastise that old hatred.

To proposals that they ask for peace terms, the Assisani, though encircled by combined military groups from which there was no possibility of escape, responded that "they would eat their children before coming to terms with the Peroscini." Finally, on a dark

November night, the city was taken. No restraint was placed on the sacking. The fearful cruelty displayed can be read on the pages of the chronicler. The victor's hymn rises above the fires and the blood in savage joy:

Alfine aveva Iddio deliberato
questa cittade mettere a sterminio
per penitenza d'ogni loro peccato.

At last God decided to destroy this people as punishment for all its sins.

Still, in the hearts of the people of Assisi, who, in the poet's words, were subjected "to the swords' cutting edge," hate was stronger than defeat and disaster, even stronger than certain death. The example of Assisi women in this war is famous in the history of the struggles of Italian communes.

A great number of them took refuge in the Basilica di Santa Chiara, wives, mothers with their children, young girls. The candles on the altar had been lit. The nuns lay prostrate, with their foreheads on the floor, praying for a miracle. The door was suddenly thrown open and Piccinino entered. With him was a large group of his men, eager to get on with the annihilation of the Assisi people.

But let the chronicler who lived through that night of horror do the talking: " . . . The captain, seeing so many women and girls taking shelter there, said to these women, and especially to the nuns of Santa Chiara, that this was no longer a good place for them, and that they should choose where they wanted to go, because he would have them sent there safely. He named all the nearby areas, and at last suggested that he take them to safety in Peroscia. But when they understood him to suggest Peroscia, the nuns first and then the other women replied: 'We would rather burn than go to Peroscia.' Whereupon, hearing this reply, the captain immediately said: 'Sack, sack'; and thus everything was put to sack; the convent with the nuns, and the girls, and everything."[21]

But nothing was changed. In the second half of the same century, Maturanzio, the Perugian chronicler, shows us the Assisi militia in turn invading Perugia: "Ascesciani, warlike men and accustomed to arms, all wicked and desperate . . . And they kill and they loot . . . and thus keep the city of Peroscia in continual tribulation."

Everyone in Assisi, he said, was born armed and grew up armed. And homicide is a term of honour to them; and he who has not killed at least one of his enemies "thinks his life has served no useful purpose. . . . They are monsters who have killed as many babies and women as they have of their worst enemies."[22]

The warlike tradition is confirmed by the records of the time. In wills, for example, arms are bequeathed with the same care as are useful household articles.

In a will dictated June 2, 1276, by a Leonardo di Scescio is a bequest for his soul, enough for the making of three candles of three pounds each, to be used to light the altar of the church in which he will be buried. There is also a bequest for the lepers' hospital, another for the church of San Rufino for the tithes not paid and the first fruits not turned over, another to clothe the naked poor and to give them some bread and a plate of fava beans on the first day of December each year after his death. To his wife Benricevuta he restores her dowry of one hundred pounds and gives her the clothes that she wears, the bench, the *soppedana* or chest for the foot of the bed, the kitchen kneading trough, the fire chain, a kettle for oil, the cupboard, the large pin, and the combs for hemp fibres. To Giovannolo di Gilio go the farm in Litorta, also the breastplate and the gorget [for protecting the neck]; to the sons of Pietro, the vat, the keg, the large urn, the shield, the buckler, the *cervelliera* [a steel cap worn under a helmet for protection of the head], the sword, and the knife.[23]

The City's New Power

Since Perugia was a papal city, Assisi, in the struggle between the church and the emperor, had to be imperial.

We find the evidence in the records, from which more shades arise: a procession of men with sonorous names and troubled faces, who move against a noise of constant battle.

There are new bishops: Agino,[24] Giorgio,[25] Agino,[26] Dragone. This last bishop was forced to flee from the city and take refuge in the monastery of Fonte Avellana, where on March 28 of an unknown year (we are very likely in the early years of the twelfth century) a monk writes his name in the Book of the Dead: "Dragone, bishop of Assisi, who found asylum with us, passed from this life."[27]

There are new priors of the cathedral: Bernardo, Leto. They have allied themselves with the emperor and feudal lords and are fighting openly with the bishop. The records show them very busy receiving donations of new lands and houses in the city and in the surrounding territory, on the mountain and on the plain.

We find that the city had by now come out of the struggle between

Emperor Henry IV and Pope Gregory VII[1] with an imperial rescript
that guarantees its independence. Reference is made to it in a later
diploma of Frederick Barbarossa: " . . . That the city be free from
every authority, as it was from the time of Henry IV to this day."[28]

And then we find other bishops: Rainerio, Clarissimo. Other priors:
Vidone, Tebaldo. By this time the canons of San Rufino are presuming to ordain priests without the participation of the bishop. Clarissimo, indignant, appeals to Rome, where a college of cardinals and
bishops rules in his favour.

And we come at last to Prior Rainerio, in whose term of office in
the twelfth century the city extended its rule beyond the confines of
the old *comitato.*

Again the cathedral plays a major role. By the time of Rainerio, the
cathedral that Ugone built was no longer adequate. The *buoni uomini*
decided to build another, on the same site as the old one, but to the
rear of it, nearer the Roman wall, so as to allow more space for the
piazza in front, which was the place of public assembly. This is the
intention pervading a noteworthy document of 1134 in the cathedral
archives,[29] in which the owners of the land between the Roman wall
and the basilica declare their intention to cede it, "to the end that
there will be sufficient to build there the church and all that to the
church will be necessary." The Latin phrase expresses marvellously
well that feeling of expansion and strength: *Ut bene sufficiat.*

We are now less than fifty years from the birth of Saint Francis, and
it would be well to look attentively at these families living about the
cathedral. They are noble, linked in a consortium, an association for
mutual aid, and are pleased to define themselves as *adiutores et defensores ecclesiae sancti Rufini,* "associates and defenders of the church of
San Rufino."[30] They form the nucleus of that part of the city where
the flower of the feudal world will one day bloom: Saint Clare.

In the consortium are the sons of Alberto: Gerardo, Ugolino, and
Berarduccio.

Adamo di Itta di Ampa with his sons and Gerardo and Suppolino,
sons of Guittone. A grandson of Guittone appears in a later docu-

---

1. This was a part of the long struggle over lay investiture. Pope Gregory VII forbade simony
and lay investiture; Henry IV, enraged at losing the privileges of his predecessors, refused to
obey and tried to oust the pope. Gregory VII then excommunicated him and released his
subjects from allegiance to him. Under pressure from the great feudal lords and the bishops,
Henry submitted to Gregory at Canossa in 1077, in the scene familiar from numerous paintings
that show him standing (for three days) barefoot in the snow, clad only in a shirt. The peace was
short-lived, however; Henry continued to hand out abbeys and sees as he chose and to fight
Gregory with every means at his disposal: repeated invasions of Italy, the stirring up of local
discontents, the election of an anti-pope by German bishops.—Trans.

ment of 1226.[m] He is called Guittone della Bona Madre. (This was the name, as has already been said, by which the ancient Roman temple on the site was known. Now, ten centuries later, it is still being used to designate the place where it stood, where the cathedral, San Rufino, now stands.) In Clare's time, then, this family still had its house, located, as the record notes, on the valley side of the land ceded to the cathedral (where the corridor of the sacristy is now located).

And finally, Berardo of the *quondam* Tebaldo, with his son, Tebalduccio. The son of Tebalduccio is to become one of the most intransigent exiles in the time of the war with Perugia. The army raised by the Assisi consuls is to move against him. His holdings, which by then extend all the way to Nocera territory, are to be confiscated. But with the signing of the Pact of 1210 the family would reacquire its old power. A grandson of Tebalduccio, who is to cross swords with Francis, will become in 1233 the *vexilliferus* of the cavaliers,[n] and his daughter, Margherita, will find peace with the Poor Clares.[31]

This illustrious family had its palazzo along the road that leads from San Rufino to Piazza Nuova. It was on ground that became the canons' garden, between the apse and the ancient Roman mausoleum called the Torrione. (Even today people call it by that name. At one time it was covered with massive blocks, but today only the inner concrete covering remains.[32])

The citadel of San Rufino is made up of this belt of towers, gates, and walls that extend to and embrace San Giorgio. In it are the *contrade* of San Rufino, the Prato, and Parlascio.[33] The *contrade* of Colle and San Giacomo[34] remain under the control of the imperial ambassador, who lives in the great fortress of Rocca Maggiore on top of the hill. The central piazza or *forum* is a neutral zone, surrounded by the houses of both feudal lords and merchants. However, San

m. The *"vocabolo* Bona Matre where the church of San Rufino is built" is mentioned in a record of a donation in 1085 A.D. in the cathedral archives (fasc. 1, no. 105). Another paper recording the donation of goods to the cathedral in 1226 again uses the term "Bona Matre," thus proving that the name was still being used in the time of Saint Francis. *NV* 3:35, 259, 307.

n. In the commune being a citizen was inseparable from being a soldier. The city's army was made up of companies from each of the city districts; each was under the command of a leader called the *vessillifero* (Latin: *vexillifer*). A number of the guilds also had their own armed companies, and there was also a special company of archers and crossbowmen. Commanding all were, first, the consuls; later, the podestà.

The Compagnia dei Cavalieri was the strongest and most prestigous of all the commune's companies; it was made up of *milites,* the noble knights who had moved into the city, and of merchants successful and rich enough to keep a horse for the commune and purchase the costly armour, also with enough leisure time to devote themselves to knightly training and exercises. It, too, was commanded by a *vessillifero* and administered by a *camerarius,* called also the *connestabilis militum* or *connestabile,* of noble rank, both. Francis, as will be seen, was a member of this select company. For detailed information about the commune's army: *NV* 3:183–87.

Rufino also holds some houses near the church of San Nicolò, as well as a tower as an outpost.[35]

These three parts of the city—San Rufino, the episcopal hill, and the imperial fortress—are in this early twelfth century linked to form the city government. All these divisions, however, struggle against one another in a tangled knot of overlapping jurisdictions, both ancient and new, and of privileges, immunities, and tributes.

Government belongs solely to the noblemen, the *buoni uomini.* At its head is the prior of the cathedral, San Rufino. However, for some time now a coalition of the lower classes has been taking place and is uniting the men of all districts against the upper classes—the *homines populi* against the *boni homines,* the *minori* against the *maggiori.* Each group is affected by the fluctuating fortunes of both the imperial party and the papal party.

The evidence is overwhelming of the noble status of the families grouped about the cathedral. It leaves no doubt of the aristocratic and feudal nature of the first municipal government or of these families' close relationship with the cathedral. Those who had donated land for the new structure speak of it as "their" cathedral, a thing of their blood associated solely with their own lives.

In that spring of great dreams for the future, the old formulae seem no longer adequate to express the new life and impetus in the city. Instead, a poem is written to memorialize the beginning of its construction. We can still read it today, on the outside of the apse. In it are all the names that must be mentioned—the prior who initiated the work and bore the expense of it, the maestro who designed the new cathedral and supervised the building. But in the cadence of the Latin octameter and in the ingenuous assonances and imagery, there is also an elation and a hint of a return of the springtime sun that transform such everyday realities into the stuff of legend and dreams.

> ANNO DOMINI MILLENO
> CENTENOQUE QUADRAGENO
> AC IN QUARTO SOLIS CARDO
> SUUM EXPLET ILLO ANNO
> DOMUS HAEC EST INCHIOATA
> EX SUMPTIBUS APTATA
> A RAINERO PRIORE
> RUFINI SANCTI HONORE
> EUGUBINUS ET JOANNES
> HUIUS DOMUS QUI MAGISTER
> PRIUS IPSE DESIGNAVIT
> DUM VIXITQUE AEDIFICAVIT.

In the year of our Lord 1140 and at the end of the fourth month of April, this house was begun and carried forward, the cost being provided by Rainerio, prior, in honour of Saint Rufinus. Giovanni of Gubbio, who was the maestro of this house, was responsible for the design from the beginning, and while he lived, built it.

Two months go by. In July 1140, once again we find ambitious Prior Rainerio, standing on the cathedral piazza. With him are his people, and his proud dream, and his drive for liberty and power. It is all in a paper more than 800 years old in the cathedral archives. The bitter odour of mould arises from it as it is unrolled, and along with it, the sensation of being in that vanished world.[36]

We are among a throng of diverse people, excited and boisterous—men in blue sackcloth, women with long heavy hair escaping from white wimples, important citizens wrapped in ermine mantles, knights with their escorts.

The trumpet gives the signal for the *arengo,* the citizens' assembly. The piazza falls silent.

Prior Rainerio speaks first. He declares that never before has there been so great and solemn an assemblage. All the free people of Assisi are present: *In presentiam totorum Asisientium civium, qui ibi aderant.*

It is the first recorded general assembly of all the citizens.

Offreduccio di Ugolino, *signore* of the *castello* of Morano, comes forward and makes a submission. " . . . Free men and ecclesiastical men shall obey you and be subject to you, also the *castello* with its curia, the lands cultivated and uncultivated, the forests, the pastures, the swamps, the mills, the streams, the serfs. And they shall all be in your jurisdiction, Prior Rainerio, and that of your successors. And the price I ask is defence by all the people of Assisi and the prayers and suffrages of all your congregation." And such an act shall return *ad onorem et protectionem totius ascisinati populi,* "to the honour and protection of all the people of Assisi."

The castle of Morano holds the road that leads from Assisi to Gualdo, and the mountain pass between the castle of Montecchio, the forest of Gazzano, and the *pieve* of Osculano—a formidable defence and offence position outside the boundaries of the city, especially important against the constant menace of the Perugini.

In this document we see that the free city has now become the equivalent of the feudal lord. In it are the act of homage and its characteristic obligation of obedience, given in return for the lord's duty of protection.

Again, among those who sign it, are the usual faithful names: the lord of the palazzo of Bona Madre, Berarduccio di Tebaldo; a Matteo, son of Rainerio, who calls himself the count of Assisi, *ascisiensis comes;* Guiduccio, son of Count Rainerio; Taccone di Guittone, the other owner of the house next to the cathedral; Gualterolo di Tignoso; Ugo di Giovanni; Petruzzano di Ugone; Berarduccio di Ugolo.

The Noble Lords Who Rule Assisi

The men who control the city are the descendants of the city's ancient nobility, whose ranks by this time have been augmented by feudal lords who have moved into the city from rural areas. They have usually done so to seek a more secure haven or a quicker way to riches; also, many of the lords who had castles in the countryside liked to have a house in the city as well, and they usually spent a good part of the year there.

The process of urbanization, developing for the most part in the eleventh century, brought into the city the consortiums mentioned earlier, which were a typical institution of the great landed families, the families of the manors or *signorie fondiarie.* From the most ancient documents we find that these associations flourished in every corner of Assisi territory. Possibly they were the remains of ancient Roman communities, or perhaps of Italian or German groups; more likely, however, they were derivations of Lombardian *farae,* groups of noble families linked by blood or by common property rights, by work or by place of residence.[37]

With the passing of time the economic element in these associations waned. Common ownership gave way to individual ownership. Even so, however, the goods of all the members of the group remained available to the consortium, the latter retaining the right to pre-empt them. It also maintained a common responsibility for the payment of obligations and taxes. At times some goods were divided among individual members, while others remained common property. There was often a prohibition against selling, buying, or giving goods as a pledge, except among certain pre-determined persons.

On the other hand, with the transfer of many of the families into the city, the political and family aspects of these groups took on even greater vigour; the consortiums became transformed into true political families or associations, whose principal aim was military organization. They stayed ready to attack or to defend themselves against anyone who threatened their entrenched privileges. Generally the members lived in the same part of the city. They owned some buildings in common and these buildings served as war arsenals in the city streets. Each had a fortified tower that served as a place for all to gather in the hour of battle. On reaching his eighteenth birthday, each of the consorts took a prescribed oath to be "one in blood and war."

As the new classes rose, the family consortiums opened membership in their ranks to other members of the nobility. They also made a place for new consortiums, which were established by the drawing up of a document, subject to the approval of the imperial authority. Hence, as Ricordano Malispini wrote in his *Storia Fiorentina,* "there were consorts by blood and consorts by paper, and they made pacts for mutual defence, which often was offence."

A document in the cathedral archives makes it clear that (as noted in chap. 1) the little church of San Damiano belonged to one of these consortiums.[38]

The noble consortiums took in these new members so as to close ranks as a class against the threat of the rebellion of the lower classes. Forthcoming battles were sensed in the very air. Each great house stood like a fortress in the labyrinth of narrow streets, where danger was always lurking. The feudal oath to be "one in blood and war" caused the skies above the city to be darkened by new and intricate fortifications—battlements and machicolations, barricades and bartizans.

The cathedral—the *duomo* or house of the people of Assisi—was affected by the growing number of consortiums and the increase in fortified structures. It, too, worried about making plans—how to expand, how to defend itself.

The canons did not want the cathedral to be subject to any of the adjacent war arsenals, and they were also determined that the church should maintain its military and political supremacy in the *contrada.* Therefore, in 1148 they made a pact with the encircling nobles of the San Rufino consortium, which was daily growing in numbers and in power.[39] Some of those who signed this pact will participate in a little while in the tumult that will give birth to the Franciscan movement.

Let us look at some of them:

Rolando and his son Rainuccio. A nephew, Ranieri di Bernardo, was the husband of a near relative of Saint Clare and a frequent visitor to her family's house. He will testify in the canonization proceedings for her, recalling her gentle adolescence and the chaste beauty that shone over the twisted spirits in her house.[40]

Pagano and his sons, Pietro, Marescotto, Mendico. A haughty family,[41] which for two centuries will raise sword and war cry in protection of the cathedral, in whose shadows generations of the family took refuge in life and in death. Even in 1086 an ancestor of Pagano, who bore the same name, Paganello, had a house near the church, *iuxta eglesia,* facing the piazza. Another Paganello, descendant of the one who appears in the 1148 document, will make an impassioned protest a century later against the ceding of San Giorgio church (owned by the cathedral chapter) to the nuns at San Damiano so that they could build on the site a new basilica in honour of Saint Clare. He was procurator of the cathedral at the time.

Offreduccio di Bernardo, Saint Clare's paternal grandfather, and his brother, Rinaldo.[42]

These families promise in the interests of the church of San Rufino, *unanimiter atque communiter,* not to allow the number of their consorts to grow. "From now on we shall neither sell, nor lease, nor give as a pledge, nor in any manner cede to any person, nor make a gift, except between ourselves, as named above, or among our heirs, and we shall not put our goods in common."

Also in the consortium was Rodolfo, son of Guelfo, and his sons. A family of judges, notaries, and knights.[43] *Ego Rodulfus iudex,* we see in that 1148 legal paper, which he drew up. The writing is precise, very neat and clear. The signature is followed by a seal: three S's, long, upright, decisive, like three grappling hooks of the kind thrown in battle, tied together with a slim hieroglyphic. Their house was on the San Rufino piazza, across from Saint Clare's family. These two families (linked by kinship since the time of Rodolfo's grandfather, whose name was also Rodolfo and who was the notary of the 1118 document in regard to Count Monaldo, son of Offredo), were always together, on festive occasions and in times of mourning, in the cultivation of Chiagio lands taken in emphyteusis from the canons, during pilgrimages to famous sanctuaries, in overseas enterprises. And on the road of holiness, they were still to find themselves travelling together. A granddaughter of Rodolfo, Bona di Guelfuccio, accompanied Clare to her meetings with Francis before her conversion; one of her sisters, Pacifica di Guelfuccio, escorted Clare on the night of her flight to Porziuncola and with her entered religious life.

These families promise to do nothing that would damage the church of San Rufino and its possessions. If such a thing should happen, God forbid, they will make amends for the damage within fifteen days of being requested to do so. They will not raise any fortification (*edifitium*) on either their lands or their houses, unless they have permission to do so from the canons or the prior or by any six of the *maiores.* And if it should happen that any such fortification should be built in contempt of the pact, the land or house on which it was built shall fall under the control of the church, which shall have the right to demolish the work done.

There is a special obligation affecting Saint Clare's grandfather and his brother: "And we, the sons of Bernardo, Offreduccio and Rinaldo, will not raise our house, which is bounded by the church and the street, above its present height."

Thus San Rufino, in the heart of a district bristling with fortifications, continued to stand as free as if it were on a plain cleared in the middle of a forest. Some of these somber great houses near the cathedral remain standing yet to testify to the nature of this epoch.

Such is the old consular palace, located on the road that leads from the cathedral to Santa Maria delle Rose. A little farther on, a corner tower rises obliquely, the corner of it facing the street, placed to break a rush of assailants (perhaps this is the same tower that can be seen immediately behind the profile of the Minerva in Giotto's fresco in the upper church of the Basilica di San Francesco, the one depicting the donation of a mantle to a poor knight).

And then, a little farther still, the church of Santa Maria Minore or Santa Maria delle Rose (sometimes also called Santa Maria del Sopramuro—Saint Mary of the Walltop—from the fact that a Roman wall serves as the foundation for it and the houses of the area). It has a façade with the remaining portions of a white curtain wall and a small campanile over an ancient arch, which is resting on blocks probably brought from a nearby Roman temple.[44] Ancient loopholes for arrows are visible in this church, and a coat of arms with the cross. A little door opens under an arch, which has an architrave and posts bearing a primitive bas-relief of the Carolingian era.

But the true phantom from this lost world is the Torre del Pozzo, the Tower of the Well. It rises below San Rufino, beside a dark *cavalcavia,* a structure bridging a street. Beyond the *cavalcavia* is a little piazza, called even today the Piazzetta del Pozzo della Mensa, the "Little Piazza of the Well of the Altar." (This name recalls the ancient *mensa canicorum,* and shows that it was once a possession of the bishop, later assigned to the chapter of San Rufino.) About the middle of the twelfth century this structure no longer belonged to the cathedral chapter, but to a consortium, which was called, appropriately, the consortium of the Torre del Pozzo. Here, too, at the base of the tower are the outlines of a typical Roman structure, strong, square in form, sinking into a well. Over it the consorts raised their tower. The primitive Roman wall of red stone, made with blocks about two meters thick, can be seen from the piazzetta. The tower was lopped off later, when the people's faction was in power.

A cathedral document of April, 1151, stipulated by the same judge, Rodolfo,[45] recalls for us some of these consorts: Panzo, son of

Ugone, with other members of his family named Severio and Vecclo, sons of Oliviero; Sabatino and Malatesta, sons of Testa; Marco; Ascarello; Girardo; Rainuccio, son of Bernardo. These, on behalf of all the other consorts (*per consensum seu per notitiam de totis consortibus nostris*), declare their intention to cede to Oliviero and Bertramo the eighth part of "one of our properties, consisting of a piece of ground having on it a tower, which is located within the city of Assisi and which is called the Tower of the Well." These consorts, as usual, are the owners of the houses that border the tower on three sides; the fourth side is bounded by the street. In the paper is the usual promise required by the consortiums: "We shall admit no other associate in the above mentioned structure without the consent of all; and if together we shall acquire anything useful for the structure itself, without fraud you shall have the part that belongs to you. And we, the aforesaid Oliviero and Bertramo, shall not alienate our portion without the consent of all the associates."

The contract is for the tower still standing today, *turris putei,* the Tower of the Well. Beside it, on the side nearest the *cavalcavia,* was the house of the sons of Gente—Oliviero, Bertramo, Rolando, names from poems of chivalry. Its warlike walls were the witnesses to knightly prowess and to vigils, slaughters, arson, attacks with rocks and arrows. They echoed from the dark water to the top of the tower with the din of city fights.

All these preparations being made by the *maiores* are clear indications of their preoccupation in this half of the twelfth century with the danger of an uprising of the lower classes, the *minores*— merchants, artisans, and workers in the fields. Many of them lived in the city and suburbs by this time, and more were constantly coming in. These new classes were solidly united against the tolls levied by nobles and the intolerable, odious system of forced labour.[o]

At long last no one is talking about the separate citadels of the bishop and the prior of San Rufino. Their disputes, if they had not vanished altogether, have gradually diminished. A new movement, basically a social movement, is maturing against the head of the feudal system, the emperor. A new political and economic order is coming into existence, one of a bourgeois and anti-feudal character, in which the commercial enterprises of the merchant are to be substituted for the production of the *curtis,* associations of producers and merchants

---

o. For the *maiores* or *buoni uomini,* see n. ff, chap. 1. The *minores* or *uomini del popolo* were those in both countryside and city from whom the *buoni uomini* claimed forced labour, gifts, fees and tolls. They were, for the most part, former serfs who had moved into the city and become artisans and free farmers. NV 2:131–32.

are to triumph over the noble consortiums, and the work of free men is to prevail over the work of serfs.

The regional and state unity of the Carolingian epoch is by now decisively shattered. The city itself has become the state, a true state, with all the attributes essential to sovereignty. It is a government that is being expanded to include all classes. It is flaunting its own laws and magistrates, even though the empire and the papacy have not formally abdicated their rights over the new arrangements.

In the second half of the twelfth century comes the imperial reaction, forcefully moving against this development, which is a precursor of true rebellion.

Assisi and Frederick Barbarossa

When Frederick I Hohenstaufen became emperor on March 5, 1152, the Italian cities were in full flower. Otto of Freising wrote: "There is not a powerful man anywhere who does not obey the laws of the city; and the city, while expanding in every way its authority over the neighbouring territory, does not shrink from conferring knightly dignity itself on young men of inferior condition and even to artisans, to those, that is, whom other people think it their duty to keep as far away as the plague from every superior activity and dignity."[46]

The restoration of the feudal regime was the principal end in view when Frederick came into Italy for the first time, in 1154. On his return from Rome, where on June 18 he had received the imperial crown, he burnt Spoleto, judged guilty of rebellion for having imprisoned his faithful vassal, Count Guido Guerra.

With the decrees of the Diet of Roncaglia in 1158, the feudal order formally again took on its ancient vigour and both the bishops and the cities were made to acknowledge that every right of sovereignty came from the emperor.[p]

In 1160, when conflict between Pope Alexander III and Barbarossa erupted,[q] Assisi was one of the cities that the emperor made an

---

p. During Frederick's second expedition into Italy to subdue towns to his rule, he summoned doctors in law from Bologna to his court at Roncaglia to rule on his legal rights; they, in this Diet, revived Roman law and ruled that he held absolute authority over everything and everyone in the empire, owned all property in it, and could modify or abrogate private rights whenever he thought it best for the state. This new concept of law was rapidly transmitted into practical action: commissioners were sent into every town to put it into effect, especially the right of the emperor to name the governor of each city. Hughes, *History of the Church*, 2:305–6; *Encyclopaedia Britannica*, s.v. "Italy."—Trans.

q. Pope Alexander III, elected in 1159, in 1160 repudiated Frederick's claims, fearing the church would become an imperial fief; and when Frederick insisted, he excommunicated him. In the struggle between them, which was long, bitter, and complicated by Frederick's promot-

effort to win over to his cause through the concession of privileges over and above those of rival cities and even of the pope himself.

November 21, 1160, he issued the diploma that is the earliest extant formal document of Assisi history. It begins: "In the name of the Holy and One Trinity, Frederick, with the favour of divine grace Emperor of the Romans and always Augustus. Be it noted by all the faithful of our Empire, both future and present, that the city of Assisi, with all its *comitato* especially and freely belongs to our imperial jurisdiction; whence we order that it also should not answer to any power except to the person of the king or to our trustworthy envoy, and to our successors; that it may thus remain free from every other authority, as it was from the time of Henry IV until today; and that it shall be at the head of all the *comitato;* neither shall it be lawful for anyone to build new castles or cities against the will of the *comitato.*"[47]

The diploma was designed to meet the principal preoccupations of the cities: the danger of being subjugated to powers other than the imperial authority, the constant threat from the network of *castelli* that menaced the government of the cities and also impeded the movement of trade, and the fear that other cities in the same territory would develop as rivals in size and importance.

It goes on to describe the boundaries of the *comitato:* from the Luparia gully on the hill that overlooks Valtopina to the forest of Gabbiano toward Spello, from the river Timia to the castle of Pomonte, from Collemancio to the Tiber, from the hill of Monteverde to Coccorano, from Giomici to Mount Luciano above Poggio Morico, and from here through Pietra scritta (*per petram scriptam*) to the Luparia gully.[48]

The Tiber, which lies in the plain between Assisi and Perugia, had marked the border between Tuscia (the land of the Tusci or Etruscans) and Umbria both before and after the Roman conquest of the area. Later, it divided the part of Italy c_cupied by the Byzantines, in which Perugia lay, from that subject to the Lombards, in which Assisi was located, a part of the duchy of Spoleto. This boundary, sanctified by age-old history, was responsible for the fact that the cities lived as advance look-out posts on a border "march" or frontier, with peoples profoundly different in customs, language, and traditions—peoples always ready to set traps and to defend themselves, peoples harassed by the continual fluctuations of occupying powers and habituated by all this to consider themselves enemies and rivals.

---

ing the election of two anti-popes, the terms Guelf (for those supporting the pope) and Ghibelline (for those supporting the emperor) first came into use in Italy. Formerly they had been applied to parties supporting rival families for the throne in Germany. Hughes, *History of the Church*, 2:303–10; *Encyclopaedia Britannica*, s.v. "Guelph and Ghibelline."—Trans.

The most ancient documents of San Rufino show us that a vast strip of land between Ospedalicchio and Collestrada, a *castello* a short distance from the river, was a part of the *comitato* of Assisi. It was owned by Assisi citizens (among whom will be the family of Saint Francis). This strip was known as Campanea, Campania, or Campagna. Even today there is a Campagna road, a *vocabolo* of Campagna, a Campagna farm, a Madonna of Campagna. We know (as is also attested by documents of other Italian cities) that the *campanea* was a public property of the city[49] and it can be supposed that this public property later became divided or alienated among individual citizens.

In the Assisi-Perugia wars during the eleventh century, perhaps even earlier, Perugia occupied this territory and added it to its own *comitato.* The Assisi victims of this usurpation never lost hope of reclaiming it. Diplomas of popes and emperors fed this unfulfilled aspiration and were used by them to bring Assisi to their side—a very important factor to understand when considering all the details of the war in which Saint Francis, in his youth, was called to participate.

There was in the imperial diploma of 1160 a perfidious promise designed not only to win the good graces of the people of Assisi but also to encourage them in their continuing struggle with Perugia, which, as we have seen, was in the orbit of papal politics: "Moreover, we order that whatever the citizens of the aforesaid city have with justice acquired or shall acquire in other *comitati* shall be held by them under our protection, which is secure for all and through all the imperial jurisdiction."

There was, in addition, the need to keep the city safe from pestiferous legal actions brought by small and large feudal lords overtaken by the new times: "And since it is in truth our firm will to hold the aforesaid city, and all the *comitato,* always subject to our authority and to that of our successors, and in our hands, and at the service of the Empire, we order, with our authority, that in no way whatsoever shall they be called to legal action or in judgement by a duke or *marchese* or count."

One hundred *libbre*[r] of gold was fixed as the penalty for anyone foolhardy enough to break the commands, half to go to the royal exchequer, half to the city.

---

r. The *libbra* (also *libra*) or pound was a standard weight of gold and silver that varied greatly according to time and place. It was very likely that the *libbra* spoken of here was somewhat lighter than our own, perhaps about twelve ounces in comparison to our sixteen. Money based on this unit naturally also varied greatly in value; in medieval times, the *libbra lucchese,* in which one *scudo* equalled one libbra, was among the most valuable. Fabbi, *Umbria Antichità,* p. 375—Trans.

The diploma carries at the bottom the seal of the Holy Roman Empire. It brings to our ears the cry that echoed on the bloody fields of Lombardy: *Hail to Caesar! Hail to the successor of Trajan! Glory to Frederick, invincible Roman Emperor!* Along with the years of the incarnation of our Lord are recorded the sire's felicitous nine years of reign and six years of empire. *Regnante Frederico Romanorum Imperatore invictissimo.*

Nine years of reign and six years as emperor—a great deal of anguish is called up by that notation, certified by Chancellor Ulrico di Rinaldo, archbishop of Cologne, in the emperor's headquarters at Pavia: *Datum Papie XI Kalendis decembris.* For Italy they were years of destruction and death, filled with the weeping of dispossessed peoples, wandering and homeless, amid constant battles and burnings of cities.[s]

In the same year of 1160, Frederick's armies destroyed Crema. After the horrors of a long siege in which hostages were tied to the war machines, prisoners butchered on the wall in front of the besiegers, and a great number of innocents hanged all through the countryside, the city surrendered to the emperor. The inhabitants received orders to leave the city with only the things they were wearing. And thus, their last good-byes said to cherished places, they appeared before their conquerors, carrying their dear children on their backs, consumed by hunger and disease. At their sides were their wives and their relatives—multitudes of exhausted and miserable people. One could not have said which was stronger in them, hatred of their enemies or hopeless love of their lost home. The men of Cremona, who fought in the imperial army, sacked the city, burned it, and destroyed it to its foundations.

There never would be an end to this chapter if all the wars that flared up in every city and *castello* in the second half of the twelfth century were no more than listed. All Italy was an immense battlefield. Fighting went on incessantly. Powerful cities, precipitated in an instant into dust, were raised again like lightning by a vitality fed on thoughts of coming revenge.

In 1164 Assisi fought Perugia. A tragic and dark silence lies around this war, of which nothing remains but the tired lament of a citizen returned to his home after the torments of imprisonment in Perugia.

All the rest has vanished, all become quiet except for the muted thread of weeping that one can hear in the surviving record[50] of a

---

s. Frederick I made five expeditions into Italy in his determination to reduce the peninsula to a province of his empire. City after city was destroyed by his armies and Rome itself was taken and sacked during that thirty-five year period.—Trans.

prisoner who has been delivered from violent death, but is condemned to die from illness contracted in the squalor of his long imprisonment.

Bernardo, son of Figura, aware of his destiny, divests himself of all his earthly goods in favour of his relatives, Gualterolo and Bartolo di Suzzolo, who for his sake had gone to the enemies and with them discussed and reached an agreement on ransom: " . . . So that from the congregation and company of the sick prisoners, among whom I had stayed for a long time in the city of Perugia, they took me and liberated me."[t]

At one time there had been a bitter quarrel between Figura, the prisoner's father, nicknamed Lupo, and the grandfather of his rescuers, Albertuccio di Bernardo, over a piece of land located above the church of Sant'Angelo di Litorta, along Rivo Torto. Albertuccio, in the arbitration that followed, had lost out and had had to hand over the land. But when Bernardo was taken prisoner and news of his illness had arrived, these same relatives devoted themselves to saving him. Perhaps the sum paid for ransom had been very large and the ex-prisoner, not being able to pay it back, felt it necessary to give away his goods, the property in Litorta—the object of the old litigation, also a vineyard in Colderba and another piece of ground located in Campo d'Argento. The relatives committed themselves to provide him with board and food and lodging for the rest of his life. Or perhaps the certainty of his fate had taught him the useless weight of all earthly goods. *In Christi nomine, ab incarnatione Domini anni sunt MCLXIIII, exiente mense octubris . . .* Autumn would soon come to an end. Leaves were turning yellow on the tops of the trees. Death was coming nearer. Of that use was old hatred? Of a struggle for each hand's breadth of land?

Again, Destruction

By now the Italian cities, even those that had taken the imperial side, had begun to open their eyes. They could not hope to have liberty under Barbarossa. Unless they wished to return to the ancient system of servitude, they were going to have to fight the German, his armies, his supporters.

The new classes were stirring toward rebellion. Masses of rustic serfs were deserting the country and seeking refuge within city walls, drawn there by the developing guilds. Serfs were ignoring their tradi-

---

t. This document will have some special importance in understanding an episode in the life of Saint Francis.—Trans.

tional obligations. But the feudal lords allied with the emperor were demanding the full restoration of their ancient rights and protection against the cities' interference.

Guiseppe Ferrari writes:[51]

> In 1162 the nobles of Milan went to the Emperor and asked that they not be subject to the power of the city of Milan. The next year, when Milan had succumbed to the vengeful fury of the League of Pavia, directed by the Emperor, the feudal lords stamped down the smoking ruins of houses and palaces and believed themselves again secure for centuries to come, now that the agglomeration of townsmen, who wanted light and space for Milan worthy of Rome, had vanished. In his last descent (into Italy) in 1184, Frederick instantly wiped out in Florence all the consular victories that had been gained over the nobles of the surrounding territory. Siena evaded the (imperial) reaction, refusing him entrance into the city.

Certainly the feudal lords of Assisi carried the same sort of grievances to the imposing assembly called in 1172 in Siena, one well managed by Christian, archbishop of Mainz, chancellor of the emperor. Attending were the prefect of Rome, the *marchesi* of Ancona, Corrado, *marchese* of Monferrato, Count Guidone, Count Aldebrandino, a great multitude of counts, captains, and vavasours or great vassals, consuls of the cities of Tuscia, the March, the Spoleto Valley, and Latium, also an enormous number of other people. War was declared against Pisa and the people of Genoa were ordered to have fifty galleys ready for the service of the emperor by the Easter octave.[52]

The chancellor, the excommunicated archbishop Christian, waged war through Tuscany during all of the year 1173. In the early part of the following year he entered Umbria. He destroyed Terni and captured Spoleto and Assisi.

Only eight years remained before the birth of Saint Francis.

Romualdo of Salerno refers to this conquest in his chronicle, in which he notes that Christian of Mainz, "coming into the duchy of Spoleto and into the Marches, laid waste and took many *castelli* of that region. He put the people of Assisi and Spoleto under his rule."[53]

In the local documents there is nothing but a name and an adjective to indicate this time (*quo haec terra capta fuit*) when the city was captured:[54] *captio capitalis,* in Italian, *la presa capitale,* the capital or mortal conquest.[55] *Capitale* is the word used for something dreadful, mortal, fatal, inhumanly cruel. This designation of time was used for many years. The words suffice to indicate the terror that the event brought to the people of the city.[u]

The word, with its association of something frightful, was one that Francis must have heard in his cradle. It may have given him his first impression of war and the heartbreak of the loss of those untimely slain.

In truth, the memory of the baleful figure of the archbishop, who was Frederick's principal instrument in his struggle with the communes, would never be erased from the memory of those who had lived through those dreadful years. A vivid page written by a historian the year after the archbishop's battle against the people of Bologna in 1172 has been handed down to us: "Enclosed in a helmet resplendent with gold and the remainder of his armour covered with a sky-blue surcoat, he spurred his charger wherever the fighting was the most dangerous. Whirling an enormous bludgeon, he encouraged his men more with blows than with his voice. That day he killed or laid prostrate nine knights. He was the victor, and he pursued the men who had fled all the way to the walls, where they were overcome by the terror. The morning after his victory he ostentatiously showed up at a church not far from the city. There he dared to go up to the altar in pontifical vestments and celebrate the Mass. Finally he went away. He left the region for the mountain, taking with him gold, hostages, and an infinite amount of booty."[56]

By perusing an ancient chronicle, we learn opinions of him of the kind that must have filled the house of Pietro di Bernardone:

"He was a Christian in name only, not in fact."

---

u. In the Pact of 1210 (Arch. Com., M 1, fol. 7; *NV* 3:575) we find that all those who lived in Assisi or its suburbs at the time of the *captionem capitalem* of the archbishop of Mainz, or three years before or after that conquest, were absolved from all the obligations of servitude. The period indicated with the phrase *captio capitalis* can refer to nothing but the capture of the city by the archbishop of Mainz, given that from 1174 to 1221, there is no record of any other conquest of the city.

[The meaning of the phrase *captio capitalis* has mystified a good many historians; Cristofani, in fact, wrote, "I confess that I do not know how to make a guess at its significance." (*Storie di Assisi*, p. 166.) And in 1977, Waley, at a meeting in Assisi of the Società Internazionale degli Studi Francescani, questioned both Fortini's explanation and whether he had accurately transcribed the phrase. He suggested that the correct version surely must be *captio capitolii*, with the word *capitolii* referring to Assisi's fortress, Rocca Maggiore. The phrase must refer, he said, to the period before the destruction of the Rocca, that is, prior to 1198. ("Le istituzioni communale," *Assisi al Tempo di San Francesco*, pp. 53–78.)

The Franciscan historians Lino Temperini and Raffaele Pazzelli, who examined the original documents in the Archives of the Cathedral, say that there is no possibility of a mistake in the transcription of the phrase. In fasc. 7, no. 1, the phrase in the third paragraph is very clearly *a tempore capitalis*, and in the same paragraph is repeated but abbreviated as *post presam cap.* In fasc. 7, no. 14, the term is used again, abbreviated in the last paragraph but clearly meaning the same thing. For a description of these records: *NV* 33:338, 346–47.—Trans.]

"He should have been called the Destroyer, considering the terrible things that happened to the *castelli,* villages, and cities in the path of his army."

"He was like a kite, which lives on prey."

" . . . and like a crow that eats dead things. That is how he lives—on the spoils of his victims."[57]

Others praised this archbishop as a generous and pleasure-loving knight, a bon vivant. He kept a harem of women famed for their beauty behind the scenes in all his enterprises. He spoke several languages and was quite eloquent in all of them. No one could resist him. They said that the mules in his retinue were better fed than the emperor's soldiers.[58]

The reaction of the feudal lords to his victorious campaign, both during and after it, was so unrestrained that the effects would be felt for years. Many tenant farmers who had come into the city were arrogantly forced back to the lands of their old lords and made to serve them again. Others had to bind themselves formally to arbitrary and oppressive service. The violent measures taken and the threats were such that few dared resist.

Three years later Barbarossa himself arrived in Assisi, after having made peace with Pope Alexander III, who had excommunicated him, and also after having suffered the disastrous defeat of his forces by a league of Guelph cities at Legnano. Four diplomas written by him attest his stay in Assisi from December 19, 1177, to January 3, 1178.[v] He went up amid universal homage to Rocca Maggiore, the castle on top of the hill, and there he took up residence.

One can still see the dark ruins of this manor, which was destroyed at the end of the twelfth century, in the remains of the castle built over it by Cardinal Albornoz about two centuries later.[59] There is a clear division, running parallel to the ground along the skeleton walls, about two metres from the grassy soil. From it we can obtain a precise picture of the two epochs, the two historic climates, in which the two structures were built. The upper portion is an ornate edifice, richly decorated with coats of arms, plumed crests, a coquetry of little arches and modillions. The lower part is built of the austere black stone blocks of the feudal period. This was the castle *par excellence,* designed to rule over the people of the city, the castle with which all the feudal lords of the *comitato* associated themselves.

v. With the first (December 19, 1177), he confirmed to the monastery of San Severino the investiture of Cesano; with the second (December 20, 1177), he granted a privilege to the monastery of Valfabbrica; the third (January 1, 1178) is addressed to the city of Fermo; and the fourth (January 3, 1178), to the count Manente di Sarziano. Stumpf, *Die Reichskanzler.*

The gold eagles of the emperor were raised on its bastions in the Christmas season of 1177. Yet a new spirit of hope had been born. Five months earlier, on July 24, Frederick and Pope Alexander III had formally signed a peace treaty in Venice, in a ceremony famous in history. The doge came out to meet the emperor with a great escort of boats and bucentaurs. They escorted him all the way to Saint Mark's, where the pope, vested in his pontifical garments, was waiting for him. With the pope were all the cardinals, the patriarch of Aquileia, and many bishops and archbishops. The two exchanged a kiss of reconciliation. A solemn Te Deum, rising up from the crowd by common consent, sealed the pact between the two.ʷ

Then the emperor had come to Assisi to spend time in meditation before the great Christian festival promising peace to all men of good will. For him, at the moment marking the birth of Jesus, the prior and the canons of San Rufino had made the old Ugonian church ring with the moving salute, *Magnificatus est Rex pacificus super omnes reges universae terrae*, "Great is the peacemaker king, exalted above all other kings of the whole earth!"

On that night in which it seemed that the noise of battle must surely have forever come to an end, the bishop who was the successor to Saint Rufinus raised his hand in blessing. This bishop, too, was named Rufinus, as the records show, *magister Rufinus*. He was one of the first commentators on Gratian's *Decretum,* a popularizer of the gloss, and the author of a *Summa decretorum* that even today is held in great respect by canonists.[60]

In the church, in the piazza, along the streets, the acclamations had risen up. They still echo in the documents of the cathedral:

"Hail Frederick, Emperor of the Romans!"

"Hail to Caesar Augustus!"

"O Invincible! O great and glorious!"[61]

In that same year of 1177, the prior, Conte, with the assent of his nephews, Fortebraccio and Girardo, sons of Ugone, sold the person of Pietro di Berarduccio, with all his goods, to the church of San Rufino. Adamo, son of Rainuccio, gave to the same church his house in Assisi and some lands in Albano, contiguous to the property of Offreduccio di Bernardino, Saint Clare's grandfather. Pietro di

---

w. This treaty, signed after Frederick Barbarossa had been decisively defeated at Legnano by the Lombard League of cities, which was supported by the pope, brought to a formal end the conflict between Frederick and Alexander III (see n. q of this chapter). Frederick acknowledged Alexander as the rightful pope and knelt before him begging for absolution. Agreements were reached of one kind or another—there were apparently many weasel words—on lands subject to the pope as head of the Papal States and those under Frederick's control. Hughes, *History of the Church,* 2:310; Waley, *Papal State,* pp. 16–19.—Trans.

Girardone signed the document as witness. In 1179 a brother of Pietro di Girardone, Maccabeo, sold to the canons a property in Castelnuovo adjoining that of the sons of Suzzolo, the liberators of the prisoner of Perugia. Giorgio di Ugo di Tebalduccio, the *signore* of the *contrada* of Parlascio, and Clarissimo, Guelfuccio's brother, were among the witnesses.[62]

Frederick, after leaving Assisi, travelled on to Genoa and from there to Borgogna. In Assisi imperial envoys had begun governing in his name. Yet the movement to gain freedom from feudal servitude continued to gain ground. Many now openly refused to render acts of homage or perform the required services. Others simply ran away from their lords and thus won freedom.[x] The two classes, *maggiori* and *minori, buoni uomini* and men of the people, are closing ranks for an inevitable violent showdown.

The same wind is blowing through every city. Again, everyone, fearful and fascinated, talks of war.

In Assisi a stranger appears on the streets and cries out two words, famous words that are still repeated today.[y]

"*Pax et bonum!* Peace and every good!"

By day, in assemblies and markets and during festivals; by night, when the third stroke of the bell forbids anyone to be on the streets, the people of Assisi hear his hoarse and impassioned voice, anxious and terrible, incessantly pleading.

"*Pace e bene!* Peace and every good!"

Silence meets the cry of the visionary in this year of the birth of Saint Francis: 1182.[z]

1182: Days of Defeat and Famine

During Epiphany (of 1182) a violent storm struck. In the chronicle of the Anonymous Benedictine monk of Monte Cassino it is noted: "In the three days that followed the Epiphany octave, a furious wind

---

x. According to the Pact of 1210 (Arch. Com., M 1, fol. 7), those who lived in the city and suburbs who had been serfs or forced to perform the obligations of serfs in the period from 1171 (three years before "the capital conquest") to 1177 (three years afterward) had to be liberated. (See n. u.) In the "Peace Paper" of 1203, those in the city or suburbs who had not fulfilled the obligations of a serf since 1179 had to be declared exempt from them, even if they were in the class from which these obligations were required. These provisions are verification of a notable slackening of the performance of these feudal duties from 1179 on. For the two treaties in full: *NV* 3:556–59, 574–78.

y. This episode is found only in *3 Soc.*, 8.

z. The year of Francis's birth is derived from the Chronicle of Albert of Stade, who entered the Friars Minor in 1240 (*MGH, Scriptores,* vol. 16). Others have thought the date to be 1181; but this opinion is based on uncertain evidence, obtained by calculating time according to Francis's illness and conversion. It has now been definitely discarded by present day scholars. See *NV* 2:112–13.

storm raged all through Italy, killing many men and animals, uprooting trees, destroying crops clear to their roots. For the next five years, and even afterward, there was such bitter famine in Italy that in many places one could not find a *salma*[aa] of grain, not even if an ounce of gold were offered for it. The land produced no fruit at all and many men, forced by unbearable hunger to eat wild grasses, died."[63]

In papers of the Assisi archives this period is described as *il tempo della fame capitale*, "the time of the capital (or deadly) famine."

Many years later, to establish in legal actions the time in which certain taxes were paid, the judges asked, "In what period was this?" And the witnesses replied, "In the time of the capital famine." It was understood that they could mean only that period that lasted through the infancy and adolescence of Saint Francis.[64]

Tenants, no longer able to pay the taxes on their sterile lands, gave them back to their masters. *Et hoc fuit,* the witnesses continue to repeat, *tempore famis captualis.*[65] Feudal lords surrendered their goods at ridiculous prices.

In 1182 Fabressa, widow of one of the consorts of Torre del Pozzo, sold her best piece of land to the church of San Rufino. The legal paper is still in existence, notarized by Forzulo, notary of the Imperial Curia: "We, Fabressa and Gisluzio, have asked that this paper of sale be written because neither I, Fabressa, nor the son that I had by Filippo di Oliviero, has been able to earn a living in this time of terrible famine."[66]

April. The spring sun shines vainly on the burnt fields. We are in the house of the canons, next to San Rufino. The baptismal font waits in the dim light. The step on which the angel is to leave a print still has no mark. Into the waiting silence comes the sound of excited voices from the neighbouring cloister, arguing over a price. Prior Conte is there, and the *camerario* (treasurer) of the chapter, Tebaldo di Armuiaffo, the priest Ugone, the canon Mosè, and the witnesses, Gionata, Alegio di Tebaldo, Bernardino di Tignoso, Golavento. When the argument is settled, this tearful cry, preserved through all the centuries, rings out: *Aliter vivere tempore maxime famis non valebamus* ("We could not get along any other way in this greatest famine!").

Then the notary reads in his sing-song voice the relevant data about the property being sold. Vocabolo Colle. Locality in lower Grippa. Borders on the sons of Filippo and *castrum,* the castle. A light

---

aa. A *salma,* in measuring grain, was a variable quantity depending on the place. According to figures given in Trecanni, this probably meant about eight bushels.—Trans.

dawns—this is the field of Collestrada, where the carefree youth of Saint Francis will be shattered in battle.

In the same year of 1182, Leta di Bernardo di Bernardino ceded his property along the Strada Francesca to Raino, presbyter of the San Giorgio hospital. Other well-known names appear. The lords of the bordering lands are Davino di Matteo, the irreconcilable feudal lord of the *castello* of Montemoro; Morico di Passanante; the sons of Rainuzolo di Gisluzio. The witnesses are Lanfranco, Cesare di Manzano, Ugolo di Raino, Benencasa di Bernardone (perhaps a paternal uncle of Saint Francis). Also present are the husband of the woman selling the land, Benedettolo di Martino, and her brothers, Arnebaldo and Lorenzo. And again there is that sad refrain of this time of famine: *pro famis aliarumque rerum maxima necessitate ("on account of the greatest need due to famine and other circumstances").* [67]

In July [as tradition has it] the merchant Pietro di Bernardone left for Champagne. His relatives and friends had vainly tried to hold him back, since Pica, his young wife, was in her seventh month of pregnancy. He could not possibly be back for the birth of the baby. Pietro was a man of the new times, in which commercial affairs had to be put ahead of everything else. So he did not hesitate to set off. He left with his wagon by the Sant'Antimo gate and took the old road across the Sementone field to the Strada Francesca at the foot of the hill, where Ospedaletto is located. There he would meet the caravan of merchants from Orvieto with whom he was to travel. Noon passed, and still no one had come. He ordered his servant to unhook the horses and wait under an olive tree at the edge of the field.

Not a breath of air stirred in the great heat, not a voice rose up from the deserted fields. The windows of the leprosarium were closed, the doors barred.

The merchant searched the city rising high on the scorched hill for his own house. He saw nothing but a forest of towers, watchful under a burning sky.

·3·

THE YOUNG YEARS

The birth of Saint Francis is known to us only through legend. No documents or old papers in archives tell us of the event.

According to the legends, Pica, destined to become the mother of a saint, came to the end of her term. In astonishment her intimate friends and the women of the neighbourhood began to count the days still passing. Yet there was no sign of the expected event. Then, a stranger came to the threshold of the blessed house and gave the young wife the mysterious message that she would not be able to give birth to her baby except in a stable, in the same way that Mary bore Jesus. So Pica was taken to the stable next to the family house. There, on the straw, the baby who would become Saint Francis first saw the light of day.[a]

At the moment of the birth, all hell was agitated and the demons quaked. At the same time the voices of angels singing were heard below Assisi, on the plain, over the tiny church of Porziuncola.[b]

The day of baptism came and the baby was carried to the cathedral, San Rufino. While the priest prepared for the sacred rite, the stranger who had appeared earlier at the door of Pica's house arrived and asked permission to hold the baby at the sacred font. He was allowed to do so. Immediately after the ceremony, he knelt on the step of the

---

a. This is a legend that arose from the desire to show that the life of Saint Francis paralleled that of Jesus; it certainly cannot be dated earlier than the second half of the fourteenth century. See Golubovich, *Storicità della stalletta*, pp. 11 ff. The *stalletta* or "little stable" where he is said to have been born was made into a chapel, open to this day to the public. For a review of the strongly-held opinions, pro and con, about the authenticity of the *stalletta* (today called San Francesco Piccolino), *NV* 2:21–36.

b. Told by Bartholomew of Pisa in *De Conformitate* (AF 4:56, 58, 98, 109; AF 5:326–27). This is a lengthy fourteenth century work written to demonstrate the likenesses between the life of Jesus and that of the Poverello. Significantly, it does not include the story of the *stalletta*, which certainly would have been used had the author known of it.

altar. When he rose, there was a miraculous print on the stone, a print that may be seen to this very day. Then he disappeared.[c]

This venturous mother was still in her bed when a poor beggar came to the house to ask for charity. (This is a story told repeatedly by Fra Nicola of Assisi, among others. He had heard it with his own ears from his mother, who had been present when these things happened, since his family house was joined to Francis's.) The beggar was given a bit of chicken left over from Pica's dinner, but he did not appear to be satisfied with it. He asked, growing more and more insistent, that the baby be brought to him. When finally it was done, he took him into his arms, hugged him against his heart, and said, "Today in this *contrada* two baby boys were born. One of them will be among the best of men, the other among the most evil."[d]

The Mother Who Foresaw the Future

No one has identified these mysterious men, who passed through the city. The legends call them angels.

They appear in the stories told by the people of the city who lived in that time. They stored up their recollections, no matter how trivial, as if each had been of supernatural, divinely ordered origin.[e]

It was probably the latter part of September.[f] This is a gentle season, with mountains and plain bathed in radiant light, the burning sunsets a drama no less than the splendid dawns, the skies full of stars that seem near enough to touch. Even today many a visitor feels in Assisi's beauty a touch of the divine. It is not surprising that throughout the centuries poets, writers, and persons of all walks of life have described the city in such extravagant terms as "a foretaste of Paradise," and "a suburb of Heaven."[g]

---

c. About this legend, which Wadding also relates, see Marinangeli, "Sulle orme," p. 159. It is another one of the many stories of marvels that blossomed about Saint Francis's birth.

d. *3 Soc.,* 2. The same episode is related in *Liber exemplorum,* 116 (*Antonianum* 2:262–63). The compiler of this manuscript, usually dated in the late thirteenth or early fourteenth century, is unknown. The evidence suggests, however, that it was probably Francesco di Bartolo of Assisi, who had ample opportunity to collect the materials included in this work. Fra Mariano da Firenze also includes this episode in his unpublished sixteenth century *Vita di San Francesco* and quotes as his source "maestro Francescho de Assisi." Fra Mariano also says that "maestro Francescho" identified the wicked man as Azolino de Navata, who is otherwise unknown. *NV* 2:53–56, 59–62.

e. The compiler of *Liber exemplorum* (see n. d), for example, tells of an old Assisi craftsman who had known Saint Francis personally and who told him a great deal about his earliest days. *Antonianum* 2:250.

f. There is a note in *24 Generals* (*AF* 3:1, n. 4) that Francis was born September 26, though no concrete evidence is offered to verify the fact. In the seventeenth century Assisi celebrated this as his birth date.—Trans.

g. Cf. the remark of Pope John XXIII: "Here, with Saint Francis, we are truly at the gates of Paradise. Why did God give Assisi this enchantment of nature, this aura of sanctity, almost suspended in the air, which the pilgrim feels almost tangibly? So that men will learn to

Pica was pious and fully attuned to the things of God. She had given her son the name of John in homage to John the Baptist, who baptized Jesus in the Jordan River. Mysteriously, in her heart she kept hearing the words of Zechariah: "And you, O child, shall be called prophet of the Most High; for you shall go before the Lord to prepare straight paths for him, giving his people a knowledge of salvation in freedom from their sins. All this is the work of the kindness of our God; he, the Dayspring, shall visit us in his mercy to shine on those who sit in darkness and in the shadow of death, to guide our feet into the way of peace."[h]

The Biblical imagery of the sun—in the words of Zechariah, of Isaiah, of Saint John the Evangelist's vision on Patmos—will be used in many ways in centuries to come by poets and saints called to write of what Dante called *la mirabil vita,* Saint Francis's wondrous life: a sun brighter than the one rising from the Ganges; the angel from the east "holding the seal of the living God."[i]

The people of the city believed that Pica had the God-given grace of being able to foretell the future. Because of this and because she had given her son the name of John, which means in Hebrew "one who is in grace," they compared her to Saint Elizabeth.[j]

In the dawns that came over the summit of the Subasio, did this prescient mother also foresee that because of her son, Assisi would be called the new Jerusalem "clothed in light"?[k] The new East—the city

---

recognize the Creator and to recognize each other as brothers." For this and many similar comparisons, see Brown, *True Joy from Assisi,* esp. pp. xxv, 131–33, 195–202. Others will be found throughout the book.—Trans.

h. Luke 1:76–79. That Pica named her son Giovanni or John is reported in *2 Cel.,* 3, and in *3 Soc.,* 2. All early biographers are in agreement about her piety. The meaning of the name John is given by Saint Jerome in *De nominibus hebraicis* (PL 23:New Testament, sec. 91).

i. Rev. 7:2. Saint Bonaventure called Francis this angel from the east (*Leg. Maior,* Preface), and the image was afterwards employed by others. See Stanislao da Campagnola, *L'Angelo del Sesto Sigillo.* The "seal of the living God" was interpreted as the stigmata. Dante borrows this imagery (see also n. 1) and underlines the splendour of the mystical image by his reference to the Ganges. The upper Ganges river crosses the Tropic of Cancer, the line of the summer solstice; therefore, the sun is at its brightest when it "rises from the Ganges."—Trans.

j. *2 Cel.,* 3. Elizabeth, too, had named her son John despite family opposition (Luke 1:59–61) and had the gift of prophecy (her greeting to Mary in Luke 1:41–43). To strengthen the parallel between Pica and Elizabeth, Fr. Conrad Harkins, director of Franciscan Institute, points out, was another reason that early biographers so frequently used the imagery of the sun. Zechariah, approving the name John for his son, calls God "the Dayspring." And Francis is therefore described by almost all early writers as one who, like John, showed forth God's light: "Francis shone forth like a brilliant star in the obscurity of the night and like the morning spread upon the darkness" (*1 Cel.,* 37). "He was a light for those who believe . . . (he) shone like the day-star amid the clouds . . . ." (*Leg. Maior,* Preface). "Resplendent as the dawn and as the morning star, or even as the rising sun . . . Francis was seen to rise as a kind of new light" (*3 Soc.,* 1). "As the sun rising on the world were Francis's life, teaching, and miracles" (Bernard of Bessa, *De Laudibus*). Cf. also the legend *Quasi stella matutina* of John of Celano.—Trans.

k. This paragraph is a condensation of several pages of Fortini's original work, in which, almost as a separate literary piece set into the text, he pours out a hymn glorifying Assisi as the

of God, who is the sun that never sets? That it would be described in Isaiah's words: "The nations (will) march toward your light and the kings to your sunrise . . . your sons also shall come from afar, your daughters walking beside them leading the way"?[1]

What were Pica's hopes and dreams as each morning, the sun broke over the horizon and very near, the bells of San Nicolò began to ring?

The Bernardone House

Pietro, Francis's merchant father, became exceedingly angry when he returned from France and found that his wife had named their son after that saint and ascetic, John the Baptist. In the Middle Ages much importance was attached to the selection of a name; it was thought that it would influence the life of the individual.[1] It was unthinkable, according to Pietro's way of thinking, for his son to have as a model the desert hermit who had dressed in sackcloth, satisfied his thirst with water from a river, and eaten only locusts and wild honey.

Pietro was not a man to give in to his gentle and fragile wife. He sought for another name that would establish the future destiny of his son, the road he was to follow, the qualities that would make fortune smile on him. The hot-headed merchant decided that there was no better solution than to name his son for the country in which he had been able to make a fortune through his dealing in wool and silk materials.

It is believed also that Pica herself, sweet, innocent Pica, came from

New Jerusalem and applying to it the lyrical verses of Isaiah 60. In the knowledge that to many English-speaking readers, this literary style would seem unduly sentimental or even tedious, a paraphrase of the text has been substituted. Readers interested either in exploring literary traditions associated with Assisi or the study (devotional or otherwise) of the religious thinking embodied in these majestic and mystical views of Assisi would do well to study these pages: *NV* 1:108–10; also Fortini, *Assisi nel medio evo*, pp. 213–61; Brown, *True Joy from Assisi.*—Trans.

1. Isaiah's exalted description of the splendour of the New Zion was applied by many early writers to the Assisi of Saint Francis. For instance, Dante recalls both the image of Francis as "the angel of the Sixth Seal" coming up from the east (see n. i) and Isaiah 60:19: "No longer shall the sun be your light by day . . . The Lord shall be your light forever" in his famous lines:

> From it, at that point where the mountainside
> grows least abrupt, a sun rose to the world
> as this one does at times from Ganges' tide.
>
> Therefore, let no man speaking of that place
> call it *Ascesi*—'I have risen'—but rather,
> Oriente—so to speak with proper grace.

Dante was very likely also inspired by the *Leg. Vers.* of Henri d'Avranches (*AF* 10:408): "The native soil of this Francis is bathed in a light like the sun; and Assisi, ancient city, flowers anew, covered with glory by the new splendour of so great a son."

France. Perhaps the merchant met her there on one trip or another, a young woman who must have resembled those statues of the Virgin so often placed on the pinnacles of the cathedrals of Picardy.[m]

So the baby was called Francesco—or as we know him, Francis.[n]

It also must have been by divine will, though, that he was given that singular and unconventional name,[o] one that was a proclamation of the qualities most admired in that century, and that by this name he should find everlasting glory.[p]

Pietro's house stood between the churches of San Nicolò and San Paolo, on the extreme side of the large piazza of the city. The remains of it, with sturdy walls, robust arches, huge basements, an outline of what must have been a beautiful entrance of rough-cut stone, attest its opulence and its considerable size, qualities suitable for the very rich merchant.[q]

---

m. In the early manuscript edited by Fierens, *Anonyma Bruxellensis* (*Revue d'Histoire Ecclésiastique* 8:290) the writer says that the wife of "Pietro Bernardone, citizen of Assisi" was named Giovanna (Johanna or Joan). If this is correct, Pica, the name given to her in all the earliest biographies, must have been a nickname. We do not believe, as has been suggested by some, that it came from a word meaning a bizarre desire of a pregnant woman, such as Pica's reported wish to have her baby in a stable might have been described. More likely (as was often the custom) it referred to her native land; and, in fact, the French word *pique* was used for the inhabitants of Picardy. According to various sources (not earlier than the sixteenth century, but drawing on older material), Francis's mother did indeed come from Picardy. Given the fact that it lay between Champagne and Flanders and so was a meeting place for the merchants of the world, it is certainly a possibility. The fact that the Bernardone son was called Francesco ("the Frenchman") gives the story additional weight. The name Giovanna recurs in succeeding generations of the family: Francis was, of course, first named Giovanni; his brother, Angelo, named his son Giovanetto, who in turn had a daughter named Giovannella and a great-grandson named Giovanni. *NV* 2:94–101.

n. The name Francesco also appears in succeeding generations of the family: Francis's brother Angelo had a grandson named Ceccolo (a derivative of Francesco), great-grandchildren named Francesco and Franceschina (who became, respectively, a Friar Minor and a Poor Clare), and a great-great-grandson Francesco.

o. The names "Franco" and "Francesco" occur in earlier notarial records in Assisi, so we can assume it was not so strange as some early biographers seemed to think it. In the cathedral archives, for example, the name "Franco" appears in these records: fasc. 2, no. 17 (1106 A.D.), fasc. 2, no. 24 (1110 A.D.), fasc. 2, no. 109 (1155 A.D.); see *NV* 3:270, 272, 289. The name "Francesco" is in a record of 1119 A.D., fasc. 2, no. 53; *NV* 3:278.

p. Thomas of Celano saw the name as a symbol of Francis's qualities and made a word play on it: "Truly Francis had a frank (*francum:* bounteous, open, free) and noble heart." *1 Cel.,* 120.

q. The author is the first to identify this house between the churches of San Nicolò and San Paolo as the paternal house of Saint Francis, a conclusion to which he was led through his extensive research into surviving records of the periods. Space prohibits giving the full account of his discoveries in this much-debated issue, but a summary of the principal factors in his identification follows:

In 1228–29, two years after Saint Francis died, the central piazza in Assisi was enlarged; the new portion was called *platea nova.* Several houses on that side were demolished, and a special tax to pay for the costs of this civic improvement was levied on the owners of the houses that were then facing the piazza—a very desirable location. Among those who paid were the sons of Angelo di Pica—Francis's brother, who was a merchant like their father. Presumably his house (and shop) would have been also Francis's house, for the merchants were grouped in one quarter of the city. (In fact, the name of the street on which the house is located, Via Portica, comes from an arcade that was once over the shops.) The questions on which there have been disputes have been: what part of the piazza was enlarged? And where was this house?

The most striking thing about it, however, is the formidable wall of cyclopean boulders on which it rests, a wall that it seems fate must have decreed should survive the devastations of the centuries, while everything around it toppled. It is the most impressive of all the walls that the first unknown inhabitants erected along the steep slope of the hill in order to build the city of the sun. They themselves saluted the city as Assisi, City of the Altar, City of the Eastern Sun.[r]

Fortini, from the descriptions in the records, says the piazza was enlarged on the west side, away from the mountain, and that therefore the house must be found there too. Unexpectedly, his opinion was fully corroborated in the last few years, when in a considerable remodelling being done on the Convento di San Antonio on Via San Paolo, excavations uncovered the remains of the walls that formed this *platea nova,* now covered by the Torre and Palazzo of the Capitano del Popolo, the Costanzi house, and the Convento itself, all built later. These walls are now open to public view. (See Andreozzi, "L'Ubicazione della 'Platea Nova' di Assisi," *Pace e Bene* 24:41–43).

A second major clue in the search for the house is a note in *Liber Exemplorum* that the author had gotten a great deal of information from a Fra (Brother) Nicola of Assisi, whose family's house was joined to that of Francis's family. Fortini identifies this brother as Nicola di Giacomo, a prominent notary in Francis's day who joined the order after a successful professional career. His house was next to the church of San Nicolò, and a number of his notarial records were drawn up there.

Two other documents and a strange set of circumstances even more dramatically speak to the identification of this house, which in all details fits the description given in the tax record. In 1280 Francis's nephew Piccardo (Angelo's son) bought two-thirds of the house of which Fortini speaks, which by that time had passed out of the hands of the family. He paid what was at the time a shockingly high price of 200 *libbre* (pounds) for it. *Three days later* he handed it over to Nicola di Giacomo, who owned the remaining one-third. He offered him the longest lease allowed by law—to the third generation—for a rent of a *piccolo denaro,* an insignificant coin, to be paid each year on the feast of Saint Francis. He surrounded the rental by restrictions: only direct heirs could hold the lease; only direct heirs could live in the house; it was not to be alienated. The penalty for any violation was the full purchase price of the house, 200 *libbre.* The lease was solemnly signed in unusual circumstances in the Basilica di San Francesco, with friars and leading citizens in attendance.

Two years later, in 1282, Piccardo took further steps, this time to provide a substitute for himself as landlord, for he was aged and unmarried. He gave the house to the Benedictine monks who owned the church of San Paolo, which was next door, with the provision that all the terms of the lease were to be honoured.

Piccardo was for many years a devout member of Francis's secular Third Order and had kept an oratorio in his own house in memory of Saint Francis. He also had served the Friars Minor for years as their procurator. Given the devotion he had for his uncle, the only sensible explanation for these elaborate arrangements is that he wished to preserve this house in his uncle's memory, in an era when there was not the slightest interest in any official quarters in anything concerning the human side of a saint—his family, his house, or whatever. (The same sort of attitude explains why for so many centuries Saint Clare's family and house could not be certainly identified. And much the same can be said of a lesser known Assisi saint of the nineteenth century, Saint Gabriele dell'Addolorata.)

Such attitudes surely also explain why Piccardo's well-laid plans went astray. The house comes into view again only in the fifteenth century when it was rented to the shoemakers' guild by the Santa Lucia monastery, an uncloistered branch of the Poor Clares, which Nicola's granddaughter Bibola is known to have entered. Presumably by that time, with all the principals dead, the terms of the lease had been forgotten or were ignored. She transferred title to the order when she entered it. That order was suppressed in 1475 and the house disappeared from history.

For all the many details involved in the identification of the house and a full discussion of other houses in Assisi that have been previously identified as "the paternal house of Saint Francis," see *NV* 2:21–90; also Brown in Englebert's *Saint Francis,* pp. 407–19.—Trans.

r. According to modern philologists, the name Assisi (Lat., *Asisium*) could have been derived, like the word Asia, from Açu, meaning east, in that it is to the east of Perugia. It was often the custom in very ancient times to adopt the local names used by nearby peoples.

Propertius, the Roman Callimachus, in a poem in which he has a prophetic spirit address him, refers to this gigantic sloping rampart:

> . . . steep Asisium's wall climbing towards the peak—
> the wall to which your genius has brought fame.[2]

These memorable lines strikingly capture the image of this massive structure of boulders that the Umbrians joined by human strength in an extremely remote time. A city of superimposed arches, an immense stairway open to the plain. A powerful acropolis for human battles, a lofty temple for soaring spirits. In the Franciscan story these last contrasting traits—so marked in the very look of the city—would be played out in a drama that would leave its imprint on the city forever.

San Paolo, the Church Next Door

When the city was being rebuilt on its ancient pattern, the same wall was used as the support for two churches on the central piazza, San Nicolò and San Paolo.

The church of San Nicolò was erected about the year 1000.[s]

The church of San Paolo owes its existence to an abbot of the monastery of San Benedetto, whose name, Aginaldo, recalls the rude devotion of the Lombardians. The date of its foundation and consecration, April 6, 1071, were solemnly recorded for posterity in a tablet on the external door of the cloister. It was still in evidence up to a century ago. The monastery on the mountain was following the current fashion of establishing a house in the city, just as the feudal lords did—their way of life, their power and riches, were the model for everyone.[t]

However, Luigi Ceci, in a discussion of the etymology of Umbrian names, suggests that the name *Asisium* is related to the Umbrian word *asa* (Latin, *ara,* altar), a word that recurs often in Umbrian inscriptions. In fact, one sees in the Eugubine tablets *puote asiane fetu* (Lat., *pone in ara victimas:* "place the victim on the altar") in Tablet I, a, line 25); also *pir ase antentu* (Lat.: *ignem arae imponito:* "place fire on the altar") in Tablet III, lines 22–23. The root *as* for *ardere,* to burn, occurs in all Italian dialects, and, of course, it was on the altar that the victims were burned. If we accept this etymology, Assisi becomes "the city of the altar"—"the holy city." See Elisei, *Della città natale,* pp. 381 ff.

s. The merchants of Italy had a special veneration for Saint Nicholas, so it is logical that a church in his honour should have been built in the Mercato. Of the church as it was in Saint Francis's day, only the crypt remains; it is the entrance to the underground Roman museum. Today the post office stands on the site of the church. The small open chapel at the side was built in 1927 by the city so that the fourteenth century painting of the school of Simone Martini, the *Madonna del popolo,* which was once on the façade of San Nicolò, could be returned to its old location. The altar of the chapel is made from the rock of La Verna. For more about the history of the church: *NV* 2:13–15.

t. This church, still in existence, is now used only as a meeting place for a confraternity. For a more detailed history: *NV* 3:15–16.

Between the two churches is the house in which Saint Francis was born. In the first half of the twelfth century it stood in a cleared space cluttered by the ruins of a Roman structure demolished in the invasions.

In Assisi, as in many other Italian cities, the marketplace of the city had been established around the ancient forum. The merchants also had their houses around the piazza; shops, showrooms, and storerooms for merchandise were attached to them. In an earlier time the street that leads from the piazza toward the *contrada* of San Giacomo (now Via San Paolo) took its name from the nearby Mercato or Market. But then the constantly expanding monastery, with its church, its cloister, and the living quarters of the monks and abbot, had finally imposed its influence and its name on the whole district, which came to be called "Badia," the *contrada* of the abbey.[u]

The Bernardone house was, like others of its time that still exist in the city, tall and turreted, with both upper and lower balconies. The principal entrance to the house was on Via San Paolo. The shop, on the other hand, faced Via Portica. A short, steep passageway, through which a gutter ran, linked the two streets and separated the house from the church of San Nicolò. In the middle of the passageway there was an entrance way, long and dark, covered with pointed arches, which ran below Francis's family house. It emerged into a spacious street (today closed), that was parallel to and between the streets of Portica and San Paolo and led to the church of San Giacomo.

On the mountain side of this intermediate street were the buildings of the monastery—fortified towers, provided with arrow slits. They stood on the exposed Roman wall that here extends quite some distance and encloses this side of the street. Perhaps the knowledge of the Sacred Scriptures that Francis was to show in his lifetime came from his having frequently been with the monks of the abbey in the years of his adolescence. Events to come will confirm an old affectionate relationship with them.

From the merchant's house one could hear the bell ring to convoke the chapters in the abbot's quarters. They dealt with appointments of priors and of sub-priors, proxies for sales and leases, quarrels with feudal lords and with the larger monasteries, arbitrations. The monks,

---

u. The forum is first described as the market, among surviving Assisi records, in 1093 (Arch. Cath., fasc. 1, no. 124; *NV* 3:264). At an earlier period the merchants had their places outside the city walls; as trade increased, they came into the city to build their houses and shops about the Mercato. *NV* 2:38; 3:11–12.

slow and solemn, would cross the cloister wrapped in long black cloaks.

Before the abbot Aginaldo had put his hand to the new construction (San Paolo), the monastery had been established in the temple of Minerva, on the piazza of the same name. The upper part of the pronaos had become a sort of aerial citadel, with windows looking out on the street between the superb fluted Corinthian columns.[v] The monks of Mount Subasio even found in the Mercato an outlet for their principal products. It was another tie—and perhaps not the only such—between the monastery of San Paolo and the shop of Pietro Bernardone.

Pietro's business affairs went well. The trips to France were frequent and the merchant always returned with new materials and news.

Notwithstanding the difficulties of communication, no period in the past was more effective in drawing people together than the Middle Ages. Next to the Crusades, for which warriors came together from every part of Europe, the Champagne fairs were responsible for a great diffusion of cultures, customs, religious and political ideas. The merchants learned of extraordinary events taking place, and on their return they told their fellow citizens about them. One can understand why many Assisi people would have loved to linger in the shop on Via Portica.

There Pietro undoubtedly indulged himself in stories about exotic places, exciting ports on fantastic seas, legendary castles on top of inaccessible mountains, plains crossed by great rivers.

He would have talked about the Cistercian abbot who, when asked by King Richard if Jerusalem would be liberated, replied that the moment had not yet come for that consolation.

He would have brought back the report that the King of Sicily, Tancred, had celebrated with great magnificence the wedding of his son, Roger, and Irene, daughter of the emperor of the Greeks.

He would have said that in Champagne there were knights whose prowess surpassed that of all others. When they went out to war, led by their lord, Thibaut, count of Troyes, their armour shone so that the whole region seemed to be burning. Thibaut's brother had taken

---

v. In Saint Francis's time, the Roman temple of Minerva was called San Donato by the Benedictine monks of Mount Subasio, who owned it. They built rooms or dwellings across the upper part of the pronaos; the holes for the beams that supported them can still be seen. The exterior of the temple, which has been called "the most complete and best preserved Roman temple in Italy after the Pantheon," is today the original Roman structure; the inside, however, was rebuilt in the seventeenth century in a baroque style. The temple is now the church of Santa Maria sopra Minerva. *NV* 3:12–13.

the cross and become king of Jerusalem. A short distance from Troyes, on the top of a rocky hill, in sight of a valley through which a great river ran, stood a castle called Brienne. There lived Count Erard, married to Agnes de Montbéliard; they had two sons, Gautier and Jean. Erard had also gone on the Crusades and had died in the siege of Saint Jean d'Acre. It had fallen to his son Gautier to gather up his bloody body and bury it with his own hands. Gautier was the son most famous for audacity, grace, courtesy, loyalty, good sense.[3]

In the shadows, the velvets and the damasks spread out on Pietro's counter gleamed. There, too, the heart of the listening boy went out to this marvellous and distant world.

San Giorgio, Francis's First School

Francis was put in school in the church of San Giorgio, run by the canons of the cathedral. It must certainly have been one of the episcopal schools teaching grammar and rhetoric maintained in that time by every cathedral chapter.[w]

Numerous documents of the Assisi archives make it possible for us to reconstruct with considerable accuracy the church itself, one that played a large part in Saint Francis's life and death.[x]

From the Piazza Minerva, San Giorgio was reached by way of the street that was called then, and now is called again, Via del Ceppo della Catena ("Street of the Block and Chain"). It stood in a large open space at the lower end of the city, lying outside the San Giorgio

---

w. Thomas of Celano wrote that Francis was buried where he had begun his learning (1 *Cel.*, 23); in *Legenda ad Usum Chori* (13) he specified that the place was San Giorgio. Saint Bonaventure confirmed his statements (XV, 5).

The church, with its priest's house and *ospedale,* was a dependency of the bishop and the cathedral chapter of San Rufino. The hospital had earlier been located near the cathedral in the section called "*fossa* ('depression') di Perlici." As were most of the hospitals of the time, it was a place of asylum for pilgrims, the poor, and the victims of disaster as much or even more than for the sick.

The schools of the Middle Ages were decidedly ecclesiastical in character. At a very early period, as a result of the Council of Vaison of 529 A.D., there were parochial schools in Italy, in which a priest (the *scholasticus*) taught both lay and clerical boys how to read and to serve at the altar. There were also capitular and episcopal schools where grammar and rhetoric were taught, even to the laity. See Manacorda, *Storia della scuola,* 2:60 ff., Salvioli, *L'iztruzione in Italia.*

These episcopal schools expanded greatly after 1000 A.D., so much so that as feudalism and the empire declined, the schools became not only in fact but also in law an emanation of the episcopal authority.

We can say, then, that the school of San Giorgio was both capitular and episcopal in character. These schools were usually held in the atrium or portico of a church.

x. In Saint Francis's time San Giorgio stood outside the city wall. It is now incorporated into the Basilica di Santa Chiara. The crypt, where Saint Francis was first buried, is in the living quarters of the nuns. Before September 1948 the only part of the church of San Giorgio open to the public was the third "crossing," where the present chapel of the Sacrament is now located. In that year the other two crossings, which had formed the choir of the nuns, were also made accessible, so that today one can, by means of a great glass window between the chapels, see the ancient church in its entirety. NV 3:54–60.

gate, the site today of the Basilica di Santa Chiara. When construction on the basilica began, around the middle of the thirteenth century, a good many of the ancient buildings in the area were destroyed. The church itself, however, was preserved and is incorporated in the new edifice, where today it serves as a side chapel.

An old fresco still remains on the wall. It depicts the ancient legend of gallant bravado and holiness: Saint George, on horseback, buries his lance in the neck of the dragon, while the princess looks on at the mortal duel. The armour of the knight is all white, and white, too, is his rearing horse. The dragon, already felled, lashes his tail furiously. The young woman watches, marvelling. Her hands and her snow white neck stand out against the purple of her dress. At the back of the church, a short staircase led to the crypt.

Where today the entrance to the living quarters for the nuns is situated, at that time three streets came together: the one from the Piazza Minerva (or Piazza del Commune), another that went up to San Rufino, and a third that led down to the Moiano gate. The place was called, therefore, the *trivio* or trivium of San Giorgio. The Moiano street was flanked by a wall for its entire length, all the way to the house of Giorgio d'Agrestolo. From that wall a structure for internal defence opened, a narrow, walled corridor lined with slits called the *carbonara vecchia* ("the old coal cellar") because of its shape.[4]

On both sides of the wall were the gardens of the canons of San Rufino, to whom the church was subject with all its pertinences. San Giorgio was the parish seat and had next to it the *ospedale* or hospital that the canons had transferred there from the Parlascio hollow. It was called the Ospedale di San Rufino and also the Ospedale del Trivio di San Giorgio. Some remaining portions of the numerous tenant houses that made it up may be seen still in the Romanesque building with stromboid windows beside the arch leading to Borgo Aretino.[y]

The rector of the hospital, who was also called the prior and the hospitaller, supervised both the church and the school. From surviving legal records we know that in 1194 the rector was Giovanni di Sasso. He was the owner of vineyards and fields in Panzo and Correggiano, and he fought with the *buoni uomini* against the men of the people, who burned his house.[5] Some years later we find a canon of San Rufino named Guido named in the cathedral papers as rector. He

---

y. These remains of the old *ospedale* are incorporated into the present guest house of the sisters, at the rear of the Basilica. *NV* 2:157.

was the cleric who, according to the account in the cathedral lectionary, was rewarded for his piety and his devotion by having revealed to him the place where the relics of the Martyr Bishop, Saint Rufinus, had been hidden.[6]

These, then, according to the old records, were the first schoolmasters of the young Francis.

Lessons were begun after Easter, the beginning of the season of good weather, in the atrium of the church. April would be gilding the houses and walls. Festoons of green climbed up the arches and columns, decorating them for the approaching feast of Saint George, on which it was customary for the knights of the city and the surrounding *contado* to hold jousts and tourneys. On the eve of the feast day, large red and blue banners began to flap in the field of Sementone.[7] Horses neighed, trumpets sounded, bells rang out gloriously under the spring sky.

It was time for the old hospitaller to tell the ancient tale again, as he did every year, in the same words and with the same imagery.

" . . . And there was in that realm a terrible dragon, who came out of the sea and came into the city and killed many persons and ate them. And one day all the people of the city armed themselves, the people and the knights, and went out after that dragon. And the dragon was so terrible to look at that all the people began to run away. And the knights, more than two thousand of them, also ran away, so that the king, in order to appease the fury of the dragon, ordered that a maiden be given to him, and that the choice of the maiden be made by lot. After a long time, it happened that the lot fell to the daughter of the king, who was the most beautiful maiden of the time. And the king, held to his duty by the people, wept bitterly. But since there was nothing else he could do, he had his daughter dressed nobly, like a bride, with a crown on her head, like a queen. He pressed her to him, then with terrible sorrow and weeping he sent her to the island where the dragon who was to devour her could be found. And she, left alone, so adorned and so beautiful, waited, trembling, for the dragon."

The scholars listened, spellbound, overcome by that unaccustomed flood of poetic rhetoric.

"And then the blessed George appeared on his great horse, and he was the handsomest young man to be found anywhere, and wearing beautifully decorated armour. He went to the princess, who was crying, and said to her: 'Gentle maiden, why are you crying here all by yourself?' And she replied: 'O most noble young man, I am waiting for the dragon who is to devour me. I beg you in courtesy to go away at once, so that you do not have to die with me, because it is to me that this cruel fate has fallen.' At this point the dragon came out of the water and hissed loudly and came toward her. Saint George ran to meet him and gave him a blow with his lance that immediately knocked him down. Then he called the maiden and had her take off her girdle and put it on the neck of the dragon, and thus the young princess drew it along behind her, like a lamb, all the way to the city. And all the people greatly marvelled, in seeing such courage and such wisdom in so young a knight."

Beyond the open atrium, in bands of light and shadow, gardens shone in the golden dust that enveloped the peach trees, cypresses, and fragrant lavender hedges. A lazy humming of bees filled the air whenever the story-teller paused.

"And the king was so happy that he could not express his joy, seeing his daughter escaped from so cruel a death. And when the dragon was in front of the king, Saint George killed it, and six pairs of oxen were required to drag it out of the city. Then Saint George preached the Christian faith to the king and to all the people. And through the miracle that they had seen, all were converted and believed perfectly in Jesus Christ. And the king had churches built in honour of God and in reverence for Saint George. And when everyone had been taught how to serve and to love God, Saint George took leave and left the realm. And before leaving, he gave the noble horse that he had been riding, and his knight's armour, which was nobly and richly decorated, to the poor for the love of Christ."[8]

It was a tale that nourished the mind of the young Francis. One day he, too, would set out, by an unknown road, for a distant land, in search of a gentle princess to whom he would offer his arms and his life. His look ran beyond the wall studded with slits, beyond the fortress-like door to the path that went down through green fields, by San Masseo and Fonte Galletta, to the Strada Francesca, the road of merchants and troubadours, of pilgrims and warriors.[9]

But the story had a relevance closer home. The *ospedale* sheltered about ten of the poor, with whom the students often talked. They were mild and sad, cowed and silent. The boy, amidst his daydreams, thought that nothing, neither the victory over the dragon, nor the love of the princess, nor the wonderful conversion of the people, was so great as that last gesture of the generous knight, in giving up his splendid arms for the love of the poor.

The Feast of Fools

Certainly Francis must have received his first religious instruction in his parish church of San Nicolò.

Nothing remains of it but the bare crypt, unearthed several years ago. It is divided into two naves by squat pillars, topped by rudely carved capitals. A wall of thick travertine blocks from the Roman period divides it from the adjacent forum.

Here Francis knelt. Here his lips opened in prayer, and here, perhaps for the first time, he received Jesus as the words were whispered from the altar, "This is my body." Is it not likely that memories like this were in Francis's mind when he spoke of "the good priest of the church of San Nicolò"[10] to his first two companions on the day that he wished to consult the Gospels about the way of life they were to follow?

Every year on the sixth of December the school boys of the city met in that church to celebrate the feast of Saint Nicholas, their patron. This custom, which was still alive in Assisi at the beginning of the seventeenth century, was in the medieval period an uproarious and licentious celebration.[z] On that day the boys chose among themselves an *episcopus puerorum,* or, as it was commonly called, a boy bishop. Like a real bishop, the mock bishop went into the church dressed in episcopal vestments and was served by acolytes chosen from among his companions. He celebrated the Mass, sang the hymns and the antiphons, and led the singers.

According to the *Ordinarium* of Parma, this extremely ancient custom was practiced *ad instar humilitatis,* to instill humility—superiors were to make themselves subjects and subjects were to learn not to desire high office. But there is no doubt that the people went to this grotesque ceremony of fun and frolic solely to have a good time, and often enough, to abandon themselves to the most deplorable excesses. Finally the feast became a bacchanal in which, by mutual consent, all inhibitions were abandoned. These orgies were surely derived from the pagan Saturnalia, which was called, for good reason, *libertates decembris,* the "December liberties." As in the ancient Saturnalia, the hierarchial order was overturned, the power of

---

z. The *Guida dei Pellegrini* edited by Salvi in Assisi in 1618, discusses the church of San Nicolò (p. 46) and touches on the "impressive celebration that the Scholars celebrate there on the day sacred to their Advocate" and on the music performed.

On the *Episcopinus* or *Episcopellus,* cf. Roberti, "La cerimonia dell'Episcopello," *Arch. Stor. Ital.* 31:172–75; De Bartholomaeis, *Origini della poesia,* pp. 177–92. In some Italian cities the boy bishop celebration was being held still in the fifteenth and sixteenth centuries. Traces of it were found in Sicily until 1736.

class structure upset. It was a good thing for the lords to know, just once, what it was like to serve, and for the servants, by putting themselves in the place of their masters, to do a little paying back as revenge for the fate that had forced them to obey others.

All restrictions, even of the moral order, were shattered. To read in the contemporary chronicles the history of those days, which were blasted in vain by popes (Innocent III's edict of 1207 is famous), is to be astonished.[11] We are transported at once to the strange, eccentric, paradoxical Middle Ages, a time full of contradictions, furies, and bizarre practices.

Lewd priests, libertine men, and half-dressed women joined the rowdy youths. They danced in the sacred place, they sang bacchic songs amid an uproar of cymbals, castanets, and sistra. The altar was used as a table for a profane agape at which, in sacrilegious mixture, great and lowly guests, true and mock canons, men and women, were seated. Quantities of food were served, along with fine wines.

Afterwards the orgy overflowed into the streets. Carts went about carrying half-naked women crowned with flowers, their hands and feet tied. An auctioneer sold them to the highest bidder.[12]

The song, "Dic Tu, Adam," which Fra Salimbene criticized so greatly, arose—the song of vengeance against woman, despised and desired, invoked and hated, enemy and mistress, scourge of the world, image of sin, destroyer of the mind and of the body:

> *Paradysi pulcra cella*
> *sum expulsus pro puella*
> *que splendebat veluti stella.*
> *Ne mulieri credite.*

From Paradise's beautiful hall I was thrown out because of a girl who shone like a star. Do not believe a woman!

And the bacchic chorus responded with a violence that made the tall houses tremble:

> *Recedite, recedite;*
> *Ne mulieri credite.*

Free yourselves, free yourselves! Do not believe a woman.[13]

The rule of the boy bishop lasted until the Feast of the Innocents (December 28). On that day he went on horseback to the house of the real bishop, accompanied by canons, preceded by school boys with candles and censers. We have a record of this strange ceremonial.[14] The antiphon resounded: *Sinite parvulos* ("Let the children come to me"). The bishop appeared on the threshold to welcome the mitred boy. Both were censed. Afterwards everyone sat down. The boy bishop subjected the real bishop to an interrogation, asking him for an accounting of the revenues and other ridiculous questions. Finally he ordered wine to be brought and all drank. At last he gave a caricature of a benediction, and the procession went back into the church.

This account supports the well-known words of Thomas of Celano about the environment of corruption in which Saint Francis grew up. It is useless to think of his words as mere rhetoric. He was always scrupulously exact, even in insignificant details. Here, then, is the passage that opens Thomas's *First Life:*

"In the city of Assisi, which lies at the edge of the Spoleto valley, there was a man by the name of Francis, who from his earliest years was brought up by his parents proud of spirit, in accordance with the vanity of the world; and imitating their wretched life and habits for a long time, he became even more vain and proud. For this very evil custom has grown up everywhere among those who are considered Christians in name, and this pernicious teaching has become so established and prescribed, as though by public law, that people seek to educate their children from the cradle on very negligently and dissolutely. For, indeed, when they first begin to speak or stammer, children, just hardly born, are taught by signs and words to do certain wicked and detestable things; and when they come to be weaned, they are forced not only to speak but to do certain things full of lust and wantonness. Impelled by a fear that is natural to their age, none of them dares to conduct himself in an upright manner, for if he were to do so he would be subjected to severe punishments. Therefore, a secular poet says well: 'Because we have grown up amid the practices of our parents, we therefore pursue all evil things from our childhood on.'[15] This testimony is true, for so much the more injurious to their children are the desires of the parents, the more successfully they work out. But when the children have progressed a little in age, they always sink into worse deeds, following their own impulses. For from a corrupt root a corrupt tree will grow, and what has once become wickedly depraved can hardly ever be brought into harmony with the norms of uprightness. But when they begin to enter the portals of adolescence, how do you think they will turn out? Then, indeed, tossed about amid every kind of debauchery, they give themselves over completely to shameful practices, inasmuch as they are permitted to do as they please. For once they have become the slaves of sin by a voluntary servitude, they give over all their members to be instruments of wickedness; and showing forth in themselves nothing of the Christian religion either in their lives or in their conduct, they take refuge under the mere name of Christianity. These miserable people very often pretend that they have done even worse things than they have actually done lest they seem more despicable the more innocent they are."[16]

We do not, of course, have to assume that Francis was guilty of all this unrestrained brutality or that he succumbed to base forms of sensuality. People who knew him said that he had innate good breeding and displayed a gentility of sentiment and behaviour.

But it is not without importance, in this question that has bothered all his biographers, ancient and recent, that the first authors reproduced Thomas of Celano's narration without any reservations. Furthermore, Henri d'Avranches, who wrote a life of the saint in verse before 1230 with the intention of warning the devout against the insidiousness of the principal vices of his time and of all times, offers us a picture of wantonness that surpasses those painted by all other biographers, both those who wrote in Latin and those who wrote in the vernacular.

He also believed that in his early years Francis was dominated more by the flesh than by the spirit, more by the strength of his senses than by the light of his intelligence. And he concludes that to find the meaning of true love, he had to climb from an abyss of concupiscence to spiritual peaks, rid himself of impurity, banish his obsessive drives. He weaves an assonant verse full of word plays on the subject, one characteristic of the poetic taste of the time:

> *Dum servire parat, saevit, dum ludere, laedit;*
> *Si quem vult lenire, linit; si quem satiare,*
> *Sauciat; in primis Venus est, in fine venenum.*

It [concupiscence] seems to obey you and instead rages against you; it seems to amuse you and instead wounds you; it seems to be balsam but is, on the contrary, filth; it seems to placate you and instead tortures you. Sweet pleasure it seems in the beginning and in the end becomes deadly poison.[aa]

---

aa. *Leg. vers.* (*AF* 10:417). Henri, after having spoken of the grave dangers to which man is exposed through sensuality, which leads astray the sense of reason and constantly alternates from burning attraction to sickening repentance, goes on to speak of the offspring of this sin:

At the end of the last ceremonial the boy bishop took off his vestments. The torches were extinguished. The songs of the orgy died away. In the mud of the road lay the crowns of flowers, the festoons of myrtle, the branches of box.

In the grey winter day the piazza was again sunk into a sullen silence. A few persons went by, wrapped in large mantles. A cold, slow mist veiled the great houses of the nobles that stood around the market and the abbey—the house of the sons of Bernardo Dodici, *signore* of Collestrada; the house of the sons of Sanguigno, *signore* of Bassiano; the houses of Incalzolo, Uguccione, the *signore* of Villarotta, Marangone.[17]

It was an expanse of fortresses, barricades, battlemented parapets. They continued to keep watch, suspicious and menacing, in the fog.

Communes vs. the Feudal Regime

The year that Saint Francis was born, 1182, had been a critical one in the struggle between the emperor, Frederick Barbarossa, and the Italian communes.

Formally, the preliminary agreements of the Peace of Constance in June, 1183, put the communes under the imperial vassals and defined the power of the consuls as an emanation of the sovereign power of the emperor. They also defined certain rights claimed by the communes as privileges granted to them by the emperor, especially those of war, *regalie* [rights traditionally considered as pertaining to the king], the free practice of ancient customs both inside and outside the walls, civil and criminal jurisdiction, and the raising of armies and maintaining of forts.

The emperor reserved to himself the right of judging appeals in trials of major importance; but these trials had to be defined according to strict territorial jurisdiction "by a nuncio appositely resident in the cities or in the episcopacies." A loyalty oath to the emperor had to be taken every ten years by all citizens from the ages of fifteen to seventy. Also the consuls, who would have to receive investiture from an imperial nuncio every five years, had to take the oath.[18]

But the close observer would have seen the men of the communes

---

"An innumerable swarm is unleashed bearing the marks of lust: Voluptuousness, which a million times arouses disgust in sick hearts and as many times returns to soothe them. Broken painful sighs and feelings that plead for satisfaction. Insinuating words. Little signals. The humble murmurs that follow a brief quarrel that only rivets the chains more strongly and serves as a diversion to drive away boredom. Silent tears. An ingenuous expression, true or feigned, to arouse tender compassion. A dear image ever-present. A desire to please, used to put on a show of gifts that to the person nature has denied. From all these things, beginning and continuing, springs Love, which is nourished on folly and fear: anxiety, embraces and kisses, seductive softnesses, desires, flame and adultery, adultery and raging flame, adultery that is the ruin of conjugal laws, incest that dissolves natural laws and releases even more serious things."

give a large sigh of relief. They had a sense of having gained a victory and of having imposed terms of peace upon the emperor. In reality the consuls continued to exercise the absolutely free government typical of the communes, while at the same time they made ready to fight the feudal regime.

The fact that the communes now had the upper hand increased the suspicion of the feudal lords. Consider the sinister name that appears in a document of 1186, Lupone (Big Wolf) di Tiberio.

Lupone declares that it is his intention to give the church of San Rufino a site next to one of his fortresses, to be used to build a church named for the knights' special saint, Michael the Archangel.[19]

His own fortress, dark and menacing, stands on the edge of a cliff that drops vertically to the Tescio and alongside the gorge below Costa Tre Case ("Slope of the Three Houses"). Near it runs a sluggish muddy stream named, from its occasional furies, Fossa del Maltempo, Bad Weather Gully.

Despite all his devotion, Lupone is suspicious and wary. He specifies that the canons may not put towers or fortifications on the new church.

All the *buoni uomini* are suffering from suppressed anger.

Here is Medico, a doctor and notary, who always ostentatiously stipulates his noble rank: *Ego bonus homo Medicus complevi et rogavi,* ("I, Medico, *buon uomo,* was responsible for and notarize this").[20] He watches the rise of the plebian people, his disdain barely contained. His pride bleeds at seeing armed ranks of citizens march by in the summer of 1186 under the eyes of Duke Conrad of Spoleto, on their way to succour Orvieto, under siege by the emperor's army for its crime of having refused the podestà sent by the emperor.[21]

Another notary, Bernardo, makes a notation in a paper of 1187 of the event that will be the cause of a new conflict between the emperor and the pope. It was a development approved by the *buoni uomini: Regnante Frederico Romanorum Imperatore una cum Enrico Rege filio suo* ("Frederick, Emperor of the Romans, reigning together with King Henry, his son").[22]

It is the beginning of a drama that will turn Italy upside down and will affect the life of the young Francis.

One of Barbarossa's most ambitious schemes was to marry his son Henry to Constance, daughter of Roger II of Sicily. The king of Sicily at the time was William II, Constance's nephew, who in 1166 had succeeded his father, William I, Constance's brother. William II was without heirs, and he had made a promise to his vassals that at his death he would recognize his Aunt Constance as successor to the throne.

Pope Urban III fiercely opposed the marriage of Constance and Henry. Traditional church politics held that the autonomy of the south was necessary to prevent the excessive expansion of both the Holy Roman Empire and the Byzantine Empire to the detriment of the Papal States. The church also relied on the Normans of the Sicilian kingdom for protection against the German emperors.

For all that, the emperor succeeded in his scheme. On January 27, 1186, Henry and Constance were married in the church of Sant'Ambrogio in Milan. At the same time the patriarch of Aquileia crowned Henry king of Italy.

Urban III suspended the patriarch and the other bishops who had attended the ceremony. Henry replied by invading the lands held by the church. Barbarossa laid siege to Verona, where the pope was secluded.

Again there was war. Once more the feudal lords whose power had been threatened or usurped hoped for a full restoration of the feudal regime. The emperor encouraged their hopes by annulling at a stroke all the territorial and jurisdictional gains of the communes and he restored to the feudal lords all their ancient privileges.[23]

The Fall of Jerusalem, 1187

It is natural that the family of Pietro Bernardone finds itself involved deeply in this struggle, since the merchants, above all, represent the new class of the towns. Pietro Bernardone is, according to the ancient writers, a perfect example of a man of the commune.

The merchants are the most directly involved in the war against the feudal lords, who are closing commercial roads, attacking caravans, imposing tributes, and exacting tolls. Pietro cannot have escaped the passions of these bitter conflicts, he who is not only the richest merchant of Assisi but also so important a participant in public affairs as to be designated *reipublicae benefactor et provisor* ("financial backer and benefactor of the communal state").[24] It is easy to imagine the talk that goes on in his shop—rumors, accusations, recriminations, resolutions, threats.

But in that same year of 1187, a piece of news falls like lead to crush the spirits of everyone, nobles and commoners, great men and small, supporters of the pope and vassals of the emperor. October 2, 1187, after eighty-four years of Christian rule, Jerusalem fell to Saladin, ruler of the Moslems.

Such was the general consternation that even Francis, then five years old, must have felt the effects of it. The strong feelings that are to make him a pure-hearted and unswerving Crusader must have originated in that time, when in the Assisi streets, piazzas, and churches, as in all other cities, there was the sound of weeping, laments, invocations, prayers.

The word "Jerusalem" was on everyone's lips; it was an obsession. The people went about dressed in sackcloth. Large paintings were exhibited that showed the Holy Sepulchre being trampled on by horses and Jesus Christ overpowered by Mohammed. Everyone thought of his own misdeeds and felt guilty of the disaster. Minstrels left off singing about love to lament the cruel blow that had fallen upon Christianity. It was a common opinion that the welfare of the faith and even the glory of God depended on the preservation of Jerusalem.[25]

Churches remained open night and day. Priests, by order of the pope, continually repeated the mournful and vengeful psalm of the people of Israel: "O God, the nations have come into your inheritance."[26] Great throngs prostrated themselves amid the columns in what are now the dark crypts of Assisi churches to raise this prayer of all betrayed and defeated peoples:

"O God, the nations have come into your inheritance; they have defiled your holy temple; they have laid Jerusalem in ruins.

"They have given the corpses of your servants as food to the birds of heaven, the flesh of your faithful ones to the beasts of the earth.

"They have poured out their blood like water round about Jerusalem, and there is no one to bury them.

"We have become the reproach of our neighbours, the scorn and derision of those around us . . .

"Pour out your wrath upon the nations that acknowledge you not, upon the kingdoms that call not upon your name . . .

"Let it be known among the nations in our sight that you avenge the shedding of your servants' blood.

"Let the prisoners' sighing come before you . . .

"And repay our neighbours sevenfold into their bosoms the disgrace they have inflicted on you, O Lord . . . "

Gloria Patri et Filio et Spiritui Sancto . . . .

The emperor himself, Frederick Barbarossa, now reconciled with the new pope, Clement III, took the cross and left with a formidable army for the Holy Land. After defeating the sultan of Iconium, he made ready to march on Jerusalem. But June 9, 1190, while crossing the river Salef, he was swept away by the current.[27] And with his death, the old struggle between the pope and the emperor, now Frederick's son, Henry VI, who succeeded his father, was rekindled.

The preceding year, 1189, the king of Sicily, William II, had died. The Sicilian Norman party feared that the Germans would get the upper hand if Constance, his aunt, succeeded him, as he had intended. With the backing of the pope, they had proclaimed as king Tancred of Lecce, illegitimate son of Roger, duke of Apulia.

By the end of March, 1191, Clement III had died, and it fell to his successor, Celestine III, to crown Henry and Constance in Saint Peter's. Immediately afterwards, Henry, now the emperor, moved against Tancred. However, a terrible pestilence destroyed almost his entire army and forced him to return to Germany. Constance, who had taken refuge with the people of Salerno, was betrayed by them and sent to Tancred. He held her prisoner until May, 1192.

These events brought a period of freedom to the cities, the heavy imperial hand having been removed from them. They lost no time in embarking on a policy of expansion. In 1193 Assisi, ignoring the borders set for it in the diploma of Frederick I, occupied Nocera and Assisi people settled themselves within its walls.[bb]

Tancred died February 20, 1194. The Sicilian Normans, again with the approval of the pope, proclaimed his young son, William III, king of Sicily. In response, Henry returned to Italy in May. After being assured of the support of Genoa and Pisa, he marched on the south.[28]

The anxiety with which Italian cities followed the new war is attested by a document of the cathedral of Assisi that contains an account of the fall of Salerno in September 1194 to the imperial army, which was led by Guglielmo *marchese* of Monferrato. The feudal lords rejoiced, foreseeing a return of Frederick's days. The capture of Salerno was held up as a salutary example to all the enemies of the emperor or his vassals.

The ancient Norman capital, *totius principatus quasi metropolis,* "the most metropolitan of all the cities ruled by the prince," the beautiful city that had seen the splendours of the court of Robert Guiscard, became nothing but a heap of ruins. Horrible things were told about the numbers of men murdered, women raped, palaces destroyed, hostages sent to Germany.

Thus the emperor washed away Salerno's betrayal of his wife, Constance.

Birth and Baptism of Emperor Frederick II in Assisi

All these events are reflected in a paper drawn by that snob Medico, who once again records his own pedigree: *Ego bonus homo Medicus notarius, rogatus* ("I, *buon uomo* Medico, notary, *rogatore*").[29]

---

bb. That this happened can be deduced from the act of alliance stipulated in 1223 between the commune of Assisi and the *milites* of Perugia, reproduced in its entirety, NV 3:604–6.

The legal document deals with the sale of a piece of ground by a certain Ciccatto to the Ospedale di San Rufino, attached to the church of San Giorgio. Representing the hospital are the prior of San Rufino, Mosè, and Giovanni di Sasso, Francis's schoolmaster.

Medico believes it opportune to go over the story of the business. Giovanni di Sasso had sold another property to Medico himself and is using the money received for this new acquisition. Medico does not record the usual information—the day, the month, the year, the indiction, the name of the pope or of the emperor—only the notation of the great happening of the time, one that marked the imperial restoration: *Anno quo Salernum fuit captum,* the year that Salerno was taken.

The contracting parties and the witnesses meet in the cloister of the cathedral, *in claustro sancti Ruphini.* (It was the cloister built in 1029 by Bishop Ugone. The remains of it may still be seen:[30] a colonnade supported by primitive pillars, whose wide arcades were closed in recent structural changes, a staircase leading to the piazza, a short corridor leading to the crypt, fragments of sculptured stone, old walls on which wild plants grow. In the middle, an ancient well, wide and deep, overlooks the rest.)

The prior, Francis's schoolmaster, and the other canons listed in the document, Tebaldo di Bernardo, Rinaldo di Sopercle, and Giovanni di Randolo, listen to the old spiteful notary give vent to his feelings:

It is time to put an end to this business of the flouting of laws by those seditious upstarts who claim the right to destroy the ancient practices of imperial law. Once everyone kept to his proper place, the vassal and the lord. Today, you could not distinguish by clothes or behaviour a *milite* from a man of the people. The merchants go about wearing silk clothes and carrying swords at their sides and even aspire to knighthood. Feudal obligations mean nothing. Workmen today are insolent and rebellious and try to get out of the service they owe. They expect to be exempt from tolls when they go over the lord's road with their loads. They never show up on Christmas, or Easter, or on the feast of Saint Rufinus with their customary gifts for their lord.

Let the example of Salerno be a warning to them. The emperor was always at the helm, generous with his faithful subjects, ruthless to the rebellious—they should remember that, these newly rich boors who claimed to be above paying him the usual levies, the *fodro, placito, denaro, dativa, albergo.* [cc]

---

cc. The *fodro* was a mandatory levy to pay for food and supplies for the emperor and his troops when they were on the road; the *dativa,* a tax on lands and flocks, also the collection of straw, hay, water and wood for the feudal army on the march; the *albergo,* lodging that must be

The *buoni uomini* are indeed trying to bring about recovery of their positions by requiring more services, by depredations, and by seizing those who rebel and keeping them in servitude until they fulfill their obligations.[31]

Another faithful servant of the empire, Conrad di Lützenfeld, comes to Assisi and is seated in Rocca Maggiore, the fortress on top of the hill. He is to become notorious for the bad government of the territory entrusted to him, which includes the cities of Rieti, Spoleto, Assisi, Foligno, and Nocera. He is called Mosca-in-cervello, Fly-in-the-brain,[dd] a nickname that in the region means extravagant, capricious, or raving mad.[32] But he is one of the most renowned captains in the imperial army. In the war against Tancred in 1191, he laid the siege to Capua. In 1193 he was commander-general of the army and acquired a sad kind of fame for his destruction of Monte Rodone, where he left scarcely one inhabitant alive. He fought bravely in the defence of Perugia.

Personages of his court are mentioned in documents of the cathedral; we see them bowing almost to the ground in a show of obsequious devotion: "I, Forzulo, notary and scribe of the Curia of the Duke Signore Conrad . . ."[33]

According to the chronicle of the German monk Albert of Stade, who became a Friar Minor and died after 1261, in 1195 the empress Constance was overcome by labour pains while she was on her way to join her husband in Sicily. She went to Assisi and stayed for a time with Conrad, who was a kinsman of the emperor. In Assisi her son was born, the future Frederick II.[ee]

---

provided for the lord when he travelled; the *denarium*, a tax assessed for the expenses of maintaining an army; the *placito*, the sum collected by a lord for the administration of justice. *NV* 3:135.

dd. Baluze, *Vita Innocentii III* (*RIS* 3:486).

[Historians (see App. VI by Brown in Englebert, *Saint Francis*, pp. 421–22) differ as to whether the man appointed to govern Assisi was Conrad di Urslingen or Conrad di Lützenfeld, called "Mosca-in-cervello" (see above citation, also Muratori, *Ann. d'Ital.*, 1172 A.D., in which Abbas Urspergens is quoted, and 1195 A.D., when Henry VI is reported to have named him duke of Spoleto. Pietro da Eboli also identified the duke as Lützenfeld and explained his nickname). The two have often been confused. Both came from Swabia. Both served in the emperor's armies under the infamous Archbishop Christian of Mainz. Both earned a reputation for cruelty and oppression in their government of conquered territories. Each of them has been called the duke of Spoleto in various sources. Many historians now identify the duke of Spoleto as Conrad di Urslingen and the duke of Ancona as Conrad di Lützen or Lützenfeld. Fabbi (*Umbria Antichità*, p. 143), perhaps to make everyone happy, combines the names and says that "Corrado Lützen d'Urslingen was chosen duke of Spoleto." Fortini follows Baluze and Pietro da Eboli, also Muratori, compiler and editor of both *RIS* and *Ann. d'Ital.*, in identifying him as Conrad di Lützen or Lützenfeld. Some other Assisi historians believe that this is correct.—Trans.]

ee. *Chronica* (*MGH, Scriptores*, vol. 16). This thirteenth century Franciscan wrote that he was born in *valle Spoletana in civitate Asis*. The fact that he mentioned the Spoleto valley means that he was not guilty of an error in spelling when he wrote "Asis" instead of "Iesi," a city in the

Some of the ancient biographers of Saint Francis who picked up this information point out how singular is the fact that in the same city were born both a great saint and an emperor who was one of the most complex and original men history has ever known—sovereign, *condottiero,* a man both generous and cruel, a poet and a diplomat, a polished man of the world and a thoughtful searcher after things of the spirit.

Frederick was baptized in the cathedral of San Rufino. The canons lined up at the door of the church to greet the procession from the Rocca, solemn men whose names live on in the notarial documents: Prior Mosé, Tebaldo, Greco, Latino, Bartolo, Eugenio, Silvestro, Crescenzio, Manno. The splendour of the ceremony reflected all the imperial glory of the past and all the imperial hopes for the future. The same German monk reports that fifteen prelates were present, among them cardinals and bishops. It is not surprising, considering the fact that the pope was at the time negotiating with the emperor for a new Crusade.

Francis, the Tradesman

Certainly Francis, who was delighted by pomp and ceremony, would have watched this solemn event, one that stirred all the city by its proud splendour, the rich ceremonial, the parade of symbols and emblems.

He was then thirteen years old.

When he was fourteen, his father took him into the shop, initiating him, according to the medieval custom, into his own trade.[34] And so we now see Francis as a very young merchant, discussing purchases and sales, prices and markets, materials and colours, all in the terms of the latest news in fashions from France.

Everything is rigorously, meticulously, governed by regulations established by the statutes pertaining to trade. The seller is forbidden to send out his cloths, but "to show them in front of the shop, as far as the middle of the street."[35]

Marches of Ancona that is generally held to be his birthplace. As Albert goes on to say, Frederick II was baptized in Assisi at the age of three "in the presence of fifteen bishops and cardinals." Since the duke Conrad [both of them?] was a kinsman of the emperor, it seems very likely that the baby was left in his care for the first years of his life so as to spare him the hardships of travel and the dangers in which he would have been placed had he been with his parents. See Fortini, *Assisi nel medioevo,* pp. 157–58.

[Still alive in Assisi, this translator found, is a story that Frederick II was not the child of Constance at all, who—according to the Assisi story—was too old to bear children at the time of her marriage to Henry VI, but of the wife of an Assisi tradesman, probably a butcher. The conventional story of his birth, in this ancient gossip, is an elaborate deception to cover up the true facts. The author told me that he took no stock in it.—Trans.]

The shop is still there, today a room for cards and games. This is where the people who passed saw him move about the materials from Flanders and Brabant, pass the *canna*[ff] on the selvedges, notched to indicate prices, and make hurried notes of expenses, duties, tolls, costs of transport. "He who sells foreign cloth must put the cloth in a showcase or on a counter, spread out to show good faith, and then put the *canna* beside the selvedge and put a mark at the top of the *canna* and then cut . . . " The precious cloths were heaped up on the large wooden counter: embroidered samite, soft velvets, green damasks, cloth of silver threads.

Not far away is the piazza of San Rufino, silent and tranquil in the shadow of the solemn cathedral. Here he used to come on the eve of the feast of the Patron Saint to offer his votive candle.[36]

The cathedral church of Giovanni of Gubbio was not yet finished. Too often the workmen had had to put down their chisels and pick up their swords and rush to defend the city walls. But already the pointed arches were marching toward the old apse, where the new façade would be placed.[gg]

On the vigil of Saint Rufinus, the main portal was thrown open to the sparkling piazza. The burning candles on the altar could be seen dimly at the back of the church. The altar-cloth, scarlet in memory of the blood the Martyr had shed for the faith of Christ, was already on the altar. The bells rang from the high tower, pouring a metallic wave of sound into the sky, which, with evening coming on, would be already losing its light and becoming an even diffused blue.

The crowd pressed close. The herald called out each name, one by one. The *camerario dell'arte* offered his candle first, according to the statute that required of him a wax candle of two *libbre*. Those on the rolls followed him, each with an offering of a candle of one *libbra*. Each had his candle burning as he was presented.

---

ff. The *canna* (perhaps originally a cane or reed?) was a standard measure of length that varied from one city to another. In Assisi the official measurements were 0.583 metres (23 inches) for silk; 0.743 metres (a little more than 29 inches) for wool; 1.040 metres (nearly 41 inches) for linen. Metal rods of these official *canne* are still embedded in the wall at the base of the Torre del Popolo on the Piazza della Minerva. Medieval authorities ordered them on display, along with blocks showing other measurements legally set by the commune, so that the citizens could assure themselves that they were not being cheated. *NV* 3:182; Fortini, *Corporazioni Artigiane.*—Trans.

gg. The arches of the twelfth century cathedral designed by Giovanni da Gubbio and built by Bishop Ugone are indeed pointed, though the construction is of a time when only Roman arches are thought to have been in use. They can still be seen today above the baroque shell that was placed inside the ancient structure in an unfortunate remodelling of the sixteenth century. The pastor (in 1972), Don Elmo Antonini, is of the opinion that the arches probably were Roman in the beginning, and that they were rebuilt in some forgotten time of repair or reconstruction.—Trans.

The merchants' guild, since it was the most important one, would have been the first to make an offering. The name rang out in the sultry air: Francesco di Pietro Bernardone!

There was a simple man in the city who must have been inspired by God to hear what others did not hear and see what others did not see. Whenever he met the son of the merchant, always he took off his mantle and spread it under the young man's feet. To those who wondered at this unusual homage, he would say, "He is worthy of every reverence, because he will accomplish great things in the future and for them will be magnificently honoured by all the world."[37]

Mysterious words that no one, certainly not young Francis himself, understood. The people of Assisi remembered this strange prophet and told Saint Bonaventure about him when he came to Assisi to search for material for his life of Saint Francis. They also told Giotto, who worked on the frescoes of the upper church of the Basilica di San Francesco, near the end of the thirteenth century.

The great Florentine artist opened his series of paintings with this episode. This fresco, besides being one of the most powerful of creations, is a true historical document.

Francis has come out of his house, a few steps behind him, and is going toward the center of the piazza. As he comes even with the first column of the old Temple of Minerva, there is the man in front of him, bending to throw down his pallium, making of it a carpet that Francis will have to pass over. The prophet is completely enthralled by Francis. He is looking up at him from below, his face in profile, the chin, decorated by a sparse beard, jutting out, an enigmatic face.

The usual idlers hanging about the piazza (young nobles with placid faces, hooded merchants with sour faces) question each other as to the meaning of the gesture, one that should be ridiculous and yet has aroused both their admiration and suspicion.

The old Roman temple serves to express a certain timelessness, a symbol overlooking the scene from its position over the old Roman forum that has been underground now for centuries. Francis is in front of those well proportioned columns with their elegant leafy capitals. He is dressed in beautiful blue clothes, sure of himself, radiant with youth. The eloquence of his hands emerging from the ample folds in a gesture of astonishment is extraordinary.

This painting of Francis fits well with the description left to us by those who knew him in this first period of his exuberant youth and who spoke of his joyful vivacity, his uncalculating liberality, his great extravagance, his showy elegance.

For him the paternal shop was emptied of sumptuous cloths, soft silks, gleaming velvets.[38] The young men looked to him to know the latest fashions from France. The gossipers said that he was a cocky fellow who thought himself better than his position warranted.

In truth, at this time he never in the world would tolerate being second to anyone in anything.[39] One day some busybody who went often to the merchant's house took occasion to tell his mother what everyone was saying. The informant was taken aback by her reply. Pica had not changed her opinion or her dream that her son would be the herald of grace.

"What do you think he will be?" she retorted. "Certainly my son will be a son of God."[40]

The Misery of the Poor

Despite all his swaggering, Francis was profoundly disturbed and saddened by the poor—and had a vague feeling of being drawn to them.[41]

The great famine continued.

Names well-known to Francis come to life again in the documents. Names of those who in vain asked his inflexible father to postpone the payment of a debt, who languished from starvation on the doorsteps of their desolate houses. The unmoved notary continued to record the laments of these heartbroken people with pale and emaciated faces and weakened, consumed bodies.

In a deed of April, 1184, written in the church of San Rufino,[42] Albasia di Rainuccio di Pietro, her husband Appatrino consenting, sells to Eugenio di Peppone, *pro famis necessitate* ("compelled by the famine"), a property in Castelnuovo. There are familiar names here. One of the neighbours is the *signore* of Porta del Parlascio, Tancredo di Ugone di Tebalduccio. A witness is that Gualterio, son of Suzzolo, who freed his relative, Bernardo di Figura, from the Perugia prison. And could the "Pietro di Bernardo" who appears also among the witnesses be Francis's father?

In another document of 1202, Bona, daughter of Ugolino, who lived near the house of Saint Clare, sells, *causa famis,* a property in *vocabolo* Spina.[43]

It happened that beggars often went into the shop on Via Portica. Their clothes, falling in tatters from their backs, were in great contrast to the background of luxurious fabrics heaped on the shelves over the great wooden chests. They wept, telling about their misfortunes, showing their skin crumpled by long starvation. All suffered from dreadful hunger. Sometimes they hung about for long periods, leaning against the door, eyes closed, covered with their rags, without stretching out their hands or making any appeal, overcome by a torpor that was like death. Francis watched them drowse in the tepid sun enveloping the whole street, where over the campanile of the cathedral, the mountain shone in its beautiful green mantle.

Generally he was generous enough with alms, for all that the family fever for money was in his blood and many times drove all other thoughts out of his mind.[44]

One day, when he was in the shop, absorbed in thoughts of materials and prices, a poor man came in and asked him for charity in the name of the Lord. Francis, annoyed, sent him away without giving him anything. But after the man had gone, it seemed to him that he had committed a great villainy. He reproved himself bitterly, "If that poor man had come in the name of some count or baron, certainly I would have listened to him. How much more I should have done, then, seeing that he spoke to me in the name of the King of kings and the Master of us all?"

He vowed, therefore, never again to turn down those who asked in the name of so great a lord.[45]

Pietro Bernardone: Rich Merchant

In contrast to such poverty, Francis's family prospered, for his industrious father took advantage of the new and ever-growing mercantile trade.

We cannot on this point dismiss certain very precise expressions of the first biographers. The Three Companions said that Francis's parents were "rich." Thomas of Celano described Francis with the adjective *praedives,* "extremely rich."[46]

One has only to look at the magnificent way of life of the young man to be convinced of the truth of the matter. He continued to dazzle his fellow citizens and to feed the gossip of the malevolent. He had reached such a point that when he sat down at table, under the portico by the garden, he looked with indifference on the usual foods and would eat only especially prepared delicacies served on the finest china.[47]

One of the characteristics of this period was the feudal lords' widespread conversion of land into movable goods, which could then be converted more easily to cash. At the same time, the merchants, both through expropriation of the land of their debtors and through the desire for investments to offset their necessary commercial risks, were acquiring great estates.

This was certainly true of Pietro Bernardone. The records allow us to reconstruct his extensive holdings on Assisi's mountain and plain.

By this period, middle-class families like Francis's had country houses in which they spent some months of each year.[48] To know Francis better, we must search out these places familiar to him, in which he spent a great part of his adolescence and youth.[49]

Land in Campagna, toward the *castello* of Collestrada, near the Tiber—the most fertile part of the plain and also the most harassed, contested in constant battles with Perugia. Even supposing that Assisi people protected their legal rights over property owned there, it was an area politically subject (as we have seen earlier) to the enemy city.

A large strip of Mount Subasio, including, among other places, the fertile pastures of the Sermolla slope, made up of pleasant hills and agreeable valleys inclining toward San Giovanni di Collepino and La Madonna della Spella. The area is called by the same name today, from the plant *sermolla,* thyme, that flowers here in great quantity and changes this stretch of green meadow into a sweet-smelling garden lying open to the sun.

The olive groves of Val Canale, between the Tescio and the hill of San Bartolo, the old Benedictine priory where the ruthless murderer who was the founder of the church of San Giacomo sought peace.

The field of San Martino d'Argentana, between the women's monastery of Sant'Angelo di Panzo and Rigo Secco [the name means "Dry Stream"]. This property bordered the land of Tancredi, sons of Ugone, the powerful knight of the Tower of Parlascio.

(Rigo Secco is the trough that descends from the Carceri. It is no more than 400 metres from the San Martino field. It is so named both because there is no water in it and because its gravelly margins run in a gorge between the two mountains in a desolation of burnt rock. Tradition explains that it became dry through a miracle of Saint Francis, who, while meditating at the Carceri one day, had his concentration disturbed by the sound of running water and so commanded it to disappear. Since then—according to the legend—absolute silence has reigned. Sometimes the stream reappears for a brief hour and in anger runs its turbulent course. This rare violation of Francis's ancient order is thought to be a sign of disaster and imminent calamity.

This legend does not fit the spirit of the man who elsewhere made springs gush out and had pity for every hardship, even those of inert things. As a matter of fact, the name appears many years earlier. It is in a document preserved in the cathedral dated 1132, a record of its age-old dryness.)[50]

In contrast, on the other side, toward the monastery, the documents describe for us a kind of garden place, with grassy stretches (the *pratali*), pools of water (the *mollie*), perennial springs, gentle streams. A limpid spring murmurs there; a copious supply of water flows out, and from it another brook takes its course down to the plain between tall rows of poplar trees. It is noted in a document of September 1129 with the phrase *rigale unde aqua currit* ("a furrow in which water runs").[51]

This stream, called the Camerata *fosso* or brook, gave its name to another property of Pietro Bernardone in the same area and called the Camerata *podere* or farm. At the edge of it, downstream, was the old Spello road, called then the San Martino road, from which the Sentiero della Mollie ("Path of the Pool") goes up to the monastery of Sant'Angelo. From here the streamlet crosses the Camerata road, the main road of the area and still in existence. It continues by the Todero bridge, crosses the old Strada Francesca at the point where the tower of San Savino stood, and finally empties into Rivo Torto at the Fontanelle bridge.

In Fontanelle, so-called because of the many springs bubbling up there, the family owned other plots of land, which were called, appropriately, Strisce di Fontanelle ("Fontanelle strips"). At this point their property became an extensive holding, rich in roads and water. At the right, toward Perugia, it extended to the church of San Pietro della Spina. It continued to the crossroads formed by the Fontanelle road, the Strada Antica ("Ancient Road") that came from Porziuncola, and the Strada Cupa di San Petrignano ("Dark Road of San Petrignano"), which came from San Damiano. Then, following this last road, the boundaries of the property extended back to the intersection with the Strada Francesca, where there was another family place, no more than four hundred metres from the church of San Damiano, called the Stradette farm.

On the other side, toward Foligno, the family land included the watery field of Gorghe ("the place of eddies or whirlpools"), also the property called Basciano or Bassano, in the direction of Castelnuovo along Rivo Torto (it took its name from the fact that it was on the lowest part of the plain; today on the site there is a group of houses along the railroad), and finally, land in Litorta near the church of Sant' Angelo.

These, then, are the places where Francis found from his earliest days that fascination with free and pure things that was so much a part of his interior life. From the days of his happy infancy, he liked to feast his eyes, always avid for beauty, on them. The description of the first and best of all his biographers, Thomas of Celano, tells the story. He was drawn, Brother Thomas writes, by "the beauty of the fields, the pleasantness of vineyards, and all that is beautiful to see."[52] One can say nothing more.

But even in the blessedness of these peaceful fields there were reminders of human greed, men always lying in wait to spy out the passing of wagons of merchandise on the smooth roads so as to claim duties and tolls. These transit rights on determined obligatory crossing points, derived from royal rights (*regalie*), were one of the chief attributes of feudalism. Along the roads most used by merchants and pilgrims, tolls were collected with exasperating frequency. They were the cause of great conflict between the feudal lords, who had no intention of renouncing this comfortable means of getting money, and the cities, where the merchants played a predominant role.

The Strada Francesca was a road particularly infested. It is calculated that on the brief stretch of this road between the Po at Piacenza and the Arno at Fucecchio,[hh] the merchants had to pay tolls no less than eleven times, a cause of great irritation as well as of annoying delays.[53]

Famous in the territory of Assisi, as we have seen earlier, was the fortress of San Savino, never called anything but "the Tower." It stood at the cross-road of the Strada Francesca and the road from Panzo, which followed the course of the Camerata stream (situated a little above the modern group of houses of Osteriola). Even after "the Tower" was torn down, its phantom continued to dominate the *contrada,* so much so that a century later, when it was necessary to specify that particular point in the *balìa*[ii] of San Savino, it was described as *ubi fuit turris* ("where the Tower was").[54] It belonged to a consortium of very powerful knightly families;[55] the documents speak of the families of Adenolfo, Carsedonio di Tommaso, Monaldo di Armanno, and of the sons of Davino.

Farther down, at a distance of a kilometre by today's measurements,

---

hh. Along the old Strada Francesca, this was a distance of 287 kilometres (a little over 172 miles), according to the Italian Automobile Club (ACI) of Rome.—Trans.

ii. The *balìa* was in the time of Saint Francis a territorial division of the *comitato;* it had replaced an earlier division of the territory in which each inhabited rural center had been known as a *locus.* At the head of each *balìa* was a *bajulus* or *bailo,* who represented the authority of the commune in his area. He appointed three custodians and a syndic (*sindaco*) to serve under him. The *bajulus* was required to wear a red cap with the arms of the commune on it at all times. There were fifty-one *balìe* in the commune, according to a census of 1232. *NV* 3:72.

there was the strong castle of Bassiano, first mentioned in documents of 1075. It stood beside the property of Pietro Bernardone and along the Rivo Torto. From that position it held the crossing at the intersection of the road of Spina (another very important means of national communication that terminated at Via Flaminia) and the Strada Vecchia, the old Porziuncola road. This fortress must have been a real nightmare to Pietro Bernardone, who would have been forced to pay the toll there even to take the yearly supplies of wine, grain, and oil into his house in the Badìa area of the city.[56]

By now the propitious moment was being awaited to wreak summary justice on this tower, together with all the other towers and fortresses of the *comitato.* On this goal, merchants and artisans were united. They were joined also by nobles of the city who no longer benefited by forced services and tolls or who were prepared to accept the demands of the *minori,* holding it useless and dangerous to quarrel with them any longer.

That same year of 1197 marked a reprise of imperial horrors in southern Italy. Jailers and executioners devoted themselves to the invention of new tortures. The boy king, William III, son of Tancred, was blinded and then atrociously mutilated. The tomb of Tancred was violated. Margaritone and the archbishop of Salerno were killed, together with many of those loyal to them. Some of them were sawed in two, others crowned with crowns of red hot iron. The savage slaughter was carried on in a frenzy of blood and torturing that could only be matched, in the opinion of Gregorovius, in the history of certain oriental sultans.[57]

Meanwhile, in the distant abbey of Hoemburg, in Alsace, the wife of Tancred, Sibilia, and her three young daughters lived as prisoners by order of the cruel German emperor. Many pleas were made on their behalf. It was said that the princesses were extremely beautiful, that they were loaded down with chains and living in a secret prison, that no one was allowed to come near them. Their names were Albiria, Madonia, and Costanza. Perhaps a knight, handsome and proud as Saint George, would one day take on the task of liberating them. Such extraordinary dreams appealed to hearts avid for heroic enterprises and fed on legends of chivalry.

Suddenly, on September 28, while preparing to rejoin his army for the new Crusade, Henry VI died of malignant fever in Messina. The news must have reached Assisi the following month, together with the refrain of a little song composed by Giovanni da Ceccano. It began, "Everything rejoices with the pope over the death of the tyrant."[58]

The revolt long brooding in Assisi was about to explode and the approaching winter served to deepen bitter resentments. The feudal lords prepared to fight a last desperate defence. The tower of San Savino and the castle of Bassiano increased their bands of armed men, who remained for entire days with their eyes glued to the slits, fearing the approach of a citizen army. No one dared walk on the road that ran across the desolate fields. After sunset, the *stagni,* the pools of water on Pietro Bernardone's farmlands, shone for a long time in the shadow of the mountain, gathering up the very last gleam of the twilight. The people used to call these still ponds *lame,* "blades";[jj] and now the name seemed appropriate because in their motionless frozen gleaming they brought to mind the sheen of bright steel when the army stands in formation and the unsheathed swords shine around the vermilion gonfalon, unfurled for an imminent battle.

jj. In the cathedral archives, fasc. 3, no. 3 (*NV* 3:301), a certain Falamanza states that he sold to Pietro di Bernardo a vineyard located *ad Lames.* The word *lama* is found in several localities in the Assisi commune; it always refers to pools of still water, and especially, water that remains after a flood. This property of Francis's father would likely have been in Bassiano, on the plain below Assisi. *NV* 2:109–10.

·4·

WAR WITH PERUGIA

Conrad Moscaincervello, who governed Assisi for the emperor, heard the rumble of the approaching storm even from the top of his strong Assisi fortress, Rocca Maggiore.[a] The idea of fighting did not worry him, seeing that his whole life had been one of running with military companies, keeping armed watches, laying sieges to cities and castles, launching assaults, scaling walls, imposing ransoms, laying waste to the land, killing men, making forays for women and cattle. But this time the count of Assisi thought his skill would not be enough to save the (imperial) rule, which had been put together with so much effort. Those loyal to the emperor must have been guilty of such excesses of cruelty that even the persons in his retinue and the soldiers in his garrison were terrified.

On January 8, 1198, Celestine III died. In his place Cardinal Lotario, son of Count Trasimondo di Segni, was elected pope and took the name Innocent III. His first concern was the restoration of papal rule in central Italy. Markwald, *marchese* of the March of Ancona, he won over easily. With Conrad, the negotiations were longer and harder. Duke Conrad offered his duchy [of Spoleto] to the pope and promised loyalty to the church, ten thousand pounds of silver, a yearly canon (payment) of one hundred pounds, and two hundred soldiers to keep watch for the pope between Radicofani and Ceprano. To guarantee his promises, he would give his sons as hostages. He promised further to maintain the fortress at his own expense.

---

a. One of the most important contributions made by Arnaldo Fortini to knowledge of Saint Francis and the background from which he came was the reconstruction of events, the identification of personages, and the explanations of the underlying causes of the civil war in Assisi and the subsequent war between Assisi and Perugia. In addition to the rich material in this chapter, more detailed information will be found in *NV* 2:131–219.—Trans.

The terms were good and Innocent was on the point of accepting them. But his willingness to do so caused great scandal. Many people accused him, according to Etienne Baluze, of "an intention to show favour to these Germans in Italy, who had reduced the people to great servitude with such cruel tyranny."[1] So the pope decided for "the cause of liberty" and refused the proposition.

By his order Conrad went to Narni, where the pontifical legates, Ottaviano, bishop of Ostia, and Gerardo, cardinal deacon of Sant'Adriano, were awaiting him. In their presence, in a solemn assembly of bishops, barons, and citizens, the old *condottiero* swore on the Gospels, the relics, and the cross that he intended to fulfill all the orders of the pope. He absolved his vassals from their obligation of obedience. Finally, to demonstrate his sincerity, he turned over to the legates the fortresses of Gualdo and Cesi.

The people of Assisi laid siege to the Rocca as soon as they received news of Conrad's departure. Messengers from the duke arrived and ordered them to halt the siege and turn the fortress over to representatives of the pope. But the people had no desire to let slip such a good opportunity to get rid of this hateful instrument of tyranny, continually at the service of one power or another. And so, under the eyes of imperial and pontifical legates, they took up an assault on the Rocca, and to the sound of bells, destroyed it.[2]

Thus fell the very symbol of feudalism. It was a way of life that would never rise again.

Francis was sixteen years old.

A People's Government

By now the city was ready for its independence. The new situation in the city was not affected by the bull that on May 26, 1198, Innocent III directed to the bishop of Assisi, Guido,[3] confirming his ancient privileges and proposing a unification of the diverse ecclesiastical jurisdictions. The project, which would have put an end to age-old quarrels, did not succeed, primarily because of the solid opposition of the canons of San Rufino and the monks of Mount Subasio.

Besides, the distrust of the pope that had been demonstrated with the destruction of the imperial fortress was greatly accentuated when Innocent III showed a predilection for Perugia, going there in September of that same year of 1198 and staying for fifteen days. He left Perugia October 2, and in Todi issued a brief declaring that he was taking the city [Perugia] under his protection.[4] Even though Assisi's desire to establish an independent government had thrown it against the emperor's man, Conrad, its political sympathy certainly remained imperial, if only because of its hatred of Perugia. In vain the imperious Bishop Guido fired off an interdict against all those who were opposing his plans to reclaim the old privileges. Those affected by it were little troubled; more than one person succeeded in removing himself from the penalties by swearing falsely that after having been excommunicated by the bishop, he had been blessed again by the pope.[5]

By now the development of the commune had been perfected in all necessary ways.

On December 9 of that same year we find the name of the first consul of the city, Bonbarone. He appears in the church of San Rufino to act as an arbiter in a controversy involving claims of lands.

The opening phrases of the opinions of the imperial magistrates had all referred to the authority of the emperor. Now, between the people and their magistrates, there is no one but God. "In the name of the Father, the Son, and the Holy Spirit, Amen. I, Bonbarone, its being my duty to become familiar with the controversy that has arisen between Giuliana on one side and Bernardo di Grasso on the other . . . "[6]

The consul, forceful and self-confident, makes a judgement: *Ego autem hoc modo laudo* ("I recommend this as a remedy"). Let us look well at the face of this new man who speaks with such firmness, who has leapt from the revolution in the piazza to military and political command of the city. We shall at once recognize him as the future organizer of the Franciscan mission to the East, the future minister general of the Franciscan order, the builder of the marvellous Basilica di San Francesco, the most intimate counsellor of the emperor, the man who was described by the chronicler Mariano as "armed with so much wisdom and so much prudence that he was first among the men of his time, first among the Roman Curia, and much esteemed by the Curia of the Empire"—Brother Elias.

His name, Bonbarone, reveals its noble origin. Perhaps he was among those nobles who moved into the city from the country and afterwards devoted themselves to trade (it is known for certain that he was born in a *castello* of the *comitato* of Assisi, probably Brittignano). He had attended the University of Bologna. We cannot exclude the probability that before entering the Franciscan order he was married and that the Guiduccio di Bonbarone who in 1246 was a witness in legal proceedings concerned with the sale of a house in the *contrada* of Sant'Ansuino (the legal paper is preserved in the Sacro Convento) may have been his son.[7] In this case, given the custom of calling neighbours and residents of the same *contrada* as witnesses, we can suppose that Elias's house stood in the episcopal citadel, beside the gate of Sant'Antimo, in the precise place on which the houses of the Fiumi family were later built.

Others that we already know had houses not far away, some of them parents of those who in a short time will appear dressed in poor sackcloth: Scipione di Offreduccio, father of Brother Rufino and uncle of Saint Clare; Tancredi di Ugone, Brother Angelo's father; Matteo di Paganello, a member of the family so loyal to the cathedral of San Rufino; also Leonardo di Scolante and Bernardo di Toserate.

The notary Giovanni who drew up the principal papers of this important historical period declares that he writes *pro communi mandato domini Boni Baronis* ("under the authorization of *domino* Bonbarone").

Six months later, in May of 1199, we discover that the powerful *signore* of the Tower of Parlascio, Tancredi di Ugone, has been invested with the supreme consular office. We find him surrounded by citizens agitating for the opening of a new city gate a short distance from his palazzo, near the place that the city walls penetrate the dismantled imperial citadel. In the past, the suspicious counts and envoys would never have consented to another access, especially at this place, where it would be so easy to reach the nearby Rocca Maggiore.

But on the first anniversary of the destruction of this German fortress, the new gate is there, a gate that will be especially useful to the merchants who go to the March by the Nocera and Gualdo roads. The promoters of the project, wanting their names to be transmitted to posterity, cut them on a great Roman stone brought from the ruins of a building that had been destroyed in the invasions. Their hope of passing their names on to posterity was not in vain, for after seven and one-half centuries the stone is in its place, over the arch with Roman stones at its base. This is the exact inscription:

HOC OPUS FACTŪ EST ANNO   EGIDII
D. NICAE INCARNATIONIS MCLX   TAFURINI
XXXVIIII .IN DIC II. VI KLS IUNII STU
DIO CUNTARINI BARTOLI LONBARDI
BRUNELLI + HAEC EST PORTA Q
UA ITUR IN MARCHIAM − DNO
HOC O   + TANCREDO CONSULE

+ This work was completed in the year of the incarnation of our Lord 1199, in the second indiction, the sixth day before the Kalends of June, through the initiative of Contadino di Bartolo, Lombardo di Brunello,

Egidio di Tafurino. + From this gate one goes to the March. + In the consulate of Domino Tancredi.[8] (Note that the name Egidii Tafurini has been added at the margin at the right, and at the beginning of the last line are the letters "HOC O," probably an attempt to begin the inscription.)

These names attest the fervour of an entire generation. They are to be found in various documents of the archives. Brunello, Lombardo's father, was in the cavalcade of the commune against Valfabbrica in 1206; in the same period he testified in a trial concerning a ruined house in the *contrada* of San Giacomo di Murorotto. Tafurino was a member of the San Rufino consortium in 1148. His son Egidio participated also in the 1206 expedition against Valfabbrica and in 1228 was among the arbiters chosen by the commune for the arbitration of payments to be made for houses on the piazza, among which was the paternal house of Saint Francis.[9]

The cross placed at the beginning and at the end of the inscription recalls the faith of their fathers. In the same way, the stone, which is believed to have been the base of a table once located in the atrium of a Roman house, could be the symbol of a new class come to power at the birth of the commune, a class at last victorious over the descendants of the barbarian invaders.

In fact, this memorial stone represents the historic process of adding the spirit of Rome to the religion of Christ. Here, where the cross has been cut into every stone, every ruin, every house, every place of worship, one cannot contemplate the old city gate that overlooks the wild valley of the Tescio river and reread the thrilling inscription on it without thinking of the words of Carducci: "Italy rose up holding in one hand the cross of Christ but at once stretched out the other to seek the consular fasces among the ruins of Rome."[10]

There is still another sentiment expressed in these old Gothic characters, and that is the unrest of this people, who are now asking for free roads, safe travel, new trade, profitable commerce. *Da questa porta si va nella Marca,* "From this gate one goes to the March." It was more than a simple direction. It was an invitation, a warning, an order, an entire program, summed up in these few words more eloquently than in any discourse.

From that drive for income and riches that is implicit in these words, a new war flared up, begun by the now resolute and implacable city against the castles of the *contado,* a war that in all cities inevitably accompanied the development of the commune. These wars reached their peak in this period after the Peace of Constance."[11]

Francis, the son of the city's richest merchant, could not have avoided participating in it.

Civil War Begins

The nobles made ready to fight. At the first cry of war they had left their comfortable houses in the city and gone to the cliffs so dear to their aggressive and brutal forefathers. In the great silence that ruled over summits open to the sun and gorges filled with shadows, the cadence of the hunting horn now resounded from morning until night, melancholy and strong, a summons to all the men of the ancient court, bound to mutual defence by the sacred feudal law.

The war began at Sasso Rosso, Red Rock or Red Cliff, the castle suspended between the extreme eastern slope of Mount Subasio, beyond the San Benedetto monastery, and the plain below.

At the border of the *comitato,* the castle exacted the *strata militum* [the toll that was the prerogative of knights] on the road between Assisi and Spello. The cliff on which it was built can be seen from every part of the valley; it remains to this very day menacing and sinister, as if up there in that harsh solitude the uncompromising spirits of the ancient *signori* still roam, tenaciously clinging to the stone, unreconciled through all the centuries.

They leap forth from the documents of the time, grim and angry, loudly proclaiming their rights over the people, waving the diploma they had received directly from the emperor setting forth their privileges "as it is the emperor's privilege to grant to them," boasting of their rank "since they had been honoured with knighthood."

There is the old man, Alberico, who fought with Barbarossa. And his brother, Conte, the prior of San Rufino who succeeded Rainerio and spurred the work on the new cathedral, his dreams of the glorious project alternating with participation in furious battles, where he was always in the forefront, on foot and on horseback, in going up the scaling ladders and in commanding the defence on the outer fortifications. The other brother, Ugone, with his sons Fortebraccio and Gislerio. And then the personages of the drama that is about to unfold: Gislerio, son of Alberico; Gislerio's sons, Girardo, Leonardo, and Fortebraccio; Oddo and Monaldo, sons of Leonardo; Paolo and Rinaldo, sons of Fortebraccio.[12]

Three generations of warriors are here, old greybeards and young beardless youths, all of whom fought bravely against the men of the commune. The raid came like a summer squall, suddenly, unexpectedly, in a great clamour. It is possible that even in this first battle, which the challengers—the men of the commune—fought by scaling the tangle of rocks in the face of unerring archers, Francis acquired the reputation for bravery that lives in that incisive description of Thomas of Celano: *levis animo erat et non modicum audax* ("impulsive and not a little rash").[13]

Today, going up on that cliff to which no path leads, one senses the fury that found an outlet in destroying Sasso Rosso. On the short declivity between two cliffs one may still see the results of that attack. A few lines of the old castle wall crop up among brambles. On the summit a mighty ruin remains planted among the boulders, walls all at one with the impervious and tenacious rocks that were the first natural defence of the castle. Seven centuries have passed and nothing has changed since the day following that battle. All those who search for what happened to give to the world Saint Francis and his marvellous love will find the answers up here among the rocks scattered in confusion, rocks that still bear the signs of violence and fire.

Which of them did the noble young friend of Saint Clare, Filippa, daughter of Leonardo, hallow with her sweet gaze and gentle smile?

Leonardo himself, in a new humility silencing the old pride, will be among the first to walk in the footsteps of Saint Francis, following him in a still more terrible battle, this one fought between the desert and the eastern sea.[14]

The documents attesting the claims against the commune for the replacement of the house and for damages suffered tell us how much nostalgia and how much grief were felt by these sons of Gislerio for their lonely mountain fatherland and their beautiful strong castle. The papers linger over every particular, every detail, evoke every tower and wall. The castle was square and measured thirty feet on each side. The walls were eight feet high, all built *de bono pariete grosso*—good, thick walls. The tower reached a height of twenty feet.

(Oh, the memory of the nights in which the walls remained solid against a formidable wind beating against the summit and filling the great rooms with a roaring din, like a storm at sea! The long sunsets of autumn in which the dark cliff hangs becomes lit in a deep bloody colour like a blood clot or like dark rust, a colour that had given it the name lost in the intervening centuries: Sasso Rosso. The ancient charm of those mountain meadows, where in the winters hunts were held. In the icy dawn the trumpets sound the *diana*. It is still dark. The great kitchen reflects the flame of the juniper crackling in the wide fireplace. The nimble greyhounds are leaping and barking. Outside the snow has mantled the bare oaks. And still it snows, in the great quiet of shadows scarcely broken by the glimmer of lanterns. It will be good to run all day, on the wide, white stretches, on the track of the fox and the wolf. And then Easter comes to scatter marguerites on the banks of the streams. Bright and beautiful banners fly over the towers and knights make ready to go down to the plain for jousts with noble friends. Their polished armour sends forth gleams of light.)

All had vanished in that grey tide of clumsy servants and puffed-up merchants who presumed to gird on a sword and make laws in official assemblies. The discomfited feudal lords gnawed on bitterness and in silence prepared their revenge.

War Against the Castles

After Sasso Rosso the castle of Montemoro was destroyed. The site has been called Montemoro (Black or Moor-like Mountain) since the most ancient times—a hill about 800 meters high, black with oaks, on the left of the road from Assisi to Gualdo. Also here there are ravines, precipitous cliffs, gorges and ledges, streams swift to over-flow.

These places still retain their lovely picturesque names. Colle de cerqua alta ("Hill of the Tall Oak"). Sega dei Sassi ("Stone Saw"). Pratacci ("Badlands"). Fonte dell'acqua jaccia ("Spring of Icy Water"). Genga Gioconda ("Winsome Genga"—a name probably meant to describe an area of tufa, a soft stone of the Apennines). Passo Cativo ("Bad Passage"). Forgotten names of the ancient inhabitants return: Torre di Gioacchino ("Joachim's Tower"), Casa delle Vecchie ("Old Women's House"), Monte dell'Abate ("Abbot's Mountain"), Selva della Saracina ("Saracen Woman's Woods"), Casalino di Brocco ("Brocco's ruined house"), Mulino di Cafarone ("Cafarone's Mill").

Saint Pier Damiani's story about the trap laid by the Perugini for the builders of San Rufino is verified and confirmed by the name of an area here, Valle del Trave ("Valley of the Beam").

Castrum maledictum, the cursed castle, Montemoro was called. And even today the people call it "the cursed castle"; they say, "The water that comes from Castel Maledetto, the wood to cut at Castel Maledetto."

The documents allow us to reconstruct the family of the lords of Montemoro.

The first name to be found is Matteo, who had a palazzo in the city in the *contrada* of Murorotto. He had two sons, Giovanni and Davino. Davino was the founder of the line of lords of the tower of San Savino, on the plain near Assisi. Giovanni's family retained the wildness of its mountain origin. One of his sons, Aguramonte, never forgave the men of the city for the destruction of the castle. He remained one of the bitterest enemies of the commune.

He and his brothers owned, in addition to Montemoro, the castle of Poggio San Damiano, located lower down toward the plain called Piano della Pieve. The entire Assisi slope of the Gualdo road was dominated by these two fortresses; no one who passed to go to the

March of Ancona, merchants or men-at-arms, was able to escape surveillance and paying tolls. The castle of Poggio San Damiano was also destroyed.[15]

Among other feudal lords who were swept away in the irresistible advance of the communal revolution were the sons of Morico. They were the lords of a remote hill toward Valfabbrica that took its name from them—Poggio dei figli di Morico—and also held a strong fortress on the top of Mount Luciano; the vestiges of it may still be seen. They had jurisdiction over the large territory that would later be a *balìa* of the same name, a place of hills and streams, bare mountain tops and tall woodlands, scorched fields and mutilated towers. Here, too, the names tell ancient stories, such as Fonte dei Pastori ("Shepherds' Spring"), Fonte dell'Acerra ("Spring of the Pagan Thurible"), and Valle degli Oppi ("Opium Valley").

Morico's family also lived in Murorotto; after their castles were destroyed, the commune obliged them to move into the city. Morico sat in 1212 as consul of the commune. Others of the family, after the first storm was over, preferred to return to their ancestral hill and rebuild the castle of Poggio. It is intact even today, its gate, its high walls, its towers; remains of the earlier building may still be seen. One of the family turned to the path laid out by the son of Pietro Bernardone. He became one of the first companions and one of the most admirable of all.[16]

Celino was another lord attacked by city mobs. This is that Celino del Poggio who in 1228 freed his serfs. Two sons, Bartolo and Berarduccio, were among the cavaliers in 1233. His castle, located on the hill between Petrignano and Mora called the Poggio of Bucaione, was a true fortress, famous in all the Middle Ages as *fortilitium Podii,* the Fortress of the Poggio or Hill.[17]

It is not possible to think that Pietro Bernardone, his sons, his relatives, the members of his consortium, were not involved in these events, that they failed to respond to the call of the consuls in that period when the towers that choked their properties on the plain and blocked the arterial roads were encircled and destroyed.

The tower of San Savino fell into the dust, never to rise again. Its imperious lords were the sons of Davino, Matteo, Tiberio, and Paride, who held the fourth part of the tower as members of a consortium. They were descendants of the second son of the Matteo who was the feudal lord of Montemoro. They had left the mountain to build their fortress on the plain, near the Strada Francesca and its profitable tolls. They owned fields in Bassano, along Rivo Torto, and in Fontanelle, bordering the properties of Pietro Bernardone.

They had lost the savagery of country ruffians and taken on the so-phisticated manners of the city. They wore ornate tunics, carried light arms, had numerous servants, lived in a sumptuous palazzo in Murorotto. We can reconstruct the exact boundaries of it: On the front, the principal street. On one side, the church, and on the other, the steep slope of the street to the upper gate, Via della Porta. At the back, the ancient city wall.

Of this family, Tiberio was the most resentful of the humiliation and the damage. Paride, on the other hand, quickly joined the new and tumultuous life of the commune, which assimilated him and placated him with assignments in ambassadorial missions, in caval-cades, in ceremonies marking the submission of other cities, in legis-lative assemblies. He is the first cavalier on a list of 1233 and the second on one of 1235. His sons, Gilio, Davino, Naimeruccio, and Cristiano, joined him in his new life—they pledged to keep a horse for the commune in peace and in war.

Cristiano was consul in 1210, councillor in 1228. He had three sons: Paride, heir of the name and the magnanimity of his grand-father, who was among the councillors who in the second half of this century went to take possession of the *castello* of Armezzano for the commune. Cristianuccio, who married Domina Risabella and died at an early age. Nicola, who married Angeleria.

Cristiano also had a daughter to whom he gave his name: Cristiana. She joined Saint Clare at San Damiano, where she felt her life con-soled by Clare's daily conversations with her. In the canonization procedures for Clare, she testified that she "believed that everything that could be said about the holiness of any holy woman, even of the Virgin Mary, could be said about her."[18]

The other members of the consortium of the tower of San Savino were, like Tiberio, embittered against the commune: Carsedonio, a man with warped judgement, a stubborn man, who, after the defeat of the feudal lords, did not hesitate to rebuild his fortress on the borders of Perugian territory and from there to continue to harrass the men of Assisi. Finally they once again resorted to arms to reason with him; they seized his castle and held it despite orders of the podestà of Perugia to release it. Of the same spirit were Adinolfo and Monaldo di Armanno, along with his son.[19]

The castle of Bassano also came crashing down. Its ruins cluttered the banks of Rivo Torto and crushed the hedges planted on the border of Pietro Bernardone's field. It must have done much to pla-cate the merchant's anger. No longer would he have to contend with these greedy tyrants or hear in his every hour their fearful names, like boasts of their innate warlike ferocity: Lupo ("Wolf"), the sons of Sanguigno ("Man of Blood").

This last family had taken up residence in the city in the time of the grandfather, Tiberio, who built a palazzo like a fortress in San Giacomo di Murorotto, near the church, opposite Davino's mansion. It was constructed of blocks of travertine marble, and this improbable grandeur commanded the admiration of the city people for a long time.[20] The family had another house on the Mercato or Market piazza, at the head of the street that goes up to San Rufino. Its properties extended all around the tower of Bassano, in places that would be the settings for major events in the life of Saint Francis: Fontanelle, Spina, the rocky road of Arce. Its holdings also included an olive grove in front of the church of San Damiano.

We can also know the members of this family, call them by name one by one, as Francis knew them and called them when he met them in the fields and in the vineyards in which he spent so much time: the sons of Lupo—Pietro and Paolo, the sons of Sanguigno—Offreduccio and Raniero, the sons of Alberico—Sanguigno, Gerardo, and Lupalino. A daughter of Lupo, Beatrice, was swept away by this war.[21]

To study the aspects, the events, the personages, of this convulsed period of Assisi history does not simply provide us with a background for the life of Saint Francis when he was a young man. [In that small city, where lives followed a well laid out pattern] we can, rather, reconstruct his life in that period of which the biographers give us only fleeting hints. There is no doubt that he participated intensely in each of these events. His temperament and his reputation for bravery would have turned him in that direction. His family, his class, and his guild would have ordered him to do so. Given the size and importance of this movement, neither he nor anyone else could have escaped participation.

Lord of the Merrymakers

It would not surprise anyone who knows the customs of our medieval city that in this very period of bitter civil strife, Assisi lived to the hilt another life—a life of festivals and banquets, full of songs and magnificent clothes, pretty girls and chivalrous lovers. It was a part of the restlessness of this epoch, when fickle spirits flickered from courtesy to brutality, from penitence to crime, and from gentility to vulgarity. Rhymes of love changed in a flash to shouts of hate. Pleasure over crowns of roses plaited in the spring sun gave way to exultation over blood poured out in nights of battle.

Hints of this joyful and giddy life that alternated in Assisi with war cavalcades and assaults on fortresses come to us through accounts of the life of Saint Francis by the ancient biographers.

It is best to let them speak for themselves. Thomas of Celano writes: "Indeed, he outdid all his contemporaries in vanities and he came to be a promoter of evil and was more abundantly zealous for all kinds of foolishness. He was the admiration of all and strove to outdo the rest in the pomp of vainglory, in jokes, in strange doings, in idle and useless talk, in songs, in soft and flowing garments, for he was very rich, not however avaricious but prodigal, not a hoarder of money but a squanderer of his possessions, a cautious business man but a very unreliable steward. On the other hand, he was a very kindly person, easy and affable, even making himself foolish because of it; for because of these qualities many ran after him, doers of evil and promoters of crime."[b]

The Three Companions, contrasting his traits with the stinginess of his father, say that Francis was "far more high-spirited and open-handed." And they add that "he was also intent on games and songs, and day and night he roamed about the city of Assisi with companions of his own age. He was a spendthrift, and all that he earned went into eating and carousing with his friends."[22]

The gossipers never ceased having something to say and they said maliciously that the son of the merchant went about spending money on himself and on others as if he were the son of a prince. And they rushed to whisper to his parents their envious tales, with the hypocritical pretense of doing it for his own good. But his parents, because they loved their son very much and at heart were flattered to see him so sought after and admired, always ended by letting him alone.

One time all the city was agog because the young man appeared in the piazza dressed in a new, very strange style, a garment made by stitching together the finest scarlet velvet and worthless sackcloth.[23]

---

b. *1 Cel.*, 3. Many of the early biographers of Saint Francis wrote forthrightly about his uninhibited life as a young man: Thomas of Celano, The Three Companions, Henri d'Avranches, the English Benedictine Roger of Wendover, Matthew Paris, the Dominican Vincent de Beauvais, and Julian of Speyer. Their pictures of his life are in full accord with the customs of the time. For a full discussion of this youthful period, see *NV* 2:113–16.

[Fortini seems to this translator to be of two minds about Francis's behaviour in his youth. While in the text of this biography he seems to say that Francis never really succumbed to the vices, particularly to the sexual immorality of his time, in his notes (*NV* 2:115) he writes that Thomas of Celano's description of Francis as a young man filled with violent youthful passions that made him feel "the fascination of sin and brazenly comply with the demands of his youth" (*1 Cel.*, 3) shows us the reason that people called him "the flower of the young people." Apparently, Luke Wadding was also of this opinion (*An. Min.*, vol. 1, App., chap. IV, 7).—Trans.]

However, the people loved Francis and recognized in him a superiority of courtesy and youthful splendour. They called him "the flower of the young people." And word of his singular charm soon spread outside the boundaries of the *comitato.* Those who knew him said that they never doubted that he would be called to great things. Others, seeing him go along so proud and magnanimous, surrounded by his young friends, could not resist saying that everyone was taken in by him. By now he was so much a part of his group of young people that even when he was sitting at table at home, if anyone of his companions came to call him, he sprang up instantly, not even finishing his meal. His parents never stopped reproving him for this.

He devoted himself to an enthusiastic search for the youthful pleasures possible to him. Nevertheless, the vulgarity that muddied some of his friends never touched him. No one was ever able to say that he had heard Francis say a single indecent or coarse word. On the other hand, if someone else made some scurrilous remark, he made no response.[24] He was elegant and serene, ardent and courteous, as if born to knighthood.

These descriptions of Francis by Franciscan writers may be completed and interpreted through other information about Assisi life and customs of that time, secured by an attentive examination of documents that have been in part overlooked.[25]

That lively young company who considered Francis their leader was of the kind that played so large a part in the life of our medieval cities, especially those in Umbria and Tuscany. They were usually called *societates tripudantium,* companies of *tripudianti* or dancers, from the fact that on certain determined religious and secular festivals, they performed traditional dances—tripudiations—through the streets and piazzas.

These ancient dances were usually performed to the accompaniment of songs that were, in Italian poetry, predecessors of the ballad. The leader of the company sang the song and led a chain of dancers, both men and women, who joined hands to dance in a ring. The characteristic phrase for it is *menare la ridda,* to lead the *ridda* or round dance.

Often the principal part was given to a woman dancer, who mimed the narrative and descriptive action sung by the others. The dance was intended to arouse, according to its theme, tears and laughter, sorrow and joy, the exultation of victory and the disillusionment of defeat, invitation and repulse, sacred love and profane love. Its passionate, often bawdy songs told of the sweet talk and storms of amorous conflict, the rue and unfulfilled desire of an unhappily married woman, the desolation of the abandoned lover, the pain of parting when at sunrise a furtive lover had to take his leave.

A dance famous for its licentiousness in the eleventh and twelfth centuries was Herodias, in which the dancer acted out the frenzy and the horror of the banquet to which the head of John the Baptist was carried.

The life and death of Christian martyrs was the most popular subject with the Tripudianti companies—in Perugia, for example, on the day dedicated to Saint Ercolano, its dancers enacted his story, a performance intended to nourish the fearlessness of that proud commune.

The Assisi company danced on the feast of the second bishop martyr, Saint Victorinus. A company was organized for that purpose, called the Compagnia di San Vittorino or Compagnia del Bastone—Company of the Baton, a name given it from the fact that the leader carried a raised staff to show his office. On the day of his election those in the company swore to obey him by touching this staff. Meetings were held in the church of San Pietro, behind the altar that enclosed the bones of the martyr.

From a reading of episodes told by Thomas of Celano and by the Three Companions, and from evidence in some of the documents in Assisi archives, we must come to the conclusion that Francis was the leader or *signore* of this Compagnia del Bastone.

Thus we can believe that he was the head of the boisterous group that would burst onto the piazza on the evening of June 13, in the festivities of Saint Victorinus. People thronged the piazza, avid to relive the story. At a signal from the leader, the heroic *conzone* rose up, and the young men and women threw themselves into the holy and warlike dance.

Saint Victorinus appears to a crowd of idolators and tells them of the glory of Jesus Christ. His virtuous power looses the tongue of a mute boy and opens the eyes of a man blind from birth. The mute boy and the blind man show their joy. The people cry out at the miracle and praise the true God.

Then Bishop Victorinus is taken before the Roman prefect. Disdainfully he refuses to sacrifice to the pagan gods. The bystanders rise up, muttering imprecations and loudly demanding his execution. The bishop walks toward his martyrdom, kneels, puts his head on the block. The executioner raises the sword, brings it down in the mortal blow. A jet of blood bursts forth, flows unceasingly into the riverbed. The river filled with blood expands, rises over the city walls, flows into the scarlet city, now brought again to the Saviour God. Silent in the night the pious women come, lift the precious corpse, wrap it in linen sheets, carry it away to protect it from the impiety of the persecutors. The chorus raises a funeral lament.

But now the gates of heaven open and flights of angels appear, seize the shining soul, rise again in a whirl of wings and are lost in an immensity of light. The dance grows faster, expressing the celestial ecstasy, the nuptial happiness, the everlasting glory. Hail, Light of the World, Cross wide and deep!

Often these rites took place in churches, by dint of an extremely ancient custom, despite the decrees of church councils.

On the day of Calendimaggio,[c] the dance of the Tripudianti, held in the piazza, celebrated the Bacchanalia and the return of spring. For this festival the young women came crowned with roses, all dressed alike, with belts of gold or silver, velvet overgarments, and white silk mantles flung sideways, according to the traditional style of the company. The doors of the houses were decorated with laurel and box-wood. Tapestries hung from the balconies and windows.

On this occasion either the dance of May or the dance of the beautiful Aelis was performed.

In the dance of May, the Tripudianti invited the young women not to conceal their beauty in closed rooms, but to come down to them and take part in the dance. Old killjoy husbands are sent into exile. And stingy ones. And sad jealous ones. And wrinkled and grumbling hags who force young women to spin and stir up the fire, Monna Scoccalfuso ("Dame Turn-the-Distaff"), Monna Tristalfuoco ("Dame Sad-at-the-Fire"). That day only one woman gives orders—the Queen of May, Queen Aurillosa.

> *Venite, donzella amorosa;*
> *Madonna, venite alla danza.*
>
> Come, loving damsel;
> My lady, come and dance.

And the girls, so beautifully dressed, welcomed the invitation and entered into the circle. They pretended at first not to know what to

---

c. Calendimaggio is one of the most ancient of Assisi festivals, with origins in the celebration of the coming of May in early Rome. Though abandoned in troubled times, it is now firmly re-established as the most important of the purely local festivals. The present colourful celebration recalls the medieval songs, dances, and customs described in this chapter and also is a symbolic re-enactment of the once-bitter factional warfare between the *Parte di Sopra* and *Parte di Sotto* (Upper City and Lower City). *NV* 2:125; G. Fortini, "Calendimaggio in Assisi," *San Francesco Patrono d'Italia* 50:236–40.

do. They hesitated. They seemed uncertain which steps went along with each part of the song—but in the end, cheered by all, they were carried away swiftly and lightly into the dance.

In the dance of the beautiful Aelis, the *conzone* tells of a lovely young girl who gets up before daybreak on a Sunday morning in May and goes down into the enclosed garden.

> *Main se leva la bien faite Aelis*
> *Bel se para et plus bel se vesti.*

At the beginning of the dance Aelis sleeps in her bed, but her sleep is restless and broken by frequent sighs. A blackbird begins to sing in the still-dark garden and awakens her:

> *E per un bel cantar d'un merlo*
> *La bella non può dormire;*
> *E quando dorme e quando veglia*
> *E quando trae di gran sospiri.*

All this is mimed by the dancer. Aelis rises to a sitting position, listens to the bird-call, makes a bundle of her clothes, goes down cautiously, and walks out under the flowering almond trees. She washes herself at the brook, puts on her shoes, dresses, tidies her hair, makes herself a pretty crown of roses, ready now to wait for her love. And the bird of the Forest Sauvage comes down from the trees, flies to her shoulder, and begins to talk in her ear. What does he say to the girl in a new mysterious language? She shows that she does not understand.[26]

There is an episode in the life of Saint Francis that illustrates to what extent he must have been master of this art, an act of his that could have come only from instruction and experience in youth. In the words of Thomas of Celano:

"But when at one time he had come to Rome because the interests of his order demanded it, he longed greatly to speak before Pope Honorius and the venerable cardinals. When the lord Hugo, the glorious bishop of Ostia, who venerated the holy man of God with a special affection, understood this, he was filled with both fear and joy, admiring the fervour of the holy man but conscious of his simple purity. But confident of the mercy of the Almighty, which in the time of need never fails those who trust in it, the bishop brought Francis before the lord pope and the reverend cardinals; and standing before such great princes, after receiving their permission and blessing, he began to speak fearlessly. Indeed, he spoke with such great fervour of spirit, that, not being able to contain himself for joy, when he spoke the words with his mouth, he moved his feet as though he were dancing, not indeed lustfully, but as one burning with the fire of divine love, not provoking laughter, but drawing forth tears of grief. For many of them were pierced to the heart in admiration of divine grace and of such great constancy in man. But the venerable lord bishop of Ostia was kept in suspense by fear and he prayed with all his strength to the Lord that the simplicity of the blessed man would not be despised, since the glory of the saint would reflect upon himself as would his disgrace, in as much as he had been placed over Francis's family as a father."[27]

This episode is of extraordinary interest. At the time that Saint Francis was so overcome by the love of God that his words could be nothing but burning poetry, he began to dance the dance of divine love. And those who listened to him (and they were the highest interpreters of the faith) were not able to hold back tears at this act of pure exaltation. The old *signore* of the Assisi company would never have thought that he would one day be called to dance so sublime a theme.

His friars followed his example, adapting to the service of God what had been an instrument of profane pleasure. An authoritative school of thought supports the belief that the *lauda* of the Disciplinati[d] was none other than a perfect imitation of the ballad that accompanied the dancing of the Tripudianti. Often the spiritual *lauda* was sung to the same melody as the romantic ballad. That was also a tripudiation, the highest, most luminous, most harmonious, of all.

Consider the *tripudio e l'alta festa grande,* the "exalted festival and dance" that Dante envisions, performed by the gloriously flaming souls of the twelve doctors of the church in the sphere of the sun. Three times, shining and triumphant, they sing and dance in a ring. As they stop, Thomas of Aquinas sings the greatest hymn that has ever been raised in praise of Saint Francis. And Dante, watching the shining wheel complete its turn, thinks again, with heartfelt nostalgia, of the merry dances of the companies of Calendimaggio:

---

d. The Disciplinati or Flagellants were religious fanatics who practiced constant self-flagellation in public places and in processions through the streets. A movement arising in Perugia, it spread rapidly all through Europe in the thirteenth century. Eventually the more extreme practices of the adherents were discarded or practiced only sporadically, but the religious groups or *compagnie,* which devoted themselves to prayer, penitence, and sacred lauds or hymns of praise, continued to exist. Their songs and dramatic presentations were inspired or modelled on things done by Saint Francis. From these sacred representations developed the Italian theatre. See Fortini, *La lauda in Assisi.*—Trans.

Donne mi parver non da ballo sciolte,
ma che s'arrestin tacite, ascoltando,
fin che le nove note hanno ricolte.

They stood like dancers still caught in the pleasure
of the last round, who pause in place and listen
till they have caught the beat of the new measure.[28]

Parties, Banquets, and Songs

The *signore* of this company also had to arrange banquets for the group. In this, too, Francis was better than anyone else.

According to the best usages of the day, banquets were to be held not only to satisfy bodily needs but also to enliven the spirit. To enjoy them properly, one had to be a true connoisseur. Many things had to be provided: delicate foods, fine wines, sensual perfumes, rich china, enticing perfumes, luxurious decorations, delightful music, the seductive charm of women. To preside at a banquet revealed better than anything else the liberality and sophistication of the *signore.* Usually the banquets were held in large halls, courtyards, loggias, or gardens, also in the piazzas, where the tables were enclosed by a fence covered with tapestries and floral decorations.

According to Thomas of Celano, Francis did things with generosity and elegance and had many tasty dishes prepared for his fellow diners.[29] Even here the rule given in the *chanson de geste* was observed—the best knight is one who eats well.

The company's rules made it the responsibility of the leader to determine who would pay the bill. By custom one paid for all. This caused some to spend more than they could afford and also provoked bitter arguments, because the one designated did not always take his "sentence" with good humour—a reaction that called forth joking comments from the others.

Women also attended the banquets. The most beautiful women in the city were invited, and they vied for the honour of being chosen. Again according to Thomas of Celano, the practice made these suppers of the Assisi company incentives to immorality, since everything done and said was marked by daring sensuality. Even here communal ordinances covered the situation; they forbade women to attend evening dinner parties in houses to which they did not belong, inasmuch as the night favoured all excesses. These laws were adopted in vain.

At the end of the supper the company went out through the streets, singing love songs—the principal reason for the formation of the groups. And also here there was no one who could challenge the leadership of the genial and ingenious *signore.* Nature had given Francis an extraordinarily harmonious voice. *Vox eius,* wrote Thomas, *vox vehemens, dulcis, clara, atque sonora,* "His voice was strong, sweet, clear, and sonorous."[30]

He had demonstrated almost from his earliest years such a perfect knowledge of the language and the new art of the Provençal troubadours that, according to some historians, it was for this reason, and not because his father wanted to make him a model merchant on the French pattern, that people had changed his name to Francis. Some, indeed, saw in his great facility for assimilating the form and spirit of the Provençal language a particular sign of grace.

And as in that day before the pope, when "the fire of divine love" reawakened the Tripudianti dancer, so in other moments of intense feeling, when he was inspired by Christ's great love, his lyrical passion poured forth in the language and rhythms of his old love songs. And these also were true, real tripudiations, the highest and most thrilling of all. This is how his great biographer Thomas of Celano defined them, for he recorded that these, *haec tripudia,* to which Francis gave himself in memory of the joyful and painful life of our Lord, very often dissolved in tears.[31]

The Wonderful Poetry of Provence

This poetry of Provence that the early youthful companies of the Tripudianti worshipped was none other than an exaltation of the life of perfect chivalry. It revolved around three principal themes; the love of a woman, the joy of living, the splendour of springtime.[32]

The lover must be subject to his lady as a vassal to his lord. Like a rich castle encircled and besieged by splendid knights is the damsel who resists her yearning lover.

> *Por los murs a fendre*
> *Fan engenhs e castels . . .*[33]

To break the walls one must prepare war machines and assault towers, catapults, trabuchs, mangonels; light Greek fire; make arrows fly while, below, the walls are shattered with battering rams. Nevertheless, she does not wish to surrender, she who is of gentle manner, beautiful and who brings forth joy with her enchanting face. All shout, one to the other, "On, on beyond the barrier!"

What can equal the heart's pleasure in the sweet laugh of a damsel?

> *Un avinen ris vi l'autrier*
> *issir d'una bocha rizen . . .*[34]

I saw the other day a lovely laugh come from a merry mouth, and because I had never known laughter so pleasing, an infinite exultation filled my soul. But this lightheartedness, which keeps me so joyous and happy, is but folly. In truth, when I think of you, I undergo such torment that I languish from desire. I do not want, I do not ask another joy and I think that this one will come too late.

Here is the secret of the happiness of the knight: To have money, fields of oats and wheat, flocks, and a hundred coins a day besides, a strong castle that no one can conquer, a quiet haven by a river that flows silently to the sea. To have the wisdom and prudence of Solomon. To commit no errors in words or in deeds. To be loyal, generous, and prodigal. To keep promises. To pay debts. To have a beautiful lady, pleasing, graceful, and merry. To go about with a retinue of a hundred knights.[35]

To feel lighthearted, because without joy one cannot sing.

> *Ar hai dreg de chantar*
> *pos vei ioi e deportz . . .* [36]

Now I have reason to sing, because I see pleasures and good times and joys and flirtations . . . and springs and clear streams, meadows and gardens.

One sings because the air is sweet and love is generous and the weather is festive and because the birds are warbling in the hedges and gardens.

> *Can vei la leuzeta mover*
> *De joi sas alas contral rai . . .*

> Whene'er I see the lark take flight
> And soar up towards the sun on high
> Until at last for sheer delight
> It sinks, forgetting how to fly,
> Such envy fills me when I see
> All those whom love thus glad can make,
> I marvel that the heart of me
> With love and longing does not break.[37]

But all too short are the nights of May.

> *Us cavaliers si iazia*
> *Ab la re que plus volia . . .*

A knight lies with his love, dearest thing in the world to him. And he kisses her many times, saying to her, "Oh, sweet rose, what shall I do? For the light is coming and the night is going away."

> *Doussa res, ieu que farai?*
> *Que · l iorns ve e la nueytz vai.*
> *Ai!* [38]

Alas, I hear the sentry crying, "Away! Already dawn is being followed by day."

The young singers assembled and went down a steep staircase that emerged in a dark arch, the confusion of their voices and suppressed laughter echoing from the tall sleeping houses. Lanterns threw fleeting gleams of light on the shining wood of their lutes and mandolins. The opening lines of the chorus seemed to spread out and expand to the sparkling stars, creating an invisible aura of happiness:

> *Aitant se plus viu hom quam viu iauzens . . .*

A man only lives when he lives joyfully;
to live another way is not to be alive. [39]

Then, in the suspense that comes in the pause at the end of the melody, a single voice, agile and pure, melodious and strong, a voice that everyone could have distinguished from a thousand others, began a favourite theme.

> *La nuech vai e · l jorns ve . . .* [40]

The night is going away and coming is the day; clear and serene is the sky. The dawn is on its way. Behold, it comes, beautiful and alluring.

Pica would listen to the last notes die away under the arch of San Nicolò. It was not yet that promised dawn, the dawn of truth that would rise from the new dawning east of the world. But she had no doubt that it would come. To those who came later to complain to her about her son's bad habits, she invariably replied that the prophesied glory was not far away.

The glory that now seemed to be smiling and beckoning was the glory exalted in his favourite songs, the ones that praised the new season not only as a forerunner of happy loves but also as a time when knights could go out to the field and satiate themselves on another great joy, one certainly not thought inferior to the joy of a loving woman.

> *E mala vic*
> *Qui no vol guerra e destric,*
> *Per c'om conois amic!*

Cursed be he who does not want war and hardships, through which one knows his true friend!

> *Pero be · m platz qe · l temps francs*
> *fai los brancs*
> *dels arbres vermeils e blancs;*
> *e am guerra qi · ls estancs*
> *d'aver fa · n remaner mancs . . .* [41]

Therefore, I like the beautiful season that turns the tree branches into masses of vermilion and white; and I love war, which deprives cowards of all they own.

It is good to see war tents spread out in the meadows, to hear the cry of an attack, to look at the dead lying in the trenches, pierced by the stumps of bannered lances.

> *. . . e vei los mortz que pe · ls costatz*
> *an los tronzos ab los cendatz.*

I tell you that nothing my soul can cheer,
    Or banqueting, or reposing,
Like the onset cry of "Charge them" rung
    From each side, as in battle closing,
        Where the horses neigh,
And the call to "aid" is echoing loud;
And there on the earth the lowly and proud
    In the foss together lie;
And yonder is piled and mangled heap
Of the brave that scaled the trench's steep. [42]

Another reason, indeed, for the organization of the Tripudianti companies was the holding of tournaments and jousts.[43]

Also at that time, and for a long time afterwards, bull-fighting was popular in Assisi. Originally it took place in the Roman amphitheatre. At a later time, it was held in the Piazza del Comune, where a mounted man armed with a lance faced a bull before a delirious and enthusiastic crowd. This custom persisted until a century ago—our grandfathers used to tell how on the week after Christmas, when in the early hours of the afternoon the bells of the cathedral began to ring for the canonical hour of Vesper antiphons, a bull was driven out of his enclosure in the old amphitheatre to run free in the city streets. There, dogs barking at its heels, it began to run furiously until the young men who dared, came out to fight it with swords.

Another curious custom, no less fierce, was that of fighting battles with stones and blunted arms on certain religious festivals. All the men of the city, including boys and men of ripe years, participated in them. The preferred places for these exercises were the Sementone field (land then uncultivated at the foot of the city walls, from the bishop's palace to the monastery of San Pietro), Prato del Parlascio (now Piazza Nuova), and the *borgo folignate,* the part of the city in the direction of Foligno (today Porta Nuova).

The participants divided into two sides, one made up of men from the upper part of the city, the other from the lower part. The sides took opposite ends of the piazza and street. At a call by the heralds of the field, the men who wore light arms began the fight by hurling a cloud of stones and yelling and shouting bloody insults. After a time, it was the turn of the boys, who repeated the action, trying to follow the example of their elders. Then the two sides moved forward, preceded by those wearing heavy armour, who, carrying shields, brandished clubs and lances from which the iron tip had been removed. A no-holds-barred, body-to-body fight followed, until a new signal from the heralds. And so it continued until one or the other side was driven from the field or asked to surrender.

No fewer than ten persons were maimed or killed in each of these fights. It was considered pure bad luck and relatives were not permitted to exercise the right of vendetta or of retaliation. Graver consequences followed when outsiders with arms joined the city men, in which case the warlike exercises degenerated into a real battle.

Often also the dances of the Tripudianti ended in blood. Sometimes in disregard of communal statutes, some members came to the piazza dressed in silk and brocade but with swords at the belt, indication of a deliberate intent to commit offences and "to come to the irons." Then women fled with cries of terror, leaving their broken garlands on the ground and the piazza was emptied in a flash. On such evenings the *festa* ended in the flames of arsonists.

Heroic Deeds in Distant Lands

Pietro Bernardone, when he returned from his usual trip to Champagne, had much to say about Count Gautier de Brienne, who had undertaken the arduous enterprise that was the dream of all knights: the rescuing of the widowed queen of Tancred and the young princesses. For four years they had been languishing in the dark prisons of an Alsatian abbey.[44] He had succeeded in his mission and returned to his homeland hailed as the perfect invincible knight. The freed ladies had gone with him to his castle.

In the name of her eldest daughter, Albiria, heir both to the title and material wealth of her brother, the slain boy king, William III, Queen Sibilia asked the pope to restore the ancient Norman reign of Apulia and Sicily, at that time in the hands of a sour German captain, Markwald, the grand seneschal, who had falsely sworn that it was his intention to defend little Frederick's crown. Innocent III, who was Frederick's guardian, was unconvinced. He sent Queen Sibilia to the king of France.

The king, hearing how she had been treated, called his barons to a parley. There is a verbatim record of his remarks: "If, messires, it is the king's duty to undertake the defence of the oppressed and to avenge them for the injuries of the powerful, even more is it a kingly thing, and I would dare to say, a divine thing, to bring help to women, and above all, to queens, who for their fragility and weakness are not in a position to resist aggressors with force; for where more manifest is a just right, the greater will be the glory and the praise. Here is Sibilia, who has asked our help and who promises to give her daughter—who carries as a dowry Sicily and all that region of Italy known as Apulia—in marriage to the one who will have the spirit to reconquer this land with arms and to avenge the injuries suffered. Nor should any of you hold that such a feat is impossible, because I myself judge that it can be done in a short time and with a happy outcome. And, God willing, I myself should undertake this expedition to become the avenger of kings, the saviour of the peoples, the vindicator of all tyranny!"[45]

Among all the knights present, Gautier was the first to offer his sword and his life.

So it was that this French knight had won the hand of Albiria, the young daughter of the king, Tancred. King Philip Augustus and all his court participated in the wedding, which took place immediately in Melun. Immediately it was a common saying all through the realm that this had been a marriage of valour and hope.[46]

In the consistory of the cardinals to which the newly married couple was summoned, Innocent III granted to Gautier the earldom of Lecce and the princedom of Taranto. He made him swear on the Gospels, however, that while fighting Markwald and his associates without let-up, he would do nothing to damage little Frederick and his rights to the imperial crown. In that summer of 1200 Gautier had been in the Champagne region in order to recruit knights for his mission. Then he set out by way of the Alps on his great enterprise.

Perhaps the merchants who were returning from the great fair and the little company of knights that was undertaking this extraordinary adventure travelled together. *Non multi sed strenui* ("Not many but strong") was the motto of the knights. Warriors of great renown were with Gautier: his brother Jean, Robert de Joinville, Walter de Montbéliard, Eustace de Conflans. They had again taken the cross, blessed by the pope, to signify the sanctity of the cause for which they were preparing to fight. They paid no attention to the voices raised on their way that called them arrogant and foolhardy to think of marching against the formidable army of an entire kingdom when they were so few in number.

On Mont Cenis the caravan halted to rest the horses. The ground over which they travelled was a slimy mess of rocky rubble and melting ice; not a blade of grass could be seen on the desolate peaks, burned by the cold.[47]

On their descent they had the surprise of meeting the marshal of Champagne, Geoffroy de Villehardouin, who himself bore the red cross on his shield. He was on his way to Venice to negotiate with that republic for the loan of ships to carry Crusaders to the east. The two companies greeted each other joyously and exchanged promises to look for one another as together they moved toward the supreme goal to which all had dedicated themselves, the rescue of the Holy Sepulchre.[48]

About two years earlier all of them had been together in the castle of Escry-sur-Aisne to take part in a famous joust that attracted the flower of French knighthood. Folco de Neuilly had unexpectedly got up and spoken, in tears, of the havoc in places that had seen the life and death of Jesus. Immediately those knights had left the festival, taken the cross, and declared themselves ready to leave for the Holy Land.[49]

Gautier was on his way to Rome. At his side rode the beautiful Albiria.

Francis was delighted by the marvellous tale and by the great heart needed to conquer a kingdom, trusting only to one's own courage. If the count of Brienne had taken Albiria for himself, there were still the younger sisters, waiting in the castle on the top of the rocky hill, overlooking a valley traversed by great rivers. And these were the most beautiful, the most ardent, the most unfortunate girls that a royal line had produced, the last flowering of the line. They were like those bright, unexpected flames that break forth from a heap of dying coals, or better yet, like those crimson roses that bloom in autumn on a branch ready to wither, all the splendours of the past spring concentrated in them. Their names expressed a musical magic of grace, passion, pain: Madonia, Costanza. The fanciful and yearning young man felt he was in love with them.

The lord of Blaye, Jaufrè Rudel, had thus fallen in love with the countess of Tripoli without knowing her, through reports of her beauty and courtesy by pilgrims returning from Antioch. Because of his desire to see her, he took the cross and set sail for the land over the sea. On the ship he was struck by a terrible fever, and those with him thought that he would not live. However, they saw to it that he was still alive when they reached Tripoli. And the countess, seeing him, took him in her arms and comforted him greatly, so much so that his sight and speech, which had been lost, returned to him. And he praised God greatly that such a wonderful grace had been granted to him. Keeping his eyes always on his love, in a little while he died in her arms.[50]

For these creatures of his desires and dreams, and for so many others dimly visualized in remote castles, on the landfalls of enchanted beaches, in the opulence of fantastic kingdoms, he, the leader of the Tripudianti of Assisi, the poet lover, would gladly be like that sweet singer who set forth with sail and oar to seek his death, repeating the verses of his passionate song:

> *Amors de terra lonhdana,*
> *Per vos totz lo cors mi dol.*

> O love of a far-away land
> For you my whole heart is yearning.

He, too, would leave one day and go forth to find his love of a far-off land. He would put an all-white ensign on a fine ship. He would become a Crusader. He would scale mountains covered with perpetual ice, go through seas beyond every known limit. He would conquer a splendid kingdom.

And now he mourned that he was not in the retinue of the count of Brienne on the day he had passed along the Strada Francesca at the foot of the Assisi hill, on his way to Rome and Apulia. He had their temper, their blood, even their name. He was called Francesco. In prowess and generosity he seemed to be one of them, one of those poet warriors come down from France.

One of his earliest biographers touched on the same point when he praised his holiness by speaking of his bold courage. His name was changed to Francis because of his great heart, he wrote, romantically adding that the name "Franks" comes from the word "frankness," in its meaning of fierté—pride, courage, and great spirit. "In these people," he wrote, "there is a natural boldness and magnanimity of spirit."[51]

Civil War Comes to the City Streets

The fight against the *buoni uomini* spread in a short time to the inside of the city. Judging from the lists of ruined houses that have come down to us in the records, it must have been a fierce no-holds-barred battle.[52]

The *contrada* of San Giacomo di Murorotto was among the first to be engulfed by it.

The papers of the time give us a reconstruction so precise that we can see the towers and city walls, the buildings that lined the streets, the streets themselves, as Francis saw them in that convulsed period.[53]

"Murorotto," the people still call the district, "Broken Wall." Its name, given as "Muro rupto" in the oldest records, indicates that the city wall, in an attack lost to memory, was surmounted and conquered by an invading army. Probably it happened in the invasion of the Franks, who came by the road from Gubbio and Valfabbrica to attack the city, then held by the Lombards. This road crosses the river by the bridge that even today is called Ponte dei Galli ("Bridge of the Gauls"). The name of Murorotto (or Murorutto) is found for the first time in a document of 1147.

Here in this harsh slope ascending to Rocca Maggiore, the city wall is tall, fierce, imposing.

At its base are the great boulders that our Umbrian ancestors, primitive artisans who worked with club and hammer, put together without lime or cement.[54] Over it are the stones shaped by the stone cutters of the high Middle Ages, who aspired to make works of beauty and harmony for the protection of the city people. Higher still are stones that even today the pickaxe cannot dislodge, so powerfully were they wedged into place on the eve of a battle. One can read, as in a book, the history of hundreds of generations that sought their destiny in arms. But on the top, where the black stone is crumbling in the silent relentless destruction of the centuries, great yellow and red wallflowers blow at the return of Easter. Their subtle perfume seems a resurrection of moribund aspirations for goodness and gentleness.

The truncated tower of the Porta Superiore, the upper gate, is there. We know from the notarial acts and judicial records of San Rufino the name of the artisan who, along with his men, undertook to repair it after this war that blazed up in Saint Francis's youth— Maestro Capitale.[55] He quarreled with his turbulent neighbours, now shouting complaints about the attack on the wall, now because of a loophole opened too near the corner bartizan, now because the line of the corner of the tower fell outside the wall. One Ugolo di Bonizzo has left testimony that he bought a ruined house that had once belonged to the presbyter Maria. It was later destroyed in a battle waged by the archbishop of Mainz. Another complained that the wall of a garden planted in hemp was twice ruined by city companies, and that a breech remained there. In front of it elders and wild figs now grow.

The priest of San Giacomo, Domino Egidio, who held the investiture all during Francis's lifetime, was continually before the consuls, because of quarrels with greedy neighbours who gathered and took away his olives or to draft documents of acknowledgement and donation or to complain of robbers whom he cursed and chased with shouts and stones. The huge orchard that the church owned within the ancient wall, rich with fruit and plants, was not enough for him. He laid claim to the walls of houses that had been destroyed, to abandoned lands, to slopes on the borders. We can visualize him looking out, sullen and angry, from the narrow aperture of the apse. It is still intact, with its curtain wall of rough cut stone surmounted by a crown of little arches. We see him rambling about the long and narrow church, all arches and niches and walls of bare stone, and going up to the altar, where in the shadows the splendid gold cross gleams, a cross famous for its richness and workmanship. We see him going out into the cloister, where the walls are embellished with mullioned windows. The cloister wall may still be seen, and so may the old well, with its chain and pulley. A tall pointed campanile, now gone, rose above the church on the side nearest the hill. The parish church was well provided with material goods. It had jurisdiction over thirty-eight houses of the *contrada*.

Beyond the street was a piazzale, a large piazza or square, in part today occupied by the church built later, at the end of the sixteenth century. The piazzale was flanked by great houses on two sides. At the back was the church with the priests' living quarters. The palazzo on the right, which stood on the hillside, its front facing another street (today the flight of steps leading to the monastery of Santa Croce), belonged to the sons of Matteo. The palazzo on the left, where the Tini house now stands, belonged to the sons of Sanguigno and the sons of Lupo.

The men of the people attacked and captured these two houses and burned them.

The ruins of the house belonging to the sons of Sanguigno remained on the site for many years, until in 1239 descendants gave the huge travertine blocks of the master wall to Brother Elias for the construction of the Basilica di San Francesco. An extraordinary thing indeed that the stones of a building destroyed in a war of factions and by the citizen army in which Francis fought should serve for the construction of the great shrine intended as an eternal reminder of Francis's infinite love!

In the same *contrada* of Murorotto, the palazzo of the sons of Morico, near the wall, was also destroyed and laid waste.

Other nobles' houses fell on the piazza of the Mercato, near Francis's paternal house: the palazzo of the sons of Dodici, the consortium's tower, the palazzo of Ugolino, son of Matteo. The rebels' bloodthirsty shouts shook the room where the merchant's son basked in his dream of glory. The reflection of fires lit up his sleepless nights. Flocks of archers armed with crossbows and huge shields passed by. Ranks of artisans were all about, raising axes, clubs, iron-tipped cudgels, and sharpened knives.

Still other houses of nobles came down in a chilling roar of flames, crashing walls and beams, and inhuman savage yells—the house of the sons of Gislerio in the San Rufino *contrada,* the house of Carsedonio and Adenolfo outside the San Giorgio gate, the house of Berarduccio di Tebaldo in the Parlascio *contrada,* the houses of Monaldo di Armanno, Gentile di Seguino, Celino del Poggio, Offreduccio del Negro, the sons of Pietrucciaccio, Giovanni del Sasso, Medico. And there were still many others.

These proud families, always having lived in opulence, were in danger of being left without roofs over their heads and having to beg in the streets in misery and hunger.

We can get an idea of their state of mind by reading a document of 1199. It is by the counts of Collemezzo, who had the castle and properties on the border between Assisi and Todi. In order to escape the communal revolution, which had then spread along the hill that divides the Assisi plain from the valley of Puglia, they put themselves and their goods under the protection of the powerful monastery of San Pietro of Perugia, one strong in material possessions, arms, pontifical and imperial immunities.

If it happened that any commune, or anyone at all, should attack them, the monastery promises to go out in their defence. "And if they, or their heirs or successors, or any of them, men or women, should fall into need, they and their families are to be able, freely, to have recourse to the aforesaid monastery for whatever is necessary to life, without opposition on the part of anyone. And if fate should bring them to this extreme need, God forbid, and they decide to put their nubile daughters who are called by God into monasteries, the abbot and the monks of San Pietro obligate themselves, at their own expense, to provide them with dowries to the extent necessary and to accommodate them in monasteries for women of the rule of Saint Benedict, as is suitable." Come what may, the aforesaid castellans are promised that they shall have from the monastery of San Pietro food for themselves and their families and all other things necessary and that the principal members of the family shall be received and seated at the table of the abbot.[56]

There is no peace, there is no longer a place for goodness. Around the ruins of the castles that have been destroyed, armed mobs of men lie in wait. They wait for the chance to render evil for evil, blood for blood.

Assisi's War with Perugia

On January 18, 1200, one of the lords of Sasso Rosso, Girardo di Gislerio, presented himself to the consuls of Perugia and asked for citizenship. He promised to hold his Collestrada properties as an allodial concession[e] of his new political home, thus depriving Assisi of the right to tax these lands. He assured them that it was his intention to obey in every particular the laws of the Perugini rulers.[57]

The ceremony was of particular solemnity because everyone understood the significance and consequences of this act. The consuls were seated in full assembly, wrapped in their peacock-blue cloaks: Berarduccio, *camerlengo,*[f] Gilio di Paolo, Bonagiunta, Cacciaguerra,

---

e. An entire property held in absolute ownership, as opposed to property held as a feudal benefice from a superior.—Trans.

f. The *camerlengo* in this instance was a steward entrusted with the management of revenues of the state; a synonym of *camerario.*—Trans.

Struffolo, Germanello, Gallo, Benvegnate, Sinibaldo. Many other leading citizens were also present.

Maestro Bertramo, notary of the Sacro Palazzo, rose and read the rights and duties assumed by each new citizen. In the present case, in which a knight was involved, the feudal law required that sons must follow the citizenship of the father. The consuls, therefore, ordered that they be advised within thirty days, by messenger, whether the sons would also appear to accept this additional condition.

After five days, on January 23, Girardo's brother Fortebraccio and his nephew Oddo, Leonardo's son, appeared and made the required declaration. Within a short time all the others of the family followed them.

It was an old tactic that the Italian feudal lords had learned from the emperor: to take advantage of cities fighting each other by putting themselves under the protection of the enemy commune, thus taking revenge and at the same time saving for themselves all that it was possible to save. Cities in turn opened their arms to these runaway castellans, seeing in the submissions and alliances a means of extending their own domain. Perugia revealed herself to be a master in this art.[58]

Each oppression of a stronger state by a weaker one, each unjust violence, each odious conquest, always must be draped in a mantle of apparent legitimacy and given moral and juridical justification, so that the aggressor, who in reality relies only on superiority of arms and acts solely from pride and greed, can proclaim that he is motivated only by the cause of human and divine law. It is a ridiculous hypocrisy of the wicked masquerading as the righteous. It fools no one; but for all that, in every march of invading armies, it is repeated with exasperating monotony. So through the centuries there has been a series of these dismal comedies, enacted on scenes of fearful tragedy, so that the most brutal tyrant can present himself in the guise of a celestial messenger, an avenging angel brandishing a sword of righteousness.

To declare war on Assisi, the Perugini consuls now had to do nothing but invoke an article of one of their own statutes, which obliged the commune to protect its new citizens and to help them in the defence and recovery of their goods. And that is what they did. They demanded that Assisi rebuild the castle of Sasso Rosso and pay damages.[59]

All this fitted perfectly into the political designs of the commune of Perugia, which sought to attain absolute supremacy both in influence and government in the entire region. It was not in the least disposed to let anyone wriggle out of the clutches of the clawed gryphon. It was simply an enactment of its ancient motto, whose meaning was unmistakable to anyone who knew how to read it properly: *Fertilis et fortis sum, libera prompta favore,* "Fruitful and strong am I, free, ready to grant to all my protection."[60]

The governors of the Etruscan city did not permit competitors and rivals on an equal basis, in wealth, in power, in independence. Its hymns to the liberty of the communal democracies, so high-sounding in the orations of ambassadors sent to make and unmake laws against popes and emperors, rang out, in this matter, like bitter ironies. The arrogant commune opened its arms to every city and castle, inviting them to enter its embrace. It offered protection, on condition that they become satellites of the major star.

If Assisi had knuckled under, it would have suffered irremediable damage to its prestige, its honour, even its independence. Anyway, there was the matter of the old hatred between the two cities. It stilled every voice counselling prudence.

Assisi preferred to resort to arms. The demand of the Perugini consuls was rejected, with stentorian bravado and in insulting messages. War broke out.

For more than two years it was limited to raids, cavalcades, the destruction of crops, surprise actions, ambushes, battles for places on the borders that were lost and won, the burning of old towers, the building of new towers to keep watch on disputed stretches, proclamations, reprisals against merchants and men of the *contado.* In the meantime, the two cities were preparing for the decisive blow—organizing their armies, intensifying the network of alliances and promises of aid, engaging mercenary companies.

Perugia's true anxiety in this war was made plain by the pact it made with Foligno in October 1201 "for the safety of the city of Perugia and of the men who live in it."[61]

Meanwhile, other citizens of Assisi followed the example of the lords of Sasso Rosso: Berarduccio di Tebalduccio, Alberico di Tiberio, Aguramonte di Giovanni di Matteo, Matteo with his brother Carsedonio, Ronzone, Obizzo, Brocardo, Satente, Andrea dell'Isola, and others.[62] The people promptly responded by taking apart their houses and sacking them.

The Assisi consuls, for their part, worked feverishly to collect an army. Aid was sent by Nocera, Bevagna, Spello, and Rosciano, as well as by the surrounding *castelli.*[63]

A large brigade from Fabriano, a city also in perpetual disputes with Perugia over castles on the borders, arrived by the mountain road. It entered by the new gate built by Consul Tancredi. Amid cheers from the citizens, their spirits raised by its arrival, it went down to the cathedral for the swearing-in ceremony. We know the names of some of the cavaliers: Guelfolino, Sasso's son Gentiluzio, Boninsegna of Gubbio, Egidio di Guglielmino, Pinzo. Alberto di Rinaldo, also of Fabriano, brought a full squad: twenty-five archers and six cavaliers—Todino, Raniero di Bonifacio, Raniero di Offreduccio, Rinaldo Dera, Giunta, Alberto Guelfo.[64]

Every day other cavaliers came. Some names were like a heroic poem, a war cry: Ruggero di Malcavalca ("Roger the Evil Rider") at the head of an entire company, Saraceno di Campodonico ("Saracen of Campodonico"), Vadovinco ("I Come, I Conquer") from Sommaregio, his brother Deusteadiuvet ("God Help You"). There were cavaliers of Serra, Sassoferrato, Gubbio, Trevi, Narni, and even from Apulia.

Simone della Rocca came down from his strong castle of Arce Pàida on Mount Subasio with his sons, Matteo, Giovanni, and Pietro, and with other knights of the family, among whom Paganello della Rocca is noted in the records. (Giovanni di Simone was among those who saw the stigmata before and after the death of Saint Francis.) And Bulgarello of Fossato, lord of this *castello* and also of the *castello* of Serpigliano, on the hill toward Nocera, came, followed by his sons, Raniero and Bernardino.

The poet of the *Eulistea* uses an extraordinarily vivid bit of imagery for this confusion of warriors through the streets and piazzas of Assisi. *Armorum estus,* he calls it: a tide, an ebb and flow, a coming and going of riders and archers at all hours, a restless wave shining with iron and steel, bristling with lances, ringing with shields and swords.

The Battle of Collestrada

The battle, so long prepared for, so long awaited, came in November of 1202.[g]

In its march the Assisi army went down to the plain, thrust forward

---

g. The battle in which Francis fought and was taken prisoner is mentioned in many early sources, including *1 Cel.* and *2 Cel., 3 Soc.,* the works of Jacopus de Varagine, Bartholomew of Pisa, Mariano da Firenze, Luke Wadding. A note in *Breve Annali di Perugia* notes the year precisely—1202, a date supported by information in the *Eulistea* and in records in the Perugia archives. Additional confirmation of this date lies in the fact that Francis's proposed expedition to Apulia could not have been later than 1205. The length of time required for his long imprisonment, illness, and convalescence, and for the planning and preparations for the trip would be right for this date. The record of a legal process of liberation in the early years of the thirteenth century mentions the war between Assisi and Perugia (Arch. Cath., fasc. 8, no. 1; *NV* 3:337–39).

The details of the battle given in this chapter, the name of the head of the army of Perugia, and the outcome are all taken from the *Eulistea.* For detailed discussion: *NV* 2:169–78.

beyond the cross-road, advanced into the Campagna territory, went up the hill of Collestrada, and crossed the border between the woodlands of the church and the castle.

The companies were on view in their parade from the cathedral to the Roman gate, their war standards unfurled. All the shops were closed. All the bells rang *all'arme* and *al doppio,*[h] together sounding a call to arms. The tocsin sent into the clear air of a sweet Saint Martin's summer that particular sense of solemnity and anxiety that always accompanies the departure of troops to an unknown fate.

The *contrade* filed past. San Rufino, its ensign bearing the crozier, the millstone, and the martyr's palm. Santa Maria Maggiore, the ancient people loyal to the authority of the bishop, raising a standard bearing a circle of stars, symbol of the glory of the Virgin Mary. Santa Maria del Sopramuro, the quarter between the cathedral and Capobove, where the dark houses rest on the Roman wall running behind the Minerva. Upper Murorotto and Lower Murorotto. Colle. Prato. Borgo, the new city overflowing outside the city wall between Sementone and San Pietro. San Lorenzo. L'Abbadia, Saint Francis's *contrada,* which has as its symbol the sword that severed the head of the apostle Paul.

The guilds followed: the merchants, the shoemakers, the butchers, the tax collectors. And then the flocks of archers and the cavaliers.[65]

Last of all, slowly and heavily, came the *carroccio,* drawn by white bullocks covered with red and blue caparisons. These same colours, the city colours, gleamed around the altar that from the height of the cart dominated everything else—cross shining, candles burning, the bell (called the *martinella*) striking at intervals, the great gonfalon of the commune unfurled, as it had been when the relics of the first bishop were transported into Assisi from his place of martyrdom on another day of emotion, tension, and excitement.[i]

---

h. "The moment of departure (of the citizen army) was announced by the great bell of the commune, which rang *all'arme* and *al doppio,* and by the public crier. As this bell began to ring, a lighted torch was placed at the gate through which the army would leave. He who had not presented himself before the torch burned out was punished. The citizens had to assume responsibility for their arms." NV 3:184.

i. It seems certain that Assisi, like other Italian cities, had its *carroccio;* there is a reference to a "Pietro del Carroccio" in city records, undoubtedly the keeper of this official chariot. The description of the vehicle used for the return of the sepulchre of Bishop Rufinus to Assisi (see chap. 2) is of a typical *carroccio:* a large wagon draped in scarlet cloth, drawn by six or eight white oxen of unusual size. On it was a bell and also a staff flying the red and blue flag of the commune (or, on occasion, a black flag called the *guasto,* to indicate before a battle was begun the intent to destroy totally the lands and towns). The *carroccio* was used as a sign of honour, as when city officials went out to meet kings and popes, also in solemn ceremonies. Often on it officials swore to the terms of treaties between cities. Before the communal army went out to battle, the *carroccio* was taken from the church to the piazza of the *arengo,* and every evening its bell, the *martinella,* was rung for a period to warn citizens to keep themselves in readiness. NV 3:183–84.

Stirring notes came from the trumpeteers surrounding the altar. The people burst into shouts and cheers.

Francis was with the Compagnia dei Cavalieri.[j] Bright eagerness shone in the twenty-year-old who was caracolling so gloriously toward combat. Perhaps the hand of some noble lady reached out to give him a white scarf. Perhaps some of those who had predicted a heroic life for him saluted him now, calling him by name.

To those who watched from the walls, the army, stretching along the Campiglione road, seemed like a serpent with shining scales, uncoiling in the brown fields. A gentle golden light enveloped all the countryside, washing a golden wave over the bare vines, the tranquil meadows, the poplars reddening on the banks of the rivers.

In the early hours of the afternoon a company of archers occupied the castle on the top of the Collestrada hill, where there was another lepers' hospital. The companies disposed themselves along the slope, between the woods near the church and the road to Perugia. A group of cavaliers chosen to keep watch over the movements of the enemy lay in the middle of the dense canebreaks on the curve of the Tiber in this point of the plain.[k]

The Perugini, when they learned of the occupation, were so enraged that more than half a century later, Bonifazio, the poet of the *Eulistea,* still felt the heat of that anger. Emphatically he addressed the daughter city of Rome, whose destiny was to dominate all the neighbouring peoples: "How could the Assisani pretend to be ignorant of your strength? Where does all that temerity, which makes them eager to raid your borders, come from? A rash and insolent people are these, a blind and forgetful, insolent people. They do not remember the time they prostrated themselves to kiss your feet and the ground over which you passed. They do not remember the days in which you, in order to defend them, moved against Caesar."

The sneers and the boasts with which the whole episode is embellished must have been straight from a phrase book of insulting clichés especially coined for these bitter municipal wars. Again, the poet continues, the Feathered Ones (meaning the weak, cheeping chicks)

---

j. As noted in chap. 2, n. n, the Compagnia dei Cavalieri was the elite of the city's armed companies, the *sotietas militum,* made up of knights and of prosperous merchants who could afford the necessary horse and costly armour. Even enemy cities recognized the difference between it and the foot soldiers, as biographies of Saint Francis indicate: the captured riders were imprisoned separately from the other soldiers. *NV* 2:170–71; 3:185.

k. The identification of the battlefield and details of the battle are given in *Eulistea.* The remains of the castle on top the little hill of Collestrada, between the cities of Perugia and Assisi, and near the Tiber River, may still be seen. A short distance away is the old leper hospital, now rebuilt and used as a school. It was in this hospital that St. Francis stopped to rest after his trip to Perugia to ask the pope for the Indulgence of the Pardon. See *NV* 2:172–78.

were claiming that they wanted to fight the taloned Gryphon. Certainly this miserable mob, coming under the worst omens, was looking for its own extermination. At the first blow of the lance they would turn tail, like a drove of sheep out of their minds with terror. They would kneel to ask mercy. Every Perugino is to raise his sword and harden his heart. "You have known how to conquer better enemies, and this particular enemy you have laid prostrate many times. Forward, then, with your tried indomitable courage!"

Bonifazio also reports conversations and plans of action from the Assisi camp, naturally in a minor key, so as not to spoil the effect of his artificial contrasts.

"Each is to be ready to rush with pride and spirit against these crude Gryphons. They are a vacillating lot, who will attack under their leader, Bonbarone." (This is a reference to the consul of Perugia who three years earlier had taken Girardo di Gislerio's declaration of citizenship.) "No one is to lag behind. One dies only once, and it is better to fall in these fields than to be in the power of an enemy or to fall back and flee before him."

The Perugino army advanced immediately to the other bank of the Tiber. Between the two armies there was a distance of less than half a mile. Naturally, according to the same source, the Perugini attacked first.

The battle burned over the hill. It ran over the castle and the woodlands. It even spilled into the lepers' hospital. It was fought at length, with equal fury on both sides. In the end, the Assisani were beaten. The slaughter that followed was great. The contemporary Thomas of Celano uses the phrase *non modica strages* to signify a massacre beyond every measure. Bonifazio uses more or less the same expression: *strages latissima, cedes sevissima:* "The final defeat came very late but the slaughter was very severe." The fugitives were pursued all the way to the *castello* of Isola.

Here the Veronese astrologer in high-flown language even pictures the Tescio so swollen by the blood of the killed that it overflowed its bed. Many saved themselves by hiding in the thick woodlands that stretched toward Montarone and Valle dell'Eremita. Others threw themselves down in fields well off the beaten path. Still others reached the tops of nearby hills. Some remained hidden in caves for a long time. They were sniffed out and hunted down like wild beasts.

The sight of those killed on the field where the fighting took place was horrifying beyond words. The fields that the cathedral of San Rufino had acquired from Filippo's widow, the vineyard belonging to Gislerio's sons, Marescotto di Bernardo Dodici's land—all were covered with the dead. Bonifazio crowed gushingly about it: "Oh, how disfigured are the bodies on the field of battle, and how mutilated and broken are their members! The hand is not to be found with the foot, nor the entrails joined to the chest; on the forehead horrible windows open out instead of eyes. That no prophet, interrogated before the battle, could have seen such omens! Oh, you of Assisi, what a sad day and what a dark hour was this!"

Girardo di Gislerio and Oddo, son of Leonardo, lords of Sasso Rosso, were probably lost in the battle. Unlike all others of the family, whose names crop up with monotonous regularity in later events, there is not from this time on the slightest trace of them.[66]

Assisi was appalled by the massacre. "Everywhere there was weeping, and some wept for their parents, and some for their sons, and still others mourned their grandsons. Very few escaped misfortune and no one was to be found with compassion for the people of Assisi." There was the same desolation in the *castelli* and towns who had sent their fighting men. According to the poet, it was the cruelest slaughter that the Perugini had up to that time inflicted on their enemies.

Thus, he concludes, mighty Assisi was beaten, *cecidere potentes Assisii*. These people who had not resigned themselves to their inferiority against the military skill of Perugia had paid the penalty of their audacity. The foolhardiness into which Assisi had fallen would serve as an example and would be remembered for generations. *Hoc et in etates hominum transibit et evum* ("This will remain in the ages of man for a very long time").

A great many of Assisi, according to Thomas of Celano and the Three Companions, were taken prisoner. Among them was Francis.

Francis's Prophetic Vision

That battle with all its raw ferocity and bloodthirsty pride, the sight of the dead, and the infinite grief made in Francis's warm and generous spirit a wound so deep that time never healed it. His happy-go-lucky youth was gone forever. Once again life's pain was more real to him than his fascinating dreams, his heroic enthusiasms and hopes of glory, more real than stirring fanfares, waving banners, and flashing blades, more real, even, than great courage.

Anyone who lives through the soul-searing instant of madness when meeting an enemy knows the nightmare that comes later. This must have been what Francis experienced long afterwards at Porziuncola. To brothers who were with him, he said "in a complaining voice": "The men of Perugia have done many evil things to their neighbours, and their hearts are lifted up unto ignominy. However, the revenge of the Lord is approaching and his hand is on his sword."[67]

By then, that lamentable war through which he had lived seemed to him to have been a revelation that made clear the burning words of the Biblical prophets, in their warnings of the vengeance of God on those who use and are heartless to their neighbours.

On that occasion, Francis arose after a time and, full of zeal, set off for Perugia. It was then that the brothers, seeing him so stirred up by a feverish excitement, thought that he must have had a vision in his cell.[68]

Did an anniversary fall on that day? The ache of the old wound return to make him suffer? Or did a grander and more desolate perception come to him, one that arose from the sad episode in the life of his city and expanded into his vision of the dreadful tragedies of the whole world?

In any case, he arrived in Perugia; he went to that piazza where as a prisoner he had walked amid jeers and insults.

Again many people had gathered there, between the cathedral and the bishop's palace. It was the day of a solemn feast.[69] As he showed that he intended to speak, they pressed around him with reverent devotion. He began, kindling that special feeling that made all hearts open to him. Perhaps he proclaimed the victory of love to that people against whom one day he had marched with sword in hand, in his soul thoughts of revenge and death. That had been a great sin, one of the many that he remembered and for which he humiliated himself by making extravagant amends for them before everyone.

It was the custom in those festivals for the cavaliers to come to the piazza for jousting. And so it happened that while the people were spellbound by Francis's discourse, these knights suddenly burst out with fierce shouts and clashing of arms. The words were lost in all the noise. In vain, the devout, men and women alike, pled that they stop and allow them to listen to the man of God. It seemed clear that all this activity was a deliberate act to keep Francis from speaking.[70]

The din drowned out everything. It was like a battlefield. Shields clanging together rang like anvils struck by a hammer. Swords and lances screeched as they struck each other. Horses made a deafening uproar as they galloped furiously over the flintstone as if their riders were launching an attack.

And in the midst of it, Francis's voice, which seemed so melodious to those who usually listened to it, thundered out, loud enough to rise over the deafening noise. Always it happened that he, who was so gentle, would be moved to such indignation by violence and arrogant disregard of others that he would heatedly challenge insolence.

According to contemporary writers who left a record of this apostrophe and who were perhaps present at the time, he said to the knights:

"Oh, the miserable folly of wretched men who neither consider nor fear the judgement of God! Listen to what the Lord proclaims to you through me, the poverello." He added, "And do not say: Nonsense, he's a man from Assisi!"[71]

His last remark needed explaining for those who did not live in the region and so the companions who reported the incident spelled out the reason for it: "Blessed Francis spoke that way because a great hatred divided the people of Assisi from those of Perugia."[72]

And he continued to speak, stubbornly standing up to the boors, who, like all bullies, believed that their strength gave them the right to trample over anyone weaker. They were already condemned, he said, because they carried in themselves the ill-omened seeds of their ruin. The violence that is their creed will drive them against one another and they will die, pierced by their own swords, in the worst of all punishments, fraternal conflict.

"The Lord has glorified you above all your neighbours," he said. "You should therefore be very grateful to your Creator and humble yourself not only before the Almighty but even before your neighbours. And yet your heart is puffed up with arrogance, audacity, and pride. You pillage your neighbours and kill many of them. I also say to you, if you do not mend your ways very soon and if you do not make reparation for the damage you have caused, the Lord, who does not allow any injustice to be done without chastisement, is preparing a terrible vengeance, punishment, and humiliation for you. He will set you one against the other. Discord and civil war will break out and will cause you worse calamities than those that could come to you from your neighbours.

"Wrath will teach you," he predicted, "for kindness has not taught you."[73]

All this really happened within a short time, for a war broke out between the nobles and the people of Perugia. It was fought so bitterly, so many people were killed, and there was such havoc in the city, that even the people of Assisi finally came to have pity on them.[74]

But this, concludes Thomas of Celano, is the law that governs states. Those who separate themselves from God, end by being separated from each other. On the threshold of their parliaments every people ought to cut this golden maxim: "There can be no more powerful bond in a state than pious love of God, sincere and unfeigned faith."[75]

Francis vs. the Communal Movement

Many modern biographers fall into error when they attempt to explain why Francis fought in the ranks of the common people, rather than with the nobles. They say such nonsense as this: "If he had been a vulgar soul, and in taking sides had followed only his own interests, his family's wealth and the nobility of his maternal blood would have led him to ally himself with the upper classes. But in this noble soul, love of justice, more than any other reason, prescribed the equality of all men and pity for the oppressed. It was a love that made his disdain for tyrants holy. His heart was for the poor people, his arm was ready to lend aid, even to his own danger, to claim the rights of the people."[76]

There can be no doubt whatsoever that the young merchant's place in battle was under the banner of the commune. The merchants, as has been seen, were the very soul of the new communal movement. The Italian commune did not have its origin in a vision of the rights of man or in an ideal of liberty and equality or in a love for the humble and oppressed. On the contrary, it was rooted in a mania for material gain, a desire for commercial expansion.

The wars between the free cities demonstrate that fact. They did not fight each other for the affirmation of a social ideal. When the people of one commune found another city, society of merchants, or commune in their way, when they realized that they were strong enough to take over the forest, bridge or pass near their borders, they attacked, as they had the day before attacked the castle of the feudal lord. As we have seen, the people of the communes did not hesitate to ally themselves with feudal lords themselves and with the German emperor when from this alliance they could gain an advantage over an enemy commune.

It is said that when the consuls' ceremonial wagon went outside city walls, cities would put on it, along with the cross, their relics of the saints, and the gonfalon, the books of the commune and the account books of the merchants, who were forever seeking to expand their horizons, forever asking for freer communications, always in search of a greater number of customers and more outlets for their goods.[77] This detail of history expresses exactly the spirit that animated and guided the citizen army. We have reached the new and the old motive for all wars: economic self-sufficiency, living space.[78] One fights because he has limits.[79]

Assisi's war against Perugia was fought by the middle classes and by the guilds for their own benefit. Nobles also participated, but they were feudal lords who either had already thrown in their lot with the commune or who fought Perugia for their own interests.

It is also important to note that a large group of Perugini, outlaws and rebels, joined the ranks of the Assisi people.[80]

Historians have understood the implications of this period.

Ferrari writes: "In the time of the consuls, the dualization of the city became economic. There is no longer a preoccupation with the claims of precedence or of ecclesiastical or feudal jurisdictions. Instead, claims are laid to riches, rivers, roads, and routes, all transformed into instruments of prosperity or of misery. The merchant, the manufacturer, and the rich man take the place of the Bishop."[81]

And Caggese: "Naturally, not only small rural centers, more or less fortified, were vanquished, but also the smaller communes that got in the way of a city's expansion. Conquest did not respect local autonomies; it reduced the conquered centers to the level of simple administrative structures, supervised, guided, often ruined, always forced to make heavy contributions for interests absolutely alien to them, never participants in the thousand advantages of municipal life."[82]

It is necessary to understand these true aims in this important period in the life of Saint Francis in order to follow the development of the fundamental essence of his concept. It did not at all rise in harmony with the communal movement. It was a perfect antithesis of it.

The Prisoners' Saint

After the battle of Collestrada, Francis was taken to Perugia and imprisoned with the nobles. Rank made little difference. His prison was squalid and miserable.

The young warrior from Assisi suffered. During his life, he consoled others. Even afterwards, those enduring like suffering turned to him, remembering that in a dark cell, at the age of twenty, a large part of his self-confident youthfulness faded.

The early biographers tell many stories about prisoners and miracles, and some of their stories are the subjects of great works of art. Thomas of Celano has passed on to us some of these legends.[83]

It happened in Greece that the servant of a tyrant was accused of having stolen something. He was innocent but the tyrant was convinced of his guilt and imprisoned him in the depths of a fortress that stood on the top of a high cliff with a fearful precipice below. He condemned the man to have one foot cut off. The poor man's wife, having appealed in vain to the cruel lord, prayed fervently that the Saint of Assisi help her. And her prayers were answered. Immediately Saint Francis appeared to the prisoner, freed him, and carried him miraculously to the plain below the fortress.

Also, once a poor man of Massa San Pietro owed some money to a rich knight and, not being able to pay it, was seized and taken to his creditor. He commended himself to Saint Francis and asked to be released for his sake. The knight replied that he would shut him up in a place from which neither Saint Francis nor anyone else would be able to free him. He then put him in a horrendous dungeon, with guards to watch over him. But even here Saint Francis arrived, broke the man's chains, and led the prisoner back to his house. The poor man took the shattered chains to Assisi in thanksgiving and put them in the church where Saint Francis is buried.

A similar miracle was reported about five ministers of a prince, who, when they had commended themselves to Saint Francis, saw the walls of the tower in which they were imprisoned dissolve, almost as if the stone had been changed into ashes. Their handcuffs, too, were shattered.

Alberto d'Arezzo, a very devout man and a great admirer of the Friars Minor, once was unjustly held in prison for debts. He fasted for love of Saint Francis on the eve of his feast day and gave his food to a sick prisoner. In the night, while he kept watch in prayer, Saint Francis came. Immediately the chains fell apart, the doors opened, and the roof fell, leaving no obstacles to flight.

A young man of Città di Castello, accused of arson, was saved in the same way.

But the most famous miracle, one depicted by Giotto in the upper church of the Basilica di San Francesco, happened to an Assisi man during a stay in Rome. He was accused of heresy and, by order of Pope Gregory, turned over to the bishop of Tivoli. Certain nobles who hated the bishop allowed him to escape. He was caught again and put in such close confinement that he could hardly breathe, in a narrow dark cell surrounded by high walls, closed by a thick wooden door riveted with iron. His arms were loaded down with chains, his feet fastened to huge blocks with heavy bars. On the vigil of the day dedicated to Saint Francis, Pietro pled his innocence to his great fellow citizen and asked for mercy. (This occurred to him, Thomas of Celano notes, because he had never heard of heretics abusing Saint Francis or making fun of his saintliness.) Francis appeared in the dungeon a little before daybreak, called Pietro by name, and ordered him to get up. He obeyed, not without difficulty; but immediately he was overcome with fear, called for the guard, and told him that someone claiming to be Saint Francis had come into the prison and ordered him to rise. The guard laughed at him and told him that too much fasting had made him light-headed and to keep quiet and sleep in peace. But then, toward noon, his bonds miraculously fell to earth and all the doors opened. The bishop was brought to the prison and recognized that a special grace had been granted. The chains were taken to the pope and to the cardinals, who blessed this miraculous justice of God.

Finally, there is the story of Guidalotto of Gemignano. He was accused by the podestà of having poisoned an enemy and was imprisoned and tortured. Everything was tried to make him confess: the rack, fire, boiling oil. He bore everything bravely, thanks to Saint Francis. Nevertheless, he was condemned to be beheaded. The night before the execution the Saint came to him, and the dungeon was filled with a miraculous radiance. His innocence having been thus demonstrated, he was allowed to go free.

Francis in a Perugia Prison

The early biographers have left us a surprisingly realistic description of Francis's prison.[84]

After the horrors of the battle, the harsh trials that Thomas of Celano summarizes in a few words would have weighed upon Francis, so devoted to light and freedom—massive iron blocks, constantly creaking padlocks and bolts, the weak light of lanterns in squalid subterranean cells where prisoners were crowded together, the imprecations of sullen guards, threats, jeers, hopes quickly extinguished, the shock of seeing on the face of one's companions the degradation and discouragement on one's own.

The empty weeks passed, the months passed, the seasons flourished and faded.

Francis's early biographers tell us that a great sadness ended when he took responsibility for the other prisoners during that long and empty incarceration. In the universal depression of spirits, Francis found the strength to return to his old dreams of glory. He kept the joyous serenity so characteristic of him. It revealed his courage but offended the sensibilities of his companions, who reproached him and called him crazy.

One day one of them said to him that his joy was an insult to their common misfortune. Francis answered, "Of course your bad luck grieves me. But I cannot help being happy, because even though my body is imprisoned in these walls, my spirit is free."

Suffering made the prisoners irascible and intolerant. In the forced association of antagonistic men—soldiers of both the noble and commoner classes, nobles who had for years fought one another—pride, that old sin of the feudal people, reasserted itself.

There was, according to Francis's contemporaries, who certainly learned of the episode from someone who had been in prison with Francis in Perugia, an arrogant noble, a nasty grouch, whom the other prisoners found hard to endure. Once he insulted another prisoner and the others decided to isolate him and not speak a word to him.

Francis was sorry for him. He went to him, consoled him, and induced him to make peace with his fellow prisoners. And his generous and loving gesture, besides touching the heart of the bad-tempered knight, endeared Francis to his companions, who from that time on sought his friendship.

Among the prisoners was a knight of Orsara of Apulia, who had come to fight with the Assisi men. In the long hours of idleness and tedium, he told of a marvellous thing being said in his land about Gautier de Brienne, the hero whom Francis admired so much.

Sneers had greeted Gautier upon his arrival in the realm. He had been thought mad and foolhardy, despite the fact that he and his soldiers wore on their chests the cross that Innocent III had granted to everyone who enlisted in the enterprise.[85] But derision gave way to a mixture of fear and admiration after his first encounter with the army of Diopoldo di Vohburg (on June 10, 1201) below the walls of Capua. Gautier had no more than two hundred men with him, while there were more than five thousand in the imperial army. It had been a great thing to see the French knights, their long lances couched, attack in a single file that was like a solid wall of iron and steel. They advanced with such fury that the whole German field was routed and destroyed.

It was said that among those who fled was the brave count of Fondi, Riccardo di Aquila, who jumped into the Volturno river, not being able to escape his pursuers any other way. While he was shouting that these were not men but unchained devils whom nobody in the world could overcome, he was carried away by the water of the river and miserably drowned.[86]

The victory was considered a true miracle. The count of Lecce came out of it wearing an aura of supernatural valour. News of it flashed through the realm; never had anything been seen like it.

Gautier, on horseback bearing a flaming sword, had seemed like the Angel of the Apocalypse, attended by knights who went into battle rejoicing as if at a festival.

(The echo of this admiration is still to be found today among the people of Apulia, who consider Gautier as the last paladin of Charlemagne. The chronicler who told of these magnificent deeds uses the words: *Magnificatus est comes Gualterus et clarificatus in Regno; hostes autem humiliati sunt et comprehensi* ["Esteemed is Count Gautier and illustrious in the Kingdom; his enemies, on the other hand, have been humiliated and taken prisoner"].)[87]

But before long Diopoldo sought to recover his position.

Gautier had disposed his company in the plain of Cannae. This part of Apulia is an intricate web of swamps, ponds, and fever-infested marshy ground, lying between the Ofanto river and the sea—a nasty place for a captain to defend, and moreover, said to be ill-omened, since here, under the mire, lay the remains of the army that is said to have suffered the greatest defeat in history.[1]

At dawn on October 21, Diopoldo attacked, this time taking Gautier by surprise. His force was huge, made up of all the warriors in the kingdom he had been able to gather together. But Gautier, once his first stupefaction was over, had "flown," as those who saw him said, upon his enemies; and, at a moment when things were not going well for his band, a cross of gold appeared and led him to victory.[88]

Thus a new augury prevailed over the old. The imperial forces who fled from the French drowned in the swamps or were taken prisoner. It was impossible to count the number of dead. They remained unburied for days, there were so many of them.

After this battle, castles and cities surrendered to Gautier, so that he was able to travel to every part of the realm without being challenged. He prepared to move on to Sicily.

Francis longed to follow so shining an example, to fight in the train of this *condottiero* who had never allowed his soldiers to know the shame of defeat. He imagined riding in the shimmering mornings behind unfurled banners, amid a forest of lances, under a dazzling sun that gave light to the sea, the rivers, the boundless plains, the castles, the cities. The contrast with his present misery made his dream all the brighter.

This hope, the certainty that he had found the road to future glory, was stressed by his early biographers. He would go to Apulia,[89] that

---

1. The defeat Hannibal inflicted on the Romans on that plain in 216 B.C.

fairy-tale land of brave deeds and dire tragedies, mysticism and beauty.

On the farthest hills of the Assisi *contado,* which slope toward Valtopina, had lived for more than two hundred years a people who had been transplanted from Apulia at the time of Pandolfo Testadiferro, duke of Spoleto. He fought a war in that region (in the tenth century) with the imperial army. Feudal lords of Assisi also took part. After a long struggle he defeated and subdued the inhabitants of the area between Ascoli and Bovino. A great many were taken prisoner and deported *en masse* to that harsh land above Assisi, uninhabited since the last centuries of Rome. There he had forced them to cut down forests, open roads, and establish parishes and *ville.*[90]

They were a people of another race, Byzantine in their customs, their mode of fighting, the style of their dress, their sacred rites, songs and legends, even in their language. Afflicted with incurable nostalgia for their lands and rivers, their churches and saints, they had reconstructed their lost country in that high place. To the river that flowed at the bottom of the valley they had given the name of their province, Puglia (Apulia); to the *pievi,* the names of their cities, Ascolano, Boviniano. There was a chapel dedicated to Saint Potitus, martyr-protector of Ascoli, and others to Saint Blaise and Saint Stephen, patron saints of the same city.

Francis remembered that a *villa* built by these exiles from Apulia was there. It stood midway on the road between Assisi and Nocera, below the summit of a wild hill. They had called it by the name of another of their destroyed cities: Satriano. In the middle of a thick oak forest, it was enclosed by high walls. An opening to the road was called, simply, "la Porta," or "the Gate." The houses came down the rocky slope all the way to a stream. On clear days, Assisi, with its fortress and the high campanile of its cathedral, could be seen enfolded among the circle of hills.

There was also a famous castle, the best armed in the commune, erected by these Pugliese and Byzantine people on the opposite side of Mount Subasio: Rocca Pàida. It was reached by a short path that wound along the meadows of Costa Sermolla (where Pietro Bernardone had his properties and flocks) from the streamlet called Fosso Vettoio ("Gully of the Peak") because it began on top of the mountain. In this season (April had already brought the breath of the new spring into the closed prison and at dawn the piercing cries of swallows penetrated the dark walls) the meadows were covered with flowers. It would not be long until the mowers would go up to the valley of Fieno, to Prato Pistello.

But though his spirit was able to travel beyond the dark walls that faced Assisi's plain and mountain (by climbing all the way up to the iron bars, one could see the city stretched out on the slope of its hill), his body was too delicate to sustain the life of deprivations and difficulties. He fell sick. He was taken from the dark dank underground cell and put with other sick prisoners.

Nearly a year had passed since he had fallen into the hands of the Perugini.

Strangely, though weak and exhausted, he had not lost his extraordinary joy. Thrown down on his bundle of straw, burning with fever, his eyes shone as if lit by a supernatural light. Those with him thought it was a sign of the gravity of his illness and attributed it to the delirium from which Pietro Bernardone's son now suffered.

He said things that no one could understand. He said, shut up in these walls, that he no longer had any limits on his road, that he was to win the greatest liberty that the world had ever known.

They pitied him. They wept over his fate. They repeated that he was delirious, that he was already marked for death.

He assured them that soon he would be revered by all men.

It was his fixed idea. His fever rose. It would not disappear.

Outside the bestial cries of the guards ordering silence rang out. The dying ones fell silent, exhausted. Night's shadow enveloped them.

·5·

NOBLE DREAMS

Some biographers date the peace between Assisi and Perugia in 1203. This is an error, and one that minimizes the importance of Assisi's internal and external war on the origins of the new [Franciscan] movement. The war accompanied Francis's spiritual crisis, as well as that of his first companions, who were his fellow citizens. It continued until the approbation of the rule and may well have been the factor that determined its coming into existence.

The struggle between the two rival cities was, in fact, prolonged more or less intensely until 1209.[a]

Assisi suffered immediate consequences of its defeat. Its dependent communes surrendered to Perugia. Still other prominent Assisi citizens went over to the stronger side. In the sort of thing that usually happens when a subordinate government sees its ruler defeated, Nocera, on December 12, 1202, swore allegiance to Perugia and made a commitment to make war against all Perugia's enemies.[1]

On January 10, 1203, another of Assisi's lords, Marescotto di Bernardo Dodici, recognized the full sovereignty of Perugia over the land and forest that he owned in Collestrada, according to the boundaries already mapped out on the battleground by the *baili* of the commune of Perugia. He declared that he spoke also for the entire family: his brothers Guidotto and Tebalduccio, his nephews Bernardo and Bonacquisto di Aliotto, and the sons of Magalotto. He promised to hold his goods *per concessione alliodale* of the Perugini consuls, to acquire a house in Perugia worth not less than one hun-

---

a. From 1205 to 1209 the war was seemingly reduced to raids and looting, without battles of any importance, though there are no exact records of just what happened. However, it is clear that no peace was declared and none of the old questions resolved. When the pope's success in forcing the emperor to give up claims on the papal state brought the Guelf party into ascendancy in Perugia again, the war was taken up with fresh vigour. *NV* 2:190–92.

dred *libbre* not later than the eighth day before the Kalends of May, and to go there to live according to the rule laid down by the Perugini rulers. The document was drawn up in circumstances of particular solemnity in the cathedral of San Lorenzo. As if they were even now still sitting as consuls, the frowning, severe images of the fierce Perugini magistrates who in the recent battle had captained the army against the people of Assisi emerge from the papers in the great volume bound with leather-covered boards: Gualtiero di Mezzante, Raniero, Villano, Giovanni, Amedeo, Pietro di Gregorio, Leone, *camerlengo.*[2]

Assisi, for its part, moved to reprisals against its traitorous "establishment" political exiles. Marescotto's houses on the piazza were destroyed[3] and the members of his consortium exiled. The men of the people were consumed by the thought of revenge. Ordinances, threats, and punitive expeditions multiplied.

In June of this year of 1203, the consuls of Assisi were Alduccio, Muzio, Giacomo, and Carlo.[4] They understood that if the city were to be saved, the people must be reconciled. For this purpose they named three arbiters: Tancredi di Ugone, the *signore* of Parlascio; Giacomo; and Marangone di Cristiano, who had his house near that of Pietro Bernardone. Marangone was the father of Bongiovanni, doctor and notary, who was linked to Francis from the earliest years of their youth and who would also be with him in the last days of his illness in the bishop's palace; he would tell him he was going to die.

They delivered their opinion in November, in that document known as *carta pacis,*[5] the Peace Paper: "Because there is in Assisi discord between the *buoni uomini* and the men of the people over the destruction of the castles and feudal servitude, we, Giacomo, Tancredo di Ugone, and Marangone, charged by the commune to compose a peace agreement, order [these measures] . . . ."

To compensate the *buoni uomini* for the destroyed houses, some of which had been *casamenti* [multiple dwellings often housing several generations of the same family], the commune would construct other houses for them inside the city, where they were henceforth to live. There were lists of the names of the feudal lords and of the towers and houses destroyed, the dimensions of the buildings to be erected, the districts in which they were to be built.

Those inhabitants of the city and suburbs who had not rendered feudal services for twenty-four years or more were to be held exempt from them. Others were to continue to be subject to them, and the feudal lords would have the right of depredation in case they were not fulfilled. On the other hand, those who were still living in rural *ville* remained under the authority of their lords, whose will would continue to be their law, both inside and outside the city.

One chapter forbade alliances and agreements with those not of the city, since these would bring dangers of new wars: "And thus we say that no person of this city shall make league or pact with any city, *castello, signore,* or imperial nuncio, without the common counsel of this city, and shall not work for any division within or without the city, but shall always do good and not evil to the commune of Assisi."

Another chapter laid down heavy sanctions against émigrés who had gone over to the enemy: "And thus whosoever shall leave from this city, or whosoever left at the time the commune was at war with the Perugini, and was not a man living in the country, and went over to the enemies of this city, shall have all his goods confiscated; and all the people of this city shall give their help to the consuls in punishing him. And if one of them shall come begging for mercy, he shall bear that penalty that the consuls shall inflict on him. And the aforesaid émigrés shall be banned (*messi al bando*)[b] inside and outside the city."

Still another established the treatment for those principally responsible: "And thus we say that if the sons of Gislerio, Bernardo, Alberico di Tiberio, Agurio, and all the others, should wish to put themselves into our hands, it will be reserved to us to make judgements between them and the commune and the commune shall be held to what we shall say."

Regulations follow that oblige the people to help one another maintain the laws, the material goods, and the lands, and to recuperate revenues and credits from cities, *castelli* and persons outside the commune. And if nobles or merchants of Assisi should be looted by any city or *castello,* the commune of Assisi shall be required to indemnify them; and if it should happen that an inhabitant of one of those cities or *castelli* comes to Assisi, the commune shall warn him three times, and then imprison him, if the booty taken had been over one hundred *soldi;* and if less, the matter would be put to the arbitration of the consuls. And the commune shall intervene to suspend from duty those who, from the time when Bonbarone was consul, had collected duties and taxes. Everyone who had made such collections from the time of the aforesaid consulate shall be required to explain his actions. And whoever of either faction does not observe the agreements shall pay to the other faction the sum of one thousand *libbre.*

---

b. *Messi* or *posti al bando:* The *bando* or ban was a public declaration that a person had been placed outside the law and excluded from every protection of society. See also chap. 7, n. b.

All were pardoned for damages done and offences committed. "And thus we say that pardon shall be given for all malfeasances committed in the aforesaid *castelli,* and those who received and sustained damages shall not avenge themselves on any person or anything because of them, and shall not file any complaint about them in the curia of the emperor or of the pope or before their representatives, or to a commune of this land; and they shall have, in order to ratify them, the instruments of quittance that were made and that they had made, under the penalty of one thousand *libbre;* and they shall make a final renunciation; and all the malfeasances generally shall be pardoned among the Assisi people."

The document closes with the declaration of the notary Giovanni that the *buoni uomini* and the men of the people solemnly swear to observe the aforesaid pacts.

But what end can be served by this paper? Its involved language is devised to safeguard everybody's intemperate greed. Its minutely detailed compromises give old adversaries the freedom to fight and wage war to defend their own egotistic interests and those of others. Its artificial discipline is a pretence at regulating the limits to which earthly emotions and appetites can be satisfied. Its fine words are a warning that it is going to prepare the way for new inundations of distrust and hatred and unleash new and more deadly conflicts.

And all is concealed under the name of peace. Thus it is written in the document: *Pro bono pacis.*

Francis's Illness

According to the ancient rule in Perugia that governed the treatment of prisoners of war, those who fell seriously ill could be returned to their city. Thus Pietro Bernardone negotiated for and obtained the release of his son.[c]

Francis returned to Assisi in the days when the *baili* of the com-

---

c. In *3 Soc.*, 4, it is reported that Francis's imprisonment lasted a year and that he was released after the two cities had made peace. This source also says that two years elapsed between Francis's return home and his departure for Apulia. The documents show that these statements cannot be correct. The first lull in the fighting is reported only in 1205, but no treaty was signed. If Francis were released that year, that would put his trip to Apulia in 1207—two years after the death of Gautier de Brienne, whom he set out to join. Therefore, he must have been released at an earlier time, for reasons that had nothing to do with a peace treaty. From a record in the cathedral archives (fasc. 2, no. 115; *NV* 3:537) concerning the will of a former prisoner of war, Bernardo di Figura (see chap. 2, p. 77) we find that in Perugia the prisoners of war who fell ill were turned over to a corporation called *congregatio et societas captivorum amalatorum,* which could make arrangements for their ransom. Certainly Pietro di Bernardone had the means to pay a ransom, and we know from Thomas of Celano that Francis did indeed become gravely ill while in prison. We can assume, therefore, that these were the circumstances leading to his release. *NV* 2:178–79.

mune were moving through the city streets, crying out new proclamations against the émigrés to Perugia. New trumpet blasts blared in the grey December[d] air, chill with the unmistakable portents of the first snow. New shouts reverberated in the desolate piazza, still cluttered with stones of the houses that had been destroyed. A sense of impending rebellion pervaded the city. Old and young had taken up arms.

Few paid any attention to the pallid spectre wearing a ragged tunic who came alone to the house in the Abbadia *contrada,* appearing in front of the horrified members of his family with emaciated face, tottering step, trembling hands, gasping breath.

A long, agonizing period began.

No one had the slightest illusion about the fate of the young man. He himself knew that he was doomed. A strange fever devoured him. He shook, spoke brokenly, gesticulated to the empty air. When evening came, he fell inert into sleep.[e] In his room there was that tragic silence that precedes the last hours, broken only by the metallic clatter of chains when, according to regulations set forth in the statutes, the sentry unhooked them and pulled them across the entrance to the piazza as a protection against nocturnal dangers.[f]

A sorrowful vigil began. Between dream and reality, between life and death, another world rose and fell in Francis's delirious sleep as he lay in bed under watchful, anxious maternal eyes.[6] Finally, the invalid passed the crisis. Members of his family rejoiced as over a miraculous resurrection. Neighbours, his friends and his companions in arms, came to see him, offer good wishes, and recall the terrible days they had been through. Francis was able to get out of bed and listen to their conversation. They talked of the war and the news.

In November of 1203, the same month that the Peace Paper was promulgated in Assisi, the Perugini consuls replied to it. They gathered in the church of San Severo on the piazza in Perugia, the parochial church of the magistrates who had their residence there. (The surviving arcades of the external portico may still be seen in the lower part of the Palazzo dei Priori, into which the church was at a

---

d. This would have been 1203, roughly a year after his capture at the battle of Collestrada.—Trans.

e. Thomas of Celano attributes Francis's illness to the dissipation of his life (*1 Cel.,* 3). In *Leg. Vers.* (*AF* 10:409) there is a long passage about Francis's having been "flagellated" by God with a long illness and a description of his violent attacks of fever.

f. The chains that encircled the piazza are mentioned in an arbitration of 1237 (see *NV* 3:644). The city gates were also chained. Special custodians opened these chains each morning and locked them each evening. (*NV* 3:23.) For the exact boundaries of the piazza at the time of Saint Francis, see *NV* 2:81.

later time incorporated, on the piazza of San Lorenzo.) In their response, they swore to the Assisi knights and common soldiers who had come over to their side, or who might have in mind doing so, that they would not make peace, reach an agreement, or come to a truce with Assisi until Perugia's new citizens from there had been compensated for all damages and their goods peacefully returned to them. They promised to give them houses in the city or the suburbs so that they might become permanent citizens of Perugia. They said that they would be allowed to have whatever booty they could take from the people of Assisi, unless Perugia were defeated. And they offered to compensate them within the space of one month for arms and horses lost in battle.[7]

Francis knew these proud enemy consuls. Their names had been on the lips of all the prisoners: Rustico, Ermanno, Marsilio, Giovanni, Ciacio, Simeone, Bartolomeo, Girardo, Latino, Raniero, Orlandino, Raniero, Leonardo, Ugo *camerlengo.* And knew that each had sworn to achieve the extermination of Assisi.

Despite these threats, by the end of 1203, Assisi's fortunes seemed to have improved. On the Feast of the Innocents (December 28), Bulgarello of Fossato and Albertino had journeyed to the cathedral of San Rufino to put the *castello* of Serpigliano, which held the Nocera road, under Assisi's jurisdiction [and protection]. They had fought with Assisi in the battle of Collestrada and feared the revenge of the Perugini.[8]

Francis listened in silence, seemingly absorbed in a far-away dream. The members of his family told him about the submission of Bulgarello. The terms had been more or less the same as those of all submissions. The *signore* of Serpigliano had received Assisi citizenship in perpetuity. He had promised to keep the castle as a mandate from the Assisi consuls, to make peace or war according to their orders, and to give aid and advice to them against all enemies of the city, excepting the people of Gubbio. He had agreed to claim no more than one *denaro* a load as a *pedaggio* or road toll from the men of Assisi. He was to procure a house in the city, laying out one hundred *libbre* to acquire it, according to the order of the consul of Assisi who had received his pledge, Girardo di Giliberto. Among those who had participated were many who had fought with Francis: Giovanni di Rainerio, Tommaso di Battero, Rosso di Bonafede, Zappolo, Cristiano di Paride, Scipione di Offreduccio, Ugolino di Rinaldo, Gilio di Marco, Arminateo di Giovanni, Ieronimo di Gualtiero, Morico di Angelerio, Andrea di Pietro, Vivieno, Ugolo, and many others.

These happenings, which once would have thrilled Francis, now seemed no longer to interest him. He had a serious relapse. Once again his illness was desperate. Once again there was an alternation of hopes and fears. Then a great weariness assailed him, leaving him prostrate and without strength. The doctors who were treating him talked of languor and their prognostications were again gloomy.[9]

At last, however, his youth won out. Thomas of Celano has left us a vivid description of his convalescence. Slowly, we learn, life began to pour back, the blood to flow in a tepid and beneficent rhythm, his breathing to become even and quiet.[10] But his heart was mute. Left alone, he wept, broken under the weight of his misery, feeling oppressed by the memory of a life so vainly spent.

Timidly he began to take his first steps, leaning on a stick. He managed to reach the nearby rooms, and then to look out from the upper balcony, which faced the plain. February was drawing to a close. A gentle warmth soothed the austerity of the neighbouring monastic cloister and gave grace to the hard lines of the bristling palazzi. It softened the masculine arrogance of the warrior city. Even the skeleton walls of the houses that had been destroyed, on which signs of the recent fires were still plain to be seen, seemed to rest in a benign peace.

In vain he tried to recapture his old feelings, the joyous wonder in the familiar sights of his native land.

Where was the time when he had been thrilled by the spectacle of spring. Where that peace, that joy, that ecstatic silence, so appropriate to the unfolding of dreams and the sighing of sweet songs of love?

These had been the secret joys of his early youth, the illuminations, the enchantments. Now he thought he had lost them forever.

By late April he was strong enough to leave his father's house and go to one of those places so dear to him. He reached the piazzetta of San Nicolò, now covered with the crockery of potters selling their merchandise in the area allotted to them by the statutes. (Brilliant terracotta vases painted in black designs, pots, pans, jugs, and a great variety of *scaldini*—copper warming pans—are still to be seen every Saturday near the Minerva, modern testimony of the flourishing market existing a thousand years ago.) He continued along the short stretch of road leading to the piazza, where there were the tables of peddlers, hawkers, sellers of carding combs and olive oil. He crossed the piazza, noisy with cries of the vendors of silk, wool, velvet. Beyond was the San Giorgio gate. Now he saw again the poor and the ill, warming themselves in the sun by the hospital and at the portico of the church. He went through the part of the city toward Foligno, known as the *borgo folignate.* Here a path passed through fertile fields, where the new grain, young and tender, could be seen under silvery blue olive trees and among serene rows of vines.

There were the oaks belonging to the monks, there the cross-roads of the San Potente road, the house in San Martino d'Argentana, the women with their distaffs spinning at the top of their staircases, the fountain fed by a murmuring spring, the water flowing along the pebbly river bed, the dense hedge, the field of hemp, the garden thick with laurel, the plants with violet flowers, the oxen lying on the threshing floor, the scratching roosters. And high above, the dark cliffs of Sasso di Panzo, Sasso del Maloloco.

All was as it had been, almost as if nothing had happened. But to his great astonishment, all these things that had at one time spoken to his heart today left him unmoved. What change had taken place in him? What spell held him in a painful stupor from which he could not rouse himself? Later, when he looked back at the road he had travelled, he realized that in this hour spent in the still solitude of his native countryside he sensed for the first time a call.[11] The voice was distant and indistinct, and he did not understand the meaning of it. He could not see that the infinite pain and sorrow in which he was living—both spectator and actor—had left in him a wound more enduring than his terrible illness.

The Oblates

In the early part of 1204 conditions in the city, always in a state of unrest because of the dangers from both internal and external war, made it necessary to choose a podestà. This was a new official in the government of the communes, chosen because of the need to have someone at the helm who was both outside the factions and superior to the vendettas, who was at the same time a man of the sword and a man of the law. He was chosen from among the nobles, and in the early days, from the families of the city [at a later time, in Assisi as elsewhere, it was required that he come from outside the city]. At first he was chosen in alternation with the consuls; in the end he completely absorbed their powers.[g]

Girardo di Giliberto, one of the consuls in 1203, was named the

---

g. The office of podestà was established in Italian cities because the consuls had not been able to control a growing anarchy, caused by the fact that feudal lords did not accept their former enemies as magistrates and judges, and also because the bitter factional divisions among the people coupled with the frequency of elections prevented the consuls from gaining the power to govern. Assisi documents reflect these situations, as well as the abuses of many consuls who did not live up to their obligations. *NV* 2:180–82.

first podestà.[h] But since he had been excommunicated, his election aroused the ire of Innocent III, who put the entire city under an interdict. The Assisi people refused to knuckle under, and a bitter struggle followed that lasted all that year. It was finally brought to an end by Cardinal Leone Brancaleone, the titular head of the church of Santa Croce di Gerusalemme, who was sent to Assisi by the pope to find some way to settle the matter. (This cardinal was later devoted to Saint Francis and entertained him in his house in Rome.) As a result of the agreement he worked out, Girardo and the commune were absolved from excommunication after a new podestà, Ugolino, and fifty of the leading citizens pledged their loyalty to the church.[i]

Fighting had begun again on the mountain toward Nocera. Postignano was occupied, that strong castle whose ruins even today overlook all the Topino valley from the height of a hill. Nocera was retaken.[j] The war continued to rage intensely till the end of 1204.

On November 8 of that year, the notary Medico, called by the canons of San Rufino to draw up a document of donation, followed his usual custom and wrote at the bottom of it the news of the day: *Hoc tempore erat guerra inter Assisium et Perusium* ("In this time there was war between Assisi and Perugia").[12]

The contracting parties of this document meet in the hall of the old clergy house. The windows open on the small enclosed cemetery, where the last roses are shedding their petals in the heartbreaking sweetness of Saint Martin's summer. The golden letters running along the mosaic on the front wall shine: *Omnes velut aqua dilabimur* ("All things like water flow away").

Earthly goods are worth nothing, have no value, except to obtain eternal life for those who are dead. Such are the thoughts that inspire the donation described in this document, one that brings us a vivid sense of the war in which Francis participated, of the persons and

---

h. Girardo di Giliberto had been podestà of Spoleto, where he had shared responsibility with consuls. He had then served as a consul of Assisi, the *primus inter pares*—for in Assisi, as in other cities, a hierarchy had developed among the consuls, the step toward government by a podestà.

It is not known whether Girardo di Giliberto was a citizen of Assisi, for in these early days the commune did not worry about whether its chief magistrate was a citizen or outsider. Since his name does not appear among the many earlier records of Assisi archives, he was probably from another commune. See *NV* 2:181–82.

i. The reason for Girardo's excommunication is unknown. Sabatier's opinion that he was a heretic is not supported by any documentary evidence. It is quite likely that it happened while he was podestà of Spoleto for political opposition to the pope's territorial claims; and Assisi reaped the consequences of having chosen a podestà displeasing to the pope.

By September 1204 Girardo was no longer podestà of Assisi. The post was held by Ugolino, who had as his judge Fortino, an ancestor of the author of this book. *NV* 2:182.

j. The retaking of Nocera can be assumed from an August 31, 1205, ordinance of the podestà of Perugia, which mentions the properties taken over by Assisi people. *NV* 2:182.

things that were on his lips and in his heart before his conversion. In it Raccorro di Ugolino, with the consent of his wife Bona, divests himself of his goods in favour of the cathedral, San Rufino, so that God would have mercy on the souls of the persons dear to him—his father and mother, his brother Pietro, Pietro's wife Pomeria. The canons who receive the offering are those who knew the heroic youth of Saint Francis: Bartolo, Latino, Eugenio, Crescenzio. Among the goods donated (a vineyard with a mill on the Tescio in the neighbourhood of San Giovanni in Campiglione, two properties in Clesia and in Costano) was Raccorro's own house on Via Portica, one of those extremely ancient structures where now poorly concealed black stones are showing through a recent and ignoble coat of plaster. We know those who lived on the borders of his property, the son of Rolando and Guido di Artemilia. Listed with the other witnesses (Berarduccio di Armuiaffo, his brother Baldovino, Guarnerio, Uguccione; the bailiff Armanno) is a Master Pietro, *magister Petrus*. Is it by chance the hotheaded merchant of Via Portica, Pietro Bernardone?

A sense of weariness lurks in these old notarial papers. The formulae lose their rigidity and are bent to express the emotion of lost souls who want to drop out of the world's struggles and are looking to heaven as their last hope, where perhaps those who die will at last be able to find peace.

Another donation bears the date June 25, 1203: "I, Berta, daughter of Pietro, fearing the coming of death, because this life is short and passing, filled with many miseries and tribulations, for the souls of my father and my mother and of the members of my family, for the redemption of my sins, and likewise for the soul of the one who provided me with these goods, and for that true blessed life to which all should rise again, to the end that omnipotent God will deign to have mercy on me as long as my mortal life endures; I give, consign, and concede freely and of my good will, to the church of San Giacomo, through the hand of Domino Egidio, priest of this same church, a piece of ground with olive trees located in Torre Canale between these boundaries: on the first side, the road; on the second and the third, the land of San Giacomo; on the fourth, the land that belonged to the sons of Roccio."[13]

In this same locality, situated along the hill that rises beyond the bridge of San Vetturino, Francis's family had an olive grove, as we have already seen.[14] What this parchment brings back to us from so long ago (an old torn parchment on which, for all that, the characters appear as undamaged and precise as if not a day had gone by since the sad sigh of the donor) is the universal and ancient grief that no one has escaped, that no one ever will be able to escape: "This life is short and passing and filled with many miseries and tribulations."

Old Assisi records recall many who offered themselves and their goods to a church in the hope of finding everlasting peace. They are the *oblati mortui mundo,* the oblates dead to the world—lay men and women who, without consecration or vows, wear a religious habit, live in a church and follow a monastic regime.[k]

In these papers we can reconstruct the changing fortunes of one Filippo, son of Guiberto di Biniolo. He is one among thousands affected by the anguish in the society of this epoch, so perpetually at war, so longing to find a path to salvation. There are many circumstances surrounding his personal drama—his desire for glory, his disillusionment, his flight from the world—that make it seem very similar to the first part of the road that will be travelled by the young Francis.

Filippo came of an ancient and prominent family. An ancestor, Guiberto, lived at the end of the twelfth century. Biniolo was his son, and he in turn was the father of this Guiberto.[15] They had their house in Capobove, an old road lying above the piazza lined by thousand-year-old buildings. It took its name, still in use, from one of those heads of oxen that in antiquity was placed on the façade of buildings, an ornamental motif derived from the skulls of oxen put up around the altar of the temple after a sacrifice. The family enjoyed a good income from their lands: a vineyard in Correggiano next to the church of San Bartolo, woodlands in the Tescio valley, other lands in Grotte bordering the property of Ospedale delle Pareti, lands in Colcaprile and in San Costano between the Tescio and Isola, and a part of the mill of Santa Croce. They also owned an entire family held to the hominicium with the obligation of working in the fields and vineyards and required to give two *amiscere* each year.

The last Guiberto had a son, Filippo, who in youth left to find adventure in distant lands. The father, alone in the empty house, long awaited the return of his beloved son. The years of the decline of life came and still no news came from him. Guiberto retired to the church of San Giacomo, to which he made a donation of all his goods, repeating the traditional formula: "In the name of God, for the health of my soul and of that of my relatives, for that true blessed life in

---

k. In early days, oblates were men and women who dedicated themselves to the service of a religious community, though remaining lay persons. Later, the name was applied to those who donated their goods to a monastery or church, lived in it and its dependencies, wore a religious habit and led a community life, without, however, taking vows. A variety of motives led the people of the time to follow this course: poverty, a religious spirit, a desire to escape from tyrannical lords or to avoid public responsibilities. NV 2:223–25.

which Omnipotent Lord God shall be pleased to forgive all our sins and our offences . . . "

Yet, among the lines of this document the old man's heartbeat can still be heard. It is betrayed in words expressive of a tenuous thread of hope in a revocation he prepared: *Si filius meus redierit,* "If my son should return . . . "

The son of Guiberto returned. He was tired and his heart was empty of illusion. He found that his father was dead, leaving him word of the way to soothe human troubles: *Si in ecclesia committere voluerit,* "If he wants to give himself to the church . . . "

Thus it was that Filippo himself also became, March 1201, an oblate of the church of San Giacomo di Murorotto. The document has preserved for us the text of his offering. First there is the usual consideration about the transitory nature of this life: "Because it is known that through the passage of time and through unexpected changes, in an instant the life of men is dissolved . . . " The ritual declaration follows: "I, Filippo, son of Guiberto di Biniolo, offer myself to the church of San Giacomo di Murorotto by means of the altarcloth, Domino Egidio, priest of the same church, being present; I promise that I myself and all my descendants will be men faithful to the aforesaid church of San Giacomo; and I choose the said church of San Giacomo for the burial of my body and of all my descendants . . . "

Gautier de Brienne and Dreams of Glory

Francis had returned to the shop. But even money-making, in which at one time he had shown himself to be expert, did not interest him any more. He blamed his illness for it and thought it a part of his sense of emptiness and tedium, his fatigue, the fever that even now kept on returning.

He was aroused and seemed to be brought back to his old enthusiasm by the widespread talk of the deeds of Gautier de Brienne, on whose prowess he had intended to measure his own life. An Assisi noble who was also avid for adventure told him of the reports. From that time he sought no other company than that of the young man who had talked to him, had no other thought than that of embarking on such an adventure, the kind that would surely bring him glory.[1]

---

1. All the biographers agree that it was at this time that Francis planned his trip to Apulia. Hostilities had diminished in 1205. Given the bitter fighting earlier, it is difficult to understand why any citizen of Assisi would be planning to go fight elsewhere; Francis's whole dream of going to Apulia must surely reflect his skill in and love of weaponry. *NV* 2:183.

The count had had to put off his expedition to Sicily because he had been forced to fight continuously against the imperial barons, who bitterly defended themselves. Enclosed in strong castles, they went out only for raids that left terror and death in their wake. In many cities, among them Brindisi, Matera, Otranto, Barletta, and Gallipoli, there had been false rumours of the death of Innocent III, followed by rebellions against Gautier. He had attacked and subdued them, bloodily. Afterwards, knowing that Diopoldo had reached Salerno, he marched against him and defeated him still again. Now he was vigorously pressing a siege against him at the castle of Sarno.[16]

In the meantime, he had taken the lead in reviving the court of Lecce, so splendid at the time of Tancred, and was making it a place of unparalleled luxury. Count Gautier established it as his capital and general quarters. Sibilia, Albiria, Madonia, and Costanza were lodged there, along with a large train of beautiful and noble women and French and Italian knights renowned for their prowess, among them Sire de Montbéliard, Sire de Joinville, and the count of Conflans. Here was a circle of the finest of the ancient Norman and Leccese knighthood.[17]

This court, in the grand style, was the epitome of all Francis's dreams and aspirations. The warriors went out to bloody combat, then laid down their heavy shields, cleaned their stained and dusty weapons, and entered lightly into tournaments characteristic of chivalry. They made make-believe love assaults on fairy-tale castles, where the beautiful damsels defended themselves by hurling roses at audacious lovers, who came forward waving branches, throwing sweet meats and sugar plums. Then there were swift hunts in shaded forests, appropriate for the meetings of clandestine lovers. And gala dinners, where the lords, wearing golden crowns, were served by a multitude of stewards, footmen, and waiters, bearing elaborate meats and heaps of fruit on golden platters and fine wines for jewel-encrusted goblets. And games, tarot cards and chess, with nobles and damsels sitting alternately in a circle, and all using the games as pretexts to whisper sweet secrets. And gay music. And harmonious verses. And joyous dances.

A brother of Gautier, named Jean, who surpassed him in all ways in nobility and courage, had followed him to Lecce. He had composed a dancing song in the vernacular entitled *Donna, audite como*.[18] It declared that the sweetest and most tormenting lordship is that of love; yet not to all is it given to know perfect love, only to one who has the heart of the perfect knight. The song began with homage to the radiant queen. The invitation followed, well known to one who was used to leading the dances and choruses of the Tripudianti in the piazza: *Chi è innamorato venga avanti a riddare* ("You who are in love, come dance in a ring").

> *E chi non lo sa fare,*
> *sì si vada a posare.*

> You who do not know the dance,
> Go this way and that way . . .

Fino amore—pure love—is supreme happiness and subtle pain, as one finds in the story of Tristan and Iseult the Fair. And the more one loves, the happier and more sorrowful he is.

But the woman who is loved must not resist her lover. Young girls, beautifully adorned, intercede, bringing flowers and prayers to the fascinating enemy. Surrender, O glowing spouse, O delicate damsel! Yield the closed defended castles to the tenacious assailants. Victory cannot fail to smile on the valiant ranks. The iron gates shall be opened, the banners unfurled to the wind, the triumphal anthems sung. All the beautiful ones shall bow to the one who is the most beautiful of all. All the lords of the castles shall pay homage to the bold *signore.*

The first biographers of Saint Francis did not know Gautier except by the term *conte gentile.*[m] *Gentile* here meant generous, magnanimous, courteous, all the highest qualities of the knight; they were saying, "the very noble count."

The young Assisi noble intended to join Gautier de Brienne and Francis decided to go along with him. He would thus realize his old ambition: to go to Apulia, to enlist in the service of the Sire de Brienne, to earn knighthood from him by the virtue of arms. The two young men could do nothing but talk of their projects, confide their feelings to each other, imagine their bright future. Sometimes they spent the entire night in such conversation, and the first light of day found them still intent making and unmaking their plans.[19]

---

m. There is perhaps something instructive about how information travels in the confusion over the identification of the young man of Assisi who accompanied Francis and the Count Gautier de Brienne of Apulia. Thomas of Celano, in both his biographies, says only that Francis's companion was an Assisi nobleman. Bonaventure mentions a *gentile* count, using the word as an adjective meaning "well-bred" and "magnanimous" and probably referring to Count Gautier. In *3 Soc.,* 5, however, we read that Francis wanted to be knighted by a "Count Gentile." In *Anon. Per.,* 5, we read that Francis planned to join "Count Gentile," who was leaving for Apulia, and to be made a knight by him. Some historians even identified this person as Gentile dei Paleari, Count of Monoppello, papal tutor for the realm and for the child Frederick II. *NV* 2:183.

To Francis's ardent nature, knighthood seemed the supreme goal of life. It would be the light that would lead him from the disconsolate shadows into which he had fallen. It would liberate and defend him from life's seamy side—cruelties, brutalities, vulgarities, lies, deceptions, weaknesses, betrayals, miseries—all the dirtiness of life.

To make himself worthy of it, he would wander from country to country, travel over all roads, throw his heart on roaring bonfires, spill his blood to the very last drop. To the final measure of his heart and his blade, he would avenge infamies, redeem shames, subdue cowardice. "My soul to God, my life to the king, my heart to my lady, honour for me." This was the knight's motto. This had been his soul's desire since childhood, since the days he had sat on the steps of the atrium of San Giorgio.

He would go up one day, with a great retinue, on the mountain of the Archangel[n] crowned with olive trees beside the Apulia sea. He would kneel at the foot of the altar in the diffused glow of lamps, and for him Gautier would repeat the formula of consecration: "In the name of God, of Saint George, and of Saint Michael, I make you knight. Be proud, courageous, faithful."

He would return to Assisi; he would enter by the San Giorgio gate, riding on a white charger. He would dismount amid the cheers of all, at the threshold of the cathedral, with a golden belt about his waist. The *camerlengo* of the commune would rush up to offer him the reward established by the statutes.[o]

He would fight. He would go out against any enemy. He would lead the élite group of attackers, scale the steepest wall, conquer the loftiest castle.

He would meet the lady of his soul. He would love.

He would enter into the disputes of love with damsels grown up and educated in splendid courts ruled over by women famous for their charm and subtlety: Eleanor d'Aquitaine, queen of France and of England, Ermengard of Narbonne, Marie of Champagne, Isabelle, countess of Flanders. This, too, was entirely a French science, one that the young merchant had learned from a book by Andreas, chaplain to the king of France.[20] It was a discussion of love—its essence, the persons capable of receiving it, the way to acquire it, the punishments that await women guilty of not meeting with passion the

---

n. Mount Gargano in Apulia, where Michael the Archangel is said to have appeared in the fifth century.—Trans.

o. The statutes of Assisi required that the commune pay an award of forty *fiorini* of gold to citizens who through their prowess were named knights (L. 1, r. 253).

passion of their lovers, the secrets of maintaining the fire of love and making it grow and die down, of extinguishing it.

The women asked the questions; the knights responded. The ideal queens handed down judgements.

One lady, for example, asked the much debated question: "Is it better to love with the eyes or with the heart?" The answer, according to Andreas, "All know that the heart rules over the eyes, because love expressed with the eyes is worth nothing if the heart does not feel. But the heart, without the eyes, can freely love that which it cannot see before it."

Another problem: "Which should be preferred, to follow the woman who returns your love to a solitary place and there to die in the consolation of that love, or to love her for all your life without having her love you or encourage you to love?" Francis would certainly have chosen the answer: "If you love loyally, you do not say no to such a death."

The valour of the knight could not exist without being aroused and fed by the love of a woman. Love was the lyrical force in all battles, the fervour that made all bravery sublime, the passion that changed bitter pain into joy. The fate of peoples and of kingdoms was decided on the field by the memory of a luminous smile and the rustling of a soft embroidered scarf. Launcelot of the Lake taught that the true knight must have strength, prowess, loyalty, kindness, gentleness, courtesy, generosity, prodigality, and an abundance of friends and of riches. But all this would have been like a bare garden in the middle of a winter night if it were not warmed and made to flower by the sun of love.[21]

The first biographers tell us that of these two young men of Assisi who were making ready to depart, the unknown noble was the richer, but Francis the more generous. The first was illustrious through nobility of birth but Francis exceeded him in magnanimity.

Those who are received at courts must wear rich and sumptuous clothes—wearing fine clothes is one of the prerogatives of knights.[22] Therefore, Francis, with his taste for elegance that came both from natural discrimination and experience, turned his attention first of all to the preparation of an extravagant wardrobe.

Once again all the tradesmen of Assisi and the surrounding area were put to work to provide him with clothes that would have no equal in splendour and originality of design, in quality of material, in colour and decoration. White satins and red satins, showy silks and heavy brocades, materials worked in silver and in gold, embroidered outer garments, mantles lined with ermine—all these accumulated in

Pietro Bernadone's house, together with weapons and armour of the finest workmanship.

Francis was dazzled with it all. He spent long hours looking at the soft velvets shot with silk and gleaming chiselled steel, trying to become blasé about them. In vain.

It was already April. The war was languishing. White and red roses and fresh young faces alike bloomed on every balcony. A soft spring sun (as in the Giotto fresco that depicts the episode about to be related) soothed the façade of the Roman temple, the severe campanile of the cathedral, the bishop's palace, the houses, the olive groves, the mountain, the valley.ᵖ

One day Francis rode out on horseback, leaving a wake of admiration that filled his heart with joy. Going through his mind like a familiar melody was all that had been said about his future glory. His great mantle of cloth of gold flew out behind him in his swift pace.

Outside the city he took the path leading from Stradette, one of the family properties, along the San Damiano declivity. A young man met him and greeted him. Francis knew him. He was one of the nobles of the castles ruined by the war and the overthrow of the manor system. Once he had seemed magnanimous and of great spirit, but fate had reduced him to a poor existence in his ruined tower. He was wearing miserable rags.

Francis stopped and took off his mantle. Marvellously it gleamed against the quiet rural landscape, gold and scarlet velvet, with wide sleeves of deep blue sendal. The other, too astonished to speak, looked at it in mingled admiration and rue. Slowly the would-be knight got off his horse and placed the mantle on the shoulders of this knight so reduced in circumstances. Then he took him to his house and joyously gave him all the new clothes and princely arms that he had loved so much. It was an act, say his companions, of nobility and chivalry; it marked his consecration and initiation into a new order of knighthood to which he would remain faithful all his life.²³

Thomas of Celano recalls the story of Saint Martin, who saw a poor man, like the knight, well nigh naked, vainly asking alms from those who passed by. He cut his military mantle in two with his sword and gave half of it to the beggar.

"Was what he did less than the deed of the great and most holy Martin?" writes Thomas. "If his way of doing it were different, the

---

p. Giotto, who worked on this fresco at the end of the thirteenth century, depicts the city and countryside from the east. It is probable that his painting, therefore, has a documentary value in establishing the locality where the episode took place, placed by the Florentine artist along the San Damiano hill. It will be remembered that Pietro Bernardone owned property here; to be precise, in the place called Semitae. *NV* 2:106.

intent and the action were the same. Francis first gave away his clothes and then all the rest, while Martin began by giving away his possessions and then gave up his clothes. But both spent their time on this earth as poor and humble men and rich entered into heaven. Martin, who was a knight but poor, cut his mantle in half to clothe a beggar; Francis, who was not a knight but rich, clothed the poor soldier with his entire mantle. Both, for having fulfilled the commandment of Christ, merited being visited by Christ in visions, Martin receiving the praise of a completed perfection, Francis the loving invitation to do that which yet he had not done to be perfect."

The comparison is more apt than one might think.

Young Francis must have had a great devotion to Saint Martin of Tours.

He was then the national saint of France, chivalrous and Christian France, which the son of the merchant had loved since infancy. His cult was also very widespread in Italy. Lucca had dedicated its cathedral to Saint Martin. Pisa had named a famous church for him. He was depicted on the façades of both these churches, on horseback and in the act of dividing his mantle with a sword.

In the city of the Subasio, too, the cult of Saint Martin goes back to very early times. In a property that belonged to the family of Pietro Bernardone, along the slope of the mountain near the women's monastery of Panzo on this side of Rivo Secco, the remains of an ancient church dedicated to Saint Martin were recently found; it had been important enough to give its name to the whole *balía*.[24] It was already ruined and abandoned in Francis's time; but it, like those other churches falling into ruins that he saw as he travelled about, must have aroused in him a pensive and sentimental feeling. Moreover, even the money that he counted in the paternal shop and that he generously handed out to the poor, the coins of Lucca called *lucenses* [the money then current in Assisi], carried on them a figure of Saint Martin on horseback.

Everything, therefore, in his dreams, in his recollections, in his acts of charity, spoke to him of Saint Martin's deed, which he had now repeated as he was getting ready to undertake a new and heroic life.

The Enchanted Castle

The next night Francis, still absorbed in thoughts of the forthcoming trip, was very late in going to sleep. The house was still. The white light of the full moon came through wide open shutters. All the familiar things—the bed, covers, benches, arches, walls—shone in an immaterial light, as in a dream, seeming things from an ethereal, supernatural world. And also shining in that radiance (an extraordinary thing) were the clothes, the arms, the mantle, that he had given to the poor man and that now, mysteriously, were again in the house, scattered about his room, shining as though lit by a clear flame.[25]

Then the house fades away.

A voice calls him by name, so strong, so near, so distinct, that it makes him give a sudden start. Someone, whose face he cannot make out, makes him a sign to follow. He sets out. A castle appears. It is beautiful, strong, rich, enormous, like the royal palace of a prince. There is a walkway for making patrols, a crown of battlements that runs gracefully around the walls, with a fringe of little arches. The castle is decorated as for a festival. On top of the master tower, on all the lateral towers and bartizans, banners wave, all bearing the cross of the Crusader knights.

The atrium is deserted. No one keeps watch at the guard post. No one calls out a challenge or a greeting. No one comes down or goes up the staircases. The doors open silently and silently they shut. Footsteps make no sound on the thick carpets.

Vistas of spacious rooms open before him. There are no hangings, no pictures, no mosaics, on the walls, only arms and more arms, an unbelievable quantity of shining bright arms, which seem to concentrate and reflect the unbearable splendour of a thousand polished steel plates or the glitter of a thousand mirrors struck by the sun.

Shields and bare blades sparkle, polished helmets gleam. It is formidable and magnificent armour, worthy of paladins and even of warrior archangels. Golden bucklers, laminated great shields, breastplates covered with scales, and coats of mail seem like a wave of the sea caught in a play of light and wind. The iron-shod points of the massive lances, their pennons and vamplates, the cutting blades of the axes, all shine like silver. Cuirasses, coats of mail, scaled breastplates, *coretti,* and corselets take the breath away. The gauntlets are stretched out as if in a promise of victory.

Long straight swords with cross-shaped hilts flash, as if someone were raising them in an open field in the light of a glorious morning. Saddles and caparisons await spirited warhorses. Norman and Carolingian helmets, crested helmets with neckpieces of woven steel, Crusader helmets with closed visors, bejeweled helmets blazoned with coats of arms, overflow the deserted rooms, ready for the use of an unknown army due to burst forth shortly, shouting a stirring war cry.

But now all is silent. No one speaks, no one comes out to meet arrivals. The castle lies in a circle of mysterious enchantment.

Beyond a closed gate a wide balcony looks out over the sea. A young woman is seated under an arcade. She is dressed like the princess in the church of San Giorgio in Assisi, with a long dress of purple velvet bordered in white. Her white face and neck, her white hands, stand out dramatically against the dark purple. She is very beautiful. Her beauty dims the light of all the arms.

She looks far away, out at the expanse of deep blue sea. She seems to wait for something: a message, an announcement, a prophecy, a ship spreading its sails on a sapphire sea.

She is the damsel that for so many years he has thought about, desired, loved, even though he has never known her. She is the chosen one. For her the banners are unfurled on top of the walls. For her the swords and the shields gleam, and for her exist the incomparable towers, the sky, the sea.

Who will be on that ship? Who is to cross the forbidden threshold and kneel before the promised bride? Who will lead the knights into battle and rule over this enchanted castle?

Everything is suddenly bathed in a great light, and the same strong and harmonious voice that earlier had called Francis by name rises up: "All this is for you and for your knights."

The light dims and fades away. The moon is setting on the far off hills. The room slowly falls into darkness.

The Spoleto Experience

The next morning Francis rose in good spirits, for he believed that the vision must be a good omen for the success of the enterprise. He was cheerful again; and many people, seeing him so happy, asked him the reason for it. He answered, "I know that I shall become a great prince."[26]

The day of departure came. The leave-taking from the family, and especially from his mother, must have been extremely painful; but his passionate eagerness to be off, not to speak of his certainty of a forthcoming triumph, overcame it. He mounted his horse and set off with the friend who was to share in his fortunes. A faithful squire followed him.[27]

The ancient road between Assisi and Spoleto is not the one usually taken today, which goes through San Potente and Viole, but another, now little travelled, that runs higher up along the slope of the Subasio. It leaves the present road a short distance from the city gate and crosses the entire length of that part of the commune named after the third bishop of the Roman period, Saint Sabinus.[28] The name of the area, which dates from the first Christian centuries, still survives in official papers and in the devotion of the people, who call this territory between the mountain and the plain the Costa [Slope] of San Savino.

A thousand years before Pietro Bernardone's son set out on this road toward his new destiny, the saintly bishop travelled it for the last time, the day they took him from Assisi to Spoleto to undergo martyrdom. So brave had been the blessed Sabinus under torture that he came to be considered the protector of all those who had to face up to war. This also was a good omen for Francis, and he must have kept it in mind while his horse ascended the steep gradient of the road. Many chapels stood along the road, reminding him of that saint associated with so much superhuman courage and heroic holiness, a saint whom he had venerated since his earliest years.

The regular lectionary of the Assisi cathedral has preserved for us the text of the passion of Saint Sabinus that was well known in Assisi in Francis's day. In it Saint Sabinus is clearly shown, even in the hands of his executioners, to be the true master. Venustianus, the legate of the emperor, orders the bishop to sacrifice to the gods. He replies that there is no god in all the world but the Lord Jesus Christ. The pagan has a statue of Jove brought to the place of the trial, and Sabinus dashes it to the ground, reducing it to fragments. For that his hands are cut off. The executioner tortures the deacons of the bishop with iron and fire, and the bishop bravely comforts them and urges them not to renounce their faith. Re-imprisoned, he restores sight to a blind man, converts the soldiers who guard him, and even converts Venustianus himself, together with his wife and children. All of them are decapitated by the tribune Lucius, sent by the emperor. "And at the same time the tribune imprisoned the holy bishop Sabinus and took him to Spoleto, and without trial, ordered that he be beaten to death with iron rods. And he, after having been beaten for a long time, died. A woman named Serena, who had picked up and kept his severed hands, also gathered up his body, and uniting hands and body, buried him about two miles from the city of Spoleto on the seventh day before the Ides of December."[29]

The would-be knight in a short time reached the point at which the road bordered the family estate in San Martino d'Argentana. Again he saw the fountain, the spring, the poplars, the field of hemp, the garden with laurel growing in it, Rivo Secco, the cliff called Sasso di Maloloco. He embraced with a long look those places so dear to him, the olive orchards and fields on the slope beyond the Camerata stream—San Damiano, Fontanelle, San Pietro della Spina, Rivotorto. A doubt crossed his soul for an instant, a question whether it would not be preferable to continue his life in that vernal and entrancing countryside, so promising and so delightful. He dismissed it as weakness and went on his way.

Above them the towers of the monastery of San Benedetto appeared, then the ruins of the castle of Sasso Rosso. The stream called Renaro marked the border of the territory of the commune.

They reached Spoleto, the capital city of the duke, who was now subject to the Papal State. There they planned to make a stop, perhaps to find out more about this enterprise for which the pope was granting the same indulgence as for participation in the Crusades.

Modern Franciscan historians have tried to reconstruct those days in Spoleto and to determine the places that Saint Francis could have visited.[30]

A short distance from Spoleto there used to be a basilica dedicated to Saint Sabinus, erected over the site of his burial. His body was once venerated there. From all parts of the country men who were going off to war used to come to pray before their departure. It is impossible to think that Francis, girding himself for a future that would depend on his sword, would have neglected to follow this pious custom. He would certainly have invoked the protection of the martyr whom his own city of Assisi considered one of its principal protectors.

We know of this custom through Paul the Deacon. His account, which is still preserved in its original form, was then often repeated to the gallant pilgrims to the basilica: "Ariulfo, Lombardian duke of Spoleto, having come to combat with the Romans in Camerino, and having emerged victor, wished to interrogate his men in order to find out the identity of the soldier who had fought with such extraordinary valour during the battle. His soldiers replied that they had never seen anyone fight more bravely than he himself. But he answered, 'And yet I did see someone braver than I am in every way, someone who, every time one of the enemies tried to wound me, strenuously parried the blows with his own shield.' Later the duke arrived in Spoleto, where the basilica of Saint Sabinus Martyr stood and where his venerated body rested. 'Who is it that is honoured in this grand building?' the duke asked. The faithful replied that the martyr Sabinus rested there, and that the Christians prayed for assistance there every time that they left for war against their enemies. Ariulfo, who was still pagan, demanded, 'How is it possible for a dead person to give help to a living one?' And he dismounted from his horse and went in to see the church. While others prayed, he looked at the paintings in the basilica. Immediately, as his eyes travelled to the image of the blessed Martyr Sabinus, he broke out in exclamations, swearing that the figure and the bearing of the warrior was that of the man who had defended him in battle. Then it was known that it was the blessed Sabinus who had rescued him in the dangers of war."[31]

One would suppose that Francis's prayer was not in vain. But, as he was making ready to resume his trip, fever overcame him again, that familiar shivering that returned every evening at the same hour and continued all night; so that he spent the nights in a semi-conscious state, half-asleep, half-awake, and in the morning was prostrate and worn out.[32]

His companion, the noble youth, left, promising to meet him again soon at the castle of Lecce. Francis remained alone with his faithful servant, his grief, his anxiety, his world filled with the phantoms that were again wavering about him.

Francis's eagerness to get up and leave became a torment. But the fever gave no sign of subsiding.

One night, being shaken more strongly than ever by the alternating waves of hope and of distress and discouragement, he heard a voice, perhaps the same one that had called him in his vision of the castle filled with arms.

The Three Companions tell the story of this miraculous event in these words:

"Now it happened that, after the start for Apulia, Francis felt unwell on arriving at Spoleto; and thinking with apprehension about the journey, he went to bed, but, half asleep, he heard a voice calling and asking him whither he was bound. He replied, telling of his plan. Then he, who had previously appeared to him in sleep, spoke these words:

"'Who do you think can best reward you, the Master or the servant?'

"'The Master,' answered Francis.

"'Then why do you leave the Master for the servant, the rich Lord for the poor man?'"

Suddenly, in a great flash that illuminated his soul, Francis understood who it was that had spoken to him. And in an instant much of the old Francis burned away: the turmoil of his ambitious dreams, his greed for marvellous victories, his mania for military glory, his need to be first, his day-dreaming about unknown roads and unexpected encounters. Biographers say that the miracle of Paul's vision on the road to Damascus had been repeated, that a mortal soul had been caught up in an experience of the divine that sublimated worldly traits into an overwhelming desire to offer himself to God.

The emblem of Francis's *contrada* was the sword that had severed the head of the Apostle Paul. Ever since adolescence, in festivals and in dances of the Tripudianti, in cavalcades and in battles and in prison, that symbol had been engraved in his heart. Now the blade of the sword had been turned on him, destroying and remaking him for Christ. On earth Jesus had said, "Love your neighbour as yourself."[33] To Francis he was to give a new commission: "Love your neighbour more than yourself." It was a mandate to which Francis would remain faithful all his life.

Francis asked, like Paul, "O Lord, what do you wish me to do?"

And the reply was much like the one that Jesus had made to Paul: "Return to your own place and you will be told what to do."[34]

The vision of arms, the voice continued, must be understood in another sense than Francis had thought. The arms and the palace were destined for knights very much different than those he had in mind. In a much different way, too, would he himself win honour.

Francis did not sleep any more that night. When the first light filtered into the room, he got up. Dawn was rising on the summit of Monteluco.

Now the significance of that extraordinary vision seemed very clear to him in Saint Paul's own words: "Since we live by the Spirit, let us follow the Spirit's lead. Let us never be boastful, or challenging, or jealous toward one another."[35]

Gautier's Death

Perhaps the same night, during that same hour, those besieged in the castle of Sarno made the sortie that marked the end of Gautier's great enterprise. The count was caught by surprise, possibly through the betrayal of someone of his company turned traitor. Though he defended himself heroically with his sword, in the end he fell, transfixed by an incredible number of arrows. Near death, he was carried to the castle.

All the encampment was sacked and destroyed.[36]

Giovanni da Ceccano compares this defeat to the one suffered by Roland: "The rout of Sarno is like that of Roncesvaux, when the nephew of Charlemagne, powerfully armed, was defeated in battle and betrayed by Gano and refused to call the emperor and the other knights to his aid."[37]

But very different from Roland's fate was that of Gautier, who in stories told by the people of Apulia is still saluted as the last paladin of France.

In the *Chanson de Roland,* the verses telling of the death of the hero mark the poem's greatest epic flight. All the French knights are dead.

The Saracens have fled. Roland, alone on the battlefield, blows the oliphant at last, not to call for help but to announce the completion of the sacrifice. Afterwards, he tries to break his sword so that no one else can use it, but in vain.

> Count Roland smites the sardin stone amain
> The steel grides hard, but neither breaks nor bates.
> Now when he sees that it will nowise break
> Thus to himself he maketh his complaint
> Ah Durandel! so bright, so brave, so gay!
> How dost thou glitter in the sun's rays!

Then he stretches out in the shade of a pine tree, crosses his arms on the hilt, directs his last prayer to heaven, salutes his king from afar, and surrenders. Surrenders to God. He consigns his glove to the Archangel Gabriel, who comes to him in his death agony. He rests his head on the angel's arm and dies. Dies unconquered, his face turned toward the enemy.

> He's turned his head to where the Paynims are
> And this he doth for the French and for Charles,
> Since fain is he that they should say, brave heart,
> That he has died a conqueror at the last.[38]

Gautier, on the other hand, is taken to Diopoldo, without being able to make the slightest resistance. Diopoldo sets about trying to cure him, for he calculates that he can make a great profit on a living Gautier. And when he is on the road to recovery, Diopoldo proposes that he become his ally. When the count indignantly refuses, Diopoldo flings a knife at his face, insults him, and threatens him with a miserable end. Gautier, in order not to remain in the custody of so treacherous and cruel an enemy, tears off his bandages and dies.

On the afternoon of March 19, 1937, the Friars Minor of Santa Maria della Foce, near Sarno, discovered the tomb of Gautier de Brienne in the church of San Guglielmo, which is attached to their friary.[39] The skeleton of the great warrior lay with arms crossed, head resting upon a stone—a bundle of loose bones in the damp soil. It was an hour of the final evaporation of the great dreams of glory, an hour in which, as the sons of Saint Francis rearranged the miserable remains, the truth of the words heard by Saint Francis in Spoleto became supremely clear.

The day after the vision, Francis returned to Assisi. Here he stayed, waiting to know what was destined for him.

The usual idlers, again ready to find satisfaction in his humiliation, were astonished to see that he was more cheerful than ever. They questioned him, pretending interest in the details of a trip that had gone badly. They needled him with veiled ironies that were repeated with malicious jeers in the piazza. They asked with an affected laugh whatever would he have done with a prince's throne.

He invariably answered that soon he would have his victory. This new crazy idea became the joke of the countryside. But everyone continued to court him and flatter him because he was rich and considered an agreeable spendthrift.

A few days after his return the Tripudianti had one of their usual gatherings. They wanted him to be with them at the banquet.

As usual, before going out to sing songs in the street, they had to elect a new leader, who would then have to choose someone to pay the bill. They knew Francis's generosity, which, when he had been chosen before, led him to "sentence" himself to that duty. They agreed for that reason to acclaim him again *signore* of the company.

The Last Serenata

The banquet of the Tripudianti was in full swing. The burning torches of the bronze candelabra flickered, stirring up flights of shadows on the beautifully prepared table, the trays filled with fruit and sweetmeats, the sparkling cups, the trees in the garden, the streets sinking into night.[40]

The companions were very gay. They were seated, men and women alternating, on scarlet cushions, the men bold because a little drunk, the women very beautiful (faces lit up, laughing, eyes flashing) and chosen, as the rules decreed, from among the youngest and most popular of the city. It would have ruined the reputation of the company to have a banquet not enlivened by the presence of pliant and endearing women.

Francis was at the head of the table, wearing magnificent clothes, as usual. He was quiet, pensive, his face shadowed by his hair, which was cut round and full about his head. He was neither talking nor touching the food nor drinking. His crown of roses was wilting slowly, though he showed no sign of noticing it. He was not stirred by the acclamations of his friends as they saluted his election at the beginning of the dinner, nor by the sceptre, the sign of his lordship, brought to him with great solemnity. He should have led the merry-making, lifted his chalice to the queen of the banquet, begun the singing. He remained detached and indifferent. He was a strange, taciturn *signore,* absorbed in far-away thought.

Beside him, clouds of precious incense rose into the dark sky. Moths swirled around his head, attracted by the flames of the lamps that hung from above.

A clamour recalled him. The table companions were getting up. Supper was finished. They called him, unanimously saluting him with an exultant shout. Who was best in playing the lute? Francis. Who had the most melodious voice in singing love songs? Francis. Who, alas, was most popular with the girls? Francis. Who was the most inventive poet, the bravest fighter, the most generous cavalier? Francis, always Francis.

All those young faces brightened by the celebration were turned toward him, all arms stretched to him, all promises designed to please him. A young girl brought another crown of roses and lightly placed it on his head. A page, kneeling, offered him the silver-banded sceptre.

They went out into the open, a large, singularly light-hearted group. They had lutes and mandolins.

The spring night was tranquil, a night that heightened that vague sense of sadness that comes at the end of every celebration.

All the houses were dark in peaceful sleep. The first chords caught that feeling of melancholy; it was as if a light veil had fallen on the heedless gaiety of the company and a hidden reminder of how fleeting is time had suddenly dissolved the high spirits of the party, with its good wines and lovely women and beautiful clothes. The song was a lament for lost joy, a cry of the pain that lies even in a rapturous night of love.

> *En un vergier sotz fuella d'albespi*
> *tenc la dompna son amic costa si,*
> *tro la gayta crida que l'alba vi.*
> *Oy Dieus, oy Dieus, de l'alba! tan tost ve.*

> In a garden where the whitethorn spreads her leaves
> My lady hath her love lain close beside her,
> Till the warden cries the dawn—Ah dawn that grieves!
> Ah God! Ah God! That dawn should come so soon!

At this point the *signore* of the company saw something that made him start, his heart pounding. The lady of his vision was at his side, the one who had appeared beyond the closed gate of the enchanted castle. Her face was gentle and pale, as in the dream. Even more marked was her delicate grace, the inexpressible tenderness that made her seem a stranger to all that surrounded her and turned her into the embodiment of a song of love and heartbreak.

But she no longer wore her rich clothes of purple bordered in white ermine. She was ragged and barefoot. And yet, an extraordinary thing, her beggar's garb made her infinitely more beautiful, more enticing, as if she were the princess in a fairy tale and regally superior to all the other girls in their silks and velvets.

It was impossible to say how she had come. No one had seen her before the moment in which, like an apparition, she was with them.

The singers moved on to repeat the refrain a little farther along, and she moved with them, always near the young Francis, almost touching his arm. She walked in bare feet, without making a sound. And she kept a singular silence.

At a curve she disappeared. She had not gone into any door, down any street. He searched for her desperately. The *contrada* was deserted.

Then an infinite lassitude assailed him, and he could neither talk nor move nor feel anything except a great sweetness. Later, when he tried to explain in some fashion just what he had felt, he would say that he thought himself taken outside the world, beyond earthly sensations, so that even if he had been beaten until he bled, he would not have had the strength to take a step or to raise a hand.

From the distance comes the reprise of the song:

> *Plagues a Dieu ja la nueitz non falhis*
> *ni · l mieus amicx lonc de mi no · s partis*
> *ni la gayta jorn ni alba no vis!*
> *Oy Dieux, oy Dieux, de l'alba! tan tost ve.*

> "Please God that night, dear night should never cease,
> Nor that my Love should parted be from me,
> Nor watch cry 'Dawn'—Ah dawn that slayeth peace!
> Ah God! Ah God! That dawn should come so soon! . . ."[41]

He does not listen, does not hear. He is alone with the lady who has come from the land of dreams to enter his life, there to stay forever.

The others, who have seen nothing, come back to him; they crowd around him full of questions. What has happened to their absent-minded leader? What is he up to now? Why had he left them? What is he thinking? What does he have to say?

He does not reply. He cannot reply. The voices come from afar, muffled, as if an abyss had opened between them.

Someone turns to him jokingly and asks, "Have you perhaps finally found a bride?"

This word struck him and suddenly brought him back to the company.

He replied, "It is true. I have found my beloved bride. And she is the noblest, the richest, the most beautiful bride who ever lived on this earth."[42]

They answer him with a burst of sarcastic laughter. The hilarity spreads. The mysterious enchantment of that night vanishes in the wave of unrestrained mirth. They remember the strange behaviour of Pietro's son in the Perugia prison, the peculiar business about his dream of shining armour, the trip to Spoleto.

By now it is only a short time until the break of day. The friends separate with spirits again light. Francis follows them in silence.

The serenata is finished. The *contrada* is again silent. Only the stars continue to glitter in the serene night, that night when for the first time Francis met face-to-face the damsel of his heart, Lady Poverty.

·6·

THE HERALD OF
THE GREAT KING

About the middle of 1204 the fortunes of war shifted in favour of Assisi.

A new political development had endangered the power of Innocent III, and therefore of Perugia. In Germany a struggle for the imperial crown had been going on since the death of Henry VI in 1198 between Philip of Swabia, Henry's brother, and Otto of Brunswick. Now Philip seemed to be victorious. Innocent, who had supported Otto, began to fear the restoration of Swabian rule in Italy. Philip had, in fact, sent Diopoldo of Worms to Italy in the spring of this year to reconquer the cities that had been occupied by the church. Assisi swore obedience to this legate.

As a consequence, Philip issued a diploma in favour of Assisi in Ulma on July 29. One of its clauses was this: "The Imperial Curia will not make an agreement with the Perugini and with those of Assisi who are with the Perugini, except with the counsel and consent of the consuls of Assisi; and this commune will do the same in regard to the Curia; and the Curia will help the men of Assisi to recover their rights and usages and to maintain them without fraud." The emperor declared that he intended to take the Assisani under his particular favour and to pardon them for all offences. He was ready to agree that the fortress destroyed in 1198 would never in the future be rebuilt. He also agreed to approve the commune form of government and the election of consuls, who, however, would have to promise loyalty to the emperor. He further promised to bestow upon the city many other benefits and fiscal exemptions. Moreover, he ordered that privileges be revoked for feudal lords who did not support the emperor, a provision that greatly alarmed those of Assisi who had fought with Perugia.

This changed political situation suddenly turned the tide in the war and led many of the émigrés to seek reconciliation with the commune.[a] In the second half of August, some of them, Aguramonte di Giovanni di Matteo, Andrea dell'Isola, Sacente, Monaldo, Ronzone, Brocario and Obizzo, declared that they wished to absolve the commune of Perugia from every obligation to help them recover their goods and asserted that the Assisani had compensated them for all damage.[1]

Their hasty statement could not have been true. On August 31, 1205, Giovanni di Guidone del Papa, podestà of Perugia, issued an ordinance in which, after declaring a state of peace between the cities, he ordered Assisi to make restitution to these same nobles for their properties and to rebuild their destroyed houses.

One senses that this peace is, like that proclaimed in the document of 1203, nonsense. Even the podestà understands it this way; he takes care to say that the peace he has declared will have to be *bona et firma pax,* a solid and sincere peace.

The same Perugia ordinance also sets a deadline for the Assisani for the restitution of the goods and for the rebuilding of the castles of the lords of Sassorosso and of Berarduccio di Tebalduccio. They were also ordered not to interfere with the freedom of the city of Nocera or of its territory.[2]

All these impressive orders fall into a void. No one in Assisi takes them seriously. They are intended to salvage the good reputation of the city of Perugia, which for the first time realizes it is using blunted thunderbolts and so suffers vague uneasiness.

The unsettled state of mind existing at the time may be seen in episodes involving nearby *castelli* that were forced by the change in the situation to switch allegiance from Perugia to Assisi. The men of Valfabbrica, subject to the rule of the monastery of Santa Maria

---

a. To recapitulate a little history as an explanation of the situation in Assisi: When Frederick I (Barbarossa) died leading a Crusader army (1190 A.D.), his son, Henry VI, succeeded him, an emperor who dreamed of heading a universal empire. However, he died in 1196, while putting down an insurrection in the south of Italy, which had been caused by the cruelty of his German officials. His only son, the future Frederick II, was a child of two. The German princes who elected their ruler objected to having a child on the throne, and they chose Henry's brother and Frederick's regent, Philip of Swabia, as king of Germany (certain also to be crowned emperor). Dissidents supported the Welf Otto of Brunswick (second son of Henry the Lion, duke of Saxony, and Matilda, daughter of Henry II of England) and in 1198 elected him anti-king. Otto won the support of Innocent III through extravagant promises to restore the Papal States to the boundaries of the Carolingian age. In the war that followed between these two factions, Otto suffered a series of defeats and was finally driven back to Brunswick. It was during this time that Philip "took Assisi under his favour," and it swore obedience to his legate.—Trans.

dell'Assunta, became, for the most part, citizens of Assisi. But then the partisans of Perugia got the upper hand again. As a consequence, in early February 1206 some Assisi men raided Valfabbrica and carried off some loot. Those who had acquired Assisi citizenship were outraged, and a hearing on the whole matter was held February 5 in the piazza of San Rufino, in the presence of the consuls, Tiberio, Tancredi, Somasolo, and Bernardo, *camerario*. The prior of the monastery, Rainerio, showed the paper of submission to Assisi which bore the names of several heads of families, and that led to a ruling by the consuls that "Valfabbrica men are (Assisi) citizens. They shall perform services for the city with the other citizens and are not to be considered men of the country," and "they shall respond to the authority of the city."

In this document, a picture of city life emerges from the shadows of the centuries, along with the familiar names of the leading citizens who knew Francis well: the rich lord of San Giacomo, Cristiano di Paride; the noble knight who had his house in Porta Moiano, Giovanni di Armoiaffo; also Andrea di Presbitero, Egidio di Taffurino, Bonainsegna di Rainerio, Accarino di Leonardo, Bartolo di Ingula, Martino di Lazzaro.[3]

Soul-Searching at Sasso del Maloloco

After that last supper of the Tripudianti Francis fled from his friends and sought solitude.

He takes to coming home just before dawn, as if returning from a night of carousing, his clothing and his heart disordered as he makes his way through the dark and deserted street, filled with a whirlwind of white flakes swirling in the freezing wind. If something touches him in that hour—a rooster calling in the distance, a bell ringing for the first Mass, a poor man sleeping on the steps of the church, a light shining in the room of someone who is dying—his thoughts turn, clear and sharp, to the pain in the world, too great to be stilled by any bacchic song.

Memories crowd in on him.

What great desolation and grief and how much misery he has seen; how many of his dreams have been dispersed! For the first time he thinks that the life of Jesus, who taught charity and love, must be the ideal to follow. But he shows no outward sign of this, lest his skeptical friends mock him and take it as another fantastic notion born of his inconstant nature.[4]

Only one of the old company remained faithful to him, a young man of his own age. Francis, who loved him deeply, took him as a confidant on his solitary walks. Not daring to reveal his true thoughts, he talked to him in allegories and figures of speech. He said that he was on the track of a great treasure.[b]

Thus they went about together, one excited by the thought of his new spiritual riches, the other greedy to share in the finding of worldly treasure. We are reminded of the impassioned poetry of the idyll of Francis and his Lady Poverty, *Sacrum Commercium,* by an unknown author of the thirteenth century: "Francis began to go about in the streets and crossings of the city, relentlessly, like a persistent hunter, diligently seeking whom his heart loved. He inquired of those standing about, he questioned those who came near him, saying: 'Have you seen her whom my heart loves?' But this saying was hidden from them, as though it were in a foreign language . . . "[5]

And his fellow citizens did not understand the young man's fixed idea that he was on the verge of marrying a girl whose beauty was surpassed only by her incredible wisdom.[6] When they questioned him about his plans, he replied that he would not again be going off to Apulia, that instead he would accomplish a great and noble enterprise in his own city.[7]

From the lands in San Martino d'Argentana belonging to Francis's family, the two friends went up the path alongside Rivo Secco, passed beyond the stony dark mass at the bottom of the mountain gorge called then "Sasso Cupo di Panzo" and today "Scoglio del Carabone," crossed the woodland, and reached a fearsome confusion of rocks, crags, and cliffs called in the documents of the time "Sasso del Maloloco," later the "Carcere of San Francesco," and now the "Carceri."

It is a propitious place for dreaming. A dark forest of holm-oaks spreads along the steep declivity in the rock. There is no stone so rough that it is not entwined by greedy tenaciously clinging roots, no crag so steep that its fissures do not bear a flowering of pale cyclamen, no convolutions of rock so harsh that they are not covered by spreading ferns.

The cavern where Francis went can still be seen, low and narrow,

---

b. Many biographers, including Sabatier, Pennacchi, Jörgensen, and Attal, have believed this companion to be Brother Elias, citing the warm friendship that existed between Francis and Elias, which could well have dated from youth, as the basis of their conjecture. However, there is no historical evidence of any kind to support their belief. In fact, Sabatier in time changed his mind and suggested that Brother Leo must have been this friend. But in truth the identity of the friend remains unknown. [But see p. 599 for the author's opinion.—Trans.] NV 2:302–3.

suspended between the woods and the miraculous stream.[c] His companion awaited him outside, thinking of the promised treasure.

In the great solitude the son of the merchant found a gift more precious than a treasure of silver or gold: the opportunity to explore the depths of his own soul. Nothing remained of all his youth, all his old hopes and ideals. The past was destroyed, the future an abyss from which there seemed no escape. More than ever the example of Christ, who also suffered, seemed the ultimate reality. He wept in his misery, not seeing yet what he could do to find himself, yet feeling compelled toward an unknown goal.[8]

The friend, who patiently waited for him, used to say that Francis was so drained after having stayed for a time that he seemed almost another person.

Often the treasure hunters did not stop in the cavern but continued their walk up through that ravine opening in the mountain between the hill of San Rufino and Sasso Piano called Fossa del Subasio. They reached another cliff, Sasso del Serpente, and leaving the road of Fossa Lupara to their left, clambered all the way up to the hill called Cronia. From here the path led, through Vallonica and Sasso Piano, to Sermolla valley, where Pietro Bernardone's pastures lay.

These were hours in which Francis's internal tumult was calmed in the peace of the vast radiant horizon. In spring streams of little blue flowers crossed the vast meadows where the tall grass surged like the sea and slender white narcissus trembled under the caress of the wind. In the splendour of the mornings, distant peaks rose, yearning for the sky.

And there was a small creature friend up there whose voice seemed to Francis to be a revelation of things beyond human understanding, a bird whose joyous music was a certain promise of an awaited happiness—the skylark.

It is the humblest of all birds, since it rarely lives at the top of leafy green domes but walks, like all other troubled creatures, on the earth; in the dust and mud it picks up its food. It is dressed poorly in earth colours.

---

c. There has been a great deal of speculation over the "grotto" mentioned in 1 Cel. 6, where Francis went with his companion; and a number of sites in and about Assisi have been suggested by biographers. A constant local tradition identifies it as a cavern on Mount Subasio in the area where the Carceri now stands, a hermitage built on the site where Francis and his companions once retired to small grottos and caves for meditation and prayer. A poet of the fifteenth century, taking note of the tradition, said Francis first did penance there. On this point, see *NV* 3:155–59; for a more extended history and description of the Carceri, *NV* 3:153–62.

But suddenly it will rise up, dizzyingly, desperately, and fly higher, higher, enraptured with sun and blue sky, pouring out in the astonished silence a marvellous song, moving and exultant. It is by then no more than a point in an immensity of light, a living speck in infinite space. The eyes can no longer see it and yet its invisible song still dominates the sky, the mountain, the plain. It is as if life and death alike quiver in that little heart of the songbird.[d]

The Serfs' Drive for Freedom

The consuls were now sitting from morning to evening to hear cases arising out of the Peace Paper. The criers of the commune were constantly on the run throughout the city and country. The judge busied himself researching the texts and reading the statements of accusation and defence. The notary indefatigably filled entire rolls of parchment.

Some of these judicial documents concerning the canons of San Rufino and their serfs reflect something of the frustration and bitterness of the people involved in this class struggle.[9]

Andrea di Marco, for instance, declares in a loud voice that he is a free man, no matter what the prior and canons of San Rufino say.

"We ourselves attest to the fact that we were constantly with him," declare his witnesses, Deotaiuti Smancamantello di Cannara, his cousin Bona di Peccio di Indurato, her sister Galbasia. "We solemnly swear that Andrea and his father Marco have remained free and independent, because they have been city people from the time of 'the mortal capture' (1173) until today. We have never seen them perform the duties of the serf or anyone hunt them out. Certainly we deny that they belong to San Rufino and that it has any authority over them."

"Do they no longer remember," the canons retort, "when they called us lords and we called them our serfs, and when they brought tributes to us, one for Christmas of bread and meat and another for

---

d. *Spec. Perf.*, 113: "Above all birds he loved the small lark . . . and he used to say of it, 'Sister lark has a hood like a Religious and is a humble bird, for she walks contentedly along the road to find grain, and even if she finds it among rubbish, she pecks it out and eats it. As she flies she praises God very sweetly, like good Religious who despise earthly things, and whose minds are set on the things of heaven, with the constant purpose of praising God. Her plumage resembles the earth, and she sets an example to Religious not to wear fine and gaudy clothing, but cloth of a humble price and colour, just as earth is inferior to the other elements.'" Cf. *Per.*, 110.

Sabatier, in his edition of *Spec. Perf.* (CED, p. 224) misread the species of bird as *lodola capellata* instead of *lodola capelluta*.

Those familiar with Assisi territory know that one species of this bird, the *allodola stazionaria*, is to be found only in the meadowlands of Mount Subasio.

the Feast of the Assumption of bread and poultry, and when they broke the sod of our vineyard and worked in the harvesting and gathering of olives?"

The stewards of the church support the canons. Pittarino di Benedettolo swears that he can personally verify that Marco and his son Andrea offer *amiscere* (tributes) to San Rufino. Ugolino confirms that Andrea, and his sons also, bring these *amiscere.* In his capacity as a steward he saw them in the year of the battle with Perugia working in the vineyard and leading the oxen for the millstones.

Still other witnesses support the canons. Giovanni di Santo knows that Marco and his sons have been bringing tributes to the church for a good twenty-two years. One Uguccione declares that once Andrea refused to offer the *amiscere* and that he confiscated his oxen and did not restore them until he promised to mend his ways. Furthermore, he says, he himself, Uguccione, through pity stood surety for him.

Another who claims the status of a free person is Matelda, daughter of Gilio Carraio. A man who will become one of Francis's first companions gives angry testimony against her—the canon Silvestro, whom early biographers described as avaricious and greedy for earthly goods before he joined Francis. He and the other canons say now that Matelda's father, Gilio, had been ordained a deacon and was himself a canon of San Rufino. The prior had sent him to the church of San Fortunato. But he had left the church, taken a wife, and had two children, this Matelda and a boy, Pietro. All of them had been serfs of San Rufino and had brought tributes of cheese, fish, and chickens. When Pietro died, he, Silvestro, went to the Clesia vineyard to reconfirm the obligations of servitude. The other canons—Pietro, Tebaldo, Greco, Cerebello, and Eugenio—had gone too. And everyone of the church says they have seen Gilio on the farm performing a serf's duties.

Another canon, Pietro, testifies that Gilio's son Pietro had certainly turned to the canons whenever he needed anything. The canon Cerebello had been in person in this Pietro's house in Murorotto when he died. He says that all his goods were left to the church and the matter placed in the hands of the canon Tebaldo. Indeed, he himself had gone to the vineyard and taken away some cherries without objections from anyone.

Domino Giovanni di Bernardo had heard with his own ears Gilio's son declare that he and his father had been men of San Rufino for more than forty years. He can swear that whenever they addressed the canons of San Rufino, they had always called them *padroni,* masters.

Matelda's neighbours, who testify in her behalf, say all this is pure invention. Offreduccio, Oportolo, Guarnerio, Iacoma, Rainuccina, Filippo di Arfito, and Puccio declare that Matelda had always been free. They say that she and her brother inherited the land from Gilio and Matelda had had part of it as her dowry. When her brother died she had come into possession of all of it. She had gotten married on the farm and remained there with her husband.

Another witness, Ditavino, says he knows this all to be true. But a Rufino admits that he had seen a dispute between Oddone and Pietro di Gilio, or his wife, in the court of Domino Gerardo, podestà of Assisi, and that he had seen Oddo obtain a recognition of the hominicium. He said that Gerardo gave Oddo possession of the disputed properties through his representative, Rainucio di Palmiero, who had gone with him and taken possession of the Clesia enclosure, the Traversa and Agnano lands, and all the other properties, including a house in Murorotto, where they had found Matelda and others *barrivano*-ing a great deal. All this happened when Gerardo was podestà of Assisi. He does not remember whether it was during the first or the second term, but it seems to him it was during the first; and he does not know when Gerardo was excommunicated.

Barrivano means literally, "They were screaming out the war cry (*barrito*)" used by soldiers in battle. Its usage here marvellously depicts the storm of invective, accusations, and threats that boomed through houses and public places in these fierce arguments.

Then it is the turn of Ugolino di Pagano, whom the canons also declare to be a serf belonging to San Rufino. The usual flood of protestations and accusations pour out. Avito had seen him give the usual *amiscere* at Christmas and on the Feast of the Assumption. Rolandino had seen him perform the required services "in the quality and quantity that it pleased the prior and the canons to order." Rolandino was present when Ugolino had gathered olives for the canons below the church of Sant'Anastasio. Ugolino di Filippo had been on hand when there had been a noisy quarrel between the prior Conte and the sons of Ugolo, in which the prior had broken out in bitter words and the others had replied with equal acrimony. Scescio knows that Ugolo was a man of Guidone and of Ugone di Biminello and used to give them two cakes on the Feast of Saint Stephen, also a pork shoulder and lard, and on the Feast of the Assumption, the *amiscere* of chickens. Atto does not know if these feudal dues were being performed "at the time when this land was conquered." Others remember a great quarrel when Scagno had confiscated oxen in which "many great wrongs were done to him and he was even kicked."

Arguments continue to overflow. Relatives and consorts are sucked into them. They embitter whole sections of the city and spread to the nearby suburbs. At the third hour[e] and again before vespers, when the bell of the commune begins to ring as a signal that hearings are open, crowds of sullen contenders and disputants group themselves in the piazza, masticating their bile and hatching new schemes of violence.

Francis's Pilgrimage to Rome

Francis by now felt detached from the things of this world even in the places most familiar to him.

The center of life in Assisi was then, as it is now, the Piazza del Comune. The Three Companions recall that in that piazza Saint Francis was often overcome with an emotion so joyful that he would leave those who were with him and hurry off to pray.[10]

His mother, who loved him very much and who was keeping up with his transformation, sometimes during dinner (his father was usually away) questioned him anxiously with her eyes, without speaking. It seemed a long time to her since Francis had left the dinner table to go off with his friends. Now he remained in another world for long periods. He often heaped loaves of bread on the table, saying he wished to distribute the extra food to the poor. His poor increasingly claimed his attention. Meeting them, he gave them whatever he had, his money, his hat, his belt, even his shirt. He would have liked to go alone to some distant city where no one knew him, to be with them, be one of the unimportant, humble poor, to sit with them at a church door and beg for charity.[11]

In the spring of 1206 he decided, in the phrase used then, as may be found in Assisi documents of that century, "to fulfill a visit to the thresholds of the saints Peter and Paul." These papers contain the last wishes of devout pilgrims, written before leaving on a pilgrimage to the basilicas of the Apostles in Rome. They knew the grave risks they would run on the road, where there was little safety.[12]

Francis received a benediction, and, in short cloak and with pilgrim's staff, set out on the Strada Francesca along with others from Assisi. In Rome, he was absorbed into the river of the devout converging from all the streets into the great piazza in front of the basilica. Amid hymns and chants, he went up the wide staircase

---

e. The third hour here refers to the third canonical hour—i.e., 9 A.M. The hour of vespers varied, but it is clear that audiences were held morning and afternoon. See *NV* 3:222.

flooded with sun. He sank into the shadow of the solemn naves, where in the forest of columns innumerable lamps glittered, all hanging from the architraves by small chains, lamps shaped like doves, dolphins, and ships carrying Saint Peter at the stern guiding the rudder and Saint Paul at the prow keeping watch. On the arch sparkling with mosaics over the glorious tomb, he read the words of the golden inscription, before which innumerable crowds humbly knelt: "Since under your guidance the world has risen triumphant to the stars, the conqueror Constantine establishes this church for you." He himself knelt at the foot of the altar surmounted by the powerful baldacchino that was supported by porphyry columns. He touched his forehead to that altar, silver, with cornices of gold, adorned with precious stones; he poured oil from the clay ampulla that he had brought with him into one of the lamps and lit it at the flame of the golden candelabra given through the devout munificence of the Christian emperor. He hoped to hear in that holy place, attuned to the heart beat of all humanity, the voice of his dreams.

On the front of the altar was a small window where one could look down at the burial chamber. The pilgrims threw their offerings on it, and the money tinkled on the bronze slabs. It seemed to Francis that all the offerings were small and given grudgingly.

His innate generosity, which the poor of Assisi and the young friends of the Company of the Tripudianti knew well, was aroused. He took a handful of money from his purse and threw it all into the opening.

As he went out of the atrium, he was struck by the turmoil of the bustling crowd—a spectacle, an unsavoury and unexpected mixture: penitents who because of their great sins could not enter the church asking prayers of the pious faithful, pilgrims hurrying to the fountain to wash their hands according to the rite of purification, the poor lounging about among the columns and along the stairs.

There were an incredible number of these poor; in accordance with an ancient custom, all the beggars of Rome gathered in that atrium. They pled, lamented, muttered prayers, stretched out their hands. Some of them suffered from the most repugnant infirmities— monstrous sores, maimed and crippled bodies, blindness, paralysis. They were called in the letters of the popes of this time *fratres nostri Christi pauperes,* or as one pope put it, "our poor brothers of Christ, who speaks through their mouths."[13] Chrysostom, in one of his homilies, commended these beggars in the atrium of the basilica of the Apostles to the piety of the devout, advising that they help them and thus cleanse their own souls, as with the water of the basin they had attended to the cleansing of their bodies.[14]

The *romeo* (as the medieval world described the pilgrim to Rome) from Assisi changed his clothes with one of those beggars. Dressed in these miserable rags, he also begged alms from those who passed, speaking in the tongue of Provençe. It was the language of his love songs.

In that time a special distribution of food was made to the poor on the feasts of the Martyrs. Tables were laid for them in the atrium, and the beggars came to eat food and drink wine served by deacons. Francis himself went to one of these agapae and sat with the ragged crowd. He was so impressed and moved that he used to say that he would have gone back, if he had not been held back by fear of malicious comments by Assisi people who had come with him.

Finally, taking back his clothes, he returned to Assisi, holding against his chest the ampulla that had been filled with blessed oil to light a lamp at the tomb of the Apostle.

Definitely, no new message had come to him on that pilgrimage. The voice that had spoken in Spoleto had clearly said that in his native city, and nowhere else, would the will of God be made clear. In his meditations he still prayed to God to be illuminated and guided in the way of truth. He had kept his thoughts secret, convinced that no one would know how to understand his new love. In truth, it was a time when material goods and pleasures were counted of the greatest importance.

In his restless heart he was conscious of a God-revealed truth, dimly perceived: "All the things that you have carnally loved and desired, you will have to despise and hate, if you wish to know the will of God. After you have begun to do this, those things that were at first sweet and desirable to you will become insupportable and bitter, and in those that have been horrid and exhausting, you will experience great sweetness and infinite balm."[15]

He had seen the truth dimly but had not succeeded in fully understanding it. Thinking about that hour spent with the beggars of Saint Peter's, he asked himself if the exultation he felt then meant that he would have to be like one of these deformed creatures who dragged themselves over the stones of the sacred atrium. The ugliness of suffering human flesh had always repelled him. In Assisi there was a poor hunchbacked woman, a monstrous creature who aroused everyone's disgust. His jeering spirit, reawakened in him, for a time threw him off his course by asking, sniggering, if perchance that were his model? He was frightened by the thought.[16]

Nothing, however, aroused such horror and fear in him as did the sight of lepers.

The Lepers

The hospital for the lepers of the commune of Assisi stood near the castle of Arce. As were all the old leper hospitals, it was dedicated to Saint Lazarus, the Biblical beggar covered with sores.[f]

Only in the fourteenth century, when devotion to Saint Mary Magdalen became widespread through the influence of the writers of devout lauds, was it given the name of the woman who suffered from leprosy of the soul: Mary of Magdala, who is said to have been contaminated by every sexual sin, until she found Jesus, who took her in and cleansed her from every stain.

The "infected men and women of San Lazzaro d'Arce," as they are called, file in front of us in a touching thirteenth-century document preserved in the Sacro Convento. The women have lovely names. They shine in the darkness of the lazaretto like the traces of beauty remaining on their ravaged faces and infected bodies: Domina Maria, Domina Bona, Domina Latuza Sugulla, Domina Stefania, Gilia, Rosa. They have put aside their fine clothes woven of purple and have put on the grey tunic and mantle of the hospital. Their faces are as white as those of corpses, yet they still burn with all the desires of which life is cheating them.

A chaplain is assigned to the hospital by the city. The statutes specify that he be a man "of good reputation and of mature age," *bone*

---

f. There were several hospitals for lepers in Assisi territory at the time of Saint Francis; but records and communal statutes make it clear that it was San Lazzaro of Arce (renamed Santa Maria Maddalena in the fourteenth century) that played so large a role in the life of Saint Francis. First under the jurisdiction, then under the jurisdiction and special protection of the commune of Assisi, it stood (and the chapel still stands today) about a kilometre from the present railroad station. A good many biographers have become confused in their attempts to identify the hospital and its chapel; Sabatier, for example, thought that the little church of San Rufino d'Arce, which is not far away (today a part of a farm structure, but still well-preserved), was a part of another lepers' hospital, and that it was for poor lepers while Santa Maria Maddalena was for the rich. He, therefore, thought that Francis and his companions were associated with San Rufino. In fact San Rufino d'Arce was never a chapel for lepers. [According to Padre Giandomenico of Rivo Torto, it was one of four chapels for the rural people, along with San Pietro della Spina, Trinità, and Santa Maria degli Angeli (Porziuncola).—Trans.] The truth is that all lepers under the care of the commune, both rich and poor, were assigned to San Lazzaro and subjected to the same rules and regulations. There were other hospitals for lepers nearby, however; and some episodes in Francis's life may well have taken place in some of them. Among them were the hospitals of Selva Grossa, Fontanelle, San Salvatore delle Pareti, Acquaviva, San Savino, Ponte del Chiagio, Ponte dei Galli, and Querciano.

For additional information and sources of these early episodes involving the lepers: *NV* 2:257–66.

fame et mature etatis, and that he be given board and lodging and a cloak on All Saints' Day. Every Sunday, after he celebrates Mass, he reminds the lepers that every beauty and every gift of earth are destined to fade away more swiftly than the mists of autumn. (His words are useless; in these walking dead, slimy thoughts and filthy grudges preoccupy men and women alike. They are always looking for the chance to avenge themselves for everyone's horror and hatred of them.)

By the time Francis was enjoying the sweet songs of love of the French and Provençal troubadours, the spellbinding story of Tristan and Isolde had been familiar in Italy for a number of years:

> *Isot ma drue, Isot m'amie;*
> *en vos ma mort, en vos ma vie.*

When King Mark was certain of the unfaithfulness of his queen, he ordered the guards to take her to the stake. On hand to enjoy the cruel spectacle were a hundred lepers, arriving to the sound of the clappers on their crutches, their faces devoured by disease and splotched with whitish stains, their frightening bloody eyes flaming under swollen eyelids. The queen was dressed in a light gray tunic interwoven with golden threads. Her hair, which came down to her feet, was bound by a golden cord.

Ivan, the most despicable of all the lepers, shouted to the king that the flame was too beautiful to be used as a punishment for such a crime as hers. A more fitting one for her—Isolde the beautiful, Isolde the fair—would be to give her to them, the lepers, whose evil passions had been excited by their disease. And the king consented. While the barons and knights shuddered at such a pitiless sentence, the dismal procession started down the hill toward these bestial creatures, filthy, screaming and shouting. But at that moment Tristan, who had been lying in wait, appeared on horseback, sword raised. For the knight it was a simple task to use the back of his sword like a whip to scatter the flock of diseased and possessed brutes and free his lover. From that time on, she would belong to him as his legitimate bride, since he had rescued her from a danger worse than death—the insulting, shameful, horrendous, contamination of the lepers.

The tale is proof that even in the poetry of chivalry, the defence of the weak and the suffering, which was one of the principal duties of the initiate, did not apply to lepers.[17]

Francis himself, who was moved by the appeals of the poor and did not hesitate to take off his rich clothes and give them to an impoverished lord, could not conquer the disgust aroused in him by that dark house of the dead, even when he did no more than look at it from above. He never went near it if he could avoid it. Sometimes that was not possible, for the road on which it stood was the shortest route to the family property in San Pietro della Spina. It was called the Strada di Collemaggio, and also, as we read in the statutes, "the road by which from the city of Assisi one goes to the river Tabito," that is, to the Ose. It began at the Moiano gate, went down by the Galletta spring, and through San Masseo to the Strada Francesca, from there it led to the hospital, then turned toward Castelnuovo. After a short stretch, one could turn to the left on the Via Antica, the ancient road that ran from Santa Maria degli Angeli to Foligno, and in a few minutes reach San Pietro della Spina.[18] From the height of the hill, these roads may still be seen furrowing the great plain.

When he did go by the hospital on horseback and saw on its doorstep the emaciated faces with pus dripping from them, the hideous eyes, he fearfully turned his face and held his nose, not able to bear the horrible stench. He sent alms to the patients by asking others passing along the road to deliver them, for he did not dare go close to the place.

There is nothing left of the old hospital today but the chapel, with its façade of rough cut stones and a little bell tower rising over it. The church is lonely, the countryside around it is silent. But in the evening, when the bell begins to ring in the darkening air, all comes to life again, real enough the shake the heart. The very walls, bare as in the days of the long-vanished hospital, repeat the ancient rite.

The leper lived hidden until someone reported him. We see him torn away from his house, brutally taken off to his new destiny. Then he is here, in the church, terrified and embittered as a wild beast caught in a trap from which there is no escape. He is on his knees in front of the altar for the sacred rite that will solemnly proclaim his separation from human society.

It is a rainy evening near the end of November. All the candles are lit. In the shadows, some objects can be dimly seen on a table at the side of the sacristy door. The church is comfortably filled with people—devout, curious, pious. The bell rings. The priest comes out in cotta and stole, preceded by clerics carrying the cross. He goes up the steps of the altar, turns, and with the same gesture he uses at funerals, sprinkles with holy water the one who is about to die to the world. Then he delivers his admonition:

"My brother, dear poor little man of good God, by means of great sadness and tribulation, of sickness, of leprosy, and of many other miseries, one gains the kingdom of heaven, where there is no sickness or sorrow, and all is pure and white, without stain, more brilliant than the sun. You will go there, if it pleases God. In the meantime, be a good Christian, bear with patience this adversity, and God will be merciful to you."

The terrible words fall into a silence as profound as the silence of a cemetery. The living corpse bends still lower to the ground. He seems to be looking for his grave.

"My brother, the separation has to do only with your body. As for the spirit, which is more important, you are still, as you were before, a participant in the prayers of our Holy Mother Church, as if every day you were assisting in the Divine Offices. Charitable men will provide for your lesser needs, and God will never abandon you. Take care of yourself and have patience. God is with you. Amen."

From the hands of the acolyte the celebrant takes a handful of black earth brought from the nearby cemetery; he sprinkles it on the head of the sick man.

"Die to the world, be born again in God. O Jesus my Redeemer, who made me of earth and clothed me with a body, make me to rise again in the new day."

The people respond, "My bones tremble, my soul loses its way. Alleluia. Have mercy on us, O Lord. Keep us from evil."

The Gospel is read. It is the story of the ten lepers, the one that begins: "As Jesus was entering a village he was met by ten men with leprosy. They stood some way off and called out to him, 'Jesus, Master, take pity on us.'"

Then it is time for the inexorable instructions:

"My brother, take this cloak and put it on in sign of humility and never leave here without it. In the name of the Father, the Son, and the Holy Spirit."

The tunic, made of *gattinello*,[g] is full and long, as the statutes prescribe. Reluctantly the leper puts it on. It is the ominous uniform that will make everyone he meets flee from him.

"Take this little flask. Put in it what will be given you to drink, and under penalty of disobedience I forbid you to drink from the rivers, from the springs, from the wells.

"Take these gloves. You are forbidden to touch anything that is not yours with your bare hands.

"If, while walking about, you should meet someone who wishes to

---

g. *Gattinello* was a poor and coarse cloth made primarily of cotton with some wool added.—Trans.

talk to you, I forbid you to reply before you put yourself against the wind.

"You are forbidden to be with any woman who is not of your family. You are forbidden to touch young people or to offer them anything. And from eating from anything but your own leper's bowl. And from entering churches or rectories, and from going to fairs, to mills, and to markets. And from walking through narrow streets where those who meet you cannot avoid you."

At last he is given the wooden clapper, the kind sounded in Holy Week.

"Take this *tentennella;* carry it always with you. Sound it to warn others of your presence."

A cortège forms as if the body is to be accompanied to a cemetery, the cross in front, then the clerics, the priest, the leper, the faithful. Night has fallen. The enclosure reeks of a sad autumnal fever. The *tentennella,* shaken by the leper, fills the air with its dismal, clear sound. The flames of the candles throw light along the long corridors and narrow passages, on the high columns. The procession seems to be passing through a walled cemetery, amid deathlike odors of dampness and decay.

The cell is ready. A wooden cross is on the door. The ghost enters the cell with his gravedigger. Inside are a low, mean bed, like a bier, a table, a chair, an old lamp, a strong box. An attendant hands the newcomer sandals, a camelskin hood, an earthenware pot, a beechwood bowl, a copper jug, a belt, a knife. Everything else the leper owns will go to this hospital of the commune.

Now he is required to make the proper response:

"Here is my perpetual resting place. Here I shall live. This is my vow."

Before the door is a stump for the collection of alms. First the priest puts an offering there; the other faithful follow his example.

Then the cortège, without the leper, who is left in his seclusion, returns to the church. Again the chant of the priest rises:

"Omnipotent God, who throws down the pride of the ancient enemy through the sufferings of your Only Son, give to your servant the necessary strength to bear with devotion and patience the evil that oppresses him. Amen."

The people respond:

"Amen."

Francis Meets a Leper

The articles of the statutes of the commune were even harsher than the ecclesiastical rules: "The podestà must, a month after taking office, make a scrupulous search for lepers in the city and in the region. And if any leper, man or woman, be living in the city or in the *contado,* he is to be hunted out from these places, and from the *castelli* and from the *ville.* And the syndics of the cities and the castellans of the castles shall take care to bring charges against the lepers."

The leper who risked entering the city was left to the mercy of the crowd, which hunted him down like a mangy dog: "No leper may dare to enter the city or walk around in it, and if any one of them shall be found, everyone may strike him with impunity."

These laws were inspired by the same fear of the lepers from which Francis himself suffered.[h]

One day he was riding on horseback down the road to the hospital, as usual absorbed in his thoughts. Suddenly the horse jerked to the side of the road. With difficulty Francis pulled him back by a violent jerk at the reins. The young man looked up and recoiled in horror. A leper stood in the middle of the road, a short distance away, unmoving, and looked at him. He was no different from the others, the usual wan specter, with stained face, shaved head, dressed in grey sackcloth. He did not speak and showed no sign of moving, of getting out of the way. He looked at the horseman fixedly, strangely, with an acute and penetrating gaze.

An instant that seemed eternity passed. Slowly Francis dismounted, went to the man, took his hand. It was a poor emaciated hand, bloodstained, twisted, inert and cold like that of a corpse. He put a mite of charity in it, pressed it, carried it to his lips. And suddenly, as he kissed the lacerated flesh of the creature who was the most abject, the most hated, the most scorned, of all human beings, he was flooded with a wave of emotion, one that shut out everything around him, one that he would remember even on his death bed.

As the leper withdrew his hand, Francis raised his head to look at him again. He was no longer there.

The first biographers describe this episode in poetic passages, seeing in it a revelation of the divine. "Though the plain lay open and clear on all sides, and there were no obstacles about, he could not see the leper anywhere," says Thomas of Celano.[19] And Saint Bonaventure says that the leper was Christ himself, returned among men to

---

h. Other statutes of the commune required that all the leper's goods were to be taken away from him when he entered the hospital and that all over the age of twelve were to perform the services ordered by the prior and to obey him. Harsh rules were in effect in all cities; a Perugia statute of 1279, for instance, condemned women who had sexual relationships with lepers to be flogged through the cities and suburbs, have their noses cut off, and banished permanently from the city. *NV* 2:257–61, 265.
For additional material about lepers, especially about their religious rites, cf. Chavin de Malan, *Saint François,* pp. 25–30.

fulfill the word of the Prophet Isaiah: "He was spurned and avoided by men, a man of suffering, accustomed to infirmity, one of those from whom men hide their faces, spurned, and we held him in no esteem. Yet it was our infirmities that he bore, our sufferings that he endured, while we thought of him as stricken, as one smitten by God and afflicted."[20]

Francis remounted and continued on his way. But the whole world seemed changed, and he, too. He saw that the mysterious words that had come to him earlier had now become a revelation of truth. He had opened his heart to what he had in the past held in horror, and the bitterness of it had become changed into sweetness of the same measure.

After several days he took some money and went to the hospital near Arce. He crossed the threshold that had filled him with horror, went along the dark corridors, knocked at cell doors on which the cross was nailed. The lepers gathered in a frightening assembly in the chapter hall. They waited, astonished and suspicious. To each of them Francis gave a piece of gold and a kiss on the lips.

In the course of the thirteenth century, the pope granted many privileges to this hospital, the Assisi hospital of San Lazzaro. The bull in which they were granted began: "The lepers' hospital, which stands on the site where the Order of Saint Francis had its beginning . . ." Such a statement is, even by the most rigid historical definition, exact. In that hospital a basic rule of a harder chivalry was laid down, one that required passion and valour over and beyond the measure needed by armour-covered warriors leading an attack.

That rule is *compassion*. For all the sorrowing, the troubled, the ill, the victims of disaster and those overcome by shame, misery, weariness, and oppression. Those kept down because of blindness or folly, subtle evil or hatred, lust for money or pleasures of the flesh.

To cleanse human beings from whatever leprosy contaminates them was the mission on which Francis embarked the day that he went to see the diseased patients of the hospital of San Lazzaro.

Before dying he dictated a few brief, impassioned words, part of his *Testament*, to establish the exact turning point for him. "This is how God inspired me, Brother Francis, to embark upon a life of penance. When I was in sin, the sight of lepers nauseated me beyond measure; but then God himself led me into their company, and I had pity on them. When I had once become acquainted with them, what had previously nauseated me became a source of spiritual and physical consolation for me."

The History-Laden Road to San Damiano

The road that leads from Assisi to the plain, passing the church of San Damiano, is another road that Francis would have had to travel often in order to go to his father's properties in Fontanelle and Palude. At the end of the section of the city toward Foligno, it turns to the right, and descends steeply to the church. Above the church it divides into two branches. The left branch passes near the old chapel of San Giovanni, touches the Strada Francesca at the well-known trivium. On the left of the Cannara road (along which Rivo Torto and San Pietro are located), it continues through Fontanelle all the way to Spina. For that reason it is called the Via della Spina. The other branch crosses the Strada Francesca at Stradette and continues beyond the present national road and the railroad to the houses of San Petrignano. Because it is on land that is somewhat sunken, it used to be called the Via Cupa ("dark, low road") of San Petrignano. We have already seen that in Fontanelle and San Pietro della Spina (the ancient name for San Petrignano) Pietro Bernardone owned land.

This suburban road at the time of the Roman Empire was flanked by funerary monuments from the old city gate to about half the distance to the elevation on which San Damiano stands. The remains of them could still be seen when Saint Francis lived. Today only one remains, the ruin that the people call "the sepulchre of Propertius," because tradition puts here the burial of the elegiac poets of Assisi, Sextus Propertius and Paulus Passennus. It is a tradition that cannot be totally ignored, because among the ruins of this mausoleum were found several memorial stones of the Propertius family and the funerary cippus of Paulus Passennus, whom Pliny the Younger described as a kinsman and fellow citizen of Propertius.[21]

The first Christians of Assisi used to gather near this mausoleum to hear Bishop Felicianus, as may be read in the cathedral lectionary.[i] The story, little known, is of particular interest, because it puts the birth of Christianity in Assisi along this road, a very short distance from the spot where an anguished call is to come from a cross.

Bishop Felicianus came to Assisi from Bevagna, where he had converted many to the faith. But in Assisi he found himself confronting bitter resistance. The city bristled with temples that the suspicious pontifices guarded night and day. In vain the apostle sought to convert the idolators to faith in the true God. He tried so hard that at last the pontifices, the chief pagan priests, had him thrown out of the city.

---

i. Bishop Felicianus died a martyr, probably during the persecutions of the emperor Decius in 250 A.D. According to an ancient tradition, he was the first bishop of Foligno.

Before leaving, he assembled his small group of followers, to say good-bye to them and comfort them.

This is the episode that the documents describe for us as having taken place *prope mausoleum antiquum,* near the ancient mausoleum.

Persecution was spreading in all its horrors. Municipal magistrates treated those who refused to sacrifice to the gods with great cruelty. The emperor Decius announced from Rome that imperial envoys would arrive to impose terrible punishments with iron, fire, and wild beasts.

"Manfully have the will to resist," the bishop said to his disciples. "Be strong, one for another. The threats of these wicked priests will be dispersed like smoke, and you must not pay any more attention to them than to filth found along your path. They, in the centuries to come, will die. You, after your death, will have eternal life."

He took a great cross of wood and fixed it in the earth.

"My dearest brothers," he continued, "remember to venerate and adore the cross that I place for you here, in memory of Jesus Christ our Lord. Prostrate yourselves here. Here raise to him your prayers, in the morning, and at noon, and when evening falls. Praise him and offer him your heart."

And his voice trembled because, now nearly a hundred years old, this soldier of Christ had had during that last good-bye to the souls he had gained for the Lord a vision of the glorious fate to which he was destined: imprisonment, torture, a departure in chains for Urbe where the implacable revenge of the Antichrist awaited him, the sudden falling of his old tired body, exhausted by torture, in the middle of the road.

And so Saint Felicianus, the father of the Christians, the athlete of the Lord, left Assisi.

But no one, neither those of the faithful present at the moving farewell, nor those of the innumerable generations who came later, was able ever to forget these saintly words, these exhortations, that benediction. The cross placed by the bishop martyr in front of the sepulchre of the poets of love had sanctified both life and death. And when in time the old cross disintegrated, the people of the city built a little chapel on the site and dedicated it to him. All that area, from the gates of the city to the Strada Francesca, was called in his honour, Colle (Hill) of San Feliciano.

By the grace of God there were many miracles in that place. Those possessed by demons who begged for peace were liberated. Lepers were rid of their terrible sores. Farmers who prayed for the salvation of their crops from the threat of storm saw the cloud melt away.

Every day Francis went by the reminders of these events. San Damiano was at his left as he went down on the high-banked road to San Pietro della Spina.

A Word from the Crucifix

The church of San Damiano seemed to be collapsing from old age, already beyond repair, desolate, without devout worshippers and without prayers. No one went down the worn staircase into the church. No lamp burned in front of its altar. Decrepit outer walls, cracked inner walls, crumbling bricks, worm-eaten beams, faded paintings. A low and smoke blackened vault, a narrow window, a holy water stoup covered with dust, an apse with vague vestiges of blue and gold, a cloister invaded by wild grass, a well without water. Silent, solitary, abandoned. On the travertine architrave of the door, the usual words so often found on the thresholds of ancient country chapels: *Domus mea.* My house. The House of God, tottering and derelict.[j]

The painted wooden image of the Crucified Lord that hung by the altar had survived all that decay—an image of goodness and suffering, expressing with extraordinary vividness both martyrdom and love.[k]

One day, going up to the city, Francis went into the church, knelt, and began to pray. He asked to be given light in the midst of all his darkness, to know the divine will, in accordance with the promise made during the night in Spoleto.

---

j. This little church, now under the care of the Friars Minor and serving as the philosophy seminary of the Umbrian province, is mentioned for the first time in a document of the year 1030, in which a serf is given his freedom (see p. 29–30). It was in all likelihood ancient even at that time; its great age is mentioned in *1 Cel.* 8. It seems certain that it was built by a consortium of noble families, for in 1103 a group of families gave the church to the prior of San Rufino. Still later—sometime in the early part of the thirteenth century—it was transferred to the bishop of Assisi, who in 1253 assigned it to the Poor Clares. After Clare's death and the sisters' move to the Basilica di Santa Chiara, it was entrusted to the Friars Minor; the earliest record of their occupation is in 1307.

[In 1867 an anti-clerical government expelled all but two caretaker friars, but in 1878 a British convert, the Marquess of Ripon, "ransomed" the church. For further information about it, and a list of the documents pertaining to it: *NV* 3:85–91; see also the notes by Brown in Englebert, *Saint Francis,* p. 463.—Trans.]

k. This Romanesque crucifix has been called, in a study of painted crosses by Sandbert-Valvalà, "an hieratic, sober, noble presentation, worthy of being numbered among the best of the first period in the history of painted crosses." Several other figures also are painted on the crucifix; among them, the Virgin Mary, Saint John, a centurion, Roman soldiers, two angels, and a small rooster (revealed when the crucifix was cleaned in 1938). At the top is a painting of the Resurrected Christ surrounded by angels, under the protecting hand of God. According to a late legend, the figure of Christ originally had the eyes closed; they were opened when Saint Francis heard the figure speak. See Antonio da Orvieto, *Cronologia,* p. 109; *NV* 3:90–91.

[According to late sources, Francis said this prayer in front of the crucifix: "O great and glorious God, illuminate my heart, give me steadfast faith, firm hope, perfect charity, and knowledge and understanding so that I may keep Thy commandments." Historians are not in agreement on its authenticity.—Trans.]

Suddenly it seemed to him that Jesus' gaze was fixed on him. There was no doubt about it. Those eyes had become animated, taken on life. They were speaking and expressing a burning passion. And, as in the night of the vision of the enchanted castle, the cavalier consecrated to a high undertaking distinctly heard his name being called. The words fell like a whisper, a light sigh, scarcely perceptible.

"Francis, go and repair my house, which, as you see, is falling into ruin."[1]

After a short pause, the sad call was repeated for the second time, for the third time.

Francis got up, frightened. The church was again sunk into a silence without beginning or end. He went out, sought the old priest who had custody of the place, and offered him all the money he had with him so that he might relight the lamp before the crucifix.

Then he rushed up to Assisi. He went to the shop and took down some scarlet, the noblest and most expensive cloth that then existed, used for making mantles suitable for the grandeur of kings and elaborate gowns with trains for beautiful women. Francis wanted to use it to cover the poor abandoned church in sumptuous purple.[22]

It was his intention to sell that precious merchandise and with the proceeds pay for the restoration. It would not do to transact that particular business in Assisi, since Pietro Bernardone would learn of it, equally impossible to do so in Perugia, since the people of Assisi had been forbidden to go there because of the war. Therefore, he went by horseback to the neighbouring city of Foligno, where he sold the cloth and the horse. He walked back on the same road that some months earlier he had haughtily travelled on horseback, followed by a squire. He returned to San Damiano and offered to Pietro, the priest,[23] all the money he had gotten.

The priest did not wish to accept the offering. All that money in the hands of one who had the reputation of being one of the most ex-

---

1. *Leg. Maior*, II, 1; *2 Cel.* 10; *3 Soc.*, 13. [The latter two sources imply that the crucifix spoke but once.]

When the Poor Clares left San Damiano in 1257 (*NV* 3:87–88), they took the crucifix with them and preserved it carefully for seven hundred years in the little church of San Giorgio, then inside the cloistered monastery. It was placed on public view again for the first time in Holy Week 1957, when it was placed over the high altar in a moving ceremony. We shall never forget the chorus of sisters behind the grating, their sweet voices so far away and so near, in the seventh century hymn of Saint Victor, *Crux fidelis*, in this celebration of the renewal of this ancient popular devotion. Cf. Fortini, *Settimana Santa*, pp. 21–22.

These ceremonies were repeated in Holy Week 1958, and in September of that year the Crucifix that Spoke to Saint Francis was permanently placed over a new altar in the San Giorgio chapel, now always open to the public.

travagant persons in the city made him suspicious. He also feared the well known stinginess of Pietro Bernardone.[24]

Francis tried uselessly to insist. Finally, seeing that he was not going to succeed, he threw the money on the embrasure of the window in the outer wall of the church. (That window is still to be seen in San Damiano, the opening now closed, low and narrow as the opening in a garret; it is called "the money window.")

Francis's Glorious Folly

Francis asked the priest if he might stay with him; and he, with his great charity, did not know how to refuse him.

So it came about that he became a true oblate. But while others chose, for protection in case of need, well fortified churches such as San Giacomo and San Rufino, his choice was the poorest and humblest church, with an obscure priest who certainly was not going to be able to protect him from the gathering storm.[m]

Pietro Bernardone, when he learned of his son's latest gambit, flew into a fury. It was customary at the time to call a council of neighbours and friends with each being given a chance to express his opinion about what should be done. Surely they all came to the house in the Badìa *contrada*—Marangone di Cristiano and his brother Benvegnate, the notary Gilio, the notary Riccardo, maestro Villano, Boninsegna di Raniero, Vivieno, Uguccione.[25]

It is probable that they discussed the thorny and complicated problem Francis had posed. He was now a servant of the church and therefore subject to its jurisdiction. That meant he was no longer under the authority of the family. It was finally decided that Pietro, together with some of the consorts, should go to San Damiano and talk to his son. There was also talk of threats to be made and resorting to violence in case persuasion was not effective.

Someone of the house rushed to warn Francis; consequently, those who came down and asked for him did not find him. He had preferred to avoid that trying meeting, and so hid in the underground chamber of a nearby house, a place he had prepared for just such an

---

m. In *1 Cel.* 8, Thomas, in telling of Francis's desire to stay with the San Damiano priest, used the words *ut secum morari pro Domino pateretur* ("(he asked) that he might be allowed to stay for the Lord's sake."). And he adds, *Acquievit tandem Sacerdos de mora illius* ("Finally the priest agreed to his staying"). *Mora* is the characteristic word used for oblates, in Assisi statutes and elsewhere. As for the need of protection against "the gathering storm": not only is this a reference to Pietro's anger but also to the fact that persons who were suspected of becoming oblates in order to claim the privilege of immunity from civil prosecution were apt to be judged harshly both by officials and in public opinion. See *NV* 2:223–24.

eventuality. It is probable that he hid in his own country house in Stradette, at the intersection with the Strada Francesca. It is scarcely 500 metres away from San Damiano.

A confidant, who was the only one to know his place of refuge, provided him with the necessary food. He was so much afraid of a battle with his own family that he did not dare leave his underground room.

But he surely heard from his friend tales that were being spread about.

There is nothing more miserable in little towns than that elusive phantom, public opinion. Envy feeds it, as was noted by the Franciscan Henri d'Avranches, who was a contemporary and a biographer of Saint Francis, in his fine description of this sin: "No sooner is pride threatened by the dominant position earned by others through merit, than envy enters in, until the mind burns in a wicked fire. Envy pardons no one, not even a friend. It flies into a rage if members of the family are happy, exults in their misfortune. It is accompanied by biting slander, base judgements, libelous accusations, nose-twisting sneers, green-eyed jealousy that gnaws at every virtue, the habit of damning what ought to be praised and exalting what is deserving of censure."[26]

Now the nobles whom he had wanted to emulate, the people whom he had wanted to surpass, the companions who had been humiliated by his generosity, the merchants who saw in Pietro Bernardone their most dangerous competitor—all were united in blind and deaf malice that had long been brewing.

The author of the *Vita Poetica* takes us to a conversation in the piazza of Assisi, the meeting place of all the idlers.

They talk about Francis, who had squandered his paternal patrimony and gone from one extravagance to another, all grinning maliciously. Every billygoat, every ne'er-do-well, wants to have his say.

"He must have been taking poppy juice or maybe dogs' brain and hemlock juice. Nothing but drugs could have made him change like this, all that craze for glory gone. Now he won't have anything to do with that sort of thing."

"Only the devil could make someone prefer poor things to good ones. Now Francis would rather be sad than to laugh and he seems to choose things that are going to harm him rather than help him. Obviously, he is possessed by a demon."

"He has never really recovered from the fever. The humours generated in the heart are pressing on the brain and have produced this madness."[27]

Francis had too recently been considered "the flower of youth" by his fellow citizens not to feel hurt by the malicious comments. These were bitter days and difficult to surmount. Often he wept and prayed to God to guide and sustain him. And again, from God came the ability to decide what was necessary. His weakness, his faint-heartedness, his desertion, were not worthy of one whom Jesus had chosen to be his champion. The hour had come in which the knight chosen for a great undertaking must throw himself into it whole-heartedly. It was no time to measure the risk or count the numbers of the enemy.

This is the image of Francis that Thomas of Celano draws for us when Francis left his hiding place and prepared to go back to Assisi. "He arose, therefore, immediately, active, eager, and lively; and bearing the shield of faith to fight for the Lord, armed with a great confidence, he took the way toward the city. Aglow with a divine fire, he began to accuse himself severely of laziness and cowardice."[28]

Paternal Wrath

Still, the uproar that broke out as soon as they saw him appear at the San Giorgio trivium[n] exceeded anything that he could have imagined.

When the furious hubbub of the mob struck him, he was like an oak seized by the sudden force of a hurricane. At first they were not sure of the identity of this pallid and emaciated figure, his clothes in shreds. Then voices rose to pass on the word. The cackling rose to a flood of jeers, bursts of laughter, and insults. There was bestiality in that greedy people, so quarrelsome and cruel, a meanness both repelling and terrifying.

Look at him, the man who wanted to become a great prince, the knight of the Crusades who lost his courage in Spoleto, the lover of the most beautiful woman in the world, the friend of the lepers! And they ridiculed him, shoved him, grabbed him by the tunic. It was the last of autumn and it had rained a little. They picked up handfuls of mud and hurled them in his face. Then stones began to fall, thick as a

---

n. The San Giorgio trivium was on the site of the present Pucci arch, which is between the Piazza del Comune and the Piazza di Santa Chiara. In Saint Francis's lifetime, three roads met there: one leading to the Piazza del Comune (as now), one going up to the cathedral of San Rufino, one descending to the ancient Moiano Gate. *NV* 3:55.

snowstorm. The violence that the statutes permitted the people to use against lepers was turned now against the madman who had allied himself with lepers in a monstrous familiarity.

Whatever he tried to say was lost in the uproar. The persons nearest him picked up the words, passed them on to others with roars of laughter, purposely distorting them and rolling them from their tongues as certain proof of his madness. As for Francis, he thanked God for having led him to this state and told them that he had been called to new undertakings and to new victories.

Finally he was like a broken ship at the mercy of the breakers. He fell silent, overwhelmed by the filthy hullabaloo of frothing faces, of screaming mouths, of fists raised against him. He walked alone in the middle of the tumult, showing no sign of indignation, his eyes fixed on his shining dream, moving toward it with greater courage than he had shown on that day of the attack on the Perugini, when he had gained a reputation for bravery. All his familiar world, a world that in his days of popularity had praised and admired him, was now falling into the dust, turning against him, attacking him without mercy.[29]

There was the San Giorgio road, there the Piazza del Comune, the forum, the columns of the temple, the church of San Nicolò, the church of San Donato, the chapel of Sant' Agata. There were those familiar houses that had been targets of the riots, destroyed with fire and brushwood: the houses of Marescotto di Bernardo Dodici, the sons of Sanguigno, Raino, the sons of Vivieno.[30] The restorations incumbent upon the commune had not yet been finished: intense work was then being done by the construction workers all about the ruined walls of the city. Now, on top of the scaffoldings they stopped and stretched their necks to stare. In no time at all the din spread all through the market. Sellers of wool came out of the doors of their shops, sniggering, peddlers climbed on top of their counters; potters abandoned their wares; notaries interrupted their work on documents and made room for their clients and witnesses; women appeared on balconies and ran down the outside staircases. Even the monks of San Paolo came to the head of the street, swept up in the mob spirit of that savage carnival. A group of archers hurried down the staircases of the temple and formed a solid barrier against the mob.

All of a sudden the clamour of shouts and hisses fell. Pietro di Bernardone had arrived. The people avidly prepared to enjoy a new spectacle.

Livid at the indignity, bent with fury, the merchant violently made his way through the mob. He hurled himself at his son, shook him, blindly hit him, shoved him all the way to the little piazza of San Nicolò, threw him brutally into the atrium of the house.[31] Then all the rooms rang as he exploded in anger. He heaped upon the head of his son, one by one, all the outrages, the humiliations, the injuries. He cursed his own former dreams, his vain illusions, his foolish hopes, the love he had given the son who was now ruining him, who had exposed him to the ridicule of everyone in the city. He spoke of the pained surprise, the shame, the anger, he had felt the moment he had learned of this new insult. He had been in the shop, intent on ordering certain new materials, when he heard the noise. Someone had told him that it was a madman abandoned to the abuse of the mob, as was the custom. He had never imagined the truth. As soon as he made out the name of his son, it had seemed that the earth had opened under his feet. To this he had been reduced, he, the benefactor, the *provvisore,* of the commune. So many years of a good reputation, of recognition of his astuteness—and now all, all were about to be lost.

Pietro di Bernardone, the merchant known on all the squares of Tuscany and of Champagne, from now on an object of the beastly slander of his enemies and the humiliating sympathy of his friends. All this, not to speak of the pieces of scarlet that had disappeared from the house and his terrible disillusionment. Now that his son (so changed, so emaciated, as if he had come out of a tomb) had come back into his hands in such a fashion, in the middle of the main piazza, there was nothing to do but to turn to competent ecclesiastical and territorial authorities. He would find the way to make him repent and be sensible.

The communal statutes gave a father the right to imprison in his house, in fetters, a son who had squandered the family assets.[o]

Francis, with his new and his old dissipations, with the scarlet taken from the shop, was guilty. Pietro, using his right as a pretext, shut his son up in the prison of the house and left him to reflect on what would be the expedient thing for him to do.

After some days he returned to see him and to question him, but he was stupified to find (for Pietro was one of those men who does

---

o. In Assisi, "dissipators" could be imprisoned in the commune's prison upon the request of two near relatives, according to the statutes of the time. As in other Italian towns, a father was empowered by the statutes to send a son who had squandered family assets to prison, whether that son was already emancipated or still under guardianship; magistrates were required to execute the paternal will without proof of the charges. A father could also confine such a son to the family house in fetters at his will, being obliged by the statutes only to give him food.

It may be deduced from the statutes that many of the leading families maintained private prisons in their houses.

For a full discussion of the legal aspects of Francis's situation: *NV* 2:230–31.

not admit obstacles to his authority) that Francis was more than ever determined to follow his new life. He tried to persuade him, showing him the degradation into which he had fallen and the hardships in store for him in contrast to the easy life to which he had been accustomed, because in this world nothing counted but money and success. Your dear fellow citizens, he said, who seek you out with false smiles in prosperous days, lick their chops over your misfortunes, ready to throw themselves upon you and devour you. Not in anyone's memory had any one of the family of Bernardone, which had taught the art of trade to all the duchy of Spoleto, turned out to be a slacker or a beggar.

As he saw that his son was not surrendering, his self-control went. He resorted to shouts, curses, blows. Then he fell into an ominous calm; he ordered one of his servants to bring chains for the prisoner's hands and feet. In the silence of the terrified house the blows of the hammer echoed fearfully, as if preparations were being made for a barbarous torture.[32]

A great shadow lay over the family from that day, and the life of each seemed to be tied to the muffled shambling of irons, coming from the dark prison like a somber clock measuring the nightmare of morning and evening, dinner and supper.

Pietro left on one of the usual trips necessary for his trade. Immediately Pica, the grieving mother, went down to the prison, freed Francis from the chains, consoled him, led him out herself. She tried with tears and with prayers to obtain a promise from him, but in vain.

She thought again, then, of the prophecies made so long ago; she was persuaded that he, to whom she had given the name of the Baptist, was walking toward his destiny. Thus Francis left his house, never to enter it again.[33]

Francis Is Cited before the Consuls

He returned to San Damiano; again he took up his life of meditation, now not seeking a hiding place but going about with confidence, happy at having survived the difficult trial.[34]

Pietro, upon his return, was informed of all that had happened and was again overcome by an explosion of fury that left everyone around him open-mouthed. He was infuriated at his son, who had rebelled against his authority; at his wife, who had not obeyed him; at the priest, who had lent a hand to the thefts of his oblate; at the city people, who were trying to put him, Pietro Bernardone, into the same muck as his son. They would soon know the sort of man he was, and what a difference there was between him and the Bernardone whose brain had been affected by illness contracted in the war with Perugia.

Without losing any time, he rushed down the path leading to San Damiano looking for his son. He saw him come forward without fear, calm, armed with sureness. It destroyed the last vestige of Pietro's self-control.

Again he argued, shouted. Again the solitude of the little remote refuge was torn by harsh words and threats. He should have doubled the chains and blocks, starvation, and beatings. To this torrent of convulsive anger Francis answered nothing, except to say that he would be ready to bear every torture, and that he wanted only one judge between himself and his father, who were of the same flesh, God.[35]

For the merchant, this reply rang out as an open challenge, a new and intolerable insult, an audacious provocation. His son, after having robbed him, was revolting against him. And therefore, not God, but the judge of criminals would judge this crime, for it was shattering the power given to the father over a son from time immemorial.

The statutes of the commune prescribed the same punishment for one guilty of this offence as for murderers and traitors: banishment from the city. Pietro did not wish to lay hands on his own blood. He would have him taken to trial before the consuls, have him thrown out like a mangy dog, sentenced to die of shame and starvation away from his native city, fix it so that any of the city people could hunt him down with impunity.

And he would see that he was not only banished from the city but also from his family and from gatherings of consorts and of relatives. He would have him cut off like a diseased member so that this cancer would not infect the rest of the healthy body. His foolishness must not throw a shadow on the family lineage or give fuel to the plotting of the malevolent and spiteful.[p]

---

p. Given the nature of Pietro's accusations, the course he followed, and the criminal nature of the acts of dissipation of which he accused Francis, it is clear that he was not simply demanding restitution of the money but was bringing formal criminal charges against his son. The steps that he took are those outlined in the statutes for bringing criminal proceedings, and the course followed by the consuls as reflected in the ancient biographies is exactly that set by the statutes for these. Pietro could not have been simply asking the consuls to settle a bitter family quarrel, for statutes prohibited the authorities from intervening in purely family disputes unless loss of life or of limb were involved.

Also, the statutes gave fathers the legal right to have a child banished or imprisoned for failure to obey, a law that Francis had also broken.

For all the relevant material about this episode in Francis's life, and about the procedures for bringing an accused person before the consuls and also before the bishop (where these were much the same): *NV* 2:223–37.

Pietro set out again, firm in his plan; he disappeared over the curve of the hill. San Damiano lay again in silence.

The ancient palace of the consuls, built about the middle of the twelfth century, is still in Assisi, a short distance from the cathedral, along the street that leads to Santa Maria delle Rose. Its forbidding masculine look has been preserved, as has the military character of its square façade, with outer walls marked by fire and violence. Preserved, too, are its rows of Roman stones cropping out at the base, its ancient slashed mullion windows, its remarkable similarity to a closed and massive fortification, so typical of houses of that time. Today it is occupied by Benedictine nuns of an order a thousand years old, the same one that took in Clare after her flight from her paternal house.[q] Its impenetrable walls seem to have grown more constricted and dark. Over its high, silent windows, now protective of claustral meditation, enormous grills have been placed. A lane that then went up to Perlici is now closed and turned into a courtyard for the use of the monastery. The walls of an ancient Roman house, lopped off at ground level, can be seen at the side of the old consular palace.

In the great silence now measured by the murmur of prayers flowing down the solitary street at dawn, at vespers, and in the evening, the bitter voice of the merchant still rings out, as when he went up there upon his return from San Damiano to ask that the rigours of the law be applied against his obstinate and crazy son. The consuls, sitting judicially, also the judge and the notary, listen to him.

Pietro charges Francis with rebellion and squandering. He repeats the well known facts; he tells of his anger and worry, his desperation. A son, in whom he had placed so many hopes, has revolted against him, plundered his shop, and left him at the mercy of public opinion. Now there is nothing to do but to declare the crime and inflict the penalties established by the statutes.

The communal statutes considered with particular severity the case of a disobedient son who had squandered the family resources.

"The son," they say, "who does not give obedience to his father and to his mother, at their request is to be banished from the city and from the district, and no one may give him anything to eat or to drink

---

q. When Saint Clare took refuge with these Benedictine sisters, they were in the monastery of San Paolo delle Abbadesse, along the Chiagio river on the outskirts of Bastia. After several moves, and a merger with other Benedictine sisters (of Sant' Apollinare) these sisters finally in 1881 moved to the old consular palace, which is near the church of San Rufino. The date of its construction is not certain; Cristofani believes it to have been built by Giovanni di Gubbio, architect for San Rufino cathedral, in the late twelfth century. See chap. 9, n. 25 of this volume; Cristofani, *Storie di Assisi*, p. 63; NV 2:388–96.

or help him in any way." In Rubric 58 of Book II, *de dissipatoribus et male utentibus suis substantiis,* it is established that guilty sons must be imprisoned at the request of two near relatives, and that they may not be released until such time as it would please these members of their family.

Francis fit the case. The judge who sat in that year of 1207, Egidio, ordered the notary Giovanni to give the necessary orders to the messenger: "Go, cite and search out in person, or at the place of his habitation, Francesco di Pietro Bernardone, and enjoin him and notify him to present himself on the third day before the consuls, to respond to the accusation made by Pietro, his father, and against it to say and to oppose what he will wish and be able to do, according to the form of the statutes of Assisi. With the warning that if he does not do so, prosecution of the accusation will go forward against the aforesaid Francesco according to the form of the statutes of the city of Assisi." According to these statutes, if the accused does not present himself, the citation with public condemnation shall be renewed within eight days; and if he persists in his contumacy, he must be held to be proved and confessed guilty.

The beginning of the year 1207 was famous for its intense cold and its great snowfalls. Fra Salimbene notes that in this year *fuit magna nix,* "there was much snow." The plain of Santa Maria degli Angeli was wrapped in a white shroud. The olive trees of San Damiano, rigid under their mantle of ice, looked like phantoms in the mist that hung over the land from dawn to dark. The church seemed emptier, in greater ruin, more timeworn than ever.

The cry of the messenger rose up in the icy torpor. It reached the cold room where the priest and the young lay brother waited in devout meditation: "Francesco di Pietro Bernardone! Be it known to everyone that you, by order of the consuls, are to be accused and tried!" (The statutes also rigorously prescribed that this cry be made publicly before the dwelling of someone accused of an offence.) The cry was renewed for the second, then the third time, after which Francis appeared on the threshold. The messenger met him, gave him the warrant without speaking. The paternal accusation was written there, point by point, precisely detailed as to the crimes, the facts, the circumstances of time and place.

Francis said to the messenger: "This paper of yours does not concern me. For some time, by the grace of God, I have been made free of every power of the consuls, having become a servant of the Most High."

It was a true and proper exception to lack of jurisdiction. The messenger, Rainuccio di Palmerio, rushed off to refer the matter to the consuls. (A report on the notification was mandatory according to the statutes, and criers were warned that should they report things that were not true, their tongues would be cut out.)

Such a question, in the diverse and contradictory ecclesiastical, imperial, and communal norms of jurisdiction, must have put the consuls in serious embarrassment. They undoubtedly saw in the assertion made by Francis that he was the servant of God a new reason for conflict with the inflexible Bishop Guido.

In his position as a lay brother, Francis would be considered subject only to the authority of the bishop *ratione materiae et loci,* by reason of what he was and where he was. And there was no doubt that he was now in the service of the church and lived in a place subject to the bishop. On this the imperial diplomas and the papal bulls issued during the past two centuries spoke clearly. It was enough to refer to the bull of Innocent III issued nine years earlier, directed to Bishop Guido: "No authority, or minister of any authority, shall have the legal right to cite rashly in judgement priests of your church, or any man whatsoever living in the lands of the Episcopacy, without the consent of the bishop." The penalty was excommunication. *Hoc enim omnino sub pena anatematis interdicimus* ("We forbid this completely under pain of excommunication"). The servant of God must be considered the man of the church, which represents God on this earth.

Moreover, the idea of taking arms against Francis must have been repugnant to the consuls. It was not clear that he had deliberately tried to squander the family resources and to take himself out of the authority of his native city.

The ruling that decided the question would have read something like this: "Since he has passed to the service of God, it is no longer our right to judge him." Therefore, no messenger of the consuls appeared at San Damiano for the second summons after the required eight days had passed.

It seemed the cruel winter would never end. Toward the middle of February, again according to Fra Salimbene, Saint Agatha's snow began to fall, called thus because it was natural to that time and to that season (Saint Agatha's day falls on the fifth of February). The snow was so heavy this year that the old ones of the city could not remember one to equal it—and their memories went back for many years. But even as the sun came out on all that immaculate whiteness, the first signs of the new season could be seen in the calm air.

The olive trees were swathed in snow and around each branch the snow had formed a tender and subtle filigree. The snow had laid down a great pure white carpet on the piazza of Santa Maria Maggiore and thrown a tapestry of silver on the façade of the church. An immense forest of lilies seemed to be miraculously blooming on the spiky bushes, on the thorny clumps of briars, on the naked hedgerows. The morning was all purity and light, enchantment and poetry, a morning suitable for a nuptial celebration.

Therefore, when the messenger of the bishop entered the enclosure of San Damiano and gave Francis the notice ordering him to present himself at Santa Maria Maggiore for a new trial, the young man felt that a festival was being arranged in a splendid court, where his dreams of love would finally be fulfilled.

He replied that he would obey.

"I shall appear before the bishop," he said, "because he is the father and lord of all souls."

In the Bishop's Court

The bishop came out of his residence at the third hour [9 A.M.], the time established in his constitutions for the audiences in which he sat *pro tribunali.* He appeared at the top of the stairway, stopped for an instant to consider the people who packed the piazza. His mitre was on his head. He was enveloped in a blue velvet mantle, very full, fastened with large clasps of gold. He was surrounded by his acolytes, the canons of Santa Maria Maggiore, the assessor Iacopo, the knight Tommaso di Raniero, the vicar, the notary.

The documents and the paintings of that century allow us to make a perfect reconstruction of the piazza of Santa Maria Maggiore as it appeared then.

At the top of the long and narrow piazza was an imposing palazzo, surmounted by a battlemented loggia bounded by a large tower. (Vestiges of it still remain in the black stones at the corner of the large arch that leads to the street of Macelli Vecchi.) Two rows of similar houses enclosed the other sides of the piazza, sloping along the declivity. (Ruins that date from the Roman epoch emerge from under the eighteenth century houses that now face the church and wide stretches of the ancient walls are near the arch of the street that goes up to the piazza.) These were the houses of powerful families who had remained faithful to the bishop: Egidio, Mincio, Giovanni di Ugone, Girolamo di Giovanni, Peppone, Matteo di Giacomo, Conte di Armoleo.

The bishop's palace stood at the lower end of the piazza, beside the old cathedral dedicated to Our Lady of the Assumption. Alterations made in the course of the centuries have completely modified the earlier residence. At that time, it stood strong and fortified, like a castle constructed for an imminent battle at the border of the consular city—a massive fortress, without openings. An open cloister supported by light columns led to the living quarters, which were adorned with little arches and crowned with battlements. At the corners of the palace, over the columns, under the round arches of the windows, the coat of arms bearing the sign of the cross stood out boldly against the background.

The façade of the church [Santa Maria Maggiore] was just as it is today: plain, of rough cut stones, divided by two fillets; a rose window with eight sections, made like a wheel of a cart; an ancient Roman arch over the main portal.

As the bishop seated himself in the cathedra, placed on the landing of the staircase, a bell began to ring, giving the signal for the opening of the audience. Then all talking ceased, and a profound silence fell upon the piazza, the crowds of people, the houses, the balconies— these, too, were packed with spectators. The air was limpid and sweet. Some flakes of snow still whitened the soil and were now melting under the slow caress of the morning sun.

The father, Pietro Bernardone, spoke first. In his usual irate tone of voice, which not even the solemnity of the assembly caused him to soften (many times his consorts had to hold him back to keep him from throwing himself on his son), he repeated his accusation, told of his indignation, asked punishment of the guilty. His son could no longer remain in the bosom of the family after having offended it so gravely, going about dressed in rags, thinking he could get off scot-free for all the outrageous things he had done. To give more weight to his words, he told again about the scarlet stolen from the shop, the horse sold in the Foligno market, the money offered to the priest of San Damiano.

The bishop said, turning to Francis: "You have disturbed and shocked your father very much. Give him back his money and he will be placated. In other ways God will provide for the restoration of his church."

Francis had brought the gold, which the paper brought to him by the messenger had mentioned as one of the principal reasons for the suit. He turned it over to the bishop.

"Lord Bishop," he said, "not only this money that I took from him do I wish to restore to him, with all good will, but even the clothes that he has given me."

The words were a sudden inspiration for Francis, knight of Christ. In that instant he saw again, very near, the gentle beggar maid who had been with him at his last serenata. As in that night, she was wearing ragged clothes, she was barefoot, she had a garland of fresh roses in her hair. Her eyes, now not dreamy in the rapture of music, were watching him intently, and there was love in her expression. He understood that the great hour had come to take her by the hand, lead her to the altar, and unite himself to her with a tie so strong that nothing, not even death, would be able to break it.

He ran up the stairs, crossed the arcade, went into the first room, called the *sala antica,* the "ancient room." After an instant he reappeared naked, naked and free, holding the bundle of his clothes in his hands like a cast off skin he was leaving behind. It was his great act of renunciation that freed him from all servitude to earthly things.

He was a living admonition of Saint Jerome: *Nudam crucem nudus sequar* ("Naked, I shall follow the naked cross").[36]

Silence fell at the extraordinary and unforeseen act. It won the hearts of the spectators, even though they did not understand it.

By now the whole piazza lay in sunlight. It was alive in the restless motion and mingling of white ermines, rose and white cloaks. Roundabout the walls of the tranquil gardens, the first timid flowering of almond blossoms peeped out.

Every tie between Francis and his family was now cut. Now he was alone, with only his love. Even the merchant, in anger and pain, found no words. He mechanically took the clothes that his son had laid down, tremblingly listened to his son's farewell.

"Up until today I have called Pietro Bernardone my father. For the future I shall say, 'Our Father, who art in heaven. . . .'"

The time had come for Bishop Guido to conclude the trial and give his sentence. But he remained perplexed, so much had he, too, been surprised and paralyzed by the act of ardent renunciation. Like the others, he was touched by a hidden beauty in it, but he also felt that he would never have been able to give up even one of the castles and properties that he owned in the territory. In fact, he had not hesitated to hurl sacred anathemas against those who had dared to usurp them. Like his predecessors, like almost all the prelates of the time, he was very rich and much attached to the goods of this world.

All the same he had the strange presentiment that whatever mysterious and solemn thing had been fulfilled at that moment in his court, it had been a conflict that crossed over the limits of time and place, one that was a part of a universal drama of troubled humanity, and that on this superhuman argument he had been called to put a seal in the name of Him who had said, "If anyone comes to me without turning his back on his father and mother, his wife and his children, his brothers and sisters, indeed his very self, he cannot be my disciple."

He had no more hesitation. He rose from his throne, slowly went down the stairs. He went to Francis, who was waiting, his hand held out as if to an invisible spouse. Without speaking, almost as if fulfilling the highest of rites, he took off his elaborate mantle and put it on Francis's shoulders.

Thus Francis married Lady Poverty.

The bishop and the persons of his court again climbed up the high staircase. The door of the powerful castle closed again. People dispersed, disappearing into the side streets. Now everyone was talking. They had come to that trial to enjoy the spectacle of a fierce quarrel. They left dismayed by the cruelty of the arrogant merchant. "Those present at this scene," write the Three Companions, "took the side of Francis because Pietro had left him without any clothing, and moved with pity, they started to weep over him."

The piazza remained deserted, with its dark houses, the tall towers, the roughly shaped stone of the façade of the church, the rose window like the wheel of a cart, the impenetrable walls of the bishop's palace, the flowering almond trees in the silent gardens, the flakes of snow, now melting, disappearing little by little under the slow caress of the noonday sun.[37]

Francis and the Robbers

Now, because his liberty was complete, Francis felt compelled to leave the city and go among persons who had never known him, so that he could rebuild his life. He felt it necessary to condemn himself voluntarily to that exile that his father had requested of the consuls of the commune. He put aside the rich velvet mantle; he took another one, poor and torn, from a farmhand of the episcopal court in Moiano.[r] With chalk, he sketched on the back of it a great cross, the knight's symbol that had appeared to him in his vision of the enchanted castle where he had found the lady of his heart. He left alone for the friendly city of Gubbio.[38]

He went out the lower San Giacomo gate, threading his way down the hill among the olive trees below the monastery of Santa Maria degli Episcopi, and reached the Ponte dei Galli, where the Tescio, swollen by the mild weather that had softened and loosened the snow, ran at the bottom of the mountain gorge with unusual violence.

---

r. Since the *curtis* or manor of Moiano was adjacent to and a part of the *vescovado* or bishop's palace, the farmhand who gave him his mantle surely came from there. NV 2:238.

He passed the mill belonging to the monks of Via San Paolo. No one was on the doorstep. The millstones rested immobile. A few small and contorted olive trees were mirrored in the tranquil gorge. He travelled on, along the slope of the hill that rises on the opposite side of the river between San Bartolomeo and Col Caprile. The path, extremely steep, led to the ancient parish church of San Nicolò di Campolungo, at the summit of the hill. He passed it and went down again toward Valfabbrica, the strong castle on the old road between Assisi and Gubbio.

Water was bursting forth from the mouths of all the streams, from the ravines, from the impervious and rocky gorges, pouring between rocky banks into the Boccabuto, the stream that lies beside the path—the Petrata streamlet, the brooks of Mosciole, Vallicelle, Castagna, Caberta.

On the Nocigliano heights thick oak forests again appeared, surmounted by feudal towers: Torre del Zampa, Ripa Rotàra, Casa Coppi, Torre delle Murce. The last one is a place of inaccessible, wild, forest-covered peaks, famous today for the passage of ring doves. The road that Francis travelled ran just below it, and on those heights every noise of men and of falling water was gone. He again found the silence of uncontaminated snow, not yet touched by the breath of the new spring.

The Latin accounts of the ancient biographers who collected the details of this trip from contemporaries of Francis are couched in poetic language. In translation:

Saint Bonaventure: "Now that he was free from the bonds of all earthly desires in his disregard from the world, Francis left the town and sought out a place where he could be alone, without a care in the world. There in solitude and silence he would be able to hear God's secret revelations."[39]

And Thomas of Celano: "He seeks now so to despise his own life, putting off all solicitude for it, that he might find peace in his harassed ways, and that meanwhile only the wall of flesh should separate him from the vision of God."[40]

But the most perceptive person about this particular episode in the life of Saint Francis is the poet Henri d'Avranches, who must have learned many authentic details either from the process of canonization extant in the papal Curia where he was situated or from eyewitnesses. He says that Francis, in leaving Assisi to go to Gubbio, wished from this moment on "to live like a wandering minstrel, who does not have a fixed place of abode and roams about poor and needy."

A jongleur, a vagabond poet, a troubadour who follows his dream.

This was indeed a custom of those knights Francis had at one time intended to imitate. (A contemporary troubadour of Provence, Elias Cairel, is said to have "walked a long time across the world," *anet loc temps per lo mon.*)[41] The troubadours came down from their castles at the first hint of spring and travelled about celebrating the praises of the lady of their hearts on the public squares and in the courts. For her they sang and to her they raised their entreaty: "Lady, more beautiful than I know how to say, for whom I weep and sigh . . ."

> *Domna, genser que no sai dir,*
> *per que soven planh e sospir. . .*[42]

When I do not see you, I have neither joy nor pleasure. Joy I cannot have, nor pleasure. I die unless I reach the harbour. So the long awaiting, the continual daydreams, the too long hours of watch, the little sleeping, and the desire to see you, keep my heart in such great anguish! A hundred times I pray to God, night and day, that He give me death or give me your love.

> *Can non ai loc de vos vezer*
> *joi ni deport non posc aver;*
> *non posc aver joi ni deport,*
> *peritz sui si non venc al port;*
> *que · l loncs espers e · l lonc consirs*
> *e · l trop velhars e · l pauc dormirs*
> *e · l deziriers de vezer vos*
> *me tenon si · l cor angoissos!*
> *Cen vetz prec Deu la noit e · l jor*
> *que · m do mort o la vostr'amor.*[43]

Now Francis had his own love song, more ardent than any sung by Tripudianti singers, in elaborate palaces or rich courts of the castles. His was the most impassioned song on earth. And he hurled it to the March sky, to the purity of the snow soaked in sun, to the flocks of white clouds gamboling over the tops of the hills, to the motionless oaks that watched him go by. It was a song in the language of Provence, the language of his lyrical raptures.

"Have mercy, sweet Jesus, have mercy on me and on our Lady Poverty. For her I languish, because of her I have no peace, and you know, Jesus, that you love me because of her. Despised and obscure is now the one who was your spouse. And yet with you she shivered in the squalor of the manger. By your side she fought in the exhausting battle. Like a good squire she parried the blows that were directed to you. When your disciples abandoned you, when they denied your name, she stayed always at your side.

"High, so very high was the cross, and Mary could not ascend it. But she, Poverty, our Lady, was there. More strongly than ever up there she united herself to you.

"She did not see to it that the wood was smooth and well-finished or that there were many sharp and shining nails. Three of them alone *she* made ready for your martyrdom: coarse, rough, blunted, to aggravate your pain.

"When you were in agony on the cross from your terrible thirst, she, because of her love, forbade you to have a sip of water. When your eyes closed, with a stronger embrace she held you close. When they put you in the tomb, the unguent that was sprinkled on your holy body, the sheet that enveloped you, belonged to another. The day of your resurrection, it was seen that she alone, abandoning every earthly thing, remained with you and followed you into heaven.

"Thank you, sweet Jesus, for our love. Grant that for her I shall live, that in her and with her I can die."[44]

Francis reached the little rural church of San Nicolò di Campolungo, where the road descended to intersect the Porziano road near the place called Pioppo. Exactly at the crossroads a valley opened. At the bottom of it ran the Rio Grande.

As Francis reached this crossroad, he found himself suddenly surrounded and seized by armed men, who in a threatening manner asked him who he was.

The song was shattered in the last gleam of sunset that was now throwing an ashy veil on the white snow.

Shaking him violently, they repeated their question, with a truculent air that promised no good. They were most likely members of a gang of thugs and robbers in the employ of the Perugini, lurking only a short distance from the border on the lookout for victims. The miserable appearance of the strange wayfarer could not have given them much hope for booty. They probably wanted an excuse for attack depending what side he was on or what lord he served.

Francis hesitated before replying. He had said to the messenger of the commune who had informed him that he must appear before the consuls that he had entered the service of God. By now he felt himself tied to no one but God, his servant and vassal. In a way he considered himself a faithful envoy, a messenger, a herald, like the heralds who conveyed a prince's commandments to the people. In just this spirit he had been going through the forest proclaiming the virtues of the great queen, Lady Poverty.

He replied then, in a loud voice that reverberated in the evening quiet, "I am the Herald of the Great King." And immediately added, "What is it to you?"

But the armed men believed that this crazy thing of rags and tatters who walked along singing at the top of his lungs in a dangerous place, full of traps, was making fun of them. Angry, they cursed and struck him. And they picked him up and threw him into the gully, yelling, "Die, miserable herald!"

He fell into the snow and lay stunned for awhile. He heard the harsh voices, the bursts of jeering laughter. Then even that faded into the distance and stopped altogether. Again there was silence.

He got up with difficulty, shook the snow off his back, climbed up the banks of the declivity. The shadows of twilight lay across the snow. A piercing wind had come up and he was aware that he was trembling from the cold. He made a futile search in the darkness for his torn mantle with the cross on the back. Now he realized he was poor, without a house, without a family, half-naked, numb with cold, abused, maltreated, alone in the frozen winter night.

It was the trial that he had wanted, one against which to take his own measure. He bore it bravely, sustained by the tingling warmth of the fighting spirit, like the excitement he had felt when in the cavalry of Assisi he had rushed the Perugian army. This time he had come out of it victorious and jubilant. He went on his way again, singing louder than ever.

The woods came to an end. The fields began. Dimly in the shadows the strong towers of the Valfabbrica castle loomed up, barring the road. Not a voice came from beyond the bolted gate, not a sentinel, not a light, along the wall. Francis called repeatedly, in vain. He thought then of asking hospitality for the night in the Benedictine monastery of Santa Maria di Valfabbrica to which the *castello* was subject. He took the path to the left and found himself again on the Gubbio road that bordered the Chiagio river. At the monastery's *porta caditoia,* the door with openings for weapons, he knocked and waited. There was no response.

The night had grown darker and was shining with stars. The long rumble of the river could be heard nearby, a hollow sound, extraordinarily menacing. He knocked again. He heard the tell-tale squeak of a peephole; then, slowly, amidst a screeching and grating of padlocks and chains, the door was opened. A lantern was lit and then put out again. Someone invited him to come in.

He walked into a low hallway like the corridor of a fortress. The lantern was relit. A monk, dressed in black, looked at him, stupified. It was obvious that he did not know what to make of this strange visitor, almost naked, teeth chattering with the cold, whose bruised face shone with radiant happiness.

The Warrior Monks of Santa Maria di Valfabbrica

From the time of its origin, the monastery of Santa Maria of Valfabbrica had given its name to all the area; that is, it was the valley of the *fabbrica,* the valley in which, in a very remote time, new work was being done by the sons of Saint Benedict.

In the heart of the forest the monks had created extensive tracts of cultivated land and flourishing fields. They had ploughed the soil, collected the waters of the river, established formidable dykes against the violent and frequent floods. They were under the jurisdiction of the famous abbey of San Silvestro of Nonantola and they were wont to boast of this relationship, as of a particular title of nobility that raised them above the riffraff of neighbouring castle lords. (This abbey was founded in 753 by Saint Anselmo, brother-in-law of the king, Astolfo. It was very rich and powerful, being the mistress of churches, castles, and lands, not only in the region of Modena, but also in Bologna, Tuscany, Umbria, and even, at the time of the Latin Empire, in Constantinople.)

Valfabbrica was also rich in lands and in castles, a condition that led it, from the earliest times, to quarrel with the feudal lords on its borders. These were generally held in check by the political power of the monks, who allied themselves with the imperial party, but at times when that power was weakened, the lords got their revenge by plummeting from their peaks and taking over priory lands.

Emperors had been generous to the monastery in privileges and aid.

Louis the Pious, in a diploma given from Aquisgrana on December 10, 820, forbade anyone from "molesting the possessions and rights of the Monastery of Valfabbrica, located in the territory of Assisi."

In the years before the last restoration of Barbarossa, some powerful castellans, supported by Perugia as a means of harassing Assisi, attacked the monks and succeeded in taking away from them the castle of Casa Castalda, which claimed very ancient rights, along with some flourishing *curtes.* Conrad Moscaincervello, however, saw that justice was done in the matter of these usurpations. And when Barbarossa passed through Assisi, he, with another diploma, confirmed the time-honoured preferred status of the loyal monastery, proclaiming it "to remain under his particular protection" and ordering "that it be *franco e libero,* independent and free from every unjust taxation and servitude, from any sort of violent oppression by *marchesi* and counts, and moreover, guaranteed against attacks by them under the penalty of ten thousand *libbre* of gold." However, these Benedictines, besides occupying themselves with codices and the Psalter, continued to train themselves for war. They stayed armed and ready for other cavalcades and assaults, killings and arsons.

Nor could it have been otherwise, given the fact that the monastery, situated in the territory of Assisi a short distance from Perugian land, was an advance look-out point, always overrun by invading armies when war was proclaimed. Even when there was no active state of official hostilities, guerilla plots were constantly being hatched by the feudal lords perched in their fortresses on the tops of the hills: Coccorano, Biscina, Giomici, Casa Castalda, Petrorio, Colle Alto, Santo Stefano.

And when the castellans were holed up in their gloomy manors, busy chewing over their last defeat and the next vendetta, the monks had to face another enemy, one no less dangerous and insidious: the Chiagio river.

This river, which comes down from the mountains of Gubbio, is famous for its devastating rages and violent floods. When it was in flood, the waters beat against the walls of the monastery so that the building and its towers appeared to rise from the waves of a lake. To try to tame it, the monks had dug canals, built restraining dykes, and constructed strong piers.

Accustomed to constant struggle with men and the elements, they seemed fierce and tenacious, harsh and steely, a warrior race.

When the war of 1202 broke out, the monastery entered it at once, hoping to see their powerful enemy, Perugia, at last made powerless. The monks rode out to battle in armour and mail and beside them rode bold warriors from lands adjoining the abbey. Among them was Count Ugo, lord of Sassoferrato, famed for his valour. His castle, too, was in fief from the abbey of Nonantola.

They fought formidable rivals—especially the sons of Monaldo, Suppolino and Rinaldo, the lords of Giomici. Their father had already been chastised by the imperial Swabians for taking monastery land. Fields, which had already been sown, were salted into sterile lands; roads, where bands of armed ruffians held the pass, rendered impassable.

The defeat at Collestrada seemed to dash the fortunes of the monastery, along with those of Assisi, its ally commune. Some peasants of the *castello* of Valfabbrica revealed themselves to be friends of Perugia and stirred up trouble. But only for a short while, since, as we have already seen, a brigade of Assisi cavaliers led by Marescotto di

Bernardo Dodici burst into the rebel *castello* and carried off a great amount of booty.

In the meantime the prior, Rainerio, who had governed since 1206, was succeeded by the prior Ugo, who again took the offensive. Charging out from the monastery, where the monks had barricaded themselves after the defeat, he led a series of raids and surprise actions.

In 1209 (two years after the events in the life of Saint Francis that we are narrating here) the Perugini, furious about this campaign that ate away at their men and their prestige, put together an army, attacked the *castello* of Valfabbrica, and burned it.

The prior Ugo was among those taken to Perugia. He was led before the consuls, and made to ratify in a solemn public act his submission and his humiliation. We possess the nasty document, which virtually exhales, after more than seven centuries, the harshness of that struggle, the one in which earlier the Herald of the Great King had been ensnared. Here it is in full:

"In the name of Our Lord Jesus Christ, in his year of 1209, at the time of Signore Innocent III Pope, the month of July, the twelfth day, the twelfth indiction, I, Domino Ugo, by divine mercy prior and provost of the Venerable Church of Valfabbrica, not constrained by force or by deception, but of my spontaneous and good will, corporally swearing to all this, and under the penalty of five hundred *marche* of silver, for me and for my successors, promise and obligate myself, legitimately stipulating, consenting in this with me all the men and the inhabitants of the *castello* called Valfabbrica, in your presence, Pandolfo di Segura, by grace of God consul of the Romans and podestà of Perugia, and for you in the presence of all the community of this city and for your successors who in this city will supervise in perpetuity, that we shall never rebuild this *castello* destroyed by you, and we shall never have it rebuilt, and we shall never allow anyone, or any others, to take steps to rebuild it, nor in the place where it rose shall ever return the men who lived there at one time, or any other persons. And we shall always especially defend the Perugini and their goods in these places and in all ways that we shall be able to do. And for the destruction of the *castello* done by you we shall not 'render you evil for evil' (*alicui vestrum malum meritum non reddemus* is the formula that renders valid the right of vendetta) 'nor have others render it to you' (*nec reddere faciemus* is the open allusion to the Assisani, who are simmering in the shame of their new humiliation); and always we shall hold our men gathered together inside the church, with the exception of five, who will be allowed to live on top of the hill, since you at the time of the destruction of the castle saved them, them and their goods."

This means that the men who sided with Assisi would have to live inside the monastery, that is, in the undefended valley in which the river flowed. But five men, supporters of Perugia, were to be allowed to live *in podio,* on the top of the *poggio* or hill, the Perugini having spared them, their persons and their goods.

(Even today there is a separate group of houses in that locality, then called "Poggio" and now, "Poggio di Sotto." It is about two kilometres from the monastery, on the Assisi side of the Chiagio, in Assisi territory, about one kilometre from the Perugia border, which once passed through Barcaccia. This hill also belonged to the monastery and in the old papers is called Podium Prioris, Hill of the Prior.)

These oaths, which were to have sanctioned the sentences imposed forever, had no effect but to inspire new offensives. In fact, a few years later, when Perugia was ruled by its citizen faction and at the mercy of her adversaries, large and small, the monks began their war again. The *castello* of Valfabbrica was rebuilt. The struggle furiously flared up again over all the region.

The son of Suppolino, who was called Monaldo like his grandfather, and the son of Rinaldo, who had taken the name of his uncle, Suppolino, returned to their raids through the fields and the forests, killing indiscriminately and sowing terror everywhere.

From a 1232 list of those judged guilty of crimes we find these notations:

"Monaldo di Suppolino, [and] the notary Benvenuto di Matteo, for the accusation made against them by Giovanni di Bernardo, because they killed his son Andrea in the district of Assisi and cited, did not appear, have been sentenced in absentia and publicly condemned to a fine of 110 *libbre.*"

And again, "The aforesaid Monaldo di Suppolino, [and] Suppolino di Rinaldo, his cousin, for the accusation made against them by Boninsegna di Morico, because they killed Mancia, their man and a citizen of Assisi, in the district of Assisi, and cited, did not appear, have been sentenced in absentia and publicly condemned, according to the terms of the statute, to a fine of 110 *libbre.*"

In 1257 the sons of Monaldo di Suppolino, Uguiccione and Guidone, at last sold to the commune of Perugia the castle of Casa Castaldo, of which they had remained proprietors. In 1257 Iacobuccio, count of Coccorano, took the goods of the priory. He looted it even to the furniture and the papers in its archives.

The monastery was again in danger in 1321, when Assisi was forced to submit to Perugia. Again in 1337 another lord of Coccorano, Giovanni di Biscina, subject to Perugia, enraged at the prior, Gioacchino di Maccarello and a citizen of Assisi, protested to the magistrates of Assisi. They in turn took up the matter with the abbot of Nonantola, claiming that it was no longer possible to sustain the rights of the monastery by force of arms. The successor of Gioacchino, Simone da Firenze, was stripped of power by the Perugini, who put other monks in his place. They proclaimed themselves independent of Nonantola. But Simone had the last word. He re-entered his monastery with sword in hand at the head of a company of armed men, who did justice to the Perugini and the rebel monks.

In 1546 the monastery and its goods passed to the cathedral chapter of Assisi, which still has jurisdiction over it. The church has been adapted as a parish church of the town of Valfabbrica and has annexed the cemetery. The ancient priory has become the residence of the archpriest. All the building has undergone extensive alterations, but traces of the ancient structure remain, especially on the façade of the church.

The Chiagio Flood

The prior, Ugo, to whom Francis was taken, scarcely deigned to give him a glance and made no attempt to disguise his bad humour over the arrival of that poorly dressed vagabond. Even the story of the brigands lying in ambush in the priory forest, which at another time would have roused him to fury and brought immediate orders to pursue them, interested him very little.

Prior Ugo and his monks had other things to think about that evening. With the melting of the unusually heavy snowfall, the river had risen so high that the structures on its banks were in danger of being washed away. There was anxiety about the harvests, the beasts, and the monastery itself. The serfs ran out periodically to check on the flood, and each time returned with alarming reports.

As Francis came in, the reddish moving light of the torches was returned in a multitude of shifting reflections from arms: shields, swords, helmets, corselets, lances, knives, crossbows, ironshod clubs. The monks themselves were gruff, hairy, like the wild boars of their woods. With bad grace they gave Francis a morsel of mouldy bread and a sheet to cover himself on a bed of straw in the kitchen.

Thus the spouse of Poverty spent the first night of his vagabond life. All during the night the rumble of the Chiagio could be heard, ever stronger and nearer. Rapid footsteps and excited voices continued to echo beyond the door.

By daybreak the valley was covered with water. Tops of the trees scarcely emerged from the agitated waves breaking against the bastions of the monastery on all sides. The light of the rising sun made that expanse of water glitter like a gigantic steel plate.

Certainly it was impossible to force the intruder to leave, and the monks lamented that fact as another calamity of the flood. They left him as he was, with a single shirt, without giving him even the charity of a mantle or cloak, not even a miserable rag.

Nor did it seem that things were going to get any better. A monk who was checking from the largest tower came down at intervals with reports that from hour to hour grew more frightening. The water had reached all the way to Rinaldo's oak tree beyond the mill. The Carfagna stream was also overflowing its banks. The Ravisada bridge had crumbled. Some men on the roof of a house toward the Barcaccia road were desperately asking for help.

Francis was left in the kitchen like a kitchen-boy, arrogantly ordered around, made to split wood, wash dishes, collect refuse, sweep the floor, stir up the fire.

He obeyed in silence. In the evening, still dressed in that wretched torn shirt, he warmed himself at the fire. The monks came to sit around the chimney cowl, stretch their hands toward the crackling juniper and talk of monastery affairs. Francis listened intently, not knowing what to make of the fact that these servants of God were immersed to such a degree in worldly struggles.

With a sort of exasperated bitterness that made their eyes go dark, they talked about their hatred of the thieving, usurping castellans, an emotion so constant that its observance had become a baleful rule of the monastery. They enlarged upon their feats of arms, their tricky skill in setting traps for the enemy. They swore that they would like to grind under their heels all the constables of the republic of Perugia. They described their old legal battles before law courts and papal legates over matters of jurisdiction and tithes, against rapacious ecclesiastical authorities, among whom they did not fail to place the uncompromising Bishop Guido.

Or they braggingly enumerated the churches and priories subject to them on both sides of the Chiagio: San Gregorio di Coltratricce, San Giuliano di Paganzano, San Senese del Poggio del Priore, San Rufino di Bisciolano (on a rocky hill swarming with serpents), Pieve Selvatica (a tumbledown chapel in an enclosed gorge), San Petrignano di Macriano, Santa Lucia di Poggio Morico, San Giorgio, San Petrignano della Ranca, Santa Maria delle Scalette.

They counted their forests and vineyards: San Portulo, Piaggia,

Cerqueto, the hill of Massaro, Capanna, Calcinaro, Forcola, the field of Locco, Bosco, San Giovanni.

All the same the war and the losses caused by extravagant monks made times difficult even for them. The income did not equal the expenses. To get along the monks had to impose the strictest parsimony on themselves. One time it was not so. The prosperity of the monastery was proverbial in all the region. Bushels of grain accumulated in the granaries, cartloads of hay filled the barns, casks of wine and amphorae of oil lined the spacious cellars.

But the monastery had had the bad luck to be under a monk named Bonifacio, chosen to govern the Nonantola abbey about thirty years earlier—a vain and prodigal man. After receiving his investiture in Rome, he stopped for a time in Santa Maria.

Thirty persons were with him as his escort of honour, all of them greedy snobs who ate with four jaws. They spent a month there, entertaining themselves with interminable banquets and luxuries of every kind, all at the expense of the monastery. When the time for their departure came, they bought chargers and palfries, attaching and alienating the most fertile lands at shockingly low prices in order to do so. The priors, given such an example, had not failed to grab their share; so Santa Maria had been brought to such extremes of poverty that the monks for a long time had had to live on olives and rye bread. The extravagant abbot was at last deposed and brought to trial, but the monastery had never recovered its prosperity.

It is probable that the mean treatment given Francis was a consequence of their strict regime, or possibly food had become scarce because of the flood and they had been forced to measure out provisions. However that may be, Francis, considered a useless mouth, was offered nothing to eat other than that morsel of bread that the cook had given him.

The narration of this episode by Henri d'Avranches finds even on this point full confirmation in the documents.

He writes that Francis, to appease his terrible hunger, would have been content to dunk the morsel of dried bread into the hot broth that was left over in the kitchen, but even this was denied him "because it was the custom of the devout brothers to stuff their pigs with that broth." And he concludes: "Do you think they were induced, then, to supply a man's clothes to one who was denied the supper of a pig?"

As has already been said, the Valfabbrica monks owned thick oak forests. They had a special *curtis* for the raising of swine, located on the borders of Poggio del Priore—it even had its own church, named

San Giovanni dei Porcelli ("Saint John of the Piglets"). All this part of the mountain was noted for the production of pork, which had as its center the *castello* that because of this industry was and is still called Porziano. The raising of pigs, we must remember, was the principal activity of all the Benedictine monasteries of central Italy.

Henri d'Avranches does not spare his barbs against these monks who were so pitiless to Francis. "The monk, when he is taken by the sin of avarice, ends by being ready to go to any excess. Whenever he who takes strict religious vows becomes forgetful of them, he will turn away from nothing. After the first sacrilege, he throws himself into every kind of evil deed."

The second trial was far harder than the first for Francis. Again he had seen the wretched dehumanization of men overcome by crass greed. And these were men who went up to the altar, administered the sacraments, called themselves servants of true religion!

As soon as it was possible (the river, receding into its bed, transformed the fields and roads into squalid swamps of mud and rubble), he left the monastery and continued on his way to Gubbio.

Thomas of Celano writes that much later, when the Poverello of Christ was famous everywhere for his holiness, the prior Ugo remembered his own great villainy during that time and went to him to ask pardon.[s]

Francis's Stay in Gubbio

At Barcaccia he crossed the river on a barge, passed the castle of Coccorano on the left, and farther along, that of Giomici on the right.

---

s. Though some Franciscan writers have thought that the monastery in which Francis took refuge was San Verecondo di Vallingegno (and Sabatier believed it to have been San Benedetto of Monte Subasio, which lies on the opposite side of Assisi from the road to Gubbio), a close examination of the physical details and the events described in the early biographies do not support this supposition. The only Benedictine monastery that does fit all details is Santa Maria di Valfabbrica. It is situated on a road between Assisi and Gubbio that was very important in the Middle Ages. It could be reached on foot in about half a day (and all the early sources place Francis's trip immediately after the trial in the bishop's court). Verecondo, about the same distance but on a more rugged pathway, could scarcely have been reached by the early hours of evening, given the complications of snow and robbers. Valfabbrica lies just beyond an area that was heavily wooded in the Middle Ages, exactly as described by early writers, and nearby is a ditch with a small stream (Rio Grande). It stands about one hundred metres (110 yards) from the river Chiagio, which is notorious for its violent floods. Verecondo is about three kilometres from the river and in no danger of floods. Furthermore, the road to Gubbio from Verecondo would not be blocked by the flooding river, while that from Valfabbrica would be. In every way, the description of the landscape given by Henri d'Avranches fits the surroundings of Valfabbrica. Again, Valfabbrica was a dependent monastery—a priory headed by a prior, as the early writers described the place. Verecondo was an independent monastery headed by an abbot. Also, Valfabbrica was in an area that was contested for a long time by Assisi and Perugia and constantly plagued by roving bands of marauders of one side or the other. For documentation and history of Santa Maria di Valfabbrica: *NV* 2:240–55.

He went up toward Biscina. The road bordered the Chiagio, as it does today. Perhaps the people were already saying the little rhyme in praise of the enchanting landscape of hills, forests, and rocks:

Alta Biscina, basso Coccorano,
Giomici bello, Caresto sovrano.

High Biscina, low Coccorano,
Beautiful Giomici, supreme Caresto.

After San Pietro the road leaves the river to go through Vallingegno and Mengara to Gubbio.

Gubbio: A somber city in its warlike solitude, stretched along the declivity of a steep and rugged mountain, criss-crossed by violent streams under a stormy sky. Guarded by massive towers, it broods at the margin of a silent valley. Thus the city was then, thus it is today, having miraculously maintained intact from the first communal epoch its tormented face, its harsh and turbulent spirit.

Francis knew a rich man there, one who had fought with him in the war against Perugia, one whose proud name was a testimony to his prowess in combat and to the strength of a sword devoted to the imperial cause: Federico Spadalunga ("Frederick Long-sword"). He lived in a house like a fortress, on the piazza of the Mercato. Francis went in search of him. It was Federico who at last gave him a tunic as a gift. Francis told him all that had happened, all about his renunciation, his intentions. His friend listened to him, astonished. Despite all his efforts, he could not understand what Francis was talking about.

The people of Gubbio welcomed him from the day of his arrival, knowing him to be from Assisi and having learned from Spadalunga and other Gubbio knights who had seen him in action with what great courage he had made rushes against the enemy and borne the hardship of imprisonment. (Between Assisi and Gubbio there had been for many years a tradition of good friendship and military alliance; it lasted all through the Middle Ages, cemented by an age-old struggle together against their common enemy, Perugia.[45] The city of the Ingino[t] had given to the city of the Subasio, with equal enthusiasm, architects for its cathedrals and numbers of knights for its battles.) But the people of Gubbio were distracted when Francis tried to describe the state of perfect liberty attained by a servant of Poverty. These ideas seemed to them to have an odor of utopia, perhaps even

---

t. Gubbio is built on the slopes of Mount Ingino, as Assisi is on Mount Subasio.

of Patarine heresy. They did not concern themselves about them. They simply paid no attention to what he said. His ideas struck them as reminiscent of old dreams futilely proclaimed by visionary ascetics, useless doctrines destined to be lost and certain to disappear in this swarming industrious city enclosed in its circle of walls and mountains. It was a city dedicated to warfare, trade, and government, to the building of towers and palaces, the making and unmaking of treaties with popes and emperors, the construction of castles to keep watch on the Apennine passes.

They could not even imagine a faith that was not sustained by military skill.

At the time of the Crusade proclaimed by Peter the Hermit,[u] a thousand warriors of Gubbio had crossed the sea to fight for the rescue of the Holy Sepulchre. In May of 1151, their Bishop Ubaldo himself had led them to victory in a war with Perugia and ten allied cities, all greatly damaged. This bishop, who had put aside the pastoral staff for the sword, the pallium for the cuirass, the aspergillum for the shield, the mitre for the steel helmet, remained, even after his death in 1160, the ideal leader to the Gubbio people, one who rode before the gonfalon of the commune when the army moved against an enemy. For an astounding [later] miracle that had caused a multitude of the enemy to be slaughtered, the city people, as one, loudly proclaimed him to be a saint. Rome had recognized it officially in the canonization that followed on March 5, 1192. Immediately a church was erected in his honour on the summit of the mountain, a little below the site of the imperial fortress that had been destroyed three years earlier. The uncorrupted body of Bishop Ubaldo was triumphally carried there September 11, 1194. From then on, every year on May 15, the anniversary of the battle, the Gubbio people carried votive candles to that church, to be offered there by the guilds of the city, as was the custom of the medieval communes. They were symbolic candles, gigantic, towering over the people like war machines, terminating in a pyramid on which were placed statues of saints to whom the commune recommended its salvation and its greatness: Saint George, protector of knights; Saint Anthony, abbot, protector of the people; Saint Ubaldo, symbol of the eternal glory of the city.

But the pugnacious enthusiasm of the people, carried away by the memory of his reckless courage, transformed this ceremony (which in other cities tended to be a sedate procession with pious canticles and

---

u. Peter the Hermit (1050?–1115) was an eloquent preacher of the First Crusade, which was inaugurated by Urban II in 1095.

lighted candles) into an evocation of the assault led by the bishop, who, at the head of his men, had been the first to hurl himself on the attacking forces. All the people lived again that hour of delirious heroism in a race in which all the guilds competed. They ran furiously up the steep slope with candles on their shoulders, all the way to the tomb of Bishop Ubaldo, brandishing their arms, unfurling their insignia, shouting the names of their captains. There, where he slept in his pontifical vestments, watched over by the flames of lamps, they put down in his presence the candles, symbols of ancient boldness and ancient victory. (Even today, every spring this warlike frenzy strikes again, undiminished by all the stormy events of eight centuries. It stirs up the torpor of the dead city, miraculously and unexpectedly lights up the hearts of the no-longer-powerful inhabitants. The old candles of their ancestors again are taken up the steep mountain amid trumpet blasts, spirited shouts, and the ringing of bells, surrounded by flashing scarlet scarfs and vivid black and blue tunics. Riding ahead of all are the Herald, the Captain of the Sword, and the Captain of the Hatchet.)

Francis's friend Spadalunga and the other knights preferred to tell their old comrade in arms about recent battles than listen to Francis's ideas.

A little after Assisi's defeat, the Perugini, growing bold, had made a punitive expedition all the way to the Serra castle, loyal to the Gubbio consuls. The same Perugino podestà, Pandolfo di Segura, consul of the Romans, had led them, showing how rabid he was against Assisi in the last period of the war.

A murderous engagement had taken place on the banks of the Chiagio. A vivid description of it was written by our old friend, the poet Eulistea di Bonifazio da Verona. It still survives. Pandolfo, to stir up his men, had reminded them of the defeat they had inflicted on the Assisi army. "I am amazed at the audacity of these unfortunate enemies of ours, who are unmindful of the fantastic victory that not long ago you had the skill to win over the troops of Assisi."

This battle, too, had been very cruel. "The horses fell, the helmets and the lances were broken, the shields and targes and every other weapon were broken, and the coats of mail and the shining blades." This time, too, the Perugini were victorious. "Here the Gubbio army was cut to pieces by the swords of our warriors. Here the Perugino became intoxicated on the good wine of battle."

And now the people of Gubbio, like those of Assisi, dreamed of recovering their position. They set about enlarging the city, bringing in the water of the river, building fortresses and establishing in them people who had overflowed the ancient walls. Such were the *castelli* of Cantiano, Costacciaro, Serra Sant'Abbondio. Meanwhile, the men of Cagli pined for the *castello* of Pergola and cast envious eyes even at cities of the Marches, and the rulers of Perugia picked a quarrel with the *castello* of Valmarcola. War was again in the air. Gubbio was relying on Assisi's aid.

Francis, listening to this talk, felt the depth of the abyss that by now separated him not only from the people of his native city, but also from the whole world, which he was seeing now as torn by struggles and quarrels. Here in this city he had hoped to forget and begin a new life. Now he could see that changing the place he lived would do him no good.

He thought again with nostalgia about the olive groves of San Damiano, the grottoes of the Carabone, the skylarks of the Sermolla valley, and above all, of his lepers of Arce. After a few months he returned to Assisi and took up his mission among the lepers— washing their feet, bandaging their sores, cleaning the dripping pus.[46]

Love Changes Everything

He went back to his priest at San Damiano. He had not forgotten the bidding from the Crucifix and his old intention to rebuild the church. Now he had no money, but he relied on the charity of the people of the city. They saw him pass through the streets and public squares, shouting strange things that confirmed their suspicion that he was mad, "Whoever gives me a stone will have one reward; whoever gives me two stones, two rewards; three stones, a treble reward."[47]

Some laughed at him; others were moved to pity, thinking how he had gone from a life of luxury and comfort to wallow in this misery. The San Damiano priest, seeing him come and go, panting under the weight of large stones, fretted, remembering the comfortable circumstances in which he had grown up. Sometimes he tried to prepare a special dish for him, different from his coarse every-day food.

But this did not redound to the honour of the knight of Lady Poverty. One day Francis took a bowl, and screwing up his courage, walked out to go from door to door and beg a bit of food or alms. Afterwards he mixed up all that he had been offered. It was a nauseating swill that no one could imagine carrying to his lips. (And again the people of the city were amazed, knowing in what refinement he had grown up.) With a great effort he ate all of it. And immediately he experienced a great light as he understood the secret of receiving as well as giving in love, which, as Thomas of Celano says, "softens all things to make every bitter thing sweet."[48]

For all that, sometimes the memory of his old life returned and caused him a certain embarrassment that he could not succeed in conquering. Especially was this true when he found himself exchanging a word with the old companions of his revels.

One day on his way up to Assisi to obtain oil for the lamps of the church, he passed the house of one of his acquaintances. Many men were gathered around a bench, intent on a game.ᵛ He flushed, not having the courage to ask for anything, and went on. But then, ashamed of himself, he turned around. He told them of the weakness that for an instant had overcome him. And immediately, speaking in Provençal, and adopting the manner of a versemaker as he had used to do when his spirits were high, he asked for and obtained the oil that he sought.[49]

One morning Francis, dressed in worn and skimpy garments, paused in an Assisi street, completely absorbed in prayer. It was in mid-January, and stinging air was blowing from Mount Subasio. His brother Angelo, seeing him shivering and so ragged, said nastily to someone nearby (using shop terms to point out insultingly what great benefits the squanderer had received from leaving the paternal house), "Ask Francis to sell you a few cents worth of sweat."

Angelo was one of those who prize things only according to the price they bring in the market.

The neighbour went and jokingly performed the commission. Again Francis spoke in Provençal, gaily returning the mockery, as in the shop he had returned an offer that was not acceptable: "I will sell my sweat at a higher price to my God!"[50]

Other times his brother did not limit himself to irony but attacked him in harsh words. But it was Pietro Bernardone, his father, who was least able to reconcile himself to the change in Francis. The old merchant had loved him too much and had suffered too much in seeing Francis drag himself about in such abject condition, and even more, in seeing him so worn and emaciated, almost as if he were a corpse. And so whenever he met Francis he shouted curses at him.

Francis was very much disturbed by this, and to keep up his spirits he asked a poor wretch of Assisi, Alberto by name, to go about with him. Every time that the painful scene was re-enacted, he asked the

---

v. Assisi statutes sternly prohibited games of chance but allowed *scachum seu tabulas, vel ad pioles, vel ad invitulam seu strillam*—even Fortini did not try to translate them into Italian or hazard a guess as to what they might be! We know, however, that they were played on public streets and on benches in the front of houses; they were forbidden, however, in certain places, especially in the piazzas in front of San Rufino and Santa Maria Maggiore and in or in front of the houses on the Piazza del Comune. See *NV* 3:221.—Trans.

poor man to bless him. Then he would turn to his father and say to him peaceably, "Do you not realize that God can give me a father whose blessing will counter your curses?"[51]

The people were struck by the calm with which he accepted the insults and provocations. He did not go about heedlessly ignoring everyone as he had once. When addressed, he stopped and replied with so much kindness that most people were disarmed by him.

He had finished the repairs at San Damiano, but he wanted to continue his work of restoring churches, according to the direction from the crucifix there. Near the family estates in San Petrignano there was a little church consecrated to the Prince of the Apostles, called San Pietro della Spina. It is mentioned in the documents of the Assisi cathedral from the eleventh century on,[w] but now it had been abandoned and fallen into ruin. He enthusiastically set about repairing it, to the stupefaction of the people who lived in the area and of servants who had been accustomed to flattering him and obeying him. It was the spring of 1208.

Today this chapel, which biographers have up to now sought in vain, is again abandoned, turned into a storehouse for a nearby farmhouse. Vats of wine, big jugs of oil, stores of grain, are in this holy place, which lives only on its memory of those marvellous distant days.

The ancient writers saw in the restoration of three churches by Francis a prophecy and a symbol of his work in restoring the religion of Christ. Saint Bonaventure wrote: "Like the three buildings he repaired, Christ's church was to be renewed in three different ways under Francis's guidance and according to his Rule and teaching, and the three-fold army of those who are to be saved was to win victory. We can now see that this prophecy has come true."[52]

While two of the churches Francis repaired, San Damiano and

---

w. Although Bonaventure (*Leg. Maior*, II, 7) tells us that the church of San Pietro that was repaired by Francis was farther from Assisi than San Damiano (which is about a kilometre from the city), biographers have been persistent in their identification of the church with the large and impressive Benedictine church of San Pietro that is in the lower portion of the city itself, and one which has had throughout its long history a rich endowment of lands and possessions. The true identification is surely to be found in the little church of San Pietro della Spina, about three kilometres from San Damiano, about midway to Porziuncola along the old Via Cupa di Petrignano. It is first mentioned in a 1030 document (Arch. Cath., fasc. 1, no. 93; *NV* 3:256). It remained in use as a church until less than a century ago. It is today a storage shed for the farmhouse owned by the Minciarelli family. A little bell-cote has been moved to the main part of the house, which at some point has been rebuilt; the family still has the bell, which probably was from the church. A painting (of Saint Francis surrounded by angels) from the church hangs in a nearby farmhouse of a member of the family, Signora Chiara Minciarelli. Among the residents of the area, there has been a constant tradition that Saint Francis repaired this church. See *NV* 2:266–72.

Porziuncola, are in their glory, this third church, San Pietro della Spina, is again derelict, as it was before Francis restored it. It needs someone to listen again to the words Francis heard from the crucifix—a good task for followers of the Man of Assisi to undertake.

Porziuncola

The third church that Saint Francis set about repairing, after having finished the work at San Pietro della Spina, was Porziuncola, about two miles from San Pietro.[x] One reaches it from San Pietro by a road that today runs almost parallel with the national road, called the Strada Antica.

The chapel stood in a little clearing, an open expanse in the middle of a thick woods. ("Porziuncola" means, in the old jargon used in the communes and the abbeys, "particella" or "particle," the name that is still given to small pieces of land separate from the principal body, for use in a particular situation or for the person of the proprietor, or for a particular kind of cultivation.) The forest there was tangled and wild, thick with oaks and holm-oaks; and once it was called the *cerreto* of Porziuncola ("oak woods of Porziuncola") or simply the *cerqueto* (also, "oak woods"). A document of August 1045 in the Assisi cathedral, drawn up by the notary Grifone, records the fact that the priest Arso sold to Pietro, son of Berga, some land located *infra comitato asisinato in loco qui dicitur allo cereto de Porzucle, seu allo Cerqueto*. A pig keeper lived there to take care of the herds, which were fed with acorns. Perhaps one of these keepers was the "Gorzio della Porziuncola," the only inhabitant of this place whose name was recorded in a census of the commune of 1232.

The chapel, consecrated to the Virgin (Saint Mary of the Angels) was called Santa Maria degli Angeli, but it was better known as the

---

x. The little chapel of Porziuncola can be traced back, through papal bulls listing churches dependent upon the monastery of San Benedetto di Monte Subasio, to 1145; but it was probably built earlier, perhaps during the tenth century. (The name "Porzucle" as a locality appears in 1045: Arch. Cath., fasc. 7, no. 6; *NV* 3:334.) The stories that it was built under Pope Liberius in the fourth century by hermits come from the Holy Land, who placed in it a stone from the tomb of the Blessed Virgin in the Valley of Josaphat and named the church Santa Maria di Giosafat, cannot be credited. These tales did not appear until the seventeenth century, and were apparently the invention of Fra Salvatore Vitale, who is not noted for fidelity to facts. He offered no documentation for his story and said only than an unknown and unnamed man had lent him a manuscript with this information.

The chapel, which today stands inside the huge church of Santa Maria degli Angeli, had long been held in special veneration by the people of the area. In *Leg. Maior,* II, 8, the popular and old legend that angels often visited the church is recorded; in *2 Cel.* 19, 20; *Spec. Perf.,* 55; and *Per.,* 8, 9, we read of Francis's special love for it. The little church was first known by the country people as Santa Maria degli Angeli. Later it was called Santa Maria di Porziuncola, but after Francis and his brothers took up residence in it, the older name was again adopted.

For further history and description: *NV* 3:92–99.

Porziuncola church. It belonged to the Benedictines of Mount Subasio, who had abandoned it. Before it had fallen into ruin, someone would come down from the monastery to say Mass on feast days and to receive the offerings of candles. Then, nothing more.

A poor, little, ancient, church. Here also were dangerous walls, loosened stones, broken bricks. The sky shone through holes in the roof and a ruined window. A door that no longer closed. A ruined altar, before which no one now ever prayed. A rusty lamp, never lit, tossed by the wind that blew through the place carrying flights of dead leaves. Only the image of the Virgin still remained at the back of the apse, with her corona of stars, her blue mantle, her glory of angels, her sweet sorrowful face.

Behind the chapel was a little uncultivated garden, enclosed by a vigorous and impenetrable hedge that divided the property of the monks from that of Filippo di Giacomo, an Assisi knight who also had land in Fontanelle close to the property of Pietro Bernardone. The woodland belonging to Filippo, which extended beyond the hedge, was a wicked thicket covered by brambles and thorn bushes.

Francis was distressed by Mary's abandoned house. To get on with the work as fast as possible, he moved into a hut near the church. Now he was wearing a hermit's garment fastened by a belt and wooden shoes (*zoccoli*), and he carried a heavy stick in his hand.[53]

In a short time this chapel also was ready to have Mass said in it. Again the monks made fleeting appearances in it.

On the morning of February 24, 1209, the day consecrated to Saint Matthias, Francis was in that chapel, listening to the Mass.[y]

A pallid ray of sun reflecting on the rough walls heralded a new spring, a coming sensed by the magic of trees putting forth new buds. Two years had passed since the day Francis had taken off his clothes before the bishop of Assisi.

The celebrant read the Gospel from the pages of the open Missal. His words went directly to Francis's heart. They rang out clear and distinct in the solitude of the wretched little church, totally unadorned, bare of all precious objects.

They were the instructions that Christ had given to his disciples on the eve of their preaching: "Provide yourselves with neither gold nor silver nor copper in your belts, no travelling bag, no change of shirt, no sandals, no walking staff. The workman, after all, is worth his keep."[54]

Francis listened in astonishment. Here, in the words of Christ, was described the road to truth he had discovered through hard experience. He resolved to obey the instructions in them to the letter. He flung away his shoes, put down his stick, and changed his belt for a cord.

The uniform of the Friar Minor was complete. And Francis's days of indecision were over. He was ready to go forward, a perfect knight, to win the world for his lord.

·7·

THE MEN OF PENITENCE
OF THE CITY OF ASSISI

In the spring of the year 1209 Silvestro, a canon of the cathedral of San Rufino, had a vision.[1]

The city of Assisi appeared to him in a dream, its walls completely encircled by an immense, ferocious, black dragon. The people had no hope of escape and were doomed to perish. (In the imagination of the Middle Ages, the dragon personified evil, and only holy warriors, supposedly, were able to fight against it. This dragon of Silvestro's dream was like the one described in the Book of Daniel, the enormous dragon that raged through the city of Babylon, which had rebelled against God and was immersed in every kind of sin: "There was a great dragon which the Babylonians worshipped."[2] We see in the accounts of the early biographers of Francis an insistent comparison between Babylon and Assisi, both corrupt and lost cities.)

And lo, the gates of the city were opened and a knight as alone and as brave as Saint George marched against the monster. With astonishment the priest Silvestro recognized him as the madman, the merchant's son, Francis. He remembered having given him a few stones one day for the restoration of San Damiano.[3]

In his dream the foolish beggar seemed to be playing the role of a paladin. He had no armour but his torn tunic, no helmet but a patched hood, no shield or lance. Out of his mouth came a cross of gold. It rose all the way to the sky, and the arms were stretched to the ends of the world. He did not ride on horseback but went forward lightly on bare feet, scarcely touching the earth. At his first shout the dragon fled, spreading his enormous scaly wings so that the city was completely darkened by them. Francis returned victorious into the city.

It was not difficult to guess the meaning of the vision. The city, held in evil, was near ruin, but Francis would lead it to salvation.

The situation symbolically depicted in the story finds full confirmation in the documents and in reports of contemporary writers. Thomas of Celano says that in this time Assisi was brutish and cruel, and that a kind of darkness had spread over everything, so that men could no longer distinguish between good and evil. "For so profound was the forgetfulness of God and the sleep of neglect of his commandments oppressing almost everyone that they could hardly be aroused even a little from their old and deeply rooted sins."[4]

This was the meaning of the cross of gold that came out of Francis's mouth. It was a symbol of the teaching of the Herald of the Great King, one that reached the ends of the earth and rose to the highest vaults of heaven.

The Greedy, Quarrelsome Clerics

An examination of the papers in Assisi archives dating from the time of Saint Francis also verifies that grave disorders existed in the public and private life of the city.

Innocent III (who intended to restore the complete temporal rule of the church) could not have had a more faithful executor than the bishop of Assisi. In Guido, strong and energetic, episcopal power was once again linked with old unlimited aspirations for material riches.

The papacy reached its greatest splendour at the beginning of the thirteenth century. The prestige of the Holy Roman Empire had been diminished with the death of Henry VI, and the dominant authority in Italy and the western Empire became that of the church.

For all that, no other period was so afflicted by such a swarm of heresies. The Catharist and Waldensian sects denied the authority of Catholic priests, contending that Jesus had entrusted to every man the divine power that was the foundation of the authority of the clergy. The lax morals and corruption of priests contributed to the spread of such beliefs.

To have an idea of the gravity of these abuses, one has only to see them listed in documents of the church councils of the period. The Fourth Lateran Council, convoked in 1215 by Innocent III, registers and condemns, among others, these abuses: "Many priests have lived luxuriously. They have passed the time in drunken revels, neglecting religious rites. When they have been at Mass, they have chatted about commercial affairs. They have left churches and tabernacles in an indecent state, sold posts and sacraments, promoted ignorant and unworthy people to the clerical state, though they had others better suited for it. Many bishops have appropriated the income of a parish for themselves, leaving the parish indigent. They have gone to the enormous abuse of forcing parishioners to make special payments so as to have still more income. They have extorted money from the faithful on every pretext. They have made a scandalous commerce of relics. They have allowed the illegitimate children of a canon to succeed the father in the benefice."[5]

We have already had occasion to examine the unremitting warfare waged in Assisi by Bishop Guido against those who struck at the church, but the critics became bolder every day. Certainly to this period must be dated the obligation laid upon the podestà at the moment that he assumed office, "to swear war without mercy against the heretics and the sodomites and the Patarines and to throw them out of the commune territory."[a] In an epistle of May 1198 directed to "the venerable brother Guidone, Bishop of Assisi," Innocent reaffirmed his firm intent to support bishops in their claims and "with paternal solicitude to provide for the churches in their care."[6] And he furthermore ordered that "all the goods that the church possessed, or would acquire in the future with the help of God, must remain in the hands of the Bishop of Assisi and his successors."

To safeguard the farms, courts, castles, vineyards, and forests that constituted the enormous patrimony of the diocese, Innocent III did not hesitate to threaten to excommunicate those who were bold enough to try to usurp them: "Under penalty of interdict, we prohibit whatever feudal lord, and every other person, to take away through violence, robbery, or fraud, or to subtract or alienate, those lands and possessions that belong now to the churches and the monasteries of your diocese or that will be duly conferred upon it in the future."

But Guido relies more on his imperious and violent temperament

---

a. Statutes, L. I, rub. 6. The accusation of sodomy was made especially of the Waldenses. Followers of Peter of Waldo and early known as "the poor men of Lyons," they at first practiced and preached poverty and the apostolic life; later they split into many branches with many differing practices and beliefs. Sabatier says, "Many vile stories have been told of the Waldenses; calumny is far too facile a weapon not to tempt an adversary at bay. Thus they have been charged with the same indecent promiscuities of which the early Christians were accused." (*Life,* trans. Houghton, chap. 3.)

In Italy the Catharists were known as the Patarini. Quite different from the Waldenses, theirs was essentially a Manichaen and Gnostic doctrine resting on belief in two opposing principles of good and evil; and they defined all material things as evil. Hence, they renounced marriage and property and advocated suicide, especially through starvation. After the advent of Franciscanism [and after a merciless war against them], they all but disappeared. For a description of the sects, see Sabatier, *Vie,* chap. 3; also Tocco, *L'eresia nel medioevo.* The penalty for heretics in the Assisi statutes was left entirely up to the podestà (L. III, rub. 21).

than on sanctions of a spiritual nature. His tendency is to attack rather than be on the defensive. His episcopate is full of litigations, causes, libels, arbitrations, pronouncements, sentences. On occasion, carried away by his anger, he goes down to the piazza and comes to blows with an antagonist.

Even the gloomy rooms of the leper hospital under the direction of the Crucifer Knights echo with his shouts, as when in a noisy fight he attacks the clerics over some wine in their possession. The decretals of Honorius III tell us that he high-handedly took the wine away from them; and when they protested, he went to the place, the Ospedale di San Salvatore delle Pareti, and brutally knocked them about.[7]

Several times the pope had occasion to recall him to moderation and to the observance of norms set by the councils. At times he also reproved him for his greed, which had led him to make a scene even around the biers of the faithful departed over his right to a percentage of the payment for the obsequies. In fact, in 1216, he got into a quarrel with the Benedictine monks of Mount Subasio about his claim to jurisdiction over churches dependent on the monastery and to the right to the *quarta funeraria,* the part of the funeral offering [customary at the time] that belonged to the bishop.[8] The litigation was long and violent. There were many harsh arguments, and in the course of them Honorius III took the opportunity to reprimand Bishop Guido for his never-sated appetite for new income and revenues.[9]

The desire to be first in dignity, in rights, in the ecclesiastical regulations, kept all the clerics in a stir.

The canons of San Rufino took up the struggle against their bishop with ever-growing vigour. They claimed the right to ordain without his participation[10] and the right to the tithes.

The ferocity of their quarrel is documented by a record in the cathedral archives, hitherto unknown, the judgement handed down in March 1217 by the arbiters of these controversies, Ugolino, cardinal bishop of Ostia and the future Gregory IX, and Cincio, cardinal of San Lorenzo in Lucina. The bishop and the canons of the cathedral had decided to submit their differences to arbitration in a compromise agreed upon in August of 1216.[11]

"The prior and the canons," asserts Bishop Guido, "shall promise the bishop obedience and shall observe the reverence due him and shall be subject to him in the selection of clerics and canons. And they shall take care not to renew quarrels or rebellious acts in order to deprive the bishop of half the offerings on the days on which he officiates in the cathedral, that is, Christmas, Epiphany, Ash Wednesday, Holy Week and Easter, the Rogations, Pentecost, the day of the dedication of the church of the Patron Saint, and the feast of Saint Rufinus.

"And they shall give him the donations unjustly held back, and the fourth part of the tithes, as is established in the sacred canons. And finally, they shall cease their high-handed tyranny over chapels and clerics over which they claim the right of patronage (the right to confer ecclesiastical offices or benefices), since in reality they can claim nothing."

The prior, goaded by the angry canons, retorts sharply and violently.

"It is an enormity that it is Bishop Guido himself who dares to take the shares of the churches dependent on San Rufino and to protest high-handed acts of the canons, he who has never left off harassing in every way possible the chapels of this diocese and their priests.

"Would you say, then, that it was in observance of the holy canons that he excommunicated Uguccione, who had appealed his sentence, and refused to follow the rulings of the bishop of Nocera, to whose arbitration he had declared he would submit? Would you say whether it was decorous that he consult lawless and meddling parishioners over the confirmation of clerics?

"He, who talks of moderation, usurped the canons' share of the mortuary portion of the church of San Venanzo, took away the Eucharistic offerings, and did not wish to make restitution of the expenses that the canons had incurred for his benefit on the day of the Resurrection.

"Would you say if it is also in the holy canons that he should demand overpayment to consecrate priests and churches? And whether it is just that he refuses to contribute to the expenses that have been or are to be made for the restoration of the church of San Rufino?"

It was the age-old argument, prolonged and grown sharper.

August 17, 1216, Bishop Guido and the prior of San Rufino, together with the canons Tebaldo, Bartolo, Greco, Crescenzio, Eugenio, Guarnerio, Giovanni, and Burgondione, meet in San Rufino and decide to submit the various controversies to the judgement of the two cardinals, "in the kiss of faith, true peace, and love." Present at the solemn pact are the most influential citizens: Carsedonio, Torrigiano, Leonardo Senzamercede, Rinaldo di Soverchia, Manfredino, and many others.

The arbiters seek to curb all this greed and pride. They assign one-third of the donations to the bishop—and he, they order, must content himself with that, *et illa sit ipse contentus.* They order the restitution of half the sequestered tithes. They do their best to distribute the money given in offerings between the bishop and the canons in a manner compatible with the fear of God, *cum timore Domini.* They rule that the canons are to be free to select their chaplains, provided the selection is confirmed by the bishop. They enjoin the bishop not to oppose the canons' exactions of homages and [feudal] services and the canons to do the same in respect to the bishop, exhorting all, however, to be reasonable in their demands so that the exactions will not impoverish and exhaust the patrimony of the churches. They prohibit the bishop without the canons, or the canons without the bishop, from selling and leasing things belonging to the church, including the valuable furnishings and those things destined for the divine offices. And finally, they prohibit the bishop from exacting remunerations for the conferring of sacraments, other than a modest recompense.

Rebellious Monks, Avaricious Merchants, Nobles Sinfully Proud

In this same time, the abbots of the smaller monasteries were rebelling against the large monasteries that claimed jurisdiction over them.

Here, for example, is an untidy brawl of which we have a record.[12]

The monastery of Sant'Apollinare del Sambro, located on the hills beyond Cannara in territory belonging to Assisi, had been put under the powerful monastery of Sassovivo with a bull of Pope Pascal II in 1115.[13] In the period of which we speak, however, the prior of Sant'Apollinare had proclaimed his independence, supported by some Assisi citizens. He now assumed the title of abbot of Sant'Angelo di Limigiano and was governing as a lord, free from every obligation of vassalage.

The two groups continued their bitter quarrel until Innocent III in 1208 ordered the rebel monks to return and make their proper submission to the abbot of Sassovivo. Notification and execution of the pontifical action was entrusted to the same bishop of Assisi, Guido, along with Giovanni, bishop of Perugia, and Egidio, bishop of Foligno.

They set out, accompanied by a large group of chancellors and chaplains, to fulfill their mission.

"While we were on the way," they report in a letter to Innocent III, "Enrico of the Rocca di Pizio and V., son of Pietro, an Assisi man, drew their swords and, with other armed men and certain of their cutthroats, fell upon us, putting us to flight and striking us on the head with swords and wounding our horses to death and also those of our clerics, in such a way that it is a miracle we were not killed. And they seized Master Filippo, chaplain to the bishop of Perugia, and had him taken away by two mercenaries, who dragged him all the way to the aforesaid Rocca, making him ignominiously go on foot for a good two miles, and held him prisoner for a time, and have not yet restored to him his cloak and hat."

The letter concludes with a request for the punishment of the prior of Sant'Apollinare, "who is author and leader of this ambush and this crime."

It was the sort of thing that reflected the state of mind of all the clergy. Preoccupied by donations and offerings, they constantly confounded the sacred and the profane, ready always to promise vigil lights and to say prayers in exchange for mills and vineyards.

"And if anyone tries to contest this possession with the church, he shall be cursed like Dathan and Abiram, who perished by being swallowed up alive by the earth."[14] Thus thundered the prior of San Rufino in an anathema written into a legal paper concerning a donation to the church. In many other legal contracts it was ordered that the price or the tribute or tax be placed on top the high altar over the tomb of the martyr, Saint Rufinus.[15]

The prior and the canons were continually before the judge to argue about fields and olive groves.[16] One of the canons, Silvestro, who would be among the first companions of Saint Francis, was said by the early biographers to have been especially guilty of such sins. We have already seen him in a dispute over other lands, such as an Agnano forest and vineyard.[17] He was described [by Thomas of Celano] as a man of "ravenous avarice."[18]

The same thing could be said about those of all social classes. The struggle between the nobles and the people—was it not fought for the conquest of wealth? The noble classes, the *buoni uomini,* were afflicted with *fiscalismo,* merciless money-grabbing. The merchants were obsessed with getting their share of the pie, and more. The men of the people were filled with an insatiable ambition to rise in the world no matter how.

It is clear that in the struggle between the two social classes of Assisi the pact of 1203 is nothing, after all, but an agreement to join together for the conquest of material gain, to the detriment of other classes and other people. "And thus we say that all the citizens of Assisi must help each other maintain all their goods and their things and their rights and their way of life and possessions that they have and that they shall acquire . . . ."[19] It does not, as is often thought, deal with an ideological movement. It is purely economic. "And whoever, noble or other person, of our city is entitled to collect revenues or whatever else from another city or *castello* or from any man outside our jurisdiction, all the people of the city are bound to help him come into possession of it."[20]

War thus becomes inevitable. It is the very life of the commune.

Again we cite the great Italian historian, Ferrari: "For the people of the cities, war is a natural, universal fact, almost without starting point, inseparable from liberty, contemporaneous with the consuls. To end it, it would have been necessary to overthrow the consuls, put an end to the great councils, obey the bishop, recall the *marchese*, proclaim a native king, renounce every aspiration, every prospect, in this plethora of prosperity seeking an outlet. And no one complains about war, not a groan, not a murmur. The royal cities themselves, wounded, sick, exhausted in the middle of the fray, far from sighing over memories of the realm, a thousand times over prefer war, in which their very pain makes them feel the happiness of existence, to the sepulchral peace of the ancient kingdom in which they were without life, without will, without liberty, as lost as unconscious viscera in an immense body."[21]

Thus the principal explanation of the conflict of peoples was their opposing material desires. "The political economy governed all the battles. Its calculations measured the anger, dispensed the furors, ruled over those unfathomable psychic currents that unleashed multitudes of Italians, one against another. These struggles were all subordinated to the income and expenditures, the debit and the credit, the capital and the speculations, of the merchants who chose the consuls."[22]

Pride was the second great sin of the time, after avarice.

First, there was the pride of the noble classes, an arrogance consecrated by the prestige of titles, by the traditions of the military arts, by chivalry.

Chivalry itself was the exaltation of ungovernable pride. To consider one's own person and one's own honour as sacred things, to demand cruel redress for every glance or gesture or word that might be interpreted as disrespectful, to do incredible things for a point of honour—these are among the first rules of chivalry.

When this pride is offended, nothing but blood can cleanse the stain. Each lack of respect brings this kind of redress. Judicial contests are considered "good for peasants but not for men-at-arms, acceptable to a jurist but not to one who puts his law in his sword."[23] The wars between the *castelli* and the cities often have no reason other than someone's wounded ego, an offended dignity.

And the pride of the people was born in antagonism to that of the feudal lords. They held themselves to be the resurrected Latin people, that people believed to be dead, but now fiercely rising, searching among the ruins for the sword of the Roman legionnaires.

Perhaps the young merchant son of Pietro Bernardone grieved over nothing more bitterly than his sin of pride, which the biographers defined as his "greed for glory."

When later he wished to inflict great punishment on himself before his brothers, he found no better way than to make himself face up to the humiliation of his origin. "Peasant merchant," he wished the brothers to call him.[24] During his secular life, his inferior status as "the son of Pietro Bernardone"—which even Dante put into his canto—had perhaps been thrown into his face as the bitterest of insults. Was not his whole youth full of this kind of thing?

Pride, in fact, is to become the principle on which all the factions will find they can agree. It will be the basis of a pact in 1210, in which all will swear to act together "for the grandeur of the commune and the power of all the citizens," *pro honore et salute et augmento Comunis Asisii.*[25]

This new pact shows us clearly, as did the old agreement of 1203, that civil war is not really at an end.

The two social classes remained armed, one against the other. The *maiores* are against the *minores,*[26] the nobles against the people, the *milites* against the *pedites.* The feudal lords, who have been vanquished in the country and been forced to come into the city, do not renounce combat. The dualism remains, the formulae appear empty abstractions, the ancient quarrel, determined by pride and wealth, becomes ever sharper.

The nobles despise and deride the conceit of the *nouveaux riches.* "'You see this consul,' says the great lord; 'his father begged at the doors of my castle. Look at that senator; he always falsified the bills. Notice that Cato; he robs all of us in his shop.' And epigrams of heroic comedy origin rain down upon the city people for the diversion of the knights."[27]

The nobles understand well enough that the time has now passed in which victory depends on the trustworthiness of a good sword and they finally acquiesce to the new times, in which money controls war. "The new struggle is blind and endless, like municipal war. Earlier, the people of the city could always count on their ability to destroy the *castelli.* The center was protected by the laws of war. Radiating outward (in aggressive tactics) assured them of victory over the unorganized structures in the countryside. But the day had come when they had to fight other things—the influence of riches, the feudalism of capital, the power of money, the prestige of great families, the unexpected alliances that the feudal aristocracy used to turn against the city in the name of a liberty greater than city liberty and democracy ever more drastic. Money can be captured by money, the pocketbook by the pocketbook, revenue by revenue."[28]

"And the Blood Flowed"

Moral, political, and economic misdeeds were rampant in both the public and private life of the commune.

We have the list of people of the city on whom a ban had been proclaimed[b] in the last years of the life of Saint Francis and in the years immediately following his death.

It is now a period in which the city is past the frightful anarchy into which it had been plunged by the civil war, and the government has begun to take shape. And yet, in the old records a great crowd, all sorts and conditions of men, all irate, greedy, and violent, comes to life, goes about nefarious deeds. In vain the podestà multiplies the sentences, cries out public condemnations, prepares the gallows, puts the convicted into the pillory. (It is the same pillory to which one day Francis will insist on being led, drawn with a rope like a criminal, to accuse himself of faults before the people.[29])

Futilely the podestà orders the most barbarous tortures for criminals. He cuts out the tongues of liars. He cuts off the right hands of forgers and the feet of looters. He has poisoners and those convicted of sodomy burned. He orders the quartering of traitors, who are dragged to their execution through the streets of the city at the tail of a horse and afterwards hung up in pieces on each of the gates of the city, one-fourth of the body to a gate. He blinds notorious thieves, brands them on the forehead with a red-hot iron, hangs them on the

---

b. As noted in chap. 5, n. b, a person banned was declared to be outside the law and had to be excluded from every social relationship and protection of society.

In medieval Assisi, a person accused of a crime was ordered by a crier to present himself to the podestà for judgement. If he failed to show up or, appearing, was fined or penalized and failed to pay in whatever form was required, he was *posti al bando*—the sentence of the ban was pronounced against him. His name was read out in public assembly; his goods were sequestrated; and everyone was forbidden to give him shelter, asylum, or aid of any kind, under the threat of heavy penalties.

The ban was lifted if the accused presented himself and paid the penalty to which he had been sentenced. (Fines were the usual penalty in the early medieval period, even for homicide.) If he did not pay within a stated period (usually a year), his goods were confiscated or destroyed; the penalties were greatly increased and often included corporal punishment; and a permanent ban might be declared. Lists of these *exhanditi*, classified according to pecuniary penalties or corporal punishment, were kept by the communal government and read out at intervals at citizen assemblies, as a reminder that no one must have anything to do with them. For a complete discussion, see *NV* 3:209–12.

gallows of the large towers on the Spello road and the road below Valecchie.

We hear, in a notation to the *Major Life of Saint Francis* by Saint Bonaventure, the desperate cry of a thief condemned by the judge Ottaviano for a crime of which he is not guilty. He recommends himself to Saint Francis for his salvation while he is being dragged to unspeakable torture by order of the podestà Ottone. The executioner takes time to poke about in the eye sockets of the condemned man with a knife, shell out his eyes, and throw them on the ground. The spectators, indulging their lust for blood, roll those poor dead eyeballs in the dust with sticks.

The people are present at the execution of death sentences. It is the custom to revel in the blood of the executed and, with no more feeling than wild beasts, drink in their agonies.

These are the same citizens who, when summoned by the podestà as for a ceremonious assembly, carry out his instructions to tear down the *castello* that rebels against the commune, according to the rule written into the statutes: "It must be cleared out and demolished and destroyed to the foundation, in such a fashion that the stones of the bottom are on the top and that never more can it be rebuilt."

They also destroy the houses of the condemned so that these, too, may never be rebuilt. They lay waste the fields that had belonged to them. To perpetuate the shame and infamy, they see to it that these fields remain sterile and uncultivated, everlasting evidence of the old crime.

Still, crime does not cease.

Everywhere, in the streets, in the piazzas, in the houses, one hears of murder. At night, after the bell has sounded for the third time and the people of the city are forbidden to go out of their houses, there are killers concealed under passageways at the mouths of dark and narrow alleys, waiting for their intended victims. Each morning the night custodians find bodies in the streets. Sometimes a house will suddenly go up in flames in a treacherous attempt to make enemies perish in an especially horrible way.

Gangs of killers even attack in full day on public roads. "Paolo, Pietro, Angelino, sons of Giovanni di Graziano from Castelnuovo," we read in one of the sentences of the podestà, "because they were charged and accused by Armagnenzia, daughter of messer Giovanni d'Ugolino, and by Leta, wife of the late Ventura, also daughter of Giovanni, of killing messer Ventura; and because they fled and remained contumacious; and because cited by us in their habitation after the death of the aforesaid Ventura, did not appear; their contumacy declared, we condemn them and pronounce against them the sentence of the ban and of the destruction of all their goods. We declare that they shall never be able to return to the city nor be given quarter until they have paid the commune of Assisi the sum of three hundred *libbre* of money.[30]

The nobles are always ready to raise their swords. Magistrates and envoys of the commune are insulted, struck in the public piazza, threatened with death, mocked, murdered.

"Graziano di Carlengo," (the sentence is by messer Berlengario, podestà in 1226) "because he killed Benvenuto di Berta di Gellio, *baiolo* of the commune, is sentenced to the destruction of his goods to the amount prescribed in the statutes; and because he did not pay, is sentenced to the ban and fined two hundred *libbre*."[31]

The magistrates, exasperated, allow themselves in turn to be drawn into the fray.

There are angry rows everywhere. Brawlers grab each other by the hair, knock each other down, roll about in the middle of the street. "Bartoluccio di Baroncello, because he grabbed Leonardo di Scagno di Raino by a foot and dragged him and kicked him, is sentenced to the ban; and because he did not pay, fined three *libbre*."[32]

There is always blood. After seven centuries the old records give us a bitter inkling of that fact, with the phrase that the judge does not neglect to write down to attest the gravity of the crime: *Et sanguis exivit,* "and blood flowed." When the people of the city, moved by a hard act of penitence by Saint Francis, confess their gravest sin in a loud voice in the public piazza, they will say over and over, stingingly: "Woe to us miserable ones, whose whole life is spent in blood!"[33] No one is respected, not even women and priests.

We read of arrows let fly, stones thrown, doors of houses split open with hatchets. Bared weapons glitter through the pages of the statutes, unsheathed in the market-place and even during solemn proceedings of the city council—swords, daggers, Spanish cutlasses, sharpened knives.

Suspicion robs the people of sleep. In fear one keeps a sword ready over the bolster. Robbery is common. Thieves enter houses, tie the hands of the residents, steal the livestock of farmers.

The Patron Saint, who once saved the farmer who was robbed of his cattle, sees the thieves go about with impunity among the columns of the very crypt in which his holy relics rest. Berta Olivana, the woman known as Lupaticia, the Wolf-Bitch, because of her ever-unsatisfied sexual appetite, steals the oil of the lamp that burns over the bones of Saint Rufinus, Martyr Bishop.[34]

Unfaithfulness and Violence

Deceit and immorality can be found everywhere. Episodes of rape and other violence to women are countless. Adultery, incest, and promiscuity are common. The names of sensual and bold women appear in the records: Brunetta, paramour of Guidone di Monaldo; Letizia, paramour of Simeone di Scagno, potter; Colata, paramour of Coppo. And many others—Grazia, Amata, Materosa, Fidanza. After the third sound of the bell[c] we see these women stir, eluding the vigilance of the night watchmen.

In fact, some very strange miracles are attributed to the Patron Saint himself. A girl, Berta, daughter of Ermanno, is accused by her own relatives of having sinned with a man and they threaten to kill her. She can think of nothing to do but to go to the church of San Rufino and immerse her bare arm in a cauldron of boiling oil. Thanks to the saint, she withdraws it unhurt to prove her innocence.

Another miracle is so curious that we prefer to report it in a literal translation:

"There was a German woman called Giunta, who, after the death of her husband, took a vow of chastity to God. In order to subdue the petulance of the flesh, she had her abdomen encircled with an iron hoop. For three years she had recourse to many saints. Finally, after returning from a journey to Rome, while she was lying in bed one night and beginning to go to sleep, she heard a voice advising her to go to the church of the Holy Martyr because God was pleased to liberate her from that hoop. After having heard this, the woman, who had heard much talk about wonders in Assisi, went there. She entered the church of the Martyr on the Saturday before the feast of Christmas while the canons were reciting vespers. Immediately the iron hoop broke in two parts and fell to the ground. The bystanders who had come into the church to pray saw it."[35]

All this fits Thomas of Celano's gloomy picture at the beginning of his *First Life:* parents who by example and threats become teachers of lasciviousness to their own children, people given to every kind of dissolution. And, as a matter of fact, later the people of the city will meet in assembly in the piazza and accuse themselves, in the presence of Saint Francis, of unbridled lust.[36]

On the roads of the *contado,* flocks of rogues attacked travellers.

---

c. The "third sound of the bell" was two hours after nightfall. The statutes prohibited the bell's being rung after that time until dawn; and during those hours all were to remain within their own houses, or at least no more than three houses distant, and if one had to be on the streets, a light was required for each three persons. These rules were suspended during the gathering of the grapes and at harvest time. NV 3:216.

Unpaid soldiers evened scores by raiding and looting. Men of the commune despoiled weaker communes in an effort to conquer and enslave them.

We have, for instance, the arbiters' ruling made in the war between Assisi and Bettona in 1223.

Giacomo di Anastasio, syndic, and Jeronimo, consul, of the commune of Bettona, on one side and Angelo di Pietro di Peppone, syndic of the commune of Assisi, on the other, submit the dispute to the podestà of Assisi, Carsedonio, so that he may decide "about the discord and the war and the other things and the damages caused and every other fact, between the communes of Assisi and Bettona."

One can well imagine what the nature of this decision will be. Carsedonio will nail down in every way possible the yoke imposed on the conquered commune. Bettona is compelled to renounce every exception to the fact that the decision is being made by a judge who is himself a plaintiff in the case. It must promise that it will not bring actions for crimes and damages it has sustained in any clerical or lay court. It pledges to make war against Assisi's enemies and peace with her friends and promises to select its podestà and its consuls from among the people of Assisi. These officials, as soon as they are elected, will make an appearance in Assisi with ten knights and ten infantrymen, chosen at the discretion of the conqueror, to receive orders.[37]

The same men who have bloodied the streets of the city since the time of Francis's youth play a part in this never-ending turmoil, and their sons inherit the old evils: Marescotto di Bernardo, Ugolino di Pietro, the son of Monaldo, the son of Gilio di Marco, Giacomo.[38]

According to the Three Companions, it seemed that all of existence had been reduced to three evil forces: "temptations of the flesh, cupidity of the world, and pride of life."[39]

But—on another side—beyond imagining was the misery and desolation, the degradation, pain and fear, of an unbelievable number of men and women with physical deformities and suffering terrible pain. We find some of them in stories of the early thirteenth century miracles of Saint Rufinus.

Certainly Francis would recognize them and call them by name, as he did when he met them along the dusty streets or looked at them prostrate before the altar of the Martyr. There was Broccardo, the cripple of the hospital of San Rufino; Berta, the epileptic; Savia, possessed by demons; Alberto, the dropsical; Beccario's daughter, Rita, the ulcerated; Gasdia and Doda, ill with fever; Benvegnate d'Albaguerra, the scrofulous; Guidone, the leperous priest.

It is said that Guidone had already decided to commit himself to the lepers' hospital and resign himself to his sad fate, when, in touching the relics of Saint Rufinus, his wounds were healed and his flesh became as clean and smooth as that of a child.[40]

The First Companions

No one knows the name of Francis's first companion.[41] The biographers limit themselves to saying that he was a simple and pious man who followed Francis with great devotion. He made a declaration of faith, knelt at Francis's feet, and an instant later was gone, caught up in the vortex of worldly affairs.

He never appears again in the early biographies. And yet this mysterious figure, whose face we cannot see, is to be counted among the personages of the Franciscan drama. He is a symbol of the anonymous human beings who, at a call, stop for an instant and open their hearts to the great sorrow in the world and then turn away.

Therefore, all the historians recognize as Francis's first companion another man of Assisi, one from the *contrada* of San Gregorio—Bernardo, son of Quintavalle di Berardello.

Bernardo was one of the most respected men of the *maggiori,* not only for his nobility and wealth, but, above all, for his learning. Since he held degrees in both civil and canon law, his advice was held in great esteem by all the people of the city in both public and private matters.[d] The family (we have a record of two brothers, Giovanni and Marzio) owned land in Colderba (a little hill overlooking the Tescio River a short distance above the bridge of San Vittorino), bordering that of the powerful *signore* of the *contrada* of San Rufino, Ugo di Tebalduccio. They also had olive groves in Mululla, the present hill of Viole, beside the cathedral close. One of his nephews was the podestà's judge in this first half of the thirteenth century.

Bernardo, who in his prudence searched for the reason for everything, straight and crooked, good and evil, wise and foolish, had not been able to understand the change in the merchant's son. The humil-

---

d. Records in the cathedral archives prove that the name Quintavalle is a family name, not a place name, as many biographers have thought. There is no doubt that the Quintavalle di Berardello mentioned in the text was Bernardo's father, given the medieval practice of giving a son the name of his paternal grandfather; and the identification is even more certain from the fact that Bernardo was obviously of a well-to-do family. The family must have continued to be a prominent one in Assisi for a long time; the tomb of a Nicolò Roscio di Quintavalle in the Basilica di San Francesco is mentioned in a list made in 1509. The tradition that his house is a part of the later Sbaraglini palazzo was first mentioned by Ludovico da Pietralunga in the sixteenth century (*Guida,* 8). Fra Ludovico also said a room still existed in which Bernardo watched Francis praying, using only the words, "My God and my all." For a description of all the records and sources pertaining to the identification of Bernardo and his family, *NV* 2:273–76.

ity with which Francis bore the jeers of the people astonished him. It was neither cowardice nor insanity, but something that escaped him, something that somehow gave him the feeling of a hidden grandeur. He decided, therefore, as was his habit, to look into the matter.

One evening he invited Francis to his house. It was early April of 1209.

Bernardo's house stood within the bishop's citadel. A portion of it can still be seen, its windows now walled up, standing among other centuries-old houses, its arches of rose-coloured stone (of recent construction) like reminders of ancient gaiety in their contrast to the dark colour of the façade. There used to be a piazza in front of the house called the piazza of San Gregorio. Later, a large, austere, sixteenth-century palazzo was built on the site, on the line of the old structure.

Across from Bernardo's house is the church of San Gregorio.[e] Dating from the same period, it is supported on Roman blocks that crop through the surface at the side of the street. It is reached from the Piazza del Comune by an alleyway that goes down among ancient houses that are warmed by the flames of carnations. Clumps of wild flowers climb all the way up the rough wood canopy of the majesty on the side of the church, wreathing the painted image of the Virgin in a glory renewed every season. We are in the heart of the old Roman city, where every now and then in a placid garden the pickaxe brings to light a bit of pavement decorated with scenes from old legends, pretty mosaics from a peristyle, fantastic figures, fragments of columns. Dreams and memories flutter through the peace of the narrow and tortuous street, which is lined by walled-up doors of ancient shops that one time rang with the work of artisans.

That evening the two sat down to dinner. The old leader of the Tripudianti was in the place of honour at an elaborately laid table where roses in silver vases exhaled their fragrance among the delicate foods and cups filled to the brim. Francis once again found the joy of the chivalrous knight and his old troubadour's fire. He talked in romantic terms about his adventurous life. All the ideals of his youth had been fulfilled, beyond every hope. He had won rule over the ornate castle that he had desired, the one with banners blowing in the wind and swords gleaming. A powerful king had chosen him his herald in all the lands of the realm. The richest and most beautiful lady had become his bride. Many knights would come to him in a

---

e. This church was not the San Gregorio seen today, which was built in the thirteenth century, but an earlier one, situated a little above it. *NV* 3:26–27.

little while, and he, with his valiant band, would go on to conquer the world.

Listening and watching with penetrating eyes, Bernardo felt his heart opening. For the first time he caught a vision of a new kind of world, and his previous life suddenly seemed an abyss at which he looked back in astonishment. How had he been able to live as he had? How had he, so blind and ignorant, claimed to be the master of his own destiny, not to speak of having been presumptuous enough to give advice to others?

The servants, standing immobile behind the scarcely touched table, listened in amazement to the man in the ragged tunic who spoke in such passionate language, so full of hidden meaning.

They rose, finally, to go to bed. Bernardo had ordered that a bed for Francis be prepared in his own room. But they did not sleep; they could not sleep. They were both filled with an eager happiness— Francis because of his joyous certainty and his pleasure in telling of it, Bernardo from listening to the wonderful words, asking questions, and considering truth hitherto unknown to him.

Lighted candles cast a dream-like light over these two men, who once could talk together only of war and conquests, power, nobility, and riches. Outside the windows the enchantment of a spring night held the city in a spell, its silence scarcely broken by the footfalls of the guards who passed and repassed at intervals, keeping watch.

Dawn drew near. A light breeze bent the flames and seemed to break the spell and recall each to reality. This time it was Bernardo who asked advice, putting his query in the juridical form that was familiar to him. He said to Francis, "A servant has certain goods from his lord. He has held them for many years. Now he wishes to give them up. What should he do? What is the best course for him to follow?"

Francis replied, "Certainly he should restore them to his *padrone*."

Bernardo concluded, "Then, my brother, all my substance, for love of our Lord who entrusted these things to me, I wish to restore to him, in the way that seems most appropriate to you."

They knew now the ideal they wished to follow. It remained to find how to practice it in everyday life, to lead others to know and follow it. They thought that another doctor of laws in Assisi, Pietro di Catanio, with whom Francis had held a long discussion some days previously, might join them. They left the house before the first stroke of the morning bell and went to the *contrada* of San Rufino, where Pietro lived. They called him and they all set out together.

Pietro's family was also one of the most highly regarded in the city, both for its aristocratic lineage and wealth.[f] There is a reference to Pietro's father, Catanio di Guiduccio, in the same cathedral document of 1188 in which the Quintavalle properties are named. There are several references to a brother, Tebaldo, in the records. He was present in 1223 at the treaty of alliance between the commune and the Perugini warrior class and along with his son, Guiduccio, who had his grandfather's name, was listed among the prominent men of the commune in 1233 and 1235. We also know his paternal uncles: Pietro (father of another Guiduccio), Matteo, and Giovanni (father of Angelo).

God's Word Makes a Rule

They crossed the piazza. Some shops were opening their doors, some shopkeepers arranging their counters. One of the watchmen of the commune opened the massive lock of the chain that barred the street of the Badìa *contrada* at night and fastened it to the supports on the nearby tower.

They entered the church of San Nicolò. Francis knew the priest well. He asked him to bring the book of the Gospels and put it, closed, on the reading stand on top of the altar. The priest went up the steps, then turned to the companions, who were kneeling. He would open the Gospels three times, and thus the will of God would be made known to them.

They rose after a short prayer. Francis's look embraced that church of his infancy and youth, where his heart had been opened to the revelation of grace. All his past life returned now to trouble his spirit in this moment of knowing his new destiny and that of the brothers God had sent him.

The morning light streamed through one of the high oval windows. A lamp burned over the stone slabs of the floor. Francis recognized the burial place where many of his elders slept in peace. He thought

---

f. Pietro is described as a canon of the cathedral of San Rufino in several sources, including *Spec. Perf.*, 61, and *24 Generals* (AF 3:4). However, in the extensive collection of cathedral records from that period, including the lists of canons, his name is nowhere to be found. It is not mentioned in *Per.*, 39, despite the similarity of the passage to the one in *Spec. Perf.*; and *Per.* is unquestionably the earlier source. So this seems to be an error, despite the fact that he is also called a canon in one passage of the Lectionary of the cathedral, in which there is a story of a miracle attributed to Saint Rufinus. It must have been a later addition to the text. In Giordano, *Chronica*, 11, he is called a doctor of law. In any case, all these references in the most reliable of our sources surely indicate he was a learned and able man and calls into question the picture of him in *3 Soc.*, 29, and *Anon. Per.*, 11, as a simple or even unlettered man. The suggestion by some recent biographers that he was a canon of the church of San Nicolò has no historical basis. There were no canons at this church. See *NV* 2:276–80.

of his family that was beginning its work-day a few steps away—his father, his brother, the mother he had abandoned.

The first time the book opened to those words of Christ that define true perfection. The priest read them in a loud voice, slowly.

If you seek perfection, go, sell your possessions, and give to the poor. You will then have treasure in heaven.

A period of silence followed. The book was closed and again opened. On the page was the exhortation of Jesus to his apostles.

Take nothing on the way.

The third time, the Gospels fell open to the secret of highest love.

If a man wishes to come after me, he must deny his very self.

God had spoken, confirming their thought. Francis said to those two first disciples: "Brothers, this is our life and our rule and that of all who are going to want to enter our company. And, therefore, go and fulfill everything that you have heard."[g]

Bernardo made haste to sell all his properties. It was necessary to undergo once again the formalities used to protect exclusive rights to earthly goods: the notary's bench (perhaps it was that notary Giovanni who drew up the majority of the legal papers of the time), the disputes about price, the participation of witnesses, the proper wording of the formulae.

---

g. [It is very probable that the book consulted by Francis and his first companions is still in existence and is at the Walters Art Gallery of Baltimore.

The book in question is a missal, dated by experts in paleography as of the late twelfth century. The fact that it is a missal rather than the Gospels alone by no means rules it out; like others of the time, it has only the Gospel passages rather than all the readings for the Mass, and thus a good two-thirds of it is made up of Gospel passages. The words "Gospels" and "missal" were frequently used interchangeably at the time. It contains the passages that Francis took as the rule for his new order.

Significant facts that have stirred interest in it include these: it is dedicated to Saint Rufinus, patron of Assisi, and lists the local feast days for Rufinus and for his son, Cesidio. It was made for a church dedicated to Saint Nicholas (San Nicolò) as a gift from a benefactor named (in the Latin form) Girardus Ugonis. There was indeed a Girardo di Ugone living in Assisi at the time; his name appears on at least two records in the cathedral archives (fasc. 2, nos. 129 and 132), one dated 1177, the other 1180. Fortini describes Girardo and traces his family; he succeeded in locating his father, grandfather, two brothers, and a nephew (*NV* 3:200). It was clearly written after 1172, because it lists the feast day of Saint Thomas of Canterbury, who was canonized that year, but before 1228, when Saint Francis was canonized. There are handwritten additions in the margins on October 4 ("S. Franciscus Confessor") and on July 30 ("Guido Episcops obiit 1228").

Don Aldo Brunacci, a distinguished Assisi historian, writes about it, "To me it seems there is no doubt. The missal surely belonged to the Church of San Nicolò *iuxta plateam civitatis Assisii*. It was in use during Saint Francis's youth. It is unthinkable that a little church could have had more than one missal for its use, because liturgical books, written by hand on parchment, were then very costly" ("Il messale consultato da S. Francesco," *San Francesco Patrono d'Italia* 58:82).—Trans.]

For the church of San Nicolò, which was on the site of the present post office, see chap. 3, pp. 91, 98, in this volume, also *NV* 3:13–15, 23. For this episode: *NV* 2:279–80. For the custom of locking chains across the piazza and gates at night: *NV* 3:23.

And all wondered at the lack of good sense that Bernardo was displaying. Up to that day he had been esteemed as the wisest of lawyers and the most consummate of negotiators. Now he was selling everything in blocks and in a hurry, at ridiculous prices—the best lands of hill and plain, the fertile vineyards, the rich olive groves, the great forests. It seemed in truth as if the son of Quintavalle must be on the eve of leaving for a long journey from which he would never return.

He scooped up many of the coins called *libbre lucchese,* took off his mantle and put all the gold in it, pulling up the edges to make a sack, and made his way to the piazza. Francis accompanied him. Bernardo had determined to follow the Gospel precept to the letter and give all that money to the poor. He would begin with the inmates of the San Rufino hospital.

They went out of the San Giorgio gate to the piazza in front of the church. It was Wednesday, April 16, one week before the feast of Saint George. They could hear the boys in the school singing, their voices alternating with that of the priest.

Francis thought again of the dreams and daydreams he himself had had at one time in that atrium, in that school headed by the hospitaller.

Twenty years had gone by. And all was now as it had been then: the songs, the serene gardens, the touch of a new spring, the festoons of green that climbed up to decorate the arches and columns. Yet, how many of his illusions had fallen by the wayside! What new horizons were opening!

The poor of the hospital came. Francis drew money from Bernardo's mantle and gave it out with full hands. Some money tumbled to the pavement, and he paid no attention to it. The poor were frightened. This was an incredible overturning of all that they had up until then considered the foundation and the essential law of all of life. They watched shyly, suspecting a trick. The gold shone, attracting the greedy, who crowded around to see such a bizarre spectacle.

Even the canon Silvestro was among them and he searched for a pretext to have his part. At last he thought he had found one. Without much grace, he said to Francis, "You did not finish paying me for those stones that I sold you."

Francis buried his hands again in Bernardo's mantle and drew them out, brimful of money. His good cheer was undiminished. He asked Silvestro, who bolted forward to take that unexpected supplement, if he were now satisfied. Silvestro replied that he was, but in his heart he wondered why Francis had not refused that unjust request. He found no answer. It seemed that in Francis's eyes money had lost all value.

Pietro's patrimony was not very great, and it was quickly given away. It, too, went to the poor.

So it was that the first two companions, now dressed in garments like the one Francis wore, followed Francis to Porziuncola.

Silvestro, back in the palatial quarters of the cathedral, could not get out of his mind Francis's handing out gold money as if it had been pebbles from the river. His amazement was stronger, even, than his satisfaction over having gotten some of it. He put the problem to the other canons, who had a great deal to say.

The names of these canons—Mosè, Crescenzio, Tebaldo, Pietro di Vivieno, Eugenio, Bartolo di Albertuccio, Burgondione—appear in arbitrations about incomes and lands. They were not only surprised but scandalized and indignant.

Some were of the opinion that the madness of Pietro Bernardone's son was contagious, something that by its very nature spread to the most astute, as certain fevers are most likely to attack persons of robust constitution. And others said that the old lord of the Tripudianti was still leading others astray, still being the wastrel he had been branded, even if he had exchanged his princely garb for sackcloth. Obviously, everybody who was now following him into the Porziuncola forest was cut from the same cloth, no doubt about it.

Someone complained that it was the fault of the consuls, who, to avoid trouble with the bishop, had not banished Francis and thus protected the city from the danger of his subversive ideas. Others used the occasion to vent their spleen against Bishop Guido, who had had the nerve in a public audience to justify, in defiance of the statutes, the crime of a rebel son.

Prior Rinaldo,[42] who had studied with Pietro di Catanio in the University of Bologna, talked about something that had happened to him and one of his companions named Giovanni, also from Assisi. They had gone outside Porta Ravvenate [in Bologna] for a bit of recreation when Giovanni noticed that he had lost a large purse of money that he always carried with him. The two scholars searched for it anxiously, and not finding it, asked the help of the Assisi martyr, Saint Rufinus. In the river there were some large stepping stones, and Giovanni had then jumped on them to cross to the other side. At a certain point he did not estimate his distance well and fell into the water, and, oh, wonders!, he felt under his feet the lost purse.

A similar thing had happened to him in person, Prior Rinaldo, when he went to Bologna to study, together with his brother, Andrea. They had reached Porta Ravennate on a gloomy night, and had gotten into a small boat, along with many others, to cross the river. When they were in the middle of the stream, a whirlwind rose up and upset the boat, which sank with everyone on board. It was the will of God that they had saved themselves by swimming, but they lost all their things and their money. They, too, could think of nothing to do but invoke the aid of Assisi's patron saint, and they made no mistake in doing so. He later appeared to Andrea and showed him the exact spot where the money was to be found. They returned and to their great joy easily retrieved it.

You could see, said Prior Rinaldo, that Saint Rufinus was ready to grant his protection to those who asked to find their money and not to those who deliberately threw it away.

The following night, Silvestro, not convinced by all this reasoning, had difficulty in falling asleep. Finally he succeeded in closing his eyes, and it was then he had his dream of Francis fighting the dragon. In his dream he saw himself on the walls with other city people, exultant and joyful, to acclaim the conqueror as he returned in triumph.

He woke up, found that he was in the dormitory. The light of a lamp revealed the beds of the other canons, all of whom were resting peacefully. We can imagine that he thought that the novena he had been attending every evening with his religious brothers at the church of San Giorgio, along with all the things that had happened, must have produced his dream and his confused state of mind—Saint George, the dragon, Francis, the people. He went back to sleep.

The vision came again. The monster dropped down from on high, hissing shrilly, spouting fire and flame. The knight in the torn habit faced him for the second time and routed him. Silvestro awoke again, alarmed. All this must have some profound and real significance, but what? His heart grew cold as he thought about his past life and imagined what it would be in the future. He was beginning to grow old. Perhaps the young man who had given him all that money without regret saw more justly and farther than he, for all his experience. He prayed that he might find light.

He fell again into sleep. And for the third time he saw the supernatural combat renewed. Then the dragon, furious and terrified, vanished with an enormous roar.

Silvestro got up from his bed and went down to the cloister. The portico was lit with the bluish light of the coming day, the well, its pulley immobile, was outlined against the light.

He decided to go find Francis. He would confide in him; he would tell him about the vision; he would ask him for advice.[h]

The Momentous Saint George's Day of Brother Giles

The surprise in Assisi was great. As long as Francis was the only one involved, the matter was judged as just another of his extravagant ideas, the kind that had been characteristic of him since his early years. But now two of the most acute jurists in the city, each accustomed to evaluate every act of life by the measure of ancient and modern wisdom, had elected to go the same way! Everywhere there was talk about it, opinions, judgements, censures, doubts, fears.

A young man of the city overheard one of these fevered discussions one day, shortly after it all happened. It took place in his own house, among members of his family, and there was a considerable difference of opinion about the whole thing. It was the eve of the feast of Saint George, Wednesday, April 22. In the end, the family argument had his fullest attention.

The young man was named Egidio, a name that his intimates and friends, according to the usage still current in Assisi, had changed into Gilio, or in the English form, Giles.[i] He was a passionate devotee of the ideals of chivalry, filled with dreams of glory, and eager for adventurous enterprises and deeds like those recounted in troubadours' songs. He was nourishing a secret dream of winning glory the next day, Saint George's day. He would enter the jousts to be held on the field of Sementone and win them, and afterward raise the colours of his lady over all of the other knights, those of the city and those from other places.

But now, listening to those voices, the words and details about what had happened, all about men whose lives had revolved around sales and money matters, he felt the dimensions of his own life inexplicably enlarge, almost as if a window had been opened suddenly in a dark room to reveal a boundless, unknown horizon. This could well be the knighthood he desired, the prowess to which to consecrate his life. It was the noble choice embraced by Saint George, who

---

h. Silvestro was clearly an Assisi man, as mentioned in *Leg. Maior*, III, 3; *Leg. Min.*, II, 8; 2 *Cel.*, 109; and Ludovico da Pietralunga's *Guida*, 8. He is also called a canon of San Rufino in a record of the liberation of a serf (Arch. Cath., fasc. 8, no. 2); see also chap. 6, p. 201, of this book. It is not known when he joined Francis, but it seems unlikely that he was one of the first eleven companions. According to 3 *Soc.*, 31, it was not long after he asked Francis for money for the stones he had given him; in 3 *Cel.*, 3, he is said to have been "one of the first friars"; and in *Leg. Maior* III, 5, it is reported that it was a short time after he had his vision. *NV* 2:280–81.

i. Giles is described as an Assisi man in a number of sources, including 3 *Soc.*, 32, and *Anon. Per.*, 14, and 24 *Generals* (AF 3:4). See also *Vita*, 1 (trans. Brown. *Little Flowers*). Nothing is known about his family. Since the name was a common one in the thirteenth century, there is no way to single it out in the surviving records. *NV* 2:281–82.

had thus identified himself to the emperor: "I am a knight and I have left riches and all worldly pomp in order to serve Jesus Christ, who is the true Lord."

These three men, Francis and his companions, were bringing familiar ancient legends to life in Assisi. Saints were descending from their altars to mingle in everyday life. Who could fail to see that, and accuse these men of some queer game?

The next day Giles rose early and went out. Bright hangings were fluttering along the streets and flags and banners were suspended from the windows of the great houses. As in years past, horses neighed, trumpets blared, bells exalted the glory of the day. The people hurried toward the church of San Giorgio for the Mass of the Knights. Giles joined them and entered the church, where the shining bright blades of swords mirrored the light of candles. The hospitaller Guido[j] was at the altar, dressed in gold vestments, officiating amid a forest of lances and flashing swords. Incense and hymns rose to Saint George, whose triumphant figure shone clear and distinct on the frescoed wall.

Giles kneels, begins to pray. He looks at the fresco in the chapel: Saint George burying his lance deep in the dragon's throat while the princess, marvelling, watches the mortal duel. The arms of the knight are all white, and white, too, is the rearing horse. The dragon, mortally wounded, is lashing his tail. The princess's snow-white hands and neck stand out against the purple of her regal dress.

It seems to Giles, overcome by a strange lightness and joy, that Guido is speaking directly to him when he turns to proclaim in a raised voice the words of the Mass for the day: "O Saints, O just ones in the Lord, rejoice! Alleluia!"

He trembles when again the hospitaller turns and again he seems to look directly at him: "God elects you his heirs! Alleluia!"

As he goes out of the church, he turns toward the *contrada* of Moiano. As he passes the gate, he finds himself on a path flowering with hawthorn. He begins to sing:

> *La nostr'amor vai enaissi*
> *com la branca de l'albespi*
> *qu'esta sobre l'arbre tremblan,*
> *la nuoit, a la ploja ez al gel,*

---

j. This is the same Guido who was rector and custodian of the Ospedale di San Rufino from 1198 to 1217. He was the priest who had a miraculous dream about the burial place of Saint Rufinus and is said to have been himself miraculously cured of a serious illness after touching the relics of this saint. *NV* 3:58, 236.

tro l'endeman, que · l sols s'espan
per las fueillas verz el ramel.

. . . Our love comes out
Like the branch that turns about
On the top of the hawthorne,
With frost and hail at night
Suffers despite
'Till the sun come, and the green leaf on the bough. . . .[43]

He passes the Galletta spring, goes by San Masseo, and reaches the trivium of the Strada Francesca. There, one road goes to Porziuncola by the little hospital of the Crucifer Knights, one down to the lepers of the Arce, the third crosses the ruins of the tower of San Savino and turns to Rivo Torto. No one has been able to tell him exactly where Francis is to be found. Perhaps at the hut at Porziuncola. Maybe in the hospital of San Lazzaro, helping the lepers. Or he and his two companions were known to stay sometimes in a deserted place along Rivo Torto where there is a hovel, a kind of shed, that in the past served as a refuge for banished lepers.

As in the city the bells of San Giorgio peal, Giles, with a prayer that God put him on the right road, takes the one to Porziuncola.

He goes into the still oak woods. There is the chapel, there the poor hut. He sees no one. The woods seem lit by a subdued light, as if in a vision; trunks of age-old oaks rise high and solemn, like the columns of a great cathedral. There is some trembling in the leaves, some trilling, immediately interrupted, some crackling near the clumps of briars.

He turns. Francis is coming forward on the path, though Giles has heard no steps. Giles kneels and puts his arms in a cross as he had seen new knights do in the act of investiture. Humbly he asks Francis to receive him in his company for the love of God.

Francis listens to him with tenderness. The youth, the candour, the devotion, and above all, the happiness of this new companion, move him. He has known him as one of those who, like himself, was planning to go seek his fortune and find a way to win knighthood. It is Saint George's day, an appropriate day for this high consecration.

He says, turning to Giles, who waits, kneeling, in the solemnity of the woods where incredible happenings are coming to flower along with the new buds of spring:

"My dearest brother, God has given you great grace. What you have desired is fulfilled, beyond your dream. Today is Saint George's day. If the emperor should come to Assisi to make some citizen his knight or keeper of his treasury, should you not rejoice over it? How much greater joy you must have now that God has chosen you his knight and most beloved servant, to observe the perfection of the Holy Gospel!"

He is silent for an instant, his voice a little more grave as he pronounces the words of the ceremony in which one knight confers knighthood on another. He exhorts him to remain strong and valiant in every trial:

" . . . And, therefore, be firm and constant in the vocation to which God has called you."

Francis takes him by the hand and raises him and they return to the path. It is noon. Bernardo and Pietro come with provisions. Francis tells them:

"Messire Lord God has sent us a good brother. For him let all of us rejoice in the Lord."

They begin to eat, joyous in their fraternal love.

They have to prepare the poor sackcloth habit for Giles right away, so Francis and the young man leave for Assisi. Along the road they meet a poor woman, who asks them for alms for the love of God. They have none to give her. They look at each other uncertainly. Francis suggests, "For the love of God, my dearest brother, let us give your mantle to the poor woman."

Giles's mantle is very rich and ornate, made of beautiful pale blue satin. The beggar woman is transfixed by the gift. She cannot say a word.

Giles remembered the legend of Saint Martin, who cut his mantle in two with his sword in order to divide it with a poor man he met along the road. He, who no longer has a sword, has given away his whole mantle, and the act has given him such indescribable joy that, as he says later, he feels as if he is flying straight to heaven.

They return along the same road, Giles carrying his sackcloth folded over his arm. Night is falling on this heroic day in which, as he had dreamed, he has accomplished great deeds and been a victor. They walk in silence, Francis and his new companion, feeling their hearts on fire with impatience to get on with the mission awaiting them.

In silence they plunge into the forest and disappear in the shadow.

The First Franciscan Mission

They left together, Francis and Giles, after a month, for their first enterprise. They went out of the Parlascio gate, the one that carries the notice: *Haec est porta qua vaditur in Marchiam,* "From this gate one goes to the March."

The words, chiselled ten years earlier by men of the commune restless for new markets and outlets, now had such a different significance to them! They had chosen the March of Ancona as their destination because there they would be able to travel with a certain degree of security. Since the war between Assisi and Perugia had flared up again, it would not have been prudent to venture into territory under the control of Perugia, and hence likely to be the scene of new retaliations. They followed the Tescio river to Piano della Pieve, went up Monte Moro, touched Gualdo and Fossato, reached Fabriano.

It was early June. The hills were shining with the brightness of yellow broom. The forest stretched immobile under the limpid arc of the sky. Unharvested crops lay heavy on the fields, mature for the scythe.

The Anonymous Perugian writes: "Great happiness superabounded in them, almost as if they had received an immense treasure. And in truth they had reason for happiness, considering that they had left many things that usually bring men to grief, holding them to be dung, and that they were unlike those who seek joy in transient things, only to find bitterness and sadness in worldly pleasures."[44]

They sang. Francis's full and resonant voice soared in the peace of the joyful mornings, in the evening vespers. He improvised in Provençal, in spur of the moment inspirations that magnified God, Lord of heaven and earth, and exulted in works of His creation.

Harvesters in the fields, people they met, did not know what to make of these vagabonds, so miserably dressed and so incredibly joyous. Some called them fools, others believed they were drunk. Young girls ran away at their approach.

Francis was not yet preaching, but the two often stopped to talk to people.

Francis said to them, with a simplicity quickened by a loving expression, "Love and fear God and make worthy penitence for your sins."

Giles added with engaging candour, "Do what my spiritual father here tells you, because he speaks most wisely."

According to the Three Companions, after they had gone on their way, people continued to talk about them. They asked one another, "Who are these men and what are they saying?" One day someone who had listened to them carefully said judiciously, "Either these men are following the Lord in great perfection or they must be demented, since their way of life appears desperate, with little food and going about barefoot and clad in the poorest garments."

They trudged through cities and villages, crossed harsh mountain passes, and finally reached the sea. It was July and the Adriatic stretched green and immense in perfect peace.

One evening they sat on the deserted beach, looking at the expanse of waves, and Giles, who liked similes, compared the immobility of the fishing boats to the indifference with which people seemed to have greeted their coming. They had been walking for weeks and months, but not a soul had responded to their message.

Francis replied that only those of great heart, not the masses of little men, would know how to grasp the truth of their teaching. "My son," he added, "our fraternity will be like a fisherman who throws his net into the sea and draws out a great number of fish. The big ones he keeps [lit., "puts into a jar"], the little ones he puts back into the water."

Giles was silent, but he wondered very much at this prophecy. Francis still had only three companions.

They returned to Santa Maria degli Angeli the middle of August (1209), where a great joy awaited them. Three other men of Assisi wanted to join them: Sabbatino, Morico, and Giovanni [John] della Cappella. Of these little is known beyond the name. Giovanni della Cappella belonged to a noble family; a nephew living at the end of the century was notary of the chancellor of the commune of Assisi.[k]

The seventh companion, Filippo [Philip] di Lungo, who joined

---

k. According to *3 Soc.*, 35, all three were Assisi men. In *Anon. Per.*, 17, Morico is referred to as *parvus* ("Little Morico"). Jörgensen, Sabatier, and others confused him with another Morico, mentioned in *Leg. Maior*, IV, 7, a religious in the Order of Crucifer Knights who contracted leprosy and was cured through the intercession of Saint Francis. This Morico, too, entered the order, but at a later time.

There has been considerable confusion about the name and the character of Giovanni della Cappella. It is reported that his name came from the fact that he took to wearing a hat instead of the prescribed hood (and thus the name became changed into Giovanni del Cappello). This story is surely a late bit of inaccurate gossip, no doubt related to the fact that he was cast in the role of the Franciscan Judas: he is said to have stolen the balsam that was to have been used on the body of Saint Francis and afterwards hanged himself. This must certainly have been an invented tale to try to make the life of Saint Francis conform in every detail to the life of Jesus. In a document of March 14, 1297, in the communal archives of Fabriano, a *dominus Petrus Iohannis de Cappella* is described as the notary of the chancellor of the commune of Assisi. The name occurs in a record of his having been reimbursed by the commune of Fabriano after he and his family had been attacked and robbed while they were en route to a small village in that area. This suggests that this friar probably belonged to a family named "della Cappella."

Nothing is known of Sabbatino except, according to *3 Soc.*, 35, he was an Assisi man. *NV* 2:282–83.

them a few days later, was from an area on the eastern slope of Mount Subasio called Costa di San Savino.[1]

That high place has remained as unchanged and hushed as the lives of the generations who have lived there, succeeding each other from time immemorial, lives spent in leading flocks from the sheepfold to the pastures on the heights, then back from the high meadows to the sheepfolds. Below the summit, which is linked to forgotten religions, a stream appears between Mortaro and Fossa Rotonda. Because of its bed of blood-coloured clay, it is called Fosso Rosceto, Red Gully. At the point where it leaves the bare rocks to flow through the olive groves along the road to Panzo, there is a cluster of houses built by shepherds for the shelter of flocks during the winter season. The place is called, for that reason, Mandria, or Flock. Even today the road is called the Mandria road. This is where Filippo comes from. His home can be pinpointed as the Costa di San Savino or, as the oldest texts have it, Mandria. We know the name of two of his brothers, Biagio and Giovanni.

But this still, lonely place had not been spared from desecration. This was where angry men, embittered by a class hatred more deadly than the venom of the vipers lurking on the fiery cliff of Sasso del Colubro, lacerated the great silence with raucous shouts and burned the castles and towers. The feudal lords whose strongholds were attacked were continuing to engage in altercations with the city consuls, supported, as usual, by Perugia. Filippo found peace by joining the followers of Poverty.

For him Thomas of Celano will fashion beautiful words of praise: "The Lord touched his lips with a purifying coal, that he might speak of him with great sweetness and wondrous spiritual feeling."

The wisdom and poetic gifts of visionary men, who solely through faith come to know and reveal the highest mysteries of Divine Thought, were embodied in him: "Understanding and interpreting the sacred Scriptures, though he had not studied, he became an im-

---

1. The identification of Filippo di Lungo, mentioned in *1 Cel.,* 25, has become a source of controversy, thanks to the inaccuracies of a number of copyists. In *Leg. S. Clarae,* he is said to be from Adria, which various biographers supposed to be either a village in Abruzzo (Andria) or one near Perugia (Antria). Bernardo da Bessa, however, said that he came from a village or *castello* near Assisi; and in *24 Generals* (AF 3:632), he is said to be from *Costa Sancti Savini.* A similar statement is in *Spec. Vitae,* 71, but the name is mistakenly transcribed as *Costa Sancti Serini.* Nevertheless, this clears up everything, for this is an area on the slope of Mount Subasio that is also known as Mandria or Mandria di San Paolo. The name "Longus" is an Assisi name; in fact, the name "Lunghi" is still very common in Assisi. The Blasius (Biagio) Longus who appears in a 1201 record and the Iohannes (Giovanni) Longus in one of 1215 can be assumed to be Filippo's brothers, there being no other family of the name mentioned during this period. *NV,* 2:283–85.

itator of those whom the leaders of the Jews alleged to be ignorant and unlearned."

Perugia Imposes a Treaty

On September 1, 1209, the residents of the *contrada* of Santa Maria Maggiore were summoned to an assembly very much different from the one held in their piazza two and a half years earlier, when Pietro Bernardone and his son had their day in court.

The Guelf party in Italy had gained a new advantage. As a result, the Assisi-Perugia war had been renewed. Philip of Swabia, the German king, was murdered on June 21, 1208, by Otto di Wittelsbach, count palatine in Bavaria. Philip's rival for the throne, Otto of Brunswick, had earlier gained the support of Pope Innocent III, largely by promising to respect the integrity and inviolability of the Papal States within their old, traditional borders from the Exarchate of Ravenna to Guarigliano. This was a renunciation of the ancient rights of the Holy Roman Empire to the duchy of Spoleto and the *contea* of Assisi. Consequently, Perugia, the old and loyal champion of the pontifical state, had grown bolder and decided that the moment had come to resolve the old questions with Assisi and to take care of its promises to the feudal lords who had become Perugia citizens.[45]

These lords had seen the order issued by the podestà of Perugia in 1205 fall into a void. The destroyed castles had not been rebuilt, the confiscated goods had not been restored, compensations had not been paid for the damages.

The lords of Sasso Rosso, Leonardo and Fortebraccio, could not hide their chagrin. Those gryphons who talked always of intending to subdue the world had not advanced one step in ten years of war, despite the high-sounding promises that had been consecrated in solemn assemblies and in legal acts sworn to on the Gospels. Perugia's reputation and prestige were suffering.

There was a great deal of toing and froing of ambassadors and intermediaries, and finally a compromise was agreed upon by the two warring cities: Perugia and Assisi would submit their controversies to two arbiters who would make a judgement on "all the litigations, disputes, and discords, bearing upon the aforesaid cities and their *comitati.*"

The arbiter for Perugia was Uguccione of the *quondam* Guidone di Giovanni. The other was an Assisi man, Bernardo di Domina Eufemia. Experts in these complicated affairs suspected that Assisi might try to evade the terms of the treaty by an underhanded claim that they were binding only on the faction in office at the time it was signed, a not uncommon practice in this period when parties and factions came to and lost power in quick succession. To prevent this from happening, they suggested for the sake of prudence that the head of the Assisi consuls, Marangone di Cristiano, ought to be delegated to conclude the treaty, not only by the other consuls (who were then Guido di Valentino, Tebaldo, and Cristiano di Paride) but also by the citizen assembly itself. Despite all these precautions, the two arbiters were not able to put together an agreement.

The Perugian delegate said that Bernardo, after having been given every authority and discretionary power and every deliberative faculty, could not be found and had not replied to the numerous invitations. He had thus been guilty of a true obstructionism that paralyzed every effort and rendered every initiative in vain. To end this little game, Perugia's Uguccione had recourse to one of those subtleties characteristic of students of gloss. Since the panel of arbiters had been regularly constituted, he, Uguccione, said that if they should not be able to meet together to reach a decision, then he was to be considered, not the representative of the Perugini, but the sole member of the judging panel, and as such he would represent both parties and act with absolute objectivity to protect the interests of each.

And thus, in that Kalends of September, Uguccione made a formal appearance in Assisi, in the piazza of the bishop's palace, accompanied by his notary, Martino. His purpose was to present to the Assisi consuls the summons to appear at the forthcoming ceremony. (This episode is a confirmation of the fact that the bishop's citadel was absolutely independent of the communal city and free from consular jurisdiction. It was considered a true state within a state. It is not difficult to suppose that in the revived struggle between the church and empire, Bishop Guido had got involved in a quarrel with the Assisi consuls, who were loyal to the emperor, and that he was sympathetic to Perugia, which had made itself a champion of the papal claims.)

Several Assisi men, because of personal dislike of the new consuls, accepted the point of view of the Perugian arbiter, and were present: Benincasa di Giovanni, Boverio, Boncompagno di Ugone, Moscone di Raimondino, Tiberio, Davino di Uguccio di Peritelda, Marescotto di Bernardo Dodici.

The arbiter Uguccione read his summons "to the consuls of Assisi, and that is, to Marangone di Cristiano and to Guidone di Valentino, to come on the following day to the church of Collestrada to listen to the decision, or rather arbitration, that he intended to pronounce between them and the Perugini."

His judgement was, in fact, given on the following morning, on the Collestrada heights, and more specifically, as the document takes care to note, "on the border of the forest of the church of Collestrada."

According to the arbiter, this locality, which marked the border between the two cities, was chosen because it was considered a neutral zone, "a suitable and common place." But the real reason lay in the desire to announce the decision on these hoary disputes on the very ground of the bloody battle, to recall, for their own advantage, the success of the Perugini and the defeat of the Assisani. And, in fact, in a front row position among the many Perugini who came to this promulgation of the treaty was the Perugian consul Bonbarone who seven years earlier had been head of the victorious army.

This ruling illuminates the dark side of this bitter war. It records the slaughters, the fires, the robberies, the destructions. It examines the ins and outs of the knotty issues. It establishes the amount of damages to be paid, describes the lands to be reconsigned, determines the fines for offenders, orders pledges that will guarantee fulfillment of the terms.

It commands the Perugini and the Assisani to keep the peace, not a peace of insidiousness, perfidy, falsity, a peace that is not a peace, but rather a peace of a good alliance, *bonam et puram et sinceram pacem.* "And nevermore shall anyone go against it, except that the Assisani should be able to help their allies, and the Perugini theirs."

If provocations and offences should arise from either of the parties, recourse shall be to a council of arbiters and not to arms. "If it should happen that any offence break the aforesaid peace, such offence shall be repaired within a month, in a manner set by two *buoni uomini* chosen from the aforesaid cities, and that is, one from each city, who shall swear that, the offence having arisen, they will intervene to order and impose the reparation within a month of their election; and these arbiters shall be named within the eight days following the offence."

A sigh of weariness still rises up from this paper, heavy with so much hatred, so much blood, so much violence: "And assuredly, at last, from this day forward, life shall run tranquilly, and in perpetuity peaceful remain and be maintained, and quiet and free from every dispute and quarrel."

But the peace that everyone desires certainly will not come from that political masterpiece springing from the brain of the shrewd Uguccione, who, beyond the formulae, is seeking reparations for the feudal lords and possession of some of the important *castelli* occupied by the Assisani. Arbitrations will always remain, regardless of the beautiful words with which they are decorated, nothing more than wicked means of domination and enslavement. This everyone understands to the very end, both the victors who treat the defeated as slaves and the conquered who prepare for revolt.

And in that understanding, no one from Assisi appears that day at Fratta del Colle, neither the arbiter Bernardo, nor the consul Marangone, nor the other consuls. There was nothing for the Perugini to do but to take note of this new treachery, this new affront (*venire et audire penitus contempsissent*), and declare the treaty valid anyway, "because no one ought to speculate on the absence and contumacy of those who, summoned, did not appear and no one should assume that their absence is sanctioned by God."[46]

Knights of Lady Poverty

The new disciples of Poverty did not receive a warm welcome in Assisi. Few gave when they asked for alms, and people asked them ironically if perchance they had disposed of their own substance in order to feed themselves on others? Their kinsmen bitterly persecuted them. And many, rich and poor, men and women, followed them about in order to laugh at them and treat them as fools and crazy men. "For this [their way of life]," writes the Anonymous Perugian, "their relatives and blood kinsmen persecuted them and others laughed at them, because in that time no one had been known to throw away his own things and go about seeking charity from door to door."[47]

This adverse public opinion made an impression on Bishop Guido himself, who said to Francis, "Your life seems hard and harsh to me, in that you possess nothing in the world."

Francis, whose first rule for his companions was "to pay no heed to money, wherever you find it, any more than you would to the dust under your feet," replied, "Signore, if we had possessions, it would be necessary also to have arms for our defence, because they give rise to arguments and litigations, and these things get in the way of love of God and neighbour. Therefore, we do not want to possess anything of temporal value in this world."[48]

So it was in vain that they tried in Assisi to touch hardened souls, these seven men of the city who had themselves at one time bargained over cloth and land, argued about prices, fought in wars, set fire to fortresses, and acclaimed pope and emperor in the piazza.

Francis intended, though, to spread their message in other regions.

So all the companions made ready to leave, two by two. Before their departure Francis called them together in the forest. "You," he said, "will find faithful, gentle, peaceful men, who will joyfully receive you and your words; but the greater number of those you see will be arrogant and curse you and resist you and everything you say. Prepare yourselves then, humbly and patiently to bear whatever is necessary."

And again, as they travelled about, people everywhere were amazed at their strange way of dressing and their way of life, which was thought to be like that of savages.

Whenever on their way they saw a church or even a simple cross, they said a special prayer: "We adore you, Lord Jesus Christ, here and in all your churches in the whole world, and we bless you, because by your holy cross you have redeemed the world."

When they entered cities and villages, castles and houses, on their lips was the wonderful new greeting, "God give you peace!" And some were astonished by it, and some jeered at them, and some in curiosity assailed them with arguments and questions, wanting to know where they came from and to what religious order they belonged. They always replied that they were "men of penitence" born in Assisi, and that their order was not yet a regular religious order.

Others judged them to be swindlers and madmen and refused to receive them in their houses. And so it happened that in many places, after having been subjected to all sorts of indignities, they had to sleep under the porticoes of houses or churches.

One evening Bernardo and Giles reached Florence. It was already late autumn and they searched in vain for a place to take shelter. Finally a woman allowed them to stay in a hut near her house. Her husband, when he learned of it, reproved his wife, who justified what she had done by saying that in the hut they would be able to steal nothing but wood. When it was day, the woman went to Mass in the nearby church and was astonished to find there the two vagabonds of the night, praying. A man came in and, assuming they were beggars, offered them some money. They refused to take it. Upon being asked the reason, Bernardo replied, "We are poor men, but poverty does not bother us as it does others, since by grace of God, whose commandment we fulfill, we voluntarily have embraced it."

And he told how, having had many fine possessions, he had disposed of all of them, because in them he had found no peace. The woman felt ashamed and wished that she might have someday the opportunity to entertain Giles and Bernardo in her house.

But pleasant episodes were rare.

The great and the small, accustomed to thinking of revenge as a duty of honour, considered their behavior cowardly and found such cowardice inconceivable. And they were offended by it. They treated them badly, yanking their only habits from their backs, smearing them with mud, mocking them, putting dice in their hands and inviting them to gamble, lifting them up by force, grasping their hoods and dragging them about like hanged men.

But they bore everything—even hunger, thirst, cold, nakedness, anguish, tribulation—with firmness and humility, as the blessed Francis had taught them. They did not grieve. They were not upset. They did not curse those who did evil things to them; rather, in conformity with the Gospels, they held these things to be a great reward and rejoiced in God and prayed for their persecutors.

Often people, touched by so much virtue, came and asked their pardon for having treated them unjustly. And they pardoned them with all their hearts, in the name of God.

When they returned to Assisi and found themselves all together at Porziuncola, their happiness was such that the evils they had endured were forgotten.

Three more men had joined them, all also from Assisi.

Barbaro.

Giovanni (John) di San Costanzo. This is the name of a *villa* located two miles from Porziuncola, between Isola Romana and the Tescio, called thus in homage to the first bishop of Perugia, Costanzo. At the time of the emperor Antoninus, he had been attacked by idolators in this area, received a mortal wound, and was taken to the prisons of Perugia, where he was miraculously cured by an angel.

Bernardo, son of Vigilante di Bernardo di Bellettone. This Vigilante appears in July of 1186 as a witness in a donation to the cathedral. He must have been of a prominent family, because another son of Vigilante, Bonaventura by name, is found in the list of principal citizens of 1233.[m]

Angelo, First Noble Knight to Enter the Order

In a small Assisi street running parallel to Piazza Nuova, in the upper part of the city, there are still the remains of the *casamenti* [large multiple houses] in which, at the time of Saint Francis, the sons of Ugone di Tebalduccio lived, the most powerful family of the Parlascio *contrada*.

---

m. It seems likely that Giovanni di San Costanza got to know Francis and his companions while they were staying at Porziuncola.

The name "di Vigilante" was incorrectly inscribed as "Bernardus de Vida" in 3 *Soc.*, ed. Marcellino da Civezza and Teofilo Domenichelli; in 24 *Generals* it is added to the proper form of the name. All three of these companions are named in 24 *Generals* (AF 3:4).

Amid shapeless patches, sections of the sectioned curtain wall may still be seen, built of stones to which the centuries have given a patina of dark velvet. In them are doors with pointed arches, little windows with architraves protected by grilles. The whole street preserves to a remarkable degree the fierce air of other times. No one passes, no one pauses from dawn to sunset, no one but the ghosts who keep watch on the worn thresholds from behind the stone windowsills, now flowering with red geraniums. On winter days the north wind, icy from snowy Subasio, howls unceasingly through the streets.

It is known that Ugone was one of the sons of Tebalduccio di Berardo, the pious and unruly donor of land for the new cathedral begun by Giovanni of Gubbio. Records show that he followed faithfully the family tradition, getting what he wanted by legal processes or by joining the mob in popular uprisings, whichever most suited the occasion. And he also followed the family pattern by alternately making compromises with canons and pacts with members of his consortium, preparing documents for the donation of lands to the Ospedale della Fossa of Parlascio (near his house) and laying down rules for the construction of the piazza.

But it was the Crusades that really captured his attention. We know this from the names he gave his five sons: Tancredi, Guglielmo (William), Alberico, Giorgio, Ugolino.

Already we have seen how false is the belief that one's name determines one's fate. Pietro Bernardone had changed the name of his son in the hopes of making a merchant of him. Ugone wanted his sons to become valiant and gallant like Tancred, the hero of the first Crusade. Disposed to immolate themselves for the cause of the Faith, like William, brother of Tancred, who fell at Tancred's side in the battle against the infidels. Strong and successful like Alberico, duke of Spoleto, nicknamed "the strongest Lion," who in the time of Ugone's forefathers led the forces that exterminated the Saracens at the mouth of the Garigliano. Devout, like Saint George, patron of knights.

His hopes were not deluded. In that tempestuous period of the life of the city, the lords of Parlascio were always in the forefront in counsel and in action, in the field and in the parley, in commanding the army and in arbitrations to resolve factional conflicts.

Tancredi becomes the outstanding consul of the period, the one who leads the people in the revolt of 1198. It is by his order that the new portion of the city wall is constructed. It is his name that stands on the memorial tablet over the arch of Porta Perlici, the one recording the fervour of the workmen who opened that new city gate on the eve of the civil war. Reading it there, we can still hear after more than seven centuries the concerted cry in citizen assemblies, ringing out like a stirring trumpet call as shields are struck: *Tancredo consule!* The cross that precedes the name itself attests the quasi-sacred authority with which he was invested.

Not a decisive deliberation for the fate of the city is taken in that time in which Tancredi's wise advice is not weighed. It is he who sits beside the first consul, Bonbarone, the future Brother Elias, in the trials held in the cathedral, he who dictates, with Giacomo and Marangone, the conditions of the Peace Paper at the time of the war with Perugia. An iron man, passionately devoted to the idea of communal grandeur, he is again consul in 1206, after the cavalcade of the citizen army against Valfabbrica. He receives the submission of the plundered *castello*. In the year 1209 he, with other leading citizens, certifies the copy of the diploma of Frederick Barbarossa that marks out the inviolable borders of the commune.

Ugolino, Giorgio, and Alberico also become prominent men of the commune, and Guglielmino takes part in parleys alongside his brother, Tancredi.

In the time of the events that interest us, some of the sons of Ugone are already dead; others are aged. Tancredi is about to reach his seventieth year. The young, brought up in the heated climate of war and revolution, are coming on.

Tancredi has two sons, Angelo and Bove. They are rich. They own lands and serfs with bold names—Baldanza and Gualtiero—who scorn the orders of the commune, refuse to pay their fines, and by the podestà's order are put on the list of those sentenced to the ban.

The sons of Ugolino are Ugone, Giorgio, Egidio. They fight bravely in the Compagnia dei Cavalieri, following the *vessillifero,* their kinsman.[49] Their names appear in the division of the paternal patrimony, where they list fields, enclosures, vineyards.

The son of Guglielmo was Andrea.

The son of Alberico proudly bears the name of his uncle, Tancredi. He was the *connestabile* of the cavalry and he appears in legal papers as the official who receives the oaths of those who swear to keep a horse for the service of the commune.

Giorgio has three children. The first is named Paolo, the second, Emilia. The third has a pretty name made popular by the romances of chivalry from France, Ginevra, or in the English form, Guinevere. If it were to be taken as a forecast of her future, it would mean that her life would be made joyous with love, that she herself would be like those crimson flowers that pour down from the fortified windows on the gloomy façade of her palazzo. In this year of 1209 Ginevra is fifteen years old and very pleased with the aura that her name creates around her gentle beauty. She keeps the romance of Launcelot of the Lake open on the reading desk of her room to the page with the dialogue in which the handsome lover is induced to reveal his secret love for the queen.

" '. . . And how long have you loved me so much?'

" 'From the day that I was made a knight.'

" 'Through the loyalty that you owe me, tell me from whence comes this love for me?'

" 'Lady, from you, in that you made me your friend, if your mouth did not lie.'

" 'And how did I make you my friend?'

" 'Lady, I came before you when I had leave from the king and said that wherever I went, I would serve as your knight. And I said to you, "Farewell, Lady." And you replied, "Farewell, my handsome and sweet friend." This was the word that made me a valiant man, and never afterwards was I in great danger that I did not remember it. This word has strengthened me against all my enemies, has cured me from all my ills, has made me rich in the midst of poverty.'

"The knight Launcelot was as hesitant in love as he was brave in battle, and it was necessary that Galeotto[n] lead him one day to the garden to see Queen Guinevere.

"Galeotto said to the queen, 'Lady, I beseech you, kiss him in front of me to mark the beginning of true love.' And she answered, 'For what have I prayed? I wish it more than you.' And the queen saw that the knight did not dare do anything. She took him by the chin and long she kissed him on the mouth."[50]

Through the window opening on the little garden, a pallid November sun cradled Ginevra's dreams and hopes. Beyond, toward the cathedral, lay the ruins of the Roman amphitheatre.[51] The vaults, arcades and flights of steps appeared to have been planned for defence. A long, strong wall (the same one that today can be seen descending into the underground passages of the house) formed the foundation and support of the palazzo on the side next to the Prato, the public meadow. In the back, towering above the mighty ruins,

---

n. *Galeotto* is the Italian form of the French name Gallehault and also is the Italian word for "pander." In Canto 5 of *Inferno*, Dante had Francesca call the book containing the story of Guinevere and Lancelot "Galeotto"; that is, as Galeotto (Gallehault) had been the go-between between the queen and Lancelot, so the book had driven her and Paolo into their ill-fated love affair. The very fact that Dante used this story in the episode of Francesca and Paolo demonstrates how popular and well-known the Arthurian stories were in Italy. See Ciardi, trans., *Inferno*, p. 64, n. 134.—Trans.

was the strong and turreted palazzo of the sons of Offreduccio di Bernardino, who were close friends of the sons of Ugone and owned land bordering theirs on the plain.[52]

The patrimony of these sons and grandsons of Ugone was huge. They owned lands all about Assisi, including properties bordering those of Pietro Bernardone along Rivo Torto and in Spina.

Information about them is contained in a legal paper of 1236, which is especially interesting because it shows the common ownership of land by different families. "Half *pro indiviso* of a piece of land (held in common) that we have with the sons of the former Guglielmino in the *vocabolo* (site) of Arce, near the church of San Rufino dell'Arce . . ." (San Rufino dell'Arce is scarcely forty metres from the leper hospital of the commune.) "Half *pro indiviso* of a piece of land and of a vineyard, of which half belongs to Paolo di Giorgio and the other half to the condividers, located in the *vocabolo* of Arce, . . ."

The immensely rich son of Tancredi di Ugone, Angelo, was the twelfth companion.[o]

He became one of the men of penitence of the city of Assisi near the end of the year 1209.

If one thinks of the long sojourns that wealthy families were accustomed to make in their country houses, to which we have referred earlier, it is not difficult to realize that Angelo had had the opportunity to follow all Francis's work from his help to the lepers to the

---

o. "Agnolo di Tancredo" is mentioned as the twelfth companion of Saint Francis in *3 Soc.* ed. Marcellino da Civezza and Teofilo Domenichelli. In *Per.*, 92, Angelo Tancredi is called "one of the first twelve brothers." The first writer to bring up his place of origin was Fra Paolino da Venezia, who, using sources and documents no longer available to us, said he was an Assisi man, in his early thirteenth century work, *Satyrica gestarum rerum.* He also listed an Angelo *de Reate* (Rieti) as a friar especially close to Saint Francis. In early sources these two men were clearly differentiated, but it was not long before they were confused, and soon all the attributes and episodes concerning the two friars were used to describe a single person. And so began the controversy, which has been heated, over whether Angelo Tancredi came from Assisi or Rieti. Certainly there is every reason to believe that this first Angelo in the order was the son of the influential noble of Assisi, Tancredi di Ugone, a participant in almost every event that took place in Assisi in that time, rather than of a noble Tancredus of Rieti, where at this early time there had been little, if any, opportunity for the people to know Saint Francis.

Ginevra, who as Sister Benedetta succeeded Saint Clare as abbess of the Poor Clares, was Tancredi's niece and hence Angelo Tancredi's cousin.

The story of the conversion of Angelo da Rieti is found for the first time in a late source full of inaccuracies, *Actus Sancti Francisci in Valle Reatina.*

As will be seen, Angelo di Tancredi was the friar who lived in the household of Cardinal Leone Brancaleone in Rome and was with Francis in the frightening experience when he believed demons were attacking him. Angelo da Rieti was one of Francis's closest companions and accompanied him on many journeys and was with him during some of his most stirring experiences.

There was a third Angelo in the order, Angelo di Borgo San Sepolcro, "a delicate and noble youth," mentioned in *Actus,* 29 and *Fioretti,* 26. In time, he became guardian of the friary of Monte Casale. NV 2:287-97.

reconstruction of San Pietro della Spina, and to have been greatly impressed by what he did. The ancient texts emphasize the fact that he was the first knight to enter the order. And they add that he showed himself "adorned with every courtesy and kindliness."

The shock in the Parlascio house must have been tremendous. Now that foolish fad of renunciation and humility was attacking even the noble houses!

Ginevra was particularly affected by it. So there really was a courage great enough to renounce material things? A courage greater than that of the heroes of the Round Table! And a man could have a love for a chosen lady stronger than that kindled in the heart of Launcelot of the Lake? She did not read her favourite book any more, though it remained open on the page following the episode of the first kiss: "And it was the dead of night, and the moon had risen, and become bright, so that it lighted all the meadow lands."

Again the old legends were coming to life. The Christmas moon shone in the cold serene night that had fallen over the angry shouts of her kinsmen. The wide meadow between the city walls was inundated by moonlight.

In the high silence enveloping the great house, the grace that had wrung the heart of Angelo returned, this time to touch Ginevra, the young daughter of Giorgio di Ugone.

Winter at Rivo Torto

Winter had come. It was too cold for the twelve companions to stay in the hut in the Porziuncola forest. They decided to move, all of them, to a little shack along the Rivo Torto.

Rivo Torto is the name of the *torrente* that is formed below the mountain road from Assisi to Panzo. It comes down by San Potente and Salceto, crosses the old Strada Francesca, and reaches Salette. From here it makes a sudden elbow bend and flows to Bassiano, makes another bend and passes under a little bridge called, simply, "the Rivo Torto bridge." From there it flows to Sant'Angelo di Litorta, where it pours into the Ose. The total length of its course is not more than fourteen kilometres. It was because of these sharp bends that the people called it (and still call it) "Rivo Torto," meaning a tortuous or snakelike stream. (The name is also given to another rivulet in Assisi, below the Subasio in the *balìa* of Costa della Tre Chiese.) The usual custom in this country is to name streams by their appearance and course.

The hovel stood along the first stretch of the stream, between Salette and Bassiano, by the road that leads off the Strada Francesca

to Cannara, a little above the intersection of the road from San Petrignano to Fontanelle. The records permit us to pinpoint its
location—it is precisely where the sanctuary of Rivo Torto stands
today. It was at the right of the stream, near the properties of the sons
of Ugone, Maccabeo di Montanaro, and Rinaldo, who was also related
to Brattarello; it was also near the Ospedale di San Rufino. These
succeeded each other along the road, with the stream lying beyond.[53]

Here the disciples of Poverty enjoyed their happiest days.

They told each other their adventures, the trials undergone, the
joys, the sorrows. Often they were overcome with remorse at not
having been sufficiently attentive to the needs of others or of not
having expressed with proper fervour their gratitude to their bene-
factors. They accused themselves of these things to Francis as if for
irreparable faults.

During the day they went into the fields to help the farmers with
their work; at night they remained for long periods kneeling before a
bare wooden cross.[54]

In the long winter nights they felt themselves touched by divine
ecstasy. Violent squalls of rain sometimes lashed the worm-eaten
door; it seemed that under the force of the wind those disjointed
stones would surely suddenly fly apart and crash in the darkness; yet
the low ceiling of the shed expanded for them to become the wide
sky of an immense cupola. So cramped were they that Francis noted
the assigned places for each with a chalk mark on the beams. But this
very thing filled them with joy, since they placed the observance of
strict poverty ahead of every other aspiration. They owned nothing,
not even in common, and to live they depended on the work of their
hands and the charity of the people.

During the winter season the waters of the streams overflowed and
covered the road in front of the hut so that there was no practical way
to venture out. Often their food consisted only of a few turnips, and
those not easily obtained.

An episode reveals to us the hard struggles that were fought in the
silence of those interminable winter nights. It was already very late
and the brothers were sleeping, when a tortured cry was heard in the
room: "I am dying! I am dying!" The brothers awoke, stupified and
fearful. Francis lit a torch and asked who had cried out. One of the
brothers replied that he was the one, because he felt that he was going
to die of hunger.

And Francis, with the delicate courtesy that was one of his most
beautiful gifts, immediately ordered the table to be laid; and to keep
the brother from being embarrassed, he himself ate with him and
likewise ordered all the others to eat.[55]

However, such discouragements were very brief. Great love united them and made them so solicitous for one another that those who later spoke of their memories of that blessed time said that it was like the affection with which a mother nurtures her child. And willingly each would have given his life for the salvation of the others. One day two of them met a madman, who began to hurl rocks at them. The friar not in danger immediately shielded the other with his own body.[56]

Sometimes on the road, the poor who were even poorer than they, approached them, asking for alms. These were emotional moments that suddenly revealed the depths of their love, as they gave everything they could: their mantles, their hoods, even the sleeves of their habits.[57]

The observance of Poverty and the evangelic precepts formed their rule, which Francis, according to his biographers, had finally put into written form.[58] He soon felt that this rule should have the approbation and sanction of the Vicar of Christ, so as to avoid suspicion and unjust accusations. Some of the brothers did not agree, pointing out how many difficulties they, so alone and unknown, would have in reaching the pope. But Francis convinced them by telling of a dream he had had on one of those stormy nights. He was travelling along a road and at the side of the road was a leafy tree, strong and tall. Miraculously he found that he could touch the top of the tree and without effort bend it all the way to the ground.[59] It meant, he said, that without difficulty the mighty tree—Pope Innocent III—would bend to receive his request.

Already all the oaks were greening on the sides of the consular road (it was the beginning of the summer of 1210) when the little group began its trip to Rome. Bernardo, the first companion, had been designated leader.[60]

In Rome fate brought them to a meeting with the bishop of Assisi, Guido. He was very much disturbed for fear that they were planning to abandon Assisi.[61] When he learned the reason for their trip, he presented them to the respected and powerful Cardinal John of Saint Paul's-Outside-the-Walls, bishop of Santa Sabina.[p] Once this prelate

---

p. It is quite possible that Bishop Guido was not as surprised to see Francis and his companions as the early biographers thought. According to Pazzelli, *Lineamenti di storia e spiritualità*, pp. 67–74, Guido surely had a much larger role in the foundation of Francis's religious order than he has been given credit for. A close personal friend of Cardinal John of Saint Paul, he surely was well acquainted with what was going on in the Roman Curia and understood very clearly the programmatic lines of the new Pontiff Innocent III, which had begun to evolve from the first year of his pontificate. In a broad sense these were to defend and expand Christianity through peaceful methods such as preaching and persuasion as far as possible, to turn to resolute, even violent, methods when the first were unsuccessful. He had established a new policy toward the many lay penitential movements that had sprung up: he attempted to bring

understood the principles that inspired the new apostolate, he said the same thing to them as had Bishop Guido. Hard was the way that they had chosen. Perhaps it would be better to enter one of the religious orders already recognized by the church.

But after having entertained them for some days in his house, after having listened to their conversation and seen their works, he began to love them to the point that he begged them to consider him one of themselves. He promised to support their cause before the pope. In fact, he went to the curia and said, "I have found a most perfect man, who wishes to live according to the Holy Gospel and in all things observe evangelic perfection. Through him I think that God intends to renew the holy church in all the world."

The pope, who knew the profound piety of Cardinal Giovanni, was so impressed by these words he asked him to bring Francis and his companions to him. The next day the twelve men of penitence were admitted into the throne room of the Lateran, into the presence of the great Innocent III.[62]

At the Papal Court

So it was that they found themselves facing each other, the fool of Assisi, kneeling with his ragged companions on the rich mosaic, and the most powerful of all the popes who has succeeded to the throne of Saint Peter.[63]

Innocent III, whose faith was ardent and bold, advocated a universal theocracy, with kings and peoples gravitating around it like satellites around their planet. Strong in the theology he had studied in Paris and in the law he had learned in Bologna, he held that it was not possible to guide men toward eternal salvation, life's supreme goal, without at the same time having at one's disposition the means of watching over and correcting their actions, in conformity with divine laws. Therefore, the papacy could not be anything but a *sacerdotium*

---

them back to the faith and to obedience to the church, unify them under one unique *propositum*, and cede certain points in exchange for an explicit profession of orthodox faith and respect for the hierarchy. "With the knowledge of all this," Pazzelli writes, "Bishop Guido was easily able to guide Francis among the rocks that had destroyed many of his predecessors of the penitential movement." The astonishing fact that Guido, a hot-tempered and violent man who quarreled with almost everyone, "helped" and "comforted" Francis, in the words of his biographers, from the very beginning of his religious life certainly would lead us to believe that he felt a large responsibility for shaping what he did. When we also remember that in a small town like Assisi, the bishop certainly would have known of Francis's departure for Rome, it is not too much to think that he also hurried there to continue his effort to guide Francis and to smooth the path for him.

Guido was bishop of Assisi from the probable dates of 1204 to 1228. According to Fabbi, *Umbre Antichità*, p. 199, his name was Wido or Guido II Spatalonga.—Trans.

regale, a royal priesthood, a supreme power at the head of a hierarchy of vassal states.

It was on this concept that this Roman patrician of the Conti family (the same family that built the Torre dei Conti in the Forum of Augustus, one worthy of comparison with the strongest fortresses of the Caesarean age) had embarked upon the conquest of the secular world so as to lead it to heaven. His success had exceeded his every aspiration, since kings and emperors were now coming to prostrate themselves humbly at his feet, receive their crowns from him, renounce their secular prerogatives, and obey him without argument. In truth, he was by now able to consider himself the lord of all, who at will controlled the world.

The long struggle for the kingdom of Sicily had been concluded with full recognition of the prerogatives of the church. The Marches of Ancona, the duchy of Spoleto, the *contea* of Assisi, once again were under the pope, who had reaffirmed his rule over a large part of central and southern Italy. John, king of England; Pietro II of Aragon; Kaloyan, king of Bulgaria; Ottokar, king of Bohemia; Alphonso IX, king of the Spanish kingdom of Leon; the king of Hungary; the king of Norway; the king of Armenia—all acknowledged that they were vassals of the Vicar of Christ. They put their golden sceptres down on the steps of the great throne and proclaimed that they were ready to unsheathe their swords in defence of it and its sacrosanct rights. The patriarch of Constantinople had yielded to the supremacy of the bishop of Rome.

East and west moved at a signal from him, this man who dispensed kingdoms and thundered out anathemas. To sovereigns who paled at receiving his imperious missives, he spoke in the language of the Old Testament: "As in the Ark of the Covenant of the Lord, the rod was kept near the tables of Law, so in the breast of the Pope are contained both the formidable power of destruction and the gentle sweetness of grace."

The Holy See was now the supreme political seat of the European states.

On October 4, 1209, some months before Francis was admitted to that audience, the German emperor, Otto IV, had come to Rome in great pomp for his coronation. After that had taken place in Saint Peter's, the solemn procession had marched to the Sant'Angelo bridge. There Innocent stopped it and had refused to give it permission to go farther than the river.

With a temerity that aroused the ire of the warriors from over the Alps, he ordered Otto to leave the Roman state by the next day.

More than two months later, in mid-December, 1209, the emperor and his six thousand knights, who still carried the marks of the battle fought in the streets of the Eternal City against the Romans, passed below the walls of Assisi. The noisy rumbling and the shouts of the crowd that came from the city to acclaim Caesar could be heard at Rivo Torto. But Francis had not stirred from his shack. He sent one of his brothers to proclaim to Otto, riding by in all his glory, the fraility of all earthly things.[q]

In a codex of Perugia's cathedral, there is a note by an unknown writer, perhaps one of the canons who had occasion to speak to Innocent III. He wrote his impressions of the pope: "Innocent was small of stature, but handsome; extremely learned in trivium and quadrivium.[r] In theology he surpassed all others. An extremely quick and brilliant mind. Very eloquent, fluent. A quick tongue, a sonorous voice that can be heard and understood by all, even if the tone is low. His appearance inspires reverence and awe in all."[64]

Now the pope listened attentively to the words of the man brought to him by Cardinal John. Too often for his comfort (since he himself had once written a treatise about holding worldly matters in contempt),[65] words were spoken about the concept and the principle of Poverty, on which the new rule being submitted to him for approval was being founded.

The pope had two goals beyond the establishment of the political papacy: the liberation of the Holy Land and the repression of heresy. These words about poverty brought to his mind the many heretical sects that vaunted poverty as a symbol. At that very time a crusade against the Albigenses, proclaimed by Innocent, was going on in France, and he was granting to those who participated in it the same indulgence that was given for fighting in the Holy Land.[66]

So when the saint had finished speaking, the pope pointed out with great authority and energy the usual objection.

The life that they, the penitents of Assisi, proposed to follow was

---

q. *1 Cel.*, 43. Friar Thomas says that "at that time, the Emperor Otto was passing through the place with much clamour and pomp to receive the crown of his earthly empire." But that cannot be exactly right, because, in going to Rome Otto left from Rimini and followed the Via Flaminia. In returning, however, he passed by Assisi between December 14 and 20, 1209, following the Via Francesca to go to Siena, and then to Florence, Lucca, and Pisa. (Boehmer, *Regesta Imperii*, p. 95.) The passage in *1 Cel.* must be interpreted as meaning that the emperor came by Assisi during the trip to Italy for his coronation.

r. Trivium was the medieval name for the group of three sciences constituting the inferior group of the Seven Liberal Arts, grammar, rhetoric, and dialectic; quadrivium, for the advanced group of four, consisting of music, arithmetic, geometry, and astronomy. A student had to complete his studies in these seven subjects before being admitted to theology.—Trans.

too rigid and harsh. He did not doubt their heroism, but would those who came after them have the same ardour?

Francis replied at once that ability to make a total renunciation comes as a gift from Jesus Christ.

The colloquy ended with Innocent's suggestion that they all pray to know the divine will.[67]

According to some sources, Innocent, in this first meeting with Francis, in that Belvedere gallery called the Hall of Mirrors, violently repulsed him. But it seems more suitable to stay with the first biographers, who appear to be calmer, more in agreement, and better informed.[s]

The twelve companions left the pontifical hall. They crossed other splendid chambers with mosaics and marbles, went down a wide staircase guarded by grave dignitaries, and found themselves in the great piazza, now flooded with sun. Two towers of the proud royal palace cut into the purity of the sky. In one of them was a map of the world to signify that the rule of the church extended over all the world. In the other was the bronze wolf, mother of the Romans, to symbolize that this empire was the perfect link with that of the Caesars.

In the middle of the piazza shone the golden horse of the Roman emperor whose crowning glory, a greater one even than that won by Augustus, was his having yielded to the Supreme Vicar of Christ. Near the Aventine a place was once pointed out as the spot where these two, Constantine and the pope, Sylvester, had met each other for the last time, and where Constantine had consigned to the pope the imperial insignia and the crown that he had himself received from the pope on an earlier day. Afterwards, he had exchanged with him a farewell kiss and gone away forever, beyond the sea.[t]

---

s. Wadding (*An. Min.*, vol. 1, 1210, n. 8) says that Cardinal John of St. Paul's, after having made his promise to Francis, hesitated to present him to the pope, and that Francis had to be introduced by an Assisi man assigned to the papal court. The meeting, he said, took place in the Belvedere in the Lateran, where the pope was walking. But because Francis looked so miserable, Innocent III mistook him for a Waldensian and indignantly repulsed him.

This version was picked up by Matthew of Paris who adds other unlikely details, such as that Innocent III told Francis to go join the pigs in the mud, where he belonged, and that Francis obediently did so, and that after he had rolled around in the street with pigs that were passing by, he returned to the pope, who was moved and praised him for his action. (*Chronica Maiora, MGH, Scriptores,* vol. 28.)

An addition to *Leg. Maior,* III, 9, made between 1288 and 1292 by Friar Girolamo da Ascoli, the future Nicholas IV, says that Innocent III saw Francis come in while he was walking in the Hall of Mirrors, lost in deep thought, and knowing nothing about him, indignantly sent him away.

t. This legend is contained in the document known as the Donation of Constantine, in which Constantine is purported to have given Pope Sylvester I primacy over Antioch, Constantinople, Alexandria, and Jerusalem; dominion over all of Italy and the West; and a number of other

The Pope Has a Dream

Now it happened that on the night that followed this audience, Pope Innocent had a vision.

He found himself in the Basilica of Saint John Lateran,[68] vested as on the days of solemn feasts. He walked alone between the vast rows of columns, which seemed to stretch out to infinity.

An unusual brightness was radiating from the enormous quantities of gold, silver, and bronze in the church. The metals gleamed with a mysterious internal light that filtered through the antique green alabaster columns that the original builders had taken from the peristyle of the palace of the Laterani. Between the altar and the apse the Corinthian columns of gilded bronze that the legions of Titus had brought from the ruined temple of Jerusalem were bathed in light. The tabernacle of inlaid silver glittered. The seven priceless altars, with the chalices, the ampullas, the *scifi* and the *patere*,[u] were glowing. The gilded panels of the magnificent coffered ceiling shone. The two candelabra that Constantine had placed under the magnificent architrave, one of silver and one of gold, were lit. A dark crimson carpet marked the throne on which Pope Sylvester had sat to receive the homage of the first Christian emperor. Clouds of incense rose from the tripods placed along the staircases.

It was truly the basilica of gold, the Christian royal palace, the temple *par excellence,* the wondrous cathedral of Rome and of the world. Here on this site, according to legend, Nero, monster of iniquity, had once perpetrated the horrendous farragos of the sort revived every Saint John's night in the sabbaths of witches and she-devils. But now here Jesus was triumphant, ruler and sovereign. On the day of the consecration he is said to have appeared in the apse, smiling and blessing the people. The scene was executed in mosaic on the apse and is there today. That face was not doleful, like the face of the figure in agony on the little Byzantine crucifix in the poor church of San Damiano; it was nobly serene, suffused with majestic beauty. Over it rose the cross that had been fixed on Calvary, from which four

---

powers and privileges, including the crown, which the pope is said to have refused. The document, proved to be a forgery in the fifteenth century, was probably fabricated in the Frankish Empire in the eighth or ninth century.—Trans.

u. Literally, *scifi* were Greek urns and *patere,* containers used to collect the blood of victims in pagan sacrifices or to pour libations. Some of these objects were put into use as Eucharist vessels in the early years of the Christian church. Often, also, they were used in churches for ornamental purposes. However, the author probably means here to refer to the rich cruet and basin used in a Pontifical High Mass to wash the hands of the bishop. Cf. Lemmens, *Testimonia Minora*, p. 37, n. 2: *Patera est "poculi genus, latum ac patens, unde nomen accepisse videtur."* ("A *patera* is a sort of bowl, wide and open, defined for whatever purpose seems appropriate.' " —Stephani, *Thesaurus linguae latinae.*)

rivers poured out, symbols of the Evangelists, through whom living water was poured over the world.

All these opulent mosaics also glowed in a splendour that Innocent had never known. Virgins, Saints, Angels, Archangels, Prophets, and Sibyls sparkled in blazing light. The Apostles, the keys of Peter, the sword of Paul, the head of the Baptist, glittered. The marvellous light was picked up by the mosaics depicting innumerable stories from the Old and New Testaments, high along the walls, amid windows with round arches and locks of carved marble. The whole church was like a vast silent poem in an enchanted hour—one celebrating the past and proclaiming the future; above all, in that hour, one echoing the hosannah on the apse: *Totius ecclesie pater,* "Father of the whole church."

Innocent came forward with his eyes fixed on the altar. No peals went up at his passage, no hymns, no acclamations. He was alone in the deserted basilica. He reached the altar, knelt, and collected his thoughts in prayer. According to an ancient tradition, the most precious relics of Israel were preserved under that altar, given by victorious emperors who had once passed under sculptured arches of triumph: the Tables of the Law, the Ark of the Covenant, the Rod of Moses, the Rod of Aaron, the golden seven-branched candelabra, the golden urn containing manna of the desert. He felt within him the quickening and burning of the new and the old strength, the eternal quality of the faith through centuries past, through centuries yet to come, that faith to which he had given so firm a pedestal.

Suddenly a great rumble thundered through the temple. Innocent saw the columns shake, the archivolts shudder. The walls were collapsing as the ceiling opened. The candelabra were swinging and the processions of ecstatic saints in the mosaics dizzily swaying. Everything was in violent motion as if caught up in the vortex of a dreadful whirlwind. Everything was about to be split asunder, demolished, and swallowed up in an instant, and there was no possibility of stopping it.

He closed his eyes and heard the terrible noise of crashing.

When he reopened them, he saw the basilica as it was before, unharmed, its columns again immobile. A gigantic man supported it all on one shoulder alone.

He saw that it was the beggar of Assisi, the man with bare feet and a ragged habit.

He awoke with a start, and, confused, tried to make out where he was. The night must be far advanced. The two bedroom servants, whose office it was to watch over the sleep of the pope, had themselves gone to sleep, heads leaning on the heavy wall hangings.

He was terrified. There was no doubt of the significance of the vision. The foundation of that fortress that he thought impregnable and imperishable was shattered. The substructure must have been reduced to dust. A small bump would be enough to turn all that exterior might into a mass of fragments and rubble.

The basilica of gold would tumble into a miserable ruin if its new saviour were not there to support it. That poor man whom he had dismissed was the one who by himself had prevented the collapse of the church of Christ.[v]

Approbation of the Rule

A great dispute arose among the members of the curia and the cardinals of the pontifical court when they were convoked to give a decision on the case of the men from Assisi.[69]

Some saw a disguised heresy in the privilege asked by these men. There was substantially little difference between their idea of poverty and that of the Catharists, who held riches to be evil and said that anyone who owned houses or fields or other goods was no true follower of Jesus, and that it was the duty of each to put all things in common with other men and live by the work of one's own hands.

Some called to mind Peter of Waldes, who was very much like Francis. This merchant of Lyon, greatly affected by the sudden death of a person dear to him, disposed of all his goods and distributed

---

v. The story of this vision is in *3 Soc.,* 51; *2 Cel.,* 17; *Leg. Maior,* III, 10.

The same vision of Innocent III was told about the approval of the Rule of Saint Dominic. Friar Constantino Medici di Orvieto of the Order of Preachers was the first to speak of it in the biography of Saint Dominic that he wrote between 1244 and 1245 or 1246 (Quétif-Echard, *Scriptores Ordinis Praedicatorum,* 1:28). According to this author, the vision took place in 1219, when Saint Dominic went with Bishop Fulcone of Tolosa to the Lateran Council held November 11–30 of that year.

Bihl justly observes, in a note to the Quaracchi edition of the writings of Thomas of Celano, that the bull approving Saint Dominic's order was issued December 22, 1216, not by Innocent III but by Honorius III, for Innocent had died July 16 of that year. Moreover, the story of this dream was not included in earlier biographies of Saint Dominic, such as those by Friar Giordano di Sassonia of the Order of Preachers, written certainly before July 3, 1234 (*AA. SS., aug,* 1:541–55); Quétif-Echard (*Scriptores,* 1:2–24, 93–96); and Friar Pietro Ferrandi, written between 1235 and 1241 (*Anal. Boll.* 30 [1911]:54–87). It is also not to be found in the canonization procedures for Saint Dominic in 1233 (*AA. SS.,* 30:628–43; Quétif-Echard, *Scriptores,* 1:44–58).

It would seem that the argument ought to have been resolved after the publication of *Liber exemplorum,* in which Brother Masseo is quoted (chap. 68; *Antonianum* 2:239): "And the same man (Masseo) told about Pope Innocent III, how he saw the Lateran church near collapse and that a poor man was holding it up and how the pope interpreted the vision to be about the blessed Francis, who at that time had approached him with a few brothers as companions."

Brother Masseo was not one of the first companions; he entered the order a little after the approbation of the rule (in 1210, according to Wadding). He became one of Francis's closest companions and also a chosen confidant.

[Many historians place these events and the approval of the Rule in 1209 A.D. See Brown in Englebert, *Saint Francis,* pp. 377–82.—Trans.]

them to the poor. Everyone thought he had gone mad; and he had gone about telling them, "O people of the city, my friends, I am not mad as you believe. Rather, I wanted to avenge myself on my enemies. They reduced me to servitude by forcing me to be more solicitous of money than of God." And so he went about begging at the gates from his old companions. And Pope Alexander III had approved his vow of poverty but had forbidden him to preach, since that office and the explanation of the sacred books belonged only to the clergy.

Someone else pointed out that the imperial party had a habit of making use of the illusions of reformers to gain its own ends, especially those who harped on the abused theme of corruption of the clergy, its material possessions, its secular power. And others saw a serious contradiction in the reception given Francis's request and the crusade opened against the Albigenses, who had set out by espousing poverty but had gone on to accuse the pope and bishops of being sons of the devil, even proclaiming Pope Sylvester to be the Antichrist and the Roman church, the whore of Babylon.

Other examples of heretics were brought up. That of the Manichaeans, who went about from city to city, calling themselves *pauperes Christi,* paupers of Christ, and declared that they wished to possess nothing so as to take proper care of their own souls. That of the poor men of Lyon, who proclaimed salvation only for those who divested themselves of all their possessions in imitation of the Apostles. That of the ragged Patarines.

It was necessary to take certain references to the Gospels with a grain of salt, they said, because they were being used only to accuse the church and the pope of shortcomings. This was true of Arnold of Brescia, who said that the church must return to the purity and simplicity of apostolic times and who cited the Evangelists, who would forbid the ministers of God the possession of temporal goods.[70]

At last Cardinal John rose to speak about the man who was under his protection. "He asks only that he be permitted to live according to the Gospels," he said. "If we reply that this conformity is beyond human strength, we shall be taking the stand that it is impossible for men to follow the Gospel, and we shall be accused of vilifying Jesus Christ, who inspired the Gospels."[71]

So all fell silent, every argument overcome. The twelve men, who had taken shelter in the nearby Ospedale di Sant'Antonio,[72] were sought out and again taken before the pope.

Francis spoke first, and with the poetic gift that added so much to his eloquence, told a story. There was once a woman, poor but very beautiful, he said, who lived in the middle of the desert. The king came there and, because of her incomparable beauty, fell in love with her and made her his wife.

The sons who were born were all extremely handsome. When they had grown up and been nobly educated (the king had returned to his court after a time), the woman said, "What does your poverty matter, since you are the sons of a great king? Go joyfully to court and ask for whatever you need."

They were astonished to hear this and greatly gladdened by it, and they went to the king's court and were admitted to his presence. He admired their fine appearance, and, noting how much they resembled him, he asked them, "Whose sons are you?"

They replied that they were the sons of a poor woman who lived in the desert. Then the king said, embracing them, "O my sons and heirs, do not be hesitant if there should be many strangers at my table, for it is only justice that there be a place for those who will succeed me tomorrow." And he ordered the woman of the desert to send all his children to the court, because he wished to bring them up and take care of them.

The bystanders understood the poor woman to be a symbol of Francis; the sons filled with every virtue, his companions; the desert, the world deprived of light; and the king, the son of God, who, poor himself, would not fail to welcome to his table those who greatly resembled him, that is, the followers of Poverty.[73]

While Francis talked, Innocent watched him, moved and astonished. He was indeed the beggar of his portentous dream, the saviour of the church sent by God.

He arose, and turning to the cardinals surrounding him, said solemnly, "This is truly the man who, with example and doctrine, will uphold the church of Christ."[74]

·8·

"LET THEM BE LESSER BROTHERS"

Francis and his companions were exultant as they walked back to Assisi. Everything had gone better than they could have hoped. The pope had not only given his consent to the rule but had also granted them the privilege of preaching[1] and promised his help for the future. With how much kindliness he had listened to them! With how much love he had advised them! Because God had so clearly helped them, they felt the need to reaffirm their holy intentions, take steps to prevent defections, and set an example to those who would come after them.

They left Rome early in the morning after spending some time on their knees before the tomb of the Apostles and had been walking ever since, devouring the road, exalted by their excited rush of memories, hopes, and promises.

Weakness induced by hunger brought them down to earth. Around them stretched the Roman countryside, deserted and parched in the arid dog days of summer. In vain they searched for help, for a house.

By good fortune a passer-by gave them a bit of bread, and they felt their cup was overflowing when at last they saw water, at the point near Orte where the Nera river flows into the Tiber. The place mirrored so well their high spirits, so joyous at their dream's having become reality, that they decided to stop there.

And there it seemed to the men of Assisi that they had at last found the true kingdom of Lady Poverty. In that enchanted solitude where no one came to disturb their peace, they found complete joy.[a]

---

a. *1 Cel.,* 34. Camilli, in *Memorie francescane,* has demonstrated that the locality in which Francis and his companions stopped was not, as had been previously thought, the site of the church of San Lorenzo but of San Nicolao *ad Scopulos,* some miles distant from the city.

Thomas of Celano has the emotions that stirred them. This Friar Minor, author of the greatest and most powerful hymn to Death that the world has ever known,[b] writes no less vigorously about divine love in the realistic terms appropriate for erotic human love.

He depicts Francis and his companions consummating their love with the lady of their hearts in that deserted and desolate place between the wild mountain and the solitary river. He shows them transported in ecstasy in their union with Lady Poverty, the gentle beggar maid who is movingly portrayed in the great frescoes of the Basilica di San Francesco in Assisi, ragged, her feet bare and bloodied as she walks in a thick tangle of briars, among which lilies and roses are flowering.

And each of them swears that he will never leave her embrace. Each vows to spend the rest of his life bound to the adored lady in a union beyond every thought and distraction, pain and misery, to put above everything else this union that brings the infinite bliss of their realized dream.[2]

They talked again about whether it would not be a better idea to remain there, where they found such rapture, than to return to the workaday world.

But Francis cut short the discussions. He said that God, who had died for the good of men, had not called them solely for their own good but also for the salvation of others.

So they returned to Rivo Torto.

The Franciscan Idyll

Who would have now recognized in them the astute men they had once been, greedy and savage, practiced in war and intrigue, prone to angry invective and subtle sophistry? Men who had delighted in lucrative trade and in being petty tyrants? Who had rejoiced in all kinds of pleasure and even debauchery and were noted for mockery and love of luxury?

Thomas of Celano's description of their life together is like a joyous melody. Filled with love, he describes them, ardent in charity. In their meetings and reunions, "a shoot of spiritual love sprang up" that made them appear creatures of another world, one in which goodness instinctively regulated each act, each feeling.

"Chaste embraces, gentle feelings, a holy kiss, pleasing conversation, modest laughter, joyous looks, a single eye, a submissive spirit,

---

b. *Dies Irae,* a sequence still sometimes used in the Mass for the Dead in the Roman Catholic Church, is presumed to have been written by Thomas of Celano.—Trans.

a peaceable tongue, a mild answer, oneness of purpose, ready obedience, unwearied hand, all these were found in them," Brother Thomas writes.

"They came together with great desire," he continues. "They remained together with joy; but separation from one another was sad on both sides, a bitter divorce, a cruel estrangement. But these most obedient knights dared put nothing before holy obedience. Before the command of obedience was even uttered, they prepared themselves to fulfill the order. Knowing not how to misinterpret the commands, they put aside every objection and hastened to fulfill what was commanded.

"Followers of most holy poverty, because they had nothing, loved nothing, they feared in no way to lose anything. They were content with one tunic, patched at times within and without . . . Girt with a cord, they wore poor trousers . . .

"They were, therefore, everywhere secure, kept in no suspense by fear. Distracted by no care, they awaited the next day without solicitude, nor were they in anxiety about the night's lodgings, though in their journeyings they were often placed in great danger. For, when they frequently lacked the necessary lodging in the coldest weather, an oven sheltered them, or at least they lay hid for the night humbly in grottos or caves. . . . . "

Patience and humility, humility and patience. "The virtue of patience so took hold of them that they sought rather to be where they might suffer persecution of their bodies than where they might be lifted up by favour of the world, when their holiness was known or praised. For many times when they were insulted and ridiculed, stripped naked, beaten, bound, imprisoned, they did not protect themselves by means of anyone's patronage, but they bore all things so courageously that nothing but the voice of praise and thanksgiving resounded in their mouths.

"Scarcely at all, really never, did they let up in their praise of God and in their prayers. Recalling by constant discussion what they had done, they gave thanks to God for what they had done well. For what they had neglected or incautiously committed, they poured forth groans and tears. They thought they were forsaken by God if they did not find themselves to be constantly visited in their devotions by their accustomed piety. . . .

"If, as it can happen, their sobriety were disturbed by an abundance of food or drink, or if because they were tired from a journey, they surpassed even a little the bounds of necessity, they mortified themselves very sharply by an abstinence of many days. Lastly, they tried to repress the promptings of the flesh with such great mortification that often they did not refrain from stripping themselves naked in the coldest weather and from piercing their bodies all over with the points of thorns, even causing the blood to flow.

"They despised all worldly things so keenly that they hardly permitted themselves to receive even the necessaries of life; and they were separated from bodily comforts for so long a time that they did not shrink from anything difficult. Amid all these things they strove for peace and gentleness with all men, and always conducting themselves modestly and peaceably, they avoided all scandals with the greatest zeal. . . . With their eyes directed toward the ground, they clung to heaven with their minds.

"No envy, no malice, no rancor, no abusive speech, no suspicion, no bitterness found any place in them; but great concord, continual quiet, thanksgiving, and the voice of praise were in them.

"These were the teachings of their beloved father, by which he formed his new sons, not by words alone and tongue, but above all in deeds and in truth."[3]

Meanwhile, Francis had begun preaching in Assisi, first in the church of San Giorgio,[4] then in the cathedral of San Rufino.

Perhaps these sermons had begun before his departure for Rome. It would not be surprising. The churches of the Middle Ages were not reserved for religious purposes alone. From surviving records that allow us to reconstruct the customs of Assisi at that time, we see that a great part of the public and private life of the city revolved around the altar. There discussions were held, questions explored. At the altar one encountered bitter passions and often the most ignoble sentiments. There city ceremonies were held—assemblies, gatherings of troops before and after battle. There, too, legal transactions were concluded—notarial deeds and contracts,[c] instruments of buying and selling, accusations and the defences of the accused, the sentences of judges, consuls, and podestà,[5] the submissions of defeated *castelli*.[6] There is, therefore, nothing extraordinary in the fact that from that time on Francis's voice, too, rang out there. On the contrary, the effectiveness of his words can be understood only if one realizes that he brought his message—living words about real life—to the very place of public assembly.

The images that his listeners had of him were drawn from their experience in war. Their impressions—that of a new battle fought

---

c. Many contracts, which in this period were kept in the cathedral archives, were drawn up in the cathedral or in another church. Cf. the contract of 1184 in *NV* 3:539–40.

between Francis and his people—live in the words of the ancient biographers.

The brother from Celano: "His words were like a burning fire, penetrating the inmost reaches of the heart."[7]

And from *The Little Flowers:* "His heavenly words seemed like sharp arrows shot from the bow of divine wisdom; they pierced the hearts of everyone."[8]

Generally he preached on Sundays. Saturday evening he went up to the cathedral. It was his custom to spend the night in a small hut in the garden, devoting himself to prayer and meditation and to thinking about what he would say to the people the next morning.[9]

On one of these nights, one of his companions at Rivo Torto saw a chariot of fire, surmounted by a globe of light like the sun, come into the hovel and make three turns about the room. Those who were asleep were awakened. All were sure that God had shown them that the sun in the burning chariot was their blessed Father Francis so they would be loyal disciples.[10]

He certainly exerted an extraordinary fascination on everyone around him. We have only to look at the desire and the grief with which Thomas of Celano remembered him, which he never lost all his life. His emotion breaks out in pages of beauty and emotion:

"O how beautiful, how splendid, how glorious did he appear in the innocence of his life, in the simplicity of his words, in the purity of his heart, in his love for God, in his fraternal charity, in his ardent obedience, in his peaceful submission, in his angelic countenance! He was charming in his manners, most faithful in what was entrusted to him, cautious in counsel, effective in business, gracious in all things. He was serene of mind, sweet of disposition, sober in spirit, raised up in contemplation, zealous in prayer, and in all things fervent. He was constant in purpose, stable in virtue, persevering in grace, and unchanging in all things. He was quick to pardon, slow to become angry, ready of wit, tenacious of memory, subtle in discussion, circumspect in choosing, and in all things simple. He was unbending with himself, understanding toward others, and discreet in all things."[11]

The people who had first laughed at the son of Pietro Bernardone now turned to him with enthusiasm. All the *contrade* seemed to be existing on a higher level, to thrive again. The poet biographer exults over this new miraculous spring: "The former dryness was routed and the crops sprang up quickly in the neglected field. Even the untended vine began to sprout shoots of the fragrance of the Lord and, after producing blossoms of sweetness, it brought forth fruits of honour and riches."[12]

Naturally there was no lack of those who continued to smile know-ingly and make fun of the notions about love. The attitude was found in all classes. It was not a rich man but a boorish peasant who, several months after their return from Rome, interrupted the brothers at prayer. Pushing an ass into their hut, he shouted to it in an incoherent voice, "Go on in, for we shall make a good thing of this place!"

Francis got up and said peacefully to his companions, "I know, my brothers, that God has not called us to prepare a shelter for asses, but to pray and show to men the life of salvation."

And they all went out and abandoned that place forever.[13]

Now that others had joined them, they could not take up again their wholly vagabond life. They decided they would have to look for appropriate quarters.

Francis went up to Assisi to see Bishop Guido, who heard him out attentively. But he said, "Brother, I do not have a church I can give you."

Francis next took his request to the cathedral. The old and the new canons were called together for a chapter meeting: Tebaldo, Eugenio, Pietro di Vivieno, Borgordione, Bartolo, Rinaldo, Crescenzio, Greco, Guido the hospitaller, Eugenio. (Silvestro was no longer with them, having some months earlier joined Francis and the Men of Penitence.) The discussion was long and agitated, but in the end they turned down his request.[14]

Francis then told the Benedictine monks on Mount Subasio of his need. Here, too, the abbot, Maccabeo, convoked his monks: Bret-tanino, Giacomo, Matteo, Pasquale, Pietro, Girardo, Bonbarone, Il-luminato. They decided to offer Francis the poorest and smallest church that the monastery had under its jurisdiction: Santa Maria della Porziuncola. Francis was overjoyed, for he knew from experi-ence that here one could find God.

But whether the abbey wished to remain scrupulously faithful to the juridical formulae that regulated even the simplest acts of its administration, or whether Francis and his companions did not wish to claim ownership even to that miniscule, derelict, forgotten chapel in the middle of the woods for fear of violating their rule of poverty, the recognition of the legal rights of the monastery were firmly estab-lished. Francis was to give the monks an *amiscera* of lake fish, the kind called *lasche,* every year on the feast of Saint Benedict. He was to receive in turn, through the generosity of the monks, a jar of oil.[15]

So it was that the two churches that stood on either side of the house in which he was born, San Nicolò and San Paolo, made their contribution to the realization of his great concept. In the church of

San Nicolò, the first Rule had been dictated, taken literally from the words of the Gospels. The monks of Mount Subasio, who had jurisdiction over the church of San Paolo, offered the Porziuncola chapel to Francis, the church that would become the head and mother church of the entire Franciscan order, the "lamp burning and shining before the throne of God."[16]

Peace at Last: The Pact of 1210

The political situation in Assisi now took a sudden and decisive turn.[17]

The expedients that had been adopted to avoid the acceptance of the Collestrada arbitration had not been in vain. The trip of Otto IV, the new German emperor, to Italy had brought secret hope to the partisans of the imperial party. Innocent III's success had not convinced anyone that matters were settled, not even the pope himself. And in fact, immediately after his coronation, Otto had begun to make appearances in Siena, Florence, Lucca, and Pisa. From there he travelled to Foligno and Terni in the duchy of Spoleto, that is, right in the very territory that he had recognized as being under the absolute authority of the pope.

Innocent III turned to Perugia, his faithful ally. A new agreement between them was made February 28, 1210, the vigil of the feast of Saint Ercolano, the warrior bishop who had led the Perugini in battle against the barbarians. That was not without significance. The document, the famous *promissio pape in civitatem Perusii* (promise of the pope in the state of Perugia), was ratified *ad honorem Dei et Ecclesiae Romanae,* and what is even more significant, *ad utilitatem communitatis Perusinae civitatis,* "for the advantage of the people of the state of Perugia." The city promised to take up arms for the defence of *Sancti Petri Romanae Urbis,* and it received from the pope an assurance that no matter what happened, it would be included in agreements that might be made with Otto.[18]

The emperor, on his part, lost no time in making clear his plan to take back these papal lands. He conceded the March of Ancona to Azzo d'Este and the duchy of Spoleto to Diopoldo, "as at a time it had been enjoyed by Conrad."

The name of Moscaincervello, old Fly-in-the-brain, who had seemed a tyrant twelve years earlier, sounded now to Assisi citizens like an oracle's prophecy that the city would regain its old power. All had seemed to go well as long as the duchy of Spoleto had been an impregnable barrier against conquest by Perugia, who clearly intended to subjugate the smaller cities. Assisi's bad luck had begun with the so-called era of liberty, when Perugia had been able to form a tyrannical hegemony while claiming to act on a high-sounding principle.

In the month of August, 1210, the emperor's forces savagely sacked all the *contado* of Perugia. The city trembled for its salvation. Rome itself was threatened.[19]

On October 11, Otto was in the *contea* of Todi.

The feudal lords of Assisi, who had waited in vain for ten years for a restoration of the old ways, pretty well understood by now that they had definitely lost that contest. On the other hand, their traditionally Ghibelline spirit would not allow them to fight against the emperor. So they and the commune at last came to an understanding.

In early November, imperial forces invaded Sicily. November 4, before leaving to take over command of the army, the emperor made a triumphal entry into Assisi. There is a record of two official acts he executed there. At the request of Nicola, abbot of the monastery of Sassovivo, he took under his protection the church of San Liberato of Orte. And he invested a German, Enrico, as castellan of Mugnano, near Perugia. Then he went on to San Severino.[20]

Five days later—on November 9, 1210—the people of Assisi gathered in solemn assembly to put their seal on new agreements that were to end the ten-year war. Leonardo and Fortebraccio di Gislerio, the feudal lords who of this family had survived the battles, attended. The arbiters named by the new podestà, the same Carsedonio who had some time earlier been the fiercest enemy of the commune, took part in it. All the members of the old feudal nobility loyal to the emperor were there. This reconciliation was clearly the work of Otto and his counsellors.

Thus they found themselves together, friends and enemies, after so much hatred and so much blood, to establish the new agreements that were to settle the old disputes. The arbiters named by the podestà were drawn indiscriminately from both factions: old Tancredi di Ugone, who had seen his son join Francis in the ranks of the new followers of poverty; the truculent lord of Collestrada, Marescotto di Bernardo Dodici; Tiberio di Magalotto, who would become one of the most rabid leaders of the Ghibelline party; Benvegnate di Cristiano, Bernardo, and Gilio di Marco.

The words of the invocation in the pact made clear at once that homage was due the emperor, who was mentioned along with the duke of Spoleto, immediately after God and the Virgin: "In the name of the Father, Amen. May the divine grace of the Holy Spirit help us.

To the honour of our Lord Jesus Christ and of the Blessed Virgin Mary, of Domino Otto, emperor, of Domino Diopoldo, Duke."

Such piety—with war already under way between the pope and the emperor, and only ten days before the emperor would be excommunicated!

The two factions, *maggiori* and *minori,* state their hopes for the only kind of concord that will assure peace: "This treaty and perpetual agreement for a good peace and harmony, *pro bono pacis et concordia,* has been concluded between the *maggiori* and the *minori* of Assisi."

All the evils from which the city has suffered so cruelly during these ten years have come from military alliances made by factions and individuals with external powers, large and small, to further their own interests or achieve the triumph of their particular causes, to satisfy their ambitions or indulge their own appetites. The supreme will and the interest of the Assisi republic has not been taken into account. So for that reason the treaty puts ahead of everything else a rule forbidding any one class or one faction to make such alliances. Those who disobey are to be banned and have their goods confiscated. "Separately they shall not make any agreement with the pope, nor with his nuncios or legates, nor with emperor or king, nor with their nuncios or legates, nor with any city or *castello,* nor with any important person, but in common accord they shall do all that there may be to do for the honour, safety, and advantage of the commune of Assisi."

Because the city was already allied with Otto, it is not difficult to see that this rule was directed against the Guelph party, to prevent its making agreements with the pope or his ally, Perugia, something it might well have in mind in the light of the new war.

Stirring up divisions in the city is forbidden, a rule that was substantially the equivalent of forbidding the party in favour of the church (Guelph) to admit that it existed. "And no one of the *maggiori* or of the *minori* shall work any division in the city of Assisi among the people of the city, or those living outside, or among the lower classes of Assisi, but will remain in common accord, and as a community, and in common will do those things that ought to be done for the advantage of the city, in the manner of good citizens; and if anyone of the *maggiori* (which may it please God not happen) or of the *minori* shall be guilty of a contravention of the law, there shall be a public condemnation of his person and his goods, according to the will of the consul or the consuls in office at that time; and the consul or the consuls shall be required to punish him, sentencing him to the ban, so that, therefore, this agreement shall not be broken; and if anyone of the aforesaid parties is guilty of violations, it shall be obliged to observe those things that are contained in this instrument, and to return to life in common, and to remain in community, as has been ordered."

It goes on to regulate the thorny question of feudal services and required tributes, the *amiscere*. The people of Assisi and its environs are absolved from all feudal services in effect at the time of the conquest of the city by the archbishop of Mainz, or three years earlier or later than that conquest. Certain other categories of persons subject to the hominicium or the payment of the *amiscere* are to be absolved upon the payment of a sum of money, the payment to be fixed according to the degree of feudal tributes and dues owed and to the economic condition of the subject. If the feudal lord refuses to liberate his subject, liberation will be effected anyhow, through the hand of the captain, the consul, or the curia of the city. And if the lord should refuse to accept the payment, the consul is to receive it for him and deposit it in the principal church; and there it is to be held until the following consulate, after which the consuls are to spend it for the good of the commune in the manner they judge opportune and with the counsel of the people of the city. And the commune is held to defend all those who have been freed and to preserve the records and instruments of liberation.

One provision is for the purpose of encouraging migration into the city to replace the losses that have resulted from these ten years of war: "And thus anyone not within our jurisdiction who comes to this city in peace shall remain safe and secure and shall be free within this city; and he shall not be required to render services to the commune for ten years, except for the army and the assembly."

Other provisions establish the obligation of common defence against violence to private persons, prohibit the *baili* who had been in office for a year (dating from the time of their confirmation) from holding office for the succeeding three years, except for town criers, prohibit putting *baili* of the city in the *ville* except to take custody of *castelli,* regulate the amounts to be allowed feudal lords with regard to tolls, and provide for the payment of city debts.

The document was approved by all, without argument. It marked the end of the violent period of war and of fighting between the *maggiori* and *minori* factions that was the backdrop for the new movement of Saint Francis.

It seemed to the people of the city that they had been freed from a mortal incubus, that they were coming out of a long illness in which every hope of cure had been lost. They could hardly believe their deliverance. Again they had found the sanity of an earlier time, and they turned with confidence to the future.

The *Minori* vs. the *Minori*

One must disagree with the modern biographers who attribute this political pact of 1210 to a spirit of harmony in the city inspired by Saint Francis and his first companions.[21]

Contrasted with love for all, which is ever the first and foremost principle of the Franciscan concept, this peace treaty, which was designed to increase the power of the commune, is little different from those imposed by emperor or enemy city: all meant exploitation of someone.

It is, likewise, a serious error to think that the new Franciscan movement is a consequence of the revolt of the *minori* that came in this period of Assisi history. On the contrary. The new communal society arises, as we have already seen, from a desire for commercial expansion. It sees in war the means of obtaining it. It opposes the pride of merchants to the pride of the feudal lords. It bases its major social force on wealth and on industry. It sanctions the vendetta against those who offended it. It was cruel in meting out penalties and punishments. This society of greedy, violent, quarrelsome, ambitious, brutal people was the perfect antithesis of Franciscanism, as Francis was the antithesis of Pietro Bernardone.

Precisely for the purposes of humbling himself and of reopening the old wound that he had had to suffer in his youth, Francis wanted his brothers to humiliate him by calling him "merchant," "peasant," "son of Pietro Bernardone." And he honoured those in the order who came from a higher class than he did. Thus, according to Giordano of Giano, he called Pietro di Catanio, who in secular life had been both noble and learned, *"Signore"*—"Lord." We should note that among his first companions, those from the noble classes and from powerful families were predominant.

This pact between *maggiori* and *minori* was a means of realizing the aggrandizement of the commune by solidifying its offensive and defensive strength. In it we are very far from the humility of the servants of Poverty, who saw renunciation as the means of salvation.

So, therefore, it was not from the name of a class or faction in the city that Francis took the name "minors" for his brothers. It was an adjective, used in its common significance, one that indicates, even among nobles and religious, the lowest, the inferiors, those who take orders rather than give them.[22]

This is the sense that the word "least" is used in the Gospels themselves. And it was from that source that Francis derived it, when he wrote in his first rule: *Sint minores,* "Let them be lesser brothers."

A bit later, while the rule he had written was being read in his presence, these words struck him with singular force.

"I wish," he said suddenly, "this fraternity to be called the Order of the *Frati Minori* [Friars Minor]."

Thomas of Celano commented on the name that was thus chosen.

"And indeed they were lesser brothers, who, being subject to all, always sought a place that was lowly and sought to perform a duty that seemed in some way to be burdensome to them so that they might merit to be founded solidly in true humility and that through their fruitful disposition a spiritual structure of all virtues might arise in them."[23]

The humility of Francis's Friars Minor was in absolute contrast with the arrogance of the *minori* of the commune, who revolted because they wished a part in ruling the city. Francis, on the contrary, admonished his Friars Minor to take care to avoid offices and power.

"Signore," he said one day to the cardinal of Ostia, explaining why he did not want his brothers to aspire to ecclesiastical office, "my brothers are called *minori* so that in no way will they presume to become *maggiori*—superiors. Their vocation teaches them to remain humble and to follow in the footsteps of Christ's humility, so that by this means they may at last be exalted above others in the eyes of the Saints."[24]

The Mirror of Perfection, from which this story is taken, also gives us a reason that rings true why Francis thought "it was revealed by God that his brothers should call themselves 'minors'":

"One day blessed Francis said, 'The Order and life of the Friars Minor is a little flock which the Son of God has asked of His heavenly Father in these latter days, saying, "Father, I would that Thou shouldest form and give Me a new and humble people in these latter days, who will be unlike all others who have preceded them in humility and poverty, and content to possess Me alone." And the Father said to His beloved Son, "My Son, it is done as Thou hast asked."'

"So blessed Francis used to say that God willed and revealed to him that they should be called Friars Minor, because they were to be the poor and humble people whom the Son of God had asked of His Father. Of this people the Son of God Himself speaks in the Gospel: 'Do not be afraid, My little flock. Your Father has determined to give you His kingdom.' And again: 'Believe Me, when you did it to one of the least of My brethren here, you did it to Me.' And although the

Lord was speaking of all poor and spiritual people, He was referring more particularly to the Order of Friars Minor which was to arise in His Church."[25]

There was a great gulf between Saint Francis's minors and the *minori* that formed a privileged class and faction of the commune. Franciscanism knew no social distinctions. Each who felt a call to this new life could open his heart to its grace. The sackcloth habit made all equal.

Francis does not belong to any faction, new or ancient. He is the universal saint. His concept is for all humanity.

It is an error to think that Saint Francis drew a great part of the spiritual content of his reform from the faction that fought the castle lords in Assisi. But one may certainly come to another conclusion: The Franciscan movement came into being as a reaction to that class war and to the conditions prevailing in Assisi at the time of Francis's youth.

The Courteous Knight, the Wicked Knight

There are some episodes in Francis's life that serve to confirm the assumption that there was an equal response to his new movement among the *maggiori* and the *minori,* the feudal lords and the people, knights and peasants.

One of the most appealing and refreshing chapters of *The Little Flowers* is devoted to such an episode.[26]

One winter evening Francis and one of his companions arrived at the castle of a very powerful noble, who received them joyfully. He went out to meet them, embraced Francis, washed and wiped his muddy feet and kissed them. And then he lit a great fire, prepared the table with an abundance of good food, and served them humbly with his own hands. But it pained him to see a man of God going about so ragged and shabby. He put at Francis's disposition all that he owned, and told him that if he should need a habit or cloak or anything at all, to buy it and that he, the host, would pay for it. "The good Lord has given me an abundance of worldly property," he said, "and so for love of Him I willingly give to those who are poor and in need."

Francis was deeply touched at such courtesy and thoughtfulness and thought that this gentle man would be an ideal Friar Minor. He confided his thought to his companion in words that are a eulogy of the virtue common to both his new order and the old rule of chivalry: courtesy.

"Courtesy," said Saint Francis, "is one of the qualities of God, who courteously gives His sun and His rain and everything to the just and to the unjust. And courtesy is a sister of charity. It extinguishes hatred and keeps love alive."

Because he felt a great love for the knight and wanted him so much to become a part of his company, he promised to return to the house soon. And he told his companion, "Let us pray the Lord God to infuse that desire into his heart and to give him the grace to put it into effect."

A few days later Francis and his companion did return to the house of the courteous man. As they drew near, Francis began to pray, in a place where he could be clearly seen by the nobleman. And in words from *The Little Flowers:* "While that nobleman was looking here and there, he saw Saint Francis praying very devoutly and standing before Christ, and the Blessed Christ standing before Saint Francis in a very bright light and looking very beautiful. And in that bright light he saw that Saint Francis was raised a great distance above the ground in a physical and spiritual uplifting."

The nobleman immediately ran out of the house to Francis, knelt down, and also began to pray, asking that he might be allowed to stay with Francis and live a life of penance. And Francis, in great joy, embraced him and thanked God for having added such a knight to his army. At Francis's command, the rich man gave all that he had to the poor, entered the order, and lived all the rest of his life "in great penance and sanctity and purity."

Franciscan humility so completely destroyed feudal pride that not even the name of this exemplary brother has come down to us. He is nothing but a shining soul, like thousands and thousands of others that over the centuries have spangled Franciscan heavens.

Often the feudal lords to whose houses the brothers of penance went were robbers in plumes, who used their cordon of knighthood as a hangman's halter to strangle their victims. They were looters, torturers, killers. And they were surrounded by bands of brutes, who thought any trace of pity feminine weakness. In their world violence and crime were considered marks of courage and nobility.

One evening it happened that two of Francis's companions reached a castle that was a true hawks' eyrie. The men-at-arms spent their days spying out the approach of wayfarers and caravans so as to rob and sometimes to kill them.

The brothers had little wish to cross that wicked threshold, but night was coming on. They were weak with cold, hunger, and fatigue and had no choice but to do so. They knocked fearfully and "meekly like sheep among wolves," they asked the ruffian who answered the door to tell the castellan of their presence. While waiting, they commended their souls to God.

The *signore* came with grim face, and they asked him to receive them into his house for the love of our Lord Jesus Christ. They expected jeers and an agonizing experience. But he showed great compassion for them and welcomed them as his dearest brothers. He called the servants. The candles were lit, the table laid, a bountiful feast prepared and served. Along with the brothers, his bloody gang sat down.

Supper began. The conversation was such as to make the two servants of God tremble. Those singular fellow diners competed with one another in telling horrible stories about the people they had killed, the booty they had stolen, the traps they had laid. They boasted of their deeds, spoke in thieves' jargon, made plans for the future, broke out in spine-chilling bursts of laughter. Silent, the brothers anxiously awaited the end of the frightful feast.

As the lord rose, one of the brothers went to him and thanked him for his charity. He said that he wished to return it, and asked him, therefore, to call all his household together to listen to what he was going to say. And the friar talked to them with heart overflowing with love and pity. He suffered at seeing them rushing to certain perdition, he said. The way they were living and the things they were doing was death without dying. They ought to live, to know the great happiness of life in the Lord. They ought to open their blind eyes, throw themselves on the mercy of God. They should pray.

These rough men were astonished and perplexed. At length the lord replied that he had always lived in a wild way, and he had never known what was an "Our Father" or "Hail Mary."

The friar said that didn't matter, that he himself would become a surety to Jesus Christ for the salvation of the lord's soul. And for that he wished the barbarous nobleman to do no penance other than to bring with his own hands a bundle of straw on which he and his companion could rest.

And surprisingly, the lord rushed off, his face alight, to bring the straw. With his own hands he made their humble bed in the most beautiful room of the house. Then, when they were in bed, he hid behind the door to watch them.

And lo, when the night was far advanced and all in the castle asleep, he saw the friar who had been so solicitous of his soul get up and raise his arms toward heaven, as if to ask mercy. And he said that he was offering himself as surety for the lord and that he intended to keep his promise, and he implored Jesus to have mercy on this soul that was on its way to perdition and to pardon it. And so passionate were his prayers that mortal flesh ceased to weigh him down and he rose into the air, all the way to the ceiling. Never had the lord seen anyone, even at the death of a dear one, shed such scalding tears nor sigh and lament as did that friar in his heartbreak over the lord's fate and in compassion for him.

As dawn broke, a contrite lord, completely won over, knelt before the holy man and promised that he would do whatever was asked of him. And he fulfilled his promise. As the friar suggested, he sold his goods, made restitution to those whom he had wronged and gave the rest of his money to the poor. In time he entered the Franciscan order, to the great admiration of his old companions. They, too, followed his example and changed their lives.[27]

How the Lords of Rocca Pàida Were Transformed

Records of the time show us there is truth in these devout tales.

In them, for example, we find that the castellans who lived on the most inaccessible portion of Assisi's mountain, the land lying between Armezzano and Collepino, were changed through the influence of Saint Francis.[28]

Here, on the harsh slope of Mount Subasio, ruins of once proud monasteries crop out in the oak woodlands, among hornbeams, flowering ash, and yellow broom, recalling the austere monks who once lived on these heights.

The monastery of San Silvestro, for instance. The wall still resists the centuries of disintegration. The church is almost intact, its rough apse and the dark crypt supported by granite columns plain to be seen. The foundation of the monastery is traced to Saint Romuald[d] in the early part of the eleventh century. Among its illustrious abbots were Ugolino Conti, who became Pope Gregory IX, and Bertrand de Got, who, after having become Pope Clement V, moved the papacy to Avignon.

And the monastery of Vallegloria. A refuge for devout virgins, it was built, according to a historical record preserved in a fine manuscript of its archives, about the year 560 by followers of Saint Benedict themselves.

---

d. Saint Romuald was a Benedictine monk, much travelled, who in 1012, near Arezzo, founded the Camaldolese religious order, with the desire to establish within the Benedictine order a rule for anchorites. He is reputed to have lived to the age of 120, of which (according to Saint Pier Damiani) twenty were spent in the world, three in monasteries, and ninety-seven as a hermit.—Trans.

This same manuscript records visits that Saint Francis made to these abbeys.

All the valley was then dominated by the strong castle situated on the high ground overlooking the village of San Giovanni, Rocca Pàida. Its Greek name reveals that it was constructed in remote times by the Byzantine people of Apulia who were deported there when the area was ruled by the dukes of Spoleto. The communal documents of that century show us a mighty palace, a keep, an encircling outer wall, castle fortifications, the *curtis*. They evoke the ancient wild warrior life.

It was the men of this region, the lords of Rocca Pàida and those from surrounding castles, who will go down to Porziuncola the day that Francis promises salvation to all men through the Indulgence of the Pardon of Porziuncola. They will kneel below the pulpit built of wooden tables and cry out repentance for their sins; and Francis will grant them this new pardon, first saying the memorable words, "I wish to send all of you to Paradise."

And it will be one of these men who would record his experience and his impression of that event: "The blessed Francis preached with so much kindness and efficacy that he seemed to be an angel of heaven and not a man made of flesh. . . . "

We have already met Giovanni, son of Simone, lord of Rocca Pàida, who fought with his father and brothers in the war with Perugia (was he among the imprisoned knights who were comforted by Saint Francis's high spirits?). He was deserving of so much love that Francis favoured him with a privilege given to very few: a revelation of the stigmata.

We know that another castellan of Rocca Pàida will also be at the promulgation of the Indulgence of the Pardon, Count Beccario, son of Seguino. And still another, Napoleone, lord of Armezzano.

Armezzano is even today an important hamlet of the commune of Assisi, perched on top of the "back" side of Mount Subasio, a long climb from Assisi. Some remains of Napoleone's castle still exist: the base of the tower, the gate, the massive walls with narrow windows through which the valley can be seen—a panorama of forests, streams, roads, hills, blue clouds.

Many documents in the Assisi archives refer to this important feudal lord, Napoleone, son of Ubertino. He was particularly devoted to Saint Francis and often entertained him at the castle. Here, when in June the bright yellow broom mantled the bleak stones of the mountain, the dark towers and grim walls of that fortress were enlivened by the grace of the young women of the family and the nuptial beauty of brides. The daughters of Napoleone were Elena and Angeleia. The brides of the sons of the family, who came there to live, were Bionda, wife of Ugolino, Palmira, wife of Bonconte, Aldobrandina, wife of Ubertino.

Napoleone was a domesticated leopard who was overcome every once in a while by his instincts of primitive ferocity. In the documents we see him ride out in the ranks of the commune, dispute rights to the castle of Serra in Valtopina with the cathedral of San Rufino, intrigue for the appointment of a relative as a canon of San Rufino (and for the purpose, go directly to the pope, who called him "my beloved son, noble Napoleone di Armezzano"), pledge his part of Rocca Pàida for dowries for his daughters, go into debt with members of his consortium, take part as a leading citizen in meetings in the cathedral of San Rufino to draw up agreements with neighbouring communes.

After having bowed at the feet of Saint Francis and obtained pardon for his sins, Napoleone again fell into depredation and murder. Two rascally servants, Benvenuto and Leonardo, became his personal evil agents. Their crimes are attested in the lists of those sentenced to the ban. In 1223 they were punished for being found by the night custodians wandering about the city in violation of the city statutes. In 1225 they looted some people of the city. In 1228 they were fined twenty-five *libbre* "because they killed Buono, son of Oportolo."

Ugolino preceded his father into the tomb, leaving three children of a tender age, Napoleuccio, Adeleta, Dialta. The promise of the old piety, dried up in the heart of the grandfather, flowered again in the last one. Dialta, while still a young girl, became a Poor Clare nun in the Basilica di Santa Chiara. She abandoned her worldly name, famous in love songs, to become the humble and pious Sister Lucia.

But particularly touched by Saint Francis was Michele di Berarduccio, who had his house and fields near Rocca Pàida.

We have a famous attestation (much argued about) of his about the Indulgence of the Pardon. Apart from consideration of its contents, the document is indubitably authentic. Michele's very spirit throbs through it, in all its devotion: " . . . In the name of the Blessed Virgin Mary and of all the Saints, in reverence for the five wounds that our Lord Jesus Christ received from execution on the cross, which the blessed Francis, while in sorrowful meditation, saw similarly imprint themselves in the Stigmata on his body . . . "

Michele went often to Porziuncola. He knew, one by one, all the brothers and he loved to spend time with them—Bernardo, Leo, Angelo, Filippo, Masseo, William. They showed him one winter day the rose bushes flowering with white and red roses spattered by precious blood. According to him, Pietro di Catanio turned to him to tell about the marvellous event: "Listen, O Michele, to the wonderful thing that happened a little while ago . . . "

These, then, were the devout people of Rocca Pàida, to whom Saint Francis went, with pleasure, during the time of his first apostolate in the *contado* of Assisi.

From the Carceri one reaches the Mortaro in two hours on foot. From here, the path, still left intact by the centuries, leads directly to Rocca Pàida, along the course of the stream that, because it is formed near the *vetta* or summit, was and is called the Vettoio.

Saint Francis returned to his favourite mountain with love. He came down reluctantly in the great calm of the first days of autumn. The forest of Pàida decorated itself for him with crimson berries shining in the midst of its dark leaves. The thistles glittered like silver. The sudden trills of skylarks were now answered by the lament of plovers, filling the vast meadows with sadness. Winter was coming.

Then came days of rain. It fell continuously, washing summits and valleys. There is a cavern in the valley where Saint Francis used to stop for a time before continuing the walk up to Rocca Pàida. (The people have preserved the memory of these times of meditation. They still point out the "grotto of Saint Francis" beside the steep slope on which the castle stood.) It was a place for thinking about the turning of the seasons, about death, about the infinite mercy of God.

Often night overtook him there, gently covering him and darkening the harsh deserted gorge, from which rose the great voice of rushing water.

The Man of Nottiano

It happened on one of those visits, that Francis arrived in Nottiano, a small village between Rocca Pàida and Armezzano on the road that led to the castle and was under the jurisdiction of Napoleone.

One can imagine what the life of serfs must have been like in this place, not yet touched by the new justice that the power of the city made possible. The account of the Three Companions shows them, in fact, in the blackest misery.

(The little church of Nottiano was for a long time little more than a neglected, bare, dirty barn. Had it not been for the piety of a peasant here and there who treasured the memory of the ancient event that occurred there and saw that it was passed down from father to son, the church would have already crumbled. It was long unroofed, walls propped up with wooden supports. In 1957, after repeated efforts, we were able to have it saved and restored. And thus a sweet Madonna with the face of a gentle adolescent has been returned to its place over the altar and there once again radiates that sense of humility that once moved the heart of a saint.)

When Francis one day passed that church, it was then, too, neglected and full of dust and cobwebs. Grieved to see it so, he took a broom and began to sweep it. By then everyone knew of the holiness of his life, and in short order the news of his arrival spread from house to house.

It was a clear day in early November and the peasants were in the fields, sowing. Among them was a young man named Giovanni—John. He was much loved and well known for his engaging simplicity.[e] Leaving his oxen in the middle of the furrow, he ran to the church, and, finding Francis sweeping, took the broom from his hands and finished the work. Afterwards they sat down outside and John the Simple told the man of God how, after having heard people speak of him and of all he had been doing, he wanted to join him. But he had not yet found the means of putting his wish into action, he said. Now, since he had had the luck to meet him, he wished to do whatever Francis thought best.

Seldom had the Poverello felt a joy so clear and strong flood his heart as in that moment, up there in that wild solitude where the autumn sun sifted through a floating golden dust that seemed to create a nimbus of holiness about an unexpected and miraculous event. There were only a few brothers at that time, as a matter of fact; and John, with his open-hearted simplicity, seemed certain to become a good religious.

"Fratello," said Francis, "if you wish to join our company, you must dispose of all your things and give them to the poor, as all my other brothers have done."

But what could John give away, with a family in misery, barely managing to avoid starvation by farming the stony ground of their small holding on the barren slope of the mountain?

But Francis's words were not spoken in vain, for John ran to the field where the steaming oxen waited, harnessed to the rough plough, loosened one and gave it to Francis.

"Brother," he said, "I have served my father and others of my

---

e. The story of John the Simple is told in *Per.,* 19; *Spec. Perf.,* 57; *2 Cel.,* 190. All say that he lived in a village near Assisi. Agostino of Stroncone specified that it was "Ottiano" ("Umbria Serafica," *Misc. Fran.* 2:45). The Ottiano or Octiani of the time is now Nottiano, high on Mount Subasio. Local tradition preserves the belief that this incident happened there, and the little church there is still pointed out as the church in the story.

house for several years already; and though it is a little thing in comparison to all that would be due me, I intend to take this ox as my part and give it to the poor, in the way you think best."

His parents and brothers, however, when they understood that he intended to leave them, were very much upset. The parents were old and no longer found it easy to work, and the other children were of a tender age. So all of them began to weep bitterly and to raise such pained cries that Saint Francis was moved by their grief. And he responded with the kind of delicate good breeding that it was impossible to resist.

"Get dinner ready," he said, "and we shall eat together. And stop crying, because I am going to bring you great happiness."

And the table was made ready. Surely this was a resplendent holy table, wholly Franciscan, there among those brown lands opened for the gift of the new seeding, blessed by the words of a saint who made an effort to put that troubled people at rest.

They must not grieve over the fact that their son wished to serve God, he said, because, even according to the opinion of the world, it would be to their advantage and honour. And moreover, their family would not be diminished, because all Franciscans would become from then on their sons and brothers. No one could prevent a creature from serving his Creator. It would seem just, however, that the ox, since it had to be donated to the poor according to Gospel precepts, be given to them, for no one appeared poorer and more in need than they.

All rejoiced then, and Francis left with his new companion for Assisi. They travelled on the road that even today goes down by ancient rust coloured cliffs, where the sharp screams of eagles and hawks hold sway.

The man of Nottiano, who in his profound simplicity imitated Francis in all that he did, achieved such perfection that when in a state of virtue he died, Francis, remembering the happy day of their first conversation, called him not "Brother John" but "Saint John."

From the Blood of Class War. . .

Maggiori and *minori* were becoming by now so mixed together that they looked back with stupor at the storm from which they had emerged and tried to show those still in the midst of it how to find salvation.

And every day other citizens dropped out of the life of the world to join Francis and increase the small company of his first companions.

There was Leo, the dearest of all to Francis and Francis's confessor. Juniper, the fool of the *chanson de geste* of Franciscanism. James, who in pity for lepers exceeded Francis himself. Simone, who enchanted everyone by the sweetness of spiritual contemplation. Tebaldo, whom the people of Orte saw cross over the waters of the Tiber in the midst of a storm. Agostino, whom Dante put in Paradise.[f]

These sons of Assisi remain forever the perfect heralds of the Franciscan concept. Saint Francis used to say that a good Friar Minor would be one who had the perfect faith and love of poverty of Brother Bernardo, the simplicity and purity of Brother Leo, the courtesy of Brother Angelo, the gracious look, eloquence, and natural good sense of Brother Masseo,[g] the contemplative spirit of Brother Giles, the virtuous and constant prayer of Brother Rufino, the patience of Brother Juniper.[29] These men were the bright harvest produced by the violence of the past.

The way his contemporaries saw Francis still lives in their recollections:

"He seemed already in heaven, and no longer able to look upon this earth . . .

"In all his preaching, before he proposed the word of God to those gathered about, he first prayed for peace for them, saying: 'The Lord give you peace.'"

He greeted everyone he met this same way, men and women, old and young, priests and laymen: "The Lord give you peace." And so, it was remembered, "For this reason many who had hated peace and had hated also salvation embraced peace . . . and were made children of peace and seekers after eternal salvation."[30]

---

f. Leo is called an Assisi man in *Spec. Perf.*, 1, and *Per.*, 16. The only Leo in Assisi records is a "Domino Leone"—a title sometimes used for priests—who is mentioned in one of the documents dealing with the liberation of serfs (Arch. Cath., fasc. 8, no. 3; *NV* 3:340–41). This is perhaps our Brother Leo.

There is an unbroken tradition that Juniper was also an Assisi man. See also chap. 13, n. 45. The "Giacomo" ("James") mentioned in *Spec. Perf.*, 5, is surely the *frater Iacobus of Assisio*, of *Leg. Maior*, pt. 2, VII, 1. Simone is described in *Fioretti*, 41, as "a young man of Assisi." Tebaldo, who joined the order shortly after the approbation of the rule by Innocent III, is said by Wadding to be also from Assisi; and Agostino, who entered the order in 1210, is presumed to be also. *NV* 2:297–98.

g. *Spec. Perf.*, 85. Brother Masseo was from Marignano, once a small village near Assisi which was named for the owner of the land; it is no longer in existence. He is also described as one of the *laici de Assisio* in a record in the Sacro Convento, and in still another, a list of burials there, as *olaico de Assisi*. The evidence of his origin is given additional weight by the testimony of Fra Lodovico da Pietralunga, who said that he was from Assisi, and by the fact that his nephew Marino, who also joined the order, is repeatedly described as an Assisi man. Hence, the belief that he came from a small village of the same name in Perugia territory cannot be correct. *NV* 2:298–99.

The crowds that went to the cathedral of San Rufino to hear him grew ever larger.

The Pact of 1210 had laid an obligation upon the consuls to see that the interrupted work on the cathedral be taken up again, in the light of the new era of prosperity now opening to the city after its thirty years of war and turmoil.

But the workmen had not yet returned to work. Assemblies, meetings, ceremonies, continued to take place in the old Ugonian church, still standing. And from this church, where the voices of consuls had thundered out before battles, the old cavalier who had fought on the heights of Collestrada, the poet of the company of Tripudianti, now addressed the people, challenging and summoning those who had grown up with him, fought with him, and suffered with him, to penance and peace.

Thomas of Celano gives us an eyewitness account of his extraordinary eloquence, his words a portrait more vivid and lifelike than any painter has ever achieved.

"He was a most eloquent man, a man of cheerful countenance, of kindly aspect. He was immune to cowardice, free of insolence. He was of medium height, closer to shortness. His head was moderate in size and round, his face a bit long and prominent, his forehead smooth and low. His eyes were of moderate size, black and sound, his hair was black, his eyebrows straight, his nose symmetrical, thin and straight. His ears were upright, but small, his temples smooth. His speech was peaceable, fiery and sharp. His voice was strong, sweet, clear, and sonorous. His teeth were set close together, even, and white, his lips were small and thin, his beard black, but not bushy. His neck was slender, his shoulders straight, his arms short, his hands slender, his fingers long, his nails extended. His legs were thin, his feet small. His skin was delicate, his flesh very spare. He wore rough garments, he slept but very briefly, he gave most generously. And because he was very humble, he showed all mildness to all men, adapting himself usefully to the behavior of all. The more holy amongst the holy, among sinners he was as one of them."[31]

And then Thomas breaks into an impetuous plea that must have been much like those cried out by the people under the high vault of the cathedral: "Most holy father, help the sinners, you who loved sinners, and deign, we beg of you, most kindly to raise up by your most glorious intercession those whom you see lying in the mire of their sins."[32]

During Lent of the year 1211, a young woman was among the

throngs who listened and were touched by him, a young woman who was in heart as well as in name, luminous.

From the new merchants had come the father of the Friars Minor. But it was from the old feudal people that the founder of the Second Order of Saint Francis would come: the shining girl from the world of castles and chivalry, Clare.

·9·

SAINT CLARE, LADY OF LIGHT

The sons of Offreduccio were unsurpassed both in moneymaking and in taking heroic risks, men who readily passed from executing legal documents to a fray, from the judge's bench to sentry duty in the piazza and defence of the city's walls.

Their house was at the left of the old Ugonian cathedral of San Rufino, the Parlascio side. The façade was an extension of the line of the left side of the cathedral and faced the small cathedral piazza. Behind the house ran the street that led to the old Roman gate, later called Via del Torrione from the ancient Roman sepulchral monument that still stands there.[a]

---

a. The description of the location of Saint Clare's family house is taken from *NV* 2:351–82. There has been considerable controversy, especially between Fortini and Abate, whether Clare's family lived in the house attached to the present façade of the cathedral (Abate) or on the site of the second house from the present façade, now the site of the Sermattei palazzo (Fortini). Fortini bases his identification on records bearing witness to the fact that the old cathedral (which extended much farther into the piazza than the present one) continued to stand and be used for a number of years after construction had been largely completed on the present one. Since Clare's friend, Pacifica di Guelfuccio, whose family lived on the other side of the piazza, testified that there was nothing between her house and Clare's but the piazza, Clare's house would have had to stand, in those circumstances, on the Fortini site. The house is described as next to or adjoining the cathedral and the street (*domum nostram, que est juxta Ecclesiam et iuxta viam*) in the document of 1148 in which Clare's grandfather, Offreduccio, and his brother, Rinaldo, agreed not to add towers or fortifications to their house that would rise above the cathedral. (See chap. 2, pp. 70–71, of this book.) That their house was an imposing mansion is made clear by testimony in the canonization proceedings for Clare as well as by the fact that surviving records give evidence that the members of the family were leaders in the prestigious consortium of San Rufino.

The discovery of the records of the canonization process for Clare cleared up a number of doubtful points about her life, in addition to the identification of the family house. Among them:

1. The family name was definitely not Scifi, as was reported in many earlier biographies. The witnesses, among them members of her own family, clearly identified her as the daughter of

It was a tall and proud palazzo, built on the same wall of boulders that supports the church, the wall built between the old Roman fornix and the Roman circus by the Umbrian forefathers whose impressive names are still engraved on the cistern that forms the base of the campanile.

The ancient *adiutores et defensores* of the San Rufino consortium, whom we met earlier (see chap. 2), had been dead for some time by the era with which we are now concerned. But their faith had been passed on to their great-hearted sons and grandsons, whom we find still living around the cathedral, near the prior and the canons. ·

Among them was Ranieri, son of Bernardo.

Also Rodolfo, Berarduccio's son. Pietro and Bartolo, sons of Oderisio. Paganuccio, son of Bernardo. Pietro di Girardone with his sons, among whom Ugolino stands out for his vigour. Ugolino would later become the captain of war and the captain of the gate at the time of the Saracen siege,[b] and Clare in the future would foresee through grace a reconciliation with his wife, from whom he had been separated for twenty-two years.

Bernardo, son of Suppo. Guelfuccio, son of Bernardo. Clarissimo, son of Rodolfo.

The three sons of Gentile: Gianni, Pietro, Raniero. The three sons of Arnaldo: Pietro, Gentile, Senalio. The son of Acquistardito, Clarissimo.

The sons of the sons of Ugone.

These men, like their fathers before them, spent their lives making war, building and tearing down castles, engaging in disputes on feudal services and homages, dictating the decisions in arbitrations, stipulating with canons the codicils for emphyteutic leases of forests and vineyards.

But it was the sons of Offreduccio who in the end surpassed all others in power and wealth, courage, prudence, and wisdom. There were seven knights in the part of the family that lived in the *contrada,* according to Pietro di Damiano, who gave testimony in the canonization proceedings [for Saint Clare]. They were all strong, daring, cruel, known for their bravura use of the spear and the halberd.

Favarone, who was the son of Offreduccio. Her great-grandfather was named Bernardino; her great-great grandfather, Offredo. "Scifi" was a late malformation of the name of her uncle, Scipione, who was the father of Brother Rufino.

2. Neither Clare nor her family had any connection with Sasso Rosso, where the civil war in Assisi began, as has been mistakenly asserted. There is clear and abundant documentation that the fortress belonged to the sons of Gislerio d'Albercio. (See chap. 4, pp. 124–26.)

For further information about the house and Clare's family: *NV* 2:315–82.—Trans.

b. See n. r. of this chapter, p. 362.

Despite the fact that their ancestors had assumed an obligation not to raise towers or bartizans that would rise above the nearby cathedral, their palazzo was strengthened like a fortress and provided with two doors, one for the days of truce, the other for the days of battle.[c]

Their vast possessions extended below the leper hospital, reached to Castelnuovo, went up the hill beyond Cannara, this not counting the lands of Chiagina conceded in precarium to the canons. An opulent *curtis,* capable of supplying every kind of produce, was established below the wall of Moiano, between Sant'Anastasio and the Valecchie road. They had serfs, men and women, and men-at-arms.

We see listed in the records of the time the sons of Offreduccio and their descendants: Monaldo, the violent lord; Scipione, prominent in affairs of the commune; the sons of Scipione, Rufino and Paolo; Ugolino, feudal lord of the *castello* of Corano; Ugolino's sons, Monaldo and Martino; Paolo and his son, Bernardino; Favarone.

With all the din made by iron-clad armour and long swords struck against the floors, the house must have quivered from an incessant noise of war. Even the women had a fiery devotion, tried in castle battles. It led them to take joy in enterprises overseas, in adventurous voyages on *saettìe*—sailing ships swift as arrows, loaded with arms. They were thrilled by prayers said among the sound of clashing shields as sails were loosed and the ship went flying to attack enemy vessels. They were stirred by the Crusades against the infidels.

Now it happened that after peace had been made with Saladin, some Assisi women, along with others of the city, went to Palestine. Among them was Favarone's bride, Madonna Ortolana, also of a noble house. Her companion on the journey was the young daughter of Guelfuccio di Bernardo, her relative and neighbour, who was named Pacifica.

The pilgrims who went to the Holy Land travelled by way of Egypt. They reached Damietta by galley and from there went on,

---

c. The second door of Clare's house has often been referred to as the "door of the dead," a romantic name frequently applied to the second door of Assisi houses. Such doors were supposedly used only for funerals. However, according to *Treccani,* (s.v. "Assisi") the belief has no basis in fact: secondary doors were common in medieval Umbrian houses, but one door was commonly used as a first floor entrance (usually to a shop) and the other opened onto a stairway leading to the upper floors. In another opinion, the art historian Mario Salmi says the second door (often equipped with removable steps) was really designed for protection during the frequent street fighting. ("La cosidetta 'Porta del Morto'" *Lares* 21:1–8.) Such would seem also to be the opinion of Fortini.

Curiously, however, this translator was told in the summer of 1972 by an aged native of Assisi that "doors of the dead" were in common use in her youth, and that they were used not only for taking out the bodies of dead members of the family but were also the doors through which brides left their houses for their weddings, symbolizing the fact that they were now dead to their families and belonged to the family of their husbands. "Was not this a beautiful custom?" she said.—Trans.

through Sinai and Gaza, to Jerusalem. Certainly the devout pilgrims from Assisi also took this route.

A notice that has previously escaped the attention of students of the subject bears witness to the fact that the principal attraction of this itinerary was a visit to Mount Sinai. This, too, would be true of those from Assisi. It must have been the intrepid canons of the cathedral, neighbours of the families of Ortolana and Pacifica di Guelfuccio, who promoted and led these expeditions.

In fact, in an account of the miracles that took place in Assisi in 1212 after the reappearance of the body of Saint Rufinus, the author, a cathedral canon, says that he himself had verified some of the marvellous happenings that took place in the cathedral but that some of them he had learned about from others who had been witnesses of them, inasmuch as during a certain period of the year he was far away from Assisi, having taken the cross "in order to go to visit Mount Sinai."[1]

This account was undoubtedly written by one of those canons whose names we know through the documents of the time. Perhaps it was the very one who twenty years earlier had led on this same road the group with whom the young wife of Favarone had travelled.

Pilgrims reached Sinai fifteen days after leaving Damietta, a trip made by crossing the desert with seldom-to-be trusted Arabs as guides. They did not have the advantage of a safe conduct from the sultan. Bands of mounted Saracen nomads armed with bows and lances were likely to burst upon them and try to kill them for booty. The group would have to pause while the men fought them off. While the battle lasted, the women knelt on the sand and invoked the aid of Saint Catherine of Alexandria, to whose protection the caravans were entrusted in those savage lands. Her relics were preserved in the church at the foot of the sacred mountain.

Saint Catherine was the brave virgin who had boldly faced up to her test in front of the emperor, according to the legend that every pilgrim carried in his heart on the long journey: "I am Catherine, the daughter of the king, and I have abandoned all my riches in order to follow our Lord Jesus Christ."

She was tortured and killed. Afterwards, it is said, angels came and carried her holy body to the highest peak of Sinai, where God had given to Moses his law. This mountain is all one massive and unyielding rock that cannot be marked even by the blows of a club. But lo, as soon as the angels had put down their precious burden, the stone yielded "as the candle yields to the red hot iron."

We take these tales and images from accounts written during that period.[2] Surely the girl who would become the founder of the Poor Clares must have been nurtured on them from the time of her infancy.

The pilgrims climbed that lofty peak, bloodying their hands and their feet in doing so. They looked at the stone that still preserves the imprint of the body of the martyr. Afterwards they went down to the monastery of the Greek monks, who came in procession, joyful and serene, to meet those who had crossed the desert. "There is among them," says an ancient chronicle, "admirable peace and harmony, and at the same time, abstinence and prayers, and frequent ringing out of devout psalmodies, which follow a time of sacred silence. It seemed that they must lead the life of angels rather than of men."

Then the pilgrims were taken to the church. Founded by Justinian, the Christian emperor, it was enriched like a corner of Paradise but bristling with towers and built with the strong heavy walls of a fortress. The assaults of the infidels came often and the monastery sometimes had to sustain long sieges. The sarcophagus that contained the bones of the martyr was there. A miraculous oil incessantly seeped from it and was used for the lamps. The pilgrims kissed the tomb and received from the monks in charity some bread and a candle. Then they resumed their journey.

Again they had trials and tribulations. Another fifteen days were required to cross the desert to reach Gaza. Water was scarce. Often the thirsty followed a lion's tracks on the sand to find a spring. Reaching a muddy puddle, they would throw themselves down to assuage their terrible burning thirst.

Friar Antonio dei Riboldi, who made that crossing in the early days of the fourteenth century and afterwards wrote a long narration about his experience in his *Itinerarium ad montem Sinai,* said that one time, being ready to collapse from his horrible thirst, he and his companions of the road recommended themselves to Saint Catherine, who miraculously sent the water for which they prayed. "Because of this," he continues, "the story of Saint Catherine was painted in our chapel, and the vow to do this was made by a merchant who was with us, a native of Piacenza named Giovanni De Rosal."

He told of another time when the Saracen robber bands came, seized them and were going to kill them. A trying time began, during which the travellers, sure they were doomed to die, again invoked the aid of Saint Catherine. And suddenly the murderers became humble and submissive and asked only for a piece of bread to appease their hunger. It was, says the pious narrator, again Saint Catherine who had come to their rescue. "She saved us from dying of thirst and delivered us from the hands of those Arabs, she, for whose devotion our pilgrimage was inspired. Many vows were then made, many prayers recited, many tears shed. I, for my part, made a vow that in honour of Saint Catherine, I would recite eighteen Ave Marias every day for eighteen years and make the same number of genuflections. And I also vowed to the Mother of God that on her four vigils and on the vigil of Saint Catherine I would always fast on bread and water, if, through her merits, she would take us away from the claws of those enemy dogs."

And he concludes: "There is not in all the world a pilgrimage harder than the one to Mount Sinai. If I had known that all these dangers had to be run, never would I have set foot on it. But always a ray of hope sustained my heart: Saint Catherine would not permit us to perish, because this Saint never fails to hear the prayers of those who turn to her."

Was it after making such a vow as this that the former pilgrim of Assisi gave her second daughter, the one who would become Sister Agnes, the name of Catherine? It is easy to think so, if one remembers for what reasons names were chosen for children, as has been explained earlier.

There is also a reasonable confirmation of such a supposition in the family devotion to the saint of Alexandria (a devotion that was passed on to become a pious tradition of the monastery of the Poor Clares of Assisi). Perhaps in a miraculous intervention lost to memory Saint Catherine made it possible that the lives of the daughters of the family were preserved for the good of Christians.

Saint Catherine is in the Basilica di Santa Chiara in Assisi, painted by an unknown Giottoesque painter in the early part of the fourteenth century. Dressed in azure and violet, she stands between Ortolana's two daughters who became saints.

One of the earliest monasteries of Assisi (still standing in Piazza Nuova a short distance from the old house of Saint Clare) was consecrated to Saint Catherine and for many years has been held in great veneration by the people of the city.[3]

Ortolana became pregnant after her return to Assisi. As the time of birth drew near, she often went down to the nearby church and prayed for long hours before the crucifix. One day, while she was thus in prayer, it seemed to her that she heard a voice saying, "O lady, do not fear, because you will joyfully bring forth a clear light that will illuminate the world."

A baby girl was born some days later. Because of this prophecy, on the day that the baby was carried to the baptismal font of San Rufino in a great flurry of laces, damasks, and noble guests, she was given the name of Chiara, or as we know it in English, Clare.[4]

Silver Dove

Ortolana made other pilgrimages.[d] She climbed Mount Gargano to visit the church of Saint Michael the Archangel and invoke his protection over the knights of the family. She went to the tomb of the Apostles (in Rome). She was strong and pious. And always the daughter of Guelfuccio accompanied her, affectionate and faithful.

Two other daughters were born to her: Catherine and Beatrice.

Clare was a young child when the walls of the castles came tumbling down under the blows of the people of the commune and flames roared up from the towers on the cliffs of the mountain. One of her special friends was Filippa, the young daughter of Leonardo di Gislerio, the castellan of Sasso Rosso, the political exile and sworn enemy of the commune. Through the stories of her terrified little friend, the sense of the animosity that rose from the hot ashes of the ruined castles touched Ortolana's daughter's heart.

As the war flared up, all of Clare's family took refuge in Perugia, where her uncle Monaldo had taken citizenship, according to the terms imposed on the knights who had committed themselves to fight against Assisi. The wrath of the people over this move exploded in an attack on the family house on the Piazza San Rufino, and it was severely damaged.

In Perugia, Clare again found Leonardo's daughter, and she lived in the house of a girl who would become one of her first companions, Benvenuta. She listened to the bitter talk of the partisans, still stirred up over the battle of Collestrada, and saw throngs of prisoners, humiliated and derided. She heard the lamentations of the noble women mourning over the bodies of the Sasso Rosso men, whose blood had been spilled on that battlefield.

The exile, filled with vain hopes and bitter disillusionments, lasted until 1205, when at last Monaldo and Favarone were able to return to their city. A cheerless adolescence was the fate of the girl whom it pleased her earliest biographers to depict as a delicate spring flower.[5] Because of her virtues of quiet tranquillity and modesty, the people of the city had a high regard for Favarone's daughter.

In that time of great happenings, the piazza of San Rufino daily

---

d. In Assisi, as elsewhere, the custom of making pilgrimages to holy places was well-established. Records show that Rome, Mount Gargano, Venice, and the Holy Land were regularly visited by the devout of Assisi. See *NV* 2:221–24, 343.

swirled with armed men, people of the city, magistrates. Every day the palazzo echoed to the trumpet calls of heralds, the bawling of rabble-rousers, the cry of people answering the call to citizen assembly, the pawing of the horses of the cavaliers. People constantly ran to the windows to watch. But the balcony in the house of the sons of Offreduccio was always deserted. These young women did not like to put themselves on display, and that, too, served to increase their reputation for virtue.[6]

At one moment, when evening is coming on, the coming of the night brings drama to the piazza. Shadow, descending from the mountain, envelops it little by little, until only the peak of the cathedral façade remains bright, burning intently. Then the sun makes it blaze in a vermilion that fades and suddenly goes out. The iron-grey stone turns ashen and cold. A waiting silence falls over the open square.

Clare must have looked out at the solitary piazza countless times in that hour. At the sight of the evening star rising, did a hidden pain clutch her heart? Hers was a compassionate heart. The suffering of that terrible period touched even the rooms of the rich palazzo, cast a pall on the lavish dinner parties.

Giovanni di Ventura, man-at-arms of the house, who gave evidence in the canonization proceedings for Clare, remembered: "For all that the *curtis* of the house was one of the greatest in the city and many things were bought, nevertheless, she reserved the food that she was given to eat, the kind suitable for a great house, put it aside, and then sent it to the poor."[7]

Years passed. The last exiles returned, Leonardo and Fortebraccio of Sasso Rosso among them. In ten years the little girls had become beautiful young women. Hope bloomed again in the grace of their songs and the light of their smiles. The house was lit up by the radiance of their jewels, the splendour of samite and velvet, the swift flashes of their long, heavy, blonde hair.

When Francis renounced all worldly goods before the bishop of Assisi, Clare was fourteen years old. *Columba deargentata,* her biographer calls her, silver dove.[8] She was very beautiful. Tall, straight, like the stalk of a flower.

The Making of Brother Rufino

In the year that the emperor Otto IV went to Rome, an unusual episode aroused a lot of talk in the family.

The son of Scipione, Rufino, had one day gone from the *castello* of Isola di Cannara, where his father was the *signore,* to the nearby *castello* of Limigiano, located in the place called Isola (Isle) of Scipione because three rivers surround it.

At that time Francis was with his first brothers at Rivo Torto, two of whom came into Limigiano and stopped on the piazza, arguing in a lively manner. One of them (it was Barbaro, who had entered the order only a short time earlier) became angry and said something insulting to the other, so that he flared up in turn. Rufino believed that they were on the point of grabbing each other by the hair and coming to blows. That was, in truth, the expected thing at the time. Therefore, the son of Scipione was astonished when he saw Barbaro, thunder-struck at the rage that he himself had aroused in his companion, remorsefully bend down to the ground, gather up ass's dung, and begin to chew it, saying, "My mouth, from which came the offence that disturbed my companion, shall bear the penalty and the shame."[e]

Even then Rufino knew that the brother who had humiliated himself in order to seek pardon from his companion was braver than those who took sword in hand to safeguard their honour. And he was so impressed by it that he declared he himself was ready to do anything the brothers asked him to do.

He found afterwards that the penitents of Rivo Torto loved one another to such a degree that if one of them let drop some word that might displease another, he would not rest until he had confessed his fault, prostrated himself on the ground, and asked his brother to put his foot on his mouth. Often the one who had been injured would refuse to perform such an act; then the one who had given offence, if he were a superior in the order, ordered him to do it in holy obedience. Or if he did not have the authority to give such an order, he would take up the matter with his superior and ask him to order it.[9]

---

e. In most early sources this incident is said to have happened on the island of Cyprus, which seems highly unlikely in these early days of the order. How could the friars have been so far from home at this time? And why?

A clue both as to its proper identification and the identification of the nobleman who saw the incident (not named in the early sources) is in a variant edition of *2 Cel.* edited by Rinaldi, in which it is said to have happened on *Insula Cipii,* rather than *Cypri.* It has long been the local custom to call a place surrounded by streams an *isola* or "island." Among the several so called near Assisi is an ancient *castello,* known today as Castellaccio, surrounded by three streams, the Rapace, Attone, and Timia, still called "Isola" by people living nearby.

In the early part of the thirteenth century, this *castello,* which stands near Limigiano, was owned by Scipione, Rufino's father. Since places were called after the names of their owners at the time, it would have been called *Insula Cipii.* This surely is the most likely place for this incident to have taken place.

What nobleman would be more likely to have seen the incident on this Isola di Scipione than a member of the family of the *signore*—in fact, Rufino di Scipione? And what more likely than that Rufino himself told the story to the ancient biographers when they were collecting material about Saint Francis, modestly omitting his own name? For a complete discussion of the question, see *NV* 2:383–88.

About a year later, the son of Scipione joined the company of the Friars Minor.

Not long afterwards he himself was to find out what it was like to be laughed at for performing a humiliating act in public.

Francis ordered him to go up to Assisi to preach.

Brother Rufino, besides being naturally shy, did not have the gift of words. Moreover, constant meditation kept him so continuously absorbed and rapt in God that he seemed to become almost insensible and mute. He rarely spoke. Therefore, he begged Francis to excuse him and not send him, saying that he was not eloquent and was only a simple ignorant fellow.

This disobedience displeased Francis. To punish his companion, he repeated his order and added that Brother Rufino would have to go up to the city clad only in his drawers and go into the church and preach a sermon.

When the son of Scipione went into the church and up to the pulpit as ordered, the congregation was convulsed with laughter. They said to each other, "These fellows do so much penance that they really have gone crazy."

In the meantime Francis was overcome by remorse at having given such a harsh punishment to Brother Rufino, especially in the light of the difference in their social stations. He said to himself, "How could you be so presumptuous, you son of Pietro Bernardone, wretched little guy that you are, to order Brother Rufino, who is one of the noblest men of Ascesi, to strip off his clothes and go preach to the people like a crazy man?"

To punish himself he stripped off his own clothes as he had ordered Brother Rufino to do and hurried up to Assisi. He was accompanied by Brother Leo, who discreetly carried the habits of both men. Again the people broke into jeers and laughter.

But Francis searched out the church where Brother Rufino was in the pulpit, preaching about the worthlessness of worldly things and the love of God and neighbour. And he, too, went up into the pulpit unclothed and began to speak so marvellously about holy penance and voluntary poverty and desire for the Kingdom of Heaven and about the nakedness and humiliation that were a part of the Passion of our Lord Jesus Christ that all that crowd of men and women began to weep bitterly in incredible devotion and compunction. And, in fact, there was heartfelt penitence and sorrow all through the city that day over the Passion of our Lord Jesus Christ.[10]

Brother Rufino was one of the most virtuous brothers who was ever a part of Saint Francis's order. In *The Chronicle of the 24 Generals*, he is compared to a lily: *liliali puritatis candore enituit.*[11]

One day Saint Francis, seated outside his cell, was talking with other brothers about God, when they saw Rufino come out of the woods where he had been spending time in meditation, and pass by not far away.

Francis asked then, "Tell me, my dear brothers, who do you think is the holiest soul that God has in the world right now?"

They said that they thought it was Francis.

And he said, "O my dearest brothers, I am myself the most unworthy and the vilest man that God has in the world. But see Brother Rufino there coming out of the woods? God has revealed to me that his soul is one of the three holiest souls on earth today. And firmly I say to you that you need have no hesitation in calling him Saint Rufino while he is still living in his earthly body, because his soul was not long ago canonized in heaven, as God has also revealed to me."[12]

Clare Meets Francis

Clare's seventeenth birthday came and went, and the members of her family began to talk of their wish that she get married.

"Since she was lovely to look at," Ranieri di Bernardo testified in the canonization proceedings, "the matter of a husband for her was discussed, and many of her relatives urged her to choose a husband, but she did not want to consent to it. I myself many times implored her to agree to it, but she did not want to hear of it."

Pietro di Damiano, a neighbour, remembered the same thing. "And I observed that her father and her mother and her relatives wanted her to make a marriage suitable to her noble station, to a great and powerful man. But this modest violet, who must have been seventeen years old or thereabouts, could in no way be persuaded to do it."[13]

One day, after long hesitation, Clare told what was in her heart to Pacifica's sister, Bona. Bona had always had a high opinion of what Ortolana's daughter thought and said, so much so that on her advice she had gone on a pilgrimage to Saint James of Compostella. But now, listening to her, she was thunderstruck.

Even Clare, like Rufino, had been drawn to the crazy man whom the street boys attacked with mud and stones. His remarkable humility fascinated her more than any great deed in war or in knightly tournaments.[14]

Moved, Bona secretly arranged for Clare to have a conversation with Francis. What must have been Francis's feeling when he saw at his feet, trembling with devotion and love, the daughter of the powerful feudal lord of San Rufino? The girl for whom he had longed when he had had daydreams of being a poet and a knight, the damsel for whose admiration he would have performed great princely deeds, in the end had come to him, sweet and gentle. And she reminded him of the humble figure of the girl whom he had seen in his last serenata with the Tripudianti dancers in the Assisi piazza. What Clare wanted was this: to dress in the same rough habit he did, to wear a cord for a belt, to follow Francis on his path of renunciation.

The meetings of Francis and Clare continued for nearly a year. Bona di Guelfuccio testified in the canonization proceedings that she often accompanied the young girl, who "went secretly so as not to be seen by members of her family."

Sometimes the old *signore* of Mandria, Filippo di Lungo, also came to these meetings.

The step on which Clare had long meditated was finally taken during the last days of Lent, 1211.[f] That was during the last days of March. Pilgrims had begun to walk along the Strada Francesca to Rome. Even Bona, Clare's confidante, was observing Holy Week there, in the city of the Apostles.[15]

The Break with the Family: Palm Sunday, 1211

According to her promise, Clare went to the cathedral, San Rufino, on Palm Sunday. It was March 27, to be exact. She wore her richest clothes and all her jewels, like a bride.

---

f. Cresi holds, as opposed to Lazzeri, that the flight of Saint Clare from her family house took place on Palm Sunday, 1212 (cf. "Cronologia di S. Chiara," *Studi Francescani* 50:260–67). [Brady follows this opinion: see his translation of *Leg. S Clarae,* p. 160.]

Whether Clare's father was dead when she left to join Saint Francis at the age of eighteen was one point not resolved by the canonization process. The evidence often cited involves three things: (1) the testimony of Pacifica, Clare's friend and neighbour; (2) the fact that Clare's mother, Ortolana, herself became a Poor Clare nun; and (3) the fact that Clare had come into an inheritance.

Pacifica testified in the *Processo* that she did not *vidde* Favarone but *vidde* Ortolana. That word in Umbrian dialect meant that she did not know him intimately, in the fashion of a member of the family or close friend, as she did know Ortolana. We can't be sure why: how would a young girl have described her relationship to the father of her friend? Could he have been an invalid? Away from home a great deal? Aloof and cold? Or dead?

On the second point: We do not know whether religious orders of the time would accept wives whose husbands were living, so we cannot be sure that Ortolana's entering the order a few years after Clare left home meant that her husband was dead. There could have been other reasons.

And the third: According to feudal law, the children of a family had the right of comparticipation in the family patrimony, even though the parents were still living. The report of Clare's inheritance in *Leg. S. Clarae* is derived from information given in the canonization process, and it is not at all clear from the *Processo* whether Clare had that inheritance when she entered the order or received it at a later time. Her younger sister, Beatrice, in fact seems to imply that Clare sold their two portions at the same time, yet Beatrice entered the order several years later than Clare.

It is true that Favarone does not appear in city records of the time, unless he is that Favarone who in 1229 had two serfs who were cited for their misdeeds. And it is equally true that none of the people who refer to him specifically say that he is dead. The question has to remain open.

For a much fuller discussion of Clare's family and paternal house, see *NV* 2:315–83; for persons associated with her, *NV* 2:383–426.—Trans.

The people came into the sun-flooded piazza from all directions. Velvets, mantles, and corslets shone. It was the first Palm Sunday after the ten years of war that friends and enemies found themselves together before the altar of their patron saint. The most distinguished ladies of the city were already in their places, as were the girls who were Clare's friends. The sound of the organ filled the arcades and priests in violet vestments sang *Hosanna in excelsis*. It was a glorious, happy morning, a morning of exultation and adoration.

The deacons carried in great bundles of olive branches and put them on the altar. Bishop Guido turned to the canons. In the pause between the music and the chants, the words of the prayer rose up as he proclaimed in a loud voice, emphasizing each syllable: "O God, who by an olive branch commanded the dove to proclaim peace to the world, sanctify, we beseech thee, by thy heavenly benediction, these branches of olives and other trees, that they may be serviceable to all thy people unto salvation."

Again the triumphal chorus burst out: "Holy, holy, holy, Lord God of hosts . . ."

The bishop put the incense in the thurible and a dense cloud rose and veiled the flames of the candles. The branches were incensed three times and three times sprinkled with holy water. The choir sang the antiphon: "The Hebrew children carrying olive branches meet the Lord, crying out and saying: Hosanna in the highest!"

Now the people flocked around the altar to receive the blessed branches. Among them were the sons and grandsons of Offreduccio, Ortolana, Catherine, and Beatrice. Clare remained in her place, absorbed in a dream. It seemed to her that these prayers, these admonitory words, had a meaning that she alone could understand.

The ceremony was coming to an end; the last to kneel were now arising to return to their places. Clare remained immobile, rapt. Then an extraordinary thing happened. Bishop Guido, the proud, hot-tempered powerful Bishop Guido, went down the steps of the altar and alone walked forward, majestically, carrying in his hand the last olive branch. When he reached the girl, he solemnly gave it to her, as if this were a part of the rite.[16]

The procession moved behind the thurifer, who was followed by the sub-deacon carrying the cross between two acolytes with lighted candles. Now everyone raised his branch, singing triumphantly.

As the procession went out into the piazza, a flickering silvery glitter played over the forest of branches raised in the sun. A wave of metallic light was falling from the campanile, making the bell a part of that jubilation of songs and colours.

In the empty church, where Clare remained alone, the notes of the song that the priests and the people were now singing came like an echo: "Do not fear, daughter of Sion. Here is your king, come to you."

Clare Flees to Porziuncola

Evening falls. Once again Clare watches the façade of the church flaming and rapidly fading; once again her spirit reaches out in farewell to the pure sky, the procession of peaks that closes the far-off horizon.

Night comes on. The house grows quiet. Her sisters sleep, white bands binding their hair and enfolding their faces.

She looks out between the curtains and then goes lightly through the silent rooms. It would not do to endanger herself by using the customary door to the house, opening onto the piazza, where the cross-bow archer keeps watch, stiff and straight on his bench. Better to try the other door, the one opened only in days of battle, so now closed and barred with great beams and a heavy stone column.

"Those things," said Sister Cristiana di Messer Bernardo di Suppo, who then lived in the same house, "could scarcely be moved by many men; and she alone, with the help of Jesus Christ, moved them and opened the exit. And the following morning, when many people saw that door open, they marvelled how a young girl could have done it."[17]

She finds herself on Via del Parlascio. A figure wrapped in a mantle detached itself from the corner of the piazza. It is Pacifica, Guelfuccio's daughter, who is going to accompany Clare to Porziuncola.[18] The moon of that Holy Week throws the immaterial light of a dream over the houses, the Prato piazza, the city walls. They pass the Moiano gate, go down by the road through familiar fields: Sant'Anastasio, Fonte Galletta, Valecchie, l'Ospedaletto.

From there the road runs straight across the plain. The night, rising to its zenith, is clear and transparent, suffused with mysterious solemnity.

The forest scarcely comes into view when a great glow lights up the trees and moves forward miraculously. The men of penitence are coming with lighted torches to meet their new sister. Two by two they walk, everyone, torn by emotion, silent.

The procession goes forward through the forest, night-peopled in a phantasmagoria of lights and shadows, and enters the small church, Clare's rich bridal dress shining against the rough habits.

Clare goes alone to the altar. One by one she takes off her jewels. She offers to the Virgin of the Angels the ornaments of the life she is leaving behind her—a jeweled diadem, a pearl necklace, a girdle of precious stones. She receives from Francis's own hands the poor habit of a Friar Minor.

Silently she kneels and looses her hair. A dazzling gleam shines in the flickering light of the torches and is reflected on the poor bare walls. A moment, and Clare's golden hair has fallen under the scissors; the strands lie inert on the floor like creatures newly dead.[19]

Now she is the humble servant of Poverty.

Clare takes leave of the ragged knights lined up to pay her honour, on her way to the Benedictine monastery of San Paolo delle Ancelle di Dio. It is about two miles distant, toward Isola, on the banks of the Chiagio. They go on foot, Francis, Clare, and her faithful friend.

The moon has set by now and the sky is a scintillation of stars. They pass the Tescio in its bed of dead stones. Among the canebreaks they hear the voice of the river.

The door of the old monastery opens, closes.

And never would Francis forget the joy of that Holy Monday dawn, welling up inside him, as he makes his way back to Porziuncola, like a song from his troubadour heart.

A Family Row at the Monastery

The monastery of San Paolo delle Ancelle di Dio, more commonly called "delle Abbadesse" (Saint Paul of the Abbesses), was famous through all the region for its wealth, its influence, its noble status.[20] In the oldest official records it is also called San Paolo del Chiagio or San Paolo del Fonte Tiberino, because it stood along the last stretch of the Chiagio river, which was here full of whirlpools and deep, like the Tiber, into which it flows below the *castello* of Rosciano, which at that time was under Assisi's jurisdiction.

Papal bulls have long enumerations of the holdings of the monastery: The fields on both sides of the Chiagio beyond the pool of water called in the language of the time *le moje di San Paolo,* and beyond the Ripa road. The men and lands of the *castello* of Isola Romano. Houses, cottages and gardens in Assisi in the *contrade* of Santo Stefano, Sant'Andrea, and San Pietro. Olive orchards below the walls. Vineyards in Mosciole, Fiano, and Campagna. Rights on the chapels of San Giovanni in Campiglione, San Bartolomeo del Chiagio, and Santa Lucia, the chapel of Sant'Andrea della Valle outside the city of Foligno, with all its possessions.

A bull of Innocent III dated May 5, 1201, directed "to beloved daughters in Christ Sibilia, abbess of the monastery of San Paolo of Fonte Tiberino, and her sisters," confirms that the monastery followed the Rule of Saint Benedict. "The Monastic Order, which is known to be instituted in this monastery, according to God and the Rule of Saint Benedict . . . "

The bull also proclaims special papal privileges granted to the nuns. No one could impose tithes or exactions on them. The diocesan bishop was forbidden to put their chapel under interdict. In time of excommunication they had the right to celebrate the divine offices with doors closed, without songs or sound of bells. They were able to receive free women from secular life who had been converted to their rule and to reject every objection or claim made in opposition to their entrance. There were severe prohibitions against anyone's molesting them: "And therefore we order that to no person be it licit temerariously to molest this monastery." Those who did so and persevered in their offences would, after the third warning, incur interdict and divine anathema.

Despite all this, the sisters of San Paolo suffered from a suppressed and jealous grudge against the rival Benedictine monastery of Sant'Apollinare, standing nearby, beyond the bridge at the confluence of the Tescio and the Chiagio. It also boasted ancient origins, eminent papal privileges, an abundance of lands and serfs. Near the end of the thirteenth century the two monasteries were moved into the city. They built adjoining houses near the city walls, between the palazzo of the bishop and the Sementone gate. But the bad feeling between them continued, worse than ever, and there were interminable arguments over the piazzetta and the wall that marked their common boundary and scandalous accusations that claimed the attention of Rome. The San Paolo sisters, become brazenly corrupt, made jokes about the rigid propriety of their neighbours. In the middle of the fifteenth century, Emilia, abbess of San Paolo, had to be deposed and exiled, and the not-so-holy cloister was suppressed and united to that of Sant'Apollinare. (Thus it happened that the researcher who went looking for the ancient papal bulls that shed honour and glory on the monastery of Fonte Tiberino when Ortolana's daughter lived there found them in a basket of linen fragrant with lavender in the austere old edifice housing Sant'Apollinare, now located near the cathedral of San Rufino. And there the age-old life of the Benedictine rule was preserved with vigilant love through all the happenings of the centuries.)

The first days in the monastery passed peacefully for Clare. In the morning she went down to the choir with the sisters to attend Mass. The church was small and quiet, as may be seen from what remains of it in the chapel of the Bastìa cemetery, where the apse still oversees the field of humble crosses and the dead, whose sleep is lulled by the monotonous voice of the river.

In the Mass of Holy Monday she was struck by these words of the Introit: "Judge thou, O Lord, them that wrong me; overthrow them that fight against me; take hold of arms and shield, and rise up to help me, O Lord, my mighty deliverer."

Was it a warning of what was in store for her? She knew that in the pride of her fierce relatives they would not be easily reconciled to her decision. By now what she had done would be known all over the city and would certainly have aroused their fury. And now the sisters were singing in their silvery voices, filling the air of the sun-soaked morning: "Deliver me from my enemies, O Lord; to thee have I fled. . . . "

During the Mass of Tuesday in Holy Week it seemed to her that the priest was saying especially for her the prayer of the Introit: "We ought to glory in the cross of our Lord Jesus Christ, in whom is our salvation, life and resurrection."

In such manner she was being prepared for the great battle that she felt was imminent.

That afternoon the nuns scattered about the grounds around the monastery. The 1201 document describes for us the gardens, the woodlands that went down to the river, the thick canebrake that stretched along its banks. Everything was now touched by the promise and the enchantment of early spring. The vines were in flower, reminding one of the Biblical song of the bride. The trees were crowned with buds. The cane shone like the lances of an army of fantasy. The water ran slowly, sweetly, toward the hills that enclosed the plain to the west, which, when the sun went down, burned in vermilion splendour.

Clare's relatives arrived in a group, close-packed, as if confronting a crucial danger: the seven knights of the family, the arrogant uncles, the impatient cousins. They knocked at the door of the monastery.

Perhaps that Sibilia to whom Innocent had addressed the bull ten years earlier was still abbess. Previously she had not hesitated to stand up to insolent troops and had made good use of the papal privilege. But the news of the resounding victories that Otto IV had won in Sicily had restored the boldness of the feudal lords who supported the emperor, and she could not count on the protection of Rome. She felt it best to be prudent and manage by cleverness.

After much talk, Clare's family was allowed to meet Clare in the church. Every one of them was shaken to the heart when she came in, the beautiful rose of Piazza San Rufino, the most desirable of all the noble young girls of the city—now dressed in a threadbare habit, her feet bare, her waist girdled with the cord of penance.

The self-confident relatives were so alarmed by the sight that they talked with timorous anxiety, as if they had found her mortally ill, on the point of departing this life forever. They spoke of their grief, the despair of her mother and sisters. They reminded her how much they had loved her, how much they still loved her. They pointed out that life would smile on her, that life for her was full of promises and gifts. She must come to herself, get rid of the madness that had seized her, consider the dishonour that would come to the family from cheapening herself.

Vilitas, cheapness, baseness—that was the term, according to the *Legend of Saint Clare,* that was the refrain of every argument. It was the accusation thrown at her by everyone. (The violence of the reaction of the ancient noble families to the new [Franciscan] conception of society and life is telling. It is no less savage than that of the [nouveau riche] merchant, Pietro Bernardone.)

When they saw no sign of her changing her mind, they flared up in anger. The little church resounded with their shouts. They pressed around her, threatening to drag her away.

It was the morning of Good Friday, and a single cloth was stretched over the top of the altar to symbolize the funeral sheet that had covered the body of Jesus after his death. Clare ran rapidly up the steps and seized an edge of it, making of it a shield against her persecutors. Now no one could touch her without committing sacrilege.[g]

They circled around and around her, like a pack of snarling dogs, accusing her of rebelling against the authority of the family, cursing those who had entrapped her, cursing the daughter of Guelfuccio who had been her accomplice and the nuns who had acted in contempt of the statutes and even against the papal privileges themselves.

Suddenly, as the uproar rose, she took off the cloth that enveloped her head. Her beautiful face was pale and resolute, but her uncovered head made the startled knights recoil in horror. Her rich, heavy hair, that hair that had spread around her delicate features like a hazy

---

g. Clare was evidently claiming the right of sanctuary, which usually required that the person claiming it must touch some part of the church, most often the altar. Reminders of this ancient right can still be seen in Assisi in tablets in the wall along Via Frate Elia, also in the wall beneath the meadow in front of the upper church of the Basilica di San Francesco. Each bears the word *Immunitas.* See NV 2:395.

golden light, was gone. Now, with that crowning veil of worldly beauty taken away, she seemed strange and distant.

The abbess and the other nuns came in then. They reminded the knights that it was not fitting for them to profane the observance of the Passion. And so the enraged relatives went away, grim and frustrated, but not before they had announced that they would come back soon to set to rights this incredible shame, which had humiliated them in front of the whole city.[h]

They did return, in fact, and renewed their blandishments and their threats, but in vain.[21]

The nuns, nevertheless, were dubious about the regularity of their position in a quarrel with this powerful house, and they held a chapter to discuss it. Most were of the opinion that their privilege was not enough to justify what they were doing. They had the right to refuse to surrender anyone who entered their order, no matter who asked it. But Clare had not chosen their rule. She insisted on taking vows to lead the kind of life laid down by the new [and controversial] Friars Minor.

It was decided, therefore, that to avoid complicated arguments in which the sisters might be found to be in the wrong, Clare must immediately leave the monastery.

Clare and Sant'Angelo di Panzo

Francis found a new refuge for Clare at the monastery of Sant' Angelo di Panzo, located on the slope of Mount Subasio. He himself came one morning some days later to accompany his pilgrim sister there. With him were two of his first companions, Bernardo and Filippo.[22]

This time the group of knights of Poverty who escorted their lady in the rough habit went in full sun, among verdant fields, along flowering paths. And it seemed to them all those things—free and

---

h. The violence of the reaction of Clare's family to this rebellious girl must be understood against the medieval concept of honour, in which criticism or infamy brought on by the deeds of any one member of a family or clan was held to be equally shared by all. What women did was held to be an especial threat to the family honour. Pertile (*Storia del diritto,* p. 238) writes: "For that reason one maintained guardianship over them so long as they remained at home and saw to their proper marriage or placement, for the double considerations of providing for their material support and guaranteeing the honour of the house."

Under the circumstances, one might wonder why Clare's family left so abruptly. This monastery, it must be remembered, had been placed under the jurisdiction of the bishop of Assisi by a papal bull of 1198, which had also threatened with excommunication anyone who used violence on lands subject to the bishop. Also, the Benedictine monasteries for women, organized on the feudal pattern, had armed forces at their disposal and were themselves capable of making violators pay most dearly. See *NV* 2:394–95.

fresh and innocent—were shedding a special glory on the path of the girl with the light step, whose face and smile were blessedly alight.

They left the plain behind and began the climb up the hill. Wheat gleamed in the furrows; the emerald meadows on top the mountain glistened; the sky was intensely blue.

On the San Savino road they passed the flocks coming from Maremma on their way up to the pastures of the Mortaro. The great calm was intensified by the small sweet sound of the rude bells worn by the flock. Filippo of Mandria thought again about the winters on the mountain, when fog clung to the melancholy peaks and that same sound rose from the enclosed sheepfolds in the long nights filled with the endless weeping rain.

This man to whom it was given to know by faith alone the meaning of the Sacred Scriptures was moved then to address to Clare for the first time the song that has been offered to her in all generations since: "Arise, my beloved, my beautiful one, and come! For see, the winter is past, the rains are over and gone. The flowers appear on the earth, the time of pruning the vines has come, and the song of the dove is heard in the land."[23]

But the monastery of Panzo on Mount Subasio was not the right setting for Clare's tranquil spirit. Everything there is dry and desolate, the cliff that hangs over it, forbidding in appearance and in name—Sasso Cupo ("Dark Stone"), the parched bed of Rigo Secco ("Dry Stream"), the puny olive trees that climb up the stony slope.

The only living thing in this landscape where everything seems dead and burnt is the copious spring that murmurs, wheedles, and invites with its subdued melody. It offers refreshment to shepherds who come down from the sunbaked mountain in the summer months. It soothes the soul.

And after that day when the living spring mirrored the happiness on these three Spirit-filled faces, everyone who comes here will realize the aptness of the words in which Pope Alexander IV proclaimed the sainthood of this great daughter of Assisi: "She was the new woman of the Valley of Spoleto, who poured forth a new fountain of the water of life to refresh and benefit souls, a fountain that has since flowed in many streams through the whole of Christendom and watered many plantings of the faith."

Ever since Clare's sojourn at Panzo, in fact, that spring has been called (there are records of it even in ancient laws) the "Spring of Saint Clare."

According to a legend still being told at the end of the seventeenth century, the monastery of Sant'Angelo di Panzo was named after

Saint Michael the Archangel. Once two brothers lived in their castle there, strong and bold knights. But they hated each other bitterly because of a quarrel over the division of the paternal goods. After many plots and intrigues against each other, they reached the point of a fight to the death. Fratricidal blows were already being laid on in the large court, when suddenly the Archangel shone brightly before them. Terrified, they fell on their knees and listened to the words of the heavenly messenger, who obliged them to exchange a kiss of pardon. Afterwards he disappeared. The two knights, to memorialize the miraculous event, changed their castle into a monastery and named it for their angelic saviour.

In the time of Saint Clare a great painting over the altar depicted the event. It showed two knights kneeling and embracing one another, as directed by an angel dressed in white armour.[i]

It was not difficult for Francis and Filippo to persuade these nuns to receive Clare. The two of them were well-known in the monastery and had had some influence there from the time of their secular life, since they had often spent time on lands they owned nearby.

Sister Agnes

After some days Clare realized that she had not gained very much by changing from the monastery by the river to the monastery on the mountain. The place was little more than a great farm, and the subjects discussed there were sales, rents, markets, lands, flocks, wool, cheeses.

These nuns quarreled with the chapter of the cathedral and with the bishop over the jurisdiction of the church, about the olive groves of Salcaiano and the pastures of Mount Subasio. The very air was heavy with a dull prosperity, and in it there was no room for mystic rushes of renunciation.

She found herself plunged into bitter loneliness and thought with

---

i. Details of this legend, which is still to be heard in Assisi, are taken from Angeli, *Collis Paradisi amoenitas,* in which the author also explains that "Sant'Angelo di Panzo" is a corruption of the original name of "Sancti Angeli Pacis (Holy Angel of Peace)." On the contrary, "Panzo" is a family name that appears in a good many of the ancient records.

By 1239 the nuns of this monastery, which is located a short distance outside the city of Assisi, below and a bit to the left of the Carceri, had left the Benedictine rule and changed to that of the Poor Clares. In 1270 they transferred their residence inside the city, into the building now housing the diocesan seminary. In 1476 the monastery was united with the one at Santa Chiara.

The old structure eventually passed into private hands; the owner in 1604, Duke Ferrantes Bonacquisti, rebuilt the tiny, primitive church, which may still be seen today. The remains of the old monastery are now incorporated into a handsome private villa; some of the ancient walls may still be seen. Saint Clare's spring stands next to the house. For a detailed history of the monastery and the structure: see *NV* 2:396–402.

burning homesickness about Catherine, her favourite sister, her long-time confidante in everything. Separation from her had been very painful. Why shouldn't Catherine, the person who had been closest to her in the world, join her in serving her chosen Spouse?

And her prayers for this were so effective that within a few days Catherine came to her in her new home.

This time the anger of the family knew no bounds. The next day (Thursday, April 14) twelve of them came to retrieve the fugitive, prepared to break into the cloister and take the monastery by storm. However, they knew very well how to dissimulate their intentions so that the nuns would allow them to enter without suspicion.

The scene that followed is dramatically described by Clare's biographer.

At first they reproached Catherine and angrily ordered her to leave the monastery at once. She, trembling but resolute, parried by saying that she did not wish to abandon Clare. Then a knight, brutish in nature and appearance, flung himself on her, hit her with his fists, kicked her, seized her by the hair, and tried to drag her away. They all shoved and pulled at her and finally picked her up bodily. At that she cried out, "Help me, dear sister. Do not let them take me away from Jesus Christ like this."[j]

They carried her by force along the slope of the mountain. Tatters of clothes and locks of hair caught and remained on the brambles flanking the path between the cliffs. (Afterwards it was called in memory of that event the "chioca[k] of Saint Clare.")

Clare fell on her knees. In tears she prayed fervently that her sister, so cruelly tried, would remain constant and that God would protect her from these men.

As the group of kidnappers reached the bank of Rigo Secco, the hubbub of shouts and curses suddenly lessened. The peasants who were working in a distant vineyard ran up in a great frenzy. Amazed and terrified, they gathered around the group.

The young woman had fainted. They had laid her down on the ground and stood about looking at her, shaking in impotent fury.

For an instant nothing happened.

The feudal lord who led these brutes, the old rebel against the commune who fought in the ranks of the Perugini, Uncle Monaldo, had sworn to bring her back dead or alive. Intending to keep his

---

j. It is possible that the family was trying to prevent Catherine's seizing the altar cloth, as Clare had done, and so claiming the right of sanctuary.—Trans.

k. In the language of the region, a chioca is a narrow path boxed in by steep banks. See NV 2:402.

word, he raised his arm to kill her. It remained rigid, as if paralyzed by an arrow, and he could not even lower it.

They remained for a long time discussing the situation, consulting each other, trying to think what should be done, and Clare overtook them. She convinced them that they must entrust her with Catherine's fragile, unconscious body. And so they went away, mute, heads hanging, without the strength to utter a prayer or a threat.[24]

Later, the monastery of Sant'Angelo di Panzo was among the first to change from the Benedictine rule to that of the Poor Clares. More than a century later a great-granddaughter of Angelo, Francis's brother, became a nun there with the name of Sister Clare and was abbess of the monastery. At the same time one of her sisters, Sister Franceschina, was among the religious there.[25]

The First Poor Clares

Francis himself cut the hair of the new Lady of Poverty and, in recognition of her having been as brave as a good knight, gave her a new name, one that recalled the bitter battle from which she had so miraculously come out victor: Agnes.

"In truth," it is noted in the *Chronicle of 24 Generals,* "for the innocent *Agnello* (Lamb), and that is for Jesus Christ, who for us was sacrificed, valiantly she resisted and openly stood up to combat."

Several days later Francis took Clare and Agnes to San Damiano.[26]

The abandoned old church seemed to revive and take on new life from their pure and holy youthfulness, in the same way that ruined walls of an ancient manor again throb with life when white roses flower over them. San Damiano, with its poor rooms, its tiny windows, its rude beams, became the true Castle of Poverty, destined for ladies of a heavenly court.

In the early days, Francis gave them a rule of life, as Clare recorded in her Testament: "Afterwards he wrote for us a form of life, especially that we should persevere always in holy poverty. Nor was he content while living to exhort us by many words and examples to the love and observance of most holy poverty, but also gave us many writings that after his death we would in no wise turn aside from it, even as the Son of God while He lived in this world wished never to desert this same holy poverty. And our most blessed Father Francis, following the footsteps of Christ, never while he lived departed in example or in teaching from His holy poverty, which he had chosen for himself and for his Friars."[27]

One by one, the friends of her youth joined her. Among the first were Pacifica di Guelfuccio, Benvenuta, Filippa di Leonardo di

Gislerio—those who with her had shared the sufferings and anxieties, the hopes and struggles, of that terrible period of their infancy and adolescence.[28]

Then it was the turn of Ginevra, daughter of Giorgio di Ugone. She entered San Damiano in 1214 and changed her name to Benedetta.

In that same year Clare had, on Francis's order, assumed the office of abbess.[1] After her death, Benedetta succeeded her and to her energy and devotion is due the construction of the basilica where Saint Clare now lies. She planned it and saw it through after a frightful struggle with the canons of San Rufino—a struggle in which this descendant of the lords of Parlascio showed herself worthy of her blood and of the devout and pugnacious tradition of her family. She is buried in the basilica and her figure may be seen in the thirteenth-century painting on the great crucifix of the apse, wrapped in the ample folds of the cloistral mantle, her delicate face expressive of inspired prayer. On it is the ancient inscription: *Benedicta post S. Claram prima Abbatissa me fecit* ("Benedetta, first Abbess after Saint Clare, made me").

In the next few years other women of the most influential families of the city also joined Clare.

Among them was Cristiana, who had lived with Saint Clare in the house on Piazza San Rufino. She was the daughter of Bernardo di Suppo, one of the members of the consortium of the cathedral.

Agnese, daughter of Oportolo di Bernardo, a greatly esteemed feudal lord who was podestà of the commune in the last years of Saint Francis's life.

Benvenuta of Madonna Diambra, sister of that Pietro whom Rainuccio di Paolo killed by burning his house in Assisi, so making his enemy burn to death. So different from the peace of San Damiano were the things that went on outside!

---

1. Originally Clare and her sisters lived under the personal direction of Saint Francis, who, as reported in the text, had given them a short written rule. Like the original rule he prepared for the Franciscans, it has been lost. The willingness of Clare to accept the title of abbess probably meant that her order was now separated from the Friars Minor and under her own direction. It may also have meant that Clare accepted at least in a formal sense the Benedictine Rule, though it was not until a year later that regulations adopted by the Fourth Lateran Council would have required her to do this. We know that in 1218 or 1219 a version of the Benedictine Rule, in which the "Privilege of Poverty" was completely omitted, was given to the Poor Clares by Cardinal Ugolino (later Pope Gregory IX). This rule was confirmed by Pope Innocent IV in 1245, but two years later he gave them a new rule and bound all Poor Clares to it. This rule of 1247 expressly allowed common ownership of movable and immovable goods. Clare, it need hardly be said, was unhappy with all these rules, and especially the last one, since they diverged from the Franciscan ideal of poverty. See Introduction, *Leg. S. Clarae*, trans. Brady, pp. 4–5.—Trans.

Balvina, from the *castello* of Porziano, on the hill between Assisi and Valfabbrica.

Massariola, daughter of messer Capitanio da Collemezzo, who, upon entering the monastery, changed her name to Francesca.

Collemezzo was a *castello* located on the old border between Assisi and Todi, on the outskirts of Casalalta. The family was noble and strong. Buonconte, son of Capitanio, at the end of the twelfth century founded the Benedictine monastery of San Vito in Val d'Oppio. Capitanio had three brothers, Bonifazio, named bishop of Todi, Ugolino, and Guido, the father of Bernardino, who was in turn the father of Vanna, bride of Jacopone da Todi.

Vanna was devoted to her aunt, called "the Blessed Francesca," and in her memory wore a hair shirt under her beautiful worldly dress. Francesca herself held a special place in Clare's affections. Pietro, brother of Sister Francesca, was a very influential citizen. His house stood along the street to San Rufino. On March 29, 1229, he was among those who presented the donation that Simone di Pucciarello had made of woods and other lands to Brother Elias for the building of the Basilica di San Francesco.

Cristiana, daughter of messer Cristiano di Paride, the consul, the wise counsellor of the commune.

The great houses of the city, the fortresses of the countryside were being emptied of their most famous beauties. The romance of feudalism, which exalted the knight who offered song or sword in return for a smile, a glance—the beautiful romance that was the stuff of dreams in a hundred castles on mountain and plain, solitary cliff and riverbank—was resolved for these women in the peace they found in the poor church standing amid olive trees on a hill that gently sloped to the wide silent plain, that church from which there had once been a cry from the crucifix.

Also among them were the granddaughters of the lord of Renara Valley, Domino Giovanni Renaro, Grazia and Completa.

The Renaro is a *torrente* that usually carries not water but dry sand. It descends from Fontebregno of Mount Subasio between steep banks that mark the border between the commune of Assisi and the commune of Spello. On the Assisi bank stands Gabbiano, a castle of a whiteness and bizarre shape that call to mind a storm-loving sea bird. A little below, where the rows of olive trees begin, is a group of houses called Renaro and the ruins of an ancient tower, this perched on a precipice called Sasso Palombo. There Giovanni had his castle, a short distance from the overhanging cliff of Sasso Rosso.

Like the daughter of Leonardo di Gislerio (of Sasso Rosso), Grazia and Completa became Poor Ladies of San Damiano. They changed their names to Illuminata and Agata.

Also the daughters of Tomassino, *signore* of the castle of Monteverde above Valfabbrica, embraced the new rule. Named Matilde and Agnina, they became Sister Iacopa and Sister Chiarastella.

Clare's own family dissolved in this call to sanctity. Balvina, daughter of Martino, came early, then Beatrice, Clare's younger sister, followed her. And finally Ortolana, Clare's mother, also became one of the Poor Clares at San Damiano.

Martino, lord of Corano, had another daughter, Amata ("Beloved"). Never was there a sweeter name for a sweeter face. Even the officious old biographers, in speaking of this relative of Saint Clare,[m] had something sentimental to say about her delicate loveliness and about the admiration that she aroused in all who met her.

She liked, they say, precious jewels, beautiful clothes, the flattery of young knights. They say that when she went down from her silent castle on the mid-slope of the hill beyond the Tescio valley, outside Porta San Giacomo, all the brooding landscape seemed to lighten— the dark forests and the steep desolate banks of streams, as the flowering of a single peach tree in March on the top of a remote hill will imbue a whole region with light.

Amata—she loved, she was loved. Already a white wedding gown had been made ready for her, and already the rose bush in the garden that would supply roses for her bridal crown was in flower, when one day she went to San Damiano. She was so touched by the humility she found there, by the luminous peace, the high and serene joy, that she never left it.

She was a witness in Clare's canonization proceedings: " . . . And this witness entered religious life through the admonition and exhortation of the saint. (Saint Clare) told her that she had asked that God give her grace so that she would not be deceived by the world and remain in secular life."

Clare's fame spread. Others to become her sisters arrived from

---

m. Some earlier biographers identified Amata and Balvina as Clare's nieces, daughters of a sister named Penenda, who was married to the count of Coccorano (a *castello* near the borders of Assisi, Gubbio, and Perugia). However, according to testimony in the *Processo,* Clare had but two sisters, Catherine (who became Sister Agnes) and Beatrice, who also entered the order. Amata and Balvina both described themselves as *nipoti carnali* of Clare's, a term meaning "of the same blood" and applying to a variety of family relationships. A diligent study of all surviving records makes it clear that their father was Martino, the nephew of Clare's father, son of her uncle Ugolino. He was lord, not of Coccorano, but of Corozano (also called Correggiano, Coriano, and Corano), a *castello* a short distance outside the city gates. Martino was, therefore, Clare's first cousin; Amata and Balvina, her first cousins once removed. The elusive Penenda is nowhere to be found in the records and early sources; she may be the invention of fantasizing genealogists of the last century. NV 2:334–39.

nearby villages and from famous cities: Cecilia, daughter of Domino Gualtieri Cacciaguerra, from Spello, Angeluccia, daughter of Domino Angeleio, from Spoleto, Lucia from Rome, Illuminata from Pisa, Anastasia, Andrea from Ferrara.

Virtue and sweetness—in many cases we feel them again today in just the music of a name. Thus, from the worn reading desk in the poor choir of San Damiano a tender melody pours out in the names of Clare's first fifty sisters, recorded (from a 1238 document)[n] on an old wooden tablet: Agnese, Filippa, Giacoma, Illuminata, Cecilia, Egidia, Agnese, Anastasia, Agnese, Cristiana, Giacomina, Balvina, Mansueta, Amata, Benvenuta, Bonaventura, Benvenuta, Benricevuta, Consolata, Andrea, Aurea, Leonarda, Agata, Felicita, Angeluccia, Felicita, Massariola, Maria, Gregoria, Maria, Giovanna, Benedetta, Giovanna, Bennata, Giovanna, Lucia, Elia, Mattia, Chiarastella, Lea, Beatrice, Bartolomea, Prassede, Erminia, Daniella, Chiarella, Pacifica, Vertera, Patrizia.

What Makes a Saint?

Assisi, the lost city that early writers called a "new Babylon," was changed as these sisters gathered at San Damiano. We have only to hear some of them in the canonization proceedings, which took place in Assisi three and one-half months after Clare's death.

On November 24, 1253, those who survived her came to the cloister to appear before Bartolomeo, bishop of Spoleto, who sat with the other investigators, people who had known Clare in her youth, those who had spent their lives with her. Their great love for her pulses through the humble and simple words, spoken in the rude and strong language that Assisi people speak even today. It spread through the quiet air where the pale November sun beamed on the last chrysanthemums, which had been dear to the departed mother.

---

n. In 1625 Wadding published a document from the cathedral archives bearing the date June 8, 1238, and signed by Clare and her sisters (*An. Min.*, 1238, n. XIV–XV). The paper in question was a power of attorney granted to Oportolo di Bernardo for the sale to the cathedral of a piece of land belonging to the monastery. From this document comes the list of names of the first fifty sisters that are inscribed on a wooden tablet now resting in the ancient choir of San Damiano.

The document is no longer in existence and there has been much debate as to its authenticity. These reasons lead us to believe the document, therefore the list of names, authentic: The form and substance correspond to other such legal instruments granted by the Poor Clares at the time. Oportolo di Bernardo was a real person and the father of one of the sisters. The land in question lies near other lands held by the cathedral, which was likely seeking to enlarge its properties during that time. The names of many of the sisters are confirmed from other sources, primarily in *Processo*. The name of the canon in the document (Cillenio Benigni) is correct. It is unlikely that anyone attempting to pawn off a spurious document would have known all these details or taken the trouble to find them. For a full discussion of the subject: *NV* 2:417–24.

SISTER BEATRICE: "Her sanctity was in her virginity, in her humility, in her patience and kindliness, in the necessary corrections and gentle admonitions to the sisters, her steadfast prayers and contemplation, her abstinence and fasting, in the harshness of her bed and clothing, in her contempt for herself, in the fervour of her love of God, her desire for martyrdom, and most of all in her love of the Privilege of Poverty."

SISTER PACIFICA: "When she ordered her Sisters to do something, she gave the order with much timidity and humility, and most of the time she would more readily do something herself than order others to do it."

SISTER BENVENUTA: "She was very diligent in prayer by day and by night, and around midnight in silence she awakened her Sisters, with certain signs, to praise God. She lit the lamps in the church and often she rang the bell for Matins. And those Sisters who did not get up at the sound of the bell, she called through her signs."

SISTER AMATA: "When she returned from prayer, her face seemed more luminous and more beautiful than the sun. And her very words had in them such sweetness that her life seemed entirely celestial."

SISTER FILIPPA: "She despised herself above all and made herself the inferior of all the other Sisters, serving them, giving them water for their hands and washing the toilet chairs for the sick Sisters with her own hands, and even washing the feet of the servant Sisters.º And it happened one time, when she was washing the feet of a servant Sister, she wished to kiss her feet, and the other drew back her foot and did not do so in a discreet way, and in thus drawing back her foot, she struck the holy Mother in the mouth with it. Nevertheless, in her humility, (Clare) did not stop at this, but kissed the sole of the foot of the aforesaid servant Sister."

They said that she knew how to read the heart of each like an open book. One time Francis sent five new sisters to her to be received into the order. Among them was Gasdia, daughter of Taccolo di Aregnato and sister of Andrea, a greatly esteemed knight and a distinguished man of the commune. Clare, when she saw her, said that she would stay in the monastery for only a short time and thus it happened.[29]

---

o. The "servant sisters" (*servitiale*) were probably externs who went outside the monastery to seek supplies and handle whatever business was necessary. It has also been suggested by Father Salvatore Butler, who as a long time resident of San Damiano has made special studies of materials pertaining to the life of Saint Clare, that they may have been peasant girls who joined the order, as contrasted with Clare and her noble friends. A short time after the sisters settled at San Damiano, the Friars Minor took over the task of obtaining food and other supplies for them.—Trans.

They said feverish youngsters had been carried to Clare and she cured them with a simple sign of the cross. One of them was the son of Domino Gianni of Maestro Giovanni, who was a councillor of the commune and the procurator of San Damiano.[30]

Brother Leo and Brother Angelo, who also attended the inquiry, heard the laments for her rise up all over again. Each had an episode to tell about, one that she had seen with her own eyes, one that she would never forget.

SISTER BENVENUTA: "She treated her body with such harshness that she was happy with one half-wool habit only and one mantle. And if at any time she saw that the habit of a Sister was poorer than the one she wore, she took off her own and gave the Sister the better one."

SISTER FILIPPA: "Always she was happy in the Lord and never was she upset, and her life was all angelic . . . and she had the grace of many tears, having great compassion for the Sisters and for the afflicted . . . And so much was she a lover of Poverty that when those who asked for alms for the monastery brought back whole loaves of bread as alms, she reproached them, saying, 'Who gave you these whole loaves?' And she said this because she preferred to receive as charity broken loaves rather than whole ones."

SISTER ANGELUCCIA: "When she sent the servant Sisters outside the monastery, she told them to praise God when they saw beautiful trees, flowering and leafy."

SISTER CECILIA: "Willingly she would have undergone martyrdom for the love of God, and she demonstrated this when she heard that in Morocco certain friars had been martyred and she said that she wished to go there. . . ."

SISTER AGNES: "She had a straw mat for a bed, and a bit of straw under her head, and with this bed she was content. . . . After she was sick, on the order of Saint Francis she had a large sack of straw."

This wave of grief was echoed four days later, November 28, in the voices of citizens called as witnesses in proceedings held in the church of San Paolo on the piazza: Domino Andreolo di Bartolo, Iannello di Benvenuto of Lucca, Domino Angelo di Pelco, Bonamancia di Barbiero.[31]

Mystic Joy: Easter, 1232

Strange things happened.

Brother Filippo of Mandria had been the visitor[p] of the sisters from

---

p. The visitor in a religious order is one who makes periodic and official visits for the purposes of inspection and supervision.—Trans.

the earliest days. During the Easter Octave of 1232, just before dawn, he spoke to them in the little church. Twenty-one years had gone by since Clare and Agnes had left their paternal house.[32]

The choir of sweet voices had begun singing the antiphon of the feast day: "I am the shepherd of the sheep. I am the way, the truth, the life: I am the good shepherd and I know my sheep, and they know me. *Alleluia.*"

When that song was finished, an inexpressible rush of tender feelings and memories awoke in the friar's heart, for his own life gave special meaning to the divine words. His poetic temperament made him see in his sisters in Christ the simple life of a flock, as he himself, Filippo, had known it long ago among the flocks in the sheepfolds below the mountain pastures.

Early in the morning the shepherd comes and takes away the bar that closes the sheepfold. The night is short for the shepherd and full of shadows and fears. Thus Jesus said, "Whoever does not enter the sheepfold through the gate but climbs in some other way is a thief and a marauder."[33]

All night the shepherd, who is ready to give his life for his sheep, has kept watch. And as they see him enter and as he calls them by name, one by one, they all turn to him. Jesus also said: "(The shepherd) walks in front of his sheep and the sheep follow him because they recognize his voice. They will not follow a stranger; such a one they will flee, because they do not recognize a stranger's voice."[34]

He who follows the good shepherd will find sweet meadows and flowing springs and will not be caught by the wind-driven storm over the peaks or overtaken by night before reaching the sheepfold. This is written in the Gospel: "Whoever enters through me . . . will find pasture."

It was at this point in Brother Filippo's sermon that Sister Agnese, the daughter of the podestà who was devoted to Saint Francis, saw the Baby Jesus appear by Clare. And it seemed to her that all the brilliance of the stars was concentrated there in those last moments of the dying night to form an aureole of light around their dear mother.

Brother Filippo continued his explanation of the beautiful figurative language. He said that to take upon oneself the yoke of a humble and gentle shepherd was to acquire peace of soul. For this Shepherd is the one who said, "Come to me, all of you who find life burdensome, and I will refresh you."[35]

Dawn was breaking and a vermilion reflection from the window of the apse came to rest on Clare's grey habit. She, so many years earlier, had been moved to accept the high teaching. To Sister

Agnese's rapt eyes that gleam seemed to grow in intensity until it became an incandescent flame giving off vivid rays of light. The sweet face, whiter than the white wimple, bent in prayer, was illuminated by it as if it reflected a supernatural fire.

The Lady of the New Knights

It pleased Clare to call herself the "little plant" of her Holy Father Francis (*parva plantula sancti patris Francisci*).[36]

She also said that she considered him her nurse, because from him she had drunk sweet milk at the time she had been reborn to life.

One time she had a dream. She, of noble descent, came to him as a humble servant, carrying hot water in a basin and a linen towel to dry his hands. And she was happy in this submission, this abasement, this humbling of herself for love, so much so that though she was going up a very steep stairway, she went as lightly as if she were walking on level ground. In the words of Suor Filippa, who told of this dream: "And when she had come up to Saint Francis, he bared his breast and said to the virgin Clare: 'Come, take and drink.' And when she had done so, the Saint admonished her to drink again; and that which she drank was so sweet and delightful that she could in no way describe it. When she had finished, the nipple remained between the lips of the blessed Clare, and taking in her hand that which remained in her mouth, it seemed to her of such pure and shining gold that she could see in it her own reflection, as in a mirror."[37]

In the traditional view, women were little more than objects associated with the sensuality of the love songs.

For instance, the poetic tournament of Sire di Maulon (already well known in Italy at the time of the youth of Saint Francis) put to knights *tres jocs enamoratz,* three questions of love.

A woman had three lovers yearning for her, and finding herself with them at a banquet, she tried to show each of them how she felt. She looked at one with intense passion, she furtively pressed the hand of another, she playfully touched the foot of the third one. To which of them, it was asked, did she show the greatest favour? The poets, in finely drawn distinctions, explained what they thought. All their answers show that a woman was considered only a delicious plaything.[38]

Another noble poet, Guglielmo della Torre Bianca, composed a sirvente in which he flaunted his opinion of the most pleasing women of his time, a celebration of the qualities that made these women famous in all the courts of love: Beatrice d'Este—highly esteemed, Emilia of Ravenna—fickle, Sandra of Soragna—courteous, Donna Berta—brave and beautiful, Donna Mabilia—skillful, Donna Emilia di Ponzone—gentle-spoken, Donna Aquilina d'Arco—ardent, Donna Bruna di Castello—gracious, Donna Verde di Cossano—careful to maintain honour and a good relationship.[39]

Again, here are some verses of the song of the troubadour of Gapençais:

> En amor trob tant de mal seignoratge,
> tant lonc desir e tant malvatz usatge,
> per q'ieu serai de las dompnas salvatge . . .

In love I find such bad lordship, such long waiting and such bad behaviour, that from now on I am against women. And they should not believe by now that I sing of them. In truth, having been their vassal and squire and having exalted their worth and their valour, I found nothing in the end but pain and injury. Tell me then if I should sing again of love.

I shall not sing of love nor desire for myself a beautiful lover, gallant and courteous, because I have found nothing but deceit, lying, falsehood, untruth, betrayal. When I think that I have her all to myself, I notice that she becomes more contrary and wicked. He is very foolish who trusts women and I have had my part in this folly.[40]

The credit for elevating the position of women and transforming all this phosphorescent frivolity into quite a different poetry may be attributed to the Poverello of Christ, who used the language of chivalry to embody high concepts. This is reflected in the bull of canonization of Clare of Assisi, the greatest of all the tributes to this particular lady, this saint, that has been made in these past seven centuries.

"She was the lofty candlestick of holiness that burned brightly in the tabernacle of the Lord, to whose great radiance many have hastened, many are hastening, to light their lamps from her light."

This is a description that fits the story of Francis and Clare and their spiritual banquet.

Francis, in the early days, went often to San Damiano to advise his new sister. At one time she had a great desire to eat with him at the poor table of the Lord, but Francis never wanted to allow this.

His companions did not approve of his refusal and, according to the account in *Fioretti* said to him, "Father, it seems to us that this strictness—that you do not grant the request of Sister Clare, a virgin so holy and dear to God, in such a little thing as eating with you—is not in accord with divine charity, especially considering that she gave up the riches and pomp of the world as a result of your preaching. So you should not only let her eat a meal with you once, but if she were to ask an even greater favour of you, you should grant it to your little spiritual plant."

Francis asked them then, "So you think I should grant this wish of hers?"

And they replied, "Yes, Father, for she deserves this favour and consolation."

And so Francis decided, "Since it seems so to you, I agree. But in order to give her even greater pleasure, I want this meal to be at Santa Maria degli Angeli, for she has been cloistered at San Damiano for a long time and she will enjoy seeing once more the Place of Saint Mary where her hair was cut and she was made the spouse of Jesus Christ. So we shall eat there together, in the name of the Lord."

On the day set, Saint Clare came from San Damiano with one of her sisters and, escorted by companions of Saint Francis, went to Santa Maria degli Angeli. She knelt before the altar where she had made her vows of renunciation and prayed devoutly to the Virgin. Then the companions walked about with her since it was not yet time for dinner.

Francis had the table laid on the bare ground, according to the usual custom. The knights and the ladies of Christ seated themselves alternately, according to court usage in castles: first Francis, then Clare, then one of Francis's companions, then Clare's companion, and then the other brothers, all taking their places with great humility.

And as the first course, Francis began to talk of God, so sweetly and profoundly, in so moving a fashion, that they were all overcome by a flood of divine grace, and all became rapt in God, imparadised, and so they remained, eyes and hands raised to the sky.

In the meantime the people of Assisi and Bettona and of all the countryside round about saw Santa Maria degli Angeli, all the forest and all the surrounding area in flames; and they came with great haste to put out the fire. But when they arrived, they saw nothing burning—only Francis with Clare.[41]

Francis, nevertheless, understood the necessity of lengthy separations to prevent people from uncharitable talk, and to that Clare reluctantly resigned herself, though she felt that her known virtue would overcome malicious gossip.

One day (this is a new and modest "little flower" gathered from people now living in the *contado* of Assisi) Francis and Clare were walking along opposite sides of a river in flood. Francis wanted to try to cross the river but was impeded by the powerful, eddying current.

He was troubled because treacherous water kept him from joining the sister after his own spirit. But suddenly Clare threw her mantle on the water, stepped on it, and in an instant walked across the river. The blessed Francis, full of awe and devotion, said, "See, Sister, you are more in favour with God than I am."^q

In the last years of his life Francis thought many times of the sadness of Clare and her sisters when the day came that he would no longer be with them. One day, in the church of San Damiano, while the sisters were gathered waiting for him to speak, Francis remained for a long time silent, eyes raised to heaven. Then, having some ashes brought to him, he made a circle of them around himself and sprinkled his head with them, while at the same time he sang in a loud voice the *Miserere,* Psalm 51, which begins, "Have mercy on me, Lord." Then he went away without adding a word.

All understood what he had meant. His body was nothing but miserable dust that in a brief time would be dispersed.[42]

Clare and the Privilege of Poverty

Clare knew that she would be able to serve Francis in no better way than to remain faithful to his great principle, Poverty. Therefore, in contrast to other monasteries that asked the pope the concession of special privileges to safeguard their vast possessions, she asked Innocent III to grant them the privilege of possessing nothing. The pontiff observed that never had such a privilege been asked of the court of Rome.[43]

With his own hand he wrote out the text of this Privilege of Poverty: "Innocent, Bishop, servant of the servants of God, to the beloved daughters in Christ Clare and the other handmaidens of the Church of San Damiano of Assisi, both present and future, professing in perpetuity life according to a rule.

"As is manifest, you, wishing to dedicate yourselves solely to God, have renounced every desire for temporal things; and to that end, having sold all your goods and distributed what was gained to the poor, you propose to have no possessions in any way, wanting to follow the footsteps in everything of the One who for us made himself poor, thus becoming the way, the truth, and the life. And you are not frightened by the lack of necessary things in this intention, so long as the right hand of your celestial Spouse is under your head to support the weakness of your body, which you have disciplined to be

---

q. This story was faithfully transcribed by the author from the narration of some of the country people of Rocca Sant'Angelo.

subordinate to the rule of your will. After all, he who feeds the birds of the air and clothes the lilies of the field will not fail you in both food and clothing, until such time as you gain eternal life, when he will minister to you himself, and his right hand will reach out to embrace you most joyfully in the fullness of his sight.

"And, therefore, as you have asked, we with apostolic favour approve your aim of highest poverty, granting, with the authority of this writing, that by no one may you be forced to receive possessions.

"And if any woman does not wish or is not able to observe this aim of highest poverty, she need not remain with you but may be transferred elsewhere."[44]

The usual threatened sanctions against usurpers of ecclesiastical goods followed.

Pope Gregory IX, who was so fond of Clare that he often visited her, suggested to her one day that she accept some goods that would allow her and her companions to live without anxiety for the future. To this, an abrogation of the privilege of Innocent III and also a suggestion in accordance with a kind of thinking that had already appeared in the first rule sanctioned by Honorius III on August 27, 1218, Clare objected with a ferocity unimaginable in a creature so sweet and delicate.

The pontiff managed to tell her that if it were her vows that impeded her from accepting goods, he had the faculty of dissolving them. The memory of Francis must have turned Clare's heart upside down in that moment, for she, not without a quiver of contempt, replied to the head of the church: "Holy Father, release me from my sins but not from the vow to follow our Lord Jesus Christ."[45]

On another occasion, Pope Gregory IX wished to forbid male friars visiting the sisters. She replied by sending away even the friars who had been going from door to door to beg on behalf of the convent.

"If we can do without spiritual bread, we can also do without material bread," she said. Again the pope was forced to give in.[46]

There were traits in her that remind one that she was the daughter of feudal lords, knights, and warriors. As a matter of fact, she liked to compare her San Damiano to a "fortress of Poverty."

When, in September 1240, the Saracens of Frederick II surrounded and threatened the monastery, she assured her sisters that she would be their sentry. She did not hesitate to confront the Saracens but had herself carried out to meet them. They, frightened and confused, retired in disorder.

The following year, when Vitale d'Anversa encircled Assisi with the imperial army, it was she who on the night of June 21 sprinkled her head with ashes and prayed with her sisters in the little choir of the church for the salvation of the people of the city. And with the help of God, the city people attacked the enemy camp at dawn and put the imperial forces to rout.[r]

She was grateful for the help that she daily received from the city for the support of the convent. During the siege she said to her sisters, "From this city we receive every day many supplies. It would be impious if, when there is need, we should not come to it in aid, according to our ability to do so."[47]

Reflecting the city's opinion that great benefits were brought to the city by the sisters is an unpublished document of 1233 listing among the Christmas donations made by Matteo di Andrea, *camerario* of the Compagnia dei Cavalieri, one for "the work of San Damiano."[48]

Her body wore out. For twenty-nine years she was confined to her bed,[49] in pain and consumed by illness. The sisters raised her to a sitting position by putting cloths behind her shoulders, so that she could use the distaff and spindle. She spun wool, like the good mother of ancient times who managed the house. She made corporals for the churches of the city and the countryside around Assisi. There was not a church on plain or mountain that did not have one spun by

---

r. The two episodes referred to here are undoubtedly the most famous in the history of Saint Clare and her order, and the first is one of extraordinary drama. According to the testimony of several witnesses during the canonization proceedings, as well as to *Leg. S. Clarae,* the Saracen armies of Frederick II, waging a war to conquer the Papal States, swept down upon San Damiano on a Friday morning of September, 1240, after having already destroyed a good many other monasteries lying outside the city walls. Before the attack began, according to Sister Filippa, Clare comforted her sisters in the words reported in the text. As the Saracens began climbing the walls enclosing the grounds of San Damiano, Clare called two of her sisters (Francesca and Illuminata of Pisa) to carry her out to meet the Saracen army. She ordered that they be preceded by the ivory and silver casket in which the Eucharist was kept. At the same time she tearfully prayed for help in defending her sisters, and, according to Sister Francesca, was reassured by "the voice of a little child" who said, "I will always defend you." Clare then prayed for the city, and the sisters again heard the voice, "It will suffer many afflictions but it shall be defended by my protection." Afterwards, Clare told her sisters to trust in Christ and assured them they need fear no more. And in the confrontation between the Saracens and Clare with the Sacrament, it was, as Fortini reports, the Saracens who turned and fled. The episode is cherished by her order, who see in it a symbol of Clare's devotion to the Eucharist. It is the basis for the traditional image of Clare bearing the Eucharist (though someone else, probably the chaplain, actually carried it); and it is the source of the motto of the order, *Ego vos semper custodiam* ("I will always defend you").

On June 22, the anniversary of the victory of Assisi over the imperial forces led by Vitale d'Anversa in 1241, a colorful festival (Festa del Voto) is held each year in Assisi. City officials, clergy, the cathedral chapter, confraternities, and citizens go in procession to San Damiano and to the Basilica di Santa Chiara for special ceremonies in which long wax candles are presented to the churches as a symbol of the everlasting gratitude of the city to Clare for its deliverance through her prayers. The custom was allowed to lapse in 1860, but was happily revived in 1924, while Arnaldo Fortini was mayor.

For detailed accounts of these episodes, see *NV* 2:404–5; Fortini, *Assisi nel medioevo,* pp. 157–212. Cf. *Leg. S. Clarae,* 21–23, and *Processo.*—Trans.

her blessed hands. The brothers carried them at her request to the most remote chapels. Priests came to the monastery to ask for them.[50]

From that humble recess the fame of her holiness spread through the world. We cite again the bull of canonization: "How great was the strength of this light! How overwhelming was this light of splendour! It was hidden in cloistered walls, yet shed abroad its shining rays; it was confined in a narrow convent cell yet spread throughout the wide world. It was kept within yet streamed forth without. In truth Clare was hidden, but her life was known to all. She was silent, but her reputation cried out. She was enclosed in her cell but famed in all the cities. Little wonder indeed that a light so burning and shining could not be hidden but would break forth and illuminate in clear light the house of the Lord, that a vessel of such fragrance could not be kept closed but would be diffused and fill with perfume the house of the Lord."

The struggle for the defence of Poverty was the drama of Clare's life. To the second rule given the sisters by Innocent IV on August 27, 1247, which mitigated the severity of the first, she opposed a stubborn resistence.[51]

What Assisi Thought of Clare

To the eyes of the people of Assisi she appeared already filled with fearless holiness, so that a great many people entrusted responsibilities to her, even in matters of a juridical character, in order to be certain that works of charity would be performed and legacies in favour of the poor fulfilled.

Interesting in this respect is an unpublished testament from the archives of the Sacro Convento, drawn up in the year 1247, a paper that also shows us that the life of the commune, even after Francis's great creation, continued to be stormy and violent.

The sons of Presbitero, Andrea and Stefano, had been companions of Saint Francis in his youth. We find them listed in the military companies, in the cavalcades, in the records of submissions of *castelli* to the commune.

Stefano assisted the podestà in his sentences. He was one of the councillors and a cavalier. One of his sons, Tancredi, became a Friar Minor, the other continued, like his father, to live in the family house on Prato di Perlici, to negotiate, and make money from his farms of Fontanelle, la Spina, Pariete, San Masseo, Vico.

In 1247 he was among those who fought against the men of Foligno and Spello, who were allied with the imperial forces, then led by one of the most valiant captains of Frederick II, Marco da Eboli. These were the same barbaric and hard-fighting warriors who five years earlier had tried to destroy Assisi—Cuman Saracens, Blachi, Agareni.[s] "It was," said Bonifazio da Verona, "the imperial army in all its full efficiency, cruelty, and fraudulence, the immense infernal power of the tyrant enemy of God."

Assisani and Perugini, this time allied, put together a large army and laid siege to Foligno. Besieged Foligno decided to give battle. Its men marched out at the exact moment of the arrival of the imperial forces that were coming to their aid. They met in a frightful clash near the walls of Spello. Attacked on two fronts, the Guelphs (Assisi and Perugia) were overcome in a short time. Fra Salimbene and Bonifazio described vividly the fury of the combat. So close-packed were the combatants that scarcely anyone could move enough to make use of his weapons. There were fearful cries from the barbarians; horses reared above knots of combatants. Arrows and javelins rained down from everywhere like water and hail during a storm. Some men became so exhausted that they could no longer raise their arms. Others, having lost their weapons, surrendered and were made prisoners.

The slaughter was very great. Assisi soldiers told Brother Elemosina about the painful sight of dead and wounded scattered everywhere over the fields.

Iacopo di Stefano di Presbitero asked himself if all this had not been heaven's punishment for the violence and pillage that men in God's ranks [papal forces] had committed against the people of Foligno, brothers in Christ before the battle. And so in his will he wished to make amends for his own ill-gotten gains and for all the looting of which he had been guilty. Worried, too, about the usurpations he and his parents had committed, he entrusted himself to Clare, to "the lady who presides over the monastery of San Damiano near Assisi," naming her to serve with his blood brother (*fratello di carne*) as the testamentary executrix. He asked that the nuncio of the commune proclaim publicly after his death that whoever had suffered wrongs done by him or his father or mother make claims for restitution upon his estate. If he had no sons, whatever was left was to go to

---

s. "Agarini" in the medieval period was a synonym for Saracens, who, according to Saint Jerome, were the descendants of Abraham's concubine Hagar rather than his wife, Sara. The "Blachi," who are mentioned in the *Processo* of Saint Clare and also in Elemosina's manuscript in the Assisi library, were Tartars from the region of Valacchia in Romania. See *Treccani*, s.v. "Saraceni"; Fortini, *Assisi nel medioevo*, pp. 164, 204.

the poor. It was his will that the fulfillment of all these provisions be entrusted to her, *dicta domina Sancte Damiani.*[52]

The Last Privilege

Until her death Clare fought to obtain a rule that would give official recognition to the Privilege of Poverty, the ardent vow to which she had devoted her life. Sister Filippa recalled how, feeling her strength fail, she desired nothing more than that a pontifical bull confirming the rule she had written be granted to her, "so that one day she should be able to press it to her lips, and the next, to die."[53]

The sisters gathered around her bed, in the bare poor room, the room with the door that opened onto a silvery sea of olive trees. Some could not refrain from tears. It was a Friday of August 1253, three days before the feast of San Rufino. In the calm light of sunset could be heard the far-off clamour of bells.

This was the moment of the vision that Sister Benvenuta told about in the canonization proceedings. A multitude of virgins dressed in white, with shining golden crowns, silently entered the room through the half-closed door and took up the whole room. The brightness was such that every corner of the house was inundated with it. One of the most beautiful of all, wearing a crown greater and brighter than any of the others, came forward. She went to the bed and there she stretched over Clare a veil so thin that it covered her without hiding her. Then she bent down and put her face near that of the dying woman.[54] And with that the vision disappeared, and the room was again in shadow.

On Sunday a friar came, carrying the papal bull that had been issued August 9 from Assisi, where the pope and his court were staying. It contained his approval of Clare's rule:[t] "Moved therefore by your humble supplications, we confirm that form of living and that

---

t. Clare began the composition of a rule soon after 1247, the year in which Innocent IV had given the sisters a rule that pleased no one. She gained approval of it by the cardinal protector of the order in 1252, but would find no peace until the pope himself issued a papal bull in which the rule was given official approval. Her rule, said to be the first to be written by a woman in the history of the church, stresses the Gospel foundation of the life of the sisters, insists on absolute poverty, and prescribes work, mendicancy, love and compassion for the erring. It is a rule full of the Franciscan spirit. For an excellent discussion of the various rules given to the order and to Clare's own rule, see Introduction, *Leg. S. Clarae,* trans. Brady pp. 4–8.

Pope Innocent IV visited Clare twice during her last illness, the last time probably during her last week of life. Brady thinks it likely that Clare, encouraged by this unheard-of privilege, asked him for the fulfillment of her most ardent wish during one of these visits, probably the second one, and that he gave her on her death-bed oral confirmation of her rule. Very likely he had the bull prepared immediately upon his return to his residence at the Basilica di San Francesco and dispatched a friar with it as soon as it was completed. Ibid., pp. 6–9.—Trans.

mode of holy union and of highest poverty that the Blessed Father Saint Francis gave you in speech and in writing to observe in perpetuity, for you and for all who shall come after you in the monastery . . . " Clare took the document without speaking and carried it to her lips.[55]

She died the next day, toward evening.[56] With her were the faithful companions of Saint Francis, Brother Juniper, Brother Angelo, and Brother Leo.[u]

Her childhood friend, the girl of the castle of Sasso Rosso, Filippa, who arranged her body, remembered Clare's death in these words: "Passed from this life to the Lord, Madonna Clare, truly clear without stain, without shadow of sin, into the clarity of eternal light."[v]

---

u. *Leg. S. Clarae*, 45. [According to *Leg. S. Clarae*, 46, just before dying, Clare said (in words especially treasured by her order), "Go forth without fear, for thou wilt have a good escort on thy journey. Go forth, for He who created thee has sanctified thee. He has protected thee always as a mother does her child and has loved thee with a tender love." To one of her sisters who asked to whom she was speaking, she replied, "I am speaking to my blessed soul. . . . Does thou, daughter, see the King of glory as I do?"—Trans.]

v. *Processo* (AFH 13:459).
Some of Clare's present daughters and other admirers who have read the translation of this chapter in manuscript have missed some of the famous episodes of her life as told in early sources. These have been covered extensively by the author in other books, but it seems worthwhile noting some of these here, especially the accounts of the many visits made to her by popes—surely an unusual happening in any age—and her gracious reception of them in her fortress of Poverty, and the episodes that tell of the tender yet increasingly difficult relationship with Francis as time went by. Especially missed is the puzzling physical and psychological phenomenon that took place on the last Christmas of her life. Too ill to go with her sisters to midnight matins at the Basilica di San Francesco, which lies about two kilometres (a little over a mile) from San Damiano, she lay alone in her room and, according to *Leg. S. Clarae*, 29, heard all that went on, including all the music and psalms. At the same time she had a vision of the manger of the Christ-child. Three of her sisters, Filippa, Amata, and Balvina, testified to this in the *Processo* (AFH 13:465, 462, 469). This strange episode, along with the prophecy to her mother that Clare was to be a light to illumine the world, led to her being designated the universal patroness of television by Pope Pius XII in 1957.—Trans.

·10·

TIME OF RECONCILIATION

For Assisi the year 1212 was a time of great works and ardent hopes.

The waters of Moiano were reactivated.[1] These springs had been famous since Roman times. The luxurious baths fed by them had decayed during the invasions, but impressive ruins still existed. Some of them remain yet: The rectangular basin in the bishop's garden, its concrete side fortified by nine buttresses (in the twelfth century it was utilized by the city as a protective wall for the defence of the first city wall). Some rows of the stones of the tepidarium, on which today a farmhouse rests. The vestiges of the superb aqueduct. An arch of squared travertine blocks from which a wall leads off and continues downward to extend below the garden of the monastery of Sant'Apollinare.

Here, as we saw, was one of the properties belonging to the family of Saint Clare—an olive grove encumbered with wreckage and ivy-covered fulcra or mounds, formed from ruined structures that were called in the language of the time *casalini*.[a] The consuls of that time, Cristiano di Paride, Tebaldo, Marangone, and Guidone, acquired one of these *casalini* in 1210 from Scipione di Offreduccio. It was their intention to retrace the lost vein of water and rebuild the fountains so that many people would be attracted to the city again. They hoped, too, to expand the sale of the wonder-working water outside the city. The project must have been realized, at least in part, because in the following centuries the tax on the water of Moiano was one of the principal sources of revenue of the communal treasury.

It happened that in the course of the work the operations were

---

a. Documents describe a *casalino* as walls and ground of a structure in ruins. *NV* 2:139.

extended to another *casalino* located immediately outside the Moiano gate, this one belonging to Giorgio di Agrestolo. He complained to the commune that the work had been done without his consent. The consuls in office in February of this year of 1212, Morico, Marescotto, and Rinaldo, settled with him for twelve *libbre lucchesi*. (The family of Giorgio di Agrestolo was among those devoted to Saint Francis. One of his brothers, Andrea, who held the highest government office of the city, in 1228 presented the donation of Simone di Pucciarello to Brother Elias.[b] Another member of his family, who was also named Giorgio, entered the order of Friars Minor when he was already advanced in age.) When work on the fountain was finished, the people of the city framed an invitation to use it in magniloquent words that still trumpet out over the ancient structure: *Benedicite, fontes, Domino. Bibete, aegri, et valete* ("O fountains, bless the Lord. O ye sick, drink and be healed"). The message was renewed on the eighteenth-century stone tablet now standing above the ancient structure, now a public wash house where women do their laundry.

In the month of May work was begun on the new city hall, the Casa Comunale. The Roman temple on the Piazza Minerva had been chosen for this purpose. The monks of Mount Subasio ceded it to the consuls of the commune, and we still have that document. It was drawn up by the notary in office, Giovanni, in the presence of some of the principal citizens: Taccolo di Aregnato, the chancellor Gilio di Guittone, Guiduccio di Celato, Pietro di Zello, Andrea di Agrestolo, Oderisio di Mazzo, Agresto di San Savino, Pietro.

"We, Domino Maccabeo, abbot of the monastery of San Benedetto, Domino Brettanino, Domino Giacomo, Matteo, Pasquale, Pietro, Girardo, Bonbarone, Illuminato, monks of the same monastery, of our full will give, offer, and concede to you, Gilio, Pietro di Giulia, Leonardo di Giovanni, Baldovino, Leonardo di Dontavino, consuls of Assisi, in the name of the Commune of Assisi, a *casalino* located on the piazza from which to make the house of the Commune of Assisi, such *casalino* belonging to the church of San Benedetto and called San Donato.

"We concede it for the Commune to you and to all your successors for the period of one hundred years, at the end of which, the consuls, or else the consul, or else those who will be in charge of the government in that year, shall give to the monastery of San Benedetto twenty *denari;* and the monastery will confirm to them the said *casalino* for another hundred years, and thus for all time to come, as

---

b. Simone gave Brother Elias the travertine blocks that had formed the walls of his family house for the construction of the Basilica di San Francesco. NV 2:152.

long as the Commune of Assisi shall be pleased to hold it. And you, and those who shall succeed you in the consulate, each year, on the Feast of Saint Benedict, shall give the church of San Benedetto twelve *denari* as income.

"You shall not have the faculty to sell, commute or alienate, but always shall hold the *casalino* in accordance with the right of the monastery. We further reserve to us the houses and the rooms that are between the columns."[2]

The consuls and the monks are looking into the future and they are sure that the commune will endure forever. The recognition of the monastery's right was surely thought to be hardly necessary, since it was required only once every hundred years. *Et sic omne tempus currat.*

Thus the first Palazzo del Comune rises in Assisi, one of the worthiest and most significant of those being built in Italian cities during this time, extraordinarily fitting for the spirit that was animating the resurgent Latin people. The atrium between the columns became the hall of justice,[3] where the magistrate sat on the bench every day, morning and evening, to render judgement to the petitioners and to try criminals brought to him from the nearby prisons. (Giotto, in one of the frescoes of the Basilica di San Francesco, depicted the little external window of the prison, covered by iron bars, slightly above the height of a man. According to the statutes, it had to remain open at all hours as a means of allowing the citizens to check on the presence of prisoners.)

In every official act, in every display, there was a harking back to Roman days. The signatory ring of the consuls, used to authenticate and to seal the public record, bore the figure of an armed Minerva holding up the statue of [the Roman goddess] Victory. A great augury and a great prophecy—to be fulfilled on the day in which the supreme magistrate of the commune would place this ring in the sarcophagus containing the body of Saint Francis, a victor then in glory.

But the principal event of this year of 1212 was the rediscovery of the relics of Saint Rufinus, Assisi's patron saint. Here is what took place, according to the prolix narration of the event in the manner of the time, which is still preserved in the cathedral archives.

As was the custom during all the Middle Ages, the sacred bones had been kept hidden to protect them from the dangers of invading armies. Where they were was known by one person alone, who in his dying moments had to select a successor to whom to confide the inviolable secret. The responsibility of maintaining silence had been rigorously maintained for many generations.

In July, 1212, while work on the new cathedral that had been ordered in the Pact of 1210 was continuing rapidly, the hospitaller Guido, Francis's old teacher [according to this narration], had a vision. The martyr bishop Rufinus appeared to him and, handing him a mantle of many colours, instructed him to go down into the crypt where his body lay and wrap the mantle around it. He did not limit himself to giving directions. He took him by the hand and led him to the place. There the priest saw the blessed bones floating on stagnant water in the subterranean part of the church.

The vision was renewed three times, always with the same details.

The canon Tebaldo was then guardian of the secret. The hospitaller went to him and, without speaking, led him to the crypt and indicated the mysterious burial place. Tebaldo was terrified but, after learning of Guido's experience, went to the bishop to ask advice. These events, when they were made known, stirred the whole city. The consuls came, the canons, and many of the people. Preceded by the cross and carrying burning torches, they went down into the crypt, excavated in the mire, and immediately the sarcophagus appeared. Opened, it revealed the precious treasure.

The new altar was ready, and it was immediately decided to put the venerated relics there. In great pomp the solemn translation followed some days later, on August 3, with bishops, abbots, and other prelates participating.

Even before the revelation, there had been reports of miracles in the city, almost as if the coming event were being foretold. A German pilgrim, Brocardo by name, sheltered in the Ospedale di San Rufino, had badly contracted hands and feet. When he invoked the aid of Saint Rufinus, he was miraculously restored to health. A child of the *contado,* knocked down by an oxcart, escaped death.

But after the relics were brought to light, we are told that the miracles could no longer be counted: Berta, the possessed; Domina Savia, the raving mad; Alberto, the dropsical; Albaguerra's daughter from Bevagna, the scrofulous; Ricca, daughter of Beccario, suffering from a fistula; the little girl born with two heads; Gasdia and Doda, suffering from fever—all were healed solely by going up to the altar that held the bones of the martyr saint.

A young man named Giacomino, riding a horse, fell into the Chiagio at a very dangerous point near Costano. On the point of being swept away, he invoked the aid of Saint Rufinus and was able to regain the bank.

Bishop Guido himself attested to the truth of these miracles. We recognize his ample style, his weighty and imperious manner:

"Since certain works of men are noted down for the purpose of preserving the memory of them, there is stronger reason to register, for their special character, the acts of God, and especially the miracles. Above all, those that regard the merits of the Saints need to be shown, either to reveal their glory or to bring us strayed ones back to the right way of truth. It is for that reason that we, Guido Second, Bishop, and we, canons of Assisi, have selected some among many of the miracles of the Blessed Martyr Rufinus, seeing that there are so many of such that they cannot be included here; but given that we have seen and have heard these, we write so that every falsity about them will be removed by our words; we have thought to be obliged to narrate them for posterity and for its admonition."[4]

Another confirmation of them is found at the bottom of the account [in a note from the canon we have met earlier]: "To these facts he who wrote of them, for having taken the French cross and departed to visit Mount Sinai, bears faithful witness, having seen many in person. For those he did not see, he has ascertained the truth of them by interrogating all, clerical and lay persons, and above all the persons who were participants in them."

Seven days after the translation, on August 10, came the observance of the Vigil of Saint Rufinus. An immense crowd, people from every *balìa* of the commune, filled the cathedral piazza. Everyone carried a burning candle in his hand in order to make the offering established by the statutes. Only a blind man, Pietro by name, was not provided with one, having come from the distant *castello* of Chiagina. Many were sorry for him and spoke to his companion about it. A young man named Leonardo, moved to pity over his plight, split his candle and offered the upper part of it to the blind man, keeping the truncated part for himself. Suddenly his stump of a candle lit up by itself. In the same moment the devout blind man, who had been taken up to the altar, recovered his sight. The people cried out at the miracle. The canons hurried to see.

The ancient fire was returning—the fire through which Saint Rufinus had passed safe and sound, the light that had blazed forth on the muddy waters of the river to reveal his body. Each heart that had pity on the pain of another was capable of receiving that light. Each blind person who believed could be illuminated by it.

The New Duomo

This new ardour was transfused into the master workmen who supervised the work on the new cathedral, these sons who received it as a precious heritage. The cold stone was warmed by it. He who wishes to know the people of this land and this time, the people from whom came Saint Francis, should examine this façade.[5]

A silent song set the rhythm of the hammers and chisels that cut out and connected the living stone. Surely these people had an overwhelming passion to tell of their life and to pass on the wisdom of the ages.

They began with the Creation: God the Father reigns supreme in the arch of the main portal, seated on a throne between the moon and the stars. They finished with the latest happening in the history of their city—perhaps an act of homage to the emperor (on the extreme left of the festoon, a man bows to kiss the feet of a potentate).

Christ the Saviour triumphs everywhere: lamb with the cross, lion crunching death, expiatory victim of the sacrifice, fountain of purification. With him are the symbols of the four evangelists: the eagle, the winged man, the ox, the lion. Peter appears, speaking with wide gesture. Paul shows the opened volume of his epistles. Bishop Rufino is there, pressing the book of the Gospels to his heart. The heads of the martyred holy deacons bring back the horror and grief of their execution.

The story of the Christian martyrs is brought back to life, and the triumphant rise of the religion of Christ is told in all its characteristic symbols: the Virgin and the Baby Jesus, the three kings with their gifts, the priest who baptizes and the priest who purifies, the seraphim who offers incense to God, the angel guardian who keeps watch over one from birth until death.

And the creatures of life have not been forgotten, the good ones and the evil: lions, eagles, wolves, calves, the dog and the fish, the stag and the hen, the camel and the owl, the serpent and the peacock. And there are figures of fantasy: imaginary animals—dragons with long tails, winged and scaly gryphons, horses with human heads, incubi and succubi—they fight each other, bite each other, twine about each other—frightful and ferocious monsters that signify the devil, expressions of the fearful fascination of hell. And also there are symbols of the rewards of those who follow the truth, elegant garlands made from slender branches of leaves twined about with flowers, figurines holding hands and dancing in sign of joy.

We also see the life of the ancient medieval city on that façade. It returns to us in little sculptured figures, miniatures in stone. The archer draws his bow, the musician is intent on his instrument, the seller of grapes offers a basket filled with fruit.

An arcade extends above all, light and elegant with a beautiful flight of columns. Above it are three magnificent rose windows.

Such is the *duomo* built by this people of warriors and merchants, emerging from a time of darkness and pain—a yearning for transfiguration, a mystic poem chiselled in the stone of their native mountain.

Francis on the Road: 1212–1215

"God revealed a form of greeting to me, telling me that we should say, 'God give you peace.'" Saint Francis, just before he died, said this. It is part of his *Testament*. And in so doing, he summed up the origins and purposes of his teaching.

It had been a new salutation, absurd, outrageous, one that astonished most people and made others angry—those who could not understand its purpose and the comfort it might give. After all, everyone knew the necessity of rendering evil for evil, washing away blood with blood and avenging death with death.

"What does your greeting mean?" someone angrily responded to Francis one day, when the order was just beginning. His companion, one of the first twelve, was embarrassed and asked Francis to change it to another.

But Francis said, "Let them chatter, for they do not understand the ways of God. Don't feel ashamed. One day the nobles and princes of this world will respect you and the other friars for this greeting."[6]

He was right. In time people came not to mock him but to listen with reverence and devotion.

The local movement of the men of penitence of the city of Assisi soon spread through the surrounding countryside, cities, and even into distant regions. The first poet biographer, Thomas of Celano, uses a beautiful image: "Like a plenteous river of heavenly grace, the holy man of God watered the fields with streams of gifts; he enriched the field of their hearts with flowers of virtue . . . "[7]

We have reason to think that in the first half of 1212 Francis was again in Rome to inform Innocent III about the progress of the order and to obtain his consent to projects that were maturing. This is the occasion on which he met Giacoma dei Settesoli,[c] the blessed lady who, along with Clare, played a large part in Francis's life.

---

c. Giacoma (or Jacopa) dei Settesoli was of a noble Roman family of high rank, the descendant on her father's side of the Norman knights who had conquered Sicily. Her husband, Graziano, was a member of one of Rome's great families, the Frangipani. They were believed to be the descendants of Flavius Anicius, who in 717 A.D. saved the people of Rome from famine by giving them bread and so was given the name *Frangens panem*. The family also traced its descent from Aeneas, son of Anchises, the Trojan hero whose emigration to Italy is told in Virgil's *Aeneid*. The name of Settesoli came from the Septizonium, the imposing structure that the Frangipani acquired in 1145 from Camaldolese monks. Thomas of Celano speaks of her

Giacoma was also of a noble family (it is said that she was descended from the Normans). She had been married to Graziano Frangipani, owner of the remaining portions of the extraordinary edifice built in Rome by Settimo Severo, the Septizonium. From it came the family name: *Septemsolia* or Settesoli. She had perhaps listened to Francis speak in one of the piazzas of Rome, for he was indefatigable in his work there. In any case, his words of peace had been balm to her heart, which had been saddened by the recent loss of her husband. Giacomina was then very young, not more than twenty-two, alone, and with two fatherless children to bring up. From then on, between the Poverello and the lady existed a holy friendship that lasted until death, indeed, beyond death.[8]

At the end of this same year Francis, after a brief stay in Assisi, embarked for Palestine, his old and passionately desired missionary goal. However, contrary winds blew up, and the ship on which he travelled was driven onto the shores of Slavonia. Only after great effort did he persuade some of the sailors to take him back with them to Ancona.[d]

In Ascoli, to which he went at this time, his efforts and words were so successful that more than thirty men from there entered the order.[9] In the spring of 1213, he was in Romagna.

During this same year he went to Spain, intending to go on to Morocco, ruled then by the famous Sultan Mohammed-ben-Nâser, called the miramolino. The details of this enterprise are not known. Some say that he reached Spain and visited the sanctuary of Saint James of Compostella and that he also founded several friaries there. Others deny that he ever reached Spain. In any case, his sojourn must have been very brief, since (and on this all the early biographers are in agreement) he fell ill and had to return.[10]

It is thought that on this return journey he passed through Piedmont and Lombardy, and stopped in Milan, Oreno, Treviglio, Bergamo, Brescia, also on the island of Garda, which had been given to him as a place for friars to live, and in Cremona, Mantua, and Pavia.[11]

---

illustrious origin, great wealth, and many virtues; he also tells us that one of her sons became a proconsul of the Romans and a count of the papal palace. See *3 Cel.*, 37–38; *NV* 2:453–56 (also Englebert, *Saint Francis,* p. 259).

d. On this trip Francis and his companions, according to *1 Cel.,* 55; *3 Cel.,* 33; and *Leg. Maior,* IX,5, stowed away on the ship returning to Ancona because they did not have enough money to pay the fare and the sailors refused to take them "for love of God." Bonaventure said that this trip occurred "in the sixth year of his religious life." Both biographers say that on the trip a storm blew the ship off course and that Saint Francis, coming out of hiding, saved the crew from starvation by sharing his small store of food, which was miraculously stretched to take care of the needs of all.

He returned to Porziuncola (it was by then 1214) where a group of nobles and literary men awaited him, among them Thomas of Celano. He admitted all of them into the order. The same sort of thing happened everywhere he went. There was no doubt God was with him.[12]

During this period he also made a trip to Tuscany with a new companion who had entered the order, a man from a little village in the *contado* of Assisi called Marignano: Brother Masseo.[e]

They had been walking for some time, the two of them, when they reached a crossroads from which three roads led, one to Florence, one to Siena, and one to Arezzo. They had not decided just where they were going, so Francis thought to learn the will of God by having his companion turn around rapidly, as children do in play, and to continue to do so until ordered to stop. Brother Masseo obeyed, spinning so long he fell down several times from dizziness. Finally, when he was spinning faster than ever, Francis ordered him to stop. At that moment his face was turned to Siena, and the two of them set out on that road.

Brother Masseo marvelled at being treated like a child and made to go around and around in front of other travellers, but from reverence for Francis, did not dare to say anything about it.[f]

In Siena they received a triumphal welcome. As it happened, at the time that they were escorted into the city, some men had gotten into a fight and two of them had been killed. Francis, through his extraordinarily effective preaching, brought them all to peace and harmony. The bishop of Siena paid great honour to the two brothers and invited them to be his guests for the night.

The following morning Francis got up very early with the intention of leaving with his companion without the knowledge of the bishop. And again Brother Masseo was astonished, thinking that Francis was behaving very rudely. But then, thinking of the effects of his holy preaching, he repented of his thoughts and decided his judgement

---

e. Evidence that Brother Masseo was from Assisi is found in a 1350 list of the relics of the Sacro Convento; among the bones of Francis's first companions are those of "Massei laici de Assisio." Again in a list of 1509 is found the name "frate Masse olaico de Assisi." Fra Lodovico da Pietralunga also mentioned the relics of *Frater Masseus de Marigniana de comitatu Asisii.* Other evidence is found in records concerning his nephew Marino, who also entered the order. The village of Marignano no longer exists in the Assisi *contado,* but the name is a common one in several areas, having been originally the name of the proprietor. See *NV* 2:298–99.

For this episode, cf. *Fioretti,* 11; *24 Generals* (AF 3:115–21). The episode probably took place at the crossroads of Poggibonsi. The bishop of Siena from 1189 to 1215 was Buono.

f. It seems to this translator that there is more to this episode than the attempt to inculcate a childlike spirit. Could Francis have used such tactics to train his friars not to be bothered by the attitudes of the people around them, no matter what they did in carrying out their mission?

must be unjust. Francis, who knew what was going on in his mind, lovingly reproved him, warning him that his complaining was inspired by the devil.

Brother Masseo had not by then understood the true meaning of this chain of events: the need to recover the simplicity of children, rid ourselves of both calculation and malice, and abandon ourselves trustingly to the love that supports and provides, if we would bring peace on earth.

On another of his journeys, Francis happened to be passing through Arezzo at a time of serious disorders, when people were fighting in the streets. He said he could see that above the fighting men there were exultant devils, dancing on the city towers. He sent Silvestro, who was with him, to order them out in the name of God. Soon thereafter peace returned to those who had hated each other.[13]

All the towns of Italy now saw remarkable happenings as the result of the work of the Friars Minor: Ascoli, Terni, Greccio, Stroncone, Ancona, Gubbio, Alessandria, Città di Castello, Gaeta. Disappointments, however, were also not lacking to the new messengers of peace.

Francis himself was discouraged at times and sometimes found himself assailed by tormenting doubt. Should he continue to follow this exhausting road, or would it not be better to retreat to a life of solitary contemplation and colloquy with God?

One day in 1215, while staying in the hermitage of Sarteano, he was so agonized over what road to follow that he decided to ask the advice of the sister of his soul, Clare, and of the first priest to enter the order, Silvestro.

Again, it was Brother Masseo to whom he entrusted the errand. He directed him to go first to Clare at San Damiano and then to see Silvestro at the Carceri, where the old canon of San Rufino was spending time in meditation, now so holy, it was said, that whatever he asked of God would be granted. After long hours in prayer (Clare also consulted her sisters), the reply of both was the same, and very precise: God wishes Francis to continue his preaching, because he has not called him for himself alone but for the salvation of others.[14]

The Perverse Leper

By now the lepers no longer arouse the least sense of repugnance in Francis. He has compassion not only for their horrible physical sores but above all for the mental suffering bred of terrible physical pain and despair. From his relationship with them comes this story:

There is in the hospital of San Lazzaro a leper known in all the territory for his bad temper. He continually cursed and burst out in fits of anger, so much so that the friars had decided they could not care for him any longer and must abandon him to his fate. Francis himself goes to the perverse leper and greets him in his usual fashion: "God give you peace, dearest brother."

His answer is fury. "What peace can I have from God, who has taken from me all peace and everything that is good and has made me rotten and stinking?"

Francis says, "My dear son, be patient, because the weaknesses of the body are given to us in this world by God for the salvation of our souls. So they are of great merit when they are borne patiently."

The sick man replies, "And how can I bear patiently the continual pain that tortures me night and day? And it is not only my illness that afflicts me. I am sorely wronged by these friars. Not one takes care of me as he should."

So Saint Francis, after spending some time in prayer, tells the leper that he himself intends to take care of him.

"All right," the unhappy man agrees. "But what more can you do for me than the others?"

"I will do whatever you want me to do," Francis replies.

The leper wants to be washed all over, because he smells so bad that he cannot stand himself. Francis immediately heats water with many sweet-scented herbs, undresses him, and begins to wash him with his own hands.

And love, we are told, wrought a miracle. Not only does the leprosy disappear wherever Francis touches his body and the flesh heal, but an even greater thing happens. While the body is being cleansed externally, the soul within is also washed. The leper weeps in thinking over how nasty he has been to the friars and how blasphemous to God. He perseveres in his repentance for fifteen days, after which, falling ill with another infirmity, he dies a holy death. Francis is greatly solaced by the conversion of this man; even more so some time later, when this saved soul appears to him while he is praying in the forest and thanks him: "Blessed be your soul and your body, and blessed be your words and your deeds, because many souls are being saved and will be saved by you in the world."[15]

But human laws aimed at impeding the spread of leprosy were not in accordance with Francis's marvellous acceptance.[16]

It happened that, upon returning to Porziuncola after a long absence, Francis found Brother James of Assisi in company with a badly ulcerated leper. He had entrusted to this brother the responsibility of looking after and taking care of the lepers but told him not to take them outside the hospital, lest he arouse public opinion. But James was of such simplicity and innocence that he had gone back and forth with them, between the hospital of San Lazzaro and Porziuncola, as if he had been walking with his religious brothers.

Francis said to Brother James the Simple, "You must watch yourself in taking the Christians about (this is what they usually called the lepers), for it is not expedient for you or for them." But scarcely had he said these words than he repented of having done so, for it seemed to him that the poor sick man found them mortifying. Wishing to make amends for what he held to be his great offence against charity, he saw to it that the leper was placed at the common table to eat from the same bowl as himself.

Brother Leo, present at the time, attested to the shiver of horror mixed with compassion that all felt on seeing that poor leper immerse his fingers, contracted and dripping with blood, in Father Francis's bowl, allowing blood and pus to trickle inside it.[17]

The Poor Man Who Hated His Master

Other events in Francis's life show that nothing in life can remain forever deaf to the voice of goodness—though some need a little special help.

One day three murderous thieves showed up at the friars' place in Monte Casale. They asked for something to eat, but the guardian, aware of their crimes, refused them admittance and reprimanded them harshly. What presumption for sinners brazenly to ask for food that had been given to the servants of God!

That same day Francis came back, carrying a sack of bread and a little jug of wine that he and his companions had begged. And when he learned what had happened, he was very much grieved.

"Sinners are led back to God by holy meekness rather than by cruel scolding," he said. "For this reason Jesus Christ, whose Gospel we have promised to observe, says that a doctor is not needed by those who are well but by the sick and that he did not come to convert the just but the wicked."

He imposed a penance on the guardian: to take the sack of bread and jug of wine, search out the thieves, and offer them all of it. Then he was to kneel at their feet and ask their pardon for his cruelty. And afterward he was to implore them to do no more evil for Francis's sake, and to fear God, and to tell them that if they should promise these things, he, Francis, would provide for all their needs.

The thieves, furious when they left the friars' place, were taken aback at seeing the guardian. He did everything just as Francis had ordered; and the robbers, once they had eaten their fill and listened to the humble words, began to consider just how villainous they had been, though up until that moment they had never felt the slightest remorse.

They decided to go back to Francis and ask him if even they, who were guilty of such great crimes, could still hope for God's mercy. Francis welcomed them with kindness and he assured them that the goodness of God is infinite. As a result of someone's caring what happened to them and taking the trouble to teach them, the robbers became Friars Minor.[18]

On another day Francis went through Collestrada, the territory held by Marescotto di Bernardo Dodici. A man that he had known in his youth met him, looking so ragged and beaten down that Francis asked him what had happened.[19]

He flew into a rage and began to curse his master, saying, "Thanks to him, may God curse him, I can have nothing but misfortune, because he has taken away everything I have."

Francis knew that his deadly hatred for his master would be also fatal to him.

"Brother," he said, "pardon your master for the love of God so as to free your own soul, and it is possible that he will give back all the things he has taken from you. Otherwise, your goods are lost and your soul as well."

But the other, obsessed by his wrongs, kept on swearing that never would he pardon his master unless he first had back all that was due him. Francis, not knowing how else to placate him, took off his mantle and put it on him.

"Here," he said, "I am giving this to you. But, I beg you, forgive your master for the love of God."

The man could no longer resist Francis. He forgave his master.

Francis's popularity reached a point where those who no more than touched his garment counted themselves lucky. "When he entered any city," Thomas of Celano writes, "the clergy rejoiced, the bells were rung, the men were filled with happiness, the women rejoiced together, the children clapped their hands; and often, taking branches from the trees, they went to meet him singing."[20]

In November of 1215 Francis was probably present at the Fourth Lateran Council,[21] where some historians believe he had his first meeting with Saint Dominic.[g]

---

g. Gerard de Frachet, *Vitae Fratrum,* p. 7, puts the date of the meeting in 1216. Others think it can only be said to have taken place sometime between 1212 and 1221. [See Moorman,

At the end of this year he was again in Assisi and remained there until the summer of 1216.

This is the time of Jacques de Vitry's famous letter, one that throws a great light on the extraordinary development of the order. This French bishop came to Perugia on July 16, the same day that Innocent III died there. The pope had been en route to northern Italy, to press for peace between Genoa and Pisa and then to initiate a new Crusade.

"From Milan," the bishop wrote, "I went to the city named Perugia, where Pope Innocent III had died but had not yet been buried. During the night some robbers had stripped him of his valuable clothes and left his body, which was lying in the middle of the church, almost naked and giving off a nauseating odor. I went there and saw with my own eyes how brief, vain, and ephemeral is the glory of this world."

The conclave, which immediately assembled in Perugia, named Honorius, "a good and pious old man," according to the same bishop, "very simple and affectionate, who has given to the poor almost everything that he had."

In contrast to his dismay over many of the things he saw in this journey, he was very much impressed by the new order of Friars Minor. He wrote, "In my sojourn at the pontifical court I saw many things that saddened me greatly. All are so taken up with secular and temporal affairs, so involved in lawsuits and trials, and so preoccupied by everything that has to do with kings and realms that it is almost impossible to get a word in about religious matters.

"I nonetheless found consolation in seeing many persons of both sexes, rich and worldly, who have renounced all their possessions and left the world for the love of Christ: 'Friars Minor' and 'Sisters Minor,' as they are called.

"They are held in great esteem by the Lord Pope and the cardinals. They are totally detached from temporal things and have but one passion to which they devote all their efforts: to snatch from the vanities of the world souls that are in danger and to prevail upon them to imitate their example."

The letter concludes with his conviction that through these simple and poor people, many souls would be saved.[22]

History of the Franciscan Order, pp. 29–30; Hermann in *Omnibus,* pp. 600–601, n. 234; Brown in Englebert, *Saint Francis,* p. 474, n. 9.]

According to *2 Cel.,* 148–50, Saint Francis met Saint Dominic at Cardinal Ugolino's residence. Both these founders of orders told him at the time that they did not wish their brothers to accept any high position. Saint Dominic also proposed to Saint Francis that the two orders be combined under a single rule.

The Porziuncola Pardon: 1216

This compassion for everyone, no matter what he was or what he had done, inspired the great Franciscan Indulgence of the Pardon.[h] According to the story told by some of Francis's companions, the Indulgence was preceded by a miraculous vision in the Porziuncola chapel on a night of July 1216.

Francis was praying, kneeling before the altar, when an extremely bright light shone all about. In the great splendour Jesus and Mary appeared, with a multitude of radiant angels. They bade Francis ask for whatever he thought best for the salvation of human souls.

And Francis replied:

"Since it is a miserable sinner who speaks to you, O God of Mercy, he asks you to have mercy on his brothers who are burdened with sin. And he asks that all those who, repentant, cross over the threshold of this place, receive from you, O Lord, who sees their torment, pardon for their evil deeds."

His prayer would be answered, he was assured. However, the fulfillment of it would have to be sealed by the pope, the Vicar of Christ.

Then the divine light disappeared and the song of the angels faded away.

When the first rays of dawn broke through the small window crookedly cut into the wall at Porziuncola, Francis rose and called Brother Masseo, and together they set out for Perugia. They presented themselves at the San Lorenzo palazzo, where the papal court

---

h. For a list of documents pertaining to the Indulgence of the Porziuncola Pardon and an identification of witnesses to it, see *NV* 2:53–56, 427–45.

[There has been a lively controversy over whether it was Saint Francis who originated this Pardon, since it is not mentioned in any of the earliest biographies. That it existed from the mid-thirteenth century on is indisputable. According to Englebert, the silence of the earliest biographers can be explained by the conditions at the time. He recalls that then a pilgrim, according to church teaching, could earn a plenary indulgence (complete remission of temporal penalties for forgiven sins, through the merits of Christ and the saints) by making pilgrimages to only three places: the Holy Land, Rome, and Saint James Compostella in Spain. Such an indulgence could also be earned by taking part in the Crusades. To put the Porziuncola chapel on the same footing as these famous shrines would lower their status and their revenues. To elevate Porziuncola over innumerable other well-known shrines would create resentment and jealousy. To give the same privilege for a pilgrimage to Porziuncola as for participation in the Crusades would damage enlistment in the Crusades. It was, therefore, natural that most prelates would oppose it; and it was also natural that Saint Francis, always reluctant to oppose the clergy, would have refrained from asking for written confirmation of it and counselled his companions not to proclaim it.

By 1277, however, the Friars Minor were strong enough "to shout from the housetops a secret already out," and they began to collect notarized testimony about the Pardon. Pilgrims were already streaming to Porziuncola; and in 1308, the bishop of Assisi, Tebaldo Pontano, had a solemn diploma drawn up to put an end to all the doubts. It reproduces the testimony collected by the Friars Minor, adds that of Brother Masseo's nephew, Brother Marino, and says that it had for years been openly preached before the Roman Curia. See Englebert, *Saint Francis*, pp. 209–11.—Trans.]

was lodged, and asked for and obtained permission to be received by the new pontiff. Francis briefly explained his request, but we are told that for humility's sake he kept silent about the miraculous vision of the preceding night.

"Holy Father," he said, "some time ago, with God's help, I repaired a church dedicated to the Virgin Mary. I ask that you grant an indulgence to it and announce it on the day of its dedication, without the obligation of an offering."

By custom the granting of every indulgence and remission required an offering of a good piece of land. But Francis exerted so strong a fascination on all those who listened to him that Honorius, like his predecessor, did not have the strength to refuse. He asked, then, for how many years should the indulgence be valid.

"I do not ask for years but for souls," Francis replied. The words summed up his prayer in the solitude of Porziuncola. The pope, however, did not understand.

"I ask," explained the man in the torn sackcloth habit, his eyes still shining from his night vision, "that all those who, repentant and absolved, shall visit this church, shall obtain remission of their sins, in heaven and on earth."

The pope was of a gentle nature, disposed to heed requests, but this was unprecedented.

Francis said, "It is not I who ask you this, but he who sends me here, Jesus Christ."

The pope arose, and three times he said, "In the name of God, this indulgence is accorded you."

To the cardinals it seemed that Honorius, through inexperience or weakness, had allowed himself to be carried away and had made too much of a concession. They observed that the new indulgence, if put into effect, would destroy the indulgences granted for pilgrimages to the Holy Land and to the basilicas of Rome.

The pope did not want to renounce his decision. He modified it, however, by limiting it to the anniversary of the day of dedication, from vespers of the vigil to vespers of the feast of dedication.[i]

Francis turned to leave, but the pope recalled him, smiling over his simplicity. Did not the founder of the order of Friars Minor know

---

i. In 1921 the Pardon was made exactly what Saint Francis wanted: a plenary indulgence valid every day of the year. However, since 1967 this same privilege is obtainable at every church. Present church practices play down the role of places or things in the granting of indulgences, emphasizing, rather, religious practices and virtues. A plenary indulgence is available to all who, free from attachment to sin and having recently received the sacrament of penance, go to church, receive the Eucharist, and pray especially for the intentions of the pope.—Trans.

that every concession required a special diploma with the papal signature and the seal?

To this Francis made a characteristic reply.

"Your word is sufficient," he said. "This indulgence is God's work, and God himself will reveal it. Let then the Virgin Mary be the document, Christ, the notary, and the angels, witnesses."

It is difficult to find a suitable reply to such faith, and the papal audience came to an end.

Francis and Brother Masseo went down the dusty incline, under the noonday sun, the glare scarcely broken by the weft and woof of light woven by the olive trees on the burnt earth. Francis was overcome with fatigue, and when they reached the plain and crossed the river, he asked to rest.

In the lepers' hospital of Collestrada, the custodian, who loved them for their zeal in the care of the sick, gave them a room and a couch, where they collapsed, exhausted.

As soon as Francis closed his eyes, a tumult of memories began to spin dizzily in his head. So vivid were they that he felt his blood draining away, as if the old forgotten wounds had suddenly reopened in that empty hour of summer heat.

This was the hill on which he had fought in a tragic battle. He saw again the summit flashing with swords, the ensigns of the *contrade,* the white *carroccio,* the flocks of archers, the mounted soldiers with whom he had attacked the Perugian army. He heard the dreadful frenzied war cry rise up again, the noise of clashing blades, the desperate groans. Again the mad, mocking hymns of victory rose up, songs built on human suffering.

He was no longer seeing just the communal battle but the fighting of all time. What could be important enough to justify it?

With God's help, there is always hope of reconciliation [Francis thought]. But not so long as anyone seeks satisfaction in hurting and humiliating others. One must pardon in order to be pardoned.

It was then, we are told, that it seemed to Francis that the voice he had heard in the night rose up again to assure him, there on top of that bloody hill, that the indulgence granted on earth by the vicar of Christ had been confirmed in heaven.

The Proclamation of the Indulgence

The proclamation of the new indulgence followed after a few days [on August 2, 1216]. In front of the Porziuncola chapel a platform was built of wooden beams, and the bishops who, by order of the pope, had been convoked from the nearby cities were on it: Bishop

Guido of Assisi, Bishop Giovanni *de Comitibus* of Perugia, Bishop Bonifacio of Todi, Bishop Rinaldo of Nocera, Bishop Villano of Gubbio, Bishop Egidio of Foligno, Bishop Benedetto of Spoleto.

Many other people had foregathered from Assisi and nearby towns. There were nobles grouped together, all devoted to Saint Francis. Though he had not changed their lives, they regarded him as an extraordinary man, unquestionably sent by God. The records that preserve the details of the famous ceremony allow us to know who they were, among the anonymous kneeling crowd, and see them as they were depicted three centuries later by Tiberio of Assisi[23]— standing, enveloped in long cloaks, elaborate headgear shadowing their hawk faces:

The castellans of Rocca Pàida and Armezzano, Napoleone di Ubertino, Beccario di Seguino.

Gilio, son of Marco, who was among the arbiters of the 1210 treaty and who sat as one of the consuls in the year that the monks of Mount Subasio gave the temple of Minerva to the commune.

Giovanni di Pietro di Tebalduccio, who had his palazzo on Prato di Perlici, to whom the commune had assigned heavy responsibilities in the settlement of the payments to the cavaliers who had fought with Francis in the war with Perugia. (One of his relatives, also called Giovanni, entered the order of Friars Minor toward the middle of the same century.)

Bernardino, one of Clare's bold and proud cousins, a son of Paolo, Favarone's brother, converted by now to the new cause of the followers of Poverty.

Pietro di Zalfano, the noble who owned land next to the properties of the sons of Ugone. He lived long enough to be called to give testimony about the event in which he had participated, at the time of the heated quarrels over whether the story of the Pardon were fact or fiction.

Biondo di Armuiaffo, the *signore* of the Perlici fortress.

Francis's friend, the man who put together the famous account of this indulgence, Michele di Berarduccio. Matteo di Benintesa, who, like Michele, lived on the mountain in Spello territory and later became an Assisi citizen.

Bonaccorso, son of that Ugone who in 1203 received, with other leading citizens, the submission of the castle of Serpigliano. He was among the consuls in 1228; in 1237 he presided at the drawing up of the arbiters' ruling in which Brother Elias participated about lands on Mount Subasio. His house was in the *contrada* of Santa Maria Maggiore. His devotion to Francis was such that he was allowed to see the stigmata, before and after his death.

Giovanni, son of Gualtieri, who was also among the citizens who conquered Serpigliano. This Giovanni was the father of that famous knight Girolamo whom early biographers of Saint Francis compared to the Apostle Thomas because of his doubts.[24] His descendants were the kind of men who (during the fourteenth century) often took over the government of the city; and their times of rule are records of heresies, slaughters, tortures, and arsons.

Other nobles had come from other places in the surrounding area: Andrea di Tiberio, lord of Montemelino; Pietro; Ugolino di Crispolto from Bettona; Corrado di Revinaldo; Andrea from Bevagna; Napoleone from Foligno.

Francis spoke from the improvised pulpit. It was the hour of *mezza terza,* half-way between prime and terce, seven-thirty in the morning. Pietro di Zalfano summarizes his words.

"I wish to send all of you to Paradise, and I announce to you the Indulgence that I have obtained from the lips of the Highest Pontiff. And all of you who have come today, and all who will come each year on this day with open and contrite heart, shall have pardon for all your sins. . . ."

Others added that he spoke "with so much kindness and with such effectiveness that he seemed a celestial angel, and not a man made of flesh."[25]

Thousands of pilgrims have climbed the Assisi hill on the day of the Pardon since then. Their knees have worn away the humble threshold of Porziuncola. Each of them has surely heard the song of the angels again in the words of the hymn that has been attributed to Brother Leo:

> *Hic fuit arctata*
> *veteris mundi via lata,*
> *et dilatata*
> *virtus in gente vocata.*

> Here the broad highway of the old world changed
> Into the narrow way to life eternal;
> And to the faithful, called from every nation,
> New grace was given freely by the Father.[26]

The First Chapters: 1216, 1217

By now the Friars Minor were walking to the ends of the earth, taking their message of love to people everywhere. But from the first days of the order, Francis had made it a rule that all the brothers must assemble at Porziuncola twice a year, on Pentecost and September 29, the feast of Saint Michael the Archangel.[j]

When the number of friars attending made these reunions affairs of considerable importance, they were called "chapters." This was the word used for the assemblies of knights; and indeed, Michael the Archangel was the great tutelary saint of chivalry. And these men dressed in sackcloth belted with a cord, who travelled the roads of the world on their own quest to gain souls to the Lord, were truly errant knights.

Their hardships were piercing and the lack of understanding they met, bitter. But no knight's heart, in anticipation of seeing again the face of the lady always in his thoughts on the long roads, was more uplifted than theirs at the thought of being together again in the Porziuncola chapel. They repeated to one another Francis's words, when he had assured them that every prayer said in this holy place would be heard and that the deeds that profaned it would be punished.[27] They murmured their own song of glory:

> *Sanctus sanctorum*
> *Vere locus iste locorum.*

> Holy of Holies is this place of places,
> Rightly deemed worthy of the highest honours![28]

Each May, as Pentecost approached, the Friars Minor turned back to Porziuncola. They left cities rich in palaces and cathedrals, descended from remote places made for prayer and meditation—little cells on the edges of forests and on the brows of rocky mountains where the snow had not yielded to the new sun. They walked over

---

j. We have already recorded how, from the first days of the order, Saint Francis loved to reunite his brothers periodically. The French bishop, Jacques de Vitry, in a letter written at the beginning of 1216, said, "Once a year, in a place on which they agree, the men of this Order assemble to rejoice in the Lord and eat together; and they profit greatly from these gatherings. They seek the counsel of upright and virtuous men; they draw up and promulgate holy laws and submit them for approval to the Holy Father; then they disband again for a year and go about through Lombardy, Tuscany, Apulia, and Sicily." (Trans. in *Omnibus*, p. 1608.)

In *3 Soc.*, 14, we also read about these chapters, which the companions say go back to the time that the Benedictines of Mount Subasio gave Porziuncola to the Franciscans. Their narration begins, "After blessed Francis had been given the sanctuary of Saint Mary of the Angels, the Portiuncula, by the abbot of Saint Benedict, he decided that twice in the year, at Pentecost, and at the feast of Saint Michael in September, all the brothers should gather there and hold a chapter.

"At the Pentecost meeting the brothers discussed how to observe the rule more perfectly; and some of them were appointed as preachers and others were assigned to the different posts in the various provinces."

mountain and plain, exulting in the thought that in the same hour, from everywhere, near and far, their brothers were also walking toward their own holy celebration at Porziuncola.

As they walked, cypresses would be shining like votive candles on the peaks of solitary hills, and even the waters of rivers in spring flood would be singing the praises of the Lord. The wide meadows had decorated themselves in golden flowers, as if they were arraying themselves in rich fabric to mark the great feast. The Umbrian people did not call it "Pentecost" but—as they do today—*Pasqua rosa,* "Easter of the Roses."

And each would be thinking of the red and white roses of Porziuncola, which (according to an Assisi bishop) lost their thorns the day Francis, tormented by sexual desire, threw himself naked into the spiky bushes to drive it away. Since then, it is said, all the roses in that garden have been thornless and all the leaves reddened with a drop of blood.[k]

For the Saint Michael's chapter in September, on the other hand, autumn would have strung wide festoons of purple and gold on the Porziuncola woods to greet their arrival. They met in the open, where the sky shone through the trees as between the columns of an enchanted portico. And in the evening all the trunks flamed in the red reflection of sunset, almost as if they were reflecting the burning spirits of these men, dedicated to becoming martyrs for their faith.

The first chapter was held at Porziuncola on Pentecost of 1216.[29] The best method of applying and observing the rule was discussed and missionaries were chosen for various places.

---

k. Cf. Little, "Un nouveau texte," *Oriente Serafico,* 1916–17:107–14.

Corrado, bishop of Assisi in 1335, wrote that Saint Francis "in fervour of spirit, knowing the false allurements of the devil, stripped new-born naked, left his cell, and forcibly pushed into a large and thorny hedge, gravely wounding his whole body on the spines and big thorns of the hedge, and saying in a loud voice: 'Better by far that I know what the passion of Christ was like than obey the false allurements of the enemy.' And when Saint Francis was in the forest so scratched and bloody, a great light appeared around him, and the wild briar patch became full of beautiful roses, white and red." See Faloci-Pulignani, "Diploma del Vescovo Corrado," *Misc. Fran.* 10:86–93; also Francesco Bartoli, *Tractatus,* chap. 8; Bartholomew of Pisa, *De Conformitate* (AF 4:163).

[Brown, in Englebert's *Saint Francis,* p. 476, n. 15, suggests that this story is probably a legendary accretion to the Porziuncola Indulgence, born in the controversy over its authenticity.

As to the roses that have been forever after without thorns, Cicioni, in a botanical study of the plants, expresses the opinion that lack of sun combined with poor soil and growing conditions are responsible for the plants' spineless and rather stunted growth. He found specimens of what is apparently the same species in other locations that are both sturdy and equipped with thorns. He believes the rose is not a native of Italy but a hybrid, perhaps introduced even so far back as when the Benedictine monks had the chapel. The rose is an unusual form, distinguishable from all others, he says; he suggests that it be called *Rosa assisiensis* because of its association with Saint Francis and the Porziuncola chapel. See Cicioni, "Le rose," *Misc. franc.* 18:3–7.—Trans.]

In the chapter of 1217, which Saint Dominic also attended,[1] these missions were definitively organized; and Italy and the other regions were divided into provinces with a minister at the head of each.[30]

About sixty friars pushed all the way to Germany (following this chapter), led by Giovanni della Penna. They had a very hard time of it. The chronicler Giordano of Giano, with moving naïveté, records how they, not knowing the language of the country, would answer only *Ja, ja* ("yes, yes") to those who asked them questions. They answered this way when they were asked if they were heretics, and so they were subjected to severe punishments. Thinking to placate these people, the friars took off their mantles and gave them away, and then also their habits, their hoods, even their underclothes. But that did not stop the abuse.[31]

Francis, in that same chapter, told the friars they could not escape exertions and humiliations, hunger and thirst, when they went as missionaries to lands outside Italy. After having asked God's guidance, he also announced that he himself would go to France.

To go to France was his old dream, both as knight and apostle. It was the land of the dreams of his youth, the land of the language he loved to use in his moments of most intense joy. It was the land where Jesus was greatly venerated in the Holy Eucharist,[32] the land in which he had many times thought it would be good to die.[33]

He chose the friars who would accompany him and gave them their rule for the journey, which he warned them would be long and difficult: "Take the road two by two in the Name of the Lord. Be humble and sincere. Keep silence from dawn until after terce, praying to God in your hearts, and do not indulge in idle and unprofitable conversation. Although you are travelling, let your words be as humble and devout as in a hermitage or cell. For wherever we are, or wherever we go, we always take our cell with us; for Brother Body is our cell, and our soul is the hermit who lives in it, constantly praying to God and meditating on Him. If the soul cannot remain quiet in its cell, then a cell made with hands is of little value to a Religious."[34]

When they reached Florence, they found Cardinal Ugolino, bishop of Ostia, (later Pope Gregory IX), who had succeeded the cardinal of

---

1. Saint Dominic's presence at a chapter is described in *Actus,* 20; *Fioretti,* 18. They say, however, that it was the "Chapter of Mats" (see chap. 12, pp. 475–79). Some historians have dismissed these stories as legendary only; but Jean Olivi speaks in his *Lectura super Lucam* of twice hearing an elderly Franciscan Bernardo Barravi, who had formerly been a canon regular of the cathedral at Carcassone, tell of having heard Saint Dominic describe seeing Saint Francis and also thousands of his brethren at a chapter in Assisi, to which many city people unexpectedly brought provisions. Scholars do not agree on the date of the chapter that he attended. Perhaps he was present for several. See *Fonti Francescane,* 2:2171–72; Brown, in Englebert, *Saint Francis,* p. 477, n. 5.—Trans.

Saint Paul in the protectorate of the order. Ugolino, when he learned of Francis's intention, heartily opposed it. He spoke of the inevitable opposition that could be expected from many prelates. He assured Francis that if, however, he remained in that province, he and all the curia would in every way protect and support him.

But Francis was reluctant to follow his advice.

"Bishop," he replied, "I should be very ashamed if I sent my brothers to distant provinces, while I remained here without sharing any of the hardships that they have to suffer for God's sake."

The cardinal remarked that there was no reason to send the brothers to undergo such sufferings. To which Francis replied, "Do you imagine that God has raised up the friars solely for the benefit of these provinces? I solemnly assure you that God has chosen and sent the friars for the benefit and salvation of the souls of all men in this world. They will be welcomed not only in the countries of the faithful, but in those of unbelievers as well, and they will win many souls."[35]

This was a new concept, a mission then undertaken by no other order. The future pope was astonished and filled with admiration. But he still was opposed to Francis's going, so Francis had to name someone else to head the little company that would continue on its way. Francis chose Brother Pacifico.

The King of Verses

This friar, Brother Pacifico, is so intimately tied to the life of Saint Francis he merits more than a brief biographical sketch.[36] He was born in the March of Ancona, where everyone knew him as the "King of Verses."

In the picturesque and fantastic Middle Ages, there were kings of rhymes, kings of amorous girls, kings of arms, kings of cross-bow archers. There was no lack even of kings of canons, kings of minstrels, even kings of knaves. The title was bestowed by popular acclaim, and often a formal confirmation of the popular choice was made by official authorities.[37]

Brother Pacifico was the singer of light-hearted songs or, to use the words of Thomas of Celano (who in few chapters so ardently pours out his own great lyrical gifts as in the one about this poet touched by grace), he was "the most outstanding of those who sang impure songs and . . . a composer of worldly songs."[38]

His was the kind of poetry then in style, in which Unhappily Married Wife weeps over the suspicions of her Jealous Man, and Daughter asks Mother for a Husband, and Lady in Love fidgets and yearns in the torment of desire.

Oi lassa innamorata!
cantar vo' la mia vita
a dire ogni fiata
come l'amor m'invita . . .[39]

What a shame that we do not have even one line from the poet of San Severino! The early biographers liked to call him "a master of noble and courtly song," since he not only composed but also sang with masterly skill and grace.[40] In short, he was so famous that Emperor Otto IV himself, when he came to Italy, was pleased to crown him "with the greatest pomp."[41] And thus it happened, still according to Thomas of Celano, that "so high had worldly glory raised him" that he "gave himself completely to vanity."

A young woman of his family had been attracted to convent life rather than to the plaintive ballads of her glamorous cousin, a "cloistered poor nun" of the Benedictine monastery of San Salvatore di Colpersito in the city of San Severino.

One day the poet came, dressed in scarlet, wearing on his head the garland of roses designated for him by imperial decree, to a festival at the monastery's church. With him was a large following of noisy and merry friends.[42]

Francis was there, too, with his silent companions standing like a faithful and proud old guard. The two companies faced each other. They eyed each other. Francis then spoke from the altar.

The King of Verses listened first distractedly, then attentively, and finally with a certain inquietude that induced him to think vaguely about a change of life. All of a sudden he was struck with wonder and felt that all the blood was rushing from his veins.

That fascinating beggar, that stranger, turned to him, looked deep into his eyes, and talked in sweeter, more persuasive words than he had ever imagined in even his most impassioned songs.

What did Francis feel at finding himself before the phantom of his own youth, standing in that flock of singers, so like the ones he had led through the streets of Assisi? Did he remember the night of the last serenata in which the lady who was the most beautiful and alluring of all those on earth had appeared before him? Did he see himself all over again in that young man entranced by earthly glory?

Perhaps someone had told him about the celebrated troubadour who had been honoured by the emperor, and Francis wanted to convince him that another emperor existed, head of a kingdom greater and more powerful than any earthly kingdom, one in which he could win rewards greater than garlands that flowered and fell in a single morning of May.

Certainly whatever he said must have been extraordinarily impressive, because, at the height of the discourse, the King of Verses saw with his mortal eyes two swords crossed over Francis's thin body. Two glittering swords, gleaming more brightly than any had ever shone under a hot sun on the day of battle. One of them went from his head to his feet, and the other across his breast, from one hand to the other as he stretched them wide in a gesture of appeal. A cross of shining steel against a worn and ragged habit.[43] And those swords cut as well as shone, and the poet felt them plunge into his own flesh and penetrate his heart.

Then he recognized Francis as that Assisi man who was said to be so hard to resist. Rising almost with anger, he burst out, "What need is there for more words? Let us come to deeds. Take me from among men and give me back to the great Emperor."[44]

The next day, dressed in brown sackcloth, he followed Francis's group of penitents, undisturbed by the comments of those who had admired and envied him. He had found his peace, and Francis, therefore, called him Brother Pacifico.

From then on he accompanied Francis on many travels.

One evening they arrived together in Trevi, the master and the disciple. Here too there had been a war and the city was reduced to a heap of ruins. A short distance from the crumbling walls stood a small, out-of-the-way church, San Pietro di Bovara, and Francis went to it to mourn and to pray. Brother Pacifico was to leave him alone and return the following morning.

Biographers say that the night was filled with infernal spirits, the only victors in war, who thundered about the territory like its masters. Francis heard a swarm of them on the roof, rampaging and making a great noise. He hastened to the threshold and drove them away—undoubtedly with words about the power of the spirit to change those whose pride drives them to violence.

At daybreak Brother Pacifico, who had spent the night in the nearby lepers' hospital, returned. Francis did not answer when he called him; and Pacifico saw him prostrate before the altar, lost in ecstasy.

And Brother Pacifico, awe-struck and admiring, had a vision. He saw the heavens open. And there he saw many thrones, and among them was one of great splendour, adorned with precious stones—the throne of Lucifer, the rebel angel cast out of Paradise for his demonic pride. And a voice said to him, "This throne belonged to one of the fallen angels, but now it is reserved for the humble Francis."[45]

It is easy to imagine Brother Pacifico's exultation when Francis chose him as his companion for the journey to France. Perhaps it was then, in a flowering of his creative gifts, that he saw on Francis's forehead, in vivid colours, the Tau of knights.[46] However, the order to lead the difficult mission to France must have seemed daunting at first. But he faced up to the difficulties, which were not few, with serene spirit.

They were mistaken for Albigenses, because the word "poverty" constantly rang out in their sermons. The bishop of Paris, Pietro Chambellan di Nemours, felt he had to convoke the masters of the Sorbonne to decide whether they were heretics. He also sent a query to the pope. Before a reply came from Rome, Brother Pacifico had succeeded in overcoming all doubts and had gained wide sympathy.[47]

The Missionaries

Also in that chapter of 1217 the name of the blessed land *Terra Promissionis* was mentioned for the first time—the land that aroused the anxiety of all Christians, from popes preoccupied with its rescue to those youngsters who had marched on a children's crusade a few years earlier: the East, the Holy Land. The Franciscans decided to make it a province. This enterprise was entrusted to the man who within a short time would fill the pages of history books with his deeds and his formidable genius—Brother Elias.

As we have seen, the citizens of Assisi were so impressed by him that they chose him, while he was still young, as consul and leader of the commune at the first outbreak of the civil war. Under his leadership, the city's soldiers, cavaliers and infantry, had attacked the fortresses of the feudal lords.[48]

But quite a different conquest was asked of him in the 1217 chapter, this time in the name of love. The province of Oltremare [literally, "Beyond the Sea"] would include Constantinople and its empire, the Greek islands, Asia Minor, Antioch, Syria, Palestine, Cyprus, Egypt, and all the rest of the Near East. Elias would go there with only a few companions, with no means of support. They would have to live alone in infidel kingdoms with merciless armies, to preach the virtues of Poverty and to be ready to face martyrdom.

Brother Elias did not hesitate a moment. He left at once.[49]

In the chapter of 1218, other new missions were decided upon. Brother Egidio and Brother Eletto went to Tunisia, Brother Benedetto of Arezzo to Greece.

The mission to Tunisia failed, because the Christians of that area feared reprisals from the Moslems for the presence of missionaries and themselves forcibly put them on a boat to Italy. Only Eletto

remained in the country, and he was captured and suffered martyrdom. He met his death on his knees, pressing the rule of the order
against his heart. He was a young lay brother, so delicate that only with
difficulty had he been able to bear fasting on the required days.[50]

In the Pentecost chapter of 1219, held at Porziuncola, a new mission was undertaken, one to bring both sadness and glory to the
order. Saint Francis, hearing that Christians were being greatly persecuted in Morocco, chose six brothers to send there: Vitale, Berardo,
Pietro, Adiuto, Accursio, and Ottone. We know nothing about them
but their names. Their place of origin, their secular life, their entrance into the order—all have been forgotten.

Someone who was present preserved Francis's words said in the
hour of leavetaking.

"My dear sons, God has commanded me to send you to the land of
the Saracens to preach and to stand up for His faith and to fight
against the law of Mohammed. And I, too, am going to go to infidels
elsewhere, and I am going to send other friars through the world."

Those who had been chosen bowed their heads and replied,
"Father, we are ready to obey you in everything."

Moved by their ready obedience, Francis tenderly continued: "My
dear sons, so that you may better fulfill the commandment of God,
look to the health of your souls and see that there is peace and
concord and a link of indissoluble charity among you. Flee from envy,
the beginning of the road to damnation. Be patient in tribulation,
humble in success, and thus always in battle be the victors. Be im-
itators of Christ in poverty, obedience, and chastity. And truly the
Lord Jesus Christ was born in poverty, lived in poverty, taught poverty, and in poverty died."

And he added other words of praise of those blessed virtues [of
poverty, obedience, and chastity] that Giotto depicted in the great
allegories on the walls of the Basilica di San Francesco in Assisi.

But at last emotions overwhelmed the serene counsellor and
teacher, and a flood of words poured out, so loving that each kept the
memory of them until his last moment of life.

"O my sons, even though I rejoice in your good will, all the same
my heart cannot escape a certain loving grief over your departure and
at separation from you, but we must put the command of God before
our will. I beg of you always to have before your eyes the sufferings
of our Lord, to strengthen you and inspire you to suffer for him."

The brothers in reply reaffirmed their obedience. They did not
disguise the dangers of that extraordinary mission. They were young
and had never been outside Italy. They knew neither the language

nor the customs of the people among whom they would be going, only that they bitterly hated all Christians. They knew the ridicule they would meet because of their poor clothes.

There were other words and some tears, and finally the six set off to their destiny.

They reached Spain where the leader, Vitale, got sick and had to leave his companions. The others, after numerous difficulties, were able to reach Morocco. Here they were benevolently received by Don Pietro, Infante of Portugal, who had been placed by the sultan, Abu-Yâqub, now the miramolino, at the head of his army. But the miramolino, going through the streets one day, happened to hear one of the brothers inveighing against the religion of Mohammed, and he immediately ordered them to leave the country.

However, the brothers managed to return and again began their preaching. Surprised again by the miramolino, they were taken into custody and subjected to frightful torture. But they had the strength to maintain their faith, and with such tenacity that the prince, beside himself with anger, decapitated them with his own hands. It was January 16, 1220.[51]

And an even more dramatic mission was to be undertaken. After the chapter of 1219, Francis made ready to leave for Damietta. It was the center of action of the Fifth Crusade, which was being led by King Jean de Brienne, Leopoldo, duke of Austria, and William of Holland. In May 1218 they and the Christian armies sailed from the port of Acre, to go to Egypt in an effort to demolish the Moslem power. They disembarked on the north bank of the second mouth of the Nile and at once laid siege to Damietta. Several engagements took place, on the whole favourable to Crusader troops. But Damietta was still holding out and the campaign was at its peak.

·11·

DAMIETTA

The exact place from which Francis embarked for Damietta is not known. Perhaps it was Ancona;[a] perhaps in one of the ports of Apulia, which Innocent III had established as the assembly point for soldiers of the Crusades.[1]

Once news of his extraordinary mission was known, brothers flocked to the port, hoping to be able to go with Francis. But there were only a limited number of places on the ship; and Francis, knowing how eager each was to go and not wanting to make anyone unhappy, called a little boy who happened to be there and had him pick out his companions for the trip.

Twelve were chosen.[2] The five whose names are known are all from Assisi. Three are among his first companions: Pietro di Catanio, Barbaro, and Sabatino.

The fourth is the once high-tempered feudal lord of Sasso Rosso whose castle the people of Assisi had destroyed, the bitterest foe of the commune of all who had gone to Perugia, the father of the girl who had been a childhood friend of Clare and who, like Clare, had

---

a. Golubovich (*Biblioteca,* 1:92), Sabatier (*Vie,* chap. 13), and others believe that Francis sailed from Ancona. Their opinions are based on the *De Conformitate* of Bartholomew of Pisa (*AF* 4:481), who was the first (1385) to mention this city; but certainly nothing in the records or in the most ancient biographies serves to confirm this thesis. Angelillis, in *Un punto inesplorato,* observes that the standard route to the East across the Adriatic began from the ports of Apulia, Barletta, Bari, and Brindisi. From the time of the earliest Crusades, the religious orders of knights—the Knights Hospitallers, the Templars, and the Teutonic Order—were established in these ports. They had the specific responsibility of equipping the ships that transported the huge numbers of Crusaders and also of re-supplying them as needed. See Carabellese, "La Puglia e la Terrasanta," *Rassegna Pugliese,* vol. 17, no. 10. We also know from *24 Generals (AF* 3:77–78) that Brother Giles, who visited the Holy Land in 1215, spent some time in Brindisi awaiting the ship on which he would sail. Innocent III, in announcing the Crusade in 1205, informed all Christians that the assembly of the troops would take place in Brindisi, from which they would embark for Constantinople and Jerusalem.

396 · FRANCIS OF ASSISI

now found peace within the walls of San Damiano—Leonardo di Gislerio.[3]

The fifth, coming from secular life, has taken a name that is almost a poetic expression of the light that had been found by the Knights of Poverty—Brother Illuminato. The oldest sources have preserved for us the name of the place from which he came: Arce, the castle that at one time was on the plain between Rivo Torto and Porziuncola, the fortress *par excellence,* the bastion whose shadow lay over the places that saw Saint Francis's first works of charity.[b]

They sailed in June, 1219.

They touched the island of Candia and probably also Cyprus, at that time a kingdom of the Crusaders.[c] Finally the ship docked at Saint Jean d'Acre.

Francis stayed in Syria only a few days. It is believed that he met Brother Elias and that he assigned his companions to various places in

---

b. Saint Bonaventure had high words of praise for Brother Illuminato, whom he knew in person, as is made clear in a thirteenth century Vatican codex. He identifies Illuminato as having been with Saint Francis in the Holy Land and with him on his visit to the sultan; he says Illuminato was also with Francis on La Verna when he received the stigmata. It was perhaps his being singled out by Saint Bonaventure that led Dante to put him in his heavenly company (*Paradiso,* Canto 12).

Nonetheless, there has been a lively dispute about the place of origin of this brother, in part because of a confusion with another Brother Illuminato from Chieti—a secretary of Brother Elias who eventually became bishop of Assisi (1273–1282), and in part because of a confusion arising from references in the early texts, particularly in the introductory letter to *3 Soc.* In some he is called Illuminato of Rieti; in others (and the oldest), of Arce. This dispute has been compounded by a subsidiary one over whether Arce was a district of Assisi on the plain near Porziuncola, on whose borders the leprosarium was located, or whether it referred to Rocca Accarina near Rieti.

According to Wadding, Illuminato entered the order about 1210, as did Brother Agostino of Assisi, whom Dante places with Illuminato in paradise. At this time Saint Francis was living at Rivo Torto. It was the time, as Thomas of Celano tells us, "that many of the people, both noble and ignoble, cleric and lay, impelled by divine inspiration, began to come to Saint Francis, wanting to carry on the battle constantly under his discipline and under his leadership." It seems likely that Illuminato was one of these. According to an ancient tradition, he died about 1266 in Tolosa.

For further details about Illuminato dell'Arce: *NV* 2:303–6.

c. Mariano di Firenze gives us this itinerary, saying that Francis left from Ancona "and in a short time reached the island of Chandia (Crete), where he stayed a few days preaching penitence and the passion of Christ. Afterwards, he sailed on to Syria and reached port in the famous city of Acre."

Some writers have thought that Francis stopped at the island of Cyprus on this voyage, because in some (but not all) early manuscripts of *2 Cel.,* 155, the incident in which a nobleman saw Brother Barbaro eat asses' dung as a self-imposed penalty for having spoken angrily to another brother is placed in *insula Cipri.* However, this certainly took place near Assisi, in an area called even today Isola or "Island" and once known as the "Island" of Cipii or Scipione; see chap. 9, n.f, of this book and *NV* 2:383–88.

The island of Cyprus is mentioned in early biographies only in reference to this incident, and none of the accounts of Francis's trip to Egypt and the Holy Land says that he disembarked on Cyprus. Fra Mariano writes, "After some time Sancto Francesco returned to Acre, and boarded a ship, and sailed to Egypt to the city of Damietta, where the army of Christians had then gone; and they were laying siege to the city of Damietta."

the region. Then he hurried off to Egypt, taking with him the friar of Arce, Illuminato. Toward the end of July he reached the Crusader army that was encamped in front of Damietta.[d]

The Siege of Damietta

The siege of Damietta[e] is one of the most dramatic events of the thirteenth century. This may be clearly seen in the rude and devout chronicle of an unknown crusader who wrote to record the events in which he himself had participated:[4] "The joys, the tribulations, the passions, the abandonments, the various torments, borne by the militant Christians in that army, we propose, as best we can, to tell to you who read and listen. . . ."[5]

All this is crucial to understanding the life of Saint Francis. To reconstruct the events of that siege, especially from August 1219 to February of the next year—the uninterrupted period that Francis remained in the Crusaders' encampment—allows us to relive a good six months of his life.

The Crusaders had undertaken the siege with an enthusiasm that had been fed by memories of stories about the place. From the city of Damietta had come Saint Mary of Egypt who, in order to make a pilgrimage to Jerusalem to adore the Holy Cross, had become a prostitute to sailors of the ship on which she sailed. There, between the desert and the sea, the pharoah's daughter had found the basket in which the newborn Moses had been placed. And they said that right

---

d. If one keeps in mind that on the eve of the battle of August 29, 1219, Francis was already in a position to judge perfectly the military situation and the conditions of the Crusader army and that he was already held in high regard by the legate, the king of Jerusalem, and the other leaders, then it can be deduced that he must have reached the camp a good many days earlier, toward the end of July.

e. The siege of Damietta (1218–19) marked the opening of the Fifth Crusade, which, after a peaceful period of forty years, was proclaimed by Innocent III at the Fourth Lateran Council in 1215 and scheduled to open four years later. Its object was the recovery of Jerusalem from the Moslems, a goal on which Innocent III had set his heart.

In 1215 Innocent III designated Egypt as the place to be attacked and ordered that during the years of preparation a Truce of God must be observed in Europe and that all trade with Egypt and the Levant would cease. An enormous number of warriors from all over Europe took the cross. It was decided that they should begin with a siege of Damietta, then a major commercial center and one of the richest cities in Egypt. The Crusade began to move in 1217.

Jean de Brienne was first chosen as the leader of the Crusade; after 1218 he was displaced by the cardinal legate Pelagius. The Crusaders rejected generous terms offered at the outset by the sultan, Malik-al-Kāmil. As we shall see, dissension between the leaders was a major problem for the armies, which nonetheless fought fiercely to take the city.

The Damietta of that time was above the mouth of the Nile, on the eastern branch of the river, between the east bank and Lake Menzala. In the mid-thirteenth century it changed hands several times in repeated battles. That Damietta was razed by order of the sultan Bibars and the mouth of the Nile was blocked to prevent further attacks. Bibars then had a new Damietta—the present one—built about four miles farther from the sea.

See also n. q of this chapter.—Trans.

on the shingly edge of the river where the army had disembarked, Jeremiah had been born, the prophet who had cried out the shame of his people; they even pointed out his house.[f]

Adventurers of every race had come, and murderers, to gain absolution for frightful crimes. Corsairs and grasping merchants were found shoulder to shoulder with proud and austere men, in a heterogeneous throng perennially animated by piety and ambition, heroism and jealousy, holiness and brutality. There were bishops, princes, Templars, Hospitallers, priests, dukes, counts, marquises, men-at-arms of the land and of the sea.[6]

When, toward evening, the *libeccio,* the hot southwest wind of the Mediterranean, rose from the mouth of the Nile, carrying the oppressive sultriness of heat and miasma of the swamp, banners of every imaginable kind fluttered from the masts of ships: pennants, ensigns, flags of every pattern and colour, flags of France, Germany, Brittany, Spain, Frisia, Holland. Companies, knights, and infantry of the Italian republics were there, equal in arms and in courage to the most powerful kingdoms: Venetians, Genovesi, Pisani, Lucchesi (led by their consuls Ubaldo and Rumone), Bolognesi with their captains, Bonifacio and Buruffaldino. There, too, was a company of Crusaders of the Spoleto Valley.[7]

The Florentine chronicle of Ricordano Malispini gives us an idea of how much enthusiasm there was for this Crusade in all the cities of the peninsula. For example, it records the death below the walls of Damietta of one of the *maggiori* of the city, Fazio dei conti Alberti, who, along with his brother, Alberto, was in the company of the Marquis d'Este. "Still other nobles of Florence made this crossing," he writes, "and also many of the people of Florence."[8]

White and crimson crosses shone on silk and on steel, on the castles of ships and on the mantles of knights of a multitude of orders. It

---

f. Milioli, p. 1085. These legends that spread among the Crusaders do not correspond at all to historical reality.

The only knowledge we have of Saint Mary of Egypt, which comes from the legend handed down to us by Saint Sophronius, is that she was born in Egypt, at twelve years of age went to Alexandria and became notorious for her licentious life, and later turned to a life of penitence.

Moses, whose existence no critic doubts, was born, according to the Biblical account, of the house of Levi at a time that the Israelites were undergoing persecution in Egypt. But no authority ever said that he was born in Damietta.

Jeremiah was a native of Anathoth (today Anàtha), a village northeast of Jerusalem (Jer. 29:27). According to a late tradition that was reported by Epiphanius in *De vitis profetarum* (PG 43:400), he was killed at Tafni in Egypt.

After disembarking, the Crusaders made camp along the left and western bank of the Nile, today the site of Ras el Bar. On the opposite bank, about a mile by sea, was Damietta. The camp of the sultan of Egypt, Malik-al-Kāmil, was in a place called Al-Adilija. al-Maqrìzì, *Histoire d'Egypte* (*Revue de l'Orient Latin,* 9:468, 473).

blazed out on the habits of monks and the garments of priests. Everywhere there was the flaming emblem that was a symbol of the passionate feelings of those souls who had come here, as the chronicle puts it, "from beyond the sea, to liberate, defend, and hold the Holy Land from the enemies of the Holy Cross."[9]

There Francis must have heard the name of Brienne ring out like a trumpet call, that name he had dreamed of serving under in his youth—for the army was led by Jean, king of Jerusalem, the brother of the Gautier de Brienne who had fought in the interests of Innocent III.

Not one, among the hundred thousand warriors serving under him, could hope to surpass him in courage or exemplary living.[10] Fra Salimbene, who knew him, shows him to us: "large and heavy, tall in stature, robust and strong and so expert in the art of war that he was considered another Charlemagne, son of the king Pippin. When in combat he struck here and there with his bludgeon, the Saracens fled as if they had seen the devil or a lion ready to devour them. In his time there was no knight in the world braver than he."[11]

He was as devout as he was brave. When he was armed to go onto the field of battle, he trembled like a bulrush in the water, according to Fra Salimbene. And he was often asked why he should tremble when in battle he was an invincible fighter. He always replied that it was not for the fate of his body that he was afraid, but because he feared that his soul was not sufficiently prepared to meet God.[12]

The Tower of the Chain

Damietta was fearfully fortified. Two high walls encircled it on the side facing the river, and three on the landward side. There were twenty-two gates, one hundred and ten towers—some equipped with two or three testudos, forty-two castles, a large navigable moat, barbicans and bastions. Iron chains crossed the river to impede the passage of enemy ships. Engaged in the defence was a multitude of infantry, archers, crossbowmen—the flower of the nobility and of Saracen prowess. Supplies had been accumulating for more than two years.[13]

The first engagements were disastrous for the Christians. Soon, however, heaven itself came to their aid. The fighting men told each other amazing stories.

There was, for instance, the affair of the attack on the Tower of the Chain, which rose, huge and strong, in the middle of the river and was defended by more than four hundred archers. When an assault was made August 24, 1218, Saint Bartholomew's Day, the scaling ladders loaded with Crusaders crackled like twigs under the rain of sulphur and Greek fire. The Christians on the other bank had given up hope of success, when, no one knew how, on top of the tower appeared a banner with the sign of the cross.[14]

The Christians were victorious in this assault. Afterwards, their prisoners, taken to the king, asked to be allowed to see again the warriors in white who had climbed to the top of the tower and the captain in red armour who led them. Accordingly, proclamations were made throughout the camp calling all who had participated in the battle to present themselves to Jean, the king. But the Saracen prisoners recognized no one. They described their marvellous unknown assailants as swift and strong, clad in white clothes and white armour. They mounted the tower as if they were flying, they said, and had no need of scaling ladders. The splendour of their shining armour was such that it blinded them and deprived them of strength.

Then, concluded our good chronicler, it seemed clear that angels had fought with the Crusaders, and the brave leader in red armour could be none other than the apostle whose feast was being commemorated on that day.[15]

It was said that God dispersed the fog and rain that impeded the Christians from engaging the enemy; he led to salvation ships that were in danger. One time the Saracens retired because of a plot of the emirs against the sultan—in the Christian camp the story went around that Saint George had come in person, ordered them to flee, and threatened to exterminate them.[16]

Still, there were days of tedium and discontent when the Crusaders thought they would all die on that squalid sandy shore, days when the armies were divided, opinions at odds and gloomy.

Cardinal Pelagius, who had come to the field as papal legate in September [1218], accompanied by a great number of nobles and Roman barons, was undoubtedly bold. (In the battle that took place on Tuesday [October 26, 1218], the feast day of Saint Demetrius, he was seen advancing ahead of all the others, raising the cross and invoking victory in a loud voice. Immediately the enemy attacked furiously, with a great noise of trumpets and cymbals. So bloody was their defeat that for many days the bodies of the dead contaminated the water of the river.)[17] Yet, the cardinal had had no practice in the art of war. Only his arrogant egotism, which had already led him to quarrel with the pope himself, accounted for his presuming [as he did] to take into his own hands the general command of the army.[18]

To these low spirits were added, during the winter, incredible sufferings from the cold and the spread of a strange epidemic, a disease that caused some to lose their nails, others, their teeth. A sixth part of the army died. Many, discouraged, sailed back home.[19]

But the first sun of March was enough to reawaken confidence and revive the call that became the rallying cry in all future battles: *Si Deus pro nobis, quis contra nos?* ("If God is for us, who is against us?")[20]

On Palm Sunday [March 31, 1219] there was bitter fighting from dawn until late at night. The women in the camp were on the field of battle with the Crusaders, taking them water, wine, bread, and stones for their weapons. Priests followed to recite the prayers of the day while bandaging and blessing the wounded. The chronicle of Francesco Pipino says that "on that holy day the only palms carried by the Christians were crossbows and bows, arrows and lances, swords and shields."[21] The Saracens lost five thousand men and thirty ships.

Warriors of twenty nations were joined in this campaign and the contrast in their languages and customs, arms, and very different dress made a vivid and picturesque scene. For instance, in the [August 1218] assault on the Tower of the Chain, a Dutch boy, almost an adolescent, confronted a Saracen standard bearer and hit him with a club like those the peasants of his land used to beat grain—a flail tied to a stick with short chains. He succeeded thereby in taking possession of the yellow flag of the Sultan.[22]

The squire Ernoul, not so impartial as many historians like to think, was put off by the unfamiliarity of the men of the Italian maritime republics. He criticized them for superficiality. "The men of Genoa, Pisa, and Venice say that they certainly would have conquered the city with four ships with ladders fixed on them. 'But they did not belong to the family of those men to whom it was granted to achieve Israel's salvation.' They wish only to make a name for themselves, coming forward with a great show of trumpets, salutations, banners." When he saw them reach the walls and slaughter the enemy, he must have changed his mind, although he continued to complain that such heroism had done nothing but arouse retaliations by the Saracens and induce them to strengthen their defences. As a result, he was of the opinion that "Damietta cannot be taken except through Divine virtue."[23]

The Lombardians made a nice contribution to the colour when on Pentecost, 1220 [1219?] they brought out their *carroccio* for the first time. It aroused great enthusiasm, and all the army promptly followed suit. On top of the altar fluttered the insignia of the cross, and the warriors marched about the *carroccio* so that it appeared to be encircled by a forest of lances. It brought fear and uncertainty to the infidels, who thought that the unknown enemy god must be mysteriously hidden inside. All of them ran to the walls and, astonished, remained gazing at the strange spectacle from morning until the ninth hour.[24]

Saracens contributed to the exotic quality. Soldiers of the Christian faith said that a strange book written in Arabic had been found. Its author wrote (among other things) that he was not a Christian or a Hebrew or a Saracen, and he prophesied that Damietta would fall and that the man with the black eyes and saffron standards (the Sultan of Cairo in person, according to some interpreters) would lose the war. And very much talked about were the Assassins and their leader, the Old Man of the Mountain. They fought the Christians by throwing open knives at them in battle.[25]

By the spring of 1219 the Crusaders were in control of all the western bank of the Nile. In February of that year they had crossed to the other shore and attacked Damietta by land. They made their principal camp between the eastern walls and Lake Menzala, which was at their backs. The city was thus surrounded on all sides.

A bridge of ships linked the shores of the Nile, distant from one another by almost a mile. The two united armies of Malek-el-Moadden and Malik-al-Kāmil fell back to the nearby isle of Mehalle.

This was the situation when war came back into Francis's life, in dimensions much greater than he had ever known.

The Brave Crusaders of Italian Maritime Republics

The friars arrived in the last part of July of 1219. Francis was there when, shortly afterwards, came an attack on the city. It opened in the early hours of the morning with a great noise of mangonels, trabuchs, scaling machines, and catapults. A rain of stones and fire was poured over the walls.

The honour of making the first assault on the designated tower fell to the Pisani. They came forward with a huge ladder, propped it against the wall and began to go up. The whole Christian army, immobile, hearts in throats, followed the action. And it was beautiful, in the first rays of the sun breaking forth in that clean shining summer morning, to see the flag of Pisa, red with a white cross, slowly rise, and the swords and shields flash, and the wan faces of enemy archers appear briefly among the black stones as they hurled flaming arrows and sulphur and bitumen. Scarcely had the first soldier of the Cross touched the parapet, which was bristling with blades, and courageously jumped inside with raised axe, than the battle was joined. It spread in a frenzy of shouts, clashing of arms, a hail of arrows. The wounded fell, assailants and defenders together, with a great noise of iron beaten into scrap.

The Pisani were alone, and, says the chronicler, no one could help them but God. Their ladder was set on fire, and they had to come down, not, however, without having wounded and killed many of the infidels.

It was then the turn of the Genovesi, the men of Genoa, who, as they swarmed up the tower and the walls next to it, astonished the whole field by the superhuman valour with which they remained fighting without quarter until evening. Their ladders burned, and they tried in vain to put out the flames by throwing wine and vinegar on them. It seemed that not one would be able to return to earth. The Christians below lamented on their knees. Amid tears, they called upon God (the unknown Crusader did not fail to note even these desperate prayers with scrupulous exactitude):

"O glorious Lord Jesus Christ, you who are powerful above all, help your servants, liberate them from that fire and from the hands of the Saracens through your most holy virtue. For you are the creator of the heavens and of the earth; you, who live and reign, world without end. Amen.

"O Lord Jesus Christ, who for us was made flesh, and sustained death and passion, and rose again on the third day, and after forty days ascended into heaven, do not look at our sins and our evil deeds, but consider the cause that leads us here.

"Help us, O Lord; as no fruit can put forth shoots unless it remains attached to the vine, so we are not able to fight without the help of God; and as lambs without a shepherd tremble among the wolves, so we are not able without your help to overcome the insidious infidels."

At last it pleased God to heed these ardent prayers and the Genovesi were able to retire safely from the fray. All on the ladder, however, were lost.

In the meantime, the sultan's army reached the bridge of ships on the Nile with many armed boats and set fire to one of the two galleys placed as a guard. The other resisted vigorously, with the help of soldiers who rushed to its defence.

This was enough to restore the spirit of the Crusaders, who in great numbers returned to the walls. This time they boldly established themselves there.

There was a great outcry from the inhabitants of the city, all of whom, mounted soldiers and infantry, women and babies, believed themselves now in the power of the conquerors. And Corradino and the sultan, seeing so grave a danger, consulted one another about what to do. At last they decided, "What shall we do? Well, we must now go forward. Either all will escape or all will die; but the Christians won't be able to capture and kill us, our men, our sons and daughters."

And so, blinded by grief and rage, heads lowered, the defending army made a rush into the trench that encircled the Crusaders' camp, and five thousand of them reached all the way to the first fortifications and destroyed five bartizans. An emir preceded them, crying out, "Mohammed is God, not the son of Mary!"

Hearing these words, the Templars, knights of Christ, were outraged and an immense roar arose among them:

"O Christ!

"O Holy Cross!

"O Holy Sepulchre!

"O Saint George, take the standard of the Holy Cross!

"Come to our aid!

"Succour us, for love of Him who for us hung on the cross!"

And thus the soldiers of Christ went out against the infidels that day, and fighting manfully, gained a great victory. The one who shouted about Mohammed was dead, with another fifteen mounted soldiers and fifty of the infantry. Many Christians also fell, and many others were wounded.

Night fell, and the dead lay on the sand. From severed heads, wide-open eyes looked into the shadows. Blood flowed from terrible wounds.

All the Crusader camp resounded with lauds until morning.[26]

What did Saint Francis think about as he lived through the barbarous events of this day?

Just three years ago the Indulgence of the Pardon had been established, his great dream of the feast of love for all men, reconciled in the shadow of the cross. And now the cross was flaunted as a banner of war! And over the horror of suffering creatures!

Saint Francis Predicts a Defeat

The day of the Transfiguration of our Lord, August 6, the Christians tried to fill up the moat that protected the city; and they brought up a war machine of great size called a cat, a kind of movable penthouse and battering ram, which was supposed to accomplish wonders against the city walls. But the people of the city, helped by the Sultan's troops, made a foray and burnt the machine. "On that day," the historian noted, "many Christians were killed and wounded. And, therefore, the spirits of the Saracens were raised and the Christians were saddened."[27]

An atrocity that must have made Francis shiver took place the day after the feast of the Assumption.

In the night eight Saracens were captured in the act of swimming the river and carrying papers, fire, and homing pigeons. They were the sultan's spies, trying to reach the city. When it was day, their noses were cut off, their arms, their lips, their ears, and one eye was cut out. Reduced thus to bloody scarecrows, half of them were forced to take the road to Damietta and the other half put on display outside the fortifications.

The Musselmen raised great shouts of fury. And for revenge they sent the same kind of frightful messenger into their adversary's camp, a Christian with the same horrible mutilations.[28]

August 24 a new assault was prepared.

For the purpose the Christians armed many cogs, galleys, and other ships; so that with a great number of ladders on them, they could reach the walls that overlooked the river. But the Nile was low in the great heat, there was no chance of its rising again, [and the attack could not be made]. That was well enough, because at the time there were great disorders among the *popolani,* the commoners in the Crusader army. They accused the princes and knights of being traitors, and they said that their treachery was the true reason that they did not want to advance to the walls.

They went about shouting that they alone were called on to fight while the others, the nobles, stayed in their tents all day. And that when they were sent out, it was like being sent to the butcher, because no one had taken the trouble to warn them about the kind of enemies they had to march against and what risks had to be taken. And that the war would never be finished.

These are the grey hours of armies, in which fatigue, discontent, and suspicion try the patience of the soldiers and the poison of unjust accusations affect even the most fearless.

And so in this excited and undisciplined multitude, old bitter divisions and fierce quarrels recurred, knights versus the infantry, nobles versus the people—in short, to use the very words of Ernoul in defining the two factions into which the Crusaders were divided: *maiores* and *minores, maggiori* and *minori.* The old tenacious hatred was still riding the backs of these soldiers of the faith. Again they squared off, again they raised accusations of treachery and called for death, re-enacting on the beaches of the African sea scenes from the piazzas of their faraway cities.[29]

Very quickly, then, a new battle plan was drawn up. One part of the army would remain in custody of the camp; another would attack on the river side; a third would attack the city by land.

Other friars from Assisi had by then reached Damietta—Leonardo di Gislerio, Elias Bonbarone, Pietro di Catanio.[g] They, with Francis and Illuminato, heard with disbelief and bitterness those familiar deadly terms echoing again, as they had in the *contrada* of Murorotto and on the plain of Collestrada.

They knew from experience to what extent discord was fatal to an army moving against an enemy. Moreover, the dangers of this battle plan were manifest, coming as it had from anger and offended pride yielding to the pressure of an impatient and ignorant mob.

After a night spent in prayer, Francis said to Illuminato, "If in truth the battle is undertaken, I see, by divine grace, that it will not go to the advantage of the Christians. But if I say so, I shall be called a fool. And if I keep quiet, not having spoken out will be on my conscience. What do you think I ought to do?"

The brother from Arce, listening to those words, could only smile as he thought about the time when everyone in Assisi had sneered at the son of Pietro Bernardone and called him crazy and out of his mind.

"Father," he replied, "I think that you ought not to pay any attention to the judgement of men. It will not be the first time that they accuse you of foolishness. Go, then, and do what your conscience tells you to do, because it is clear you ought to put more weight in what God says than in what men say."[30]

And so Francis went to the papal legate and to the king, Jean;[31] he talked to the great and to the small, to captains and privates, advising against the battle and predicting defeat.

It is said that the king and the most expert captains recognized the wisdom of his words and wanted to rescind the orders. But the troops

g. There is no doubt that members of the order other than Francis and Brother Illuminato were present in Damietta. See *2 Cel.*, 40: "At the time when the Christian army was besieging Damietta, the holy man of God was present with some companions."

Also, Etienne de Lusignan, in *Chorografia* (Golubovich, *Biblioteca,* 1:394), says that from 1217 on there were in Acre "many religious of the new Dominican and Franciscan orders."

As for Brother Elias: see Giordano, *Chronica,* 9, in which there is the note that Brother Caesar of Speyer, "a great preacher," joined the Crusaders in 1217, and that afterwards, "crossing the sea after the usual journey, he was converted to the order by the preaching of Elias." The Rhenish and the Frisians (with whom Caesar sailed) left in the spring of 1217 on a strong fleet of 300 sailing ships under the command of Giorgio of Wied and William of Holland. After having fought the Moors in Portugal, they docked at St. Jean d'Acre in March and April 1218, and from there went immediately to Damietta with Jean de Brienne. There could not have been enough time for Caesar to come to know Brother Elias in Syria, and it certainly seems that their meeting must have taken place outside the walls of Damietta. See Golubovich, *S. Francesco e i Francescani in Damietta*, p. 19.

immediately raised a great uproar and said that it was ridiculous that anyone should put faith in that humble unknown friar.[32] And no one dared discuss the matter further for fear of being accused of treachery and cowardice.

Milioli wrote that "Monsignore the Legate, the King of Jerusalem, the Patriarch, and all other noble and powerful men of the Christians were disturbed and agitated over the revolt of the common people, and they also feared very much their perfidious rage."[33]

The battle was fought on August 29 [1219], the day of the Decollation of Saint John the Baptist.

It was the anniversary of the martyrdom of the saint to whom Francis was particularly devoted, the saint whose name his mother had given him, the saint who was seer and prophet. His first biographer says that he celebrated the days dedicated to him with particular solemnity. But surely never did the word of God as brought to us in the pages of the Evangelist seem so fitting as in the early morning hour when the troops were on the way to take up their positions in advance of the battle in which so much blood would be poured out. All seemed very real then: the decorated table, the dance of the graceful young girl, the mad frenzy of the diners, the incredible request, the astonishment of Herod Antipas, the head carried in on a golden platter stained with blood. The words of Ambrose, used in the office of the day, seemed on that fatal morning gruesomely appropriate: "Drink the blood ceaselessly pouring out from the open veins of the severed head."

In closed ranks the Crusader army went out from the fortifications and advanced near Kāmil's encampment. And he, putting into effect a strategem decided upon earlier, ordered his army to strike the tents and begin a retreat.

The Christians followed. The Saracens continued to retreat until they reached an arid, deserted area favourable for an attack. There they stopped and lined up, showing their intention to fight.

The captains were not agreed as to what to do about that surprising about-face. Some said that they must carry on; others, that it would be best to turn back. Tempers flared up again. Everyone was improvising strategies and putting forward his own plan. Great battles of words and empty speeches were fought there at a time when it was essential to prepare for battle.[34]

Time passed. The strong August sun rose into a sky of flame. Cuirasses, helmets, and armour heated up alarmingly. The fierce, dizzying heat confused desert, river, and sea in an immense storm of light.[35]

Suddenly, though no order had been given and not a single enemy sword had been raised, the ranks of seditious infantry opened, broke, and became disordered (it was said that the devil himself entered into their midst to punish them for their sins).[36] Immediately the Saracens moved forward and attacked the right flank, assigned to the knights of Cyprus. After a weak attempt at resistance, they took to flight, which then became general, tumultuous, irreparable.

Francis had remained in camp, over which a few sentinels kept watch. Anxiously he had already sent Illuminato once to a small elevation to try to see the outcome of the battle. But Illuminato had looked in vain, in the dazzling light of that incandescent noon.

This was the time that the patriarch of Jerusalem took off the cross that he was wearing and held it up against the horde of deserters, beseeching them to turn back in the name of the most precious blood that had washed that holy wood. Uselessly. Only the king and a few other brave spirits—Templars and Hospitallers, both French and Pisani—stayed to try to oppose the advance of the infidels.[37]

According to the accounts of those who escaped, more terrible than the swords and fire of the Saracens in that battle was the agony of thirst—a horrible thirst, abnormal, bringing hallucinations and delirium. Crazed men threw away their arms and, completely naked, danced in the midst of a rain of arrows. Others suddenly fell as if they had been struck by the blows of an invisible club.[38] Without a thought of the danger that they were running, many ran to the river and threw themselves in, men and horses together in great confusion. At the beginning a small band protected them, fighting with desperate bravery, then the enemy overcame them and even went into the water after them.

A great devil of a Saracen, wearing three cuirasses, one on top of the other, was in front of all, carrying two enormous clubs, one in each hand, with which he fractured and broke into bits the Christians' helmets and armour. When he came near, everyone fled or met instant death.

But the king of Jerusalem, already badly burned under the bursts of Greek fire, awaited him with feet firmly planted. As he saw him come close, he raised his huge sword and delivered such a stroke that the ogre was split in two, from the head to the kidneys.[39]

In the meantime, Brother Illuminato, at Francis's order, had returned for a second look. But he could see nothing of the tremendous defeat because the Roman barons and Latin Crusaders were bravely holding in the very midst of the enemy host, forming a sort of wall against which the wild fury of the assailants was breaking.[40]

Then even they slowly folded, always fighting, in the midst of a cloud of arrows.

At the hour of vespers Illuminato returned for a third time to report to Francis.

The battle was irretrievably lost.[41] The Saracens had reached the Christians' trench. If it had not been for the great valour of the king, Jean, and of the Hospitallers, Templars, and Alemanni, all the Christians would have been killed or taken slaves. At the news, Francis was overcome by profound compassion. Thomas of Celano says he especially grieved for the Spanish Crusaders, who because of their bravery had fallen in great numbers.[42]

Then came other news. Fifty knights of the Templars had been beheaded. Thirty of the Alemanni. Thirty-two of the Hospitallers. The chamberlain of the king of France and his son were dead, also the bishop of Belvaio and his brother, John of Asse, the count of Belino, Andrea da Pisa, Anselmo di Luni, the provost of Sant'Omero with eighty knights. In all, five thousand Christians had fallen and a good thousand had been taken prisoner.[43]

Night came and the river was covered with a dense curtain of fog. Now all the Crusaders who had come out unscathed had before them the image of the severed head of John the Baptist. "Saint John," we read in the same chronicle, "must have wanted to have a lot of companions, since so many Christians had had their heads cut off, just as he had been beheaded for God."[44]

The Friar Minor had been right. The man of piety had seen what seven sentinels stationed on the heights had not succeeded in seeing.[45] And it was said that the defeat was a punishment from God, "because not in fear of him, but in rage, they had gone into battle."[46]

In this chronicle we can still hear the cries of pain and desperation that threw a black veil over the Christian encampment. "Day of Decollation of Saint John the Baptist, marked by tears and prayers. And truly this was a day of wrath, calamity, and misery, a day of death and pestilence, a leaden day and very bitter to the Christians."

But then an enchanting vision dreamed in the first light of dawn suddenly becomes the stuff of legend as it is reported in the lofty style of the lectionary of the martyrs: *Audite, fratres carissimi* . . . "Hear, my dearest sons and brothers, how Christ welcomes his martyred saints. A certain German had been left for dead. As night came on, he opened his eyes and saw a great man, dressed in white. And with him was an infinite multitude of angels, singing over the bodies of the dead and saying, 'They are the ones who have survived the great period of trial; they have washed their robes and made them white in the blood of the Lamb; they died for the faith and love of Christ.'"[47]

A Bishop Remembers Francis

Meanwhile, the sultan was sending sacks of flayed heads through all the provinces. On market days a herald stacked them in town squares and proclaimed, "If anyone wishes slaves, come get ready to take your pick, because the princes of the Romans are dead and those who remain are thinking of flight."[48]

These were dark days for the Christians. A deep exhaustion weighed upon the soldiers of the faith, who by now were sure that the war was lost and that the Crusade had ended miserably.

There was great talk of peace between the sultan and the Christian leaders, but it was all debates and useless words to hide the secret thoughts of each. One side was by now convinced of the inevitable dissolution of the Crusade army; the other was counting on promised aid, especially from Italian cities.[49]

In the meantime "the time of passage" was drawing near, the season in which ships customarily arrived and departed. The Crusade pilgrims seemed much like migratory birds that cross the sea. At the first shiver of winter they took flight to the countries of the sun. They returned with the warm breath of spring. (It happened often enough that they made their crossing together, flocks of swallows and men who had taken the cross. The birds settled themselves on the masts, the yards, the crows' nests; and their twittering united with the songs that floated over the blue expanse of waves.[h])

By now most of the fighters had succumbed to discouragement and homesickness.

The threats of the clergy and the memory of the heavy punishments that had fallen upon deserters a few months earlier now meant nothing, not even in the face of the news that six thousand (deserting) Britons had been shipwrecked on the coasts of Italy and that whole regions in Holland, whose pilgrims had *en masse* abandoned the siege, had been submerged by the ocean, which had broken the dikes, covered entire cities, and killed more than a hundred thousand men.[50]

On the very day of the feast of the Exaltation of the Cross, in what

---

h. "According to ancient custom, voyagers fixed two times a year for crossing the sea. Pilgrims embarked almost always in March and September, both to go to the East and to return to Europe. This caused them to be compared to birds of passage that migrate at the beginning of a new season and at the end of good weather." Michaud, *Histoire* Bk. 12. [According to Sabatier (*Vie,* chap. 13) the trip at that time required twenty to thirty days.]

seemed an incredible profanation, the Roman barons, the bishop of Hungary, Count Gualterio, Count Oremigio, and a good twenty thousand Crusaders departed for home. It looked as if the field were going to be deserted, and the Christians were terrified at the thought.

And all during this time, false messengers of peace were going back and forth between Cardinal Pelagius and the sultan. In their colloquies they pretended to discuss the various articles of the treaty, while all the time, in all the Muslim countries, as far away as Baghdad, heralds kept on shouting themselves hoarse in the arrogant announcement that must have drawn many a Mussulman into the army: "He who wishes to acquire Christian slaves, come join the ranks! Let it be known to everyone that almost all the Christians are dead or have fled! Those who remain cannot in any way escape from the hands of the sons of Mohammed!"[51]

Illuminato, Elias, Leonardo, and the other brothers of Assisi who had come to join Francis must have been reminded of the "good and sincere peace" that the commune of Perugia had one day offered to their city.

The first sign of rescue came from Genoa, whose ten galleys arrived, led by two noble citizens, Giovanni Rosso della Volta and Pietro d'Oria, together with the galley of Alamano, count of Syracuse, and three more, led by the noble poet of Provence, Savaric di Mauleon, who was accompanied by many pilgrims. And once again the white banner marked with the red cross of Saint George seemed to bring such new hope from across the sea that many who had been about to leave and had even already boarded ships, took courage and stayed.[52]

When the sultan believed the moment had come to put an end to postponements, he called his soldiers together and said:

"O my loyal men, so strong and warlike, rulers of all the world, it is finally given to you to know what is written in our law: the sons of Mohammed will cross over the mountains and the seas and will subdue even the empire of the Romans. Do you not see that almost all the Christians are dead or have run away? Fight like men against them and you will conquer their fortresses, their gold and their silver, and all the other things that are in their camp. I command you to swarm over their trench and enter it."

And so they rushed the trench. But the Christians ran to defend it and forced them to retire with heavy losses. They then returned to the sultan and said, "Lord, these slaves are ruthless and cruel, and they brought four mangonels against us and killed as many of us as they could."

But the fable of easy victory and copious booty, spread to the four winds by Saracen chauvinists, had in the meantime produced its effect: people of every race, men and women, poured in to reinforce the ranks of Malik-al-Kāmil.

The attempt against the trench was renewed several days later. Because few Christians were on guard, it seemed at first to succeed ; but soon the small company of defenders, with great valour and sacrifice, again drove back the invaders. They had to fight all day long, without even eating. The forces that had been repulsed returned to the sultan and said ironically, "Those slaves are very rude and wicked to us."[53]

One morning near the end of September, just before dawn, the river appeared to be burning. (It was the day dedicated to Saints Cosmas and Damian, patrons of the little solitary church in Assisi where Clare was praying.) Four enormous *geremite,* the name given to floats covered with brushwood, dry wood, straw, and a mixture of oil and tar, had been launched by the Saracens to burn the bridge of ships that linked the two shores.

Flames stretched upward like fiery branches against the reddening sky. Instantly a rumour spread that the bridge had burned and the enemy had succeeded in forcing the siege and was carrying grain and other edibles into the city. But, as it pleased God, the Crusaders succeeded in suffocating the flames. Also that day no one rested and no one ate until night.[54]

There came days in which treachery walked in felt shoes. The Christians were no longer able to read the hearts of their brothers. No one felt safe in his tent. Mania for gold was the reason, and not even the cross of Jesus, who had abandoned his very clothes to the executioners, could overcome it.

Nine Crusaders to whom the sultan had secretly made great promises of gold and silver, while on duty at the bridge, stealthily spent their time in ruining it so that the Saracens' swift warships could take aid to the city. But one of the traitors repented and revealed the plot to Cardinal Pelagius. The others, realizing they were discovered, took refuge with the enemy. "And thus," concludes the chronicler, "our Lord Jesus Christ Crucified freed the Christians from the snares of the enemy. *Laudemus et benedicamus Dominum nostrum natum de Virgine Maria.*"

The next night a man from Genoa who had cut the chains for the Moslems after being paid six thousand *bisanti* was captured. And then a Spaniard was discovered who had sold bread to the Saracens for a *bisante* a loaf. Both of them were tied to the tail of a horse and dragged through the camp.[55]

However, the Christians had by now recovered their decisive superiority. In one engagement on the bank of the river, up to five hundred dead and wounded enemies were counted; and Corradino, who was beside the trench, had not dared take part in the battle. "Corradino and the sultan," notes Milioli, "became very sad, because it did them no good to resist the Christians nor to try to rescue those who were dying in the city."

Anguished appeals reached these two brothers from inside the city, where eighty thousand inhabitants suffered from both war and famine. The Moslems used the most desperate expedients to send any kind of provisions to them. Often they threw sacks made of skins full of provisions into the water so that they would float under the walls and the besieged could draw them out with grappling hooks. Sometimes they used cadavers wrapped in funeral sheets, with bread hidden in the folds. But the macabre strategem was soon discovered and thwarted. The defenders no longer had the strength to raise a sword or draw a bow. Some of the inhabitants fled to the Crusaders' camp and asked for mercy.

In desperation, the official in charge of the defence of Damietta had its twenty-two gates walled up to keep the inhabitants from leaving. Thereafter, no one, neither the Crusaders nor the sultan himself, could get news of the besieged. A dismal silence fell on what had been the pearl of Egypt. Damietta, according to an Arab writer, "was no more than a closed tomb."[56]

We have an account of this siege written by Jacques de Vitry, who had been in Perugia at the time of the death of Innocent III. He had been named bishop of Acre [in 1216] by Honorius III. This old canon of Namur had not hesitated a moment to leave his beautiful cathedral opening on to the sea, where on solemn occasions his flourishing talents as a poet in the style of Saint Augustine had enraptured the people of his diocese. He at once followed the Crusaders to Egypt.[57]

There he observed and he made notes. And the thing he found most moving, most edifying, in the midst of this ferocious clash of cultures, was the goodness of the Friars Minor.

"The master of these brothers, who is also the founder of the Order, is called Francis; he is loved by God and venerated by all men. He came into our camp . . . burning with zeal for the faith. . ."[58]

Even one of the monks who had come from Acre in the retinue of the bishop had not been able to resist the wonderful teaching of the Poverello of Christ. "Sire Rainerio, the prior of Saint Michael, has just entered the Order of the Friars Minor . . . . an Order that is making great strides through the whole world. . ."

According to Jacques, God himself was responsible for the establishment of this new rule in order to restore life to religion, which was declining into a time of sunset. "They are called Friars Minor. They are lesser and more humble than all present-day religious by way of their habit, their poverty, their contempt for the world . . . . they draw from the pure waters of the fountains of the gospel with such thirst and spiritual ardour that they are not satisfied with carrying out its precepts but work hard at observing its counsels in every way, thereby reflecting trait for trait the life of the apostles. They give up all that they own, renounce themselves, take up their cross, and naked, follow the naked Christ. Like Joseph, they leave their tunic behind; like the Samaritan woman, their water jar. They run unimpeded, relieved of every cumbersome weight. They walk before the face of the Lord without ever turning back. They forget whatever they leave behind them, straining and always marching toward the goal before them. . .

"These poor men of Christ travel about with neither purse, haversack, bread, nor money in their belts; they have neither gold nor silver; they wear no sandals. No brother of this Order has the right to own anything. They have neither monasteries, churches, fields, vineyards, animals, houses, property, nor anywhere to rest their head. They have nothing to do with furs and linen, but use only woolen tunics with a capuche; they have neither capes, mantles, cowls, nor other garments. . . ."

So free, so released from every human impediment were the friars, the good bishop said, that "they fly like a cloud, like doves to their cote."[59] Even as he wrote, this ancient prophecy was being fulfilled, so far were the friars above the dark tangle of bastions and towers, the never-idle field, the turbid river, the sea and desert, and the human impediments of hatred and fury, greed, hunger, and death.

The last attempt that the sultan of Egypt made to communicate with the city showed clearly that, even as the emirs were going to and fro in his name to discuss peace, he had nothing in his mind but fraud and deceit.

It came on the night following the Feast of the Dead.[i] While the Christian camp slept, six hundred Saracens divided into three squads came silent as shadows, slipping along the river swamp and seeking to get to the walls. "But," the historian relates, "a woman heard them and began to shout, 'To arms! To arms!' And it happened that by chance the Templars and the Hospitallers were already up that morn-

---

i. November 2, All Souls' Day.

ing; and they, in the name of Christ, feared neither fatigue nor death nor any arrow. And they ran and they killed two hundred of the Saracens and took ninety of them prisoner. The others fell back, and so God confounded the enemies of the cross."[60]

The Christians hurled the severed heads of the defeated into the sultan's camp with a catapult, and they placed the bodies in front of the moat that encircled the city as a mockery, to inspire fear, as a warning. But no one responded on the barricades, on the gates, on the towers. The city remained closed in its dismal, mysterious, terrible silence.

Fearing that some other devious scheme was afoot, the Crusaders felt impelled to keep an alert watch and take steps to shatter, once and for all, this nightmare. It was creating more anxiety than hard battles openly fought.

The City of the Dead

On November fourth and fifth, preparations were made for a general assault. A flock of heralds shouted the proclamation of the king and the cardinal legate through all the camp.

"First command: He who abandons the fortifications shall be tortured on the rack.

"Second: If he is a knight, he shall lose his arms and his horse and all his possessions. If an infantryman, his hand shall be cut off and he shall lose all his things. If a merchant or a woman, of those who are in the army, he shall lose a hand and all his things.

"Whoever, man or woman, shall be found without arms, unless he is sick or a child of those who look after the pavilions, shall be excommunicated.

"He who turns back while going up the scaling ladders or on the cogs and other ships to make the assault shall lose his hand and all his things.

"All those who enter the city and find gold, silver, and all other things, alike shall put together all that they find in three or six houses that will be designated. If anyone steals, he shall lose his hand and the part of the booty that belongs to him.

"And those who have been ordered to swear, shall swear to punish those who do not observe the prescribed rules."

The whole army was gripped by an obsession like the savage passion of rapists, their warrior's ardour strangely mixed with barbaric and almost carnal frenzy. The beautiful intact city, enclosed in its garland of towers, seemed like a pale virgin yearned for long and feverishly: "In the name of the Father and of the Blessed Virgin Mary we shall force open the city and with the help of God put it in our power."

The multitude responded with a single voice: *Fiat, fiat.*[61]

Dark and troubled, the November evening came on. Large clouds rose slowly from the sea and rested silently over the condemned city. Darker, more deserted in their dead dreariness, rose the hundred towers crowned by the cloud.

The storm broke in the dark, while the first ranks were being ordered up. It came on in an unspeakable noise of wind and water and great bursts of lightning. The roar of the river, flooding over its banks, in short order added to the din. The trenches defending the camp and those excavated in front of the city were flooded, and everywhere the water gushed back and overflowed; encampments, pavilions, shelters, war machines, were inundated and then submerged.

At midnight some Florentine and Roman Crusaders, chosen from among the bravest (yet whose hearts must have been shaken by the enormous risk and the hidden danger), fixed ladders on a bridge leading to the wall. The first to reach the rampart was a Florentine, Messer Buonaguisa dei Buonaguisi, who planted the red and white flag of his commune on the conquered barrier. (He was greatly honoured for it and given the title of knight with the escutcheon of the half-eagle; from then on, on the feast of Saint John, that flag is always displayed in Florence.)[62]

An uncertain shadow rose to fight and was beaten down by the first blows. The assailants could not believe that these men were vigilant in defence. The gate and the tower were taken. The wind whistled across the undefended loopholes. The rain beat on empty fortifications. Not a shout, a fire, a sign, a clank of arms.

In surprise the Romans exultantly summoned the troops:

"Hurry up, brothers, and come, for the land is ours!"

And then, amid an overflowing of emotion, the cadences of the litany of Loreto broke through the storm raging in the skies and on the earth as if they were falling from on high, from an invisible temple suspended in the shadows:

Kyrie eleison.

Christe eleison. . . .

The combatants responded in a unified shout that rose above the din of rain and wind, of the river and the sea:

Gloria in excelsis Deo.

There was a confused clamour of commands, exclamations, prayers. The Cardinal praised the omnipotence of God. The Hospitallers raised their battle song, *Sancta Crux, et Sanctum Sepulcrum, intercede pro nobis.* Some hurled themselves on the external walls, the bartizans. A gate was burned, another shattered by axes.

"Thus," concluded the old chronicler of the Crusade, "through the grace of God, Damietta was taken."[63]

As soon as it was morning, the Crusaders advanced toward the city, swords raised, shields slung on. Between the first girdle of walls, already taken, and the second, which was an extremely strong bastion, a vast field stretched out, marked by innumerable furrows. It seemed that the ground had recently been worked. The attackers stopped, horrified. The field was covered with shallow graves that the torrential rain of the night had opened. The dead were emerging: heads, hands, feet, from an immense, macabre, horrendous cemetery.

Only these putrifying corpses were on duty to defend the city from the soldiers of the cross.

Beyond the second wall, in the streets, in the city squares, on the thresholds of the mosques, there were only the dead and the dead and the dead, lying naked. Men, women, children, killed by hunger and by pestilence, their faces deformed, their frightfully contracted limbs partially devoured by dogs. And in the houses there were more. No one had been strong enough to remove them. Three, four, for every bed, the dying stretched out beside the dead.[64]

The few survivors were ghosts. Sunk in a deathlike torpor, they did not stir at the entrance of the Christian army.

The good Bishop Jacques, present at that terrible entrance, offers us some statistical data in a letter written some days afterward. In February, when the Crusaders crossed the Nile, there had been eighty thousand inhabitants of Damietta.

"After nine months, therefore, on that November fifth when the city was taken, scarcely three thousand were to be found, among whom only a hundred would have been in condition to fight to defend it. And in truth, God, striking down the enemies with pestilence, bared the sword over them so that when we entered the city, we found a great many cadavers above ground, because the few remaining alive had not been able, for the intolerable stench, to bury such an enormous quantity of dead."[65]

Francis also entered the dismal city of the dead. Surely, he shed horrified tears, more scalding than those he had shed on the day of the army's defeat.

No, it was not, it could not be, as the bishop of Acre thought, the vengeance of God that had caused such horror and pain. This had come from the dark and evil drive that Francis himself had known, one that only followers of Poverty had found how to put to rout.

But Francis was not the only one who suffered.

Something happened in that entry of the Crusaders into Damietta that no one could have foreseen. All those warriors who had come thirsty for blood were seen lowering the weapons they held ready to kill, their faces streaked with tears.[66] If in the field there had been long prayers for victory before the assault, there, in the cursed city, the hymns of jubilation were hushed. An anguished silence ruled over everyone and everything, the living and the dead, the conquerors and the conquered, the men of God and the sinister Assassins.

Nothing remained of a war proclaimed with so much bombast, initiated with so much enthusiasm, fought with so much ferocity, won with such fanfare, but that immense, unconquerable, painful pity.

The Booty

Compassion lasted but an instant. As it is written, men shut their eyes again, even after they have seen great truths. The greed of the sack, which the leaders tried in vain to control, burst out more violently than had the storm on the night the city was taken. Damietta was rich beyond the fantasy of adventurers and plunderers.

An eyewitness who saw the fabulous booty that was taken wrote: "In the city the Christians found gold and silver, precious stones, purple, samite, ornaments of the highest price, and vases of gold and silver without number, and a good four hundred asses and mules, and wheat and barley and biscuits and many vegetables."[67]

Another asserted that after the sack one would have thought, judging by the enormous booty, that the Crusaders had conquered Paris and the Indies.[68] So many things were taken that even the women and the children of the fighting men had a share.[69] On the other hand, the goods that were put in common to be divided equally among all, in obedience to orders, reached scarcely two hundred thousand *scudi*.

Jacques de Vitry describes starved children clinging to the bodies of their parents and begging for bread. Not even these children were spared the greed of the invaders, who sold them along with the other prisoners. The bishop bought back several; but almost all, after having been baptized, died.

How the sultan of Cairo learned the news of the fall of the city is described by Milioli.

"Early in the morning some Saracens came and saw well-armed Christians singing *Kyrie eleison* and *Gloria in excelsis Deo*. So one of the Saracens asked, 'O Christians, why are you so exultant?' The Christians replied, 'Do you not see that our Lord Jesus Christ this night gave us the city of Damietta?'

"At once the one who had asked turned around and took the news to the others, who in turn carried it to the sultan. When he heard it, he immediately lost the power of speech. By gesture, he ordered that the messengers of the bad news have their heads cut off, which was done without delay. After having remained for two hours prostrated in great sadness, he arose, drew the sword that he carried at his side and cut off his beard and his braids. Then he cut off his horse's tail and mane.

"The other Saracens followed his example. They raised their voices in lament, all crying out, 'O Damietta, until today you were the ever-burning torch of the sons of the Prophet, and now for us you are extinguished. From today you will be the light of the Christians.

" 'Why did not I, miserable wretch that I am, die in the womb of my mother! Why did I not die before the virgin Damietta was taken in this reign by the Christians!' " [70]

Meanwhile, the horrors of the city and the fear of contagion induced the Crusaders to return to their encampment, where interminable disputes arose over the division of the booty. For weeks, the commissioners named by the legate devoted themselves to estimating, weighing, discussing, and apportioning, all according to the right of each and to the part that each kingdom, city, religious order, and individual had played in the enterprise. Bitter quarrels drove everyone to the end of his tether.

The city's districts, its houses and churches, its walls, castles, and towers, were assigned. The cardinal proposed, and the assembly unanimously consented, that the most beautiful and the strongest fortress, which was called at one time the Tower of Babylon, be given to the Church of Rome and renamed the "Roman Tower." Another fortress went to the new archbishop of Damietta. [71]

The men of penitence of Assisi were not forgotten. If it had been possible, the conquerors of Damietta would have given them (who for no inducement on earth would have exchanged their humble habits for all the precious materials accumulating on the appraisers' counters) nothing less than the bed of Solomon. [j]

---

j. A reference to Solomon's bed is made by Jacques de Vitry in chap. 32, *Historia orientalis.* According to Fortini's interpretation, he means that nothing was too great for the friars' share, not even the bed of Solomon as it is described in Song of Songs 3:7–10, "coming up from the desert like a column of smoke, laden with myrrh, with frankincense, and with the perfume of every exotic dust," made of wood from Lebanon, silver, gold, purple, and ivory. Others (see *Omnibus,* p. 1613) think the good bishop is likening the friars to the "sixty valiant men" mentioned in the same passage who are the guards of such a king, as he also compares them to Jerusalem's watchmen of Isaiah 62:6: "Upon your walls, O Jerusalem, I have stationed watchmen; never by day or by night shall they be silent." The entire sermon is full of Old Testament allusions.—Trans.

And in truth no one had surpassed them in courage.

They were (it is again Jacques de Vitry, the bishop of Acre, who speaks) the new militia called up by God in that day and time "to battle against the Antichrist, the son of perdition, and against his unbelieving henchmen." They were the *fortes Christi milites,* "the valiant men of Christ," who, as it was written in Isaiah, had been chosen as watchmen upon the walls of Jerusalem—"defenders of the ramparts of Jerusalem, for day and night without interruption they devote themselves to praising God or to preaching. They shout for all they are worth and raise their voice like a trumpet.

"They do not withhold their sword from blood. They fight, they travel through the city in all directions, they know how to bear up under hunger like wandering dogs. They are, as it were, the salt of the earth, which seasons food and transforms it into nourishment of sweetness and salvation, preserves meat, does away with the decay of worms and the stench of vices. They are the 'light of the world' that sheds light in order to lead to the truth, that inflames and enkindles fires to propagate the fervour of charity. But this Order of perfection and this cloister whose dimensions are worldwide cannot, it seems, be fitting for the weak and the imperfect. These, in fact, sailing the sea in ships and trading on the deep waters, would be shipwrecked if they did not prepare themselves. . ."[72]

Francis and his friars were assigned to a church in the quarter allotted to the Crusaders of Bologna and Lucca, on the road that divided that section of the city from the area given to Cyprus. This church can be considered the first Franciscan friary in the East of which we have certain documentation. A notarial document of that same year of 1220 shows that it was located amid two fortresses—one large and one small, an arch, and a ruined palace. Beside it stood the houses assigned to men of the archbishop of Milan and the lord of Beirut.[k]

The city was put under the rule of the king of Jerusalem, to whom everyone was to owe obedience.[73] But then fierce opposition was raised by those who wanted a free government. The cardinal [Pelagius], who could not share command with anyone, blew on the

---

k. In a document of June 19, 1220, a street is described as *iusta ecclesiam in qua abitant Fratres Minores* ("in the jurisdiction of the church where the Friars Minor live"). Another, of August 27, 1220, records that a doctor Roberto of Lucca was invested with a piece of the property "beside the house given to the nuncio of the Bologna Crusaders and the Friars Minor." The doctor promised to carry out for the city the service that was due from the Bologna Crusaders to the king, a significant record of how the city was ruled after its fall. See also n. 7 of this chapter. Salvioli, *Annali Bolognesi,* 2:431–32, n. 487; 442–43, n. 493.

fire. The discord, fed by lack of discipline, spread through the entire army and the disputants were not far short of coming to arms.[74]

It took nearly three months to clean the city. Finally, an official, solemn entrance was set for Candlemas.

In the grandiose procession, after the legate and the patriarch, the bishop of Acre, Jacques de Vitry, had the position of honour, and with all his clergy, he followed the cross of our Lord. Under his episcopal mantle he wore the surcoat of his armour. Other bishops in the procession were also vested in a manner suitable to their warrior faith. Cuirasses clanked under holy vestments, long swords lifted up the edges of sumptuous episcopal copes. Strong they were, like those lions that support the doors of their cathedrals, brave, on horseback and on foot. All but two of the bishops from Hungary had died in battle.

Jacques de Vitry, in a letter to relatives and associates, describes the unending line of Crusaders carrying burning candles, the lights, the hymns, the canticles, the lauds of thanksgiving.[75]

The cardinal celebrated Mass in the largest mosque, which had been reconsecrated as the metropolitan church of the Christian city and dedicated to Mary. It was the richest, most majestic temple imaginable, famous in all the East. Square in form, it had one hundred and forty-nine marble columns, seven portals, and a cupola so high that it could be seen from the sea.

Four altars had been raised—the central one dedicated to Mary, the others to Saint Peter, the Holy Cross, and Saint Bartholomew (in memory of the victorious day when the Tower of the Chain had been taken).[76]

Some idea of the magnificence of this Feast of the Purification is given us by those who saw it and who forever after remembered it as a dream glowing with gold, silver, and steel, with rich draperies, silks, and velvets. The gleaming shields reflected the myriad candle flames lit in honour of the Virgin in this Candlemas ritual of purification— flames to purify the city, and after it, everyone's heart. The incense rose from the thuribles up through the magnificent columns. The song of a hundred thousand Crusaders echoed under the vast vault, shook the arcades, and poured out into the crowded plaza.

But this elevated celebration lasted only one day. Afterwards the Crusaders turned to brawls, brutal appetites, and violence. The enemy had been conquered. One would have thought that there was not a single infidel to fight in all the East.[77] The season was mild. Swarms of prostitutes poured in from everywhere, alluring and brazen, like those who at one time had come to the desert to tempt anchorites in their solitude.[78] Their eyes were circled with antimony, their hair tinted blue. They oozed sweet oil. To the sound of cymbals they could dance on steel balls with the lightness of the wind.

Francis and the Prostitute

From these circumstances comes the story of how Saint Francis, when he was in the East, went into a house to rest one day and found a beautiful woman there, who offered herself to him.

He did not rail against her or heap imprecations on her head. Without horror or fear he looked at her from the depths of his own parched eyes and accepted her proposition.

She started to lead him to her bed when he stopped her. There was already a bed prepared for pleasure, he said, a very beautiful one, the woman had only to follow him.

And he took her to a great fire burning in the house, and in great eagerness stripped naked and threw himself on an enormous incandescent brazier, telling her to undress quickly and come lie with him in that splendid and wonderful bed, already well shaken up and nicely made. The woman, astonished and trembling, looked at him, while Saint Francis remained happily in the great fire and neither burned nor turned brown. And according to *Fioretti,* "she not only repented of her sin and evil intention but was perfectly converted to the faith of Christ and through the merits of [Francis] she became so holy in grace that she won many souls for the Lord in that region."[79]

This little tale is related to undeniable historical facts.

It is known that great numbers of prostitutes joined the Crusader armies, no matter how often they were denounced by the leaders. And it also happened often enough that women were taken as loot and added to the booty along with gold and precious cloths, then sold to the highest bidder.

But the major scandal was caused by Christian women (among whom were young women of the highest lineage, whom we know about through satirical little poems composed by the Crusader troubadours themselves), who had come along in the retinues of their husbands, brothers, and fathers. Daring and combative to the point that they rode on horseback, fully armed, into battle and faced up to the most formidable dangers,[1] they did not, for all that, run away from

---

1. References to the women who fought with the Crusaders abound in the writings of Arab chroniclers. 'Imad-ad-dīn: "Among the French there are women knights, with cuirasses and helmets, dressed in men's clothing, who have been going into the very thick of the fighting and performing like very knowledgeable men; there are delicate women who have made this their usual practice, believing it all to be a pious work through which they would assure themselves

amorous intrigues that provoked all sorts of passions, violent jealousies, and bloody feuds. For that reason the historian Guatiero Vinisof considered women in that expedition the cause of all the crimes, *fomes delictorum.*

Luigi Marcili, in a letter to his sister Domicilla, said that the demon exulted when he heard the Crusade preached, "because in the pilgrimage of the cross a host of noble women turned themselves into so many prostitutes, and thousands of virgins lost their innocence."[80]

Fra Fidenzio of Padua, living in the second half of that century, wrote about Crusaders: "So much has by now this contagion of lechery taken root that many are infected, clerics and laymen. The pilgrims should guard against this evil and do all possible to be preserved from it, because the vice of lechery in the countries overseas is very widespread and there are evil and vicious women there."[81]

The Arab chroniclers themselves wrote some very lively pages on the indecency that reigned unchecked among the Crusaders.

'Imād ad-dīn reports that one day a ship arrived loaded with three hundred Frenchwomen "adorned with youthfulness and beauty," who proposed to alleviate the discomfort that forced continence had produced in [the Crusader] warriors in the field. They were all, the historian testifies, licentious and mocking, sinners and seducers. "Enchanting and bewitching, exposing themselves to public view and arrogant, fiery and exciting, dyed and painted, desirable and appetizing, exquisite and lovely, they ripped and patched, slit and mended, roamed about and flirted, broke into things and stole what they could. Seductive and languid, desiring and desirable, giddy and amusing, drunken and youthful, amorous and willingly becoming prostitutes, impertinent and ardent, loving and passionate. Red of face and impudent, eyes black and made up, rich of buttock and bold, voice nasal and legs plump, hair tinted a pale ash grey, squanderers and

---

of bliss. Praise be to Him who has induced in them and has led them from the path of wisdom! On the day of battle more than one woman was in evidence who was modelling herself on knights, and had the endurance of a man, notwithstanding the weakness of the sex. Dressed in nothing but coats of mail, they were not recognized until their armour was stripped from them and they were made naked. Some of those who were discovered were sold as slaves, and every place was full to overflowing with the old ones. These were at times strong and at other times weak. They made a lot of speeches and stirred everybody up. They said that the cross allowed only resistance to the bitter end, and that the fighter would have life eternal only if he sacrificed his life, and that the tomb of their god was in the power of the enemy." Gabrieli, *Storici arabi,* p. 194.

And Ibn al Atir, telling of the defeat of the Christians at Acre in 1177, records: "Among the prisoners there were three French women, who fought on horseback. When they were captured and their armour taken off, they were recognized as women." Ibid., p. 177. Jean, sieur de Joinville, notes that in the second capture of Damietta (1250), prostitutes had their tents a stone's throw from the pavilion of Louis IX.

fools. Each wears a train on her gown and captivates whoever looks at her with her brightness, bends like a sapling, is as noticeable as a strong castle, quivers like a small branch."[m]

A great many Moslem warriors were so attracted by their reputation for wantonness that they deserted and renounced their religion.[82]

This is also the sleazy picture given by the historian Marino Sanudo, who writes that Saint Francis did wonders, after the fall of Damietta, to end "the adulteries, the robberies, the murders."[83]

The men of Assisi must have remembered the days when their own city was compared to another Babylon in the laxity of its morals. Now the true Babylon was being revealed to their eyes in all its perversity. Their mission began again and again it was remarkably successful.

The bishop of Acre continues to speak of the Friars Minor with devout admiration. He did not, however, dissimulate his own displeasure over having lost, by way of conversions, so many competent members of his own clergy to the Franciscans. "Colin, the Englishman, our clerk, has also entered this Order along with two other companions of ours: Master Michael and Dom Matthew to whom I had entrusted the parish of the Holy Cross. . . . And I am having a difficult time holding on to the chanter, Henry, and a few others. I am worn-out and have a heavy heart; nothing more do I desire than to finish my life in peace and tranquillity."[84]

It was the very sigh that was rising from Francis's own heart after bitter disillusionment.

But from all Francis's experiences in Damietta—a bitter reality that could not be disguised by any sort of window-dressing—his dream emerged intact. It is the only thing that survives of all that fighting, all those tumultuous events.

Today beautiful, strong, rich Damietta is a heap of ruins that hardly rises above the soil on the bank of the sacred river. Nothing, not a stone or wall, records the victory that then seemed so marvellous and caused all Christian people to rejoice.

Only in the Basilica di San Francesco in Assisi, where Saint Francis rests, a king also sleeps on his marble bed, under the loving gaze of the Virgin. He is wrapped in purple and on his head is the imperial crown. This is the tomb of the leader of the Christian army of

---

m. Gabrieli, *Storici arabi,* p. 192. These lively happenings are often placed in the territory ruled by the Saracens, but chroniclers were understandably anxious to avoid taking note of the corruption in the Christian camp. Another misstatement in some of these chronicles is that Saint Francis, while he was with the Sultan, had so many friars with him that he could send them two by two into the various districts of the infidels. It is even less likely that the sultan would have given him permission to such an effort to spread the Christian religion.

Damietta, the king of Jerusalem, Jean de Brienne, who died in the habit of a Friar Minor, in the wish to find peace near the man he knew and loved. Nearby, along the base of the tomb, between the columns, appears the shield with the cross, the sign under which millions of warriors marched bravely to victory and to death.[85]

It is the only monument that records the Crusade in which Francis took part.

Francis's Strange Request

After the fall of the city, Malik-al-Kāmil's army, after having burned the encampments and the bridge on the river, retired to the south.[86] About sixty kilometres south of Damietta the Nile divided into two branches: one descended to the city, the other turned east and, passing below the walls of Ashmun, flowed into Lake Menzala. Kāmil followed the Nile upstream and encamped opposite the village of Talkha, which is on the left bank, immediately before this fork. It was a formidable position, both barring the victor's way to Cairo and providing easy access to reinforcements.[87]

Every day that passed increased his consternation and his mortal hate of the Christian usurpers. His anger was hardly diminished by the news that on November 23 the Crusaders had also occupied Tanis, without meeting resistance. A very strong city, of great memories, had been Tanis. Located to keep watch over Lake Menzala, it had seven powerful vaulted towers, a double moat, and a barbican. As it is today, the lake was rich with fish and birds that produced an annual revenue of four thousand *marche* of silver; its famous salt works supplied all the kingdom.[88] The colossal ruins of the metropolises of the pharoah were there: ruined temples, overturned columns, fallen statues, empty sepulchres that had held kings and queens, strange inscriptions with long processions of slaves and dancers—all the proud images of the grandeur of thousands of years, now crumbled into dust. What destiny [he must have thought] was now being prepared for this land that in another age had fallen subject to the power of the Roman armies?

Kāmil was sending out desperate calls all over the Mussulman world. The heralds, who had earlier arrogantly proclaimed the annihilation of the Christians, hurried now in great agitation from one place to another, shouting out that "all Mussulmen will take up arms on pain of death."[89]

As a sign of defiance the sultan began the construction of a new city where the army was encamped to compensate him for the grievous loss of the one that he had loved above all others. And to this new city, which was intended as a testimony in all the centuries to come to the definitive triumph of the Muslim people, he gave the name of Mansura, "Victorious."[90]

Under the hard blow he had suffered, his innate ferocity rose again. He shed the outer garment of knightly courtesy and generosity that had earned him the title of "The Perfect Prince." He became the ancient barbarian, who, like all his fathers, wanted Christian blood. And he ordered his heralds to proclaim to the four corners of the earth a cruel decree: whoever brought him the head of a Christian would be rewarded with a *bisante* of gold.[91]

It is easy, then, to imagine how stupefied the Crusaders were, as Ernoul describes it, when the news was spread about that two clerics had presented themselves to Cardinal Pelagius and asked permission to go preach to the sultan. These two were Francis and Illuminato.

The Spanish cardinal had allowed his pride to grow to such an extent since the taking of Damietta that in letters sent to Christian princes, he had not hesitated to present it as his personal accomplishment.[92] Now he was studying military plans for an attack on Cairo, the city that under the dynasty of the Ayyubid had reached a prosperity and splendour that vied with that of Baghdad itself. With vain self-satisfaction, he often recalled a prediction made in his youth that he would be the future conqueror of Mohammed and the supreme champion of the Faith of Christ.[93]

So the prelate listened attentively to the strange request of the man whose ability to foresee the future he had experienced at his own expense on the day of the battle of the Decollation of Saint John the Baptist. And his answer was a blunt refusal. He knew all too well that if the two friars were to go, they would not come back.

Against such an enemy [he said], no good Christian should march except with lance in hand. No vice existed that was not found in the followers of the false prophet; they were treacherous, carnal, cruel, greedy, malicious, brainless, falsehearted.[94] It would serve no good purpose to expose oneself to the sinful blasphemies of those who swore that Christ was man and not God, who often attached a cross to an ass's tail to show contempt for it, who forced Christian youngsters who fell into their hands to spit on the symbol of the Redeemer. They were all in foulness up to their eyes. This alone would be enough to bring about their extermination. The whole earth would be purged of them in time as, by the miracle of omnipotent God, Damietta had been. It was as Saint Paul says, ". . . all who do such things deserve death. . ."[95] Those who did such things were indeed worthy of death, and not only those who did them but also those who made them possible.[96]

Many more words were poured out and to all of them Francis replied only that he wanted to go to accomplish a great good, if he could. It was impossible to keep on resisting an entreaty made with so much fervour and with such humility.

"Signore," the cardinal finally said, "I do not know what thoughts you harbour in your heart, whether they are good or evil. But if you go, remember to keep your heart and your thoughts always turned to God. In any case, all this is to be your sole responsibility, because certainly I shall not be the one to send you to certain death."

"And so," Ernoul concludes, "the two clerics left the Christian army and went away toward the army of the Saracens."[n]

Sultan Malik-al-Kāmil

As on the day in a robber-infested forest he had proclaimed himself the Herald of the Great King, Francis went forward singing. He sang

---

n. Ernoul, *Chronique* (Golubovich, *Biblioteca,* 1:12–13).

Modern biographers of Saint Francis have often put the visit to the sultan before the Christians' capture of Damietta. An examination of all the sources seems to make this opinion untenable. Giordano, *Chronica,* 10, is often quoted in support of this theory: ". . . since he could not harvest any fruit among them . . . he was led at the order of the sultan by an armed guard to the Christian army that was at the time besieging Damietta." But Brother Giordano uses the word *obsedit,* the historical past tense, to speak of the siege; it serves only to indicate the fact that it took place, which could well have been before their visit. It would have another meaning altogether if he had written *obsidebat;* that would indicate that it was going on at the same time. In reality, he says nothing about the time.

Bernard the Treasurer also seems to put the event during the siege (see Golubovich, *Biblioteca,* 1:13–14). We know, however, that the work that goes under his name was put into Latin by Pipino (see n. 18), who summarized and often altered Ernoul's chronicle. In any case, the only thing said is that Francis and his companion, when they betook themselves to the sultan, "were in the Christian army in Damietta." Fra Paolino, in the chapter of *Chronologia* entitled "De Obsidione Damiate" (Golubovich, *Biblioteca,* 2:87), says that Francis, after the fall of the city into the hands of the Crusaders, was nauseated by their sins, left the Christian camp, and went to the sultan's camp.

Marin Sanuto says the same thing in his work *Secreta Fidelium Crucis,* published in 1332. He, after speaking of the lax morals of the crusaders (see n. 83), remarks on the pleasure of having the holy preacher stay for a time and says that he even went to the sultan, "exposing himself constantly to danger."

Finally, Fra Mariano asserts that the Poverello went to the Saracen camp while the "sultan with his army was encamped against the city of Damietta, so that the Christian army would not pass farther in the direction of Cairo; and he was greatly embittered and was piling cruelty upon cruelty upon the Christians . . . for having taken Damietta." *Libro delle vite* (Golubovich, *Biblioteca,* 1:78).

There seems no doubt, therefore, that this important episode in the life of Saint Francis took place after the capture of Damietta.

This is also the opinion of Boehmer (*Analekten,* p. 101, and in his edition of *Chronica Fratris Iordani,* p. 9); of Golubovich (*Biblioteca,* 2:280–81, and *S. Francesco e i Francescani in Damiata,* p. 15); and of Iacopozzi, the distinguished former custodian of the Holy Land ("Dove sia avvenuta la visita?" *Frate Francesco* 2:379–93).

the psalm that David sang while his sheep grazed in peace beside still waters. He addressed God with the same faith that the lamb puts in his shepherd: "The Lord is my shepherd, I shall not want."[97]

The river along which the two brothers walked was not still. The waters, swollen by the rains, roared along swiftly and spread out into an immense troubled expanse stretching to the horizon of the desert. Not a house was to be seen, not a plant, a cultivated field, a living person—everything had been burnt, sacked, destroyed, in the furious haste of the retreat.

But above the noise of the swirling river rose Francis's strong voice, filling the forbidding emptiness: "Yea, though I walk through the shadow of the Valley of Death, I shall fear no evil, for thou art with me."

They found two sheep browsing tranquilly and believed them to be a sign sent by divine providence. Francis, as Illuminato later told Saint Bonaventure, rejoiced over them and said to his companion, "Place all your trust in God, because the words of the Gospel will be fulfilled in us, 'Remember, I am sending you out to be like sheep among wolves.' "[o]

The wolves fell upon them a little farther along. Warriors of the sultan's army attacked them, seized them, shouted incomprehensible threats, and beat them so savagely that the two travellers believed that they had been called to receive the palm of martyrdom they so much desired. Amid all this, they incessantly called out the name of the sultan, and the Saracens finally decided that they must be ambassadors with propositions from the leaders or Christians who wished to

---

o. See *Leg. Maior*, IX, 8. Authoritative sources for Francis's visit to the sultan, other than the already-cited Ernoul, *Chronique*, are as follows: Jacques de Vitry, the letter "De captione Damiatae" and *Historia Orientalis*, p. 354; *1 Cel.*, 57; also Julian of Speyer, *Vita Sancti Francisci* (AF 10:352–53); Giordano, *Chronica*, 10; Marin Sanuto, *Secreta fidelium Crucis*, chaps. 7 and 8; *Actus*, 27; *Fioretti*, 24.

The Arab chronicles do not speak of Saint Francis or of this episode. However, Massignon, followed by Roncaglia, in "Fonti arabo-musulmane," *Studi Francescani* 50:258–59, holds that a Moslem mystic, Fakhr-al Farasi, counsellor of Malik-al-Kāmil, was acquainted with Saint Francis. Indeed, this is the inscription on his tomb: "He has many well-known virtues. And his experience with Malik-al-Kāmil, that is, the things that befell him owing to the monk (*râhib*) are very well-known." This inscription is taken from Yusuf Ahmed, *Turbat al-Fakhr al Farasi*, and from two other authors of the fifteenth century, Al-Sakhari and Al-Zaiyat.

The "monk" must have been Saint Francis. This identification is rendered probable by the fact that Arab specialists in the history of the Crusades "do not know a native Christian monk who would have been talked about so much during that period. Whoever wrote the epigraph on the tomb of Fakhr-al Farasi obviously did not believe any other details were necessary. Also, in the history of the Coptic church there is no mention of such a monk."

The advanced age of Fakhr-al Farasi at the time of the meeting of Saint Francis and the sultan cannot be an obstacle to the admission of this identification. Gabrieli calls this evidence "a tenuous trace" (*Storici arabi*, p. 251).

abjure their faith. So they tied them up securely and led them to Kāmil.[98]

And that is how it happened (perhaps for the first and only time in the history of the relationship between Christianity and Mohammedanism) that the leading exponents of the two religions and the two civilizations, so long and so incessantly at war with each other, found themselves face to face. One of them was seated on a throne in luxury, surrounded by ministers, chamberlains, captains, and women of pleasure—the last great sovereign of the splendid Ayyubid dynasty that had extended its domination over all the Mohammedan world, the recognized head of a powerful political, social, and cultural system, the ruler who aspired to universal supremacy and the domination of all peoples by virtue of the sword. The other one, even stronger in courage, was led in by guards—Francis of Assisi, ragged, barefoot, the founder of the new rule that proposed to make all men equal under the miraculous law of love.

Ernoul's narration is so precise and detailed that it must surely have been taken either directly or indirectly from the report of someone who was present at that famous meeting, which immediately became legendary in all the Crusader camp. It is best not to mar the dialogue with corrections or rewriting but to reproduce it in the appealing style of the Christian squire, with the repetitions, the ingenuousness, the mix-up of Christian and Mussulman titles and functions so common at the time.

Francis and Illuminato, brought before the prince, saluted him and he responded to their salute. Then he asked the reason for their coming, whether they were messengers or Christians who wished to become Moslems.

Francis replied, "Moslems we shall never become, but in truth we are messengers, come from God to save your soul. If you believe in Him, we shall commit your soul to God. And we tell you truthfully that if you die according to your own law, you will be lost and God will not accept your soul. This is the reason that we have come to you. If you wish to listen to us and to understand us, we shall show you (let the wisest men of your land also come if it should please you to call them) that your law is surely false."

The sultan replied that he had many archbishops and bishops of his own faith and also good clerics, and that without them he would not be able to listen to what the two Christians were going to say.

The brothers replied, "That suits us well enough. Send for them, and if we cannot give you good arguments to show you that what we are saying is true—that is, that your own law is false—then have us decapitated."

The sultan sent for his learned men, and the most eminent and wisest men of the state came. He explained to them the reason for having summoned them.

The doctors immediately said, "Lord, you are the hope of the law and it is your duty to maintain it and to observe it. Therefore, we command you, in the name of God and of Mohammed, who gave us that law, to have these men beheaded at once. We shall not hear what they wish to say. Furthermore, we warn you about listening to their words, since the law forbids listening to anything said against it. And if someone comes burning to preach or to speak against the law, the law commands that his head be cut off. So, therefore, we order you, in the name of God, to have their heads cut off, because the law commands it."

Having said this, they took their leave.

The courtiers were silent, waiting to see what the prince would do. And the brothers were also silent and awaited the sentence that would decide their fate.

Kāmil reflected before speaking. Perhaps he thought of his great ancestor Saladin who once had asked a Jew reputed to be very wise in the things of God which of the three laws he held to be true, the Jewish, the Moslem, or the Christian. The Jew replied with a parable about three rings, so alike that no one could recognize the true from the false.[99]

Finally he said, "*Signori,* those men commanded me, in the name of God and of the law, to have your heads cut off, because the law commands it. But I shall nevertheless ignore this order and not kill you, because it would be a poor recompense for your having come here at the risk of your lives to save my soul."

Thus ended this first conversation. Francis and Illuminato remained in the camp and were treated as honoured guests.

Such magnanimity and understanding moved Francis. He was anguished over the thought that a soul so noble was surely going to be lost forever. False and foolish were those who depicted Kāmil as a monster. So, on another day Francis said to the sultan that he, humble messenger of God that he was, would willingly enter a great fire to demonstrate the truth of the law of Christ.

"Your priests shall come with me," he proposed. "Thus you may know which religion is the real one."

But the sultan replied that none of his priests would accept such a trial.

"Very well," replied Francis, "if you will promise me that you and your people will accept the law of Christ if I emerge without harm, I shall go alone into the flames. And if I burn, it will be because of my sins. But if Divine Grace should protect me, you will acknowledge 'Christ the power of God, Christ the wisdom of God' as true God, the Lord and Saviour of all."

But Kāmil also refused this proposal, saying that he feared the reaction of his people. It may have been that by this time he also had too much affection for the man who had so moved him to allow him to expose himself to such a risk. He invited him to remain with him. He promised him possessions and riches. He had precious jewels, fine cloths, great quantities of gold and silver, brought out for him. But Francis declared that he would take nothing. One thing only had he come to seek, the soul of the ruler, and that had been denied him.

Nevertheless, he agreed to stay for several days and was treated with great honour.[100]

The historians do not tell us anything else about this sojourn, and the reason they do not is easily explained, given the extreme delicacy of the situation in this epoch in which relentless war against the infidels was always going on.

Did Francis go to Cairo, where Malik-al-Kāmil had established his court? Did he debate with the wise men about perfect joy? Did he see the stone face of the Sphinx?[101]

We can hope that he did. The image of the Poverello before the figure symbolizing the power of the pharoahs is intriguing. And surely he would have solved the Sphinx's riddle of life, for its answer can only be Love.

The Sultan's Pledge of Brotherhood

Modern biographers, in speaking of this sojourn, are inclined to treat as historical two episodes that, according to a codex of the fourteenth century, were told to Saint Bonaventure by Illuminato himself.[102]

On one occasion, according to a collection of moral fables compiled by a Friar Minor of the previous century, the sultan, wishing to try the devotion and prudence of his guest, ordered that a carpet worked with a design of crosses be spread out. He said to his ministers, "Fetch that man who seems to be a true Christian. If in coming toward me he walks on the crosses of the carpet, we will say to him that he insults his Lord. If he refuses to walk on the carpet, I shall ask him why he disdains to approach me."

They called the man of God, who, without a shadow of hesitation, walked calmly over the carpet. When he was asked why he had committed such sacrilege, Francis replied, "What I have walked on is not the cross of our Lord, which is ours alone and which we devoutly adore. On the contrary, it is the cross of the thieves who were put to death with him, the false and irreligious cross that would be in your hands. . . ."ᵖ

This tale reflects the taste of the time for subtle questions, and for *belli risponsi,* clever come-backs. This pastime was very popular and much in vogue in both piazza and court, among Christians and infidels.

They were known as "flowers of speech," according to the golden book called *Novellino,* and like other stories of handsome manners, generous gifts, and delightful loves, everyone enjoyed them. "And he who has a noble heart and a subtle intelligence can acquire this gift, and from this time on can argue and speak and narrate wherever the occasion arises, to the pride and pleasure of those who do not know how and would like to know."[103]

The sultan of Egypt appears often in *Novellino* as the character who states the proposition and makes the judgements.

The ninth tale is about a Saracen cook of Alexandria who demanded that a poor man who had come to his kitchen to ask for some bread pay him for the smell of the baking bread from which he had derived great pleasure. The wise men of the Saracens long debated the subtle points of this "new and uncivil question that had never before come up," and they had various opinions about it. Finally the sultan ruled that the fumes should be paid for with the sound of a piece of money.

In the twenty-fifth tale, the same sultan orders that two hundred *marchi* be paid to someone who had brought him a large basket of roses during the winter. His treasurer, it happened, in error wrote down three hundred. So the sultan decided that four hundred should be paid to the flower vendor so that the pen of the treasurer would not be more generous than he.

It is clear that the amusing anecdote about Saint Francis and the sultan has nothing in common with Francis's impassioned devotion to the cross where our Lord died. In fact, the thought of the cross so touched his heart that he was often moved to tears.[104] Never could it have become for him the subject of an ingenious and pleasant word game.

In addition, no one has noted that this episode, which is supposed

---

p. As Raymond points out (*In the Steps,* p. 225), Francis's reported retort—a *bel risponso*—was a beautiful play on the word "thieves," since the Saracens had taken possession of the True Cross in 1187.

to have happened to Saint Francis, is none other than an enlargement and a new version of the same twenty-fifth tale of *Novellino,* in which the sultan Saladin, during a truce, invited some Christians to his encampment, where "they saw that the Saracens ate on the ground in a dirty and disgusting way." The sultan had a rich pavilion set up for eating and the ground covered with carpets, worked all over in a design of wide crosses. The foolish Christians went inside and walked on those crosses, trampling them underfoot as if they were walking on the ground. So the sultan spoke up and reproved them: "You preach the cross and yet despise it so much? It seems that you love your Lord God in words but not in deeds. I do not like your attitude. Let the truce be broken and this unfinished war again begin."

Even less credible is the second episode told about Kāmil and Saint Francis.

"God forbids you Christians, in your Gospel, to render evil for evil and tells you not to deny your mantle to him who takes from you your tunic. For this good reason you should not invade our lands," the sultan is supposed to have said.

And Francis is made to reply:

"The Gospel also teaches us that if our eye scandalizes us, we must not hesitate to pluck it out and cast it away. Let us admit that you are as dear to us as an eye. Well, then, we obey our faith in driving you back, fighting you, and invading your lands, because you have scandalized us greatly by cursing the name of God and alienating yourself from his religion."

We already know what Francis thought of this war and of those who led it.

What, on the other hand, strikes and fascinates us in this marvellous page in Francis's life is something that did not interest his contemporaries at all: the meeting of these two great and noble spirits, and the fact that at the very time Christian and Moslem armies were engaged in trying to annihilate each other, the barriers between these men fell forever and they came to understand and love one another.

One can hardly imagine the amazement and admiration of the Crusaders when, after nearly a month, they saw Francis and Illuminato reappear in Damietta, with an escort of Saracen knights sent by the sultan to protect and honour them, one as large as those provided for emperors.[105]

Still another story is told about this encounter. It is not true, but it is significant and moving in its attestation of the strength of the affection between the sultan and Francis, which lasted until death. That concerns the conversion of Kāmil told in the *Actus.*[106]

When Francis took leave of the sultan [according to the story], the sultan confided that he would willingly be converted to the faith of Christ, but that he feared to do so at that time. His men would kill him, he said, and Francis himself would be unable to escape their anger. And this would be a great shame because of all the good that he could still do.

Francis then said, "Signore, I am leaving you; but when I am back in my country, and, after I die, whenever that shall please God, I shall send two of my friars from whom you will receive holy baptism. You will be saved, as has been revealed to me by my Lord Jesus Christ. In the meantime, make ready to receive the grace of God with faith and devotion."

After the death of Saint Francis, the sultan fell sick, still awaiting the promised grace. He ordered watchmen to be placed in the ports of the kingdom to look for a ship bearing friars dressed in the habit of Saint Francis. And it came to pass that Saint Francis appeared to two of his friars in a vision and ordered them to go immediately to the sultan and secure his salvation. Without delay they set out and travelled over the sea. The sultan was overjoyed at sight of them and said, "Now I know truly that God has sent his servants to me for my salvation, according to the promise that Saint Francis, through divine revelation, made to me."

Historically, it is certain that this conversion is pure legend. But Kāmil's memory and nostalgic desire for the Poverello of Christ must have revived with great intensity several months later, when the Christian army, advancing toward Mansura, was caught by the flooding waters of the Nile. All would have perished without the generous help of the Moslems, their enemy. A Moslem poet said, "If they had conquered us, they would have spilled our blood. Now we have conquered them, and we have saved them."[q]

In Saint Francis's church in Assisi is preserved an ivory horn[107] that is thought to be a gift of the sultan to Francis. The leader of the infidels used it to call his warriors together during battles with Chris-

---

q. Reinaud, *Extraits de l'histoire*, p. 425. This defeat of the Christian army took place August 1221. Peace came as a result of it, but the Crusaders had to abandon all Egypt.

[As would be surmised, the Fifth Crusade had a sorry ending. The Crusaders failed to capitalize on their victory of Damietta; they spent the entire year of 1220 waiting to consolidate their position and waiting also for the appearance of Frederick II, who had promised to join them by 1221. Finally in 1221 the cardinal ordered a march on Cairo, though Jean de Brienne opposed the move and also wanted to accept the sultan's new offer of terms, which included ceding to the Christians a good part of the kingdom of Jerusalem, the surrender of the cross (captured by Saladin in 1187), and the restoration of all prisoners. The cardinal's attempt to extract a large indemnity in addition to these terms was unsuccessful, and the subsequent march on Cairo was a disaster. The Crusaders in the end had to give Damietta back to the Moslems and to evacuate Egypt; they gained only the surrender of the cross and a free retreat. Thus ended the Fifth Crusade.—Trans.]

tians. Saint Francis blew it, according to the legend, to reunite his brothers who were spreading the Franciscan message around the world.

The pledge of brotherhood between these two men is surely the most remarkable the world has ever seen. One can well believe that if this horn should sound again, the spirit of Saint Francis would return to us, so thoughtful and loving that no one could resist his call, ancient and ever-new.

In the Land Where Jesus Walked

Another extraordinary sign of Kāmil's kindness was the fact that he gave to Francis a safe conduct to the holy places of the Christian faith that lay within his empire.[r]

So after a short time Francis left that encampment where his spirit had been so battered and torn and set out, probably again by sea, for Syria. There he again found all that holy shore submerged in war. The sultan of Damascus (Corradino) had come from Egypt with his army, laid siege to the old city of Augustus, Caesarea, held by soldiers of the king of Jerusalem, and in a short time had succeeded in conquering and laying waste to it. However, he had not been able to conquer the strongly fortified castle of the Pellegrini (Pilgrims), held by the

---

r. According to *Actus*, 27, and *Fioretti*, 24, the sultan, after having joyfully entertained Saint Francis, "generously granted permission to him and to his companions to go anywhere and freely preach wherever they wished in all his empire. And he gave them a certain little token *(signaculum)* so that no one who saw it should harm them."

This *signaculum* would be the first firman (a decree or edict issued by a Moslem prince) given by the Moslem rulers in favour of the Friars Minor, who had and still have the custody of the Holy Sepulcher. Cf. Fortini, *Gli ultimi Crociati*.

Angelo Clareno, who knew many of Saint Francis's first companions, says in his "Prima tribulazione" (chap. 1) that the sultan gave orders that Francis and his friars could go freely and without paying tribute to Christ's sepulcher. And further along, after having said that Jesus appeared to Saint Francis to tell him about the serious problems in the order during his absence, he concludes, "After he had visited the sepulcher of Christ, he speedily returned to the land of Christians." (Ibid.)

We also know from Jacques de Vitry something about the Saracens' reception of the preaching of the Friars Minor: "Even the Saracens and men plunged into the darkness of unbelief admire their humility and virtue when the brothers come among them to preach to them without fear: they receive them very gladly and give them all they need. . . . The Saracens gladly listened to the Friars Minor preach as long as they explained faith in Christ and the doctrine of the gospel; but as soon as their preaching attacked Mohammed and openly condemned him as a liar and traitor, then these ungodly men heaped blows upon them and chased them from their cities; they would have killed them if God had not miraculously protected his sons."

It must be kept in mind that Jacques de Vitry wrote his *Historia Orientalis*, from which this passage is taken (chap. 32) in Damietta in 1221, and that Saint Francis entitled one chapter of his rule, written that same year, "Missionaries among the Saracens and other unbelievers."

The presence of Saint Francis in Syria is mentioned also in *1 Cel.*, 4; and in *Leg. Maior*, IX, 7, in which Saint Bonaventure writes that Saint Francis in the thirteenth year of his conversion (which would have to be dated by that reckoning in 1206) "made his way to Syria where he courageously surmounted all dangers in order to reach the presence of the sultan of Egypt."

Templars. And Acre had fought victoriously against the Saracens, but Saphet, the strong fortress on the mountain overlooking the lake of Tiberias, had been destroyed.[108]

We know little or nothing of Francis's sojourn in the country of Jesus. Certainly the emir of Jerusalem must have paled when he saw in the hands of that ragged and emaciated pilgrim a document with the seal of Malik-al-Kāmil, gold and threaded with red silk, where he read how effusively the powerful lord of the two Egypts recommended him, a Christian like those who had usurped Damietta, as the friend nearest his heart.

Jerusalem in that time looked squalid and abandoned. The walls had been destroyed. With the exception of the basilica of the Holy Sepulchre, the beautiful churches built by Crusaders in places marking events in the life and death of Jesus had been reduced to heaps of rubble. The people of the city had fled after the cisterns were destroyed, as ordered by Corradino.[109]

What prayer welled up from Francis's heart when he stood at the tomb of Jesus?

Early biographers say that Francis travelled all through Syria. Certainly he was accompanied by the first minister he had named to the overseas province, Brother Elias.

Near Antioch rose Mount Nera, famous for its fertility, a mountain of rivers, springs, forests, meadows. On it many Greek and Latin monks lived, in constant contention with one another. But it is said that when the Poverello went up there, the abbot and the religious of a Benedictine monastery came out to meet him in procession, carrying the cross, and that all wanted to become Friars Minor.[110]

Meanwhile, ominous things were being said about what was happening to the order in Italy. Crusaders habitually consulted seers and fortune tellers about events at home, and someone hurried to consult a famous seer named Veredica. She gave an alarming warning: "Return, return. On account of the absence of Brother Francis the order is disturbed, torn asunder, and scattered."[111]

In July a lay brother called Stefano the Simple because of his naive piety arrived from Italy in great haste. First, he knelt before Francis and confessed and asked pardon for the sin of having come secretly and without the permission of his superiors. He had searched for Francis through all the overseas province and had given up hope of finding him, and someone had told him as a sure fact that Francis was dead. But it was necessary that he, Father Francis, know how many things had happened and were happening in his absence.[112]

His true sons, the fervent servants of Poverty, were being shunted to one side. Despairing and grief-stricken over the distance between them and their holy shepherd, they were continually and tearfully praying that he soon return. Others in the order had begun to leave the way of perfection that he had shown them and were no longer constant in love and in the practice of charity, humility, and holy poverty.[113]

Also, immediately after his departure, Cardinal Ugolino, while on a trip to Perugia, had imposed on the Poor Ladies of Monticelli, Siena, Perugia, and Lucca, the Benedictine rule that Francis had steadily refused, through his brothers, to accept.[114]

In this decision the hand of Brother Gregorio of Naples could be clearly seen. A nephew of Cardinal Ugolino, he had been named by Francis as his vicar during his absence and given the task of travelling about to comfort and to keep up the spirits of the friars and to maintain the discipline of the order. The other vicar named by Francis, Matteo of Narni, was to remain in Porziuncola to receive new friars.

The old rule had specified fasting on Wednesdays and Fridays, and, with the authorization of the head of the order, also on Mondays and Saturdays. But in the last chapter at Pentecost, the vicars had multiplied formal and sterile rules about this matter. Now the brothers were forbidden to provide meat even on the days that were not fast days, though they were allowed to eat it if it were spontaneously offered to them by others. And mandatory fasts were also ordered for Mondays and two other days; and on Mondays and Saturdays the brothers were also to abstain from all milk products, unless by chance some of their faithful supporters brought some to them. And so on.

Brother Stefano had brought the new rules with him and he tearfully showed them to Francis. And also, he said, Brother Filippo had asked Cardinal Ugolino for special privileges for the sisters at San Damiano. And, finally, Giovanni della Capella had gathered together a great number of lepers, men and women, and claimed to have formed a new order. He had already gone with them to seek approval of it by the pope. Still other things were going on, too long to tell about, but in every way fulfilling exactly what the seer had said.

While Stefano the Simple talked, Francis and Pietro di Catanio were sitting at table. There was meat, and it was a day on which it was forbidden by the new constitutions.

Francis asked the former canon of the cathedral of San Rufino,[s] "Tell me, messire, what we ought to do."

---

s. In chap. 7, n. f, of this book, the author expresses the opinion that Pietro could not have been a canon of San Rufino despite late descriptions of him as one. Perhaps this sentence was an absent-minded slip.—Trans.

Pietro, for all that he was a scholar of the University of Bologna and an expert in jurisprudence, had no intention of giving advice to the man who seemed to him to be in every act inspired by God.

"We shall do whatever you want to do," he replied, "because to you alone belongs the privilege of giving orders."

"Then," said Francis, "we shall obey the Holy Gospels and eat what is put before us."[115]

Francis left at once on a ship making the autumn passage from Acre. He took with him Pietro di Catanio, Elias, Cesario of Speyer, and others, leaving some brothers to maintain Franciscan places and to continue the work of the apostolate.[116]

It was a Venetian galley. Perhaps it was one of those five hundred and fifty that, sixteen years earlier when Francis had a passion for things to do with arms, had been a part of the fleet of the nonagenarian doge when he attacked Bisanzio, one fortified with floating towers and drawbridges so that to terrified defenders it looked like a powerful city wall suddenly arising from the sea.[117]

The ship moved swiftly through the azure glory of the dying summer, the water mirroring its wide billowing sails and its fluttering banner of Saint Mark atop the mainmast—the image of a power proud of its supremacy, a fitting ship for the avaricious strong men who had used the Crusades to found a great empire nearly half the size of the Roman Empire.

Did anyone, in the midst of such greedy ambitions, such fomenting of violent enterprises, sense that the only conqueror in the war fought in the name of the cross was this little man with the rapt face, the man who had known how to dispel the hatred of an inveterate enemy with the single weapon of charity?

They touched the lands of the Republic, Crete, Greece, Albania, Dalmatia, and finally arrived in Venice, which spread out the splendours of its golden basilica, its marble palaces, its spires, cupolas, and pinnacles, like a concentrated reflection of the magnificence of the east. They breathed in all the opulence of the city's life, so full both of war and trade. They heard the roar of the crowd acclaiming the return of warriors loaded with booty.

Then a little boat gently and slowly took Francis to an isolated forgotten island to find a time of peace after the struggle he had been through and to prepare himself for the one soon to come, this one, perhaps, to be even more bitter.

The Idyll of Isola del Deserto

Isola del Deserto, Island of the Desert, is a lagoon hermitage where wide blue heavens are mirrored in still waters, an island locked in a deep spell that makes true its ancient inscription: *O beata solitudine, o sola beatitude!* ("Oh, blessed solitude, oh, solitary blessedness!").

Already the twilight had begun to veil the mirror of the estuary when Francis went there with Brother Illuminato, and rising from the canebreaks was the vespers concert of the aquatic birds. It was a marvellous thing to see how these creatures of God did not fly away at the approach of the brothers, but devoutly saluted them by stretching their necks and flapping their wings.

There was no sound of bells. Francis knelt on the grass and began the evening prayer. His companion made the responses.

Little by little, as in the crescendo of an invisible orchestra, the chorus of the swamps rose, grew in intensity, swelled ever higher, became an overwhelming paean. At last it was a hymn so great, so full and sonorous, that it brooked no competition. It ruled the air, the sky, the waters. One could distinguish in the harmony the obstinate wailing of the wild duck, the shrill call of the summer teal, the pathetic clucking of the bittern, the piercing trumpet call of the crane. The coot sighed a motif like a reed instrument. The plover imitated the sibilance of the wind; the snipe interrogated with the sweet note of the flute; the curlew lamented; the waterhen cawed.

The brothers could no longer hear each other; everything was submerged in the noise of the great echoing symphony of these mixed voices of joy and harmony.

Then Francis arose, and in the uncertain light when day is dying and it is not yet night, he spoke to his sister birds, asking them to allow the servants of God to say the evening lauds, so comforting and sweet to them after an exhausting and trying day. Immediately, as if obeying the gesture of a magic baton, the song hushed.[118] And in the great peace that reigned over the lagoon, where a red streak still remained on the edge of the waters, there was no sound but the prayer of the two *poverelli* of Christ.

·12·

PERFECT JOY

The loveliness and loneliness of Isola del Deserto were balm to Francis's troubled spirit. He felt he had finally arrived at his soul's safe harbour. One day he picked up the pilgrim's staff that he had made for himself from a pine branch during a stop on the Albanian coast and fixed it in the earth. It symbolized his desire never to leave that peaceful island. According to tradition, the wood immediately grew green again and put forth deep roots and produced leaves and fruit. It grew in the years that followed until it became a great tree, with abundant foliage that murmured in the sea breeze on calm days. Even today, three centuries after the tree died, friars who care for the hermitage of San Francesco del Deserto give devout visitors a precious splinter of the holy pine tree.[1]

But all too soon he had to leave the little beach and be on his way to settle the ever-growing discord in the order.

In early September (1220) Francis and Illuminato embarked on the fragile little boat that would carry them back to the mainland. Even the sea was troubled, stirred up by a storm that was growing in intensity. Before long their little ship seemed to be in danger of sinking and Brother Illuminato could not keep quiet about his fear. A word from Francis, we are told, calmed the winds and brought back fair weather.[2]

They stopped briefly in Verona, then went on to Bologna. Perhaps no other city, except for Assisi itself, was so much and so dramatically involved in the bitter disputes in Franciscanism's early days as this one. It was the setting for the crucial struggles of reality vs. the dream, the spirit of poverty vs. the heady excitement of learning, weighty logic vs. impassioned zeal for a cause [regardless of one's own strength and the greatness of the sacrifice it required.]

At the end of the twelfth and the beginning of the thirteenth centuries, the University of Bologna had ten thousand scholars of every nation, and doctors of civil and canon law. What swarming, what movement, what tumult there was in this large and noisy city, the world's brain! It was the maker of the theory of law; the hotbed of subtlety, disquisition, reasoning carried to extreme lengths, and the art of jurisprudence, all according to precept and human experience![3]

The students came from everywhere, homing in like industrious bees to a flowering garden: Frenchmen, Spaniards, Poles, Hungarians, Czechs, Bulgarians, Scandinavians, Germans.

Italian cities took pride in every native son who returned to his birthplace with a degree, considering it equal in dignity to knighthood. Assisi was no exception, as we see in a provision of its statutes: "All the doctors and lawyers who return to Assisi with the doctoral degree in civil and canon law shall have from the Commune twenty-five *fiorini* of gold. And this is intended for the citizens whose origins and ancient roots lie in the aforesaid city, and not for those who have come or who shall come in, named citizens according to whatever statute."[4] In a will of 1263 a certain Giovanni di Angelo di Rainuccio received as a legacy "the books of law that he had had in Bologna."[5] We have already seen that some of Francis's companions had attended the famous university.

The first companion to take the Franciscan message to Bologna was Bernardo da Quintavalle. Francis sent him there in 1211.[6]

There Bernardo had a crucial decision to make. Should he try to match the haranguing and dialectics of the decretalists to whom the emperor turned for opinions in Roman law? Should he go down to the piazza and entrust his message of faith and love to a dangerous game of ratiocination, arguing like the doctors of the university?

We see how he resolved the matter in a marvellous chapter of *Little Flowers,* "How the Holy Brother Bernardo d'Ascesi was sent by Saint Francis to Bologna and how he there took up his abode."

Bernardo goes through the busiest streets, dressed in a habit so poor and ragged that he could not help attracting attention. People stare at him, laugh, make joking or sneering remarks, say he is crazy, a lunatic escaped from the asylum. In his heart he rejoices over this ill treatment endured for the love of Christ and keeps silent. And he deliberately goes to the piazza, so that people can have an even better chance to make fun of him.

In plain view he sits in the place of the *arengo,* the site of public assembly. Men and boys come, curious and sharp-tongued, amuse themselves by making him the butt of their jokes. They howl and whistle. They invite him to make a speech. He remains patient and silent.

They walk into him and shove him about. They pull his hood over his eyes and twist it around his neck. They slap his face and throw stones and handfuls of dust at him. And the friar not only persists in his silence but seems to be made happy by all this. He returns to the piazza for several days to invite more of the same.

He becomes the laughing-stock of all those who had nothing better to do, the curiosity of the day, the public buffoon. He seems the image of cowardice, a man without nerve or spirit. Anyone can beat him up without running any risk whatsoever. He can be hit as if he were the puppet used in jousting.

But one day it happens that one of those taking part in all this has the same thought about Bernardo that Bernardo had had at one time about Francis, when he saw that he had not been disturbed by the abuse of Assisi hoodlums. Bernardo, this man reflects, must be a saint.

The man is a doctor of the university, one of those whom it would have been very difficult, and perhaps impossible, to influence through argument and syllogisms. Now he wants to know all about Bernardo, who he is, where he comes from, and why he is deliberately exposing himself to public abuse. Bernardo even then does not say a word but puts his hand in his bosom and draws out Francis's rule, which he always carries over his heart. And after he reads and rereads it, the learned doctor of law speaks out to the sneering and malicious mob, waiting on tenterhooks to hear some scornful remark.

"This certainly is the highest form of religious life that I have ever known," the doctor tells them. "He and his companions are surely among the holiest men in all the world. So those who insult him are committing a very great sin, for he should be given the highest honour, one befitting a man very close to God."

Many think that the speaker was Nicolò di Guglielmo di Pepoli, who was perhaps the messire Nicolò mentioned in a Bologna document drawn up by the canons of San Salvatore in 1194, which records him as the owner of a house of study in the *platea maiori* of the city. The account goes on to tell how he offered Bernardo a place for a friars' house and how he became the "father and special protector" to Brother Bernardo and his companions. It is known that he himself entered the order of Friars Minor and that he died with a reputation for great holiness.[7]

Thus Brother Bernardo became so dear to the people of Bologna and was held in such great honour that the person who could get close to him and speak to him considered himself blessed.

But this was exactly what the disciple of humility was anxious to avoid, fearing that "worldly honour would interfere with the peace and salvation of his soul." So he left Bologna and returned to Francis, to whom he told all that had happened. A place was now being made ready for Franciscan brothers in Bologna, he said; and he urged Francis to send other brothers since he feared that he could no longer do any good there because the people held him in too great esteem. He was afraid that he would lose more than he would gain and even forfeit his own peace.

Here begins the Franciscan argument over Learning vs. Humility. These two values were arrayed against one another, both of them with good justifications, both of them potent. One came from the culmination of the experience of a hundred generations; the other was without such credentials and strange but invested with youthful enthusiasm and drive. Francis's companions were divided over which would be more effective.

It all brings to mind those sculptured figures on the sides of sepulchral monuments in the churches of San Domenico and San Francesco in Bologna—scholars in their cowls and gowns, solemn doctors, their grave and furrowed faces under hoods of vair seemingly still bent to an annotated book.

Yet not all truth can be found in the texts of Roman law. Very often the devil himself becomes a doctor of laws and goes about arguing with great acuteness, as in that "little flower" about the evil spirit that entered into the body of a woman of Massa San Pietro and "made her speak so intelligently in Latin that she defeated all the learned and educated men who came to debate with her."[8]

We can understand Francis's indignation, therefore, when he came to Bologna and found that another famous doctor of the university, Giovanni da Sciacca, who had become a Friar Minor, was holding a chair of jurisprudence and teaching in a Franciscan house in the same manner that he had done in secular life. At Francis's order, all the brothers had to leave that house, even those who were sick. Before they could re-enter, he insisted that Cardinal Ugolino declare publicly that he owned the house. Brother Giovanni was severely reproved.[9]

"You want to destroy my order," Francis told him. "I desire and intend that my brothers, following the example of my Lord Jesus Christ, pray rather than read."[a]

---

a. In *Spec. Perf.*, 6, it is noted that "one of these friars, who was sick and obliged to leave the house, is still living today, and has written this account." According to Sabatier, this was Brother Leo. CED, pp. LXIV–LXV.

A stiffer test was awaiting Francis two years later, in August 1222, when he had to return to Bologna.[10]

It was a sad time in the city. All the ideal rules of government propounded in the university had failed to spare the people from the tragedy of bloody factional fights. Miraculous signs were proclaiming the coming of Divine wrath. A great comet with more than one tail, red like burning coals, had appeared in the early days of that same month of August and shone in the sky many nights. It flamed like a sword of fire over the tower of the Asinelli, dimming the brightness of all other stars. The people of the city were seized by terror of what it portended.

Francis preached in the same piazza in which Bernardo had been subjected to such shameful treatment eleven years earlier.

A great crowd gathered to listen to him. Attracted by his fame, the professors of the university were there, stately in their red mantles with hoods and costly chamois gloves. They were gruff, stiff, and straight, as at examinations, not being able to reconcile themselves to the fact that a man without learning thought to move such a crowd. There was a throng of students.

From his first words, everyone was captivated by him.

We have the word of one of the scholarly listeners, Thomas of Spalato, for this:

"Being in Bologna on the feast of the Assumption, I, Tommasso da Spalato, archdeacon of the cathedral of that city, saw Saint Francis preach in the piazza in front of the little palazzo. Almost everyone in the city was there. The subject of his sermon was 'Angels, Men, Demons.' He spoke so well and with such eloquence and precision about these three classes of spiritual and rational beings that even the scholars in the audience were amazed at this untutored man. Yet, he did not speak in the manner of a preacher; rather, he in simple fashion exhorted the people to put an end to hatred and restore peace.

"His clothes were wretched, his person was insignificant, he did not have an attractive face. But God conferred so much power on his words that he reconciled nobles who had been slaughtering one another for generations. And so greatly were the people devoted to him that men and women flocked to him, and whoever could touch or tear off a piece of his poor habit counted himself blessed."[b]

And again from *Little Flowers:*

---

b. Boehmer, *Analekten*, p. 106. Thomas, archdeacon of Spalato, specifies that this sermon took place the year that the city of Brescia was destroyed by an earthquake. From several chronicles it is now known that there was such an earthquake in Brescia on Christmas Day, 1222. *Annales Brixienses, Cremonenses, Bergomates* (*MGH*, vol. 18).

"At one time while Saint Francis was travelling, he came to the city of Bologna. When the people heard about his arrival, they ran to see him, and there was such a crowd that he could hardly walk. For they all wanted to see him, as a new flower of the world and an angel of the Lord, so that he had a hard time to reach the city square.

"And when the entire square was filled with men and women and students, Saint Francis stood up on a high place in the center and began to preach what the Holy Spirit dictated to him. And he preached such marvellous and astounding things that he seemed to be not a man but an angel. And his heavenly words seemed like sharp arrows shot from the bow of divine wisdom, and they pierced the hearts of everyone so effectively that by this sermon he converted a very great multitude of men and women from a state of sin to remorse and penance.

"And among them were two noble students from the Marches of Ancona. One, whose home was in Falerone, was called Pellegrino; and the other's name was Riccieri from Muccia.

"Among others whose hearts had been touched interiorly by divine inspiration through the sermon, they came to Francis, saying that they had an intense desire to leave the world and receive the habit of his friars. . . . "[11]

Wine, Women, and Song

We know a little about these two scholars who, up until the time they heard Saint Francis, had been drawn by the glamour of empty dogma and worldly pleasures. Pellegrino was "a very learned scholar and well-known as an expert in Roman law."[12] Riccieri had left no stone unturned in his pursuit of youthful pleasures.[13] Francis pointed out to both a better path: humility.

As a result Brother Pellegrino never wanted to become a cleric but remained a lay brother all his life.

A beautiful tribute is paid to him in *Actus:*

"And he really was a pilgrim. For the love of Christ, which he always had in his heart, did not allow him to find peace in any creature or to attach his affections to any temporal thing, but he always strove for his heavenly home and looked to his heavenly home, and he climbed from virtue to virtue until he was transformed from the lover into the beloved."[14]

The fleeting reference to the dissolute youth of the scholar Riccieri is sufficient for us to recognize him as one of the goliards famous in the Middle Ages for their licentiousness. [They were flourishing in the time of Saint Francis.]

Their lively and crackling poetry tells us a great deal about the corrupt customs of the time.[15]

When the scholar first arrived in Bologna, he was greeted by a rhyme:

> *Huc accedant sitientes*
> *Dogma gratum cupientes*
> *Et argentum habentes.*[16]

Dogma is a precious thing. But money is better. Nothing in the world is outside its power. And this verse was followed by a host of others, rapid, facile, trilling, that rained on prelates, the Curia, monks, like a volley of arrows. Equivocation, double meanings, raillery, irony—these marked the impudent songs, which mocked every idealism, every institution, every good rule of life.

Isn't it true that the world is nothing but buying and selling? (the scholars sang). Everywhere you find people who ask for money. One pays and pays again; there is no end to paying. And if you wish to get anywhere, there is only one rule: give to those in charge and give again, unto your uttermost farthing:

> *Das istis, das aliis, addis dona datis.*[17]

It's a mercenary world. Look at the dignitaries who chase after money, the judges who barter justice, the asses with doctor's degrees who think of learning as a commodity only to be sold.

Let us have no talk, then, of ideals, heroism, faith. What have you got when you have shed rivers of tears over the plight of the Holy City? Believe me, a sensible man lives for the moment and for all the pleasure he can get in it.

It was impossible for a scholar in Bologna or Pavia, surrounded, as he was, by so many enticements and so many beautiful and easy young women, to remain chaste.

> *Quis in igne positus igne non uratur?*
> *Quis Papie demorans castus habeatur?*
>
> Would you sit amid the fire?
> Will the fire not burn you?[18]

In such manner these libertine singers, all dedicated to scandalous folly, explained themselves in their audacious and obscene songs, which parodied sacred texts, scholastic rules, the rhetorical arts, mercilessly and mordantly ridiculed and mocked everything. Better for you than all the glosses, they sang, are the rapture of love, gaiety from wine, bated breath at the gaming tables, the pride of winning and the satisfactions of cheating, a life of heedless liberty.

A fool is he who refuses to taste the pleasures of youth:

> *Dulcis amor*
> *Qui te caret*
> *Hoc tempore—fit vilior.*

> Ah, that love!
> Whoso now is robbed of thee,
> Wretch is he.[19]

Phyllis with the full lips is beautiful, and Flora of the flashing eyes is no less beautiful. Spring is the time to steal away with them into the friendly shadows of the woods; in the winter the silvery peal of a young laugh will give you joy as you lie together beside a roaring fire.[20]

Woe to you if you get sentimental about women! It is not good to be too truthful. *Habere, non haberi:* Conquer, and don't let yourself be dominated. Take betrayal with indifference; banish jealousy from your heart. And if sometimes a cloud settles over the brain, remember that a cup of good wine helps to restore the spirit.

> *Vinum dulce gloriosum*
> *Pingue facit et carnosum*
> *Atque pectus aperit.*[21]

The dice also offer their consolations:

> *Ergo nos ludamus,*
> *Sorte proiciamus,*
> *Laetanter bibamus*
> *Et hoc propere.*[22]

Even the goliards, though, found that when the songs die away and the crowns of roses wither on the fair foreheads, nothing remains of all that fire but a cold heap of ashes. And so their rowdy bacchic songs include a reference to the black earth into which all must go.

Post laetam juventutem
Post molestam senectutem
Nos habebit humus.[23]

[Such must have been the background of the scholar Riccieri.] But so touched was he by Francis's preaching that, after he joined the order, he devoted himself to serving the brothers with great humility. So much so, in fact, that Francis chose him as a special confidant.

But he could not entirely forget the pleasures of his student days, and four years after his conversion he was overcome by the old passions. Sexual desire attacked him so violently that it seemed likely to destroy him in both soul and body. Day and night, while scourging himself and in prayer, the images called up by his brain haunted him. Consumed by hours of wakefulness and by grief, he came to the end of his rope and believed himself completely abandoned by God.

Then he thought about Francis and how much affection he had given him. He decided to go to him. If Francis happily welcomed him, it would mean that he could hope that God would still have mercy on him. If not, nothing remained to him but to give up and die.

So, at the end of the summer, we find Riccieri setting out to see Francis, who by now is lying gravely ill in the bishop's palace in Assisi. Still driven by his inner turmoil, he trudges alone on roads worn by a relentless drought. Finally he catches sight of the steep city on the Subasio, and it seems to him that already, under the clear arch of the Assisi sky, a first breath of coolness refreshes his exhausted spirit. He is astonished, as he passes through the Perlici gate, to see Brother Leo and Brother Masseo coming to meet him. They embrace him and greet him in the name of Father Francis; and they say, as Francis has told them to do, that of all the brothers in the world, Francis has a special love for him, Riccieri.

Riccieri falls on his knees in the middle of the road with his arms in a cross and such relief sweeps over him that he almost loses his senses.

Together they all go to the bishop's house and into the room where Francis lies ill. But when he hears Brother Riccieri, he gets up, goes to meet him, and embraces him warmly. And he repeats, "My very dearest son, Brother Riccieri, among all the brothers in the world, I have a special love for you."

And after that, he makes the sign of the cross on his forehead and lovingly kisses him there. And wonderful to say, as soon as Francis finishes saying these words, Brother Riccieri feels his troubled and guilty thoughts leave him and it seems that he had never had them.[24]

Brother Riccieri, who led a holy life until his death in 1236, certainly must have been thinking of all this when he said, "In some fashion every man can readily attain real knowledge of the truth and attain perfect peace."[25] He teaches that everyone who wants to achieve this goal "must above all free himself from attachment to every creature."

This is the secret of humility—"and what is humility but the light of truth?" Beside this light, place a hundred of the most alluring damsels in the world, he says. They will arouse nothing but distaste, because the divine light within you will always extinguish worldly brightness.[26]

In recognition of his special light, Francis ordered Brother Riccieri, a scholar who could have become a priest, to remain a lay brother and humbly to serve his brothers.

Why Francis Distrusted Intellectual Pursuits

In the story [of Ricciero and his failure to find satisfaction in the purely intellectual life and in the pleasures of sex and riches] we can begin to see the explanation of Francis's dim view of learning. Worldly learning was to him a thing to be opposed: philosophy was to him the academic discipline of frivolous curiosity. And jurisprudence, the science of vanity and of oppression, fallacious by its very nature, betraying its very mission of justice through what seems to be impeccable reasoning, too often putting human reason at the service of the most evil passions. In similar fashion, Dante, preparing to celebrate the life of Saint Francis and contrasting it with the "worthless exercise of reason" that makes the little mortals of the earth "beat their wings into the ground," puts in the same class the tyranny of the lord and that of the logician, physical violence and moral violence, the brutality of war and the insidious cruelties of the sophist.[27]

We can understand Francis when we remember how many peoples have been led astray, overwhelmed and reduced to servitude by the lies of an evil demogogue. How many times in the administration of human justice has an unscrupulous counsellor been able to subvert the truth and win the unthinking assent of a judge? How many tears and how many innocents have been sacrificed to a false divinity in a scholar's cap and gown who loudly proclaims himself to be above ordinary men and claims the right to judge vices and virtues, innocence and guilt, honesty and depravity?

This is surely the explanation of the will made by a doctor of laws, Domino Giacomo di Samuele,[c] who lived in Assisi in the same cen-

---

c. The Samuele name appears for the first time in the city records in 1235, when the father (*Iacobus Samuelis*) of the prominent citizen who is mentioned here was a witness in one of the

tury as did Saint Francis. Dying, he directed that in reparation of the injustices he had committed, all his books of law should be sold and the proceeds distributed to the poor. "He wishes and directs that in reparation for his illicit acquisitions, his bad advice, his negligence, the sentences unjustly pronounced by him . . . all his books of civil and canon law, and that is to say, the *Codex,* the *Digesta* (new and old), the *Institutiones,* the *Liber Authenticarum,* the *Infortiatum,* the three books of the *Codices,* the *Apparati* with the *Apparato di Accursio,* Rofredo's book on civil law, and Goffredo's *Decretali, Apparati,* and *Somma,*[d] should be freely consigned and put into the hands of the Custodian of (the Basilica di) San Francesco. And this Custodian shall sell them and distribute the proceeds to the poor."

So all this explains why Francis used to say that to the sons of the secular world must be left this "prideful and foolish learning," fed on "wordy circumlocutions, ornaments, and embellishments, vain displays and curiosities" and instruct his friars to seek "not the bark but the pith, not the shell but the kernel, not the many things but the much, the greatest and the lasting good."[28]

Yet, though he had made action and preaching the basis of his order and believed these necessary to lead the world back to the Gospel, Francis himself could not, especially after the enormous multiplication of his followers, ignore or oppose "the divine science." Those who like to present Saint Francis as an ignorant man, uncultured and deprived of all intellectual accomplishments, are wrong.[29] His knowledge of theology was so profound that many thought it a

---

quittances granted to the city by the knights who fought in the war with Perugia (Arch. Com., M 1; fol. 2; reprinted in *NV* 3:580–82). He also served as a councillor of the commune in 1228 (M 1, fol. 8). Giacomo was in 1237 a councillor named in the arbitration settlement made by Brother Elias (*NV* 3:641). In 1255 he was a judge (Perg., B 14–P 4). In 1257 he appears as a witness in a notarial deed (B 14–P. B 6); in 1271 he took part in the sale of the castle of Armezzano to the commune (B 15–P.B 15); in 1275 he again appears in the record of the sale of a house to the commune (B 15–P.B 19). In 1278 he made his will (Str. 1, no. 40); reprinted in *NV* 3:480); from the text it seems that he had a sister named Bionda, who was married to Ugolino, son of Napoleone, lord of Armezzano (see *NV* 2:431). From the will we know that he served as a judge in Norcia and that he had a son named Mello.

d. The *Codex,* the *Digesta* (or *Pandectae*), and the *Institutiones* are three of the four works included in Justinian's *Corpus iuris civilis.* The *Liber authenticarum* is the designation for one of the three known copies of the fourth work included in the *Corpus,* the *Novellae Constitutiones;* it was the copy most widely used in the west in the Middle Ages. After the foundation of the law school of Bologna, copies made of the *Digesta* were divided into three parts; the *Digestum infortiatum* is the second one of these divisions, made up of Books 25–38 of the *Digesta.* (The other two divisions are *Digestum vetus,* Bks. 1–24; and *Digestum novum,* from 39 on. Copies of the *Digesta* so divided are designated *littera Bononiensis,* after the school in Bologna, or *littera vulgata.* The *Codex,* in manuscripts after the thirteenth century, is also divided into three parts.)

The *Apparato* or *Glossa* on the Justinian law written by the famous jurist Accursius was the indispensable book for lawyers in the first half of the thirteenth century. Also necessary were the books on canon and civil law (*libelli de iure canonico et civili*) by Roffredo Epifanio da Benevento, the decretals of Gregory IX, and the compendium of those decretals by Goffredo da Trani, the *Summa super rubricis Decretalium.*

gift from God.[30] And, moreover, his enthusiastic spirit gave life to his words, so that even in the most difficult arguments he could put the most knowledgeable theologians in the shade.

Thomas of Celano depicts these gifts of his magnificently, uniting, as he usually does, precision of language and poetic expression: "For his genius, free from all stain, penetrated the hidden things of mysteries, and where the knowledge of the masters is something external, the affection of one who loves enters within the thing itself. At times he read the sacred books and what he put into his mind once he wrote indelibly in his heart. . . . "[31]

A great theologian who had listened to Francis talk of God said, "My brothers, the theology of this man, based upon purity of life and contemplation, is a soaring eagle, while our learning crawls on its belly on the ground."[32]

And it was Francis, we must remember, who wished brothers chosen to preach "to give themselves to the study of spiritual things . . . not hindered by other duties." For these, he used to say, have been "chosen by a certain great king to deliver to the people the edicts that proceed from his mouth."[33] Had he not himself once proclaimed that he was the Herald of the Great King?

But learning, he always insisted, must not hinder prayer and the contemplative life. *Primo unctio et postea speculatio.* Above all, learning must not weaken humility, which remained, along with poverty, the foundation of Franciscanism. This Francis believed, this he constantly repeated. He believed also that one must have humility to understand the divine mysteries. "He often said that the man who would easily move from knowledge of himself to a knowledge of God is the one who would set himself to study the Scriptures humbly, not presumptuously."[34] Otherwise, even holy doctrine would grow arrogant and pedantic and would end by being just like secular and "pagan" science.

And here, on this subject, is another great page of Thomas of Celano: "Francis once said that a great cleric must in some way give up even his learning when he comes to the order, so that having renounced such a possession, he may offer himself naked to the arms of the Crucified. 'Learning takes from many people their docility,' he said, 'and does not permit them to bend to humble practices. Wherefore I want the learned first to make this petition to me: "Behold, Brother, I have lived in the world a long time and I did not truly know my God. I beg of you, give me a place that is removed from the noise of the world where I can think over my years in sorrow, where, recollecting my distracted heart, I can bring my soul to better things."

"'What kind of man,' he said, 'do you think he will become who starts out in this way? Surely he would go forth unto all things strong as an unchained lion, and the blessed moisture he has tasted at the beginning will increase constantly in him. He may be assigned confidently to the true ministry of the word, for he will pour out what is bubbling up within him.' "[35]

The brother who could master this true learning would realize the ideal set forth by Jesus: the simplicity of the dove united to the cunning of the serpent.[36] It was exactly in this way that the scholar Riccieri shone.

In this lay the beauty of Saint Francis's order: the wise learned from men of great piety and zeal and the simple learned from cultured men, who could have held a post anywhere in the world but who had chosen to live the same humble life as they did.[37]

[In Bologna these matters eventually resolved themselves.] In the same city where the school of Irnerius had been located, a Franciscan house of studies was established; and it grew and prospered. Here the greatest of Francis's brothers, Anthony of Padua, was the foremost lecturer in theology. He taught with Francis's consent.[e]

Famous jurists who had one day heard Francis's message and had never been able to forget it began to come there, their hearts open to the idea of being detached from worldly things so as to be free to ascend to the stars. Nicola da Pepoli had made a first donation of a site to the friars. A second was made by Maestro Bondi, chaplain of the bishop of Bologna.[38] And when this place was not large enough for all the friars who came in constantly increasing numbers, the most famous professor of Bologna, the great Accursius, who was called the Glossator, gave the friars a house he owned on the outskirts of the city, Villa Riccardina.[39] He, and after him, Odofredo [Denari, thirteenth century jurist and glossator], Marsilius of Padua [physician, lawyer, and philosopher, whose works on church reform and liberty of conscience are credited with playing a role in England's breach with Rome], and other great jurists chose to be buried in the church of San Francesco.

---

e. In *24 Generals* (AF 3:132), there is this letter written by Saint Francis to Saint Anthony of Padua: "To Brother Anthony, my bishop, Brother Francis sends greetings.

"It is agreeable to me that you should teach the friars sacred theology, so long as they do not extinguish the spirit of prayer and devotion over this study, as is contained in the Rule. Farewell." This letter generally has been held authentic. See Felder, *Storia degli studi scientifici,* pp. 143ff.

[Irnerius, a jurist of the late eleventh and early twelfth centuries, was famous for glosses of Roman law; it was under Irnerius that the University of Bologna acquired prestige as a school for the teaching of Roman law. He is sometimes described as a founder of the University of Bologna, but the school certainly existed before his lifetime. See Treccani, s.v. "Irnerio," and "Glossa e glossatori."—Trans.]

Perfect Joy · 453

And in a way, this, too, was a confirmation of the teachings of the Poverello. An hour of tribulation will come, he said, when useless books are thrown out the window and forgotten.[40]

Giving Up the Order

After he left Bologna, Francis went to Florence, where he visited the monastery that a woman of the Ubaldini family had opened at Monticelli. At his direction, a few months later Agnes, Clare's sister, was transferred there and assumed the office of abbess.

On his way back he sent to the sisters at San Damiano a message that reflected his constant anxiety and melancholy thought: "I, little Brother Francis, wish to live according to the life and poverty of our most high Lord Jesus Christ and his most holy Mother and to persevere in this to the last. And I beseech you, my Ladies, and I exhort you to live always in this most holy life and poverty. Keep close watch over yourselves so that you never abandon it through the teaching or advice of anyone."[41]

He went on then to Orvieto, where Honorius and his court were staying. This was the occasion on which in the presence of the pope and the cardinals, among whom was Ugolino, he preached that memorable sermon in which words could not contain the wave of immense happiness that overwhelmed him, and he ended with a dance of Love.[f]

Those who see in Ugolino an enemy of Franciscanism should reread the pages that Thomas of Celano wrote about him: "The blessed father Francis had chosen him, with the consent and will of the lord Pope Honorius, to be father and lord over the whole religion and order of his brothers inasmuch as blessed poverty was very pleasing to him and holy simplicity was held in great reverence by him. This lord conformed himself to the ways of the brothers, and in his desire for sanctity he was simple with the simple, humble with the humble, poor with the poor. He was a brother among the brothers, the least among the lesser brothers; and he strove to conduct himself in his life and manners, in so far as it was permissible for him, as though he were one of the brothers. He was solicitous about planting this holy religion everywhere and the widespread fame of his renowned life greatly enlarged the Order in remote places.

---

f. As indicated in chap. 4, pp. 134–35, of this book, Francis may have been unconsciously re-enacting the traditional dances of the Tripudianti and the custom of dancing in the churches. See *NV* 2:128. In both *1 Cel.*, 73, and *2 Cel*, 25, this incident is said to have taken place in Rome; a note in Giordano, *Chronica*, 4, however, says that Honorius was staying in Orvieto at the time.

"The Lord gave him a learned tongue, with which he confounded adversaries of truth, refuted the enemies of the cross of Christ, brought back to the right way those who had gone astray, made peace with those in discord, and bound together with the bond of charity those who lived in concord. He was a lamp burning and shining in the Church of God and a chosen arrow prepared in a seasonable time. O how often, having put aside his expensive garments and having put on mean ones, and with his feet unshod, he would go about like one of the brothers and ask the terms of peace. This he did solicitously between a man and his neighbour as often as was necessary and between God and man always."[42]

He was so much in accord with Francis's ideas and feelings that at the end of this famous speech, Francis asked of the pope, and was granted, the appointment of Cardinal Ugolino as the official protector of the order. To him Honorius "graciously made over his own authority over the order of the brothers."[43]

Francis also asked that the privileges wished upon the Poor Clares be withdrawn and that the petition of Brother Giovanni della Cappella be turned down.[44]

But this struggle against internal intrigue, for which it had been necessary to turn to external authority and which could not help having an adverse effect on even the greatest love, was repugnant to Francis. [He did not wish to wield a club.] He intended, in his humility and his faithfulness to his own concepts, to remain always the *minore,* the least of all, the servant and subject of his brothers. This had been his chosen role even in the first trip to Rome to ask for approbation of the rule, when he had chosen Brother Bernardo to head the expedition.

He used to say that those in the order who aspired to high positions, often without having the necessary qualities for them, did not seem to be true Friars Minor. Even a desire to rise to an office was enough for him to judge them as friars fallen from their vocation, not to mention those who were upset when they were removed from office, thus showing very clearly that in their hearts, it was not the responsibility that was important to them but pride in the position.[45]

One time, near the time of a chapter, he said to the brother who was accompanying him, "I would not seem to myself to be a Friar Minor unless I were in the state I will describe to you. Suppose I, being a prelate among the brothers, should go to the chapter and preach and admonish the brothers, and at the end this should be said against me: 'An unlettered and contemptible person is not suitable for us, therefore, we do not want you to rule over us, because you have no eloquence. You are simple and unlettered.' At length I am thrown out with reproaches and despised by all. I say to you, unless I listen to these words with the same face, with the same joy, with the same purpose of sanctity, I am in no way a Friar Minor."

His concluding remark, expressed beautifully, as usual, in Thomas of Celano's incomparable Latin, was this: *In proelatione casus, in laude praecipitium, in humilitate subditi animae lucrum est.* ("In office is found occasion for a fall. In praise, an occasion for complete destruction. In the humility of being a subject, an occasion for profit for the soul.")[46]

On September 29, the feast of Saint Michael, Francis was back at Porziuncola, where the brothers had assembled for the chapter.

The rapid growth in the numbers of brothers was now making it necessary to organize the order. Therefore, Honorius issued a brief in Orvieto on September 22, directed to all "priors" of the brothers (in Franciscan terms, the guardians), to be read at that chapter. It established an obligatory novitiate of a year before admission to the order, and prohibited the brothers, once they had made their final profession, to leave it.[47]

Did this necessary transformation, which [turned him into a supervisor] and imposed precise and arduous duties of administration and exacted a heavy sacrifice of time for meditation, lead Francis to take the unexpected step of giving up leadership of the order?

Thomas of Celano has preserved for us a vivid description of this moving event:[48]

Francis said, "'From now on I am dead to you. But see, here is Brother Pietro di Catanio, whom I and all of you shall obey.' And bowing before him, he promised him obedience and reverence. The brothers, therefore, wept . . . when they saw themselves, in a certain way, to be deprived of such a father. But Francis, rising and with his hands joined and his eyes raised to heaven, said: 'Lord, I commend to you the family that you heretofore have entrusted to me. But now, because of my infirmities, as you know, most sweet Lord, I am unable to care for it and so I entrust it to the ministers. Let them be obliged to render an account before you, Lord, on judgement day, if any brother of them perishes because of their negligence, or example, or harsh correction.'"

In truth, the trip to the Mideast and the hardships of the battlefield had caused an appreciable worsening of his physical condition, already damaged by his illness in the Perugia prison. And it was also true that he had suffered from the inevitable contradictions between having to exercise authority as head of the order and his own need to make himself the least of all.

Later, when he was lying sick and near death in the house of the bishop of Assisi, a brother reproved him for his lack of firmness toward those who had not scrupulously observed the rule. He replied that it had been easy with word and example to obtain perfect obedience from the brothers when there were but a few, but that when the friars, "through lukewarmness and lack of zeal," began turning aside from "the right and sure way by which they had once walked," he had not been "willing to become an executioner, and use punishment and flogging like some podestà."[49]

And in that same chapter he asked Pietro di Catanio to assign to him a special guardian whom he would "cherish as his superior," and he promised to obey him devoutly.

In Praise of Humility

He always thanked God for his desire to live under the direction of another, a trait so marked in him. He considered it a great gift.

"I would obey a novice of one hour, if he were given to me as my guardian," he used to say, "as carefully as I would obey the oldest and most discreet person." And he added that in his opinion, the more contemptible was the one who gave orders, so much the greater was the one who obeyed in humility.[50]

Brother Thomas, the poet who always longed for Francis, says about his humility:

To hear him talk, there was no sinner greater than he. Everything that made others venerate him as a model of holiness in his opinion had no importance whatsoever and must not be thought important; rather, he accused himself of the most terrible shortcomings. "He was humble in dress, more humble in conviction, most humble in reputation. This prince of God was not known as anyone's superior except by this brightest jewel alone, namely, that among the lesser he was the least. This virtue, this title, this mark indicated that he was the minister general. All lofty speaking was absent from his mouth, all pomp from his gestures, all ostentation from his actions.

"In many things he had learned his opinion from a revelation; yet, conferring about it, he would set the opinions of others ahead of his own. He considered the advice of his companions safer, and the view of another seemed better than his own. . . . He preferred to hear blame spoken of himself rather than praise, for the former would lead one to amend his life, the latter to a fall." He summed this up in a lovely sentence, "Humility is the guardian and ornament of all virtues."[51]

Francis possessed this virtue in such abundance that it was easy for him "to show mildness to all men, adapting himself usefully to the behaviour of all. The more holy amongst the holy, among sinners he was as one of them."[52]

So no praise ever pleased him more than that given him by one of his dearest companions, Brother Masseo. At the time they were both living at Porziuncola. One day Francis was returning from the woods, where he had been in prayer, when he met Brother Masseo, who had been waiting for him, as he wanted to find out how humble he was.

Masseo said brusquely to Francis, "Why after you? Why after you? Why after you?"

Surprised, Francis replied, "What do you mean, Brother Masseo?"

"I mean," said Brother Masseo, "why does all the world seem to be running after you, and everyone seem to want to see you and hear you and obey you? You are not a handsome man. You do not have great learning or wisdom. You are not a nobleman. So why is all the world running after you?"

Francis rejoiced greatly on hearing this, and he raised his face toward heaven and stood for a long time. Then he knelt and gave thanks to God, and "in great fervour of spirit," he turned to Masseo and said, "You want to know why after me? You want to know why after me? You really want to know why everyone is running after me? I have this from the all-holy eyes of God that see the good and the evil everywhere. For those blessed and all-holy eyes have not seen among sinners anyone more vile or insufficient than I am. And so in order to do that wonderful work which He intends to do, He did not find on earth a viler creature, and therefore he chose me, for God has chosen the foolish things of the world to put to shame the wise, and . . . the base things of the world and the despised, to bring to naught the noble and great and strong, so that all excellence in virtue may be from God and not from the creature."[53]

This episode is a prelude to the song that will truly summarize and express the glory of Franciscanism: the Canticle of Brother Sun. The fundamental theme, *maestoso,* already appears here, ready to be developed and explained in the full symphony in which all created things show forth the glory of God.

Francis feared very much that the very excellence of his brothers' lives would make them boastful and full of pride.

At a time he was living in a solitary place with his first companions, among whom was the same Brother Masseo, he put him to a test by appointing him doorkeeper, collector of alms, and cook. Brother Masseo readily obeyed, but the other brothers were disturbed over the fact that a man so gifted as he should have to do all the burdensome work in the place. Francis praised them for their concern and then divided up the duties among all. But first he preached holy humility to them, teaching them that the greater the gifts and graces given to us by God, the greater is our obligation to become more humble, because without humility, [no one can know God,] no virtue is acceptable to God.[54]

At another time when Francis was preaching in Terni, the bishop of the city said to the people, "In this latest hour God has glorified his church in this poor and despised, simple and unlettered man." Francis, hearing these words, fell at his feet, saying, "In truth, lord bishop, you have done me a great favour, because you render to each his own, attributing to God the praise, to me the worthlessness."[55]

The Friar Minor was supposed to run from every form of honour. Taking pleasure in doing good, accepting and enjoying praise from others, even the attempt to achieve holiness, were considered grave dangers, especially because these things are so insidious that it is not easy to guard against them. As when Francis, going through Assisi, was stopped by a poor old woman asking alms of him for the love of God. Having nothing but his mantle, he took that from his shoulders and gave it to her. And because he seemed to feel an inner joy because of this charitable gesture, he immediately confessed before all that he was guilty of vainglory.[56]

Very often, he used to say, we think we do something because of love, but egotism is our true motive. A good appearance and the approval of the world are enough for us. Easily we adapt ourselves to our own lack of goodness. "We cannot bear not to seem good, not to be thought good. And thus we live completely amid the praise of men, because we are nothing but men."[57]

A Winter Day on the Assisi Piazza

After the chapter of September 29, 1220, Francis stayed at Porziuncola.

Autumn was slowly giving way to winter, and already all the forest was mantled in a funereal sheet of grey fog. Francis grew steadily sicker.[g] His fever, which rose rapidly in the early evening hours,[h]

---

g. It seems clear that this illness came in the year suggested here. All the writers tell us that Francis in this period was seriously ill, and indeed some specify *maxima infirmitate*—"a very grave illness." (*Spec. Perf.*, 61; *Per.*, 39.) These texts add that Francis "suffered for a long time from his liver, spleen, and stomach, right up to the time of his death. In addition to that, in the course of the voyage to preach to the Sultan of Babylonia and of Egypt, he had contracted a very serious disease of the eyes caused by fatigue and especially by the excessive heat he had to endure both in going and in returning." (*Per.*, 37; *Spec. Perf.*, 91.)

There is no doubt that it was these illnesses that induced him to turn the governing of the order over to Pietro di Catanio. ("Because of my infirmities which Thou knowest, sweetest

induced confused visions in which he saw his brothers scattered throughout the world, constantly encountering wicked people, exposed to dangers of every sort. He would have liked to be near all of them, to share with them their hunger, thirst, abuse. Little by little his hovel would fill with shadows. Beyond the opening in the wall, the skeleton trees swam in the dripping sea of fog like phantoms. Inside, there was a great silence. Even Brother Leo, who sat beside the poor bed of the sick man, finally dozed off. In such a half-asleep, half-awake state, Brother Leo saw a great river and many friars, bearing heavy loads, going into its turbulent waters. At a certain point, they lost the struggle against the violent current because of their heavy loads and were swept away and drowned. Brother Leo grieved for them.

Then other brothers arrived carrying no load or burden of any kind. And they went into the river and crossed over without any trouble at all.

Brother Leo awoke with a start. The room had grown dark but he felt Francis's eyes upon him. Sensing that Leo had had a vision, he asked him what he had seen. And after he had told him, Francis said, "What you have seen is true. The great river is this world, and to pass through it, the brothers must get rid of all carnal things. But those who went across without danger are the friars who are content following Christ naked on the cross. And every day they joyfully take up the burden of the cross and the light yoke of his holy obedience. And thus they easily pass from the life of this world to eternal life."[58]

His illness was long and painful. To combat the extreme weakness to which he was reduced, Francis was induced by those who cared for him to take a little broth and meat. But having done so, he was afraid he had been guilty of hypocrisy.

Earlier in this winter, which had been very cold, the guardian Pietro di Catanio had assigned to him noticed that his emaciated body was covered only with a badly mended habit and had ordered him to sew a piece of fox fur on the inside of it. He obeyed, but only on

---

Lord, I now entrust it to the Ministers, for I no longer have the strength to care for it." *Spec. Perf.*, 39.) The opinion that Francis's resignation took place as early as 1210 or 1212, as Golubovich has suggested (*Biblioteca*, 1:122) cannot be sustained. It cannot have happened earlier than 1220, after Francis's return from the east; it cannot have taken place later, since Pietro di Catanio died March 10, 1221.

Since the episode that took place on the piazza in Assisi is related to this serious illness that afflicted Francis during the winter, and since it also involved Pietro di Catanio, who had already been chosen by Francis as minister general (*Per.*, 39; *Spec. Perf.*, 61), it is certain that it happened during the winter of 1220–1221.

h. We are told that Francis suffered from quartan fever in *Per.*, 39; *Spec. Perf.*, 61; and *Leg. Maior*, VI, 2—translated simply as "feverish" in *Omnibus*, p. 672.

condition that another piece of fur be stitched also to the outside of his habit (so as not to hide this "pampering" of the body).[59]

And so, scarcely was he on his feet again after this illness, and still suffering from fever, when he went up to Assisi with Pietro di Catanio and many other brothers and called the people together in the piazza.[60] The weather was still very cold; it was one of those winter days in Assisi when the piazza is swept by the cutting north wind from snowy Subasio.[61] But the news of Francis's summons were enough to bring people out to listen to him, despite the frosty cold. He talked then about contempt for worldly things and the consolations of pure love, then suddenly breaking off his sermon in the middle, he asked everyone to wait for him. He went up the street that leads to the cathedral of San Rufino, and there he went down into the crypt.[62]

The pagan sarcophagus in which Saint Rufinus had lain was still there, still bearing its enchanting story about nymphs and cupids.[63] But its sensuality was a weak fire compared to this burning spirit. By now, according to Brother Thomas, "the warmth of his spirit had already so spiritualized his body, that with his soul thirsting after God, his most holy flesh also thirsted, O how many ways."[64]

Francis appeared to be consumed by this sort of rapture at that moment, when he turned to Pietro and asked him if, through obedience, he would do whatever he asked him to do.

Pietro replied, "I can and ought not to desire anything but your wish in what concerns both of us."

What Francis wanted was that Pietro tie a cord around his neck and lead him before the people, all the while shouting out like a herald, "Behold the glutton who has grown fat on the meat of chickens, which he ate without your knowing about it."[i]

Moaning, Pietro carried out the harsh order, and his distraught companions, who followed him down the short sloping street, were

---

i. *1 Cel.*, 52. Thomas omits the scene on the piazza and tells how Francis, "when he had come to the gate of the city, . . . commanded a certain brother who was with him to tie a rope about his neck and to drag him in this way like a robber through the entire city and to shout in the voice of a herald, saying, 'Behold the glutton . . . '" Also *Leg. Vers.* (*AF* 10:451) says that the brother who was leading the saint by a rope through the city streets had to call out like a public crier, "Behold, O citizens, a voracious parasite, an ill-humoured hypocrite, who praises fasting in your presence but really hates it, and who loads his greedy belly with fat chickens."

It is probable that this was done while Francis and his companion were going down the sloping street from San Rufino to the piazza.

In the time of Saint Francis, forgers and those who made false statements were led about the city while mockery and opprobrium of every sort was heaped upon them; and then they were exposed on the pillory. Fines were also levied against those who gave false testimony or falsified public documents; if they did not pay promptly, their right hands were amputated. See *NV* 3:220.

also anguished. And in that far-off winter day, men and women ran to the doors and windows of the dark houses that still stand along the ancient street to look out at Francis led by Pietro, who cried out in a broken voice, "Run, people, come and see the greedy scrounger, the hypocrite, who preaches fasting to your face and behind your backs gulps down fat chickens!"

When they got to the crowded piazza, Francis got up on the stone where criminals were exposed to public ignominy,[j] and turning to the people, he said, "You think I am a holy man, as do those who, on the basis of my example, leave the world and enter the order and lead the life of the brothers. Well, I confess to God and to you that during my illness I ate meat and some stew."

Many who heard him wept, seeing him so exposed in the cold, when he was not yet over his fever. Others thought this fresh proof of his saintliness. And many struck their breasts, conscience-stricken, and said, "This holy man accuses himself with deep humility of having taken care of his health when he so clearly needed it. We who know his life so well, we know that it is because of his excessive abstinence and austerity since his conversion that we see him live in a body that is almost dead. What shall we do, wretches that we are, we who live according to the pleasure and desires of the flesh?"

And among those who carried on like this were people who had been bragging of their wicked deeds, murderers whose lives had been spent in killing, bullies guilty of every kind of high-handed behaviour.

Reports of this episode close with a favourite theme of the early biographers: "It is a lesson in true humility and shows the true follower of Christ that he is bound to disregard all earthly praise and

---

j. Only in *Leg. Maior* do we read of Francis's getting up on "the stone where criminals were punished." What was this punishment? From the text, and especially from Bonaventure's use of the verb *collocari,* which indicates a continuing state, it seems clear that he was speaking of the penalty, so frequent in the Middle Ages, of the pillory. It is thus clear that Francis's intention was to expose himself to public scorn as one who made false statements, in the method prescribed by the laws of the city. And because he was thin and weak, the bitter cold would have been an additional punishment.

Thus this is a living cameo of the life of that time, and an encounter between Francis and his people on the site of the old forum, the place in the city so full of memories and of historical associations going back to the time of Saint Rufinus, and before.

[One cannot help wondering, too, about the human side of all this: Were Francis's mother and father still alive? They lived nearby; did they see this harrowing event? What were Francis's thoughts about that?]

While this book was being completed (April 1959), excavations brought to light again some of the Roman columns that once encircled the old forum, sections of the Roman city walls, pieces of the ancient stairways. The portico of the Palazzo dei Priori of the early fourteenth century stands on the Roman paving that was uncovered, freed today from the rubble that used to surround it. The Palazzo dei Priori itself was once a palatial house; it existed in Francis's lifetime. On September 12, 1317, the city bought it from its private owner, Vagnozzo, and converted it into its seat of government. See *NV* 3:21.

subdue the displays of bloated pride while renouncing all lying pretence."[65]

With February the first timid sun of spring returned. It was the season in which the desire to carry on his apostolate, always so alive in Francis, seemed to make him unfurl his wings, like swallows that at dawn are eager to fly to the sun.[k] And so the brothers saw him leave again, on foot as always, free and light, toward a distant destination. But it is recorded that among those who came to salute him in that hour was one who would not see him again on this earth. On March 10, 1221, Pietro di Catanio died at Porziuncola. His companions buried him there, in the place that by now held so many memories and hopes. Here a simple memorial stone on the outside of the chapel records the holiness of this man who set out to base his life on earthly wisdom and soon discovered the frailty of that goal, the man who was the first among the heroes of the great drama to ascend to the throne of God.[1]

The Rule of 1221: Take Nothing for the Journey

Despite the fact that with Francis's return from the east, calm had settled over the order, he felt troubled over all that had happened. It was enough to make him think of his death and what would happen then. Would the building, constructed with so much fervour, be threatened by ruin? Would chronic complainers, quibblers, those who distorted the rule, find grounds for changing it? Above all, he was disturbed at the thought that someone might seek to mitigate the principle of absolute poverty and arguments and dissensions arise about it.

One day one of his brothers asked him what had been his intention in basing the rule on the Gospel precept: "Take nothing for the journey."

Francis remained for a moment absorbed and thoughtful before replying. And he saw again that Mass in the empty church on the Assisi piazza, when God had revealed to him the way to follow. No other word had been said; everything seemed so clear and simple.

---

k. Thomas of Celano records that Francis's "willing spirit, that devoted spirit, that fervent spirit that dwelt within him" enabled him to make a circuit of four or five *castelli,* and often whole cities, in a single day; and "edifying his hearers not less by his example than by his word, he made a tongue out of his whole body." *1 Cel.,* 97.

l. The memorial stone mentioned here is on the outside wall of the Porziuncola chapel. It bears in rude lettering this inscription: ANNO D.NI MCCXXI VI ID. MARTII CORPUS FR. P. CATANII QUI HIC REQUIESCIT MIGRAVIT AD DOMINUM ANIMAM CUIUS BENEDICAT DOMINUS. AMEN. ("In the year of our Lord 1221, six days before the ides of March, Frate Pietro Catanio who rests here returned to the Lord. May the Lord bless his soul. Amen.")

Now, to form his brothers into perfect lovers, he had to make long speeches, argue, split hairs.

Finally he said, "Those words mean that the friars should possess nothing but a habit, with a cord and an undergarment. And anyone compelled by necessity may wear sandals."[66]

He was often terrified by the thought that when he was gone, even this basic concept, so precisely stated, could be deformed and diminished, at the mercy of any theorizer. Therefore he decided to put into writing a true and proper rule, based on the old admonitions and requirements, but amplified, explained, annotated, divided into chapters, validated with citations of sacred texts, brought up to date with the new precepts and regulations that had in the meantime been enacted.

The rule that he was to write as a result of this decision is known as the Rule of 1221 or the *regula non bullata* (because it was never submitted to the pope for approval). It is none other than a further development of the Rule of 1209, the primitive nucleus still unchanged. [Though that does not survive,] this is made plain by the first words of it: "This is the life Brother Francis asked to be permitted him and approved by the lord Pope Innocent. The Pope granted his request and approved the Rule for him and for his friars, present and to come."[67]

Francis needed someone versed in the Sacred Scriptures and he thought of the new brother that he had brought from the east, Brother Cesario.[68] He was a native of Speyer, where he had studied theology as a deacon under a famous preacher of the Crusade, Maestro Corrado. Before he entered the order, Cesario had edified everyone by the power of his oratory and the austerity of his life. And he was so eloquent that one day, in preaching contempt for worldly things, he had induced some of the women of Speyer to renounce the luxury of jewels and ornaments. Their husbands were outraged, accused Cesario of heresy, and asked that he be condemned to the stake. With difficulty Maestro Corrado saved him. Afterwards he followed the Crusaders to Syria. There he became acquainted with Brother Elias and, at his urging, became a Friar Minor.[69]

It was he, then, whom his contemporaries called "a man of great doctrine and of excellent morals," who collaborated with Francis in the compilation of the Rule of 1221.

One can imagine what these two must have said to one another in the quiet of the solitary hermitages during that spring of rebirth when Francis's great concept was brought to a second splendid flowering, revitalized by the trials it had undergone. Never so much as now, in this time of struggle, had Francis felt so greatly the love that had made him, when he was still a young man, rush off to do battle for his "dearest lady."

Thomas of Celano's beautiful imagery, which Dante was to borrow, captures this feeling:

" . . . he longed for poverty with all his heart. Looking upon poverty as especially dear to the Son of God, though it was spurned throughout the whole world, he sought to espouse it in perpetual charity. Therefore, after he had become a lover of her beauty, he not only left his father and mother, but even put aside all things, that he might cling to her more closely as his spouse and that they might be two in the spirit. Therefore he gathered her to himself with chaste embraces and not even for an hour did he allow himself not to be her husband."[70]

And so like a solemn vow are the first words of this new rule, drawn not from man's words but from Sacred Scripture: "The Rule and life of the friars is to live in obedience, in chastity, and without property, following the teaching and the footsteps of our Lord Jesus Christ who says, 'If thou wilt be perfect, go, sell what thou hast, and give to the poor, and thou shalt have treasure in heaven; and come, follow me.' "

And it continues: "Elsewhere he says, 'If anyone comes to me and does not hate his father and mother, and wife and children, and brothers and sisters, yes, and even his own life, he cannot be my disciple.' "[71]

Now, after this new consecration, which took him back to the headlong dedication of his early youth, he could look back with peaceful tranquillity at the road he had travelled. What lack of comprehension there had been! What fear and discouragements! He remembered the novice at Porziuncola who asked repeatedly for permission to own a psalter. He had sought to dissuade him: "Once you have a psalter, you will want a breviary. And when you have a breviary, you will sit in a high chair like a great prelate, and say to your brother, 'Bring me my breviary!' " The novice seemed resigned, but after a time he repeated his request. Francis, who dodged arguments, finally told him to see the minister general and let him decide the matter. He immediately regretted his words, and calling the novice, he said, "Come back and show me the place where I told you to do as your minister directs about the psalter." And when the other, astonished, had done so, he knelt down before the novice and said, "*Mea culpa,* brother, *mea culpa.* For whoever wishes to be a Friar Minor should possess nothing but a habit with a cord and undergarment, as the rule allows him."[72]

Another time, again at Porziuncola, he forbade Pietro di Catanio, who was worried about the great number of friars who were coming to visit and had nowhere to say the Office, to complete the building of a small house. It would be, said Francis, a bad example for the rest of the order.[73] But some brothers were going about criticizing the whole idea of poverty and making great plans to reform the rule.[74] Using the growth of the order as an excuse, many urged that it was necessary to own property in common.[75]

And while he was re-writing the rule, several friars were sent to him to cite somebody else's authority or other rules of ancient vintage. This, in fact, had happened during the preceding winter, when he had been lying ill at Porziuncola. They had caused him such anguish that, ill as he was, he raised himself in bed and passionately cried out, "Who are these who have torn my order and my friars out of my hands? If I come to the general chapter, I will make my intention clear!"[76]

His intention, clear and immutable, appeared now in the rule that he and Brother Cesario were working out. From the very first article, the rule is a resolute affirmation of the basis of the order: Poverty.

The first article puts forward the thought that it is preoccupation with worldly goods that creates a barrier between people and love, people and goodness of life. Riches [it implies] are at the root of selfishness, depravity, and degradation. They can give rise to filthy behaviour, betrayals, and repudiations—all the things that degrade human dignity, throw brother against brother, bring broken hearts and suffering. Therefore, each and every postulant, down to the very last, is to follow the example of the first Friar Minor, who himself following the example of Jesus Christ, stripped himself of all possessions.

The stage was thus set for the second article, concerned with the reception and the clothing of men who asked to join the order. Ministers are to explain clearly the requirements: "The minister, for his part, should receive him kindly and encourage him and tell him all about our way of life. When that has been done, the candidate should sell all his possessions and give the money to the poor."

Recognizing that impediments might exist for some friars, however, the article also states, "If anyone who seeks admission to the Order cannot dispose of his property without hindrance, although he is spiritually minded to do so, he should leave it all behind him, and that is enough."[77] In other words, the necessary thing, Francis taught, is not so much an act of renunciation performed before all the world, but the renunciation each must make within his own soul.

It happened in the Marches of Ancona that a man who had asked to join the order thought he could get out of this inflexible obligation of the rule by giving all his goods to his relatives rather than to the poor. When he came back and boasted of his generous liberality, Saint Francis laughed at him and said, "Go on your way, Brother Fly, for you have not yet left your home and your relatives. You gave your goods to your relatives and defrauded the poor. You are not worthy to be numbered among the holy poor. You have begun with the flesh, you have laid an unsound foundation on which to build a spiritual structure." And so, Thomas of Celano tells us, "That carnal man returned to his own and got back his goods which he did not want to give to the poor and for that reason he abandoned his virtuous purpose."[78]

The uniform of the Knights of Lady Poverty was to be always the one Francis had donned after his dramatic audience before the bishop of Assisi: a sackcloth habit.

When the habits wore out, according to the rule, "[The friars] can patch them with pieces of sackcloth and other material, with God's blessing."

Francis thought again of the insulting remarks made to him and to his first companions. And he added, "And even though people may call them hypocrites, the friars should never cease doing good. They should avoid expensive clothes in this world in order that they may have something to wear in the kingdom of heaven."[79]

The Rule of 1221: The Love of Money Is . . .

But the principle most in need of being nailed down was repugnance for the thing that stood for man's worst characteristics, the instrument of evil: money. Francis described it as worse than mud and the friars were to consider it dung.

On a certain day at Porziuncola, which to Francis and his companions was Lady Poverty's own fortress, a devout man came in to pray. When he left, he put some money beside the cross as an offering. When he had gone, one of the brothers picked it up [thereby violating the rule against touching money] and threw it at the window. His act was noticed; and the brother, being found out, rushed to Saint Francis, threw himself on the ground, and asked pardon. The punishment meted out by Francis was that "the friar was to lift the money from the window sill with his mouth and to place it with his mouth on the asses' dung outside the walls of the place."[80]

A number of such occurrences are reported by the early biographers stressing the relationship of evil and money, as when one day two friars, walking along the street, saw a coin on the road. One of them wanted to pick it up and offer it to the lepers. Says Thomas of Celano: "His companion forbade him, lest he be deceived by false piety, and quoted to the rash brother the words of the rule from which it is very clear that a coin that is found is to be trampled on as though it were dust. But he hardened his mind against the admonitions, for by custom, he was always a stiff-necked person. He spurned the rule, bent down and took the coin. But he did not escape divine judgement. Immediately he lost his speech and though he ground his teeth, he could not speak."[81]

Another story instructs how in money evil hides, like a snake. Francis and one of his companions, walking along a road in Apulia, near Bari, found a money belt. His companion urged Francis to take it and give the money to the poor. Francis refused, and called the whole business a trick of the devil. They went on their way, but since the companion continued to argue Francis finally consented to turn back. On the way he called a young man, who was sitting on a well, to come along with them as a witness. When they reached the money belt, they saw that it was filled with money. Francis forbade any of them to touch it until he had retired for a short distance and prayed. Strangely, the brother did not want to pick it up when Francis returned and ordered him to do so, and he would not do so until ordered in the name of obedience. And when he took the purse in his hands, "behold, a not very small serpent jumped out of the purse."

It was then that Francis gave his well-known definition of money, as reported by Brother Thomas: "Money to God's servants, Brother, is nothing but a devil and a poisonous snake."[82]

Chapter 8 of the rule, therefore, lays down the proper attitude of the friar toward money: " . . . And so all the friars, no matter where they are or where they go, are forbidden to take or accept money in any way or under any form, or have it accepted for them, for clothing or books, or as wages, or in any other necessity, except to provide for the urgent needs of those who are ill. We should have no more use or regard for money in any of its forms than for dust. Those who think it is worth more or who are greedy for it, expose themselves to the danger of being deceived by the devil. We have left everything we had behind us. We must be very careful now not to lose the kingdom of heaven for so little. If ever we find money somewhere, we should think no more of it than of the dust we trample under our feet, for it is vanity of vanities, and all vanity (Eccles. 1:2).

"If any of the friars collects or keeps money, except for the needs of the sick, the others must regard him as a fraud and a thief and a robber and a traitor, who keeps a purse[m] unless he is sincerely sorry. The friars are absolutely forbidden to take money as alms, or have it accepted for them; so too they cannot ask for it themselves, or have others ask for it, for their houses or dwelling places. It is also forbidden to accompany anyone who is collecting money for their houses.

"The friars are free to engage in any other activity which is not contrary to our Rule, with God's blessing. But if there are lepers in urgent need, the friars may beg alms for them, only they must be on their guard against money. So too, they should not undertake long journeys for mere temporal reasons."[83]

The materialistic spirit, which invites corruption, was the dangerous river of Brother Leo's dream. And to cross it is indeed necessary to jettison these heavy burdens.

No anxiety, greed, or vanity, therefore, is to be a bar to the friars on their journey. They are to take as their own the counsel of the Apostle, "Having food and sufficient clothing, with these let us be content."[84]

Cardinal Ugolino's Banquet

Friars, also according to the rule, have to support themselves with work or, that failing, depend on the compassion of their fellow men. In other words, beg alms.

"(Friars) should be glad to live among social outcasts, among the poor and helpless, the sick and the lepers, and those who beg by the wayside. If they are in want, they should not be ashamed to beg alms, remembering that our Lord Jesus Christ, the Son of the living, all-powerful God, set his face like a very hard rock (Is. 50:7) and was not ashamed. He was poor and he had no home of his own and he lived on alms, he and the Blessed Virgin and his disciples.

"If people insult them and refuse to give them alms, they should thank God for it, because they will be honoured before the judgement-seat of our Lord Jesus Christ for these insults. The shame will be imputed to those who cause it, not to those who suffer it. Alms are an inheritance and a right which is due to the poor because our Lord Jesus Christ acquired this inheritance for us."[85]

The business of begging alms from door to door must have been very hard for the new knights, since so many pages of the early biographers are devoted to Francis's encouragements and admonitions on this difficult part of the rule. In the beginning, Francis, following his innate generous impulse to bear the suffering and struggles

---

m. "A traitor, who keeps a purse"—i.e., Judas.

for everyone and take on the hardest jobs himself, would go out alone to beg alms.[86] But later he had asked everyone to take part and not draw back because of shyness. Like a captain who watches a soldier new to combat tremble with fear at the beginning of battle and yet remain firm and undaunted so as not to disgrace himself by cowardice, Francis was moved by the blush that "mounts the modest forehead" and he praised those who did not allow themselves "to be confused by shame."[87] One day he saw one of the friars who had been collecting alms in the city break forth in song and in praises of God as he was coming down the road from Assisi to Porziuncola. It made him so happy that he ran out to meet him, kissed his shoulder, and took the sack from him to carry himself. "Blessed be my brother," he said, "who goes our readily, begs humbly, and returns rejoicing."[88]

These were the hours in which his love for his bride had risen joyously from an overflowing heart. "If (my brothers) embrace my Lady Poverty," he said, "the world will provide for them, because they have been given to the world unto its salvation."[89] Brother Thomas writes, "Therefore, bound to the Lady Poverty by an indissoluble bond, he looked for her dowry not in the present life but in the future."[90]

Francis, "so that he might not offend even once that holy spouse," had followed the practice, when he was invited to dine by rich lords, of first going to the houses of neighbours and begging some scraps of bread so as to go to table "enriched by want." Asked why he did this, he would say, "It is poverty that makes us heirs and kings of the kingdom of heaven, not your false riches."[91]

One evening when he was a guest of Cardinal Ugolino, he went out before dinner and begged for some scraps of black bread. When he returned, he placed them on the bishop's table. "When the bishop saw this," according to Brother Thomas, "he was somewhat ashamed, above all because of the newly invited guests. The father, however, with a joyous countenance distributed the alms he had received to the knights and the chaplains gathered about the table."

Some of them ate them, and others kept them "out of reverence," the account continues. But after dinner was over, the bishop took Francis aside and gently reproved him. "My Brother," he said, "why did you bring shame on me in the house that is yours and your brothers' by going out for alms?"

And Francis said to the bishop, "Rather I have shown you honour, because I have honoured a greater lord. For the Lord is well pleased with poverty, and above all with poverty that is voluntary. I then deem it a royal dignity and a mark of nobility to follow the Lord who, being rich, became poor for us."

And the bishop said to the saint, "Son, do what seems good in your eyes, for the Lord is with you."[92]

Rule of 1221: Franciscan Poverty

The results of Francis's insistence on poverty can be readily seen. The Holy Doctor [Saint Bonaventure] admirably describes the beauty and strength of their spiritual pilgrimage:

"Poverty, which was all they had to meet their expenses, made them ready to undertake any task, while giving them strength for any kind of toil and leaving them free to travel without difficulty. They possessed nothing that belonged to this world. They loved nothing, and so they feared to lose nothing. They were free from care, with no anxiety to disturb them or worry to distract them. Their hearts were at peace as they lived from day to day, looking forward to the morrow without a thought as to where they would find shelter for the night."[93]

And indeed these knights errant were marked by peace and happiness and loving kindness, as they roamed from place to place for the love of their Lady, their "lover of a far-away land."

One of the loveliest chapters of *Little Flowers* tells of a banquet in her honour. They had reached a village, Brother Francis and Brother Masseo. As they were quite hungry, they went begging for bread, according to the rule, Brother Francis along one street, Brother Masseo along another. [The account continues:] "But because St. Francis was a very small and insignificant looking man, and therefore was considered a common little pauper by nearly all who did not know him . . . he received nothing but a few mouthfuls of food and some small pieces of dry bread. But to Brother Masseo, because he was a tall handsome man, people gave plenty of good large pieces and some whole loaves.

"When they finished begging, the two came together to eat somewhere outside the village. They found nothing but the dry ground to put their begged food on, because that region was quite bare of stones. However, with God's help, they came to a spring, and beside it there was a fine broad stone, which made them very happy. And each of them placed on the stone all the pieces of bread he had acquired. And when St. Francis saw that Brother Masseo's pieces were more numerous and better and bigger than his, he was filled with intense joy because of his longing for poverty, and he said: 'Oh, Brother Masseo, we do not deserve such a great treasure as this!' And he repeated those words several times, raising his voice each time.

"Brother Masseo replied: 'Dear Father, how can this be called a treasure when there is such poverty and such a lack of things that are necessary? For here we have no cloth, no knife, no dish, no bowl, no house, no table, no waiter, no one to serve.'

"St. Francis answered: 'That is what I consider a great treasure— where nothing has been prepared by human labour. But everything here has been supplied by Divine Providence, as is evident in the begged bread, the fine stone table, and the clear spring. Therefore I want us to pray to God that He may make us love with all our hearts the very noble treasure of holy poverty, which has God as provider.' "[94]

At times Francis spoke about the nature of that treasure, the same one he had searched for and praised while still a young man. It lay in poverty of houses and furnishings, he said. Nothing on the table, nothing in the utensils used, should bring back memories of the world. "Everything," he said, "should show forth our state as pilgrims, everything speak our exile."[95]

It was also in poverty of bedding and beds—a few half-torn rags over some straw at best. During the chapter of 1219, Cardinal Ugolino came to visit the brothers, along with a crowd of knights and clerics. When he saw "how the brothers lay upon the ground" and "that their beds might be taken for the lairs of wild beasts," he wept. "See, here the brothers sleep," he said to all. And he added, "What will become of us, miserable as we are, who [wallow in luxury]?"[96]

Francis also wanted the brothers to live in poor houses, built of wood and not stone, small, humble places. He used to remind his brothers, "The foxes have dens and the birds of the air have nests; but the Son of Man has nowhere to lay his head."[97]

Even books were to be few in number and not elaborate or highly ornamented.[98]

He was jealous of his poverty to the point that when he saw someone poorer than he, he was saddened. One day he met a man so poor he was going about almost naked, and he was humiliated. He unburdened himself to the brother accompanying him: "For my wealth, for my spouse, I chose poverty; but see, poverty shines forth more brightly in this man."[99]

He would never allow others to speak disparagingly about the poor. On an occasion when he was feeling very sorry for a poor and infirm beggar, one of the brothers said "Brother, it is true that this man is poor, but it may also be true that nowhere in the whole province is there a man who is richer in his desires." Grieved by the words, Francis rebuked the brother and ordered him to take off his habit, cast himself at the feet of the poor man, and ask him not only to forgive him but also beg him to pray for him.[100]

Begging alms itself must not be done to accumulate supplies or put something aside. One day Brother Bernardo went begging for alms but brought back nothing. Worried, he cast himself at Francis's feet and confessed that he had eaten what he had received because he was dying of hunger. France embraced him and exclaimed, "Oh, my dearest son, you are more blessed than I. You are a perfect observer of the Gospel, because you have accumulated nothing and nothing have you put aside for tomorrow, and all your thoughts you have been directing to God."[101]

But the joy of giving was to be considered infinitely superior to the joy of receiving. Everyone, no matter how poor, has something in his life to contribute when an appeal for charity is made to him. He remembered the time of great famine in Assisi, when many who had once been in easy circumstances did not have enough to eat, and he remembered how sad he had been at seeing them. Now he no longer has a rich mantle to give, as he had when he rode about the countryside on horseback. But even his poor habit, and those of his companions, the only goods they possess, can do someone some good.

In Celano, he gave a woolen cloth "folded like a mantle" to an old woman to make herself a dress;[102] in the village of Le Celle near Cortona, he made the brothers buy back his own mantle so that the poor man to whom he had just given it might buy another;[103] in Porziuncola, he directed that the brothers' only breviary for saying the morning prayers be given to a poor woman whose two sons had entered the order.[104] These were but some of the occasions in which Francis demonstrated his desire to put no limit or measure on giving or compassion for a fellow human being.

When brothers raised objections to his giving because of practical considerations, as they sometimes did, he settled the matter with this unanswerable argument: everything the Friar Minor had belonged to the poor; and if the poor needed it, it must be given back to them. To do otherwise, he said, would be robbery.[105]

Moreover, even when depriving themselves of necessary things, they were not to dwell on the matter because (and Francis inserted these words in his rule) "everything people leave after them in this world is lost, but for their charity and almsgiving they will receive a reward from God."[106]

He covered other essential matters in this Rule of 1221: the daily prayers required of the friars, the fasts to be observed, the various duties of the ministers, the correction of friars who had erred, the care of sick friars.

Directions are laid down for travelling [they are "to take nothing for the journey" and they are forbidden to travel by horseback, except for rare necessity]. Rules are also given for preaching and working as missionaries in pagan lands.

Friars are told they "must love one another."

They must be Catholics and receive the sacraments of confession and the Eucharist as prescribed.

Those who have a trade are directed to work at it, if it is no obstacle to their spiritual progress and creates no scandal. Friars are permitted to work for and serve others [but are not to be in charge of money or of the cellar, and they may take no positions of authority; they are to be "the least and subordinate to everyone in the house"].

In each section of the rule is an appropriate maxim, thought, exhortation, or recall of previous events. Reading it, one seems to hear the very words exchanged between Francis and Brother Cesario, both caught up in an outpouring of faith and of the fruit of their shared memories.

One can imagine what it must have been like for these two, the apostle of Assisi and the deacon of Speyer. Together they had travelled through remote countries, blazing deserts, contested seas. Together they had prayed before the walls of cities about to die, been stricken by the horrors of battle and the sight of unrestricted slaughter. Together they had seen unbridled ambition, the agony of the innocent, the unbelievable frenzy of looting, the fury and greed when booty is divided.

With good reason, they therefore exhorted the friars to remember the only words that could bring an end to such horrors, the words of Jesus, "Love your enemies, do good to those who hate you."[107] These had been since the earliest days the basis of the new Franciscan movement.

And friars of all places and all times are reminded: "Our friends are those who for no reason cause us trouble and suffering, shame or injury, pain or torture, even martyrdom and death. It is these we must love, and love very much, because for all they do to us we are given eternal life."[108]

It is said that the last touches in the redaction of the rule were completed by Francis in the hermitage of the Carceri,[109] the scene of the anguished struggle of his youth, when he had searched in despair for his dream.

May would have come, and its light would touch the fern-covered avenues in the forest and the flowering cyclamen along the bitter stream. Now he and his Lady Poverty were passionately united, free to come from the shadows . . . free to remember that there his first painful cry had rung out, "Have you seen her whom my soul loves?"[110] There the voices of demons had risen from the stony depths, the demons who always appear when there is love.[111] There the strength of their love had repelled them. As another mystical saint once wrote, "What shall we say is love, if not a fire? And sin, if not a rust? The greater the fire of love in the heart, then, the more that rust is consumed."[112]

Now the poem of his love to Lady Poverty had explained itself in life. It had expanded and risen to supernatural heights: "O faithful spouse, most tender lover!"[113]

To her, of whose beauty "the son of the most high Father had become enamoured,"[114] God had given the grace of knowing the storms of the human heart. And it was she who now dictated to Francis all over again, in the great silence on that solitary hill, the first instructions given [by Jesus] to his disciples: "Do not keep gold, or silver, or money. Take nothing for your journey, neither a bag nor a wallet nor bread nor a staff nor shoes; neither have two tunics. . . . Do not be anxious, saying, 'What shall we eat?' or 'What are we to put on?' "[115]

The time for the general chapter of Pentecost was drawing near. They would have to hurry. The brothers who were coming from far-away lands were already walking toward Assisi for the meeting.

On the day that the last word of the new rule was written, Francis and Brother Cesario added to it their prayer. It was perhaps one of those early mornings drenched in blue, when all the rich tapestries of this palace of Poverty—lush green of trees, vines, grass—hung from sloping rocks and stretched over the worn threshold of the little chapel, while flowers carpeted the grottoes hidden in the foliage.

The two brothers knelt for a long time in the sun. Their prayer was for all human creatures. It named them, one by one: "priests, deacons, subdeacons, acolytes, exorcists, lectors, porters, and all clerics and religious, male or female . . . all children big and small, the poor and the needy, kings and princes, labourers and farmers, servants and masters . . . all virgins and all other women, married or unmarried . . . all lay folk, men and women, infants and adolescents, young and old, the healthy and the sick, the little and the great, all peoples, tribes, families and languages, all nations and all men everywhere, present and to come."

In the name of their order they prayed: "We Friars Minor, servants and worthless as we are, humbly beg and implore everyone to persevere in the true faith and in a life of penance. There is no other way to be saved."[116]

The Chapter of Mats

Francis did not return to Santa Maria degli Angeli until the eve of the chapter.

An unpleasant surprise awaited him. The Assisi commune, after some discussion, had decided to put up a large building a short distance from the little church, to lodge the friars who would be assembling. It had gone up rapidly and it was an imposing structure. Francis was pained by it. Not only was it contrary to the rule but he also feared that friars from the various provinces would use its existence as an excuse to build fine places to live. Porziuncola, after all, was supposed to remain always a model and an example of humbleness for all the order.[117]

So he and other brothers immediately went up to the roof of the new building and began to throw down the tiles, intending to take it apart to its very foundations. The men from the commune, not understanding why he was behaving in such a fashion, firmly stopped him.

Among the cavaliers in the service of the city, there at Santa Maria degli Angeli, was Francis's own brother, Angelo. The city had named him seneschal, and his responsibility was to be the provider for the chapter.[118]

"This house belongs to the commune, and we are representing it," Angelo and his company told Francis. "We forbid you to destroy it."

No one could go against these words; and Francis replied, "If the house is yours, I do not intend to touch it."

But even the commune's large structure would have been too small to house the enormous number of friars who came from everywhere to that chapter. A good five thousand of them arrived.[119] They camped on the plain that surrounded the church, separated into groups according to their provinces.

On May 30, Pentecost Sunday, the bells rang *a festa* in the great sun of early morning, sounding out the joyous notes of a celebration. And the field was transformed into an immense temple, where the brothers prayed, mourned over their sins, and discussed the health of their souls. There were no huts, tables, or benches. For shelter, screens of rush matting had been put up, with other mats on top of them to form roofs, and for this reason this assembly was called the Chapter of Mats.[120]

Crowds came to gape at the unaccustomed spectacle—noblemen, counts, knights, barons, priests, commoners. Even Cardinal Raynerius [bishop of Viterbo] came, accompanied by a great number of bishops, abbots, and other religious; and he marvelled at so much holiness to the point that he could not keep back tears. Turning to his companions, he said, "Truly this is the camp and the army of the knights of God!"[n]

Among the great crowd was an unknown friar who would become Francis's greatest disciple—Anthony of Padua.

Little is known of the discussion that took place in this chapter. Certainly the articles of the new rule would have been presented, discussed, and adopted. Brother Elias was named minister general, filling the vacancy left by the death of Pietro di Catanio. Francis was very weak from his constant agonizing illness. He remained humbly seated on the ground at the feet of Brother Elias; and when he wished to say something, he tugged at Elias's habit. Elias bent to listen to him and then repeated his words to the brothers.[121]

Francis found the strength to preach, however, in the words of *Little Flowers,* "with fervour of spirit (explaining) the word of God and of life to that holy flock . . . (preaching) to them whatever the Holy Spirit made him utter." He said, "My little sons, we have promised great things, but far greater things have been promised to us by God." He added, "Brief is the world's pleasure, but the punishment that follows it lasts forever. Small is the suffering of this life, but the glory of the next life is infinite." He spoke of the love that should exist among the brothers, urged them to have patience in the adversities of the world and temperance in prosperity. He exhorted them to remain in peace and harmony with God, with men, and with their own conscience. And especially he urged them to the love and fervent practice of holy poverty.[122]

When the sermon was ended, the five thousand knights of Christ fell to their knees, crossed their arms, and gave themselves up to prayer, in the great silence that lay all about as twilight fell and a slow golden haze drifted over the field. The watching people were also silent, moved by this spectacle of great devotion.

[Francis had ordered that no friar was to have care or anxiety about anything to eat or drink on this occasion, each was to concentrate on prayer and praise of God. Many had criticized him for his imprudence,[o] but that] he was clairvoyant in this instance was proved. A

---

n. In *Fioretti,* 18, this remark is attributed to Cardinal Ugolino. The account in *Fioretti* may have combined the events that took place in several chapters. Despite the report of Giordano (*Chronica,* 16) that it was held in 1221, some historians have thought that date an error. In any case, in 1221 Ugolino was in northern Italy and was replaced by Cardinal Regnierio Capocci. Cf. Brown, in Englebert, *Saint Francis,* p. 477, n. 5.

o. Possibly among those who criticized Francis's imprudence was Saint Dominic, who, according to *Fioretti,* 18, and *Actus,* 20, was present at this chapter. Which chapter he attended is a matter of dispute among Franciscan historians, however. Fortini believed it to have been the chapter of 1217—see chap. 10, n. 30.—Trans.

multitude of people from surrounding towns, the same ones who in the past had cruelly closed their doors on the faces of the brothers, arrived with loads of food and provisions. They flocked down from the hills, came by dusty roads from the *castelli* on the plain, descended from the hilltop cities—Perugia, Spoleto, Foligno, Spello, Assisi. They carried tablecloths, plates, glasses, pitchers, and everything that such a crowd would need. Knights and noblemen were among the first to offer their services.

For a long time nothing else was talked about in that part of the country but that memorable event. Strange and fantastic tales were also told about it, such as Bartholomew of Pisa's account of how devils flew up in a frenzy, disturbed by all that holiness in San Salvatore delle Pareti.[p] These tales, however ingenuous, do serve to show us how touched people were by that great and humble gathering of a kind never before seen.

A vivid description of the Chapter of Mats has been left to us by one of the brothers who was there, Giordano of Giano, a small town on the hills of Montefalco, facing Assisi. Brother Giordano himself was involved in an event there that determined the course of the rest of his life.[123]

The chapter was about to end [Brother Giordano tells us], when Francis remembered something very important that had not yet been dealt with: the great hostility that had driven the brothers out of Germany. Again he pulled at Brother Elias's habit, and Brother Elias repeated what he said to the friars:

"Brothers, thus says The Brother (meaning Blessed Francis, who was called that by the other brothers to indicate he was the friar *par excellence*), there is a certain region called Germany, where there are devout Christian people. You have often seen them pass through our country, carrying large staves and great burning torches,[q] and sweating in the sun's heat as they go on their way to visit the shrines of the Saints. But the brothers who were sent to them were treated badly and returned. Because of that, The Brother does not compel anyone to go to them; but to those who, inspired by zeal for God and for souls, may wish to go, he wants to give an even greater mandate than

---

p. Bartholomew of Pisa says that when this chapter took place, the demons, alarmed at the holiness of the friars, also held a chapter "at the Crucifers' hospital of (San Salvatore delle) Pareti, on the (then) existing road between Assisi and Santa Maria degli Angeli, where there were eighteen thousand demons." One demon said that nothing could be done against the friars so long as they were obedient to the rule, but it would be easy to overcome them if their practices were relaxed. *De conformitate* (AF 4:161–62, 445). Cf. *24 Generals* (AF 3:27–28); *Leggenda Antica*, ed. Minocchi, p. 22.

q. Fortini follows the manuscripts in which the Germans are spoken of as bearing *cereis* (candles). Glassberger and Wadding use the word *ocreis* (leggings, boots).—Trans.

that customary for the overseas missions. If anyone here wishes to go, let him rise and step to one side."

Immediately, Brother Giordano says, about ninety brothers, all zealous for martyrdom, stood up and gathered in a group aside.

Brother Giordano was amazed by such a response, because he himself had asked God to keep him away from both the people of Lombardy and the Germans. He was sure that those who volunteered could be considered already dead and buried. He remembered how he regretted not having known the brothers who were martyred in Spain, and he decided to make sure he did not let this opportunity slip. So he went from one to the other, asking each who he was and where he came from. He thought how great it would be for himself if, in case they were martyred, he could say, "I knew this one, and I knew that one."

In the group there was a brother named Palmerio, a deacon, "an amiable and cheerful man" from Monte Gargano in Apulia. When Brother Giordano came to him, he gave his name, then grasped Giordano and drawing him close, he said, "And you too are one of us and shall go with us."

Giordano protested and struggled; but the other, enjoying his game, drew him to the ground and made him sit with him among the others.

And at that point Brother Giordano's name was called, and he was assigned to a different province. But he could not reply because at the very same moment Brother Cesario of Speyer, who had been named the minister of Germany, arrived and began his selection.

Uselessly Giordano wore himself out repeating that he did not wish to volunteer, that a mistake had been made. In the confusion no one paid any attention to him. Brother Cesario, not understanding what it was all about, took him to Brother Elias. But here, instead of being cleared up, the situation grew increasingly entangled, since Giordano remained silent and all the others talked. Brother Cesario insisted on taking him along. The friars of the province to which he had been assigned joined the argument and strove to keep him because he was weak and they did not think he could stand the harshness of the German climate. Finally Brother Elias said impatiently, "I command you, Brother, in holy obedience, to decide finally whether you wish to go or to be released."

Brother Giordano was wildly confused at this peremptory order. He did not want to seem pusillanimous; yet, he did not want to make a choice. On the one hand, it would look as if he were following his own will; on the other, he did not want to volunteer because he feared that the suffering he might have to endure from the Germans would make him lose his patience and thus imperil his soul. In his dilemma, he resolved to ask the advice of another brother, one who had suffered many tribulations in other missionary journeys and so was considered the veteran of the group. And this brother advised him to go to Brother Elias and put the matter in his hands, so that he would not have any regrets whichever way it went.

And Brother Elias decided that Brother Giordano should go.

Twenty-seven were chosen, of various nationalities, twelve clerics and fifteen lay brothers.[124] Among them were Thomas of Celano, Simone, described as the son of the countess di Collazzone, the deacon Palmerio, Giovanni di Piancarpine, who later was sent as a missionary to the Tartars.

Brother Giordano remained in Germany more than forty years and died there in (it is thought) 1262.

As for Francis: this was the high noon of his life. Everything for him at the moment was shining and splendid. The others felt it. Just to go near him, receive a glance or a few words from him, listen to his prayer, was to move into a radiance. It seemed that his life was such that it drew heaven to earth and made them one.

Poverty and Joy

Chivalry required joy. It ranked as equal in importance with valour. "The knight," according to an ancient regulation, "must be joyous, because this is the life of warriors: happiness in the field and joy in the castle. *Car d'armes est li mestier liex. Bruit es chans et joie a l'ostel.*"[125]

No one could be considered truly gallant who was not light-hearted and joyous, *gais et ioios.* The highest valour was deemed that silently practiced in the face of tribulations and sufferings. Ill temper reveals weakness, sadness is but a disguised form of cowardice. The poets of feudal chivalry, the troubadours of Provence, say that one does not talk of great anxieties, such as illness, unrequited love, defeat, dishonour, betrayal, death.

They recognized, though, that it happens often enough that a man who fights with spirit in battle is unhorsed and conquered by a little disappointment in domestic life. And the prior of Montaudon, who composed tensons and sirventes between 1180 and 1213, enumerated the things that could disturb the serenity of the knight:

> The gabby man whose pledge is idle
> the man who's much too homicidal
> (and all the) steeds that pull on bridle,

a youth whose shield is always slung
but never a blow against it rung,
priest and monk with whiskers hung,
and gossips with a cutting tongue . . .
a woman poor but ungracious . . .
a man with wife he loves tenacious . . .
I don't like the knight effete
who boasts outside his country seat,
and yet at home no charge can meet . . .
cowards waving flags with mettle,
hunting hawks in sorry fettle,
skimpy meat in a mammoth kettle;
I hate, by good St. Martin's sign,
a pint of water drowning my wine! . . .
Long abstinence I've always hated,
and meat cooked hard, almost cremated . . .
a vile man heaped with joy through vice,
to run when roads are caked with ice . . .
a sorry fiddler in fine court nested,
a small estate with heirs infested,
too many peers in one domain,
rich lords who seldom entertain . . .
large tables spread with cloths too little,[r]
a scabby lackey carving victuals,
a gross hauberk of mail that's brittle . . .
(to have) to wait outside the door
when weather's bad and showers pour,
a poor jade feigning she's offended,
a youth admiring his legs as splendid . . .
to ride with no cloak when it's raining,
to find a sow with my horse, draining
his trough of all the grain remaining,
a saddle with wobbly horn, not strong,
a buckle that has lost its prong,
a wicked man at home day-long
who can't behave or speak but wrong.[126]

This emphasis on outward composure is also reflected in another well-established custom of the Provençal troubadours, one that

---

r. According to Bianco, long table cloths were considered desirable because they hid the remains thrown under the table and served also to clean the face and hands. *Asti Medioevale,* p. 262.—Trans.

lasted until the time of the poets of the *dolce stil nuovo:* to compose a last song at the moment of death.[127] The practice was a noble and courtly way of dictating one's spiritual testament, showing one's true mettle. The count of Poitiers, who led the Crusaders in 1101, did just this; and in his last hour he wrote the delicate poem, *Pos de chantar m'es pres tolentz* ("Because I am being taken, I wish to sing . . . ")[128]

He says farewell to the things that are dear to him, the companies of knights, fine clothes trimmed in vair and sable, the fabulous courts of love: "Never to be love's obedient in Poitou or in Limousin."

He fears for the fate of his lands:

> Now into exile I will go.
> In peril, in frightful woe,
> I leave my son to face war's throe
> And the wrongs my neighbours do.

It is the traitorous Gascons and Angevins whom he fears, and he invokes the protection of the king for his son.

He asks pardon of those whom he has offended:

> Mercy I beg of you, dear friend.
> If ever I wronged you, make amends.
> To Jesus enthroned, I pray: defend!—
> In Provensal, in Latin too.

He thinks about his funeral:

> At my funeral, friends, I pray:
> Gather around, shout your praise,
> For I've known many happy days
> Far and near, and in Poitou.

But uppermost in his mind to the end was that rule of prowess and joy to which he had been faithful all his life:

> *De proeza e de joi fui . . .*
> O, I was a man of prowess and wit,
> But now I renounce each single bit;
> I'll go to Him Who sin remits
> Where men can end renewed.

He has been true to the rule of chivalry:

Mont ai estat cuendes e gais . . .
Yes, I was a jaunty lord, and gay,
But another lord points another way.
Now these shoulders, burdened, sway
As my end looms in view.

Francis made use of the knight's obligation to be joyous. It was transposed from chivalry into the new order of Friars Minor and invested with a new spirituality.

A cheerful manner was one of Francis's most marked characteristics, from the time of his uninhibited youth (one remembers the episode in the Perugia prison and the meeting with the robbers of Valfabbrica) until the day of his death.

For him sadness was an illness of the soul, one of "the thousand snares and wiles of the enemy." He used to say, "Then the devil rejoices most when he can snatch away spiritual joy from a servant of God. He carries dust so that he can throw it into even the tiniest chinks of conscience and soil the candour of mind and purity of life. But when spiritual joy fills hearts, . . . the serpent throws off his deadly poison in vain. The devils cannot harm the servant of Christ when they see he is filled with holy joy. When, however, the soul is wretched, desolate, and filled with sorrow, it is easily overwhelmed by its sorrow or else it turns to vain enjoyments."[129]

His joy was contagious. A word, a glance, from him was enough to make shadows fly away, to lighten even the most troubled heart. When he travelled about the countryside and people crowded around him, he seemed to radiate peace and holiness, and it soothed and stilled every restlessness.

This joy never left him, not even when he was exhorting his listeners to repentance or when he wept over the passion of Jesus.[130] He was still, as he had been earlier, the podestà of the Compagnia dei Tripudianti, a leader who now had been given a happiness unknown to worldly poets: "The breath of the divine whisper which his ear perceived in secret would burst forth . . . in a song of joy." He no longer had his troubadour's lute, but it was not necessary for these new songs of love. "At times, as we saw with our own eyes," Thomas of Celano writes, "he would pick up a stick from the ground and putting it over his left arm, would draw across it, as across a violin, a little bow bent by means of a string, and going through the motions of playing, he would sing in French about his Lord."[131]

Artists who depict the saint from Assisi sunk in meditation over grinning skulls or bent to gaze sadly at the earth that encloses the dead do not understand this part of Francis's spirit. He was heaven-drunk. His life was a hymn of joy, a flight into the sun.

Nor did he allow his friars to wear peevish and sad faces in public, saying, "It is not becoming for a servant of God to show himself sad or upset before men, but always he should show himself honourable. Examine your offences in your room and weep and groan before your God. When you return to your brothers, put off your sorrow and conform yourself to the rest."[132]

The new knights were always to be joyous in the Lord. He put this principle in the rule: "They should let it be seen that they are happy in God, cheerful and courteous, as is expected of them, and be careful not to appear gloomy or depressed like hypocrites."[133]

The chapters held by the friars were always enlivened, as Giordano of Giano wrote, by a *fraterna jocunditas,* "brotherly cheerfulness."[134]

Francis also used to say that to fight the Babylonian evil there was no remedy more efficacious than prayer. "The Babylonian evil" to him meant sadness that rusted and wore away the spirit. It is, he said, like the rust in the cauldron in Ezekiel's parable about the taking of Jerusalem by the king of Babylon.[135] "If the servant of God," Francis would say, "as may happen, is disturbed in any way, he should rise immediately to pray and he should remain in the presence of the heavenly Father until he restores unto him the joy of salvation. For if he remains stupified in sadness, the Babylonian stuff will increase, so that, unless it be at length driven out by tears, it will generate an abiding rust in the heart."[136]

Poverty is happiness, because it is liberty. Francis had given his brothers the motto *Paupertas cum Laetitia,* Poverty with or for the purpose of Joy, or more simply, "Poverty and Joy."[137] Humility is also joy, because the injuries that have hurt us the most, that we keep most secret, are those that dig at our pride.

The knight of true prowess knows how to change pain into pleasure, troubles into exultation. This [ability to find joy in pain and sorrow] is the heroism of Francis's rule, the heroic quality that the saint defined as "perfect joy."

Perfect Joy

Francis was walking with Brother Leo along the road from Perugia to Santa Maria degli Angeli. It was the Via Dolorosa of his twenties, at the time of the war with Perugia.

Old memories returned to him: the ranks of the commune army crossing over the wide gravelly stream at the foot of the Colle dell'Inferno, the first shouts of the lookouts resounding in the *castello* of

Isola on the bank of the Chiagio, his own trembling as he realized that battle was imminent, the furious raging of the battle on the hill beyond. And he saw again the summit flashing with swords, the banners of the *contrade,* the white *carroccio,* the flocks of archers and masses of cavalry. He heard the blood-curdling shrieks, the clash of iron against iron, the desperate groans under the spine-chilling songs of victory that mocked and exulted in suffering.

A little farther along on the wooded banks of the Tiber, was the bridge of San Giovanni, where he had stopped on his way to Perugia as a prisoner to look at the river, which flowed along as indifferent to his own tragedy as it had been in all the centuries, when frightful forgotten disasters had taken place on its banks—that muddy river whose very name was associated with domination and empire and the ships of victors returning to the city of the Caesars laden with slaves and booty. He remembered how he, disarmed, humiliated, his hands tied, finally began the hard ascent to the city of the clawed gryphon, trudging along a road snaking through the hills, and how merciless brutes shoved him into the middle of a crazed mob. How long ago it all seemed! And now surely no one could distinguish between victor and vanquished.

A different song of victory is about to rise up on that bleak winter evening. We are in the month of December, 1221.[138] The fog is lying motionless on the bare plain. It is cold and it is raining, a lacerating plash that beats down on the deserted road, still covered with muddy snow.

As told in *Little Flowers:* "Saint Francis called to Brother Leo, who was walking a bit ahead of him, and he said: 'Brother Leo, even if the Friars Minor in every country give a great example of holiness and integrity and good edification, nevertheless write down and note carefully that perfect joy is not in that.'

"When he had walked on a bit, Saint Francis called him again, saying: 'Brother Leo, even if a Friar Minor gives sight to the blind, heals the paralyzed, drives out devils, gives hearing back to the deaf, makes the lame walk, and restores speech to the dumb, and what is still more, brings back to life a man who has been dead four days, write that perfect joy is not in that.'

"Going on a bit, Saint Francis cried out again in a strong voice: 'Brother Leo, if a Friar Minor knew all languages and all sciences and Scripture, if he also knew how to prophesy and to reveal not only the future but also the secrets of consciences and minds of others, write down and note carefully that perfect joy is not in that.'

"As they walked on, after a while Saint Francis called again forcefully: 'Brother Leo, Little Lamb of God, even if a Friar Minor could speak with the voice of an angel, and knew the courses of the stars and the powers of herbs, and knew all about the treasures in the earth, and if he knew the qualities of birds and fishes, animals, humans, roots, trees, rocks, and waters, write down and note carefully that true joy is not in that.'

"Going on a bit farther, Saint Francis called again strongly: 'Brother Leo, even if a Friar Minor could preach so well that he should convert all infidels to the faith of Christ, write that perfect joy is not there.'

"Now when he had been talking this way for a distance of two miles, Brother Leo in great amazement asked him: 'Father, I beg you in God's name to tell me where perfect joy is.'

"Saint Francis replied: 'When we come to Santa Maria degli Angeli, soaked by the rain and frozen by the cold, all soiled with mud and suffering from hunger, and we ring at the gate of the Place and the brother porter comes and says angrily: "Who are you?" And we say: "We are two of your brothers." And he contradicts us, saying: "You are not telling the truth. Rather you are two rascals who go around deceiving people and stealing what they give to the poor. Go away!" And he does not open for us, but makes us stand outside in the snow and rain, cold and hungry, until night falls—then if we endure all those cruel rebuffs patiently, without being troubled and without complaining, and if we reflect humbly and charitably that the porter really knows us and that God makes him speak against us, oh, Brother Leo, write that perfect joy is there!

"'And if we continue to knock, and the porter comes out in anger, and drives us away with curses and hard blows like bothersome scoundrels, saying: "Get away from here, you dirty thieves—go to the *ospedale!* Who do you think you are? You certainly won't eat or sleep here!"—and if we bear it patiently and take the insults with joy and love in our hearts, oh, Brother Leo, write that this is perfect joy!

"'And if later, suffering intensely from hunger and the painful cold, with night falling, we still knock and call, and crying loudly beg them to open for us and let us come in for the love of God, and he grows still more angry and says: "Those fellows are bold and shameless ruffians. I'll give them what they deserve!" And he comes out with a knotty club, and grasping us by the cowl throws us onto the ground, rolling us in the mud and snow, and beats us with that club so much that he covers our bodies with wounds—if we endure all those evils and blows with joy and patience, reflecting that we must accept and bear the sufferings of the Blessed Christ patiently for love of Him, oh, Brother Leo, write: that is perfect joy!

"'And now hear the conclusion, Brother Leo. Above all the graces and gifts of the Holy Spirit which Christ gives to His friends is that of conquering oneself and willingly enduring sufferings, insults, humiliations, and hardships for the love of Christ. For we cannot glory in all those other marvellous gifts of God, as they are not ours but God's, as the Apostle says: "What have you that you have not received?"

"'But we can glory in the cross of tribulations and afflictions, because that is ours, and so the Apostle says: "I will not glory save in the Cross of Our Lord Jesus Christ!"'"

The Free Men of Assisi

"Love your enemies, do good to those who hate you"[139]—this Gospel teaching is incorporated into the rule. Because of it the men of penitence of Assisi go about their native city free and happy.

These men (like their contemporaries), had once been carried away by hatred, taken sword and club to the piazza, shouted for death to other men in bitter battles, lain in ambush, shattered doors with axes, spent sleepless nights over unsatisfied revenge, looked forward to killing. [Now they lived the life of mystics:] they were absorbed in thoughts of God and conversed with angels.

There was Brother Simone of Assisi, for example. He walked in such light that he was constantly visited by special blessings [or, as we now say, he enjoyed constant charismatic gifts].[140]

And Brother Rufino. The devil had put Brother Rufino through such a time of sadness that he lost all his faith and his love for Francis. But Jesus appeared in the forest of the Carceri to the son of the old consul from Piazza San Rufino and said to him, "As long as you live, you will never again be sad or depressed." And when he went away, Brother Rufino had "such joy and peace of soul and inspiration of mind that he was absorbed in God day and night."[141]

Brother Leo. In the Basilica di San Francesco in Assisi, the blessing that Francis wrote for him (on La Verna) is still preserved. This humble little lamb of God carried it over his heart as long as he lived. On it are a few wavering lines, uneven, faded, in the handwriting of Saint Francis. At the bottom Francis wrote the wish, infinitely touching, coming, as it did, at the dawn of his own new life in the spirit: *Deus det tibi pacem* ("God give you peace").[s]

---

s. Brother Leo, who was with Saint Francis on Mount La Verna in 1224, asked him for something written in his own hand, to help him in "a painful spiritual trial." Francis wrote the well-known benediction from Numbers 6:24–26 ("The Lord bless you and keep you! The Lord let his face shine upon you, and be gracious to you! The Lord look upon you kindly and give you peace!"); and Brother Leo, until his death, carried it always (*2 Cel.*, 49; *Leg. Maior*, XI, 9). This paper is preserved in the sacristy of the Sacro Convento in Assisi, enclosed in a silver reliquary of the seventeenth century. On it are the words in Saint Francis's handwriting:

The first companion, Bernardo da Quintavalle. Someone who knew him in the last years of his life and saw his face always raised toward heaven, compared him to the swallow, in that he flew so high, "with his mind utterly freed and detached from earthly matters." According to *Little Flowers,* "And sometimes for twenty days, sometimes for thirty days, he used to stay alone on the tops of mountains, contemplating heavenly things."

To Brother Bernardo, as well as to Brother Masseo, it was given at last to know the treasure the Poverello of Christ had searched for in his youth. Brother Bernardo, having been overcome by ecstasy during Mass, came out of his rapt state and went all through the friars' Place shouting in a voice filled with wonder: "Oh, Brothers! Oh, Brothers! There is no man in all this country, no matter how great and noble he is, who, if he were promised a very beautiful palace full of gold, would not willingly carry a sack full of the most filthy manure in order to obtain that very noble treasure!"[142]

Brother Giles used to say, "All our times and years are like three days." The one who blindly pursues a goal always beyond his reach rarely notices how swiftly time flies until the moment he is on the brink of the final precipice and unable to turn back. Giotto depicted just such a moment in the Basilica di San Francesco, in his painting of the Intruder who enters unexpectedly and sits down at table with a knight, who drops to the ground, surrounded by the grief-stricken women of his family.[143]

Indeed, the man who makes material things his chief goal is condemned to keep on running always, a fact noted by Brother Giuliano da Spira: *illa erronea et intermina cupiditatis via.*

This was not the way taken by Brother Bernardo, who gave away

---

Benedicat tibi Dominus et custodiat te, ostendat faciem suam tibi et misereatur tui. Convertat vultum suum ad te et det tibi pacem.

Following the benediction is the dedication, written also by Saint Francis: *Dominus benedicat, F. Leo, te* ("God bless, Brother Leo, you"). At the end is the signature—a Tau, symbol of the cross, drawn on the profile of a mountain that most believe to represent Golgotha. There are additional notations by Brother Leo, written in red ink: "Two years before his death the blessed Francis kept his fast in the locality of Alverna in honour of the Blessed Virgin Mary, Mother of God, and of the holy Archangel Michael, from the feast of the Assumption of the Holy Virgin Mary up to the feast of Saint Michael in September; and after the hand of the Lord came over him on account of the vision and allocution of the seraphim and of the impression of the stigmata of Christ upon his body he made these praises written upon the other side of the paper and, giving thanks to the Lord for the benefit conferred on him, wrote this with his own hand." Below the blessing he wrote, "The Blessed Francis wrote with his own hand this blessing for me, Brother Leo." And under the signature: "He also with his own hand made this sign Tau with a head (skull)." Eng. trans.: Jörgensen, *Saint Francis,* pp. 286–87.

Today, after many exhaustive disputations and studies in depth by able historians and paleographers, no one now doubts the authenticity of this document. For an examination of the question, see Boehmer, *Analekten,* pp. 69–70; Faloci-Pulignani, in *San Francesco,* 4:193.

all his goods so as to love his brothers in freedom. At the hour of his death, he said that if he had to do it all over again, he would not have chosen a different path. "And after he had said those words and given some other good advice," we are told in *Little Flowers,* "as he lay back on his bed, his features became very radiant and joyful, to the great amazement of all the friars present. And in that same joy his blessed and most holy soul, crowned with glory, passed from this life to the life of the angels and the blessed in the victory which had previously been promised to him."[144] The perfect joy of Brother Bernardo was such that unnoticing and unnoticeably he rose to Paradise.

Brother Giles of Assisi, too, was often lost in joyous contemplation. It was said that like Saint Paul, he was caught up to the third heaven. No spiritual poet or tract on ascetism has given us so beautiful a description of contemplation as did this brother. It is, he said, a fire, an unction, an ecstasy in which the soul is rapt and withdrawn from the physical senses. It is also a marvellous sweetness in which the soul rests and a glory that refreshes the soul—"to contemplate is to be separated from all and to be united to God alone."[145]

In the Franciscan story, Brother Giles and Brother Juniper are eagles placed on earth. Alike, "the mystic knight" and "the fool of Christ" rapidly shifted from contemplation to action. In them Franciscan joy is seen in all its splendour.

·13·

THE MYSTIC KNIGHT
AND CHRIST'S FOOL

All Francis's early companions, it is safe to say, were remarkable men, united by their view of life and of God. They would have had to be, to join Francis in the unconventional way of life he felt necessary to express their beliefs. It was a way that allowed a great deal of individual freedom in service, even of eccentricity. Consider, for example, two of these early Franciscans: Brother Giles and Brother Juniper.

To Brother Giles (whose homely words of wisdom were collected by his companions in a work known as the *Sayings of Brother Giles*), Franciscanism becomes life itself. Practiced every day, he says, it gives life to all that human beings do. This he constantly repeats, shouts out in piazzas and on ships sailing the seas and in rich and prosperous ports.

However, he, like Brother Bernardo, finds his greatest happiness in the mystical ecstasies of solitary prayer. He compares them to the joys of married lovers. On the wedding day a husband likes to see his bride elegantly dressed in a train, veils, jewels, a handsome sash, a crown. But when it is time for love, all these ornaments are cast aside and she alone will be for him alone. And in the same way, good works, which are the ornaments of the soul, are in contemplation cast aside at the hour of union with the beloved.[1]

This thought was his own troubadour song of love. When a brother went to him to find out in what way he could make himself most acceptable to God, Brother Giles made no reply. But the following morning he led him to the garden, took up a stick, and with it began imitating a man playing a viol. Walking about and singing like a true minstrel, he repeated over and over again two words alone: *Una uni, una uni,* which can be translated, "She alone for him alone. She alone for him alone." Finally he stopped, left off singing, and said to the brother, who was gaping in astonishment, "Do this and you will please God."

And since the other showed that he did not understand at all, he explained, "The soul alone, that is, without any intermediary, must give itself to God alone."[2]

Often he engaged in good-natured teasing and banter with Brother Bernardo, who would sometimes say to the other brothers, when he observed Brother Giles spending much time in prayer in his cell, "He keeps himself shut up in his room like a girl." And then, when Giles arrived, he would egg him on by saying, "But now let's see you go on out among men, talk with them, ask for bread for the brothers and everything else that is necessary."

And Brother Giles would say, no less good-humouredly and with great humility, "Brother Bernardo, it is not granted to every man to eat like the swallows, as you do."

This he said because as the swallow is said to feed while flying, so Brother Bernardo seemed nourished only by his soaring flights to ecstasy in times of contemplation.[3]

In reality, Brother Giles does spend time among people. More than any other brother, he lives their life, enters into their activities, talks as they do, sits down at their dinner tables, sleeps under their roofs. We see him go out to the forest for firewood, sweep rooms, wash dishes, move haystacks, cut canes, fetch water. He is the apostle in workman's garb—God's own worker, the proletarian of the Franciscan story, the man who accepts labour as both a joy and a purification.

Brother Giles dislikes the empty words of so-called apostles who fill piazzas with sterile rhetoric and believe that with this they will help their neighbours. He believes that perfection is constantly doing good. One day a brother asked his blessing before going out to preach in the piazza in Perugia, and Brother Giles responded, *Bo, bo, molto dico e poco fo* ("Boo, boo, much I say and little I do").

Another time, while he was living in the hermitage of Monteripido, to which he had retired after the death of Saint Francis, he heard in a nearby field a worker in the vineyard exhorting the peasants, "Don't talk, but do, do." Immediately Giles hurried to find the other brothers; and while still far away he began to shout, "Just listen a bit to what this man is saying: 'Don't talk but do, do.'"

He even attributes such thoughts to strange natural voices: the rustling of the forest, the murmuring of the river, the crackling of the fire, the wind's cry, the birds' song.

On a spring morning he is struck by the shrilling of the quail. After listening silently for a long time, he turns and says joyously to the invisible singer, "O madonna quail, I must come to your abode and listen to the praises of the Lord. I want to remember that you do not say *là, là* but *qua, qua*—that is, not there (*là*) in another life but here (*qua*) in this life we must do good works."[4]

From his earliest days in the order, Brother Giles spent long periods of time in Rome, where he lived by the work of his hands. He would get up early in the morning, listen to Mass, then go out to a forest eight miles from the city to make bundles of wood. One time when he was returning with a bundle of this sort on his shoulders, a woman asked him the price. He proposed that they split the wood fifty-fifty, and Brother Giles carried the wood to the woman's house. Then, however, her conscience bothered her because she knew him to be a holy man, and so she insisted that he at least take more wood than the half agreed upon. But the friar refused. He did not wish, he said, to be overcome by the vice of avarice. Indeed, he ended by taking only one quarter of the wood and with that he was content.[5]

Another day (it was in early October and nut-gathering had begun), while he is quietly sitting in a piazza, he hears someone offer a man a job knocking down nuts. The man makes all sorts of excuses. The road is too long. It is too dangerous to climb to the top of the tree—he has lots of excuses. Brother Giles says, "Friend, if you will give me part of the nuts, I shall go with you to knock them from the tree." And so, being agreed, together they go out to the field. The tree is very tall, but Brother Giles is not discouraged. He makes the sign of the cross, climbs up, and not without a certain tremor of the heart, begins to knock down nuts. At last so many nuts fall that he cannot carry them all. He takes off his habit, ties the sleeves and hood together to make a sort of sack, puts the nuts in it, and bent under the weight, returns to Rome and with great happiness gives his share of nuts to the poor.

At harvest time Brother Giles goes out to glean with other poor men. If anyone offers him a handful of grain, he replies, "My brother, I do not have a granary to put it in." And most of the time he gives away all he gleans for the love of God.[6]

The story of his life, as told by his companion and fellow citizen, Brother Leo,[7] seems to glow with this earthy piety and holiness, in which the dirtiest labour is redeemed by the Franciscan-inspired renewed dedication to God. He even speaks as a man of the fields, with examples, proverbs, metaphors, but the old folk wisdom is shot through with a new meaning. In his words the grain in the stalks, the fruit of the trees, the buds on the flowers, exist only to record the beauty and the goodness of God and his work.

"Look at the fruit of the earth, which cannot be had except after long work and in the proper season. In like manner God will not give you grace until your soul is prepared and the right moment comes."

The Sayings of Brother Giles

The joy of grace, once it is attained, is so great that everyone forgets how much it costs. To demonstrate this, Giles uses this comparison: "It is as sometimes happens to a farmer who sees a forest of trees and briars on a section of his land which he wants to cultivate and sow with grain, but he [must put in] much labour and sweating and trouble before he can gather any grain there. At times he is almost sorry he undertook that job on account of the work and worry it brings him. But if he perseveres until harvest time, he stores the grain away with great joy, almost forgetting the hard work, because of the rich harvest that it finally brings him. And he endures many other labours besides these, and he blesses them all on account of the joy that the sight of the good harvest gives him."[8]

Failures and defeats are not important. "Although a tree has grown, yet it is not large all at once. And if large, it is not in bloom. And if in bloom, nevertheless it does not immediately bear fruit. And if it bears fruits, they are not large at first. And if they are large, yet they are not ripe. And if ripe, nevertheless all of them do not reach the mouths of those who eat them, but many fall down and rot away or are eaten by pigs or other animals."[9]

And keep this in mind [he also says]: "No sinner should ever despair of God's mercy as long as he lives. For there is hardly a tree so thorny and knotted that men cannot make it smooth and beautiful. Likewise there is no sinner in this world so bad that God cannot adorn him in many ways with grace and virtues."[10]

He continues, "Don't stop doing good because of the temptation to vanity. For if a farmer wishing to throw seed on the ground says to himself: 'I don't want to sow this year because, if I sow, birds may come and eat that seed,' and if therefore he does not sow, he would not have any produce from his land to eat. But if he sows, although some of the seed perishes, still he will have most of it. That is the way it is with the man who is tempted to vanity and fights against it."[11]

Prayer is of more value than good works, but to have consolation in prayer you should try to free yourself from all that is blameworthy.

"If you had some good wine in a glass and some sediment was under the wine, would you shake the glass and mix the wine with the sediment? That is not the thing to do."[12]

The supreme virtue, says Brother Giles, is obedience. "As long as the ox holds its head under the yoke, it fills the barns with grain. But the ox that does not hold its head under the yoke and wanders around may think it is a great lord—but the barns are not filled with grain. The great and the wise humbly put their heads under the yoke of obedience. But the foolish withdraw their heads from under the yoke and do not want to obey."[13]

When harvesters rest in the shade of oaks and on the sun-drenched fields cicadas sing, when nut-gatherers gather in a circle around a burning fire in an olive grove, when the miller is grinding the grain that has been carried in sacks to the mill and the peasants are sitting on the low parapet along the mill-stream to wait and the water is rumbling and rushing into the turbine, Brother Giles talks. To each he uses the simple words that find their way into the heart.

It was the old slaves of the land to whom he spoke, the oppressed serfs who just yesterday had rebelled against the feudal lords.

Through the knowledge that he gains of the human soul and through his life in common with the humble who work and earn their wages with sweat and tears, Brother Giles becomes the incarnation of a basic precept of Franciscanism: purity of soul is not a privileged state of grace given to some, but a prize to be won in struggle and with strength of will. It is a painful battle for those who are too much attached to worldly standards. "If someone walked well in the way of the Lord, he would not feel tired or bored, but in the way of the world he feels tired and bored to death."[14]

Knightly Rules

Brother Giles also told stories in the language of chivalry, using the glittering life of castles and courts as the setting for his allegories, fables, stories with a moral, symbolic tales. His words then appear in quite a different garb; but unchanged is both the ardour that inspires them and their purpose—to demonstrate the truth of the Christian faith. His "sayings" reflect the prime Franciscan concept: that all persons in all social classes must be loved equally.

When man leaves off sinning, he will find that the greater his efforts, the greater his rewards. The secret lies in will power and God will not fail to help the faithful servant in this fight. Here is his story.

"Suppose a king has two servants, one of whom is armed, but the other is unarmed, and they have to go to war. The one who is armed goes bravely to war, but the other who is unarmed says this to his lord: 'My lord, as you see, I have no weapons. But because I love you I will go into battle even without weapons.' Now the king on seeing the faithfulness of that servant says to his attendants: 'Go and prepare armour to adorn this faithful servant of mine, and place on all his armour my own emblem.' So too if someone goes into the battle of prayer as if without arms, because he feels dry and lacking devotion, God sees his faithfulness and places his own emblem on him."[15]

This is characteristic of many of his stories—all romantic flashes and gleams and talk of the bravery of knights, blazing armour, clashing shields, shining swords, waving ensigns, pawing horses, battles flaring up under battlemented walls. Frequently the emperor, the royal court, the paladins of France, appear in them. Perhaps it was for this reason that Francis used to call Brother Giles his knight of the Round Table.[16]

Here is how Giles says that the man who suffers and fights off temptation wins more merit than those unassailed by problems: "My brother, I am of the opinion that much more prowess has the lord whose castle is being besieged and attacked by his enemies, and yet who defends himself so bravely so as not to allow a single enemy to enter, than the one who remains in peace without any quarrels and obstacles."[17]

In a struggle everyone must hold firm and never yield a step. Whoever gives up prayer because of difficulties "is like a man who runs away from battle."[18] Brother Giles believed that the good knight does not immediately leave the battlefield when he is wounded or struck by the enemy; rather, he continues to resist vigorously to win, so that by winning, he can rejoice and be cheered by the victory. A knight who left the fight as soon as he receives a wound or blow, he said, would be confused and ashamed and disgraced.[19]

The rule of the Friars Minor he compares also to the code of knights: "A truly obedient religious is like a well-armed knight riding on a good horse who passes safely among enemies and no one can harm him. But a religious who grumbles at obeying is like an unarmed knight riding on a bad horse who, when passing among the enemy, falls and is immediately captured, chained, wounded, imprisoned, and sometimes put to death."[20]

Both the feudal lords who fight in the name of a pride that they believe consecrated by the concepts of chivalry and the Benedictine monks with whom Brother Giles stays for a time and for whom he works as a water-carrier listen with amazement as he shapes the rules obtaining in castles to express the courage that must inspire the disciples of Poverty.

In battle strong armour will do no one any good if courage is lacking. In the same way, it is useless for a Friar Minor to put on the habit if he cannot fight unceasingly to defend and to win spiritual rewards.

On this matter Brother Giles says: "Many enter the religious life and do not practice those things that are a basic part of the religious life. And they are like a farmer who would put on the armour of Roland but not be capable of using it in battle. For not all men are able to ride the horse Bayard, or if they rode it, could keep from falling off."[21]

He adds: "I don't think it is much to enter the court of a king, nor do I think it much to receive gifts from a king. But I do think it is a great thing to know how to remain in a royal court by doing the right thing. The court of the Great King is the religious life—to enter it and to receive some gifts from God in it is not much. But to be able to live in it by doing the right thing and to persevere devoutly and conscientiously in it to the end is a great thing."[22]

Spiritual Vagrancy

All those who aspired to be perfect knights longed to be consecrated to Christ in the land where every rule of chivalry is at the same time a religious vow; every daring, holiness; every death, martyrdom. In 1215 Brother Giles, with Francis's permission, left on a pilgrimage to the Holy Land. He first went to Brindisi to wait for a ship. While staying there, desirous of living by the work of his hands, he begged a jug, filled it with water, and went through the city crying, "Who wants water?" For his labour he was given bread and other necessary things.[23]

When he had nothing else to do, he went to the harbour to look at the sea. Ships, big and little, were constantly arriving, sailors landing and unloading the merchandise. He rejoiced in everything and saw in everything a reflection of the thoughts and feelings with which his own heart was running over: "What good does it do a man to fast and pray and beg for alms, if he does not reach with firm perseverance the port of salvation? Sometimes a ship appears on the sea that is beautiful, large, new and full of rich treasure. But some disaster happens to it and it does not reach port safely but sinks miserably—what good did all its excellence and beauty do it? Again, sometimes there is a ship on the sea that is small, ugly, old, contemptible, and not full of treasure. And with great difficulty it escapes the dangers of the sea and safely reaches port. That alone is worthy of praise. This happens also with men in this world."[24]

Finally the ship for the journey was readied, and in it Giles reached the Holy Land. He was the first Franciscan to put foot there in the country of Jesus, the herald of the many brothers of the cord who for many centuries after the Last Crusade have stood guard at the Holy Sepulchre.[25]

He then visited Jerusalem and the other Holy Places, and on his return he stopped at St. Jean d'Acre. Here, in order to get along, he made reed baskets and also carried the dead to the place of burial. When everything else failed, he turned to what he always called the table of Jesus Christ: begging alms from door to door.

He is the spiritual vagabond, the eternal traveller, an apostle of the high road, a perpetual pilgrim. One day Giles asked Francis to send him to a Franciscan Place so that he could be given assignments and live under rules like the other friars. Francis replied, "For you a place is always ready. Go where you will."[26]

Brother Giles avails himself of this privilege. He had already visited Sant'Angelo di Monte Gargano and San Nicola in the city of Bari. He pushes on even to Saint James of Compostella in Spain.[27] When fatigue and hunger overtake him and he cannot go on, he sleeps under a hedge at the side of the road. Sometimes upon awakening, he finds half a loaf of bread nearby, a sign that some good soul had had pity on his rags.[28] Barefoot and having only his habit on his back, he does not hesitate to take off the hood of the habit and give it to someone even more ragged than he. He talks with everyone he meets, men and women. He speaks of God and of Holy Poverty. They laugh at him. They tell him that they would prefer to renounce their part of Paradise than to go about as he does. They call him under the pretence of wanting to help him, then make fun of him by putting dice into his hands and inviting him to play for money. Never upset, he replies humbly to all who insult him, "May God forgive you."[29]

Often he likes to walk without a goal or a fixed itinerary—just to travel on through the world, in the sun, the rain, trusting in the will of God.

One morning (it is the season of Lent and the winter had been extraordinarily severe; everyone is huddling in a corner in the depths of the house because the grey sky promises snow) he wants to leave to go in search of an out-of-the-way place where he can meditate on the passion of our Lord. The cardinal from whom he asks permission to go, for himself and a companion, does not know how to conceal his astonishment.

"Where do you wish to go?" he said in a pitying tone. "You seem to me like birds without a nest."[30]

But Brother Giles pushes along to get on with his venture, he and his companion. They walk deserted roads and pass strange villages. As night falls, they find themselves on top a bare mountain where they can see the ruins of an ancient castle. A poor, sad-looking church stands nearby, and they go in and begin to pray. And then in the middle of the night it begins to snow. It snows all night and all the next day, and then for another two days and nights. The icy cold north wind blows through the unhinged shutters. There is not a twig, not a particle of bread. They try to see out from the threshold but are driven back by the storm, their faces sprayed by a whirlwind of ice and snow. They fear they are going to die from cold and hunger.

Finally Giles remembers an old story of monks who found themselves in the same danger and prayed in a loud voice and were miraculously heard and rescued. So, as the storm grows worse, the two sing lauds in voices so strong and trumpeting that they might have been singing compline on the feast of the patron saint. And sure enough, after a time someone knocks at the door and a man enters, covered with snow. Inspired by God, he has traversed the pass, heard them, and brought them wine and a bit of bread.

The Pilgrim King

A mystic of the fourteenth century wrote that Jesus came "like a lover and an armed knight" to save souls.[31] The same sort of description would apply to Brother Giles. And to him, according to legend, homage was paid by the most intrepid, the most battle-tried knight that the world has ever known: Saint Louis, king of France. The king, humbly dressed and with few companions, is on a pilgrimage to shrines throughout the world. Hearing reports about the wonderful holiness of Brother Giles, who was among Francis's first companions, he determines in his heart to visit him.

He arrives at the brothers' Place of Perugia,[a] where Giles is living. He knocks at the door and asks with great eagerness for Brother Giles, without telling the brother porter who he is. The porter hurries

---

a. The Bollandists deny that this story has any historical value and say that there is no evidence that this king ever came to Perugia. But it is a well-known fact that *l'argumentum a silentio* cannot be trusted. It is especially so in this case, in the light of the circumstances in which the king went on the pilgrimage. Moreover, this story is found not only in *Fioretti*, 34, but also in *Actus*, 46, *Speculum Vitae*, 109b, *De Conformitate* (AF 4:210), and, most importantly, in *24 Generals* (AF 3:90–91), a source of indisputable historical value. It is also included in *La Franceschina*, 2:272–73, an account especially important because the author is Padre Giacomo Oddi, a Perugia native who was guardian of the Perugia friary of Monteripido (where it is said to have taken place) in 1460 and who died there June 25, 1487.

to Brother Giles and tells him that a pilgrim is at the gate asking for him. Immediately Brother Giles knows "in spirit" that it is the king of France. With great fervour he rushes from his cell and runs to the gate. Without a word to each other and though neither has ever seen the other, the two embrace, kneel together, and kiss each other with as much affection as if they had been old and intimate friends. Neither speaks but they remain embraced in silence.

After staying like this for a long time, without a word they part, and the king continues on his way and Brother Giles returns to his cell.

When the friars learned (from one of the king's companions) who the unknown pilgrim was, they reproached Brother Giles for not having said a word to this great king who had come all the way from France to see him and listen to him.

Brother Giles replied, "Dear Brothers, do not be surprised that neither he nor I was able to say anything to each other, because in the moment when we embraced, the light of divine wisdom revealed his heart to me and mine to him. And so by God's grace we looked into each other's hearts, and whatever he thought of saying to me or I to him, we heard without sound even better than if we had spoken with our lips—and with greater consolation. For if we had wanted to explain with the help of our voices what we felt in our hearts, because of the defect of human language, which cannot clearly express the secret mysteries of God except by mystic symbols, that conversation would have saddened rather than consoled us. And so you should know for sure that the king departed marvellously consoled."

Perhaps we can see in this "Little Flower" the inspiration of Jacopone da Todi's passionate laud, "O mute love, that cannot speak!"

What Is Perfect Love?

The years pass. Brother Giles' hair turns white, his back is bent, he supports himself on a stick. Despite the fact that he, in his humility, has asked God not to be given the power to perform miracles, a sense of the miraculous surrounds the hermitage of Monteripido, where he waits to close his eyes in peace. Laymen, ministers and novices, even the general of the order—the great Saint Bonaventure,[32] come from afar to be illuminated and consoled, to learn from his white-haired saintliness the paths of heaven and earth.

Tired and ill, Giles receives them in the garden, where he spends a great part of his time. From there the two hundred towers of the warrior city and its powerful walls from Roman times can be clearly seen[33] [—a contrast to the] old stone seat in a quiet meadow spangled with anemones, a well with a pulley, an ancient marble tomb that protected the relics of a Christian virgin, and in the background the forest of meditation and prayer.[34]

One who climbed the hill, anxious to be inspired by the wisdom of the man of God, asks him about good and evil, truth and falsehood, short-lived beauty and eternal beauty, the way of salvation and the road to perdition. Brother Giles does not reply at first, seemingly absorbed in a far-away thought, perhaps lost in one of his frequent ecstasies, when he was transported to another world. (One time[35] a friar asked him if it were possible for the soul to leave the body during contemplation. And Brother Giles had replied yes, and added that there was a man on this earth who had experienced this. Said the friar, "I think when the soul re-enters the body there must be much sorrow." And Giles sighed and replied, "You have said the exact truth.") The seekers keep on pursuing him like buzzing bees. "What is prudence in holy spiritual teaching?" "How will the soul in its journey through life be able to defend itself from the subtle assaults of material and immaterial enemies?"

At last Brother Giles, speaking slowly, replies:

"If you want to see well, pluck out your eyes and be blind. If you want to hear well, be deaf. If you want to walk well, cut off your feet. If you want to work well, cut off your hands. If you want to love well, hate yourself. If you want to live well, die to yourself. If you want to make a good profit, know how to lose. If you want to be rich, be poor. If you want to enjoy pleasure, afflict yourself. If you want to be secure, always be afraid. If you want to be exalted, humiliate yourself. If you want to be honoured, despise yourself and honour those who despise you. If you want to have good things, endure evil things. If you want to rest, work. If you want to be blessed, desire to be cursed.

"Oh, what great wisdom it is to know how to do this!" he continues. "But because these are great things, they are not given to all."[36]

He who lives in this way does not need to go to Bologna or Paris to learn theology. As Brother Giles says: "If a man were to live a thousand years and not have anything to do outside himself, he would have enough to do within, in his own heart." He still would have to travel there a long way to know perfect love.

One day he and the other friars argue about perfect love. Some of them say that love is only a passion of the soul that has the power to make the lover also the beloved. That is why the wise men say (they reason) that the soul is greater when it is with what it loves than it is by itself. Even Saint Augustine said that the soul ever seeks what it loves. It was intended, in fact, that lovers remain always together, and if it were possible, live together in a single body for a more perfect union.[37]

But others in the group say that love is an appetite, peculiar only to human beings and angels, each of whom desires and begs for it. After all, what do people seek if not love?[38]

According to Brother Giles, however, perfect love is none of these. Perfect love, he says, has nothing to do with satisfaction to self.

"If you love, you will be loved. If you fear, you will be feared. If you serve, you will be served. If you treat others well, others will treat you well.

"Blessed is he who loves and does not therefore desire to be loved. Blessed is he who fears and does not therefore desire to be feared. Blessed is he who serves and does not therefore desire to be served. Blessed is he who treats others well and does not desire that others treat him well."[39]

Sometimes Brother Giles is in such high spirits that his replies become a song. This is what happens when five ministers of the order come to visit him, and he lifts his face to the heavens, raises his arms, and bursts out in these lines:

> O mi fratello
> O bel fratello
> O Amor fratello.
> fammi un castello
> che no abbia pietra nè ferro.
> O bel fratello,
> fammi una cittade
> che non abbia pietra e legname.[40]

> O my brother,
> My fine brother,
> O Brother Love,
> Build me a castle
> Not made with stone and iron.
> O good brother,
> Fashion me a city
> Not built of stone and wood.

Only love, in other words, can give us walls formidable enough, towers high enough, fortresses strong enough, to guard us against every attack of enemies and assure us of safety and salvation.

Giles used rhymes to demonstrate the transitory quality of all earthly power and show how many great ones had fallen:

> *Lasciami giacere.*
> *Se io non salisco in alto,*
> *non posso cadere.*[41]

> Let me lie low.
> If I do not rise high,
> I cannot fall.

Again and always, humility is the great teacher: "The way to go up is to go down."

"All the dangers and great falls that have happened in the world," says Brother Giles, "would never have happened except for holding the head high, as can be seen in him who was created in Heaven and in Adam and the Pharisee in the Gospel and many others. And all the great good that has happened has been done by bowing the head, as can be seen in the Blessed Virgin, the publican, the good thief, and many others."[42]

This kind of vivid, telling imagery shows us that he is a poet even when he does not speak in rhyme. Here, for example, is how he addresses himself to the purification of the soul through humility:

"Humility seems to me to be like lightning. For as lightning strikes terrible blows and afterwards none of it can be found, so humility dissolves all evil and is the enemy of all sin and makes a man look upon himself as nothing."[43]

We are told that sometimes there was no need for him to make use of imagery in speech; as if in verification of a truth he had spoken, starry lilies and fragrant violets sprang up miraculously in the meadow where he was sitting.[44]

Giles's Last Prophecy

His ecstasies became ever more frequent, his joy more intense. His companions now do not always succeed in understanding what he says, so far love has raised him to another plane.

One day he announces to one of his favourites, "I have found a great treasure, so splendid that it cannot be described by human tongue."[45]

At that moment no one knows what he means. But the meaning shines out clearly to all the brothers the day they see him down on his poor cot, devoured by fever, eyes shining among the wrinkles in the withered face—those clear eyes, still pure and blue as those of a boy, open now to the diffused light of the spring evening.

It is April 22, 1261, the vigil of the feast of Saint George.

The news runs swiftly among the people, touching every house, moving all hearts: the Blessed Giles is about to die.

The night is already late when the friars who are keeping watch in the poor cell, lighted only by a weak lantern, hear in the great silence of waiting the noise of arms and cadenced steps. Soldiers have been sent by the commune, which has also posted guards at all the gates, so that the venerated body would not be taken from the city of Perugia and carried to Porziuncola, as has been whispered about.

Giles is already far away, totally absorbed in the splendour of heaven that is opening to his prostrate body, his tired old body. But that noise, those conversations in a low voice, those schemes, bring him back. He says (and the friars have to bend down to pick up the sigh from his lips), "Let the Perugini know that neither for my canonization nor for my miracles will they ever ring bells."[46]

And the reply of the Perugini is equal to the grandeur of that moment of death. They say, "It is no matter. We want him for himself and not because he is a saint."[47]

Thus they, a violent, overbearing, proud, cruel people, have been won by love. Now no one thinks in the same way as he had on the day that Francis went down to preach on the Perugia piazza, when everyone wore a label: friend or enemy, fellow citizen or outsider, follower or rebel, soldier of one flag or soldier of another.

The serene, calm night follows its course, a tepid breeze blowing through the wide-open window. The old companion has one last return to earthly life. He sees himself again in his youth, when he was full of dreams and eager for heroic enterprises. He sees another sleepless night like this one, also on the vigil of Saint George. He got up early, as one with a long road to travel, and went to the church of Saint George in order to say the prayer of a new knight. The streets of the city were full of life on this day before the warriors' tournament. The pennons waved in the Sementone field.

Now Saint George, in his shining armour, is guiding his soul, free at last, through the pathways of the countless stars.

The brothers kneel. Dawn is on its way.[48]

Who is Brother Juniper?

Which of the ancient citizens of Assisi of whom we read in contemporary records hides behind the name of Brother Juniper? Certainly it was not this friar's original name, but one taken upon entering the order.[b]

The absolute silence of all the sources closes the door on investigation. It is known for certain that he was among the first who followed Francis.[49] And the name, which served both as a uniform and a password in the battle he was undertaking, confirms what we read in the most ancient stories about him, that is, that this Franciscan wished to base his spiritual life on humility and contempt of self.

The juniper is a lowly shrub that grows among brushwood and dunes. As is true of all creatures who live a life of humble love that persists even beyond death, it, after being consumed by fire, keeps in its ashes the heat of the flames longer than any other wood, even the most prized. Although its sharp leaves remind one of the sackcloth of mortification, it is always in flower. And when in the dark dawns of December the thrushes rise like arrows among the groves of the Subasio, its intoxicating fruits shine like an offering in the utter desolation.[c]

This well describes Brother Juniper, an impassioned soul in the brown sackcloth of penance, his life a perpetual immolation of his entire self. His flesh, his spirit, even his kind of holiness, was a confrontation to the frightening selfishness of the world. They called him "God's fool" because in him there was a frenzy of love, a madness for the good, a foolishness of the cross, that make him appear to us as a fighter so foolhardy as to be absurd, one contemptuous of every sensible rule of prudence and suitability. His charity and zeal knew no limits, so much so that Francis used to say that the good Friar Minor will be one who can attain the same contempt of self and of the world as Brother Juniper.[50]

The Pig in the Porziuncola Forest

In the beginning Brother Juniper had a much harder battle than he could have possibly imagined. Untamed pride reared up at an unexpected rebuke. It is certainly true that in this world it is much easier to be poor than to be humble in the sense of knowing how to cope

---

b. The constant tradition is that Brother Juniper was from Assisi. See *NV* 2:298.

c. This lovely picture of Brother Juniper is presented in Wadding: "Francis, admiring his simplicity, said to those standing there, 'Brothers, would that we had a whole forest of junipers like this.' He was alluding to the etymology and the properties suggested by the name, because, according to Isidore, just as juniper preserves burning coals longer than any other wood, and just as the juniper is sown by bees and, according to Jerome, always flourishes, always bears new fruit, and never loses its green, so this man, by his severe penance as well as by his austerity, preserves within himself the verdancy of divine love."

with wounded pride. And this friar grew hot not only at a belittling remark but also at a reprimand from superiors. We are told in *Little Flowers* of his solution: "Seeing therefore that he could not remain silent and refrain from answering when something unpleasant was said to him or when he was scolded, (and) realizing that his tongue was doing him much harm, he decided to remain silent at all cost. And he arranged it this way in order to observe it better. On the first day he kept silent out of love for the Heavenly Father, the next day for love of Jesus Christ, the next for love of the Holy Spirit, the next for love of the Virgin Mary, the next for love of our Father Saint Francis, and so on. Every day for love of some Saint, he remained silent and did not speak for six months. And although he suffered pain and anxiety within, nevertheless externally he forced himself not to reply, even though with great difficulty."[51]

We are also told in *La Franceschina* that he succeeded in remaining silent, but one time the physical effort was so great that his anguish caused him to spit up blood. He rushed to kneel in front of the crucifix and pour out his passion and pain: "See, my Lord, what I am bearing for love of you!" And immediately the Crucified Christ miraculously raised his right hand from the cross, where it was nailed, laid it on the wound in his side, and said, "And I—what am I bearing for you?"

From that moment, the account continued, Brother Juniper was changed into another man. Instead of suffering over unpleasant remarks, he exulted in the least sign of contempt from others.[52]

The second virtue that Brother Juniper practiced in the highest degree was charity, carried to its utmost limits.

One time at Santa Maria degli Angeli he happened to visit a sick brother. Full of compassion, he asked him if he could do anything for him. The sick man replied, "I would love to eat a pig's foot if I had one. . . . "

Brother Juniper did not have to be told twice. The account of the incident in *Little Flowers* continues: "He went and took a knife from the kitchen and ran into the fields, where he found a group of pigs feeding. He ran after one of them, caught it, and cut off one of its feet with the knife. Leaving the pig with its leg maimed, he came back and washed and dressed and cooked the pig's foot. After he had prepared it, he brought and served it with great kindness to the sick friar. The latter ate it very eagerly, to Brother Juniper's intense joy and consolation. And to entertain him, Juniper gleely described how he had caught the pig.

"Meanwhile, however, the man who was guarding the swine and

who had seen him cut off the foot, told his master the whole story indignantly. When the master heard about it, he went to the friars' Place and shouted at them, calling them hypocrites, thieves, forgers, bandits, and evil men for having with deliberate malice cut off one of his pig's feet. At all the noise he was making, Saint Francis came out with the others and very humbly made excuses for his friars, saying that he had not known about what had happened. Yet to appease him, he promised that he would make good the damage. But the man would not calm down. Raging with anger, he continued to curse and threaten, repeating over and over that the pig's foot had been cut off with deliberate malice. He refused to accept any excuses or promises, and he left still shouting.

"While the other friars stood around chagrined, Saint Francis prudently thought the matter over and said to himself: 'Could Brother Juniper have done this out of indiscreet zeal?' He immediately summoned Brother Juniper privately and asked him: 'Did you cut off the foot of a pig in the fields?'

"Then Brother Juniper, acting not as if he had done something wrong but as one who believes he had performed an act of great charity, answered joyfully: 'Dear Father, it is true I cut the pig's foot off. And now listen compassionately to the reason. I went to visit that sick friar . . . ' And he told him the whole story.

"On hearing it, Saint Francis was saddened. His face flushed, he said: 'Oh, Brother Juniper, why did you bring this great disgrace on us? That man is quite right in being angry at us. Right now he is probably complaining about us and spoiling our reputation throughout the town—and he has good reason to do so! Therefore I now order you under holy obedience to run right after that man until you overtake him. Throw yourself on the ground before him and admit your guilt to him. And promise to make good the damage—and do it—in such a way that he will have no more reason to complain against us. For this certainly has been a most serious wrong!'

"Brother Juniper marvelled that anyone should be angry over an act of charity. To him all material things seemed like nothing, except if they were put to use in practicing charity. And he replied: 'Father, you can be sure I will quickly give him full satisfaction. But why should he be so angry when something that belonged to God rather than to him was used to perform such a real act of charity?'

"Then he ran off and overtook the man, who was still so angry that he had not an ounce of patience left. With intense joy and fervour Brother Juniper told him all about the amputation of the pig's foot, as though he had done him a great favour for which he deserved a reward. The man's anger only increased, and he shouted that he was a fool, a lunatic, and the worst kind of criminal—and he almost struck him.

"Brother Juniper was amazed at these ugly words, although he rejoiced at receiving the insults. And because he thought that the man had not understood what he had said (which seemed to him a matter for joy rather than anger), he told the same story over again. And he embraced the man, explaining how it had been done only out of love, and urging the man to congratulate him for doing such a good deed, and even inviting the man to give the rest of the pig for the same purpose.

"Then that man was overcome by so much simplicity and humility. And recovering his senses when he heard that the cause of the deed had been an act of charity, he knelt down and wept and admitted that he had been wrong in insulting Brother Juniper and the other holy friars. He acknowledged that perhaps he was greedy and ungrateful to God for the good things which he possessed. So he went and caught and killed the pig and had it cooked and well dressed. And with great devotion and weeping he brought it to Santa Maria degli Angeli and gave it to those holy friars to eat as compensation for the wrong which he had done them.

"Now Saint Francis, considering the simplicity and self-contempt and patience under adversity of that holy Brother Juniper, said to his companions and the other friars who were standing around: 'My Brothers, if only I had a great forest of such junipers!'"[53]

Brother Juniper's Cooking

However, in situations concerning himself and the other religious, Brother Juniper did not understand why so much time had to be lost in the preparation of food, which seemed to him a great loss of hours better spent in meditation and prayer.

One day, while he was living in a small friary, all the brothers had to go out for some reason, and they told Brother Juniper to prepare a little something for them to eat when they returned.[54] Brother Juniper promised, but after they had gone, he began to think the matter over, especially how much bother it was to have to spend time in the kitchen to the neglect of prayer. And he decided to prepare enough food to last a fortnight.

"And so," we are told in *Little Flowers,* "he eagerly went to town and begged some cooking pots and collected some fresh and some salted meat and chickens and eggs and different kinds of vegetables. And he gathered and lit a lot of firewood. Then he filled all those pots with water and put them on the fire, and he put everything into the pots—chickens with feathers and eggs in shells and the vegetables, one thing after another—so that they should all cook together.

"Meanwhile, one of the friars who was a friend of Brother Juniper and used to his simple ways, came back and was let in by the Brother. On entering the kitchen and seeing so many large pots boiling on the roaring fire, he sat down and watched what he was doing. And he saw how he kept anxiously running from one pot to another, stirring their contents with a stick, and bringing more firewood and blowing on the fire and constantly keeping busy cooking, without a moment's rest. And because, owing to the intense heat, he could not get close to the pots to skim them, he took a board and tied it tightly to his body with a rope in order to protect himself from the heat. And then he jumped from one pot to another in a thoroughly entertaining way.

"Meanwhile all the other friars returned. And after watching him with great amusement, that certain friar went out of the kitchen and said to them: 'Brother Juniper certainly is preparing a wedding feast!' But they thought he was joking.

"Then Brother Juniper took his pots off the fire and rang the bell for the meal. And when the friars had gone into the refectory, he came in with all that food he had cooked, red-faced from his exertion and from the heat of the fire. And he said to them: 'Have a good meal—and let's go to pray, and no one need bother about cooking for the next fortnight because I have prepared enough today to last more than two weeks.'

"Then he set down on the table before the friars that hodge-podge of his, which not a single hog in the city of Rome would have eaten, no matter how hungry it was. And he served them dishes of eggs in the shell and chickens partly covered with feathers. And the friars found on their plates the feathers which had fallen off when the chickens were boiled. Then, seeing that the other friars were not eating anything, Brother Juniper took a chicken with feathers and put it to his mouth, and without cutting it he tore it apart with his teeth. And he praised what he had cooked, like a salesman selling his wares, saying: 'Such chickens are good for the brain—and this mixture will keep the body in good condition. Eat it—it will do you good!'

"But though the friars admired his simplicity and considered his self-control a sign of wisdom, the guardian was angry at his foolishness and wastefulness. He scolded Brother Juniper severely. Poor Brother Juniper threw himself on his knees before them all and humbly admitted his fault, declaring that he was a very bad man. He recited the sins which he had committed when he was in the world, and said: 'A certain man committed such and such a sin, and they tore out his eyes, but I should rather have my eyes torn out. Another man was hanged for his crimes—I should rather be hanged for my evil deeds, because I have wasted so many good things of God and of the Order!' And he went out, repenting bitterly, and would not let himself be seen by any of the friars all day long.

"But the guardian said to the friars: 'My dear Brothers, I wish Brother Juniper would waste as much every day—if only we had it—so that we might be edified like this. For it was his great simplicity and charity that made him do this.'"

Charity vs. Obedience

There were times that Brother Juniper could not give rein to his charity because it was held in check by obedience. At such times he, to escape the duty that had been laid down for him, resorted to various sophistries that would make us laugh if it were not for the fact that the thought of a love that conceived of daily life as a sacrifice brings tears to our eyes.

Brother Juniper, whenever he met some poor man, bare or badly clothed, would immediately take off his habit or rip off his hood and give it away in charity. Finally the guardian ordered him under obedience not to give away any more of his clothes, either his whole habit or a part of it, to anyone.

A few days later he met a poor man, almost naked, who begged Brother Juniper to give him something for the love of God. Brother Juniper was extremely embarrassed. On the one hand, he was full of compassion, but on the other, he did not wish to disobey his superior. Finally he said to the beggar, "My dear man, I have nothing to give you except my habit—and my superior has forbidden me to give it or part of it away to anyone. But if you pull it off my back, I certainly will not prevent you."

He was not speaking to a deaf man, we are told in *Little Flowers*, and the beggar immediately pulled the habit off inside out and left, leaving Brother Juniper naked. When he returned and the other brothers asked him what had happened to his habit, he replied, "Some good person pulled it off my back and went away with it."[55]

Brother Juniper's charity led him not only to give away his habit but also books, ornaments for the altar, the cloaks of other friars, and whatever else he could lay his hands on. For this reason the friars would hide the things they wanted to keep so Brother Juniper could not find them, "for he used to give everything away for the love of God and for His praise."[56]

His love of poverty and charity was matched, however, by his love of humility. [Indeed, he went to extreme lengths in his naive efforts to make himself the lowliest of men.]

One day in Viterbo, to expose himself to the greatest possible contempt of the people, Brother Juniper stripped, tied his clothes in a bundle, put them on his head, and walked to the main piazza. There he remained for a good part of the day, completely naked. Children and boys mocked and insulted him and threw stones at him. Toward evening, when he returned to the friary, the friars scolded him and threatened him with such things as prison and hanging and being burned at the stake. And Brother Juniper listened cheerfully and answered joyfully, "You are right. I deserve all those punishments and still greater ones for causing such scandal."[57]

He did the same sort of thing another time, when he walked stark naked from Foligno through several villages to Assisi to a solemn festival. The general rebuked him harshly and concluded his scolding by saying, "Your fault is so great and serious that I don't know what penance I should give you."

And Brother Juniper answered, "I'll tell you, Father. Since I came here naked, as penance I should go back naked along the same road to the place from which I came to this festival."[58]

[Through this same desire to be the least,] Brother Juniper desired that after he died he would not be remembered and venerated but greatly despised. One day he asked a brother what sort of death he preferred. The brother replied that he would like to give up his last breath in a friary surrounded by many brothers, praying for his salvation.

Said Brother Juniper: "On the other hand, I would like to give off such a stink that no one could come near me and for that reason they would throw me in a ditch and leave me there in solitude and abhorrence, without burial, until the dogs devour me."[59]

The Tyrant Named Nicolò

Francis had taught Brother Leo how to achieve perfect joy, but Brother Juniper pushed the matter of bearing maltreatment in patience and joy to absurd lengths.

There was a cruel tyrant named Nicolò, lord of a castle and village at war with Viterbo. And it happened that the devil, wishing to find a way to make Brother Juniper suffer, went to him and denounced Brother Juniper. (It is said that the devil, in order to give vent to his impotent hate, often assumes the role of an informer. His bestial face hypocritically takes on the mien of an honest man, the mocking grin becomes an indulgent smile, the talons of a filthy beast disappear into a pair of pure white gloves.)

In this way the devil went to the lord Nicolò and whispered, "Sir, watch out for this castle of yours, because soon a great traitor will be sent here by the men of Viterbo to kill you and set fire to your castle. And I give you these clues that this is true. He goes around dressed like a poor man with tattered and patched clothes and a torn cowl hanging on his shoulders, and he is carrying an awl with which to kill you, and he has with him a flint and steel to set fire to this castle. And if you do not find this to be true, punish me any way you wish."

The lord ordered guards to watch with diligence and told them that if anyone arrived fitting that description, to seize him at once. In the meantime Brother Juniper arrived, his habit cut off because he had given half of it to the poor, his hood torn, looking like anything but a Friar Minor. And with a great brouhaha the guards seized him and took him to Nicolò. They searched him and found in his sleeve an awl with which he mended shoes and a flint and steel, which he carried because he lived often in forests and other deserted places and needed it to light a fire.

Seeing that the facts fit the accusation, Nicolò ordered them to twist a rope about Juniper's head and tighten it with a stick, and they did so with such cruelty that the rope cut into the flesh. They then tortured him on the rack and pulled and wrenched his arms and tore his whole body without mercy.

And all that time they asked him who he was and what his name was. He replied, "I am a very great sinner."

They asked if he had come to betray the castle and give it to the people of Viterbo. And he said, "I would do even worse things if God permitted it."

That was enough for Nicolò. In a rage and without further investigation, he condemned Brother Juniper to be tied to the tail of a horse, dragged to the gallows, and hanged.

And still Brother Juniper made no excuses and gave no sign of distress. Rather, he looked like someone who finds joy in miseries. He did not even complain when he was tied by the feet to the horse and dragged over the ground like a lamb being taken to the butcher. And in the meantime, the people were rushing up to see the execution of this stranger, so quickly and cruelly sentenced to death.

But one compassionate man who saw all these happenings ran to the Place of the Friars Minor and said: "For God's sake, please come quickly, because a poor man has been arrested and immediately sentenced and is being dragged to execution! Come, so that he can at least commit his soul into your hands—because he seems like a good man to me and he has not had time for confession. And they are taking him to be hanged—but he does not seem to care about death or the salvation of his soul. Please come quickly!"

The guardian immediately went, but he found the square so crowded that he could not get through it. So he stood and waited; and while he was waiting, he heard someone say, "Lay off, you rogues, that rope is hurting my leg."

The guardian thought he recognized a familiar voice. He threw himself into the middle of the crowd, raised the cloth that covered the face of the condemned man, and was petrified to find that it was Brother Juniper. And Juniper, paying no attention to his own pain, smiled and said, "O Guardian, how fat you are!"

The guardian, moved to tears, took off his own habit to cover him; but Juniper continued to joke, "O you wicked man, you are very fat and don't look well without a habit. I don't want it."

The guardian begged the executioners and all the people to wait for pity's sake, so that he could go to the tyrant Nicolò and ask him to have mercy. And, believing that he was a relative, they agreed.

The compassionate guardian went to Nicolò and in tears said to him, "Sir, I can't tell you how amazed and how sad I am, because I believe that today in this place a greater sin and a greater wrong has been committed than was ever done in the days of our ancestors. But I believe that it was done through ignorance."

Nicolò listened patiently and asked what was this great evil. The guardian replied, "One of the holiest friars in all the world, living in the order of Saint Francis (for whom you have a special devotion) has been sentenced by you to a very cruel punishment—I fully believe without justification. . . . and that is Brother Juniper, the companion of Saint Francis!"

The tyrant had indeed heard of the famous Brother Juniper. He paled, rushed to the place where the execution was to take place, released Brother Juniper, and, weeping, threw himself at his feet. "I believe truly that soon I shall have an evil death," he said, "because I have tortured this holy man in such a manner without any reason."

And this really happened to him, because a few days later he was cruelly killed by the sword.[60]

The Lord's Jester

Even Brother Juniper's love for his brothers had something frenetic about it, something of both sweetness and savagery. It was moving, terrifying, nurtured on macabre fantasies outside normal limits in both religious and community life. At one time he had a companion named Amazialbene, whom he loved. Brother Amazialbene was a model of the virtues of patience and obedience, so much so that if he had been beaten all day, he would not have raised a single complaint. And because of his virtues, he was often put with others who were very hard to get along with. Brother Juniper could persuade him to laugh or cry, whatever he wished.

Now this Brother Amazialbene died, in an odor of sanctity. And when Brother Juniper heard of his death, he was overcome by the greatest sadness he had ever known. He went about saying, "Alas, I have nothing good left in this world! Everything has fallen apart in the death of my dear and beloved Brother Amazialbene!"

He said, "If it were not for the reprisals that the friars would take against me, I should go to his tomb and take his skull and out of it make two bowls. One of them I should use for eating in memory of my continual devotion to him, and the other I would use for drinking whenever I am thirsty."[61]

Even his visions, whatever high significance they might have, had something out of the ordinary about them. One day, while at prayer, it seemed to him that he saw a hand in the air and that he heard a voice warning him, "O Brother Juniper, without this hand you can do nothing." And he immediately got up and went all through the friary with his eyes raised to the heavens and saying, "Indeed that is true! That is very true!"[62]

His life was like this in the several friaries in which he lived: in Assisi, Gualdo, Spoleto, Viterbo. At last he was sent to Rome.

Perhaps it was Pope Innocent IV himself who made the suggestion, thinking that the presence of Brother Juniper would increase the devotion of other brothers in the order. The pope and Brother Juniper had met in 1253 in Assisi. And certainly they understood and loved each other. The papal court had been in residence in Assisi since the Octave of Easter of that year, in the Gregorian Palazzo of the Convento di San Francesco. According to the Chronicle of Matthew of Paris,[63] the people of Rome were making a great noise at the time about the absence of the pope. They were even threatening the people of Assisi and declaring that they were going to come with an army, take the city, take possession of the person of the pope and by force take him back to the deserted Lateran palace. And sometimes they railed against the pope, saying, "Come now or never come again!" Legates from the senator of Rome, Brancaleone, came and went, beetle-browed, to the apostolic residence to repeat these demands.

But Innocent had decided not to give in. His firmness was as great as his piety. Nicola da Calvi [also called Nicolò da Curdio], who was in his retinue, wrote: "Being in all his acts counseled by piety, he made himself humble with the humble, meek with the meek. And the brothers, regarding him more as a true and loving mother than as a father, constantly went to him. He encouraged them with his persuasive words and his discourses."[64]

This was the time that Clare, sweet Sister Clare, lay dying in San Damiano. Innocent went to see her, and from this visit she drew great consolation.

Brother Juniper also went down to San Damiano. The Blessed Clare had no more than a few hours of life remaining. She was in great pain. But, as she saw Brother Juniper enter, her face shone with joy and she saluted him: "Here is the great jester of the Lord."

She knew all his songs. She asked him if he did not have something new in hand.

And Juniper began his laud. It seemed, said the biographer, that "Juniper sent forth like sparks . . . flaming words from the furnace of his burning heart."[65]

And the Blessed Clare did not suffer any more. She listened, finding "great consolation" in his words, in his strange and pure song that gave her a mysterious happiness that lifted her above the pains of her body and spirit, a song that was a prelude to supernatural ecstasy.

In the Hallowed Halls of the Campidoglio

As soon as the news that Brother Juniper was coming ran through Rome, a great many people went out to meet him, drawn by his reputation for holiness. But Brother Juniper, when he saw all those people, wondered how he could turn their admiration into scorn and mockery.

Nearby were two boys playing see-saw on a plank set on a log. Brother Juniper quickly went over to them, made one of them get down, took his place, and began to see-saw.

The sight astonished the crowd of people that had come out to welcome him. But they greeted Brother Juniper with great respect and waited for him to stop his game and let them escort him to the friary. But Brother Juniper paid little attention.

They waited and waited. A good many of them began to say they had come out to greet a country bumpkin and a blockhead instead of a holy man, though some still said that what he was doing just proved how virtuous he was. Finally, however, they all got bored and left. And when he saw that they had all gone, Brother Juniper, well satisfied, got down from the see-saw and set out to the Franciscan friary, alone and in perfect humility.[66]

Since 1220 the friars had had a place in Rome in the area that was to be known as San Francesco a Ripa. Later they were installed in other churches: San Salvatore *in pede pontis*, Santa Maria in Cosmedin, Santa Maria del Popolo. It was soon clear that they needed a new place, something that would be, like the basilica on the hill of Assisi, both a fortress of faith and an entrance to paradise. And Innocent thought of the Capitoline citadel, where one of the twelve Benedictine abbeys of the city had its seat.[67]

The Campidoglio—the Capitoline hill—is the living heart of Rome, the symbol of its political life, ancient and modern. "If," said Petrarch, "only the naked Capitoline rock remains in the city of Rome, "the imperium will endure there forever."

But it has always been also a sacred place. Here, under the sun of the countless summers before there was a Rome, prayers rang out to Saturn, the peaceful numen of seeding and harvest. Here Romulus raised the first temple to Jove, invoking him on the coming of his warrior people. Here, according to legend, Augustus, not satisfied by triumph and by empire, yearned to know the supreme truth, which was to be revealed in the coming of the Son of God. Here he raised the first altar dedicated to an apparition of Mary: *ara coeli,* altar of the heavens, channel between earth and heaven.[d]

And now, here, the pope willed, must be established Saint Francis's new and perfect citadel [dedicated] to the salvation of the world through love. The friary was built rapidly, and by offerings from all the people of Rome.

Brother Juniper took up residence in it.

In the years that followed, Santa Maria d'Aracoeli was the meeting place for all the *rioni* ("districts") where discussions were held with representatives of the Maggiore and Minore Consiglio. In it peace and war were deliberated, public acts drawn up. In the friary, where the general of the Friars Minor lived, the Collegio dei Giudici Urbani (the body of city judges) had its seat. It often happened that the senators and the proconsuls took off their purple and steel and put on the sackcloth of the friars in order to search for peace in the humble cells. Bartholomew of Pisa wrote in 1385: "Many friars in Aracoeli were nobles of the houses of Colonna, Orsini, Sant'Eustachio, and of other Roman princes."[68]

---

d. According to tradition, on this site the Sibyl of Tivoli is said to have prophesied the coming of Christ to Augustus. In the church, the Holy Chapel is built over the site of an altar erected by Augustus as a result of the prophecy of the Sibyl.

After Seven Centuries

In this friary of the Aracoeli Brother Juniper spent the last years of his life. He desired nothing more than to depart from the desert of this world so as to enter into the flowering garden of his dream. Once he was overcome by ecstasy in the choir of the church, and the brothers left him alone. When he returned to himself, after many hours, he spoke of having seen through grace the glory of the blessed in paradise. He said over and over, "O brothers, why don't you want to endure a few troubles in order to win eternal life?"[69]

He died in peace, as if he were going to sleep, on January 6 (4?), 1258. He was buried, perhaps by his wish, in the most out-of-the-way corner of the church.[70]

After seven centuries, the translation of his relics took place, on June 22, 1958—an unforgettable ceremony.[e]

The procession crossed the solemn nave. The candle flames shone in the subdued light. Trumpet calls of Assisi heralds reached to the top of the columns, taken from pagan temples, and awoke echoes from the tombs. A great crowd, dressed in coarse gray cloth, in iron, purple, gold, came to life again, some wavering on the stones of the tombs, some lying under the baldacchini of funeral monuments, and some underfoot, worn by the steps of generations gone by. A wave of emotion ran through the vast basilica, as in the time of the passionate assemblies convoked there for war and for peace, for victory and for defeat. In the past centuries, how many of these voices have struck the hidden tomb of Brother Juniper, from the barons of Charles of Anjou to citizens caught in the attack by Henry VII, to the apotheosis of the victor of Lepanto!

It was Brother Juniper's hour again. Now his bones were receiving the glory he had wished to deny himself in life and in death. Friars and citizens, both dead and the living—all sang in chorus the words of

---

e. On May 26, 1958, in a celebration of the seventh centenary of the death of Brother Juniper, steps were taken to provide proper recognition of these relics, which had been recovered from the lower part of this pilaster. On the lead casket there was a Latin inscription; it recorded that in 1548 Padre Luca Basso, the guardian of Aracoeli, had moved to this more decorous place "the bones of Brother Juniper, which for a long time had lain in an obscure place of this noble church of Aracoeli."

On June 22, 1958, in a solemn ceremony marked by the participation of the Minister General of the Friars Minor, the mayors of Rome and of Assisi with their respective delegations, these bones were placed in the left wall of the Chapel of Saint Francis, near the tomb of Luca Savelli, the nephew of Pope Honorius III and father of Pope Honorius IV. The ancient jasper memorial stone was placed above the site; it bears these words: *Ossa Fratris Iuniperi socii S. Francisci;* and underneath these were added: *Ossa Fratris Iuniperi—rite recognita et heic reposita—die 22 Iunii 1958—septimo recurrente—ab eius pio obitu—saeculo.* On this occasion, the June, 1958, issue of *Ara-Coeli,* monthly journal of Franciscan religious life, was devoted to "Vita di fra Ginepro compagno di S. Francesco d'Assisi." The material was drawn from various sources and was the work of Padre Ferdinando De Angelis, editor of the periodical.

the gradual of the Mass of Saint Francis: *Franciscus pauper et humilis dives coelum ingreditur,* "Francis, poor and humble, enters heaven a rich man."

The hymn spreads into the piazza flooded with the midday sun. In a hush, the ringing of all the bells of Rome could be heard—a festive ringing, a medley of sound that rose from churches near and far. The Gesù, Santa Maria Nuova, San Francesco delle Stimmate, San Nicola dei Cesari, Sant'Andrea della Valle, San Lorenzo in Damaso, Chiesa Nuova, Santa Maria in Campitelli, Santa Maria sopra Minerva, Santissimi Apostoli, San Giorgio in Velabro, San Bartolomeo dell'Isola, Sant'Ignazio, Santa Caterina, Madonna dei Monti, San Pietro in Vincoli, Santa Maria in Cosmedin, Santa Maria Egiziaca, Sant'Anastasia—all are ringing out their salute. Their hosannas linger in the circle of drowsy towers, in the brilliance of the spreading light. Then little by little, all becomes still; silence again enfolds the imperial city that has paid him homage.

·14·

LOVE OF ALL CREATURES

If there is one thing that everyone knows about Saint Francis, it is that he liked birds. Seldom, however, is it pointed out that the founding of his third religious order, the Secular Franciscan Order, can be traced to the birds, specifically, to his "Sister Swallows."

Swallows are exasperating creatures. In their nests they must have reminded Francis of Clare and her sisters at San Damiano—dressed in black and white, sweet and humble. But in a most unClare-like manner, they will suddenly shoot into the air, whirl and dart about in erratic frenzy, all the while lacerating the sky with piercing cries that boggle the mind. Are they joyful or sad? Who can say?

Just such cries of the swallows filled the air the day that Francis preached in the piazza in Cannara,[a] a strong *castello* of the Assisi diocese, on the left of the Tupino river, some miles from Santa Maria degli Angeli.

It was an inaccessible place, squeezed between a swamp and a wooded hill. In Francis's time, only a few fields, planted in spelt, lay outside the walls. All in all it looked like an island, and in the records it is called the *asio*[b] of Cannara." In the winter months the waters in the gullies overflowed and lay stagnating in a large marshy stretch covered with the thick canebrakes (*canneti*) that gave the place its name. The wolves would come all the way up to the barred gates and fill the nights with their doleful howls.

---

a. Thomas of Celano says that the episode of the swallows took place in Alviano rather than in Cannara (*1 Cel.*, 59) and Saint Bonaventure follows him (*Leg. Maior*, XII, 4). Because Alviano is more than ninety kilometres from Assisi and Cannara is but eight, and because all the sources place this episode alongside the sermon to the birds at Bevagna, about eight kilometres distant from Cannara, it seems likely that the name Alviano was a copyist's error. Records in the Assisi archives prove conclusively that Cannara was in existence during Saint Francis's lifetime. See *NV* 2:456–60. In *Actus*, 16 and *Fioretti*, 16 Cannara is named.

b. The word *asio* was used to denote a short stretch of cultivated land: *NV* 2:312–13.

On the particular day with which we are concerned, it was already late spring. The canes glittered in the sun, the flowing river mirrored the clear blue sky. It was just after Francis had been advised [by Clare and Brother Silvestro] to continue in his apostolate. So again he had set out on foot, taking with him Brother Masseo and Brother Angelo, with the thought of making a new beginning from this *castello,* familiar to him since the days of his youth. He was so full of spiritual enthusiasm he devoured the road that descends from San Damiano and continues on through Castelnuovo, and he reached the Cannara bridge in high morning. Immediately the word spread and people hurried out to gather in the piazza before their parish church.

Records in the Assisi archives give us the precise and immediate sense of what these people were like. Sullen and unbending millers, wont to argue with contractors in the Assisi commune about how much was made by the mills and fulling mills, about the water conduit and the tax on the flour. Often they went so far as to engage in bloody feuds and in doing so, ruined the dams and damaged the walls and beams of the mill-race. Spelt farmers. Honers of millstones. Ox drivers and woodcutters. Wolf hunters. Wicker weavers.

As he talked, Francis saw faces smooth out, the dark diffidence give way to an expression of wonder. And his fervour grew because of that unexpected emotion. But the cries of the swallows distracted him and kept him from concentrating.

The flock fluttered back and forth between the river and the Limigiano gate, making such a racket that Francis, in the middle of his sermon, stopped. "My sisters," he said, "it is my turn to speak now. You have said enough already. Listen to God's word and be quiet until the sermon is over."

Immediately—and it was quite a sight—the swallows stopped flying about and settled down attentively. On the cornices of the houses, along the modillions of the towers, in the brackets and arcades, the ranked white breasts and forked tails of the now-silent birds shone out as when they gathered in September at the time of their migration.

But to such a miracle was added another, no less wonderful.

When Francis had finished speaking, not only some (as was usual) but all of the men and women wanted to join him.

Without regret they would leave their beloved homes, their warm hearths, the walls they had fought over, the clear water of the river, their moist furrows, their flocks and herds. All were ready to forget, just as in the hour of dying, their work, their affections, hopes and memories, their seeding and harvesting, their mill, meadow lands and woodlands, the soothing sound in the long night hours of a shuttle on the loom. They were ready to put behind them the hill fragrant with juniper, the romantic songs of May, the rows of poplars whispering along the riverbed. Joining Francis in his mission was more important than their loves and marriages, their tender little ones and white-haired old men and the dead asleep in the church. All these things they would joyfully give to bring into reality the beautiful dream that the words of the man of Assisi had opened to them.

Francis's heart was shaken by this heroic self-offering of a whole people. What he had imagined to require an unusual condition of grace had suddenly shown itself to be the deep aspiration of all human beings. What was he to do?

Silence reigned for an instant over the sun-baked piazza, the anxious people, the devout listening swallows. Finally he said, "Don't be in a hurry and don't leave, for I will arrange what you should do for the salvation of your souls."

And so it was that Francis conceived the idea of the Secular Franciscan Order [formerly the Franciscan Third Order]. And it grew out of the remarkable happening seen by these people, who were the first to dedicate themselves en masse to the new movement, when "irrational creatures recognized his affection for them and felt his tender love for them." [It was surely, in their eyes, a validation of his vision.]

Francis must have been exalted by the thought as he made his way from Cannara to Bevagna. The poetic quality of the event, the opening of an enlarged vision, brought to life his springtime spirits. The road stretched out amid fields of grain and in a short time led into a large plain that the country people called then, and call now, Pian dell'Arca. Oaks stood here and there, and Francis, raising his eyes, saw on the branches great flocks of birds; they seemed to be awaiting his coming. He called to them and immediately they flew down and settled in a circle on the ground around him, so near that some touched his habit.

It was a very special moment, surely under skies of the same deep blue that Giotto used to suggest its splendour in his famous painting of this scene in the Basilica di San Francesco.

And Francis said:

"My little bird sisters, you owe much to God your Creator, and you must always and everywhere praise him, because he has given you freedom to fly anywhere—also he has given you a double and triple covering, and your colourful and pretty clothing, and your food is ready without your working for it, and your singing that was taught to you by the Creator, and your numbers that have been multiplied by the blessing of God—and because he preserved your species in Noah's ark so that your race should not disappear from the earth. And you are also indebted to him for the realm of the air, which he assigned to you."

And it was beautiful to see that at these words the little creatures of God began to open their beaks, stretch out their necks, spread their wings, and with discreet chirps show their great delight.

Francis continued:

"Moreover, you neither sow nor reap, yet God nourishes you, and he gives you the rivers and springs from which to drink. He gives you high mountains and hills, rocks and crags as refuges, and lofty trees in which to make your nests. And although you do not know how to spin or sew, God gives you and your little ones the clothing that you need. So the Creator loves you very much, since he gives you so many good things. Therefore, my little bird sisters, be careful not to be ungrateful, but strive always to praise God."[1]

They seemed very much alike then, the joyous Poverello of Christ and the little songbirds. And in fact, there is nothing more like the Friars Minor than birds, for both free and light travel about the world, possessing nothing and entrusting their lives solely to the providence of God.[2]

The garrulous anxious swallows! Even after Francis died, the sound of his name could awake them to the old love.

Thomas of Celano tells us a story about a scholar at the University of Parma, probably one of those sceptical and pleasure-loving goliards ready to laugh at the most sacred things. He was studying diligently one day but was distracted by the continual screeching of a swallow. Impatiently he gave vent to his annoyance, saying, "This must be one of the birds that disturbed Saint Francis when he was preaching, until he told them to be quiet." Then, jokingly, he turned to the swallow and said, "In the name of God's servant Francis, I command you to come to me and keep quiet." Scarcely had he finished the words when the swallow flew into his hands.[3]

The Third Order

Several years had to pass before the promise made to the people of Cannara could be fulfilled. It happened in the spring of 1221, when Francis passed through Poggibonsi, a little town between Siena and Florence, and met the man who would become the first tertiary, Lucchesio.

He, like Francis at one time, was driven by status seeking and social climbing. But while Pietro's son had tried to make himself as grand as the nobles by prodigal spending, Lucchesio, convinced that the secret of success lay only in being rich, had gone in the opposite direction. He had thrown himself body and soul into making money by the cornering of grain. He acquired large quantities from the wholesalers and held on to it, thus preventing normal supplies from coming into the market. And he profited by the strong rise in prices that followed his manoeuvre by reselling his merchandise at the greatest possible profit. He was, in other words, a king of the black market.

His accomplice in this sordid business was his young wife, Buonadonna. Their house was cursed by all the hard-pressed and hungry.

One day they saw the folly of this miserable business and realized the uselessness of the gold they had accumulated. Lucchesio sold all his goods for the benefit of the poor, keeping for himself only his house and a small garden. But he gave even the modest income from this to those who kept on knocking at his door. Buonadonna nagged her husband constantly because the very necessaries of life were often lacking.

On one of the days her husband told her to give a poor man bread, there was not a crumb left in the house, and she was particularly provoked.

"Numbskull," she said, "anybody can see that fasting has destroyed your memory. Just where is there any bread in our house now?"

All the same, at her husband's insistence, she went to the bread bin and opened it. She was amazed to see that it was full of fresh and fragrant bread. Tears in her eyes, she knelt before her faithful companion, who seemed suddenly to have left ordinary life and become a saint. From that day onward her love was full of this kind of awe, and she showed it by continually doing good.

They asked Francis, this husband and wife, to receive them as disciples of Poverty, but without forcing them to separate, since they could not get along without one another.

It was then that Francis remembered his promise at Cannara. He saw again the piazza of the Umbrian *castello* in the distant spring morning, the swallows attentive on their nests, the people aroused by his words, the birds flying down from the tall oaks to the juniper-bright plain. And he thought of the great strength and luminous beauty of love when the union of a man and a woman is an indissoluble joining of souls. It would not be right to destroy a family, which is also a gift from God, blessed by God. On the other hand, it was only just to open his arms to everyone who sincerely wished to live a new life. Absolute renunciation is required, surely, only for an apostle.

Thus was born the Secular Order, or, to use the name given to it by Saint Francis, the "fraternity of the Third Order of Penitence," the name given to it in the rule that is generally thought to have been composed by the founder.[c] Among other things, the rule prohibited members from bearing arms, from hatred, and from taking any solemn oath except in those circumstances allowed by the church. These basic precepts can bring peace and justice. They have the power not only to destroy war but also tyranny, through the destruction of oaths of fealty on which the power to rule, however unjustly, is built.

That same year of 1221, tertiaries in Faenza refused to take up arms in the service of the emperor; and the bishop of Rimini, to whom they appealed, not daring to decide the matter himself, referred it to the pope. The reply of Honorius is clear: no one has the authority to force men to go to war, if they have made peace their life and mission. [The right of the conscientious objector was upheld.]

In the centuries since then, many great spirits have found peace in the Secular Order, beginning with the first, Lucchesio, who received the blessing of Saint Francis in his remote village church among the cypresses and olive trees, where he now sleeps in the Lord.

That spiritual union with his beloved wife that had been the spur to the establishment of the new rule received a moving confirmation at the time of death. Together they had been joined in greedy pursuits; together they had made their way up the "steep slope" of redemption; together their hearts had been lost to Francis. It was just, therefore, that together they should be, even in the final moment of life.

---

c. Just how the Third Order was founded has been a greatly disputed question of Franciscan history. Some historians believe that Francis in the beginning founded only a single lay order of men and women, which gradually evolved into three distinct orders. However, most of the early writers—among them, Thomas of Celano, Saint Bonaventure, Jacques de Vitry, Bernard of Bessa—clearly differentiate the three orders and the founding of them. It therefore seems certain that Saint Francis instituted the Third Order as a separate religious order and that he wrote a rule for it.

[There have been many unsuccessful attempts to find or reconstruct the original rule written by Saint Francis. In 1976, Father Cajetan Esser, on the basis of internal and external criteria, identified as authentic a letter written by Saint Francis to "the Brothers and Sisters of Penance"; and there is strong reason to believe that this is, indeed, the original "rule" or "way of life" for the Third Order.

The original is Manuscript 225 of the Guarnacci Library in Volterra, Italy. Sabatier first published the Latin text in 1900 under the title "Verba vitae et salutis"; until Father Cajetan's study, it had not been recognized as an authentic letter written by Saint Francis. See Esser, *Rule and Testament,* trans. Habig, pp. 219–26.

In 1289 Pope Nicholas IV, with the Bull *Supra Montem,* approved a rule that remained in force until almost our own time. Pope Leo XIII in 1883 adapted this rule to the times with the Bull *Misericors dei Filius.* For additional discussion, see NV 2:460–62. This last rule has now been superseded by a new one approved by the Sacred Congregation of Religious on June 24, 1978.—Trans.]

They became ill at the same time, and Buonadonna was the first to grow worse. In the arms of her husband, her hands in his, she, unable by now to speak, looked at him intently until her eyes, shining in the last indescribable light of farewell, closed on the marvellous vision that was crowning the fidelity of her love. And death itself bent to their desire. Lucchesio, lying down beside her dear, still body, in short order joined his wife.[4]

We know in the same legendary light the royal Franciscans that Simone Martini painted in the Basilica di San Francesco in Assisi: Elizabeth of Hungary, the young wife of the landgrave of Thuringia, who fell in the Fifth Crusade, and Louis IX, king of France, who for love of his faith underwent war, imprisonment, and death. These are the two protector saints of the Third Order, and they are portrayed with the Franciscan cord.

Over Francis's tomb the great Dante climbs a harsh cliff to a fortress guarded by armed archangels. Dante, whose life was cruelly damaged by factional wars, bears on his own body the only good and the only comfort that will accompany him into the tomb: his sackcloth habit of the Order of Penitence.[5] Passionately the poet looks at Francis, who stands above, extending his arms. In the great silence that fills the church is the whisper of his ancient prayer: *O ignota ricchezza, o ben ferace!* ("O wealth unknown! O plenitude untried!").[6]

The Rule of Fonte Colombo (1223)

Like an answer to a universal prayer are those great words of Francis in a letter to the minister of the order: "I should like you to prove that you love God and me, his servant and yours, in the following way. There should be no friar in the whole world who has fallen into sin, no matter how far he has fallen, who will ever fail to find your forgiveness for the asking, if he will only look into your eyes. And if he does not ask forgiveness, you should ask him if he wants it. And should he appear before you again a thousand times, you should love him more than you love me, so that you may draw him to God. You should always have pity on such friars."[7]

This letter, which some think was directed to Brother Elias,[8] apparently was in preparation for the new rule, written between 1222 and 1223. The rule of 1221 was proving too long and wordy. Experience was showing that its provisions should be summarized in a few articles that each friar could commit to memory. In that way, also, there would be less danger of its being destroyed by "interpreters."[9]

Again Francis searched out the solitude that so inspired him.

A brief distance from Rieti stood the hermitage of Fonte Colombo. This, too, is in a rocky landscape surrounded by an ilex forest. A *torrente* runs in the clefts of the mountain. It is a wild place, dear to the ring doves that stop here during their October and March migrations. From them came the name of the hermitage—Fonte Palombo or Colombo.[10]

But the complaints of discontented friars reached the hushed stillness of that hermitage and shook the very walls of the grotto where Francis worked with two of his most faithful companions, Brother Leo and Brother Bonizo, the latter a gifted jurist of the University of Bologna.[11] According to Saint Bonaventure, Francis had given a first redaction of the rule to Brother Elias, who lost it. There is nothing astonishing about that, when one thinks of the many who would have made it a point to look at it and the ill humour of friars who had found the provisions of the 1221 rule intolerable.[12] A new copy had been made ready, the same as the first.

Then, according to the *Mirror of Perfection,* the grumbling ministers came in person, along with Brother Elias, to talk about their objections. Francis made no reply to them. He turned, interrogating the sky. A great voice rang out, echoing from the mountain and the abyss, "Francis, nothing in this Rule is yours; all is Mine. I wish the Rule to be obeyed to the letter, to the letter, without a gloss, without a gloss. I know what the frailty of man can achieve, and I know how much I intend to help them. So let those who are not willing to obey the Rule leave the Order."

The malcontents left Francis, "confused and terrified."

Some concession had been made in relaxing the rigour of the earlier rule, but more of form than of substance. Thus, the old precept to "take nothing for your journey" was removed. The friars were enjoined, rather, "to observe the Holy Gospel of our Lord Jesus Christ by living in obedience, without property, and in chastity."[d]

The new rule was approved in the Pentecost chapter of 1223. In

---

d. Whether the Rule of 1223 was a "sell-out" of Francis and his earlier rule is another greatly disputed subject in Franciscan history. Sabatier (*Vie,* chap. 20) says that the Rule of 1223 has nothing in common with that of 1221 except the name, and that it owes its origin to the intrigue of the Apostolic See, which sought to transform and change the new movement.

This is also the opinion of Jörgensen and of many other modern biographers. It is a cliché that has no basis in the facts. A simple comparison of the two rules shows that the text of the Rule of 1223 is nothing but a faithful compendium of the Rule of 1221.

[But what did Saint Francis feel in seeing his beloved Lady Poverty downgraded? And in seeing the great words revealed to him when the Gospels were opened in the Church of San Nicolò, those passages that formed his first rule and that opened his Rule of 1221, dropped altogether?—Trans.]

November of the same year it received the sanction of Honorius III.[e] At this time, too, during his stay in Rome, Francis took lodging in the house of Cardinal Ugolino.[f] But he soon found the crowd of dignitaries and courtiers, the streets crowded with pleasure loving and quarrelsome city people, the ceremonials, the intrigues of the Curia, too much for him.

A powerful prelate, Cardinal Leone Brancaleone, insisted that he come to stay in his house. He was titular head of Santa Croce in Gerusalemme, a Roman bishop in surcoat (who in 1205 had exerted himself to remove the interdict that Innocent III had placed on the citizens of Assisi). But Francis was not willing to accept his invitation. He disliked all that princely pomp, those grand salons that were scenes of conspiracies, revels, and banquets—even if at the end of the meal the doors were opened to the poor who had been waiting patiently in the antechambers. A desire for his woodlands, secluded in the lonely greyness of the mountain winter, seized him, and he suffered from an anxiety that grew ever more acute. The cardinal, however, observed that it would be imprudent to set out on a journey in a season so inclement. It had rained for days and the roads had turned into muddy rivers.

"Brother," he said to Francis, "remain with me until the weather is

---

e. It was approved with the Bull *Solet annuere* of November 29, 1223 (*Bullarium Franciscanum*, 1:15–19). This rule, which consists of twelve articles, is the one professed by all Friars Minor today. It has been said of it: "There is no other Rule, and perhaps will never be one, that has had such and so many expositors as the Rule of Saint Francis. Among those who have commented on it either as a whole or in part are the Supreme Pontiffs Gregory IX, Innocent IV, Alexander IV, Gregory X, Nicholas III, Clement V, John XXII. Among the Friars Minor there are the four Masters of Paris, Saint Bonaventure, Ugone da Digna, John Peckam, Giovanni della Valle, Pier Giovanni, Ubertino da Casale, Bartolomeo Pisano. Among the jurists are Bartolo da Sassoferrato and Pietro Angarono." Sbaralea, *Supplementum*, p. 244.

[In our own times von Galli, distinguished Jesuit theologian and writer, argues that in the freedom of Francis's rule and in his ideals are to be seen the church of tomorrow. He quotes the Jesuit Peter Lippert: "The organizational principle that leads from Benedict through Dominic and Ignatius to the newer communities seems to have practically exhausted its inner possibilities. . . . The fundamental newness that is precisely the thing being sought today by countless souls . . . is to be found only along a completely different line: along the original ideal of Francis. In other words: in the direction of a freely chosen life style and freely chosen bonds of love; in the direction of a life that operates through spontaneous initiative of the self rather than through great constructs of the will; in the direction of a truly living and individual personality shaped by its own inner laws and standards. If God should someday deign to reveal the Order of the future to his Church . . . it will surely bear the stamp of Francis's soul and spirit." *Living Our Future*, pp. 172–89.—Trans.]

f. On this subject, we should like to call the attention of scholars to Oliger's fine monograph, "San Francesco a Roma e nella provincia romana," in *L'Italia francescana nel settimo centenario della morte di San Francesco*, pp. 65–112. He demonstrates that the residence of Cardinal Ugolino was beside the church of SS. Pietro e Marcellino, which still stands today on the corner of Via Merulana and Via Labicana. In fact, the Register of this cardinal, Ist. 101, January 14, 1222, bears the following precise annotation: *Actum est . . . in urbe Roma, in camera dicti episcopi, in Sancto Petro Marcellino.* Levi, *Registri dei Cardinali*, p. 125.

more propitious for travelling. You may eat with the other poor men who come to my table."

And since he knew his liking to meditate far removed from noise, he added, "I shall give you, if you wish, a place of solitude where you and your companion can pray and meditate without being disturbed."

Angelo di Tancredi, one of Francis's first companions, was also staying with the cardinal at the time. He turned to Francis and suggested, "There is a beautiful, high, and spacious tower, not far from here, on the city wall, that has nine rooms. There you can isolate yourself as if you were in a hermitage."[g]

This is a very precise detail that allows us to check the accuracy of the ancient authors.

There was indeed a medieval city wall, with a forest of impregnable towers, such as Torre dei Conti, Torre delle Milizie, Torre dei Carloni, Torre dei Mesa.

In the works of Thomas of Celano we find a specific description of these patrician towers, tall, without inside landings, equipped with gallery and winch where the keepers watched at night. One of them once fell from that dizzy height and was saved through a miracle of Saint Francis.[13]

They were part of an armed city that had arisen on the colossal ruins of ancient Rome. Baronial families were constantly entrenching themselves and keeping watch on one another: Stefaneschi and Ildebrandi, Crescenzi and Savelli, Caetani and Colonnesi. In the ruins of the theatre of Pompey, the Orsini had built their citadel; the Pierleoni had established themselves on the walls of the theatre of Marcellus. The bricks of the new fortifications were laid over the sculptured marble; stockpiles of arrows were heaped on the stones of glorious mausolea. Battlements crowned the crumbling structures of the Imperial Forum, where the deserted open spaces were covered by thickets, vineyards, gardens, and swamps, and great silent gardens, full of shadow, extended all about old monasteries.

---

g. According to *An. Min.*, 1210 A.D., n. 17, Cardinal Leone Brancaleone lived near the church of Santa Croce in Gerusalemme, of which he was titular head. He played a large role with Ugolino in the affairs of the Roman Curia during the papacies of Innocent III and Honorius III and died in 1228. See Cardella, *Memorie storiche*, 1:195.

The account in *Spec. Perf.*, 67, is amplified in *Per.*, 92. According to *Spec. Perf.*, the cardinal, in order to overcome Francis's hesitation, told him that he could receive his food as a beggar at the same time that other beggars were fed each day.

The precise description of the tower is found in the same chapter of *Per.*, which quotes Angelo di Tancredi. The *testuggini* mentioned in the Latin text are the vaults of the rooms; it is clear that the tower had nine vaulted rooms for the soldiers who took it over in time of war. In fact, the city wall ran then, and still runs, behind the aforesaid church. But the tower no longer exists.

Giacoma dei Settisoli

In his sojourns in Rome, including this last one of 1223, Francis spent a great deal of time at the Septizonium palazzo, where Giacoma dei Frangipani, who had become a Franciscan tertiary, lived with her fatherless children.[14]

That proud monument had been one of the marvels of imperial Rome. The emperor Septimus Severus built it, a house of regal magnificence at the head of the Via Appia, so that those who came to Rome could immediately see the greatness of the ruler of virtually the entire world. The façade was formed by a colonnade of seven banks of superimposed columns. Statues, fountains, and marble columns added to its fantastic architecture. It was said that the builders had been inspired by Ovid's verses: *Regia Solis erat sublimibus alta columnis* ("The Royal Palace of the Sun is raised on lofty columns, glittering with shining gold and flaming garnet. White ivory covers its highest pediments; the double doors of silver dazzle with their splendour . . . ").[15]

All the emblems of power, light, life, and voluptuousness were now, however, dissolving into dust and slowly sinking into the ground. The place had run wild. Some statuary could still be seen among the gardens, mutilated, corroded, covered with moss. Fragments of chiselled marble lay in heaps against the pilasters. Flocks came to drink from the basins of the ancient fountains. In the spaces between the columns, on the fallen porticoes, on the archivolts, under the ornate cornices, there were new structures—the palace was bristling with arrow slits, barricades, and bastions. Overlooking all was a high, fortified loggia. A round fortress called the *trullo* or "trullum," a cortile, and a heavily fortified tower that rested upon the tawny travertine of the Circus Maximus (called, for that reason, the Tower of the Arch), completed the fortifications. The great open space that up until the epoch of the Goths had resounded with the noise of charioteers was given over to a kitchen garden and a field of hemp (*canapa*), called, therefore, the "Canapina." The waters of a stream called the Marrana ran near the structure; they fed an ancient mill, then flowed down into the Tiber. Other towers formed a formidable belt around the Septizonium, which was known as "the citadel of the Frangipani"—a true fief in the heart of the city, between the Colosseum and the Palatine.

The names of grim *signori* of the family rang out among the discoloured heaps of stones, evoking present and past stories of violence, arsons, massacres: Cencio Frangipane, who opened the gates of Rome to the Normans of Robert Guiscard; Leone, consul of the Romans;

Roberto, grand elector of Innocent III. They were a fearless and murderous people, who could be counted on to provoke riots, plot to control conclaves, ride against mobs whose loyalties shifted without warning; they even laid sacrilegious hands on the popes themselves. They were schismatic: in the expression used in a papal bull of 1179, they "do not give peace to the Church." From this arrogant family came at last an antipope.[h] They were also lawless and seditious: in 1204 they had entrenched themselves behind fortifications in the Colosseum against Innocent III and had not hesitated to spill fratricidal blood on the holy arena that had known the agony and death of so many martyrs. Rabid supporters of the imperial faction, they controlled Marino, Terracina, Torre Asturia, Cisterna. Scarcely five years after Francis's last visit to Rome, the Frangipani were to drive from the city Cardinal Ugolino, who had become Pope Gregory IX.

The Wind in the Tower

The beauty and the piety of the Roman gentlewoman Giacoma dei Settesoli had brought a new light into the ancient Royal Palace of the Sun. The heiress of a family of warriors and the widow of one of the most powerful of the Roman barons, she was like one of the heroic blessed saints in whom courage is the highest expression of femininity and fidelity survives the flight of the years, even death.

Giacoma and Francis were friends for more than ten years. We can say truthfully that they loved each other.

Thomas of Celano wrote: "Jacopa of Settesoli, equally renowned for her nobility and her sanctity in the city of Rome, had merited the privilege of a special love from Saint Francis." And in still another passage, which reminds us of certain verses of the Song of Songs, he writes of Francis as one "whom she loved so ardently."[16]

The *Mirror of Perfection* [and also the *Legend of Perugia*] compares her to the woman who loved Jesus even to the cross and beyond: Mary Magdalene.[17]

Francis gave Giacoma in this, his last stay in Rome, a gift of great significance, a white lamb. It symbolized her innocence, flourishing within these malevolent walls, where the family coat of arms showed lions on the attack, rapacious eagles, enraged vipers. There had been a time, in fact, when the family, in boast of its feral savagery, had kept a live leopard that came and went freely through the palace. The

---

h. Lando Frangipane of Sezze, elected pope (antipope) with the name of Innocent III in 1179. He was deposed the following year. This occurred during the pontificate of Alexander III (1159–81).—Trans.

beast, overcome by its instincts, had even attacked a poor woman engaged in domestic duties and killed her.

But now the lamb ruled over life within these walls. Its tremulous, imploring voice echoed through the place from the earliest morning hours. Francis thought of it as the visible symbol of Jesus, who had said, "Blessed are the lowly; they shall inherit the land."[18]

The day would come (said Francis) when cruelty would be conquered by gentleness and no heart could resist kindness. The Lamb who had come to take away the sins of the world had declared, "Love your enemies, do good to those who hate you; bless those who curse you and pray for those who maltreat you."[19] Human beings could come to see the folly of bloodshed, war, and revenge. Evil could be overcome by good.

Giacoma listened to Francis with a humility full of grace, pervaded by a mysterious happiness that she would remember all her life. Often, while he was speaking, tears would come to her clear, intent eyes and overflow down her cheeks. At such a time it was easy to understand why Francis's companions compared her to Mary Magdalene. Like Mary Magdalene, she was capable of great love and she was also "full of tears and devotion for the love and sweetness of Christ."[20]

At the time of which we speak, it was early December, and rain pelted unceasingly. It washed the fields of ruins, the frowning walls, the uncultivated land.[21] The Septizonium itself was wrapped in a dreary cloud. The great voice of the water rumbling in the mill stream filled the room, darkening in the first shadows of evening.

It must have been on just such a stormy evening that Francis moved to the room on top of the tower that Angelo di Tancredi had prepared for him. He prayed, as was his habit, then lay down on a cot to await sleep. But, as he was dozing off, a long and noisy rumble jolted him awake. The old tower was shaking and shuddering mightily, as if the centuries-old fighting had begun around it again. From the farthest corner, from every opening, from every fortification, cries of terror and rage were breaking out. Pleas for help rose from those abandoned to the sack, along with the barbaric shouts of the sackers. Crossbows cracked, arrows whistled, beasts howled, and fires roared up. Bells clamoured the tocsin over the clashing of swords. All the voices—scornful, threatening, desperate—that had rung out there in the battles of the centuries returned on that stormy night in the sleep of the Poverello of Christ. They begged, cursed, died away, then returned with new force.

The storm grew in violence. By the light of a dying lantern, Francis saw moving shadows. Phantoms leapt to the arrow slits, ran up the stairs. All along the open galleries figures appeared and then vanished. Suddenly they joined and all together rushed Francis. They knocked him down and hit him repeatedly and savagely. He saw their flaming eyes, their contorted faces and gnashing teeth in frothing mouths.

He sprang from his bed, crying out in terror. Angelo, sleeping in another room, came running.

"The devils, brother," said Francis, "have beaten me severely. I wish you would keep me company because I am afraid to stay alone."[i]

His companion looked at him in astonishment. Francis was beside himself, every bone in his body trembling.

"Why did the devils beat me? Why did they receive permission from the Lord to hurt me?" Francis went on. And he added, "The devils are our Lord's policemen. Just as the podestà sends his policemen to punish a guilty man, so too does the Lord correct and chastise those he loves through his policemen, that is, the devils whom he permits to do this work."

He seemed delirious. It had been a mistake to imagine he could have a peaceful stay here in this place, so associated with war and violence. The Friar Minor should shun such places, should shun the palaces and courts of powerful men. It would not do to yield even to a well-meant invitation when it involved something displeasing to God.

Brother Angelo listened without replying. In the silence of the long winter night, they heard the booming of the wind as it slammed against the tower.

He had been wrong to put off his departure, Francis continued. "It is possible, it seems to me, that the Lord had me chastised by his policemen for the following reason: Surely, the cardinal was spontaneously very generous in my behalf—undoubtedly, my body needs some consideration and I can accept it without remorse. And yet, my brothers who are going through the world, suffering hunger and all kinds of tribulations, living in small humble houses and in hermitages, on learning that I am the guest of the lord cardinal, could find in this a pretext to complain against me. They could say: 'While we are enduring all sorts of privations, he is enjoying every kind of comfort!' I am always bound to give a good example. That is the reason why I was given to them."

When dawn broke, the two left the tower and went to Cardinal

---

i. It was a common belief in the Middle Ages that storms could raise devils.

Leone. And Francis said to him, "The people have great confidence in me and regard me as a saint; but, as you see, now devils have thrown me out of my prison!"

And with these words he firmly took his leave.[22]

The Christmas Crib of Greccio

Francis set out again on the roads of Umbria. Again he went up the rugged path along the woodlands of Fonte Colombo and joyously greeted the little church so dear to him.

The days that followed were among the happiest of his life. Christmas was drawing near. Pleasant weather had returned, and in the cloister formed by the wooded hills, a clear light shone in the joyful, immaculate mornings. Toward evening, the long slow notes of cornemuses rose from the valley, playing ancient pastorals. Tenderly they dwelled on the miraculous dream of the return of the son of God to earth as a baby, little and poor, clasped to the breast of the Virgin.[j]

Francis wanted everyone to share in the joy of this "feast of feasts." He wanted the poor and the hungry to sit at the tables of the rich, and oxen and asses, the humble beasts who had warmed the cold body of the baby Jesus with their breath, to be given more than the usual amount of grain and hay.

"If I could speak to the emperor," he said, "I would ask that a general law be made requiring all who can to scatter corn and other grains along the roads so that the birds might have an abundance of food on such a great and solemn day, especially our sisters the larks."[23]

A few days before Christmas, Francis sent for a noble of Greccio, a *castello* nearby, a man named Giovanni for whom Francis had a very special love because of his goodness. To him Francis disclosed the plans he had made.

It would be, he said, so good, so edifying, to call to mind the birth of the Christ Child on the night of Christmas,[k] to have "set before our bodily eyes in some way the inconveniences of his infant needs, how he lay in a manger, how, with an ox and an ass standing by, he lay

---

j. *2 Cel.*, 199: "The birthday of the Child Jesus Francis observed with inexpressible eagerness over all other feasts, saying that it was the feast of feasts, on which God, having become a tiny infant, clung to human breasts."

k. "The night of Christmas" would be Christmas Eve by our calendars, since the days were reckoned from sunset to sunset.—Trans.

upon the hay where he had been placed." His poetic gifts enabled him to give vivid life to the scene. Giovanni was enthralled.

Brothers from nearby Franciscan places were invited. Many torches and candles were needed to make a great light in "that night that has lighted up all the days and years with its gleaming star." Men and women worked unceasingly to prepare them. All had been made ready in that forest by Christmas Eve, the Vigil of Christmas: the manger, the hay, the ox and ass. Francis inspected it and was pleased. At last he had found a way to make a living presentation of the concept in which he passionately believed, in a drama that could not fail to stir even the most stolid. The lowly manger would show forth God—small, poor, humble. Greccio would become a new Bethlehem.

Night fell and obscured the dark beech trees, the steep cliffs, the hermitage, the valley. A profound waiting silence lay over the great stage. Then it began to snow, and there was nothing but an immense whiteness in the calm and peaceful night. It seemed that unseen bells were ringing out the ancient invocation: "Peace on earth to men of good will!" In the great, white quiet, every petty, malicious, and unworthy feeling died away.

As the hours passed, far-away lights appeared in the valley and began to move up to the hermitage. Again, as once before, shepherds were walking in the night to "come and adore Him."

In reading over the description written by Thomas of Celano, who certainly got his information from someone who was there, we ourselves can see the marvellous scene.

A thousand torches blaze up in the darkness, joyous moving lights, like the enchanted lights in a festival of fantasy in legends arising from the deeps of a magic forest. And still it is snowing. A whirlwind of flakes dances in the flickering flames of the torches. Great crackling bonfires add their light and voice to the jubilation of flames that shine out on the harsh and lonely mountain. The night, writes Thomas, is "lighted up like the day."

A great throng crowds about the manger, where the ox and the ass bring the ancient miracle to life again. The people, writes Thomas, are "filled with new joy over the mystery."

From the group of kneeling friars arises the mighty chorus: "Let the heavens be glad and the earth rejoice; let the sea and what fills it resound . . ."[24] The song rises to the tops of the white oaks on which reflections of the red fires dance; it expands into the invisible sky. It travels to the distant mountains.

Everything proclaims solemnity, beauty, and joy: the priest with the gold chasuble who celebrates the Mass, the altar shining with lights, the brothers in their pure white surplices, the forest ringing with the joyous hymn, the rocks that "make answer to their jubilation." A single harmony unites all things and all creatures—perhaps even the angels who sang on the night that Christ was born are singing again, too, beyond the intense light.

Francis, vested as a deacon, sings the beautiful lesson: "She gave birth to her first-born son and wrapped him in swaddling clothes and laid him in a manger . . . "

His voice rings out like heavenly music that none of those present could ever forget: "a strong voice, a sweet voice, a clear voice, a sonorous voice." The nobleman Giovanni is so overwhelmed by it that as Francis reads, he sees the baby Jesus "lying in the manger lifeless, and . . . the holy man of God go up to it and rouse the child as from a deep sleep."

"This vision was not unfitting," writes the friar, "for the Child Jesus had been forgotten in the hearts of many; but, by the working of his grace, he was brought to life again through his servant Saint Francis and stamped upon their fervent memory."

Then Francis preaches to the people, and "he spoke charming words concerning the nativity of the poor King and the little town of Bethlehem." Speaking the word "Bethlehem" (*Betlemme*), says Thomas, his voice seems to resemble the sound of a lamb.

And the light that shines in the darkness is truly the light of the dawn, the beginning of a new day for all who were there—that light that touches the faces, envelops the motionless plants, reaches into the snow-covered valley and up to the icy heights that still echo with the sound of silvery voices: *Rejoice! Rejoice!*[25]

The Weak and the Strong

The stay at Greccio, where there are no barriers to the flight of the spirit, was prolonged for several months. Francis had chosen as his cell a part of the cliff that juts out over an abyss, a true eagles' nest where no one could come to disturb his meditation.[26]

The winter was very severe, and there was snow on top of snow. The nights were filled with the howling of wolves that had been driven down from the mountain by hunger. They were so fierce that they attacked not only flocks but also human beings. All the people round about were terrified of them. After sunset the gates of the *castello* were closed, as when an enemy stalked the land.[27]

Francis had reached the state where he loved everyone, even the most wicked, even those who wantonly kill, even the animals most despised and feared. [His love is the inspiration for some of the most charming and familiar stories that have come down to us about him. As Thomas of Celano says, "In a most extraordinary manner, a manner never experienced by others—he discerned the hidden things of nature with his sensitive heart."[28]]

In everything, as the *Mirror of Perfection* points out, is a scintilla of the goodness of God, and Francis, "being completely absorbed in the love of God," clearly perceived this goodness "in all created things."[1]

One day one of the brothers brought him a little rabbit that had been caught in a trap. The frightened animal and Francis looked at each other for a moment, and Francis was moved to pity, because nothing in the world can express fright like the great melting eyes of a rabbit.

Francis took the rabbit in his arms, caressed it, then put him on the ground and said, "Brother rabbit, come to me. Why did you allow yourself to be deceived like this?"

And the rabbit returned to Francis and lay quiet in his bosom. He held it and petted it with motherly affection, then released it so that it could return free to the woods. But each time it was set on the ground, it returned to Francis, and finally the brothers had to carry it off to the nearby woods.[29]

Often Francis went down to the nearby lake of Piediluco, whose people, for the most part fishermen, greatly venerated him. In one of these excursions, while he was in a boat near the landing, someone offered him a freshly caught tench. He accepted it joyfully. Immediately he began to call it "Brother," and he put it back in the water. And when the others grieved about the loss of that tasty dish, he explained that all the family of the Lord are linked. And everyone marvelled greatly when the fish frisked about the boat, just skimming the surface of the water, as if to join in those praises of the Creator. When Francis's prayer was finished, he bade farewell to the fish, who disappeared beneath the wind-ruffled water.[30]

The little, marvellously blue lake of Piediluco, where every word spoken in the luminous silence is echoed on the beaches, is the setting

---

1. "Being completely absorbed in the love of God, blessed Francis clearly perceived the goodness of God both within his own soul, already endowed with perfect virtue, and in all created things, so he therefore had an especial and profound love for God's creatures . . ." *Spec. Perf.,* 113. *1 Cel.,* 80: "Who would be able to narrate the sweetness he enjoyed while contemplating in creatures the wisdom of their Creator, his power and his goodness?"

And *Leg. Maior,* III, 6: "The realization that everything comes from the same source filled Francis with greater affection than ever and he called even the most insignificant creatures his brothers and sisters, because he knew they had the same origin as himself."

for many stories of the saint. He often went there to spend what time he could enjoying the beauty of hills and water, air and sky.

One of these times was in early March, when the passage of wild ducks had begun. They come in high, the flocks spread out in a wide triangular pattern. They dive and circle about and fill the air with their laments. These migrants stay no more than a single night, driven on by longing for their lonely northern lakes; but even in this brief pause there is always a hunter on their track, hidden among the canebrakes, ready to lay his trap at the first light of day when the flock gathers for its departure.

A duck that had been caught like this was given to Francis while he was in a boat crossing the lake. Francis tenderly plunged his hands into the warm feathers of the quivering creature; he put it on the palm of his hand and blessed it. And the bird, so frantic for freedom, did not move. Instead, it settled down in his hand as if it were his nest.

Now Francis stood up in the boat, which was still out in the middle of the lake, extended his arms and said to Brother Bird that he was safe, no one would again take away his freedom. The bird stretched out its wings and fluttered them in farewell. Then with no sign of uncertainty, like a creature who knows his road, he rose and disappeared.[31]

The Wolf of Gubbio

We are told that as long as the people of Greccio preserved their simplicity, they reaped the Poverello's marvellous spiritual heritage and lived in harmony with the animals with whom they shared the mountain, the forest, the water, the sky. But when they reached for the easy life, they were changed, as indeed is everyone by prosperity: Thomas of Celano accurately writes that wealth and not poverty causes war, and that it covers faces "with grossness and the fat of temporal things."[32] So in time the people of Greccio, gorged and greedy, were again plagued by the wolves of Mount Terminillo. What is worse, a terrible war broke out among them. Many died, and the *castello* was destroyed.

Wolves are considered the robbers and criminals of the animal world. None of the usual violent methods can change them. Only love can accomplish it. This is the meaning of the story of the wolf of Gubbio [or Agobbio, as some of the old texts spell it]. In fact, one great Franciscan writer thought the wolf to be a symbol of the people of the Middle Ages, with their divisions and feuds, brought to love by the power of Christianity.[33]

At the time of which we speak, a huge wolf was prowling about the countryside, so strong and so daring that it would attack anyone who risked going outside the city walls.[34] People took weapons with them when they went into the country, as if they were going off to war. But no one could escape the wolf if he were unfortunate enough to meet it. Everyone was so terrified that hardly anyone dared venture outside the city gate.

[And here is what happened, as told in *Little Flowers:*]

"While the saint was there at that time, he had pity on the people and decided to go out and meet the wolf. But on hearing this, the citizens said to him, 'Look out, Brother Francis. Don't go outside the gate, because the wolf, which has already devoured many people, will certainly attack you and kill you!'

"But Francis placed his hope in the Lord Jesus Christ who is master of all creatures. Protected not by a shield or a helmet, but arming himself with the sign of the cross, he bravely went out of the town with his companion, putting all his faith in the Lord who makes those who believe in him walk without any injury on an asp and a basilisk and trample not merely on a wolf but even on a lion and a dragon. So with his very great faith Saint Francis bravely went out to meet the wolf.

"Some peasants accompanied him a little way, but soon they said to him, 'We don't want to go any farther because that wolf is very fierce and we might get hurt.'

"When he heard them say this, Saint Francis answered, 'Just stay here. But I am going on to where the wolf lives.'

"Then, in the sight of many people who had come out and climbed onto places to see this wonderful event, the fierce wolf came running with its mouth open toward Saint Francis and his companion.

"The saint made the sign of the cross toward it. And the power of God, proceeding as much from himself as from his companion, checked the wolf and made it slow down and close its cruel mouth.

"Then, calling to it, Saint Francis said, 'Come to me, Brother Wolf. In the name of Christ, I order you not to hurt me or anyone.'

"It is marvellous to relate that as soon as he had made the sign of the cross, the wolf closed its terrible jaws and stopped running, and as soon as he gave it that order, it lowered its head and lay down at the saint's feet, as though it had become a lamb.

"And Saint Francis said to it as it lay in front of him, 'Brother Wolf, you have done great harm in this region, and you have committed horrible crimes by destroying God's creatures without any mercy.

You have been destroying not only irrational animals, but you even have had the more detestable brazenness to kill and devour human beings made in the image of God. You therefore deserve to be put to death just like the worst robber and murderer. Consequently everyone is right in crying out against you and complaining, and this whole town is your enemy. But, Brother Wolf, I want to make peace between you and them, so that they will not be harmed by you any more, and after they have forgiven you all your past crimes, neither men nor dogs will pursue you any more.'

"The wolf showed by moving its body and tail and ears and by nodding its head that it willingly accepted what the saint had said and would observe it.

"So Saint Francis spoke again, 'Brother Wolf, since you are willing to make and keep this peace pact, I promise you that I will have the people of this town give you food every day as long as you live, so that you will never again suffer hunger, for I know that whatever evil you have been doing was done because of the urge of hunger. But, my Brother Wolf, since I am obtaining such a favour for you, I want you to promise me that you will never hurt any animal or man. Will you promise me that?'

"The wolf gave a clear sign, by nodding its head, that it promised to do what the saint asked.

"And Saint Francis said, 'Brother Wolf, I want you to give me a pledge so that I can confidently believe what you promise.'

"And as Saint Francis held out his hand to receive the pledge, the wolf also raised its front paw and meekly and gently put it in Saint Francis's hand as a sign that it was giving its pledge.

"Then Saint Francis said, 'Brother Wolf, I order you, in the name of the Lord Jesus Christ, to come with me now, without fear, into the town to make this peace pact in the name of the Lord.'

"And the wolf immediately began to walk along beside Saint Francis, just like a very gentle lamb. When the people saw this, they were greatly amazed, and the news spread quickly throughout the whole town, so that all of them, men as well as women, great and small, assembled in the market place, because Saint Francis was there with the wolf.

"So when a very large crowd had gathered, Saint Francis gave them a wonderful sermon, saying among other things that such calamities were permitted by God because of their sins, and how the consuming fire of hell by which the damned have to be devoured for all eternity is much more dangerous than the raging of a wolf which can kill nothing but the body, and how much more they should fear to be plunged into hell, since one little animal could keep so great a crowd in such a state of terror and trembling.

"'So, dear people,' he said, 'come back to the Lord, and do fitting penance, and God will free you from the wolf in this world and from the devouring fire of hell in the next world.'

"And having said that, he added, 'Listen, dear people. Brother Wolf, who is standing here before you, has promised me and has given me a pledge that he will make peace with you and will never hurt you if you promise also to feed him every day. And I pledge myself as bondsman for Brother Wolf that he will faithfully keep this peace pact.'

"Then all the people who were assembled there promised in a loud voice to feed the wolf regularly.

"And Saint Francis said to the wolf before them all, 'And you, Brother Wolf, do you promise to keep this pact, that is, not to hurt any animal or human being?'

"The wolf knelt down and bowed its head, and by twisting its body and wagging its tail and ears it clearly showed to everyone that it would keep the pact as it had promised.

"And Saint Francis said, 'Brother Wolf, just as you gave me a pledge of this when we were outside the city gate, I want you to give me a pledge here before all these people that you will keep the pact and will never betray me for having pledged myself as your bondsman.'

"Then in the presence of all the people the wolf raised its right paw and put it in Saint Francis's hand as a pledge.

"And the crowd was so filled with amazement and joy, out of devotion for the saint as well as over the novelty of the miracle and over the peace pact between the wolf and the people, that they all shouted to the sky, praising and blessing the Lord Jesus Christ who had sent Saint Francis to them, by whose merits they had been freed from such a fierce wolf and saved from such a terrible scourge and had recovered peace and quiet.

"From that day, the wolf and the people kept the pact that Saint Francis made. The wolf lived two years more, and it went from door to door for food. It hurt no one, and no one hurt it. The people fed it courteously. And it is a striking fact that not a single dog ever barked at it.

"Then the wolf grew old and died. And the people were sorry, because whenever it went through the town, its peaceful kindness and patience reminded them of the virtues and the holiness of Saint Francis."ᵐ

Brother Creatures

True or symbolic, this story gives us the exact details of one of those "peaces" so common in the Middle Ages, a pact that solemnly and juridically puts an end to a state of war, whether between individuals, families, or city factions. Included here are all the elements of the pact: the form, the procedure, the agreement between the parties, the intervention of the bondsman.[35] The ultimate meaning of the story, however, is that peace is possible through effort, even between men and animals.

In another "creature" story, we see Francis passing through a village of the Marches. He met a man on his way to market, carrying over his shoulder two little lambs, bound together. They bleated so pitifully that Francis was filled with pity, and he went to them and touched them with the compassion that a mother would show to her weeping child.

Francis said to the man: "Why are you torturing my brother lambs, tied up and hanging like this?"

The man replied: "I am taking them to the market to sell them, because I need the money."

Francis asked: "What will happen to them then?"

And the man answered: "Those who buy them will kill them and eat them."

"This must not happen," Francis said. "Take this mantle I am wearing as their price and give the lambs to me."[36]

In other words, the pain of human beings and the pain of animals are not divisible; we, too, must feel what they have to bear.

---

m. Is the story about the wolf of Gubbio true? There has been much discussion of this over the years; cf. Bartolomasi, "Il lupo di Gubbio," *Misc. Fran.* 10:32–36. [According to Brown (*Little Flowers,* pp. 320–22), the first clear reference to the story is in the third edition of *Leg. Vers.* (ca. 1290), which contains the statement, "It is said that through his influence one wolf especially was tamed and made peace with a town." The Franciscan Custody of Gubbio adopted the figure of a wolf on its seal perhaps as early as the thirteenth century. And a wolf's skull is said to have been found in the late nineteenth century in a small shrine. These pieces of evidence have made earlier opinions somewhat uncertain: these have ranged from outright disbelief to suggestions that the story was an embellishment of a trip Francis once made safely through wolf-infested country around the Monastery of San Verecondo or that it really referred to a bandit called Lupo.—Trans.]

There is in Gubbio a church, La Vittorina, that is said to be on the site of the meeting of Saint Francis and the wolf; and another church, San Francesco della Pace, stands where Saint Francis parleyed with the wolf in front of the assembled people; it is also said to be the place the wolf was buried.

A boy of Siena once caught a number of turtle doves in a snare. While he was carrying them alive to market to sell them, he met Saint Francis. Stirred by love and pity, Francis said to the boy: "Good boy, please give me those doves so that such innocent birds, which in Holy Scripture are symbols of pure, humble, and faithful souls, will not fall into the hands of cruel men who will kill them."

And the boy immediately gave all the doves to Francis, who gathered them to his bosom and began to talk to them: "My simple, chaste, and innocent Sister Doves, why did you let yourselves be caught? I want to rescue you from death and make nests for you where you can lay your eggs and fulfill the Creator's commandment to multiply."

And he made nests for them. The doves settled into the nests and laid their eggs and brought up their young. They stayed with Francis and the other friars, so tame that they seemed like chickens raised by the friars. And they did not leave until Saint Francis sent them on their way, with his blessing.[37]

Even the pain of creatures of repulsive appearance, creatures who arouse such repugnance and disgust that everyone feels justified in squashing them under their feet, needs to be understood and shared. Even they need love. There is no room in Franciscanism—or among any who love the world and all its inhabitants—for a false compassion only for the suffering of creatures who arouse sympathy and admiration. Slithering reptiles and slimy toads are also our companions and brother creatures on this planet.

When Francis found worms in the road, he picked them up and put them in a safe place so they would not be stepped on by those who passed.[38]

Of course, evil, hatred, violence, and treachery exist among animals as they do between man and animal. So as we see Francis quick to have pity on an animal suffering from human beings, we also see him indignant at the sow who killed a newborn lamb.[39] And worried over a nest of little robins that the mother and father robin had entrusted to the care of the friars, because one of them, stronger and greedier than the others, wanted to eat the others' food.[40]

Another time, while he was on the road to the town of Osimo, he saw one little lamb amid a herd of she-goats and he-goats. Looking at it, so innocent among the rams with long beards and twisted horns, he was reminded of Jesus among the pharisees and chief priests. He went to a great deal of trouble to rescue the little creature, and he took it to the bishop of the city, who gave it to a convent of nuns.[41]

To insects, too, Francis was charitable and generous. He saw to it that the bees were given honey or the best wine in winter, lest they die from the cold. He admired those industrious workers so greatly that he would often spend whole days watching and praising them.[42]

Along with the story of the wolf of Gubbio must be ranked the legend of the crow, told in the *Chronicle of Twenty-four Generals.*

The crow is popularly credited with bringing bad luck. Crows can be seen circling mournfully around corpses to feed on the rotting flesh. Their strident song is held to be a sign of misfortune. The crow, black and frightening, is the antithesis of the dove. It is the symbol of evil and damnation.

But Francis's crow, thanks to his master, went to choir with the brothers, ate with them in the refectory, visited the sick in the infirmary of the friary. He went with them to Assisi houses to beg for alms. When Francis died, the crow languished and would take no food. He refused to leave Francis's tomb and died there from grief and weakness.[43]

From Francis's marvellous sense of brotherhood with the creatures of the earth, with all creation, will come—as we shall see—a hymn of perfect joy.

More Creature Stories

Francis made friends with a cricket. It happened like this. In the Porziuncola woodlands one day, in the burning dog-days, a cricket breaks the empty noonday silence with its song.[44] The brothers, who had risen before dawn to recite the hours, are asleep. So now in the merciless heat the praises to the Lord are sung by the cricket. Her song is almost too much as it pours out of the fullness of her joy. The parched fields, the thirsty streams, the dusty roads, resound with it.

Francis, motionless among the still oaks, listens, enraptured. He is overcome by the desire to take into his hand this wonderful sister, who can make her wings, a weft and woof of steel, become a ringing lyre. He is delighted by this little creature from which comes such vibrant harmony, who can sing alone or, though in solitude, join a chorus of other crickets. The cricket sings for herself, for the cloud passing over the hill, for the frond stretching over the still water, for the blade of grass awaiting the morning breeze. But she falls silent when people approach, suspecting the worst.

Even this distrust was overcome when Francis calls, "My sister cricket, come to me."

And the cricket comes immediately from a hiding place in a fig tree into his hand.

Francis says, "Sing, my sister cricket, and praise your Creator with a joyful song."

And the cricket begins to sing again. She sings and sings while Francis, enthralled, listens to her and praises her. He speaks to her about his thoughts, his desires, his dreams. He speaks of God who is splendour and harmony. He talks of light and shadow, of beautiful life and silent death.

Finally he lifts his hand and the cricket returns to its tree. Eight days pass and the cricket does not move from that tree. When Francis leaves his cell, she is ready to fly to his hand, to sing or be silent according to his command. At the end of that time Francis says to his companions, "Let us give our sister cricket leave to go, for it has made us sufficiently happy now. We do not want our flesh to glory vainly over things of this kind."

So the cricket takes flight beyond the tree and is lost in the sky. It never returns.

The Contest between the Poet and the Nightingale

On another occasion, Francis himself sang in competition with another creature of song.

We are again in the Porziuncola woodlands, at the end of a spring day. Francis looks at the darkening sky. Soon it will be evening. It would be good, O Brother Leo [he says], to lay the table of the Lord near the flowering hedge of whitethorn, in the peace that comes with the first shadow of evening.

They sit down on the grass, Francis and faithful Leo. Suddenly, as they are about to eat, they hear in the twilight calm the first notes of a nightingale.

They listen with suspended hearts, these two who have walked together through these same woodlands in the squalid mud and ice of a distant winter evening, talking of perfect joy.

Francis says, "Let us go praise God together with our Brother Nightingale."

When they reach the tree where the invisible singer awaits, Francis invites Brother Leo to sing.

"Father," says Leo, "I do not have a good voice. You have a fine voice and know so many beautiful songs—you must reply to the nightingale."

So they begin to sing a tenzon or competition, in the perfect style of the Provençal troubadours, Francis and the nightingale, the man who had once led serenades through the streets of Assisi and the noble virtuoso of the woods.

Which songs, new and old, does the minstrel of God bring back from his heart's depths to compete in this new court of love? Perhaps the songs of his melancholy, when he went about through the city searching for the lady whom his soul loved. Perhaps of a love that neither iron nor fire could part. Or his newer song of devotion that begins:

> Hail, Queen Wisdom! The Lord save you,
>   with your sister, pure, holy Simplicity.
> Lady Holy Poverty, God keep you,
>   with your sister, holy Humility.[45]

The nightingale replies. He sighs in sympathy at the grief of the disconsolate lover. He exults in a joyful song of love won again. He grows humble and plaintive in prayer. He puts questions in his turn. Then he launches into a dizzying flood of nimble notes that rise and fall in a thousand tones, in a thousand swift and resonant progressions, in an immense jubilation that no one could resist sharing. And when the last passionate note dies away, everything remains still under the spell of the power and sweetness of that song.

Francis turns to Leo and says, "Brother, truthfully I must confess that the nightingale has beaten me."

They return to their meal. The nightingale comes to rest on Francis's hand. This pleases him and he says to his companion, "Brother, let us give something to eat to our sister bird, who deserves it more than we do."

Thus, all together, they share the supper.[46]

Easter at Greccio

After the Christmas at Greccio, Francis decided to spend Easter there, too.[47]

From atop his Greccio cliff, he saw spring coming on—the mountain growing green, the forest lands thickening with branches in new leaf, the plain shining in the joy of fields freed from the grey torpor of winter snows.

It was a time for remembering the Passion again, and he meditated on it, in such identification with it that his bitter thoughts brought tears. One time, near Porziuncola, he said to someone who had seen him weep like this and asked him the reason for it, "I weep for the passion of my Lord Jesus Christ; and I should not be ashamed to go weeping through the whole world for his sake."[48]

On the silent mountain, the cross that he carried in his heart dominated everything else. It obscured the splendour of spring. This was the same cross that Jesus had borne, the cross of the pains of the whole world.

Francis had composed for Lent his *Office of the Passion of the Lord,* using excerpts from Sacred Scripture.[n]

He allowed voices from ages past to be heard in it—voices full of pain, the lamentations of prophets who had lain in the dust in their sackcloth and cried out the future destruction of famous cities. In his alpine solitude, all the agony of the ages beat on him, like storm-driven breakers.

The brothers say: "Let us begin the psalms composed by our most holy father Francis, in honour, remembrance, and praise of the Passion of the Lord."[49]

We hear it now on this evening of Holy Thursday. April 11, 1224.

The poor church of the Greccio hermitage is dark. Some candles burn before the Sepulchre. Francis, in sorrowful memory, kneels on the bare earth. The first portion of the *Office,* said at compline, conveys a shadowed scene of sadness and death. It recalls suffering common to all human beings. In it the just man cries out his desperation from the prison to which the wickedness of his enemies has sent him.

"My wanderings you have counted. My tears are stored in your flask. Are they not recorded in your book?

"All my foes whisper together against me and take counsel together.

"They repaid me evil for good and hatred for my love.

"In return for my love they slandered me, but I prayed for them, those who have blackened me. . . .

"You have taken my friends away from me, you have made me an abomination to them; I am imprisoned, and I cannot escape. . . .

"Make haste to help me, O Lord my salvation!"

---

n. In *Leg. S. Clarae,* 30, we read: "She learned the Office of the Cross as Francis, the lover of the Cross, had composed it, and prayed it often with like affection." (Eng. trans., Brady, p. 40.) Historians have concluded that this Office of the Cross is the Office of the Passion, which is to be found in a number of codices. An excellent edition is to be found in Boehmer, *Analekten,* and also in Lemmens, *Opuscula.* [An English translation by Fahy is in *Omnibus,* pp. 140–55.] It is made up of a number of selected verses from the Psalms; the final portion is designed for use in the Christmas season. [No exact date can be assigned to its composition.]

To his liturgy of commemoration of the night when Jesus sweat blood, Francis added other excerpts from psalms of humiliation and confusion, solitude and abandonment, to be said at matins: "Insult has broken my heart, and I am weak; I looked for sympathy, but there was none; for comforters, and I found none.

"O God, the haughty have risen up against me, and the company of fierce men seeks my life, nor do they set you before their eyes. . . . "[50]

And grief continues in the first light of Good Friday, when at prime the words of David's plea against his persecutors rings out: "Have pity on me, O God; have pity on me. . . . "

But there is a note of hope. Faith returns: " . . . They have prepared a net for my feet; they have bowed me down; they have dug a pit before me, but they fall into it. . . .

"I will sing and chant praise. Awake, O my soul; awake, lyre and harp! . . . " After the night, the dawn will surely come.

But at terce the office is again a cry of despair: "Have pity on me, O God, for men trample upon me. All the day they press their attack against me. . . . "

And again misfortunes and evils are enumerated, counted off on the fingers: "All my foes whisper against me . . . They who keep watch against my life take counsel together. . . . All who see me scoff at me; they mock me with parted lips, they wag their heads. . . . I am the scorn of men, despised by the people . . . a laughingstock to my neighbours, and a dread to my friends. . . . "

Sext, the sixth hour, is a crying out at fate: "With a loud voice I cry out to the Lord; with a loud voice I beseech the Lord! . . . "

And the remembrance of the hours of agony on Calvary continues at none: "O all ye that pass by the way, attend, and see if there be any sorrow like to my sorrow. . . . "

Never had anyone, even among the prophets, known how true these words are and will be of all those who love, as did Francis, the imitator and follower of Jesus, on the Good Friday of the year in which he would receive the stigmata, as he mourned the death of Jesus in the words of all prostrate nations on the scabrous rock that is like a prototype of La Verna.[o]

At vespers came the final portion of the Office. Sorrow changes

---

o. "The Office of the Passion is nothing other than the expression of sentiments that the mountain of La Verna will bring to realization in his heart. It is the way of the cross of one who was so united to Christ that at La Verna he receives the Stigmata." Sabatier, *Études,* p. 300.

into the joy of the resurrection: "All you peoples, clap your hands, shout to God with joy of gladness. . . ."

On this Easter day, the brothers at Greccio took the trouble to prepare the dinner with a certain elegance, to show their joy at having Francis with them. They put a white tablecloth on the table and set out bottles and glassware. Francis, coming down from his cell, saw what they had done. In the words of Thomas of Celano, "He did not smile at the smiling table." He made his way outside without being noticed. There he donned the hat and took the staff of a poor beggar who was waiting there. After the brothers had begun to eat, he knocked on the door and called out, "For the love of God, give alms to this poor sick stranger!"

The brothers bade him enter for love of the one whom he had invoked. Though they were all greatly astonished to see that it was Francis, they gave him a plate and some bread.

It was still cold and a fire was burning in the fireplace. Francis sat down on the edge of the hearth. He said to the brethren, "Now I am sitting as a Friar Minor should sit." Turning, he added, "We should be mindful of the example of poverty of the Son of God more than other religious. I saw the table prepared and decorated, and I knew it was not the table of poor men who beg from door to door."

The eyes of many of the brothers filled with tears. And no one could say which grieved them more, the humility with which he remained sitting on the ground or his loving reproof.[51]

A few days later he left Greccio. He stopped for some months at Porziuncola. In early August, along with Brother Leo, Brother Angelo, and Brother Masseo, he set out for La Verna.[p]

---

p. Some biographers have placed on June 22 of this year of 1224 the meeting of the last general chapter in which Saint Francis participated. But Golubovich has demonstrated that no general chapters were held after the one in 1223 until 1227, the year after Saint Francis died. *Biblioteca,* 1:99 ff.

An important happening in this year of 1224 was the arrival of the first Franciscans in England. The mission, composed of four priests and five laymen, was led by Agnellus of Pisa, provincial minister of Paris. See Eccleston, also Cotton, *The Grey Friars of Canterbury.*

·15·

THE SERAPH

I n Francis's day, and for centuries thereafter, in Italy Montefeltro was a name of power and enchantment. It meant a castle atop a vertical cliff, an aerie of famous captains and courteous knights. A war cry shouted for three centuries by the bravest of all the armies on Italian battlefields. The longed-for goal of poets intent on disputes about perfect love. A symbol for courage founded upon hard rock, like the ancient ancestral manor house.[a] It was—and is—synonymous with battle and romance.

It is early members of this powerful Montefeltro family who hold the "great banquet and court festival," of which we read in *Little Flowers,* surely already an example of the princely munificence that will see its luxuriant flowering in *Il Cortegiano.*[b]

On May 8, 1213,[c] the castle opens its gates for this celebration, held in honour of the knighting of one of the young counts of the

---

a. *Castrum Montis Feretri,* "the *castello* (castle and walled village) of Montefeltro" mentioned in *Fioretti,* "First Consideration"; *Actus,* 9, no. 4), is today known as San Leo, in Romagna, a short distance from San Marino. The counts of Montefeltro came from here. In 1234, one of them, Buonconte, occupied Urbino and initiated the Ghibelline tradition of the family. Among the famous captains in the family are Guido, who later became a Friar Minor (see Fortini, *Assisi nel medioevo,* pp. 238–42); his son, Buonconte, who died on the battlefield of Campaldino in 1289 (cf. Dante, *Purgatorio,* Canto 5, ll. 85–129); Federico (died 1322); and Guidantonio (see Fortini, *Assisi nel medioevo,* pp. 381–85). Cf. Ugolini, *Storia dei conti e duchi di Urbino.*

b. *Il Cortegiano* of Baldassare Castiglione was inspired by the court of Guidobaldo of Montefeltro, duke of Urbino. The book consists of conversations during four evenings of March 1507 at Guidobaldo's court, supposedly carried on by real personages, men and women, associated with the court. The subjects include the qualities of a perfect courtier, how to put these into practice, the courtier's relationship to his prince and to political affairs, women, love, and the courtier's obligations in regard to love and beauty. It was the most popular work of the Renaissance, was translated into many languages, and went through many editions. Even by dour American Puritans it was regarded as the ideal guide to good manners and gentle behaviour.—Trans.

c. This date is known beyond the shadow of a doubt from the legal confirmation of the gift of the mountain made by the sons of Count Orlando, stipulated in Chiusi on June 9, 1274. In translation, it reads: "The Lord Orlando, count of Chiusi, boldest knight among all the knights of the emperor and father of the above-mentioned, in the year of our Lord 1213, on the day of

family. The news of it has travelled through the castles on the near and far side of the river, on the near and far sides of the mountain. San Marino, San Leo, Pennabilli, Mercatino, Sant'Agata Feltria—the names ring out over the rugged mountain chain, peak upon peak, ridge upon ridge, tower upon tower, like repeated trumpet calls in a slow and joyous fanfare sounded to summon a rendezvous at the first rising of the sun.

And the lords make haste to go to the rich and solitary castle. Women come from Rimini, bringing with them something of the luminous grace of the Adriatic sparkling in the morning light. Banners wave atop the walls, massive armour flashes, white silks and red velvets gleam. The meadow is smiling, the flowers sparkle, the tall towers keep watch, forest trees put out new branches and leaves, the blue peaks of the mountains form a distant backdrop for the events, the azure blue sky shines in reflection of the restless sea.

Among those who come to the festivities is the *signore* of Chiusi of La Verna, Count Orlando dei Catani. No desire to pay court to the ladies has brought him here, or a wish to join the others in a song of the new spring. Many enterprises, both hidden and plainly visible, link him to this Montefeltrano of Carpegna, now extending his rule over the whole region. Orlando had gotten up in the middle of the night, left with a great retinue, as was befitting such a ceremonious occasion and so powerful a lord, and ridden from crag to crag by the light of the stars. He descended into the valley to see dawn reflected on the water of the Marecchia. He followed the course of that river upward among gorges and precipices, and he was already below the cliff on which the castle stood when the first ray of sun touched the master tower, flying its proud pennons. Then he dismounted and clambered up the rocky path on foot, an exhausting climb that Dante a century later thought about in purgatory.[d]

May 8, solely for reason of devotion, gave and donated and conceded, freely and without any restriction, to Brother Francis and to his friars, both present and future, the Mountain of La Verna, so that Father Francis and his Friars would be able to live there. And on the aforesaid Mountain of La Verna we intend and the aforesaid intend (to include) all the forest land, the rocky lands and the meadowlands, without any limitation, from the top of the said Mountain all the way to its base." For the Latin text, see *NV* 1,2:258; cf. Lazzeri, "L'atto di conferma della donazione della Verna," in the special issue of *Studi Francescani* (La Verna) 11(1913):101–105.

The date of 1223 given in *Fioretti* is, therefore, a mistake. In 1224 Saint Francis went for the sixth and last time to La Verna.

d. Dante, *Purgatorio,* Canto 4, lines 25–27, trans. Ciardi:

> Go up to San Leo or go down to Noli;
> go climb Bismantova—two legs suffice:
> here nothing but swift wings will answer wholly.

Benvenuti dei Rambaldis da Imola thus describes the place: "(The fortress is) situated upon a great mountain, surrounded by a chain of mountains, also very high, in such a way, however,

Count Orlando is as brave as he is devout. The ceremony of the making of a new knight uplifts him. All has gone as would be expected from such a magnificent household: the Mass, the investiture, the bestowal of the sword and spurs, the congratulations of the guests. They are here in great number, the flower of knighthood within a radius of fifty miles, large and small feudal lords, vavasours and their vassals, knights *di scudo* and knights *d'arme*—noble squires and armour-clad knights.

Now the sound of animated voices and laughter rises from the open square facing the castle. Groups of young men and women are forming to sing, naturally, of love. Perhaps they choose one of those songs that in the drowsy midday seems to lull one on the wide bed of the Marecchia among the tall rows of poplars, in the quiet of the sun drenched countryside:

> *E lo mio cor s'inchina;*
> *Ohi, merzè v'addimando . . .*

> And my heart is bowed-down;
> Ah, mercy of you I implore . . .

Or it may be the song in which the clandestine mistress warns her dear lover not to let himself be discovered:

> *Valletto, se m'amate siate saggio.*

> My dear man, if you love me, be prudent.[1]

Or perhaps they sing in chorus the song of fragrant May [that was also a salute to a lady love]:

> *Fresca rosa novella,*
> *Piacente primavera . . .*

> Fresh new rose,
> Delightful Spring . . .

But all of a sudden there is silence. Francis has come into the piazza, followed by Brother Leo.

On his way from the Spoleto valley to Romagna, he passed by the foot of the *castello* and learning about the festivities that were taking place, has come to gather, with God's help, some good spiritual fruit.[2]

---

that on the inside it produces crops and everything necessary for provisioning and sustaining human life, just as in San Marino. Through its natural position, it is a marvellous and inconquerable fortress, four miles distant from San Leo." (*Comentum,* 3:117–18.)

About San Leo, cf. Bughetti, "San Leo of Montefeltro," *Studi Francescani* 11:81–86.

He steps up on a low wall and begins to speak. He talks of another beautiful love song, the one that begins:

> *Tanto è il bene ch'io aspetto*
> *Ch'ogni pena m'è diletto.*

> So great the good I have in sight
> That every pain I count delight.[3]

This song they all know and they live it every day. It is the song of the knight who travels the roads of the world, the image of his mistress in his heart. Every tribulation, every risk, is light to him, if he thinks of the happiness that awaits him at the end of the hard road. The strongest passion is the one that is nourished on sighs and tears, in separation and in waiting, in sacrifice and in hope. Only love can give such joy in sorrow.

There are words from the Gospels similar to this worldly song: "Your grief will be turned into joy."[4] The pains of the world count for nothing in the light of heavenly joy. And Francis, there at the festivities, speaks of the apostles who for love of Jesus underwent infinite hardships. He tells about the martyrs, who rejoiced even while being tortured because they awaited the opening of the doors of Paradise.

Orlando listens attentively, along with the others. He has heard marvellous things about the holiness and the miracles of the man from Assisi. Now that he hears him and sees him, it seems to him that it has all been understated.

When the talk is finished, he takes Francis apart and says to him, "Brother, I should like to discuss with you the health of my soul."

Francis replies, "I am glad. But now go and honour your friends, since they invited you to the festival. After you have dinner with them, we shall talk together as much as you wish."

The lord of Chiusi goes to the elaborate banquet, but somehow for him nothing is the same. Everything seems far away: the power of the Montefeltro lord, the alliances made and unmade, the banquet hall, the decorated tables, the rich food, the cups full to overflowing, the servants bringing in silver platters, the musicians and their music, the roses on the fine tablecloths.

As soon as he can, he rises and rushes off to look for Francis, to tell him what he has in mind. He is very rich and will willingly divest himself of a part of his goods for the sake of his soul. He is full of admiration when he learns that Francis and his companions once owned houses, lands, shops, and castles, and that they have deprived themselves of all these things to follow their ideal by leading a life of penitence in poverty.

He says, "Brother Francis, I have a mountain in Tuscany, which is very solitary and wild and perfectly suited for someone who wants to do penance in a place far from people or who wants to live a solitary life. It is called La Verna. If that mountain should please you and your companions, I would gladly give it to you for the salvation of my soul."

To Francis that is good news indeed. He promises to send some of his brothers to look at it. If they think the mountain is well adapted to prayer, he will happily accept the gift of this good man. Thus it was that in this May festival in the remote castle in the Apennines, between a love song and a prayer of penitence, the knight of Chiusi offers to Francis, the knight of Christ, the mountain that will see the miracle of the Stigmata.

The Great Crag

La Verna. It is a mountain surmounted by an immense cliff, rising vertically, cut off from the rest of the mountain on all sides. A thick forest covers the top. Dante described it as the *crudo sasso* ("harsh crag") between the Tiber and the Arno.[5]

It is a mass of stone surmounted by furious storm clouds. A retreat for prayer in the harshness of winter. An altar in the heart of holy Italy, between its two seas, between the sources of two of its immortal rivers, whose waters have mirrored ages of iron and bronze. It was called "the great castle of the soul" by the most passionate of all the mystics, Teresa of Avila. There are no better words for it. This mountain is truly a fortress destined for terrible battles of body and of soul.

In vain one searches for the peace that Orlando had promised to Francis. The whole gigantic crag seems tormented, wounded, and broken in some horrendous convulsion. Violent passion made grievously immobile lurks in the fearsome rock that is constantly assaulted by storms, rock that seems of another world. In winter it lies under an icy pall of snow; in the summer the stone grows scorching hot. Often it is crowned by livid lightning under flying black clouds and trembles under the long booming of thunder.

It is said that its name came from the terrible winter (*inverno*) on its heights. Sometimes in the January nights, when the cold north wind holds sway from one peak to another, from every cliff, every abyss, every inaccessible chasm, from all the lost precipices, voices not human rise up, like shackled unearthly spirits in frightful torment. It is said that even up here the demons did not give a moment's peace to Francis during his harrowing vigils.[e]

This fortress does not bring to mind angelic ecstasies. It is more a setting for a battle of titans. Covering the rocky rampart, which on all sides plunges downward in a straight line, are fearful bastions, enormous towers, inaccessible citadels, all made by the bedlam of twisted rock.

According to Francis, God revealed to him that those enormous fissures and chilling precipices were made in the hour that Jesus died, when, according to the Gospel, "the rocks split."[6] And here, where the mountain had responded to the spasm of the earth in Galilee, the wounds of the Passion were to come again in answer to a prayer, this time to Francis, the poverello of Christ.

The Thirsty Man

Several days after Francis met Orlando in the castle of Montefeltro, he sent two brothers to the castle of Chiusi, according to the agreement. Count Orlando ordered fifty men to accompany them on a visit to the mountain in order to protect them against the danger of wild beasts that lurked there. They explored it for a long time, and finally they found a small plateau. The soldiers used their swords to cut branches and tree trunks to build them a little hut in which to stay.

Francis was delighted at hearing how their visit turned out. He was getting ready to leave on his trip to Spain, however; so he put off going to the new hermitage that God and the generosity of Count Orlando had made possible.

Two years later, in 1215, after the general chapter at Porziuncola, he set out on the road to Città di Castello [and La Verna]. Angelo, Leo, and Masseo accompanied him. Between bad weather and the thoughts that were troubling him, the journey was long and fatiguing. Near the peak they paused for a time under a large oak tree. This time they did not have the men-at-arms with them and they looked to God to protect them. Sheltered by the tree, they saw—instead of the beasts that they had supposed would come from every side—a great number of birds. The birds flew around Francis, then settled down on his head, his shoulders, his arms. It was the miracle of Cannara all

---

e. We are told in *Fioretti*, "Second Consideration": "Among other times, one day during this fast Saint Francis came out of his cell in fervour of spirit and went to pray in a cavity nearby under a rock, below which there is a horrible and fearful precipice and a great drop to the ground. All of a sudden the devil appeared in a terrifying form, amid a great uproar, and began to beat him in order to throw him down."

over again, this time even more moving. Francis said to his companions, "My dear brothers, I believe it is pleasing to our Lord Jesus Christ that we accept a Place and live a while on this solitary mountain, since our little brothers and sisters the birds show such joy over our coming."[7]

They went on up to the top of the mountain, reached the hut made of tree branches, and walked about the little stretch of level ground. There, in a labyrinthian stretch of rock, Francis saw a beech tree below them whose branches stretched over a tiny grassy place.

The next day, Count Orlando, having learned of their coming, came with some men who lived nearby. He offered to send provisions and everything that would be needed during their stay on this wild and desolate mountain. Francis asked only that the count have another small hut built for him at the foot of the beech tree. It was done that very day, and in the first shadows of evening they took up abode in their houses. The brothers stayed by themselves. [Francis remained alone in his hut.]

In that cell Francis spent many mystical days—days of prayers, ecstasies, visions.

From La Penna,[f] which overlooks the regions of Tuscany and Romagna, the horizon stretches out to infinity. When he was tired, body and soul, after hours of meditation under Sasso Spicco,[g] he needed only to go up to the summit, into the forest of fir trees and beeches, and rest on the meadow flowering with cyclamens, and he was refreshed.

The brothers made other trips here in the following years.[h]

In August of 1224 Francis resolved to go again and to stay for longer than usual. At one time it had been his cherished plan to hold a chapter meeting there with his brothers on the feast of Saint Michael the Archangel and there to deal with problems in the order. This trip, however, he wanted to spend the time in meditation about the prince of the angels before his feast day. He had decided that they would spend the entire Lent of Saint Michael there in honour of the angel.[i]

---

f. La Penna is the peak of the mountain, somewhat above the area where the brothers had their shelters.—Trans.

g. Sasso Spicco is an enormous rock projecting from a rock wall. It lies in a chasm in the mountain amid fearsome tumbled stones, deep fissures, and dark caves. The area beneath the rock was for Saint Francis a favourite place to meditate and pray.—Trans.

h. It is thought that Saint Francis returned to La Verna in August 1216, in 1218, and in 1220, after his sojourn in Venice. For these trips, see Mencherini, *Guida illustrata della Verna*, pp. 286 ff.

[The account in *Fioretti* does not make clear on which trip the various episodes narrated took place. The account surely represents a composite of several trips.—Trans.]

i. Saint Francis adopted the practice of keeping a special Lent—a period of forty days of fasting—from the Assumption (August 15) to Michaelmas (September 29) because of his

After two days on the road, they reached the foot of La Verna on the vigil of the Assumption and prepared for the arduous climb. Francis was very weak, and his companions went to a peasant who lived in the area and asked him to lend them his donkey.

"Are you," he asked them, "friars of that Brother Francis of Assisi about whom people say so much good?"

The brothers replied that they were, and that it was really for Brother Francis that they wanted the donkey. The peasant, with great devotion and care, got the donkey ready, led it to Francis, and helped him mount it. Then all set out on the road, the brothers in front, and behind them Francis on the donkey, led by its owner.

As they were going over a good stretch of the road, the man again asked his question. "Tell me," he said, "are you Brother Francis of Assisi?" And when Francis assured him that he was, the peasant said, "Well, then, try to be as good as everyone thinks you are, because many people have great faith in you. So I urge you, never let there be anything in you different from what they expect of you."

As soon as Francis heard these words, he got down from the donkey, knelt before the peasant and devoutly kissed his feet. He thanked him most humbly because he had taken the trouble to admonish him so charitably.[8]

They reached the mid-point of their ascent. The sun beat straight down and scorching heat rose from the red-hot rock. Not a tree, a hedge, a blade of grass was there, only stones, desolate in the burning heat of midday. The owner of the donkey walked as if he had been blinded by the light. A dreadful thirst scalded his throat. Everything round about—parched, dried up—seemed to increase his preoccupation with his thirst. The mountain itself seemed to be pleading for water as it stretched toward an implacable sky.

The peasant began to complain. He said that he could not stand it any more, "I am dying of thirst. If I don't have something to drink, I'll suffocate in a minute!"

Francis had pity on him. He got off the donkey and knelt on the stone, under the flaming sky. In the dazzling reflections that encircled him, he seemed to be praying not only for the man of La Verna but for every poor soul in thirst. Far away, the bells of the country

---

special devotion to the Archangel Michael, who, he said, ought to be honoured because he had the office of presenting souls to God. Whether his companions joined him in this Lent is not clear from the sources; perhaps some did, as it would have served as a time of prayer and spiritual preparation for the chapter that began on Michaelmas. According to *Leg. Maior,* IX 2, 3, Francis kept three other special Lents in addition to the regular one: forty days of fasting beginning on Epiphany, before the feast of Saints Peter and Paul, and from this feast to the Assumption.—Trans.

churches rang out, announcing midday on the vigil of the feast of Assumption.

Finally Francis arose and told the peasant that God in his mercy had answered his prayer.

The man ran to the place Francis showed him and to his joy and astonishment saw a bubbling spring of clear water. It gushed from the harsh rock and ran gurgling down the slope. Eagerly he flung himself down on the ground and plunged his mouth, face, and hands into the fresh water and drank avidly.

When he had finished, it was the peasant who knelt at Francis's feet, overjoyed by the miracle that had so helped and strengthened him, and that would certainly comfort others nearby who would hear about it from him. He would tell them that it was proof of Francis's holiness.

But when he went back home on the same road, he wore himself out searching for that miraculous spring. In vain. The water had disappeared as it had come and the ground was once again as it had been earlier—bone-dry.[9]

It was already late in the day when Francis and his companions reached the summit. Bells were no longer ringing, but on the plain were glowing fires lit in honour of the Virgin.[j]

The next day Francis began his meditation. The cell by the beech tree did not seem sufficiently isolated from the others for him, so, with Brother Leo's help, he selected another place, on the far side of a fearful chasm over which they put a piece of wood to serve as a bridge. No one was to come to him but Brother Leo, who would bring him a bit of bread and some water once during the day and again at night, at the hour of matins. Before crossing the chasm, Brother Leo was to call out, *Domine, labia mea aperies* ("Lord, open my lips"). He was to go forward only if Francis replied, *Et os meum annuntiabit laudem tuam* ("And my mouth shall proclaim your praise").

L'Alter Christus

The succession of days began, distinguishable only by the rising and the setting of the sun, by the blazing and the dimming of the stars.

A great silence prevailed.

---

j. The custom of lighting great bonfires in celebration of the feast of the Assumption, as well as on other great festive days, was widespread in Italy until relatively recent years. It still survives in many rural areas.—Trans.

At evening, when the mountain reddened in the sunset, from his cell Francis heard the falcons cry as they wheeled in the cobalt sky. Then a shadow began to creep downward from La Penna; slowly it veiled the forest and filled the distant valley.

One of the falcons became his friend. It was a fierce and violent creature, the same colour as the rock. Its black eyes shone ferociously in its little grey head, its claws contracted in its instinctual rapine, the hooked beak was ready for attack. But even its predatory savageness disappeared as it was gentled by Francis. The falcon built a nest near his refuge, as the innocent turtle dove had once done. It hovered to listen to his words. In the heart of the night, at the hour of matins, it came to awaken him by repeating its cry and beating its wings nor would it leave until Francis had gotten up. At dawn it "would very gently sound the bell of its voice" to call Francis to prayer.[10]

But this, says Thomas of Celano, was Francis's victory, because his love was being repaid with love; "little wonder if all other creatures too venerated this eminent love of the Creator."[11]

At the hour of matins when Brother Leo came, earth and sky were linked in harmony and from the woods came the sharp odor of cyclamens. The woodlands were immobile in a light of dream, wrapped in the whiteness of the full moon. Dark tree trunks stood straight as the lances of an army of giants. The breeze would rise and a long murmur, like the sighing of the sea, pass over the tops of the trees.

On one of those nights Brother Leo came to the brink of the gorge and said the words agreed upon, "Lord, open my lips."

No one replied. He crossed the log and looked in the cell. Francis was not there. He went further and walked through the woods. At last he saw Francis on his knees, his face and his hands raised to the sky. Over and over he said, "Who are you, my dearest God? And what am I, your vilest little worm and useless little servant?" In the still night was a man overcome by his own insignificance as he confronted the immensity of God.[k]

Later, Leo and Francis interrogated the Gospels, as Francis had done in the church of San Nicolò, after the night he spent with Bernardo di Quintavalle. And each of the three times they sought God's will, the book opened of itself to the Passion of Christ.

On this night, it seems that the lamentations of the Holy Week in Greccio fill the silence and make it a night of anguish. Francis and

---

k. According to *Fioretti,* on La Verna Brother Leo constantly spied upon Francis "with holy ingenuity." Among the marvels that he is said to have seen are seeing Francis raised off the ground as he prayed, seeing a scroll from heaven and, later, a torch, come down and rest on Francis's head, hearing him converse with God and with the angels.—Trans.

Leo hear all the pain in the world rising like a tide against the side of the mountain.

And he who was the father of all wants to bear the cross of all. Francis has a vision of Jesus rising before him. He comes forward on pierced feet, uncovers his lacerated heart, stretches out his nail-marked hands, and repeats the words of the Last Supper: "This is my blood. Drink all of it."

He has the tender face of those who suffer and endure more than their share of pain and abuse, who must drag crosses too heavy for them up exhausting hills. They collapse under the beatings life deals out to them, get up and go on, fall again. The mountain seems to be trembling under the blows of the hammers nailing them to their crosses. It echoes with the sounds of imprecations, everlasting derision, torture, and grief. Jesus becomes every suffering creature; life, an immense Calvary.

And Francis, kneeling before his cell, lifts up this fervent prayer:

"My Lord Jesus Christ, I pray you to grant me two graces before I die. The first is that during my life I may feel in my soul and in my body, as much as possible, that pain that you, dear Jesus, sustained in the hour of your most bitter Passion. The second is that I may feel in my heart, as much as possible, that great love with which you, O Son of God, were inflamed in willingly enduring such suffering for us sinners."

Francis's prayer is answered. The life that began with a kiss to a leper, the life that has in it leper hospitals, prisons, battlefields in Arce and Perugia and Damietta, and all the places he found pain and suffering, has led now to this moment in the night before the feast of the Exaltation of the Cross.[1]

---

1. Saint Bonaventure says that the vision occurred "about the feast of the Exaltation of the Holy Cross" (*Leg. Maior,* XIII, 3); Thomas of Celano, "two years before Francis gave his soul back to heaven (*1 Cel.,* 94)." In *24 Generals* (AF 3:65–67) it is placed "early in the morning on the day of the Exaltation of the Holy Cross; and in *Fioretti,* "Third Consideration," it is also said to have been on "the Feast of the Cross."

Both history and science are today virtually unanimous in recognizing the reality of the stigmata. Among the testimonies given by Francis's contemporaries are these: the letter of Brother Elias announcing the death of Saint Francis; the benediction given to Brother Leo by Francis, on which the presence of the stigmata are noted; three surviving letters of Pope Gregory IX, who canonized Francis; other affirmations of the miracle by Popes Innocent IV and Alexander IV; repeated references by Thomas of Celano in his *First Life, Second Life,* and *Treatise on Miracles,* and also in his famous sequence *Sanctitatis nova signa;* attestations by a number of other historians, including Saint Bonaventure, Jacques de Vitry, the Three Companions, Julian of Speyer, Fra Salimbene, Thomas Eccleston, and others. Also, a document in the Archives of the Sacro Convento bears the names of witnesses to the stigmata. Brothers Elias and Rufino were among those who saw the stigmata while Francis was still living. In the Basilica di San Francesco in Assisi, the clothes that Saint Francis was wearing when he died are soaked with blood on the right side and his sandals also still show traces of blood. For a discussion of these and other details regarding the stigmata, also for an identification of the witnesses to it, see *NV* 2:446–51.

He saw the mountain covered by light, the heavens open, and a burning seraph swiftly descend. Light blazed everywhere. Every blade of grass was clear and distinct in the dazzling light.

Francis raised his eyes. The angel had his arms open, his feet stretched out. He was nailed to a cross. A living cross with six flaming wings, two raised over his head, two covering his body, and two spread out in flight.

Then he was over Francis and rays darted from the wounds in his feet, his hands, his side, to pierce Francis's hands, feet, and heart. Francis's soul was caught up in a vortex of fire. An infinite joy filled him, and also infinite pain. He raised his arms toward the living Cross, only to fall unconscious against the stone.

The whole mountain of La Verna seemed to be burning, as if the sun were high. Shepherds, taking their flocks to the pasture-lands of the sea, were awakened. Muleteers got up, thinking it was dawn, and set out on the road again.

They travelled on in what seemed bright daylight. And then they saw that immense light fade and vanish. Night returned, alive with stars.[12]

Farewell, Mountain of Angels

Afterwards, Francis suffered anguish from the wounds. His hands and his feet looked as though they had been pierced by nails. The wound in his side was like one made by a lance; blood constantly flowed from it and clotted on his habit. He was forced to confide in some of his brothers—his companion during the Crusade, Brother Illuminato, his favourite disciple, Brother Leo. Leo had the duty of changing the bandage on his side nearly every day; Francis wore one over the wound until his death.[13]

Even the falcon had pity on him. He came later every morning to awaken him so that Francis could sleep longer.

At the end of September he wanted to go back to Porziuncola, so he prepared to leave La Verna, saying he would never return there. His faithful companions remained: Angelo, Illuminato dell'Arce, Silvestro, Masseo. Brother Leo would accompany him during the trip.

Their departure was set for the last day of the month. After having listened to Mass in the little church of Santa Maria degli Angeli that had been built for him some years earlier, they set out together. Francis went first on an ass that Count Orlando sent. The others, who had decided to accompany them for a stretch of the road, followed. Everyone was silent, overcome by emotion. About them shone the light of that autumn sun. Filtered through the dark foliage of the fir trees, it radiated a sense of profound peace.

When they reached the summit of the mountain La Foresta, where it is possible to see the top of La Verna, the flood of sentiment and memories that stirred Francis overflowed. He got down, stood still, and turned to salute the mountain, the cliffs, the trees, the brothers.

"Farewell, farewell, farewell, Brother Masseo. Farewell, Brother Angelo. Farewell, Brother Silvestro and Brother Illuminato. Live in peace, dear sons. Farewell, my body is going away but I leave you my heart. I am going to Santa Maria degli Angeli and Brother Little Lamb of God will accompany me. I shall never return here. Farewell, farewell, all! Farewell, Mount La Verna! Farewell, Mountain of the Angels! Farewell, dear Brother Falcon; I thank you for your kindness to me. Farewell, Sasso Spicco, you who received me into yourself and so mocked the devil; we shall not meet again. Farewell, Santa Maria degli Angeli! Mother of the Eternal Word, to you I entrust these sons of mine."[m]

He wept, and the others, kneeling around him, also had tears in their eyes. They watched him go down the slope of the mountain until he disappeared at the bend in the path. Then slowly and silently, their faces streaked with tears, they went back through the forest, desolate now.

In the valley the news that Francis was coming had spread. People hurried from everywhere. They pressed close all along his route, seeking to kiss his hands. One woman brought him her baby whose abdomen was so swollen from dropsy that he could not stand on his feet. Another raised her ulcerated son. Farther along the way, a group arrived, dragging by main force a woman who twisted every which way, barking like a dog and with slavering mouth. All the pains, the miseries, the evils, that affect human beings unrolled before him on that road. We are told that a light touch of his blessed hand was enough to bring peace to these tortured people.[n]

They descended to the *castello* of Monte Acuto and continued on to Caprese. At Borgo San Sepolcro there was an immense crowd, which welcomed him with cries of jubilation. Many people marched ahead of him, as when Jesus entered Jerusalem. They carried olive branches

---

m. This reconstruction of Saint Francis's farewell to La Verna is found in a seventeenth century document preserved at La Verna, once believed to have been written by Brother Masseo. Though critical examination proved the document not authentic, it does recall an ancient tradition that has all the earmarks of truth. See *NV* 2:447–48.

n. The reaction of the people suggests that the brothers, despite Francis's wishes, had learned about and spread the news of the stigmata.—Trans.

in their hands and shouted, "Here is the saint! Here is the saint!" But Francis remained rapt in his dream and paid no attention to them. He seemed already separated from this earth.

From the valley of Afra they climbed to the hermitage of Monte Casale, where they stopped for several days. At Città di Castello they stayed for over a month because of his steadily worsening physical condition.[14]

They took the road again, accompanied by a farmer who had offered them his donkey. They travelled together all one day, hoping to arrive at Fratta before night.

Darkness caught them in a deserted place far from every house. It was snowing and the blowing wind was so cold that at last they could go no farther. They took shelter under an overhanging rock and waited. The snowstorm and wind grew worse, and the owner of the donkey began to complain. He said that it had not been sensible to make that ascent at that hour and in that weather, and that certainly they would never last until daybreak, seeing as how they were already so chilled. But Francis had only to touch him with his hand for him to get warm, so much so that, as he said later, he felt that he was near the mouth of a blazing furnace. He always added that he had gone to sleep immediately afterwards, comforted in soul and in body, and that he slept better that night among the stones and snow than he ever had in his own bed.[o]

They reached Santa Maria degli Angeli at a late hour on the following day.

Francis was exhausted. Furthermore, he had developed an eye disease after his return from the Holy Land, and it was now so badly aggravated that he could not bear light.

And now anxiety over complications in the order, by now far from its primitive simplicity, was added to his physical problems. Santa Maria degli Angeli had become the general quarters of a great band that was marching throughout the world. Quarrels, dissensions, and rivalries had even extended to matters concerning him, which worried and grieved him even more than his bodily suffering.

Some friars complained that he had committed himself to the care of specific brothers dear to him, who stayed with him, advised him,

---

o. The great snow and cold are mentioned in the account of the trip in *Fioretti,* "Fourth Consideration." Since the episode took place on the road between Città di Castello and Santa Maria degli Angeli, which they reached the day after this episode, we can assume that the month was now December. By taking into account the stops made in the various places, we can see that this would be exactly right. The arrival of Saint Francis is also recorded in *Fioretti.*

took care of him, and assisted him during his trips. A kind of jealousy was born of the great affection all of them had for him. The inevitable divisions characteristic of all idealistic movements were arising even in his own family—divisions between those who had entered the order first and those who had come later, between the purists and those who favoured a relaxation of the rules, between those who gave orders and those who had to obey.

He had been greatly comforted by the assistance of those affectionate and faithful companions, Leo, Rufino, Angelo, Giovanni delle Laudi.[p] But to avoid being in the middle of disputes, he told Brother Elias that he would no longer choose companions to help him. From then on, anyone who was pleased to do so could ask to accompany him. He added, not without a shade of bitterness, "Recently I saw a blind man who had only a little dog to guide him on his way, and I do not want to seem better than he."

Perhaps the matter was dropped, but he was profoundly shaken by it.[q]

It seemed to him that he had accomplished nothing truly good up until that day, and that he must begin all over again.[15] Nostalgically, he thought about the humility that had once guided every friar in all that he did.

Now many, too many, wanted authority. They served their own pride. Their goal was to win the world's approval and the praise of their subordinates. They did not take into account that it was dangerous to rule or that Francis taught it was better to be ruled.[16] The ancient idealism had become only a memory. Vainly Francis prayed that the brothers too much attached to the world might persevere in grace.[17]

He wanted to lead everyone back to the straight path by example. He himself would once again serve the lepers. He would go sit in the Assisi piazza and bear mocking remarks in patience.[18]

---

p. Thomas of Celano identifies these brothers only by their characteristics; he says he does not wish to reveal the names so as to spare their modesty. But we can easily recognize the Three Companions and Giovanni delle Laudi: "One was known for his outstanding discretion (Angelo), another for his extraordinary patience (Rufino), the third for his great simplicity (Leo), and the last was robust of body and gentle of disposition (Giovanni)".

Thomas says that Francis entrusted himself to the care of selected brothers so that "he might direct his intention more freely to God, and in frequent ecstasy, wander about and enter the workshops of the blessed mansions of heaven and present himself with an abundance of grace on high before the most kind and serene Lord of all things." *1 Cel.,* 102.

q. *Spec. Perf.,* 40; *2 Cel.,* 144. Neither source says specifically that Francis's renunciation was accepted and became an accomplished fact. Successive events, in fact, show otherwise. In another passage from *1 Cel.,* 102, we are told that these four companions, who assisted Francis in the last two years of his life, "tried with all vigilance, with all zeal, with all their will to foster the peace of mind of their blessed father, and they cared for the infirmity of his body, shunning no distress, no labours, that they might give themselves entirely to serving the saint."

Return to San Damiano

An all-encompassing love for all the world, which consumed him, kept Francis from feeling the death of his flesh.[19] For all that his body was so broken, he thought he could still (as he had before) make it obey him and somehow overcome all obstacles.[20] Thomas of Celano says of that time, "True virtue knows not a limit of time, since the expectation of a reward is eternal."[21] And Saint Bonaventure adds, "The goad of love never ceases to urge a person on to greater efforts and leaves no room for discouragement or sloth."[22]

He was seized by a renewed desire for prayer in solitude.[23] Since Porziuncola in this season is often foggy, and the humidity was aggravating his illnesses, the brothers searched for a place not far away that would help him in both body and spirit. They chose San Damiano.[r] Surely it would be good to return to the place his mission began.[24]

They built a little hut of mats for him, as he asked them to do. It stood outside the monastery, sheltered by the house of the old priest who had once taken him in, now the quarters of the four friars assigned to give spiritual assistance and to collect alms for the sisters—a priest with another cleric and two lay brothers.[s] The place was quiet, sheltered from the wind, and when the sky was clear, it got the very last rays of the sun.

Brother Elias came often to visit him. He exhorted him earnestly and affectionately to take care of himself, ordered him to see a doctor and promised to be with him and help him. But it was clear that they would have to wait for better weather before beginning treatment.

For about two months Francis stayed inside the hut, completely in the dark. The terrible pain in his eyes kept him from sleeping.[25] And

---

r. None of the suggestions that Francis stayed elsewhere can stand up to close examination, either on the basis of documentary evidence or on guesses as to more likely places. First and foremost, the two major sources for the writing of the *Canticle*, *Spec. Perf.*, 100, and *Per.*, 42, 43, say that this is where he was staying. The closest critical analyses of these texts has left no doubt as to their reliability, particularly, in this case, the second one, in which "we who were with him" give the longest, most detailed account of this period of Francis's life. The earliest known copy of the *Canticle*, MS. 338 of the Assisi library, also says that it was written at San Damiano. Though the date of this copy cannot be fixed with absolute certainty, it is certainly of the early to mid-thirteenth century. There is no documentary evidence of any kind to suggest that it might have been composed in the Rieti area or in the bishop's house in Assisi. As to the objections that it would have been improper for Francis to have stayed at San Damiano, where the Poor Clares lived, see chap. 16, n. a, of this book. For a full discussion of all the factors involved and the theories that have been advanced by others, see *NV* 2:471–543.

s. The number of friars assigned to San Damiano can be determined from *The Rule of Saint Clare of 1253.* In *Leg. S. Clarae*, 11, the sisters ask "as a favour of the Order of Friars Minor a Chaplain with one clerk . . . and two lay brothers . . . even as we have always had through the courtesy of that Order." (Brady, trans., pp. 80–81.)

if he did begin to doze off, mice running about the room awoke him with a start. There were a great many mice, and they ran about so boldly that they even climbed up on the table when he sat down to eat.[26] Yet in that dreary hovel, during that winter of pain and trial, Francis felt to the fullest the joy of a life that is totally permeated by love.

He thought of everything in creation as his brothers and sisters, even things that have no resemblance to human creatures, yet which have their own strong and mysterious life. These, too, he saw as created beings, lovely and loving, who add their voices to the eternal harmony that makes the earth an edge of Paradise.

The Friar Minor had arrived at life's highest peak—he was at one with the whole of creation. The world, the universe, were transformed by his perception. It was as if he saw all things for the first time.

"Who would be able to narrate the sweetness he enjoyed while contemplating in creatures the wisdom of their Creator, his power and his goodness?" said Thomas of Celano. "Indeed, he was very often filled with a wonderful and ineffable joy from this consideration while he looked upon the sun, while he beheld the moon, and while he gazed upon the stars and the firmament."[27]

He loved the sun, who is beautiful and who rules over all. To him it seemed to show forth the very image of God, who through the sun gives men light, heat, and life itself.[28]

He loved the moon, Sister Moon, silent and white. The virgin stars, whose brightness alternately burns and dims as they twinkle light and dark all through the night. In solitude and in silence they shine, creatures that bring to mind Saint Clare and her sisters at San Damiano, whose chaste beauty was burning hidden in their sanctuary among the olive trees, solely for the praise of God.

Those who were with him remembered that "above all creatures deprived of reason, he loved with the greatest love the sun and the fire." The shadows in which he was forced to live made him love light all the more. At each dawn he rejoiced in the sun, rising triumphantly over the top of the Subasio. Each evening his heart was gladdened by the fire blazing in the fireplace, its light reflected on the dark walls of the room.[29]

He had always been fascinated by fire. Staring at it had always been a great joy, as it rose and blazed and flickered and roared, changeable and audacious, vivid and beautiful, revealing a thousand glowing and immaterial shapes like blazing spirits. At times he had not hesitated to feed it with his own habit.[30] Always, he felt saddened when candles on the altars were extinguished after religious rites and depressed when the friars threw ashes on the fire before going to bed.

He wanted the brothers to burn wood until it was completely consumed. He told them not to extinguish half-burnt brands by throwing them to the wind, as was customary. There is happiness (he must have felt) in being given entirely to the purifying flame.[31]

Next to fire, he loved water.[32] Now he was seeing anew the liveliness of the springs gushing out along the road, their moving water satisfying the thirst, their pools, mirrors of the sky, the still surfaces alive with images of sailing clouds on a sea of blue. He thought again of the days he had spent in meditation by the sea in Venice, by the lake near Perugia, in solitary and luminous nooks beautiful with algae and canebrakes—lonely places where he had spent long hours gazing at the living looking-glass, exulting in the weft and woof of silver woven by the sun and wind on calm days, hidden spots where he had listened to the language spoken by restless waves.

Flowers, too, he loved. Not only did he consider that there was spirit in sky and sea; even the tiniest flower and the slenderest blade of grass he thought to be imbued with it. He had ordered that some pieces of ground in the friars' garden always be used for these bearers of colour and perfume.[33] Brother Flower, he said, shows God's love for men and in them he gives us a supreme sign of grace.

He was sure that flowers responded to love like other creatures. When he came across an abundance of them, he was likely to preach to them as he had one day preached to his sister birds.[34]

And another small space of the garden he ordered to be reserved for wild herbs, whose scents are more pleasing than those of all the fabled unguents and balsams of the Orient: thyme, wild thyme, mint, balm. He wanted everyone to note how they praised God with their perfume: "God made me for your sake, O man."[35]

Thomas, the biographer poet, writes: "How great a gladness do you think . . . the flowers brought to his mind when he saw the shape of their beauty and perceived the odor of their sweetness?"[36] He said that the flower that comes from the root of Jesse has by its fragrance raised thousands from the dead.[37] He was fond of recalling the passage from the Song of Songs that speaks of a green valley flowering with white lilies and red roses. It made him think of the man called the rose on the plain and the lily on the mountain slopes.[38]

He recalled the words that symbolize the suffering of the just: "For a tree there is hope, if it be cut down, that it will sprout again."[39] And he ordered that the words be taken literally. No tree that had to be cut was to be totally destroyed; all must be left in condition to sprout again. Thus they would comfort every broken creature with the hope of salvation and rebirth. So he forbade the brothers to cut down the whole tree when they cut wood.[40] He also said that trees made him think of Jesus, who died on the wood of the cross.[41]

According to Saint Paul, even the rocks recalled Jesus,[42] who was compared to a rock that cracks to give water to the thirsty pilgrim as he crosses the desert of life.[43] Thus one day water had gushed out from a rock along the steep pathway to La Verna through Francis's prayer.

On that holy mountain he had once seen Jesus, standing on top of a rock. And as the vision faded away, he had called Brother Leo and said to him, "Wash this rock with water." And the friar washed the rock with water. Then he said, "Wash it with wine." And it was done. And then he had said, "Wash it with oil." And at last, "Wash it in balsam." The friar replied, "O dear father, how in this wild place can I find some balsam?"[44]

But now to Francis, all the rivers ran with balsam. And rocks had become jasper, embedded in an earth of gold.[45]

To look with love is to find all things transformed, to find that every creature asks only to serve others through the Creator. Beauty is itself this kindness and charity: "God has created me for you, O man!"[46]

In this dissolving of individuality in the sweet harmony of life, in this divine oneness, shines the unique genius of Humility.

The Canticle of Brother Sun

One interminable night in the middle of winter, his pains became so terrible that he took pity on his poor Brother Body and prayed to God for the strength to bear them. And he found that his pain became the strong wing that bore his soul to God.

He got up early in the morning, his body worn out, his heart in tumult from his night's vision. He called one of the friars. He said to him that for every trial on this earth, there is a joy in heaven, for every bitterness, a divine consolation, for every enemy who injures us, a creature who loves us. This is the great grace and blessing given to us by God.

"Therefore, for his glory, for my consolation, and the edification of my neighbour," he concluded, "I wish to compose a new 'Praises of the Lord,' for his creatures. These creatures minister to our needs every day. Without them we could not live, yet through them the human race greatly offends the Creator. Every day we fail to appreciate so great a blessing by not praising as we should the Creator and dispenser of all these gifts."[47]

He sat down, his face alight, while he collected his thoughts. Outside, the grey morning light lay over the motionless olive trees, heavy with snow under a veiled sky. But to Francis, all things reflected the interior light that by God's grace he had been given and shone as vividly as had the cliff of La Verna on the night of the Stigmata.

On La Verna, Brother Leo had once heard him pray fervently, "Who are you, my dearest God? And what am I, your vilest little worm and useless little servant?"[48] It is not only the human being alone who sings praises to God, he had come to realize. His is but one song in a chorus of all creatures. God is best praised when all the songs are joined and all creation sings in brotherhood. His perception was a triumph over his blindness and winter's squalor and a realization of the wickedness and foolish pride of human beings, who deem themselves alone important. And the song in which he put his thought in words is one of "cornfields and vineyards, stones and forests and all the beautiful things of the fields, fountains of water and the green things of the gardens, earth and fire, air and wind."[49]

Palm Sunday's hosanna rose to his lips: "All glory, laud, and honour, to thee, Redeemer, King!" He had the words now, so he stood up, and the friars hurried to gather around him. And from his full heart, he poured out the words of his immortal song:

Canticum Solis

Incipiuntur laudes creaturarum, quas fecit beatus Franciscus ad laudem et honorem Dei, cum esset infirmus apud Sanctum Damianum.

> *Altissimu, omnipotente, bonsignore,*
> *tue sono le laude,*
> *la gloria elhonore*
> *et omne benedictione.*

> *Ad te solo, Altissimo, se konfano*
> *et nullu homo enne dignu*
> *te mentovare.*

> *Laudato sie, misignore, cum tucte le tue creature,*
> *spetialmente messor lo frate sole,*
> *loquale iorno et allumini noi par loi.*

Et ellu ebellu eradiante cum grande splendore:
 de te, Altissimo, porta significatione.

Laudato si, misignore, per sora luna ele stelle:
 in celu lai formate clarite
 et pretiose et belle.

Laudato si, misignore, per frate vento,
 et per aere et nubilo
 et sereno et omne tempo
 per loquale a le tue creature
 dai sustentamento.

Laudato si, misignore, per sor aqua,
 laquale e multo utile et humile
 et pretiosa et casta.

Laudato si, misignore, per frate focu,
 per loquale ennalumini la nocte:
 edello ebello et iocundo
 et robustoso et forte.

Laudato si, misignore, per sora nostra matre terra,
 laquale ne sustenta et governa,
 et produce diversi fructi
 con coloriti flori et herba.

Laudate et benedicite, misignore,
 et rengratiate et serviate li
 cum grande humilitate.

The Canticle of Brother Sun

Most high, all-powerful, all good Lord!
 All praise is yours, all glory, all honour
 And all blessing.

To you, alone, Most High, do they belong.
 No mortal lips are worthy
 To pronounce your name.

All praise be yours, my Lord, through all that you have made,
    And first my lord Brother Sun,
    Who brings the day; and light you give to us through him.

How beautiful is he, how radiant in all his splendour!
    Of you, Most High, he bears the likeness.

All praise be yours, my Lord, through Sister Moon and Stars;
    In the heavens you have made them, bright
    And precious and fair.

All praise be yours, my Lord, through Brothers Wind and Air,
    And fair and stormy, all the weather's moods,
    By which you cherish all that you have made.

All praise be yours, my Lord, through Sister Water,
    So useful, lowly, precious and pure.

All praise be yours, my Lord, through Brother Fire,
    Through whom you brighten up the night.
    How beautiful is he, how gay! Full of power and strength.

All praise be yours, my Lord, through Sister Earth, our mother,
    Who feeds us in her sovereignty and produces
    Various fruits with coloured flowers and herbs.

Praise and bless my Lord, and give him thanks,
    And serve him with great humility.[t]

He was happy, with a sense of completion in having found the song that expressed the truth that he had been seeking from his earliest years.

---

[t] *Canticle of the Sun.* The Italian text is that of Ms. 338 of the Assisi library; Eng. trans.: Fahy, *Omnibus,* pp. 130–31. What Saint Francis meant by the Italian word *per* has never been fully determined: does it mean "by," "for" or "through" ("by means of")? In the original sources, Thomas of Celano, in his references to the canticle, seems to use the interpretation "by," with his comparisons of the canticle sung by Shadrach, Meshach, and Abednego in the fiery furnace (Daniel 3:52–90). In *Spec. Perf.,* on the other hand, we are told that Francis wanted to move men to praise the Lord in his creatures—therefore, "for" would be the proper word. This latter point of view is the one generally followed. See *NV* 2:543.

[Ezra Pound, for one, opts for instrumentality, the third possibility, and translates the *per* as "of." (*Translations,* pp. 442–43.) Leclerc, following Desbonnets and Vorreux, sensibly points out that when a language has not yet stabilized distinctions in the words being forged, no distinction can be made in spirit. Thus, for Francis and his contemporaries, *per* meant all at the same time, "for," "by," and "through." *Il Cantico delle Creature,* p. 15.—Trans.]

He himself composed a melody to go with the words. He was so pleased with his song that he wanted to send the old king of poets, Brother Pacifico, through the world, with a few selected other friars, to sing it so as to teach everyone its urgent truth. He told them just how to do it: they were to sing like minstrels, who formed a ring in city piazzas when they sang their songs about brave knights and true loves. In this case, one of the friars was first to preach a sermon, then all of them would sing Francis's song. Afterwards, the one who had preached was to turn to the people and say, "We are the jongleurs of God and the only reward we want is to see you lead a truly penitent life."

"Who, indeed," said Francis, "are God's servants if not jongleurs who strive to move men's hearts in order to lead them to the joys of the spirit?"

In this last period of his life, his illnesses and infirmities were steadily growing worse. But always, even when he was suffering most intensely, it was enough for him to sing and have his brothers sing his song of joy for him to gain the strength to endure every pain.[50]

The New War with Perugia

He was shaken out of that ecstatic mood by a new war, a nasty little partisan war that in that moment came to impinge on his great vision. It was a war that churned up all the passions of the past—factional bitternesses, resentments over old injuries, the renewal of violent feuds.

Assisi went to war with Perugia again.[u]

In 1214 [it will be remembered] a struggle had begun between the nobles and the people of Perugia, a conflict that had been predicted by Francis. In 1217 this internal fight had broken out again. Assisi took advantage of the fact that Perugia could do nothing about it to

---

u. This new war with Perugia grew out of factional struggles in Perugia that had been going on—despite minor pauses at intervals for the signing of still another peace treaty—since 1214 (see *NV* 2:199–219). Innocent III and Honorius III both unsuccessfully tried their hands at settling it, in the interests both of peacemaking and of trying to keep the disorders from spreading and drawing in nearby cities. In 1222 Honorius had set the penalty of excommunication for anyone who was involved in the continuation of this strife; thus, Bishop Guido had little choice but to carry out this sentence against the podestà, Oportulo, who had been one of the signers of the alliance of mutual aid with the nobles of Perugia. No doubt one of the factors, as far as the commune of Assisi was concerned, was the anticlerical spirit so pronounced in all Italian communes of this time, which was a protest against special privileges of any sort. Between 1228 and 1230, Gregory IX was reasonably successful "in placating the exacerbated spirits and composing the long and bitter dissension existing between the two cities." For details of Assisi's involvement: *NV* 2:210–14; for the documents mentioned in the text: *NV* 3:597–99, 601–6, 611–12.

claim dominion over Nocera, and it had assured itself of the possession of the road leading to this city by occupying Postignano.

Postignano was a strong and beautiful *castello*. Impressive remains of it may still be seen overlooking all the Valtopina slope. Its ancient counts had been munificent in their donations of lands and churches to the Assisi cathedral, and knights renowned for their courage, skill, and bravery in combat still lived there. Saint Rinaldo, who was at that time the bishop of Nocera, was born at Postignano.

In the archives of the commune of Assisi is the treaty of submission of December 18, 1217, signed by the sons of Guitto, lords of Postignano, and the podestà of Assisi, Domino Amardo.

"The aforesaid sons of Guitto shall make war and peace with the Assisani against all persons, with the exception of the Spoletani. And in this year all will swear to observe the orders of the podestà and of the consul, in the same manner as other citizens of Assisi. And every year twelve of the principal men of Postignano with their consuls shall swear to observe the orders of the podestà or of the consul of Assisi."

Everything in the pact is minutely regulated, according to the rules learned from the years under Perugian oppression. Here are the obligation to construct new houses in the city, the payment of heavy taxes, service during war, the reprisals, and the exterior sign of subjection: "And each year the *castello* shall offer a candle of three pounds to the church of San Rufino, on the Feast of Saint Rufinus that falls in August, for the honour of the city of Assisi."

The old warriors who had been defeated at Collestrada signed the chapters of this instrument, which was drawn up by the notary Angelo: Marangone di Cristiano, Ugolino di Matteo, Pietro di Gentile, Rudolfo di Bernardo, Bernardo di Domina Eufemia.

In 1222 there was another outbreak of the war between the nobles and the people of Perugia, and again Assisi took advantage of it, this time to move against the commune of Bettona.

On April 14, messengers from Bettona appeared before the glowering Assisi magistrates in the *arengo*, held now on the Piazza del Comune [rather than San Rufino]. They asked for peace, and they touched the open Gospels in taking their oath of submission. A year later, April 10, 1223, on the anniversary of their defeat, Giacomo di Anastasio, syndic, and Girolamo, consul, of the commune of Bettona empowered the podestà of Assisi to make all decisions about the Assisi-Bettona matter.

[This is the arbitration described in chapter 7—one in which Assisi becomes complete master of Bettona.]

We recognize many of the new and old partisans in the crowd

listening to the terms being read out, as they stand in front of the columns of the Roman temple, now the communal palace:

Carsedonio di Tommasso, the podestà who dictated the unfair ruling, the old feudal lord whose hatred of the *minori* of the city led him to build a castle on Sasso del Eremita after the battle of Collestrada, in agreement with the Perugini;

Angelo di Pietro di Peppone, the syndic of the commune of Assisi, who had a house in Via Portica facing Francis's family house, on the edge of the episcopal citadel;

Pietro di Domina Giulia, the consul who had received the temple of Minerva from the monks of Mount Subasio to be transformed into the house of the commune;

Giovanni, son of Barisano, a canon of San Rufino, who was among those who saw the stigmata after Francis's death and who testified about them;

Giacomo, son of that Gilio di Marco who attended the proclamation of the Indulgence of the Pardon;

Andrea di Taccolo, whose sister Gasdia appealed to Francis in order to enter Clare's sisters at San Damiano;

Mercato di Feliziano, who was among the councillors of the commune at the time of the legal arbitration made by Brother Elias on lands on Mount Subasio;

Angelo di Brunaccio;

Marescotto di Bernardo Dodici, the hot-tempered exile of 1202, the time of the war with Perugia, who owned lands where the battle took place.

All of these were filled with pride over the terms and Assisi's new pre-eminence.

In that same year the over-bearing Perugini knights who had hindered Francis from speaking in the piazza, learned the truth of the scriptural words: "I will put an end to the pride of the arrogant, the insolence of tyrants I will humble."[51] They had fought and had been defeated in a war with the people of Perugia. Hats metaphorically in hand, it was their turn to come and ask for Assisi's support and an alliance with her to give them a chance to win their struggle at home.

Consequently a pact was made June 24, 1223, between Egidio of Maiolo and Gualfreduccio di Tribaldo, captains of the Perugini cavaliers, and Messere Oddone of Orvieto, podestà of Assisi, Rinaldo, *camerario,* and Giovanni, syndic, through the hand of the notary Angelo. The Perugini stated their intention to remain good friends and positive collaborators in maintaining the grandeur and might of the commune of Assisi.

"We give assurance that we intend to help and to support, according to our every possibility, all the men of the city, *contado,* and district of Assisi, and each one of them against every enemy, *salva fidelitate Ecclesie* ('excepting always fidelity to the Church'), according to the terms written above; and we shall do everything in words, deeds, and in every way, in good faith and without deception, for the honour, increase, and benefit of the aforesaid city, its *contado* and its district; and we shall prevent, to the extent of our powers, every prejudice and burden that would weigh upon its subjects. We shall not permit, neither in words nor in deeds, nor in counsel, nor in contract, that anyone or any others offend the aforesaid city, *contado,* and district, nor the men living in the same city, *contado,* or district."

And so on and so forth. There was an obligation not to sever Assisi from the obedience of the church. Not to foment divisions or discords in the city, but rather, in the case of internal disorders, to exert every effort to bring about a prompt peace. The recognition of all the occupations made by Assisi thirty years earlier, especially those in the *comitato* of Nocera. And even more, the formal obligation to restore land arbitrarily taken by Perugia.

This is in the usual prolix and hypocritical jargon of all treaties made between those who hate and fear each other, yet who claim to have been mistaken about each other and simulate a heart and soul pledged friendship, as they draft minutely detailed and useless clauses covering every time and circumstance.

"And if it should come about that we treat of peace with the men of the people and their party, it shall be with the consent of the podestà, the *camerario,* and of the special Council of the aforesaid city [Assisi]. And if on our side, or if some of us, amicably and through common accord reach an understanding with the men of the people, we shall swear that everything said above shall be maintained and that everything remain unchanged, and we and you shall have peace with them. If, however, before or after such a peace, the men of the people or their party intend to injure you, all of you or some of your people, by using their army to make raids or take booty, or in some other way, we shall prevent it on behalf of the Commune and we shall help you with [your] persons and with [your] things and shall wage all-out war. And we assure you that we shall exert ourselves with the people and their party to the end that they do not make war against you nor offend you, in either a general or a special way, separately or together."

The popes had always tried their best to patch up these conflicts between the factions in Perugia, despite the fact that the people's faction had never been friendly to the church because of the privileges it had granted to the clergy, especially in regard to tributes. In the archives of the commune of Assisi is a copy of a letter sent by Honorius III to Cardinal Colonna on July 1, 1222, in which the pope forbade anyone to continue to stir up discords between "the *cavalieri* and the *popolani*" of Perugia, that is, between the knights and the common people, or to lend aid to either. The penalty for doing so was excommunication. The opposition of the court of Rome to the alliance with Assisi was also noted in this pact of June 24, 1223, in which it was expressly stated that if the pope should dissolve the alliance, the Perugini knights and the commune of Assisi would obligate themselves to renew it within a month of receiving notice of its dissolution, under the penalty of two thousand *marche* of silver. And it was also established that the parties themselves would maintain the agreements "by all means possible," *pro posse,* in confrontations with the pope, the cardinals, and all the pope's representatives. The usual clauses followed providing for compensation of damages inflicted by respective enemies.

"And thus we say that if anyone of the party of *cavalieri* and of the *popolani* who are with us shall damage things or persons of one or more persons of the city of Assisi, the *contado* or its district, the captains of the *cavalieri* and of the *popolani* who are in our ranks will indemnify them within fifteen days after a request is made of them. And if, on the other hand, one or more persons of the party of the people offend the men of Assisi, its *contado* or its district, we shall do everything possible to the end that restitutions be made of the things that were taken away."

And we again find familiar names among those who are stirring up war, even names of those devoted to Francis: Tommasso di Ranieri, *camerario* of the commune at the time of Francis's death who later verified in person the marks of the stigmata, Andrea di Agrestolo, Tommaso del Vescovo (belonging to the bishop's household), who received and attended Francis in the days before his death, Pietro di Giovanni, Rinaldo di Giacomo, Pietro di Alberico, Benvenuto di Giovanni.

There was a new battle between the Perugini factions in the late spring of 1225. In the bitter civil war, the men of the people sneeringly called the nobles, who had a falcon as their symbol, "Beccherini" ("Peckers"). In turn they were called by the nobles "Raspanti" ("Clawers"), because they adopted a cat for their insignia.

We can get an idea of the bitterness of this struggle from a page of the biography of Gregory IX written by a contemporary: "But the Perugini, who are deemed among the most favoured sons of the

Church, were roused to a cruel revolt by the perfidy of the ancient enemy. The inhabitants were divided one against the other and the nobles were thrown out of the city, and it came to pass that the father raised his hand in fury against his children and they in turn hurled themselves upon their parents. Everyone rose up ferociously against his neighbour. The walls oozed fraternal blood. Houses were destroyed to their foundations, trees were flattened. Those inside the city were subjected to hunger, and those outside, to never-ending slaughter."

In June the pope, in his effort to resolve the matter, declared that the treaty between the commune of Assisi and the nobles of Perugia was dissolved. But immediately, in July, the alliance was renewed. An agreement was stipulated on July 20 in Deruta, where the Perugini knights had gathered, a place where they could be sure of the protection of Assisi, which by now ruled over the *castelli* of the hills all the way to the Tiber. It states: "Those present will swear and will reconfirm the alliance between the Commune of Assisi and the *cavalieri,* and also the *popolani* of Perugia who are with them, in perpetuity, according to the pact signed in the instrument drawn up by the hand of the notary Angelo . . . "

The war is already in full swing. " . . . And if anyone of the *cavalieri* of Perugia and of the *popolani* and of others who are [allied] with them, shall lose his goods in the struggle between the *cavalieri* and the *popolani* of Perugia, the commune of Assisi shall be obliged, if able to do so, to come to his rescue."

On the same day the podestà of Assisi swore on his part to observe the new agreements. It was an open challenge to the pope and the Papal State. Bishop Guido excommunicated the podestà.

Podestà Oportulo

Oportulo di Bernardo was then podestà of the commune, a man of great spirit and of much authority among his fellow citizens. A perusal of Assisi records[52] permits us to reconstruct the strong and extensive family. His father, Domino Bernardo, owned properties in Padule di Castelnuovo, next to those of the sons of Ugone. A brother, Giovanni, was a witness in the emancipation trials. The son of one of his father's brothers, Bernardo di Giovanni, was councillor of the commune in 1228. In turn he had a son, Giovanni, who in 1252 took part in a dowry contract made in San Paolo, together with the abbot of Mount Subasio. Oportulo had three children, Giovannello, Angelo, and Agnese.

The family had its house on the piazza. In the 1229 list, this house was listed just before that of Benvenuto di Riccardo, which was near Francis's family house.

We have the list of persons exiled by Podestà Oportulo in the year 1225, when he held the office: *In Dei nomine, amen. Isti sunt exbanditi tempore domini Oportuli potestatis Asisii MCCXXV, indictione XIII.* Resolute and decisive, he is merciless to thieves and bribers, to the sacrilegious.

It is he who at once led the communal army in support of the Perugini knights.

By his order, no one of the men of the commune must pass the short-cut, located on the border of land that is again a battlefield, as at the time of the Collestrada engagement. We find in the list those who disobeyed:

"Alessio di Fabulo, of San Gregorio, because he went beyond the short-cut after the proclamation made by the podestà, is cited for ten *soldi*. Bonaccorso di Matteo, of Ripa, through the aforesaid proclamation, because he did not pay, is cited for ten *soldi*. Bonaccorso di Ranuccio, of San Gregorio, for the same deed, for ten *soldi*. Ventura di Ranuccio, of Sterpeto, for the same deed, ten *soldi*."

We find a name along this road, which borders the stream, that recalls the ancient ambushes: Trivio del Trappola, "Cross-roads (or Trivium) of the Trap."

Others were not present when the army was in the field and the captains called the roll.

"Iacopo di Gualtiero, because he did not take part in the war of the Commune of Assisi, and did not pay, is cited for ten *soldi*.

"Berarduccio, neighbour of Tebaldo, smith, because he did not take part in the aforesaid war, and did not pay, is cited for ten *soldi*."

Others came improperly armed.

"Pietro di Alfazia, because he did not have arrows in the war, and did not pay, is cited for ten *soldi*. Rosso di Addevelo, because he did not have arrows in the war, and did not pay, is cited for ten *soldi*. Donato di Gabiolo, for the same deed, for ten *soldi*. Pietro di Albertino, for the same deed, for ten *soldi*."

Guido's sentence of excommunication made the podestà Oportulo rise up in fury. To his eyes and those of the other city people, the imperious bishop was the eternal adversary of the commune, the enemy in the house. He was deceit personified, the man who always claimed to be above the law, the instigator of the cliques that put themselves above the interests of the city.

He decided, therefore, on reprisals. As was customary then in the struggle against the clergy, he decreed an economic blockade against him. By his order, no one could sell anything or contract in any way with the bishop or with his household.

The public crier, Bonbarone, shouted out the new ordinance to the sound of trumpets through all the streets of the city.[53]

It was the end of July. The houses buzzed with those words of challenge, those trumpet blasts. On the open balconies, women leaned out to talk against a torrid sky, their faces lit up, their eyes flashing. Some leap from the lists of the year, ready of tongue and of hand, quarrelsome and uninhibited, such as—among others— Pietruccia, wife of Giovanni di Maria and Chera, wife of Latino.

Men hardened by the crosses they had to bear every day rushed to the piazza, eager to curse and to damn and to make threats. This violent and picturesque people marvellously comes to life in the old records of the communal archives, their ringing names and murderous deeds forming a strange contrast to the canticle of love that was coming from San Damiano.

In Oportulo's proclamations, we know their bloody terroristic acts:

Aliotto, the nephew of Messer Benvegnate, prior of San Bartolomeo, "cut off the hand of Ugolo and inflicted other wounds with the knife on the other hand and on the shoulder."

Boncompagno di Crisso "robbed two men on the highway."

Paolo di Uffredone and his son Benvegnate "killed Barile."

Gilio di Ranuccio di Bianco "struck Finaguerra, servant of Pietro di Guarnerio, with a club, so that the blood flowed."

Gilio and Angelo, sons of Maestro Mantolo, "struck Ammodeo and Iacopo di Bevegnate, of the wool-worker, so that Iacopo died."

Leonardo di Giovanni di Clavello "two times attacked the crier of the commune, Bonbarone, and Pietrosollo, on the Piazza del Mercato."

Giacomo di Gennaro "insulted Messere Rinaldo within his church."

Martino di Pietro di Azzo "made himself a false card of sale for half a piece of land."

Bernardo and Leonardo, servants of Napoleone di Obertino, "robbed some persons."[54]

And the same bitter feeling that drove these violent men was shared by the podestà who had judged them and even by the bishop who had made the ruling in the case involving Francis and Pietro Bernardone. *Nimis oderant se invicem,* say the sources, "there was a savage hatred between them."[55]

The Canticle of Pardon

The sound of this quarrel reached San Damiano, and caused great consternation. Bishop Guido had played a major role in the birth and development of the Franciscan movement. And the podestà, Messer Oportulo di Bernardo, was among Francis's most devoted supporters. Five years earlier his daughter Agnese, scarcely adolescent, had joined Clare at San Damiano, and Oportulo treasured the memory.

So Francis was saddened. Those who go through the agonies of hating others are as much to be pitied as those who suffer physical pain.

Even now no one was trying to be a peacemaker to the bishop and the podestà. But Francis, who had come to call his sufferings his sisters,[56] knew what needed to be done. Jesus said, "Love your enemies, pray for your persecutors."[57] Love—of God, of others—provides the strength to bear the sufferings of the body and of the spirit, to endure both illnesses and the wrongs done to us by others. It is as necessary to pardon those who injure us as it is to accept our own infirmities with peaceful spirit. As Thomas of Celano wrote of Francis, "Nor was it for no reason that his purgation was completed in this vale of tears. . . . I think the best way to understand his suffering is this: that in bearing them there is a great reward."[58]

Jesus also said, "Blessed too the peacemakers; they shall be called sons of God."[59] Blessed are those who bring good where there is evil, love where there is hatred, harmony where there is discord.

So Francis now added another verse to the Canticle of the Sun:

> *Laudato si, misignore, per quelli ke perdonano,*
> *per lo tuo amore*
> *et sostengo infirmitate*
> *et tribulatione.*
>
> *Beati quelli kel sosterranno in pace,*
> *ka da te, Altissimo,*
> *sirano incoronati.*

All praise be yours, my Lord, through those who grant pardon
  For love of you; through those who endure
  Sickness and trial.

Happy those who endure in peace,
  By you, Most High, they will be crowned.

He called one of his companions and said to him, "Go and find the podestà and tell him for me that he should go to the bishop's palace with the officials of the commune and any others he can bring along with him."

And after the brother had left, he told the other friars to go also to the bishop's residence and when everyone had gathered—the bishop, the podestà and the others—to sing the Canticle of Brother Sun.

"I have confidence," he said, "that the Lord will put humility and peace in their hearts and that they will return to their former friendship and affection."[60]

And so they all met in the enclosed courtyard of the bishop's palace at Santa Maria Maggiore, freighted with its thousand years of glory, strengthened by the blood of Assisi's martyrs, the warlike courage of its early bishops, the intellectual achievements of its annotators.[61]

We see again, in the first row, the magnates: Ugolino di Pietro, the knight who knew Clare when she was a young girl; Tebaldo di Catanio, the brother of the friar who slept in peace in the shadow of the Porziuncola chapel; Bernardo, the *camerario* of the commune; and others—Andrea di Giacomo, Andrea di Tiberio, Guelfone, Uguizzone di Guidone, Nicola di Benvegnate, Viviano di Andrea, Armanno di Ascanio.[62] Under the porticoes that went around the inside of the courtyard the people crowded around, avid to stir up the inevitable melee.

The Miracle of Love

The scene is no less dramatic than it was eighteen years earlier when Francis made his great renunciation.

Bishop Guido has aged. He is a little bent. His hair is whitening. But his masculine face is still marked with its old haughtiness. Proudly he rises up amid his canons, clad in his long pallium, decorated with scrolls of gold and reaching to his feet. The podestà is dressed in armour, as is befitting the captain of the army. When the messenger brought him Francis's invitation, he did not hesitate a moment to set out for that extraordinary gathering. The sun draws gleams from his damascened cuirass and polished steel helmet, lights up the velvets of his escorts and the shining white surplices of the clergy. In the burning summer afternoon even the dark walls are shining, as if hung with luminous tapestries.

Tension is in the very air.

One of the brothers rises (perhaps Brother Pacifico), and in the profound silence he speaks as minstrels do when they describe the theme of their story.

"Despite his sufferings," he says, "blessed Francis has composed the 'Praises of the Lord' for all his creatures, to the praise of God and for the edification of his neighbour. He asks you to listen with great devotion."[63]

And at once two of the brothers begin to sing Francis's song.

Those who listen feel a great calm, the power of a dream, come over their anguish and weariness, their ill temper and brutal appetites. All the lost relationships of Eden call out in this song—the sun, the moon, the stars, the sky, cloudy and calm, the streams that flow in flowering valleys.

The vigorous face of the podestà betrays his violent internal emotion. He again sees his dear daughter dressed in sackcloth, her gentle sweet face shining between the white fillets. They say that she remains long in prayer, along with Clare, at the sixth hour, when Jesus died on the cross. They say she wears rough, harsh cloth made of horse's hide against her tender skin.[64] He rises to his feet and joins his hands, listening with as much concentration as when the Gospel of the Lord is read in church.[65]

The singers reach the final stanza, which Francis had composed only a few hours earlier. Their voices rise and ring out stronger, transfixing everyone. They soar beyond the present moment to make the song a universal prayer. It pours out over the watchful walls and touches the tops of silent towers.

> Happy those who endure in peace . . .

Those who had hated, gone to war, and suffered with the son of Pietro Bernardone bend their heads, overcome by the wave of memories. A wish for peace has been his greeting to them. It may be his last affectionate word. Someone close to him says that he is sick beyond hope of recovery.[v]

> By you, Most High, they will be crowned.

The last notes die gently away, like an echo of a distant and invisible angelic chorus.

---

v. According to *1 Cel.*, 109, Brother Elias had a vision in Foligno, in which a white-garbed priest "of very great and advanced age" appeared and instructed him to tell Francis that he had but two years to live.

The podestà weeps. In the silence he is the first to speak:

"In truth I say to you," he cries out, "not only do I forgive the lord bishop whom I ought to recognize as my master, but I would even pardon my brother's and my own son's murderer!"[66]

A stir runs through the crowd. Everyone understands the significance of these words in the mouth of the magistrate who cried out imprecations and dealt out punishments every day on the bloodstained piazza.

They have been waiting for a duel of bitter words, a harsh clash of accusations and recriminations.[67] They are stupified to see the podestà Oportulo kneel at the feet of the bishop.

"For the love of our Lord Jesus Christ and of blessed Francis, his servant, I am ready to make any atonement you wish."

The bishop takes his hands and raises him.

"My office demands humility of me," he says. "By nature I am quick to anger. You must forgive me!"

They embrace each other and exchange the kiss of peace.[68]

The haughty and imperious Bishop Guido himself has been conquered. In this moment [at least], a centuries-old struggle for power ends.

The people, as they disappear into the darkening streets, say that Francis has wrought a new miracle.

"We who lived with blessed Francis," comments one of the friars who was present, perhaps Brother Leo, "attest that if he said: 'Such and such a thing is taking place' or 'will happen,' his words were fulfilled to the letter. We have seen with our own eyes many examples, which it would take too long to write down and to recount."[69]

·16·

THE ROUGH WAYS

Francis became a troubadour again, as he had been when he was twenty. Songs poured out of him.

He wrote one for the Poor Ladies of San Damiano, who were much distressed by his illness. In it he exalted their firm adherence to the concept of absolute poverty. He was grieved at the same time, however, by the thought that they, so fragile and delicate, had such a hard life with never an easy moment. What a shame that it has been lost!

A description of it was preserved. He bade his dear sisters to pray to the Lord, who had united them in holy charity, holy poverty, and holy obedience, and ask him to keep them firm in these virtues and in them devoutly to die. To pray to use the alms that the Lord should send them for the care of their bodies, with joy and gratitude and discretion. And to be comforted in the sad and inevitable hour when the body would lie, wasted and ravaged, in the silence, heavy with mystery, of a solitary bare cell. Happy those who endure in peace![a]

---

a. [These "lost words" were apparently discovered in 1976 in two medieval manuscripts of Verona by Padre Giovanni Boccali of Assisi. As translated by Brown (in Esser, *Rule and Testament*, pp. 217–18):

> Hear, little poor ones (*poverelle*) called by the Lord
> Who from many parts and provinces have come together:
>
> Live always in truth,
> So that in obedience you die.
>
> Do not look to the life outside,
> For that of the Spirit is better.
>
> I pray you with great love
> that you have discretion as to the
> alms which the Lord gives you.

But the time had come for him to travel on. It was best not to put off treatment any longer. In Rieti there was a doctor who was expert in eye diseases, and the friars decided to consult him. Since Francis could not bear the light of day, the brothers wrapped his head in a great hood, with a piece of woolen cloth lined with linen sewed on the front, a sort of bandage that covered his eyes. They lifted him to the back of a horse and set out. That long trip in darkness would be altogether exhausting.

News of their coming travelled before them. When they drew near Rieti, a huge crowd came out to meet Francis. To avoid a triumphal reception, he stopped in a little church called San Fabiano near the city. The priest's house was attached to it. It was a pleasant and tranquil place. Already September was gilding the clusters of grapes in the little vineyard below the house.

The quiet was of short duration. At the end of June, Honorius III,

---

> Those who are weighed down by infirmities
> and the others who labour for them,
> all of you bear it in peace,
> for you will see this labour as very dear.
>
> For each will be a queen
> crowned in heaven with the Virgin Mary.
>
> —*Trans.*]

Whether Saint Francis was at San Damiano when he composed this song, during this period of illness, has been much debated among Franciscan scholars. Arguments put forth against San Damiano include these: it would have been improper for him to stay at San Damiano, where Saint Clare and her sisters lived; the fact that he sent the song to them by messenger indicates that he was some distance away; there was no real reason for him to be at San Damiano rather than at Porziuncola or another place, such as the bishop's palace in Assisi.

But there is no doubt that this song, as well as the Canticle of the Sun, was composed at San Damiano. First of all, the two major sources for this period of Francis's life both say that the song for the sisters was composed there: see *Per.*, 45; *Spec. Perf.*, 90.

Second, there was nothing improper about his being there. Some of the brothers were in permanent residence there to care for the spiritual and material needs of the sisters, and Francis's cell was undoubtedly a part of or within their house. In fact, Franciscan friars are known to have lived at monasteries of the Poor Clares even after the life of Saint Francis; among them, Jacopone da Todi.

Third, there are sound and logical reasons for Francis's staying at San Damiano: Porziuncola, on low ground and surrounded by trees, is damp and often closed in by fog during the cold season; San Damiano, on the slope of the Assisi hill, is somewhat drier. Furthermore, the continual bustle at Porziuncola, headquarters of the order, and also at the house of the bishop would have been disturbing to the invalid. Most of all, Francis had strong emotional ties to San Damiano, where he had first become conscious of a mission; he would have been comforted by being there.

Fourth, the texts themselves give the reason why the song was sent by messenger: Francis's illness. And the texts also indicate that he was near the sisters by explaining that he wrote the song because he knew of their distress over his illness.

Finally, though as founder and spiritual leader of the Poor Clares, Saint Francis could have seen them at any time with perfect propriety, his regard for their cloistered life would probably have led him to send a personal communication by a third person. And in any case, whoever heard of a poem or poetic message being delivered by anyone other than a third person?

For a complete discussion, see *NV* 2:491–92.

compelled to leave Rome because of a rebellious uprising, had come to Rieti, accompanied by all his court, including Cardinal Ugolino. Cardinals, high prelates and pontifical dignitaries, driven by curiosity and affection, constantly were coming to see Francis. They were followed by swarms of secretaries, litter bearers, and grooms. They callously stripped or trampled down the grapes and the priest was indignant at the loss of his supply of wine for the entire year. He descended to tirades and name-calling and complaints about Francis's being there, since he was the cause of the damage.

Francis was told of it. He comforted the priest and promised him that his crop would be double that of preceding years. And so it happened. The repentant priest did not fail to tell everyone about this new miracle. Never before had he been able to produce more than thirteen *some* of wine, he said; but this year, the vineyard, so badly reduced, had given him more than twenty![1]

After some days Francis and his companions went on to Fonte Colombo.[b]

---

b. Few questions about Francis's life have been debated so much as the exact chronology of this trip to Rieti for treatment of his eye disease, again a part of the controversy over where the Canticle of the Sun was written. Fortini reconstructs the events in this sequence: Francis received the stigmata in September 1224. He left La Verna the day after the feast of St. Michael the Archangel. On the return journey he stayed several days at Borgo San Sepolcro and one month at Città di Castello. Since the roads were covered with snow when he and his companions set out again, it was probably in late November or early December. They went directly to Santa Maria degli Angeli but stayed there only a short time, because immediately afterward we find Francis lying acutely ill at San Damiano, and it was there that Brother Elias told him to seek treatment for his eyes. This must have been in early winter in the closing weeks of the year 1224.

For fifty days or more he lay in a dark cell at San Damiano, unable to bear light of any kind, tormented, too, by mice that infested the place. These must have been in the months of December 1224, January and February 1225.

During this period Francis composed the Canticle of the Sun, and also the song for the Poor Ladies.

But then, his weakened condition and the severity of the treatment to be imposed must have made it necessary to wait for a "favourable season" before undertaking the trip to see the Rieti doctor. In the meantime, Assisi, in alliance with the noble classes of Perugia, had gone to war against the people of Perugia. (We know the time through the treaty of July 20, 1225, which brought the excommunication of the podestà who signed it, Oportulo; we also know that Oportulo's term of office would have begun on the kalends of May 1225 and extended to the kalends of May of 1226: see *NV* 2:530, and, for the treaty, *NV* 3:611–12). This would have been the time, of course, when Oportulo and the bishop, Guido, would have been locked in their bitter struggle, and when Francis would have composed the new stanza for his canticle (see chap. 15, pp. 569–79). This must have meant that Francis was still at San Damiano (or at any rate in Porziuncola or Assisi) as late as midsummer 1225 and that he must have left for Fonte Colombo for the operation on his eyes about mid-August. This would have allowed him to be at the priest's house in Rieti in September, when the grapes were getting ripe. Reasons for the long delay cannot be known with certainty. Perhaps it was thought that the really warm months of summer (spring can be very chilly in Assisi and in the mountains) were best for the drastic operation; perhaps an aggravation of Francis's weakness or illness had caused a delay in plans. It seems possible to this translator that Francis may have been so distressed over the war that he was unwilling to leave until he tried his hand at bringing peace. For a full discussion of the timetable of the trip and related subjects, see "Questioni sulla Composizione del Cantico del Sole," *NV* 2:471–543.—Trans.

The famous doctor came. He recommended that the veins between the jawbone and the eyebrow, on the side of the worse eye, be cauterized with a red hot iron. It would be a very painful operation; and Francis, remembering Brother Elias's offer and advice, did not want to undergo it without him. However, the minister general was then busy with affairs of the order, and he kept putting off coming.[c]

The doctor visited him every day. He admired and respected Francis greatly, and he stayed for long conversations. Despite the fact that he was a very rich man who led a comfortable life, he sometimes sat at table with the brothers, eating whatever those who had gone out begging had been able to get—a little bit of bread, some wine, some olives.

Francis's illness grew worse. Day and night he suffered atrocious pain, and he grieved for the heavy burden that he had become to those who took care of him.[2]

Brother Elias still did not come. Finally it was decided to go on with the operation without him. On the day set, the brothers, frightened and anxious, gathered about Francis. They put the iron to be used in the ordeal in the coals and drew it out incandescent. Francis's ulcerated eyes, freed from their bandages, fixed on that live, pulsating, terrible brightness. And he broke into a hymn of praise to Brother Fire.

"My brother fire, which surpasses all other things in beauty, the Most High created you strong, beautiful, and useful. Be kind to me in this hour, be courteous. For I have loved you in the past in the Lord. I beseech the great Lord who made you that he temper your

---

c. In the many differences of opinion over the sequence of events in the last years of Francis's life, there has been considerable argument over when and where both Brother Elias and Cardinal Ugolino told Francis to have his eyes treated. Fortini believes that Cardinal Ugolino's words on the subject must have preceded Brother Elias's advice, which was given at San Damiano, according to *Per.*, 42. He finds no evidence that it was in Rieti that Brother Elias told Francis what to do, as some have argued.

Fortini also believes that Francis must have gone on immediately to the hermitage at Fonte Colombo rather than remaining for a time in Rieti, for in the mountain retreat he would have been spared the constant visits of townspeople. Given the devotion of the doctor to Francis, as reported in *Per.* and *Spec. Perf.*, it is natural to suppose that he would have gladly made the relatively short trip from the city to the hermitage to take care of Francis.

There is nothing in the texts to identify the place that Cardinal Ugolino met Francis and urged him to have his eyes treated. Only a daily journal kept by the cardinal could tell us just when and where that happened. Given his love for Francis, it is not too much to suppose that he might well have gone to see him in Porziuncola or San Damiano.

Many of the disputes over these and other matters relating to the trip are involved with the theory put forth by some biographers, notably Terzi, that Francis spent a considerable period in and wrote the *Canticle of the Sun* in the small monastery of San Fabiano near Rieti. He believed that copyists later wrote in error "San Damiano" for "San Fabiano." The fact that the theory does not rest on evidence at all convincing, as has been pointed out by Brown (Englebert, *Saint Francis*, pp. 445–57), has made most serious historians discard it. See *NV* 2:495–500 —Trans.

heat now so that I may bear it when you burn me gently."[3] And then he made the sign of the cross over the red hot iron.

And we are told that his prayer was granted, in an astounding reconciliation of man and the elements.

At his gesture, his words, all the brothers fled, too overcome with pity to stay for the painful ordeal. When they returned, Francis said to them, "O fainthearted and weak of heart, why did you flee? In truth I say to you, I did not feel either the heat of the fire or any pain in my flesh." And to the doctor he said, "If my flesh is not sufficiently burned, burn it again."

The doctor was stupefied. He said, "My brothers, I am afraid to apply so drastic a cautery to the strongest man, let alone to one who is so frail and ill. But he did not flinch or betray the least sign of pain. I say to you, brothers, I have seen wonderful things today." Thomas of Celano adds, "I believe that he had returned to primitive innocence, for whom, when he wished it, cruel things were made gentle."[4]

The wound was frightful. From the lower part of the ear to the eyebrow, the cheek and temple were horribly burned. The veins had been deeply cut.

They decided to take him to Rieti to stay while the wound healed. There he accepted the bishop's hospitality. A canon named Tebaldo di Saraceno gave up his room in the bishop's palace for him.[5]

Another doctor came to examine him there. He declared that the first one had been mistaken and that the operation had been not only useless but dangerous. And so the sick man was subjected to still another horrendous "treatment," the perforation of both ears with a red hot iron.[6]

All his pain gave him even greater compassion for the sufferings of others. For instance, another canon of the bishop, Gedeone by name, was confined to his bed with a serious kidney disease brought on by a dissolute life. With the help of others, he made his way with great effort to Francis's room. He knelt in front of him and asked to be blessed.

Francis said, "Since you lived in the past according to the desires of the flesh, not according to the judgements of God, why should I sign you with the sign of the cross?"

But then, as always, he had pity on that miserable human wreck and he made the sign of the cross over him. And immediately the man arose, healed.[d]

---

d. This miracle is reported to have taken place while Saint Francis was staying at the palace of the Bishop of Rieti. See *Per.*, 58: *2 Cel.*, 41; *Leg. Maior*, XI, 5.

Another time the doctor who attended him told him of a woman of the *contado* who had come to him for the cure of her eyes. She was so poor, he said, that in addition to treating her free, he felt impelled to add a gift of money to cover the expenses of her trip and of the medicine. That was enough for Francis, who was so moved that he sent his mantle to the woman, saying that he had taken it in loan from the poor and to the poor it must be restored.[7]

But as all this was going on, his pain from his illness was increasing and his sufferings were becoming so terrible that he doubted that he had the strength to bear them any longer.

The Unknown Music

He longed to hear music. He thought it might help him bear the pain.

One day he said to the companion who was attending him,[e] "Brother, the children of this world have no understanding of the things of God. Formerly, the saints used such musical instruments as the zither, psalteries, and others to praise God and console their soul. Now these instruments promote vanity and sin, contrary to the will of the Lord."

He was silent for an instant, and then he continued with a certain hesitant timidity, "I wish you would secretly procure a zither from a respectable man and play me some beautiful music. Afterwards, we will put words and the 'Praises of the Lord' to it. My body is afflicted with many severe pains. I would like in this way to change the physical suffering into joy and spiritual consolation."

The brother replied, "Father, I would be ashamed to go and procure that instrument for myself. The people of this city know that when I was a layman, I learned how to play the zither, and I fear that they would fancy that I am tempted to play it again."

"In that case," Francis said, "let's not talk about it any more."

About midnight he was awake as usual, and in great pain. He lay

---

These same sources tell that the canon returned to his life of dissipation and was punished by divine justice: while he was in the house of another canon, the roof fell in and killed him. All the others who lived there were saved.

Sacchetti-Sassetti (*Anecdota franciscana reatina*, pp. 38–40) has shown that a Tebaldo di Saraceno, who was a canon, truly lived in Rieti at the time of Saint Francis. The nature of the evidence suggests that he lived in the bishop's palace, as was common at the time. The opinion that his house is to be identified in the palazzo of Via San Rufo cannot stand up.

e. For this episode, see especially *Per.*, 24; also *2 Cel.*, 126; *Leg. Maior*, V, 11.

Many have thought Francis's companion to have been Brother Angelo da Rieti, who was well known to the people of that city, as may be deduced from *Per.* 24 (see Sacchetti-Sassetti, *Anecdota*, pp. 35–38). Others believe it to have been Brother Pacifico. Cf. Octave d'Angers, "Du frère cithariste," *Études Franciscains* 44:549–56.

immobile on his cot. He was alone. Even his companion had gone away.

Suddenly he heard, or it seemed to him that he heard, the distant sound of a zither, sweet and harmonious as the *tintinnìo* of a silver harp. He listened to it as it grew louder and came nearer. He did not understand from where it came, whether from the road, from the sky, or from his exhausted heart. But he could clearly hear the melody, beautiful, pure, and joyous, and it seemed to him that his spirit would melt in its loveliness. The terrible spasms of pain lessened as if an invisible hand had been placed on his disfigured forehead, on his inflamed eyes.

The music faded away, returned, grew alternately stronger and softer. It sympathized, comforted, died away in a tone of peaceful melancholy, like a wave that changes colour when a passing cloud veils it. Then it rose again, jubilant as a hymn of angels in Paradise.

And Francis understood that he was not hearing music made by man but by God. In exultation he fervently broke out in praises to the Lord, who had been pleased to grant him his desire and console him. The brothers, when he told them what had happened, confirmed what he had deduced. No one had passed on the road. Moreover, a rigidly enforced decree of the podestà forbade everyone from being abroad after the third sound of the bell.[8]

In the Alberino Friary

In the meantime other treatments were tried, poultices and eye salves, but these also were useless.[9] Winter was coming on, and the doctors again advised a change of climate. Francis left for Siena.[f] One of the doctors who had treated him offered to accompany him.

As they were nearing the city, on their way across the plain between Rocca Campiglia and San Quirico, all of a sudden three women, young and obviously highborn, appeared in the desolate countryside. Their clothes, the look on their faces, seemed identical. They stood in the middle of the road as if awaiting someone.

---

f. Sabatier, followed by a good many modern biographers, depicted Francis travelling to a number of places, placing in this time some episodes related in early sources; for example, his preaching during the Christmas season in Poggio Bustone (*2 Cel.*, 132), staying at the hermitage of Sant'Eleuterio in a cold winter (*Spec. Perf.*, 16), spending time at Greccio where two brothers came to receive his blessing (*2 Cel.*, 45) and where a feather pillow made him believe the devil was attacking him (*2 Cel.*, 64). Sabatier even has him going to the hermitage of Sant'Urbano—which is at an altitude of more than a thousand meters!—and there changing water into wine (*1 Cel.*, 61; *Leg. Maior*, V, 10). But all these episodes must be dated at an earlier time. There is no doubt that given his condition—almost blind and very ill—he could have done none of these things; he would have had to have been taken directly from Rieti to Siena. See *NV* 2:462.

As Francis drew near, they saluted him in the moving, intimate words, *"Ben venga, Madonna Povertà!* Welcome, Lady Poverty!"* Clearly, a loving greeting, and the Poverello of Christ was stirred both by wonder and anxiety. He looked at them, elated, and made ready to reply. But the three women were gone. The plain was again deserted, its bleakness even more pronounced, now that the mysterious women had disappeared. Celestial creatures these must have been, says Thomas of Celano, since earthly women could not have vanished more swiftly than birds.[10]

He stopped in the Alberino friary, a short distance from Siena. Here, during the first part of April, his illness grew so much worse that the brothers believed they were losing him forever.[11] One night he began to vomit blood, and the attack was prolonged until the hour of matins. He was so weak that it seemed unlikely that he would see dawn. His sons' sorrow, which up to that point had been kept bottled up, burst out uncontrollably, as we know from the pages of *Mirror of Perfection.* In the quiet spring night, the grief-stricken voices rose and fell like the laments made around the body of someone already dead.

"Father, what shall we do without you?

"To whose charge will you leave us, miserable orphans?

"You have been father and mother to us, for it was you who conceived and brought us forth in Christ.

"You have been our leader and shepherd, our instructor and corrector, teaching and correcting us by your example rather than by words.

"Where shall we go, sheep without a shepherd, children without a father, rough and simple men without a leader?"

Francis remained immobile, his eyes closed, as pale as if all the blood had drained from his exhausted body.

"Where shall we go to find you . . . ?

"Who now will show us blind men the way of truth?

"How shall we hear your mouth speaking to us, and your tongue giving us counsel?

"Where will be your burning spirit, which guides us along the way of the Cross, and inspires us to evangelical perfection?

"Where will you be, so that we may run to you, light of our eyes?

"Where can we seek you, comfort of our souls?

"O Father, you are dying. You are leaving us abandoned, sad, and full of despair!"

He did not reply and gave no sign of understanding. He appeared to be far away and at peace. The lament was renewed as if it would never end.

"Alas for this day! A day of tears and bitterness, a day of desolation and grief is coming upon us!

"And no wonder, for your life has been a constant light to us, and your words have been like burning torches, always lighting us along the way of the Cross to evangelical perfection, and to the love and imitation of our dear crucified Lord."[12]

His face quivered. He still had life, but it was like the weak flame of a candle that the smallest breath can blow out.

They asked him for a word, a last word, to save as a holy inheritance for all the sons who would come into the order. He spoke, but in such a low tone that it was necessary to bend down to pick up his voice. He wanted them to call the priest who often came to him for the celebration of Mass, Brother Benedetto of Pirano. When this brother arrived, Francis gasped a last testament to him:

"Write that I give my blessing to all my brethren in the order, and to all who will enter it in time to come until the end of the world. And since I cannot speak much because of my weakness and the pain of my disease, I wish briefly to make my will and purpose clear to all the brethren, both present and to come. As a sign that they remember me, my blessing, and my Testament, I wish them always to love one another, as I have loved them. Let them always love and honour our Lady Poverty, and remain faithful and obedient to the bishops and clergy of holy Mother Church."

A few days later Brother Elias arrived, having been summoned in a hurry from a distant place. Francis was a bit better, and he told Brother Elias of his desire to be taken back to Assisi. They wanted to satisfy him and so the journey started. But they had to stop before reaching Cortona. His abdomen, hands, and feet were swollen. His stomach could no longer tolerate food. They took him to the nearby hermitage of Le Celle for a time and then set out again and, travelling by Perugia, in a short time reached Santa Maria degli Angeli.[13]

And it seemed that his beloved land, where he had spent so much of his heart and life, gave him new strength. He got better, and everyone rejoiced at the miraculous resurrection. Since summer was coming on, they decided to take him to one of those mountain places so dear to him, a little friary that the brothers had recently built on the slopes of Mount Pennino, beyond Nocera, in a region famous for its salubrious air and its waters—Bagnara.[g]

---

g. There has been considerable confusion about the trips in the final months of Francis's life. Sabatier, for example, questioned the stop at the hermitage of Le Celle on the return trip from Siena to Porziuncola. But since the road from Siena to Assisi goes right by Cortona and Le

Certainly Brother Elias must have had a hand in this choice, and he must have acted in full accord with the magistrates of Assisi. The absolute rule that the commune by now exercised on all the territory of Nocera lessened the anxiety of the Assisani that the people of Perugia—partially because of the fanatic kind of devotion so frequent in the Middle Ages, partially to inflict an injury on their traditional enemy—would try to seize Francis's body after he died. The thought of the damage that would be done to the commune from such a robbery became an obsession in the days that followed.

When the news arrived that the sick man was worse and that his feet and hands were again swollen, a certain sign that the end was nearing, these suspicious thoughts were transformed into frenzied action. The new podestà, Berlingerio di Iacopo of Florence, decided he must send to Francis a solemn delegation, made up of the most authoritative knights of the city, who could convince him that he must not allow others to have the glory of his body.[14]

The Mission of the Knights

They went, they talked with rude affection, these unpolished men whose devotion was devoid of every pretence. It was known, nor could it be otherwise, that the end of his mortal life was approaching. The people of the city wished—and certainly their will had divine sanction—that his saintly soul, when freed from the flesh, ascend to the King of the heavens in the same place "where the knowledge of heavenly things was first given to him and the saving unction poured upon him."[15]

This argument, both reverent and imperious, fitted Francis's own desire, and in the end, he agreed. They left Bagnara at sunrise. Francis was so weak that he could not sit on horseback alone. It was decided that the knights should take turns carrying him as they rode.[16]

These knights were, for the most part, the companions of his youth, men who had taken part with him in the parties and merry-

---

Celle would have been but an hour's travel time away, Le Celle would be a logical stop to allow Francis to rest.

Sabatier also has the group travelling by way of Gubbio and Nocera, so as to avoid Perugia, where it was feared that the people might try to kidnap him so as to gain possession of his body. Then, he believes, they went to Bagnara, before returning to Assisi.

It is indeed likely that they went by way of Gubbio, given the war between Assisi and Perugia at the time. But to go to Nocera from Gubbio would be a long way out of the way. The trip to Bagnara surely came at a later time, after a period spent at Porziuncola. And indeed, this is exactly what we read in *Per.*, 59. See *NV* 2:462–64.

making of the *tripudianti,* who had fought alongside him in war, who with him had dreamed of heroic enterprises.

They were all stirred by a feeling of inexpressible tenderness now, in which there was something of both the old affection and a new veneration, as they travelled along carrying this dying saint in their arms like a tired child. It seemed impossible that from his wretched little body, drained by illness, could have come the soaring song that had accomplished such wonders, that encompassed the universe.

His face, usually luminous and benign, was veiled by exhaustion. His eyes, so alive and shining, were closed. His voice, which had been like a live flame enkindling those who listened, was mute. Perhaps some of the devoted knights saw in that hour (and trembled at the incredible revelation) the miraculous marks, the stigmata.

They left the ancient episcopal city and made their way down the slope. Their path rose again toward Postignano, held by the sons of Guitto and guarded by a handful of the commune's bowmen.[h] Toward midday they reached the summit of the Gazzella Hill.[i]

All the enchantment of the dying summer lay in the whitening sky that curved to the distant horizon to touch the bare peaks of the high, dark blue mountains. At the left they were overshadowed by the barren mass of Subasio, looming solemn as an altar. They began the descent of the steep slope on the opposite hill, making their way to Assisi. The road stretched ahead into the forest. The tall oaks seemed to light themselves for their passage.

After a short stretch, a rocky clearing with a stream at the bottom opened in the forest. Along the steep slope rose Satriano, a strong and ancient *castello,* subject, as were the surrounding lands, to the nearby monastery of San Benedetto di Satriano.[j] (A few years ago, in

---

h. Postignano had been taken over by Assisi while Perugia was looking the other way, occupied with its factional war. For terms of the pact, see *NV* 2:200–201.

i. The route travelled by the knights as they returned to Assisi with Saint Francis certainly must have been the wide and good road that then existed between Nocera and Assisi—and furthermore, a safe one, since Nocera was at the time controlled by Assisi. See the map for the route; for a detailed description of the road and the places through which the company travelled, see *NV* 2:464–70.

j. The identification of Satriano (which no longer exists) has also been the question of much conjecture and research. It was a *castello* northeast of Assisi, in a valley beyond Mount Subasio. It appears in the commune's records for the first time in September 1030, in which property in Satriano was given to the abbot of the monastery of Farfa. It is mentioned again from time to time up until the early part of the fourteenth century, when it was destroyed in the Guelf-Ghibelline wars. Undoubtedly the *castello,* with the surrounding woods and the valley, belonged to the monks of San Benedetto di Satriano.

Up until the identification in this book, the majority of biographers followed the opinion of Sabatier, who, in his efforts to locate it, discovered in 1897 a farm on Mount Subasio, on the Assisi-Spello border, named Satriano and deduced that this must have been the place. On this identification he based his reconstruction of the route taken by the knights from Bagnara to Assisi. He supposed that they had to avoid the dangers of the road in Foligno and Spello and so

the digging of a vineyard, the ruins of the walls and the tombs of the monks came to light again. The bones were all put together in a tabernacle in memory of the place where the ancient monastery once stood.)

They decided to stop and eat dinner. They lodged the sick man in the principal house of the village, whose owner welcomed Francis's arrival as a blessing of God.[17]

Then the knights scattered, and the brothers, as was their custom, went about begging from door to door. In a short time the knights returned to Francis, disillusioned. They said they had knocked at the door of every house and asked for something to eat, naturally offering to pay for it. But all of them had been turned down.

"Brother," they said, half-seriously and half-jokingly, "you will have to give us some of your alms if you don't want us to die of hunger."

For a moment Francis regained his old fire. He retorted, "You have gotten nothing, because you kept on trusting in your flies (this was always his term for money) and not in God. Go back to those same houses, and do not be ashamed to ask alms for the love of God. You will get what you seek."

They went around again, begging with easy conscience, as Francis had suggested. Everyone, men and women, gave willingly and in abundance.

Overjoyed, they attributed everything to Francis who, blind, saw more deeply and farther than anyone. And again they were convinced that whatever he said would always and to the letter come true.

The poet brother, who wrote about this intriguing event, summarized it in a fine expression that could serve as the motto of these reformed knights who found freedom by sweeping aside the forbidding barriers [of conventionalities and custom] that make the spirit a slave to the body: "Hunger had no power where abundant poverty prevailed."[18]

A Note about Satriano

Thus Francis's old friends found out how he had felt and what he had learned on the day that he had showed up in the midst of a party,

---

took mountain paths to this out-of-the-way place and so down to Assisi. But, as can be seen from the note above, there was no need at all to go through Foligno and Spello, and the road between Nocera and Assisi was shorter by two-thirds than Sabatier's route and totally under Assisi's control. Sabatier's Satriano is a simple *vocabolo* or place name, still to be found on military topographical maps. It designates the site of an ancient chapel dependent on the monastery of San Benedetto of Mount Subasio, called San Paolo di Satriano. See *NV* 2:465–70.

asking alms for the San Damiano lamp. Twenty years had gone by, and that lamp was still lit. In the same way, these proud knights had pocketed their pride to beg from the humble for the love of God. And the old serfs, who just yesterday had risen up in a bitter war against the feudal lords, at once divided their bread with the very men who had been their oppressors.

It is worth the trouble to tell this old story to demonstrate the eternal relevance of the Franciscan idea.

Up until the epoch of Saint Francis we see the name of Satriano in the records of the imperial notaries, Grifo and Forzulo, the clerk of the curia of Duke Corrado. Its every-day life returns to us—its entangled forest called the "Serra de Satriano," its *pieve* consecrated to the Virgin, its spring Acquaviva at the margin of the woodlands, its valley and stream, its extensive *balìa* or political jurisdiction.

For the time that Francis passed by, we can reconstruct one by one the eighty-four *focolari,* or number of hearths, thus learning the number of households. We can even know the inhabitants by name. In our minds we can see the faces that hardened when the proud knights tried to buy their hospitality but relaxed at the humble appeal to charity.

Then, suddenly, nothing more. There is a dark silence around the place in the papers of the archives and in the memory of the inhabitants. When after seven centuries a transalpine scholar interrogated the local historians in a search for information about the village where Saint Francis paused for a while on his last journey, no one knew that a place called Satriano had ever existed in the commune territory.

Sustained by a certain despairing hope, we went up there one day, to try to find records that would establish the site of the *castello* beyond question, in our search for the place Saint Francis stopped on his last trip to Assisi. Brambles and oaks occupy the lonely site. An extensive expanse of dead ruins, cropping out all along the difficult slope, are all that remains of the ancient and devout Satriano. The people indicate them with a vague and lugubrious name, *i casalini,* "the demolished houses." In the great silence of the centuries, only the spring, to which the women who knelt when Saint Francis passed came to draw water, continues to gush out and to speak.

A centenarian who had come to the place to give us the requested information pointed out the hills, the valleys, the churches, the streams. And suddenly, the harsh and pious past is revealed in a poetic short name, as the presence of an army is revealed by the fugitive flash of a blade.

"Torre di Zampitto," he said. "Colle di Balestraccio, Osteria del

Cireneo." And he continued with "Bridge of the Wolves" (Ponte di Lupi), "Gully of Stones" (Fossato dei Sassi). He showed us San Gilio, Santa Croce, Santa Lucia della Neve ("Saint Lucy of the Snow"), Frustavento ("Windlashed"), and Le Ginestre ("The Junipers"). And he mentioned Tescio dello Sperone (the place is a wide curve of the river Tescio at valley bottom that markedly resembles a knight's spurs), also several small hills—"Hunchbacked Hill" (Colle Gobbo), "Luparino's Hill" (Colle di Luparino) and "Hill of the Little Towers" (Colle dei Torricelle). Then: "Valle dei Cavalieri"—Valley of the Knights.

Here is precise information confirmed in the old papers of the Assisi archives and in the thirteenth-century statutes of the commune. The valley shown by the old man is the one that unfolds beyond the last of the *casalini*. The ruins are called "La Porta" (certainly a name from the *castello* gate toward Assisi) and are down by the ravine through which the Bisciolano gully runs. This was once the site of the old road between Nocera and Assisi, today disappeared (the statutes also give us confirmation of this: *strata qua itur ad Civitatem Asisii a Civitate Nucerii*). The *vallis militum.* In an 1198 record it is called "Gola del Bisciolano" ("Bisciolano Gorge"). But in one of 1255 it has become the Valley of the Knights. [Given the dates,] there is no doubt that it took its new name from the *milites* that early biographers mentioned who passed through here, the knights who accompanied Saint Francis.

Ancient Satriano was destroyed in the dark and tragic events of a war between the Guelphs and the Ghibellines of Assisi, who fought on these mountains in 1319. An exile, a relative of the knight named Girolamo who on the night Francis died wanted to authenticate in person the existence of the stigmata, took refuge here. The stones of the ruined houses still preserve the marks of that ancient devastating fire. We, in love of this place, caused them to be taken away from their original site and used to rebuild the Satriano church.[19]

Every year since then, on the second Sunday of September, all the people of the surrounding area come to that chapel. The revived Compagnia dei Cavalieri, which is formed by descendants both of the ancient noble families and the families of the humble people of the mountain, united once again in memory [of that day in 1226], rides on horseback up there bearing the torn habit of Saint Francis.

Then for the day the place lives again, solely because of that act of goodness in which the hearts of the bitter serfs were touched and they became reconciled with their lords. Neither the revolution of 1198 nor the elaborate Peace Paper had so great an effect.

The Return to Assisi

The procession that accompanied Francis left the hill during the early hours of the afternoon, to the ringing of the church bell. It continued to ring until the mounted group was lost to view in the valley. The sun disappeared under a thick curtain of black clouds. Darker still was the shadow in the forest through which the devoted cavalcade travelled. They went down by the Bisciolano gorge, reached the church of San Giovanni di Parasacco, and passed the bridge. At the mill of the Pieve di San Venanzo, the miller came outside and knelt down on the shingle bed of the stream. Farmers who had carried grain to be ground knelt also, uncovering their heads.

They passed the bridge of San Biagio, left the Rocca di Lupone di Tiberio behind, and arrived at the Piano della Pieve. The road from here to Assisi is cut off almost perpendicularly on the Tescio, and runs at about midway of the Subasio slope through a narrow silent valley, winding in a series of unexpected curves.

Great flashes of lightning lit up the leaden cliff, the barren hill, the flints of the *torrente*. The light seemed to create an aureole around Francis. In the stormy, still air, the pawing of the horses behind him rang out with unnatural clarity.

They passed the proud Assisi gate with its stone on which the Consul Tancredi had placed the words: "From here one goes to the March." Through that gate Francis had set out with Giles on the first journey of his apostolate. And through it he was returning on the last journey, blind, broken in health, exhausted, after having travelled many roads, after having lit up the world with the light of his clear eyes and blessed it by the benediction of his pierced hands.

As soon as the procession entered the city, the storm broke.[20] Thunder drowned out the hosannas of the crowd. The rumbling of the storm changed the festive ringing of the bells into a frantic tocsin. The knights put the horses to a gallop and advanced in close ranks. The brothers ran with hoods lowered against lashing rain.

The cavalcade rapidly crossed the Piazza del Comune and took the road of Ceppo della Catena to the house of the bishop.

As evening fell, the clouds cleared. Above the fortress that dominated the rocky cliff, a strip of sky appeared, suffused in light. It was lit up for an instant by a last red blazing of the sun that brought supernatural splendour to the wooded hill, the narrow valley, the *torrente*. Then it slowly paled and was lost in night.

In the Bishop's House

The city people rejoiced, thanking the Lord. They knew that Francis could not live more than a few days, and they were elated because now they were assured of the possession of his body.[21] But their jealous devotion took a cruel turn, and they became suspicious and mistrustful. They were afraid that the friars would take the holy body away by night and carry it to another city. It seemed to them a danger all the more possible because the bishop of Assisi was gone at the time on a visit to the sanctuary of Mount Gargano.[k]

They suggested to Brother Elias that the dying man should not be taken, as he had asked, to Santa Maria degli Angeli. They ordered guards all around the walls of the bishop's house, from sunset to dawn, in the same way that watches were kept on the city walls.[22]

The *connestabile* of the knights would come in the middle of the night to interrogate the watchmen. The commune was anxious to know who was coming and who was going, what the brothers were saying, how the illness was coming along, what Francis was doing. The watchmen, motionless against the wall of the bishop's garden, replied sotto voce in the shadows.

During these hours, some men from Lucca who wished to be received into the order came to Francis. Among them was a man of a noble family who could not hold back his tears at the sight of the saint. Francis read his heart and perceived that he wept for the world that he said he wished to leave and not for the spiritual consolation that he said he wanted to acquire. In fact, in that very moment horses were heard outside; the young man looked out the window, recognized relatives, and promptly left with them.[23]

The end was approaching. Francis was too weak to move. Someone asked if he would prefer this long illness to martyrdom at the hands

---

k. According to *2 Cel.*, 220, on the day of his death Saint Francis appeared in a vision to the bishop of Assisi, who "had gone at that time to the church of Saint Michael on a pilgrimage."

Certainly one cannot think that Bishop Guido left Assisi just when Francis was near death in his own house and all the people of Assisi were greatly stirred up over it. One must believe that he had gone before Francis reached Assisi from Bagnara.

On October 4, 1226, when Francis died, Guido was in Benevento on his way back home (ibid.). From that we can deduce that Francis's stay at the *vescovado* lasted only a few days, certainly not more than a month.

Thus, there is no cause for the pained astonishment expressed by Sabatier (*Spec. Perf.*, CED, p. 243). His interpretation of the sequence of events starts from the supposition that the bishop was at home in Assisi when Francis arrived and that this was also the time of the reconciliation between the bishop and the podestà. But this, as we have seen, cannot be right.

of torturers, and he replied that save for the fact it was the will of God, three days of his kind of illness were harder to bear than any kind of torture.[24]

Nevertheless, despite his terrible suffering and the nearness of death, Francis sang. And when he was not strong enough to sing himself, he had the brothers who were with him sing. The guards were astonished and a bit scandalized.

The weak, clear song spread in the calm night over the sleeping houses, through the gardens. It was not a song of anguish or pleading, but of pure joy, sweet and mirthful.

> Praise to Thee, my Lord,
> for Sister Moon and the stars;
> in heaven you have set them,
> clear, precious, and fair.

Brother Elias, with his experience in old and new posts of authority, tried to reconcile the outpourings of so much saintly joy with the people's need to have things done as they thought proper. He tried to put Francis on notice with a little speech full of prudent advice:

"My dearest brother, I am very consoled and edified to see the joy that you experience and manifest to your companions in such affliction and sickness. Surely the men of this city venerate you as a saint in life and in death; but since they firmly believe that your serious and incurable sickness will soon lead to your death, they could think and say to themselves as they hear the 'Praises of the Lord' sung: How can he display such great joy when he is going to die? Would it not be better to think of death?"

The dying man replied, "Brother, let me rejoice in the Lord and sing his praises in the midst of my infirmities. By the grace of the Holy Spirit I am so closely united to my Lord, that, through his goodness, I can indeed rejoice in the Most High himself."[25]

The room where his life was slowly running out had all its windows thrown open upon the valley below the Moiano gate. It was already the middle of September—a sweet and pensive season on the plain stretching out at the foot of the San Damiano hill.

The sky stretches in calm peace above it, its intense deep blue gentling to a delicate azure; in the distance the mountains rise clear and distinct. The sun becomes soft and pale. A strange spell is cast by the extravagant and regal pomp that mantles the fields and trees, the countryside preparing to die.

At evening, when the dark plain seems wrapped in contemplation of the coming night and approaching winter (already the swallows have gone away and flocks of cranes fill the air with their plaintive cries), the magnificent fire of the setting sun burns black clouds lying motionless on the horizon, over Porziuncola.

Often the wind brings sudden violent storms to the forest of olive trees. The trunks seem to split in their frenzy, the branches to scream in desperation. Large silvery waves heap up in the grey-blue sea of leaves, convulsed by the squall. But when the wind falls, a luminous silence quiets and seems to invoke mercy for all things that suffer.

Francis drank it all in as he lay there, in this time that brought back memories and images of his earliest years.

His flesh virtually consumed, he seemed all spirit, already separated from the body.[26] He had always been hard on his body, but now at last he could feel compassion for the pain-wracked thing he was about to leave behind.

One night the invalid thought parsley would taste good, and he asked the cook to go into the garden and gather some for him. The cook hesitated, saying that it was hard to find this herb in the dark. But overcome by Francis's insistence, he went out and gathered the first herbs that came to hand. Among them was parsley, leafy and tender. Francis ate some of it and was much comforted.[27]

Another time, when the brothers were pleading with him to take a bit of food, he wanted and asked for some eel. They were all embarrassed, not knowing where to go search for it in that place and in that season. But there was a knock at the door and a man came in, carrying a hamper from Brother Gerardo, provincial minister of Val di Rieti. Inside were beautiful eels and a crayfish pie.[28]

The simplest things that happened around him now had a tinge of the miraculous. Francis was aware of it. He knew, even, that after his death his mortal remains would be exalted in triumph. The thought no longer bothered him.

One of the brothers, perhaps again Brother Leo, asked him jokingly one day for how much he would sell to the Lord the rough clothes he was wearing—his patched habit, the worn bandage wrapped about his head.

"One day many canopies and silken palls will cover this little body of yours that is now clothed in sackcloth!" he told Francis.

Francis smiled and replied "with a great outburst of joy," "What you say is true, for it will be to the praise and glory of my Lord!"[29]

Brother Leo himself would have given his life to have the habit of his master and to be able to keep it in memory of him. His longing did not escape Francis, who called him and said to him, "I give you this tunic; take it that it may be yours for the future. Though I wear it while I am alive, it will be yours at my death."[30]

The Canticle of Sister Death

Another day a doctor of the city named Bongiovanni came to see him.

He was the son of the Marangone di Cristiano who was several times consul of the city in the agitated period between 1198 and 1210 and who sat with the arbiters of the Peace Paper in 1203. Marangone's brother was Benvegnate, a knight of great reputation and a councillor of the commune.

Marangone had other sons: Leonardo, who was devoted to Francis and who in 1239 took part in the agreement between Brother Elias and the sons of Offreduccio di Sanguigno about the travertine taken from the house of the latter for use in the building of the Basilica di San Francesco. Leto, also a councillor in 1228. Pietro, owner of lands in Castelnuovo. Ugolino, who in this year of 1226 served as *camerario* of San Rufino. The very powerful family was tied by family relationships to the lords of Parlascio, with whom they shared lands on the plain.

Their house stood near the Bernadone place. Therefore, it is not surprising that the ancient biographers, speaking of this Doctor Bongiovanni, say that "he was a close friend of blessed Francis," *erat valde familiaris beato Francisco.*

The friendship between the two must have gone back to the time of their early youth. It is not improbable that the young friend for whom Francis had so much love that he confided in him and chose him as his companion was this son of the consul, his neighbour.

Bongiovanni attended the University of Bologna and returned with the reputation of being a scholarly and learned man. At that time the teaching and practice of the law, philosophy, and medicine were considered all one, which accounts for the fact that Bongiovanni is described in the 1233 census of the commune as both notary and doctor. In 1223 he was *giudice ordinario* of the *curia urbana* (judge of the city court). One of his rulings, concerning an appeal to the edict of "the divine Hadrian," has even come down to us.[1] His office was

---

1. Edict of the "divine Hadrian": Hadrian, Roman emperor of the second century, had an *edictum perpetuum* drawn up that served to a great extent as the basis of Justinian's *Corpus iuris*. For the ruling given by Bongiovanni in which a provision of this edict was cited, see *NV* 3:307.

on the piazza, on the first floor of his house, where his grandsons a century later continued the same profession. He had two sons, one of whom he named for his father, Marangone, and the other for his friend, the man he had loved devotedly, Francesco. The latter became a Friar Minor in Assisi.

Like the notary Medico, the son of Marangone was pleased to boast of his rank as *bonus homo,* a noble and a man of law, and he styled himself and is called in the records *"Bonus Iohannes,"* Bongiovanni.[m]

This frailty of his was not unknown to Francis, who, nevertheless, did not like to call anyone by the name "Good" (*bonus, buono,* or *bon*) out of reverence for the Lord, who said, "Only God is good." Not wishing, however, to make a big thing about this little weakness of his friend, he addressed him familiarly by the name of his paternal uncle, as is often done yet among the people of Assisi. It also gave him a way of welcoming him with a play on words:

"How does this illness of mine seem to you, Benvegnate, *Benevenias* (lit. 'Well come'—'Welcome')?"

The doctor took up Francis's joke, continuing with a remark that both referred to Francis's illness and carried on the allusions to his

---

m. Assisi records confirm the existence of the doctor and notary Bongiovanni and identify him as a member of a family that played a leading role in the birth and establishment of the commune. His father and uncle appear frequently in public records of the time. The title of *bonus* given to Giovanni was an indication that the person was a nobleman or a prominent man of the law.

The professions of notary and physician were frequently combined in that day, when in the university the teaching of medicine, philosophy, and law were combined. Many men are described as both *medico* (or *fisico*) and *notaio* in the ancient records of Italian communes; see especially Briganti, *L'Umbria nella storia del notariato italiano,* pp. 14 and 27; Tarulli Brunamonte, "Documenti per la storia della medicina in Perugia," *DPSU* 25:177.

Bongiovanni lived with his father and brothers two houses away from the house identified in 1229 as "of the sons of Angelo di Pica"—Saint Francis's paternal house (see chap. 3, n. q of this book).

The description of Bongiovanni as a man of Arezzo in some but not all manuscripts of *Spec. Perf.,* 122, undoubtedly came about through a copyist's error. The name of Bongiovanni's father, Marangone, was frequently written "Maraçonis" or, in a shortened form, "Mareço." As not infrequently happened, a copyist, not understanding the word, guessed at it as "Areço," and transcribed it as Aretio or Arezzo.

The word *benigbengnate* or *benbemgnate,* as found in early texts, which was used by Francis in his exchange with Bongiovanni, has so confused many students that in some translations it is left out altogether. But the explanation of the word is that it is a reference to Bongiovanni's family, particularly to the name of his uncle (which was frequently used as a means of identification of individuals, in the same way the name of the father was used). "Benvegnate" was then turned by Francis into a pun meaning "welcome"—*bene veniat*—referring to Sister Death. And in fact, in Riccardi codex 1409, Francis's reply is recorded as *Bemmevengha la mia sirocchia morte.*

Bongiovanni's close relationship with Francis can be deduced not only from the nature of their exchange in the bishop's palace but also from the fact that he named one of his sons Francesco. That son became a Friar Minor; and in 1289 he served as the witness to a will in which the *fidecomissario* or trustee was Francis's nephew, Ceccolo di Piccardo.

See *NV* 2:536–42 for a detailed description of the family and discussion of all the matters touched upon in this note.

name. He replied, *"Bene erit* ('All goes well'), Brother, through the grace of God."

Such word plays were very popular at the time. They were considered the best possible form in which to express an idea or make a statement. It happened often enough that in imitation of certain verses of the Scriptures, such somber concepts as the infinite vanity of all things were expressed in elegant word games and comparisons, even in such austere sequences as the *Dies Irae.* Thomas of Celano showed himself to be a master in this art. And it was certainly a devoted follower of Saint Francis who cut into the San Damiano choir those fine admonitions in the style of love songs:

> *Non clamor, sed amor,*
> *Non vox, sed votum,*
> *Non cordula, sed cor,*
> *Psallit in aure Dei.*

> Not a clamour, but love,
> Not talking, but a pledge,
> Not flagellation, but heart,
> Make music in the ear of God.

But now Francis was insistent.

"Tell me the truth. What is your real opinion? Don't be afraid to tell me, for by God's grace I am not a *cucco* and I am not afraid of dying."[31] (*Cucco,* in the Assisi dialect, means even today a fool, a worthless, stupid man.)

And he added, "The Lord, by his grace and in his goodness, has so closely united me to himself that I am as happy to live as I am to die."

Then his friend and doctor told him, "Father, according to our medical knowledge your disease is incurable, and it is my belief that you will die either at the end of September or in early October."

Without rising from the bed because of his weakness, Francis returned to the duel of wits by going back to his original word play on "well-come" or "welcome" and the name of his friend's uncle—the same sort of thing he had done in his company of rhymsters:

"Bene veniat. And then, *ben venga* Sister Death."

He was a poet to the end.

From the group of men who loved him and were hiding their grief, a brother arose and made this little speech: "Father, your life and conduct have been and still are a torch and a mirror not only for your brothers but for the entire Church. It will be the same with your death. It will cause much sorrow and sadness to the brothers and to countless others, but it will be an immense consolation and an infinite joy to you. You will, indeed, go from great labour to great repose, from an ocean of suffering and of temptations to eternal happiness. The strict poverty that you have always loved and voluntarily practiced from your conversion until the last day will be replaced by infinite riches, and temporal death by eternal life where you will see constantly and face to face the Lord your God, whom you have contemplated in this world with so much fervour, desire, and love."

He was silent for a moment and then continued:

"Father, know in truth that, if the Lord does not send from the height of heaven a remedy for your body, your sickness is incurable and, according to the doctors, you do not have much longer to live. I am warning you of this to comfort your spirit, so that you may constantly rejoice in God, inwardly and outwardly, and so that your brothers and those who are coming to visit you may find you joyful in the Lord. They know for certain that you are going to die soon, and your death, for those who witness it or will hear it described, must constitute a memory and an example, as your life and conduct already have."[32]

At these words Francis's poetic spirit once more took fire. He thought again of those knights of Provence, crusaders with the white cross, who before dying dictated a last song to those around them.[33] Now, he too wanted to extend an ardent greeting to the good sister who was nearing, and to praise the perfect joy that had accompanied him in life and that was still with him in death.

He had Angelo and Leo called and told them to sing once again the Canticle of the Sun. Whatever tears tightened their throats, they obeyed. When they reached the last verse, he made a sign for them to stop. Then he murmured a last stanza for the Canticle:

> *Laudato si, misignore, per sora nostra*
> *morte corporale,*
> *da laquale nullu homo*
> *vivente poskappare.*

> *Gai acqueli ke morrano*
> *ne le peccata mortali!*

> *Beati quelli ke trovarane*
> *le tue sanctissime voluntati,*
> *ka la morte secunda*
> *nol farra male.*

Laudate et benedicite, misignore,
et rengratiate et serviate li
cum grande humilitate.

All praise be yours, my Lord, through Sister Death,
From whose embrace no mortal can escape.

Woe to those who die in mortal sin!

Happy those she finds doing your will!
The second death can do no harm to them.

Praise and bless my Lord, and give him thanks,
And serve him with great humility.[n]

Farewell to Assisi

He prepared himself for the great farewell. He called all the brothers,
and they came and knelt around him. He could no longer recognize
them, for he could no longer see at all. He crossed his arms on his
chest, stretched out his right hand and put it on the head of the
brother in front of all the others, on his left. He asked who it was.

It was Brother Elias. Francis, his voice catching, gave the minister
general his last blessing:

"You, my son, I bless above all and throughout all; and just as the
Most High has multiplied my brothers and sons in your hands, so also
I bless them all upon you and in you. May God, the king of all, bless
you in heaven and upon earth. I bless you as much as I can and more
than I can, and what I cannot, may he who can do all things do in you.
May the Lord be mindful of your work and of your labour, and may a
share be reserved for you in the reward of the just. May you find
every blessing you desire, and may whatever you ask worthily be
granted to you."[o]

---

n. Despite the efforts that have been made to prove that this stanza was written in some
place other than the bishop's palace, as reported in *Per.*, 100, and *Spec. Perf.*, 123, no evidence
has been offered that gives us any reason to doubt these texts and their detailed story of the
canticle pouring out of Francis's full heart after he was told death was not far away. There is no
contradiction, as has been argued, in *2 Cel.*, 217, in which Francis in his final days at Porziuncola
asks his companions to sing the Canticle to him and recalls the words of the doctor and his
welcome to Sister Death. This is obviously a separate, later episode. See *NV* 2:532–36.

o. The words of *1 Cel.*, 108, are quite precise and speak in unequivocal fashion of Brother
Elias. In *Spec. Perf.*, 107, this episode is reported as a blessing of Brother Bernardo. This must
be a substitution or an interpolation, because it is not possible, as some have claimed, that there
were two events so alike in every detail. Cf. Edouard D'Alençon, "La benediction de Saint
François," *Études Franciscaines* 9:204–7; Faloci-Pulignani, "L'ultima benedizione," *Misc. Fran.*

After a moment, he continued:

"Farewell, all you my sons, in the fear of God, and may you remain in him always, for a very great trial will come upon you and a great tribulation is approaching. Happy will they be who will persevere in the things they have begun, though future scandals will separate some. I am hastening to the Lord and I am confident that I will go to my God whom I serve devoutly in my spirit."

[Still he was not ready.] He felt he could not close his eyes in peace in a room of the old imperious palace, magnificent like an armed castle guarded by the men-at-arms of the commune. Too many shades, new and old, were about him there, too many agitated and nervous men, too much at odds with his radiant vision. He longed for Porziuncola and talked of it to the brothers: "My sons, see that you never abandon this place! If you are driven out one door, re-enter by another, for this place is holy indeed. It is the dwelling-place of Christ and his Virgin Mother. When we were few, it was here that the Most High increased us. It was here that he illumined the souls of his poor ones with the light of his wisdom, here that he kindled our desires with the fire of his love. Whosoever prays here with a devout heart shall obtain whatever he asks, while an evil-doer shall receive heavier punishment.

"My sons, regard this place as most worthy of all reverence and honour as the true dwelling-place of God, especially dear to him and to his mother. Glorify God the Father, and his son Jesus Christ our Lord, in the unity of the Holy Spirit, in this place with all your hearts and with the voice of praise and confession."[34]

Finally, the brothers came to an agreement with a devout canon of the bishop's palace, Domino Iacopo, who was very dear to Francis,[p] and made arrangements to carry him down to Porziuncola without moving him from the bed in which he was lying.

The procession went out the nearby Moiano gate and proceeded along the road of Fonte Ingaldetta, and from there through Sant'Anastasio. It went through Valecchie, the sinister village that supplied the commune with its executioners.[q] After travelling along a

---

9:107. It would certainly be likely, however, that Brother Bernardo was among those blessed by Saint Francis soon before his death.

p. Domino Iacopo appears in city records as a canon of the *vescovado* and an assessor who assisted the bishop in judicial proceedings. He was among those who saw the stigmata both before and after the death of Saint Francis. See *NV* 2:234, 448–49.

q. City statutes (L. III, rub. 113) required that notorious thieves be hanged and that the sentence be carried out only in the tower of Massacii, beyond Renaro, or on the gallows in the field near the road to Santa Maria degli Angeli, at the lower part of the district toward Spello, "where they are customarily placed . . . supplied by the men of Valecchie." See *NV* 3:217.

short stretch of the Strada Francesca, it arrived at the crossroads of Santa Maria degli Angeli and San Salvatore delle Pareti.[r]

At this name, all his past life stirred in Francis's heart, as in the moment of death everything returns in order to be dissolved. He saw again the dismal field where criminals were hanged, the funereal houses of the lepers. He thought again of the bitterness of the communal revolution, the horrors of the war with Perugia, the sneers of the people when he had first begun his apostolate. And he remembered the night spent in Bernardo's house, the first companions who had joined him at Porziuncola, Clare's pure ardour.

Now he saw clearly the miracle that God had been pleased to bring about "in these last times" for the salvation of all sinners, by granting to him, his herald and precursor, the gift of bringing from hatred, love; from discord, brotherhood; from evil, goodness. By God's mercy he, Francis, had brought from war, peace; from an accursed city, a blessed city; from darkness, the light of the "New East"; and from the shadow of death, the good news of the certainty of life.[35]

He told those who were with him to stop, to put the bed down on the ground. Then, blind as he was, he asked them to turn him to face Assisi. With weak but still vibrant voice, he blessed the city that he loved so much:

"Lord, I believe that this city was formerly the refuge and abode of wicked and unjust men of evil repute throughout the country; but I also see that, by your superabundant goodness, at a time chosen by you, you have shown this city the riches of your love. It has become the abode and residence of those who know you as they should, who give glory to your name and diffuse the sweet fragrance of a pure life, a solid faith, and a good reputation among all Christian people."

He had to stop and gasp for breath. The brothers, the ones who were carrying him, were all kneeling. On both sides of the road the fields were shining in peace. The sky seemed transparent through the leaves of the olive trees.

---

r. The exact route taken in this last procession has been a subject of speculation among Franciscan writers. Sabatier, for example, in his reconstruction, has the procession, after leaving the *vescovado,* going through the Portaccia (the Sementone gate), then through the village of Valecchie, from there down to the old Strada Francesca, from which it reached San Salvatore delle Pareti (*Spec. Perf.,* CED, p. 244). But in the time of Saint Francis the Sementone gate did not exist; it was built when the city wall was enlarged more than half a century later (see Fortini, *Assisi nel medioevo,* p. 257, n. 49).

The ancient Moiano gate would have been reached immediately after the group left the *vescovado;* from there they would have gone down to Porziuncola on the route described above. Cf. *NV* 3:32–33.

He raised his hand in a gesture of supplication:

"I therefore beg you, Lord Jesus Christ, Father of mercies, do not look upon our ingratitude, but recall to mind the infinite love that you have shown to this city. May it always remain the abode and residence of those who will know and glorify your blessed and glorious name in the ages to come. Amen."[s]

s. The most familiar text of Saint Francis's blessing is the one in *Actus*, 18, and *Fioretti*, "Fourth Consideration": "May the Lord bless you, holy city, for through you many souls shall be saved, and in you many servants of God shall dwell, and from you many shall be chosen for the Kingdom of Eternal Life." We prefer the version in *Per.*, 99, and *Spec. Perf.*, 124, and in Lemmens' *Documenta Antiqua*, 2:32. It is hardly necessary to say that these are far more reliable sources. Furthermore, the words of Saint Francis in them point up the perfect correspondence between events in the history of the city and the life of the first "men of penitence of the city of Assisi."

·17·

SISTER DEATH

As soon as Francis reached Porziuncola, he wanted to write his testament, so as to put a final seal on his last wishes. It was an intention he had been pondering for a long time. And so he dictated it—a testament[1] pervaded by a subtle melancholy. He celebrates the past in it. He pours out his grief over things loved and lost, in this time when he already lay in death's shadow.

"This is how God inspired me, Brother Francis, to embark upon a life of penance. When I was in sin, the sight of lepers nauseated me beyond measure; but then God himself led me into their company, and I had pity on them. When I had once become acquainted with them, what had previously nauseated me became a source of spiritual and physical consolation for me. After that I did not wait long before leaving the world."

The first rule of the friars had been nothing but passages from the Gospel.

"When God gave me some friars, there was no one to tell me what I should do; but the Most High himself made it clear to me that I must live the life of the Gospel. I had this written down briefly and simply and His Holiness the Pope confirmed it for me. Those who embraced this life gave everything they had to the poor. They were satisfied with one habit which was patched inside and outside, and a cord, and trousers. We refused to have anything more.

"Those of us who were clerics said the Office like other clerics, while the lay brothers said the *Our Father,* and we were only too glad to find shelter in abandoned churches. We made no claim to learning and we were submissive to everyone. I worked with my own hands and I am still determined to work, and with all my heart I want all the other friars to be busy with some kind of work that can be carried on without scandal. . . . God revealed a form of greeting to me, telling me that we should say, 'God give you peace.' "

In comparison to the idyll of those first years, the future seemed full of doubts and unsolved problems.

His pleading admonitions reveal his anxiety over whether the friars would keep faith with the lady of his dream:

"The friars must be very careful not to accept churches or poor dwellings for themselves, or anything else built for them, unless they are in harmony with the poverty that we have promised in the Rule; and they should occupy these places only as strangers and pilgrims.

"In virtue of obedience I strictly forbid the friars, wherever they may be, to petition the Roman Curia, either personally or through an intermediary, for a papal brief, whether it concerns a church or any other place, or even in order to preach, or because they are being persecuted. If they are not welcome somewhere, they should flee to another region[a] where they can lead a life of penance, with God's blessing. . . ."

He still agonized over the bitter quarrels that had arisen at the time of the writing of the Rule, and was crucified by the thought that perhaps even this last passionate appeal, straight from his dying heart, could be pulled to pieces, coldly dissected, and destroyed by the logic of interpreters and commentators:

"The friars should not say, this is another Rule. For this is a reminder, admonition, exhortation, and my testament that I, Brother Francis, worthless as I am, leave to you, my brothers, that we may observe in a more Catholic way the Rule we have promised to God. The Minister General and all the other ministers and custodes are bound in virtue of obedience not to add anything to these words or subtract from them. They should always have this writing with them as well as the Rule and at the chapters they hold, when the Rule is read, they should read these words too.

"In virtue of obedience, I strictly forbid any of my friars, clerics, or lay brothers, to interpret the Rule or these words, saying, 'This is

---

a. This phrase in the critical Latin edition of the *Testament* is *"fugiant in aliam terram . . ."* (Esser, *Opuscula,* p. 313). In *Omnibus,* the phrase is translated, "flee to another country." Fortini, however, renders *terram* as *altrove*—"elsewhere," "another place." Temperini and Pazzelli agree with his interpretation. Father Conrad Harkins, director of The Franciscan Institute, adds that the admonition comes from Mt. 10:14–15, in which the Latin is *. . . terrae Sodomorum et Gomorrhaeorum. . . ,"* translated "land" in the old Confraternity Version and "region" in the New American Bible. The word "region," he says, seems to preserve that connection with the Scriptures and also perhaps has more the connotation of an area widely removed from the place of persecution than do most others. This translator should like to add that *terra* was the word for the populated center of the medieval commune—is it possible that Francis meant, "Go to another town"?—Trans.

what they mean.' God inspired me to write the Rule and these words plainly and simply, and so you too must understand them plainly and simply, and live by them, doing good to the last.

"And may whoever observes all this be filled in heaven with the blessing of the most high Father, and on earth with that of his beloved Son, together with the Holy Spirit, the Comforter, and all the powers of heaven and all the saints. And I, Brother Francis, your poor worthless servant, add my share internally and externally to that most holy blessing. Amen."

One by one, all those whom he had loved returned to his heart. After his friars, the sisters of San Damiano.[2] He thought of Clare, first flower of the enclosed garden. He saw her again as a young woman in the rich house of Piazza San Rufino. His poet brother's words about her, one of his most lyrical pieces of writing, rang out in his soul: "Clare by name, brighter in life and brightest in character."[3]

He said to the brother who was leaving for San Damiano, "Go and take this letter to the Lady Clare. You will tell her to banish the sorrow and sadness she feels at the thought of never seeing me again. Let her know, in truth, that before she dies she and all her sisters will see me again and will receive great consolation from me."[4]

But there was another woman, the one for whom every rigid rule of cloister was to fall, a woman so dear and irresistible that from death's door he wanted to send her an affectionate message: "To Madonna Iacopa, servant of God, Brother Francis, the little poor man of Christ, sends his greetings in the Lord and fellowship in the Holy Spirit of Our Lord Jesus Christ."[5]

This was the way he addressed her in the letter that he wished his companions to write in his name.

"You know how much she has loved me since I have been an exile from the world. Tell her that I am about to die, and that if she wishes to see me again now that I am about to return to the heavenly kingdom, she must hurry without delay. And tell her to bring some cloth for a religious habit, ash-coloured, and also some of that special dish that she herself made for me many times in Rome."[6]

His companions carried out his instructions with all speed. They wrote the letter, and they searched for someone to leave at once for Rome. But when one of the friars was already explaining to the messenger how, why, and where he must go, they heard outside a great pawing of horses and a confused rumble of voices, some authoritative, some obsequious, and the clatter of swords and armour. A large company had stopped outside the door of the friary. One of the brothers rushed to open it and stood transfixed. At the door was

Giacomina dei Settesoli, Francis's "Brother Iacopa," an anxious question trembling on her sweet face.

They reassured her. Francis was still alive. He had asked for her. He wanted to see her again.

She talked agitatedly while the knights and the women of her escort respectfully stood apart. She had been praying at home when a mysterious voice inside her told her to hurry to Assisi, where Francis was, and to do it soon if she wished to find him alive, and to take cloth for a habit, the sweets that he liked so much, candles and incense for the funeral.[7]

To the Three Kings, who came bearing gifts to honour Jesus at the time of his birth, the brothers compared Giacoma, this blessed holy woman, who came with gifts to honour his most devoted servant at the time of his death, which surely would be for him his true birth.[8] They told Francis she had arrived, and he told the brothers that no rule about cloister would apply to Brother Giacomina, to bring her to him at once.

Neither Thomas of Celano nor the writer of the *Legend of Perugia*, both of whom tried to reconstruct in minute detail everything that was said around Saint Francis at that time, report anything at all of the conversation between Francis and Giacomina, in that time of waiting for death, when they said their final good-byes. There is only the report of a brother, who certainly had to have been at Porziuncola at the time, that "when she saw him, she wept."[9] But what could anyone say? Perhaps it was the only hour, of all that extraordinary and never-to-be-forgotten preparation for eternity, in which Francis's heart trembled a little.

The brothers took charge of the gifts.

A red silk cushion, with the lions of the house of Frangipane and the imperial eagles embroidered on it.[10]

The cloth for the funeral habit, woven by Cistercians overseas.[11]

A white silk veil, embroidered all over, and around, over and over again, in silk and in gold, the three letters of the lovely word that is the same in Latin and in Italian, in the language of yesterday and of today, the command that never grows old, never loses its power to relieve pain: AMA ("Love").[12]

A little casket with sugar, almonds, and other ingredients to make the sweets that the Romans call *mortaroli*.[13]

Candles for the funeral vigil. Incense to spread the perfume of the last prayer.

Her visit brought new life to him.[14] Francis seemed to light up again, like a spluttering lantern that is given new fuel. But this, alas, was nothing but a miracle of his heart's having once again found joy before stopping forever, a last dramatic response of a gracious and generous knight that caused him to come back to earth from the celestial glory to which he was already rising, back where a devoted lady was weeping for him.

He was able to enjoy but little of the food that Giacoma prepared for him.[15] In the meantime another woman whom he called Sister had arrived, the woman to whom he had addressed his last song in the bishop's house in Assisi. She came silent and alone and placed herself at his side with jealous love.

Mors, janua vita. Death, the gateway of life.[16]

The brothers had given way before her. The people of the city were waiting, impatient now to carry his body to the city in triumph.[17] Still more armed guards had been sent to Porziuncola by the commune, and they kept watch with assiduous care.[18]

There was nothing to keep her from Francis now but Giacoma's last desperate hope. With invincible faith, she still rebelled at the inevitable.

So now she proposed that she send back all that great company that had come as her escort—the knights, the ladies, the servants, the men-at-arms. She would stay with Francis and, in humble piety, care for him and serve him.

Francis heard and replied with effort. He said in a low voice, but with so much certainty that the lady felt her soul reel, "No. Saturday I shall die. Sunday, you will leave, together with all the others."[19]

The Dearest Lady

As three Marys played a part in the agony of Jesus, so a third woman was waiting for a word from Francis. And she was the lady whom he had loved the most, the one who had been at his side on every road, in every hour, since the night of his last serenata through the streets of Assisi—Lady Poverty.

Neither word nor poetry alone was adequate to show her how much he loved her in this final moment.

He wanted now to renew the wedding vows that he had taken with her twenty years earlier, in the bishop's court.

Stripping himself of his habit and of the bandage that had been wrapped around his head, he asked the brothers to put him naked on the naked earth.[20] They wept at seeing his poor wretched body, his empty eyes, the face furrowed by the horrible scars, the scrawny hand that he pressed against his heart in an effort to conceal the wound in his side.

He entrusted to them his dearest lady. He said, "I have done what was mine to do. May Christ teach you what is yours."

The guardian of the place arose and, weeping, gave him clothing. He ordered Francis, "Know that this tunic and trousers and cap have been lent to you by me, by command of holy obedience. But, that you may know that you have no ownership with regard to them, I take away from you all authority to give them to anyone."[21]

Francis allowed them, then, to put back on his body that habit of rough cloth, to let the rude hood fall over his ruined face and spent eyes.[22] He was filled with joy. They had understood his feeling, the joy of entering eternity in an everlasting embrace of the woman whom he had so long and anxiously sought.[23]

So he begged them to allow him to die stripped of everything, in a pure nudity of love. He said, "When you see that I am brought to my last moments, place me naked upon the ground just as you saw me the day before yesterday. Let me lie there after I am dead for the length of time it takes to walk a mile unhurriedly."[24]

One morning (perhaps it was the Friday preceding his death[b]), after having spent a sleepless night in the cruelest suffering, he wanted to call his brothers together again. He put his hand on the head of each, and again he blessed them.

---

b. Most biographers have thought it possible to make a chronological reconstruction of the things done by Saint Francis in the last days of his life. The episode in which he wished his brothers to put him naked upon the ground, most have held to have taken place Thursday, October 1 (Sabatier, Vie, chap. 20). The next morning, Friday, would have then been the morning that the brothers gathered at Saint Francis's bedside for a Eucharistic meal (although Sabatier, in Études, p. 325, placed this on Wednesday, September 30). [In the English translation of Sabatier's Vie, however, it is said to happen on Friday.—Trans.] This would have also been the time of the reading of the Gospel of Saint John (for all the episodes, cf. Facchinetti, San Francesco nella storia, p. 652).

These interpretations are not authorized by any of the primary sources. We can see this very clearly when we go back to Papini, who places on the last day, that is, October 3, Saint Francis's asking his brothers to put him, when he was in his last moments, naked upon the ground again, "just as you saw me the day before yesterday." (Sabatier, to explain his reconstruction, cites 2 Cel., 217. See n. 24.) It is not true that Celano says, either directly or indirectly, that Saint Francis asked this on the day of his death. He limits himself to saying that "he spent the few days that remained before his death in praise." He tells how he invited everything, even death itself, to praise God, and how he adds, "Tell me bravely, Brother Doctor, that death, which is the gateway of life, is at hand." Then he tells his brothers to place him naked upon the ground when "I am brought to my last moments." This entire narration is of events that took place in Francis's last days, without any particular determination of the day on which each took place.

In regard to the bread that he wished to share with his brothers: According to Spec. Perf., 88, Saint Francis was one night wracked by pain. When at last morning came, he called his brothers around him to re-enact the things that Jesus did in the Last Supper on Holy Thursday (quinta feria). In fact, he asked immediately afterwards if it were the fifth ferial day. "And when he was told that it was another day, he said that he had thought it was Thursday." There is nothing to indicate whether the event took place in the days preceding or following the Thursday of the week in which he died, though one must remember the Bologna manuscript that specifies that "it was then the sixth ferial day"—i.e., Friday. This source, however, is not enough to determine with certainty the actual day.

In Leg. Maior, XIV, 5, and 1 Cel., 110, the reading of the Gospel of Saint John and the recitation of Psalm 142 are placed in the moments before death. The first source, however, says the Gospel was read before the psalm; the latter, afterwards.

Brother Bernardo's presence moved him especially. He remembered that April morning in which together, in the San Giorgio piazza, they handed out his money to the poor. He told the friars that they must regard Bernardo, his first companion, with the same affection as they did himself. (But who had been even earlier? That young man, almost an adolescent, who, before everyone else, had leapt to join Francis in his hard mission, only to be immediately caught up in the busy life, the whirlwind of the world's affairs?)

He saw with extraordinary lucidity the friars who would come in future times, the immense army of knights of the habit and cord—knights who would make his name and his special view of life a symbol of irresistible love, a banner of life and of victory. He saw those nearest and those farthest in time—the peacemakers, the missionaries, the martyrs, the saints, the ascetics, the learned. He would have liked to have had every one of them beside him, so he could put his hand on each one's head, from those who would wear a crown to those anonymous friars who would live lives of pain, borne in solitude in remote forests and in desert dusts.[25]

He had them bring bread—the bread of charity, like that they had begged together, crust by crust, all along the interminable roads they had walked, the bread of sorrow that Jesus had given his disciples in farewell, when he said, "Take, eat. This is my body that has been given for you. Do this in memory of me."

He tried to divide it but could not, so great was his weakness. He took the tiny pieces that others broke for him and gave them to all as a sign of his love.[26]

He believed, and he said to them, that this must be the fifth ferial day, Thursday, the day on which Jesus celebrated the Last Supper. He had lost all track of time. The sky, the earth, all the things in which he had rejoiced, no longer had any significance for him. And perhaps he had indeed already been raised from that bed of pain in the hovel lost among the trees and, his poor worn body left behind, was walking peacefully in the evening light that reaches beyond life, already completing his first mile toward the throne of God.

Sister Death

But he suddenly returned to the world that he loved and was now leaving a few hours before his death. It was Saturday afternoon, October 3.

He felt that it was the end. He wanted two brothers to sing again for him, for the last time, his canticle in praise of all creatures.[27]

Farewell, shining sun, serene nights, autumn wind. Farewell, enchanting streams and flowering gardens. Farewell, you who remain amid life's problems and pain. For this weeping that rose from the very soul, for the life that had passed and for the one now opening, praised be you, Lord.

One of the brothers dearest to him arose and said, "Kind Father, alas, your sons are now without a father and are deprived of the true light of their eyes. Remember, therefore, your orphan sons whom you are now leaving; forgive them all their faults and give joy to those present and absent with your holy blessing."

He replied, "Behold, my son, I am called by God. I forgive my brothers, both present and absent, all their offences and faults, and, in as far as I am able, I absolve them. I want you to announce this to them and to bless them all on my behalf."[28]

He had them bring the missal and asked them to read the Gospel of Holy Thursday, telling of love enduring until death, in the words of Saint John that are used in the Mass before the altars are stripped: "Before the feast of Passover, Jesus realized the hour had come for him to pass from this world to the Father. He had loved his own in this world, and would show his love for them to the end."[29]

Evening was coming on. In the woods the trees were still glowing in a soft and rosy light, though Porziuncola itself, where everyone knelt around Francis, lay in darkness.

After a long pause of shadow and silence, Francis's lips opened on his last invocation—David's prayer in a cave, the prayer of souls sore oppressed: "With a loud voice I cry out to the Lord; with a loud voice I beseech the Lord."[30]

The brothers made the response in subdued voices: "My complaint I pour out before him; before him I lay bare my distress."

From the edge of paradise, as if on a threshold that opened to light, Francis's voice rose again. He spoke for all troubled and abused souls in the last message of his exhausted heart.

"I look to the right to see, but there is no one who pays me heed. I have lost all means of escape. There is no one who cares for my life."

He cried out in pain. His cry shook the dark walls and flowed out through the door, wide open to gather in the last light of the evening. The tops of the trees were no longer visible, but in the west the skies still burned in fire and blood.

"Rescue me from my persecutors, because they are too strong for me."

And the brothers continued with the last verse—a final hope, a final faith in goodness: "Lead me forth from prison, that I may give thanks to your name. The just shall gather around me when you have been good to me."

And then there was silence. Francis was dead.

While anguished prayer was being murmured in the darkness by the brothers, their faces against the earth, an aerial chorus rose up—a great symphony made by the beating of wings, joyous trills, cascades of melody. A song rose with stupifying abandon. It soared in intensity and filled the firmament, as if it were not an autumn night but a clear summer morning, not the time for rest but the time of awakening, as if the sun were rising again.

A multitude of skylarks fluttered on the roof of Francis's cell and sang for him, for his glory and his triumph. In the shadow of night, they poured out a paean that belonged to blue sky and sun and joy, even though mute forever was the voice that had addressed them in courteous fraternity: "Sister larks, you praise God very much by wanting with so much sweetness to become like good religious who despise earthly things and whose thoughts are always in heaven."

This unheard of happening, this impossible event, astonished the guards who, leaning on their shields, kept watch. They called to others who were waiting nearby, and they rushed up and were also witnesses to this wonder.[c]

Giacomina's Tears

Brother Elias went to the woman who was praying alone, on her knees in the chapel, and made a sign for her to follow him. They crossed the brief stretch of woods and entered the cell. Francis lay on his poor bed, in peace. His face was as white as lilies, and rapturous, like that of angels.[31]

---

c. The episode of the skylarks is found in all the ancient sources:

Leg. Maior, XIV, 6: "At the time of Saint Francis's death, when it was already dusk, a great flock of larks gathered over the building, although they normally prefer the light of day and avoid the shades of night. There they remained, flying about and singing with unusual joy, clearly testifying by the sweetness of their song to the glory of the saint who had so often called upon them to praise God."

Spec. Perf., 113: "For late that Saturday evening, after Vespers on the night when he passed away to the Lord, a great flight of larks assembled above the roof of the house where he lay. And they circled around it in the form of a wheel, singing sweetly as they flew and seeming to praise God."

An especially vivid narration of the singing of the birds is in *3 Cel.,* 32: "The larks are birds that love the noonday light and shun the darkness of twilight. But on the night that Saint Francis went to Christ, they came to the roof of the house, though already the twilight of the night to follow had fallen, and they flew about the house for a long time amid a great clamour, whether to show their joy or their sadness in their own way by their singing, we do not know. Tearful rejoicing and joyful sorrow made up their song, either to bemoan the fact that they were orphaned children or to announce that their father was going to his eternal glory. The city watchmen who guarded the place with great care were filled with astonishment and called the others to witness the wonder."

He gently picked up Francis's frail body. It was not at all rigid, but as docile as it had been on the day that the knights in Satriano had carried him on their horses along the mountain road.[32] A poor racked body, yet seemingly marvellously young, as Elias later pointed out in his message of Francis's death that he sent to the friars who were away. It was, he said, a certain sign of the promised resurrection: "While he was living, his face was not beautiful, but distorted because of the intolerable agony that did not spare any part of his body. Through the contraction of the nerves, the members were stiffened like those of a dead man. After his death, on the other hand, he became beautiful, shining with a marvellous brightness that gave happiness to all present. And the members that had been so hard took on an extraordinary suppleness, as in a tender adolescent."[d]

The former consul placed the precious burden in Giacoma's arms, saying, "See, he whom you loved in life you shall hold in your arms in death."[33]

At that gesture, at those words, her tears broke forth in a cry that knifed through the silence that had returned to the room after the last note of the skylarks was lost in the night. It was a cry of love from a creature wounded beyond repair, one who would not be able to live anywhere the rest of her life except in the place where he had died nor find repose in death except near his tomb.[e]

---

d. *Epistola encyclica de transitu* (AF 10:527). [For an English translation of the letter, which again compares Francis to a Sun and a Light and is packed with Biblical allusions: van Constanje, *The Covenant with God's Poor*, pp. 123–28.]

The date of Saint Francis's death is given to us in the letter: "At the first hour of night before October 4th, our father and brother Francis went away towards Christ." We also find the date in *Leg. Maior*, XV, 6: "Our holy father left this world on Saturday evening, October 3, in the year of our Lord 1226, and he was buried on the following day." And again in *Fioretti* ("Fourth Consideration"): "The glorious confessor of Christ Saint Francis passed from this life on Saturday, the third of October, in the year of the Lord 1226, and he was buried on Sunday. That year was the twentieth of his conversion, when he began to do penance, and it was the second year after the imprinting of the Stigmata. And it was in the forty-fifth year from his birth."

It will be noted that Francis died the evening of October 3, but in the reckoning of time in the Middle Ages, sunset marked the beginning of a new day. Therefore, in that form of dating, he died on October 4. This is the day on which the church celebrates his death.

e. The date of the death of the Lady Giacoma has been much discussed. In *Actus* and *Fioretti* ("Fourth Consideration") we are told: "But some time later, out of devotion to Saint Francis, she came again to Assisi. And there she ended her days in saintly penance and virtuous living and died a holy death. And it was her will that she be buried in the Church of Saint Francis with great devotion. And so it was done."

In *24 Generals* (AF 3:102) and *Fioretti* ("Add. Chaps.," 6), there are accounts of a visit that she made to Brother Giles in Monteripido. According to Wadding (*An. Min.*, 1239, XIV), she probably died in 1239. Sabatier, however, believes that she was still living in Assisi on October 18, 1273 (*Spec. Perf.*, CED, p. 276). He bases his opinion on a record that a Domina Iacoba de Roma received a legacy of 20 *soldi* in a will of that date. (Arch. S. Conv., Str. 1, 58). The name is also found in another legacy dated April 8, 1258.

Thomas of Celano calls the son who accompanied her to Assisi Iohannes Frigia Pennates. This was a name used by the Frangipani to indicate their descent from Phrigiis Penatibus, that is from Aeneas, son of Anchises, Trojan hero whose emigration to Italy is told in Virgil's *Aeneid*.

She wept for her dear friend who had gone on a long journey, for her own loneliness, for a diminished world. Her burning tears flowed over the cold body as she continued to hold it and to kiss it.[34] Who was it who thought in that hour about Mary Magdalene, who had gathered the body of Jesus, taken from the cross, into her arms?[35]

As she saw the wounds in the hands and feet, the pierced side, she immediately comprehended to what supernatural heights he had been raised. No need to search among the dead for the living. He who had received so exalted a sign on this earth could by now be nowhere but in the highest glory of heaven.[36] She drew new life from him, lived again in his piety, in his holiness. She was consoled.[37]

The brothers' sorrow also gave way to exultancy through the discovery of so great a miracle. While he was alive, only a few among those close to him had known of the miraculous prints. But now everyone could see them, venerate them, release their feelings in song that was both jubilation and weeping.[38]

"Singular gift and mark of special love, that a soldier should be decorated with the same glorious arms that because of their highest dignity were worthy of the son of the king!

"O miracle worthy of everlasting memory . . . in which . . . is expressed the mystery of the blood of the unblemished lamb, which, flowing from five wounds, washed away the sins of the world!

"O sublime splendour of the living cross that gives life to the dead, whose burden is so light and pain so gentle that through it dead flesh lives again and weak spirits are made strong!"[39]

The cries rose, sobbed, pled, became song, alternated, came one on top another, blended in a single outcry of joy and anguish, of sorrow and desire. "O true light of the world, shining in the Church of Christ more splendidly than the sun! O truly merciful and most holy father!"[40]

Whatever the words, they sprang unbidden from those who knelt beside Francis's spent body, kissed his inert hands, paused to collect a droplet of the blood that was continuing to flow from his side. No one would ever forget this stupendous revelation.

No one of those who saw, rejoiced, and wept, in the brief time that the incredible marks could be examined, could ever tell others about

---

Giacoma was buried in the Basilica di San Francesco. Her tomb was first in the lower church; but in 1933 her remains were re-interred in an urn and placed in the crypt, near the tomb of Saint Francis.

For information about Giacoma dei Settesoli and her family: *NV* 2:454–56; also chap. 10, n. c of this book.

that miracle without feeling again something of the shining things seen and felt in that great hour.

Brother Leo, with all his faith, gave the most beautiful account of the scene, in answer to Brother Salimbene's curiosity: "It was as if it were Jesus taken down from the cross."[41]

Others said: "For in truth there appeared in him a true image of the cross and of the passion of the lamb without blemish, who washed away the sins of the world, for he seemed as though he had been recently taken down from the cross. His hands and feet were pierced as though by nails and his side wounded as though by a lance."[42]

Another brother, fanciful like Brother Giles: "And because he glowed with such wondrous beauty before all who looked upon him and his flesh had become even more white, it was wonderful to see in the middle of his hands and feet, not indeed the holes made by the nails, but the nails themselves formed out of his flesh and retaining the blackness of iron, and his right side was red with blood. These signs of martyrdom did not arouse horror in the minds of those who looked upon them, but they gave his body much beauty and grace, just as little black stones do when they are set in a white pavement."[43]

And a poet: "The side wound was red, and the flesh was contracted into a sort of circle, so that it looked like a beautiful rose."[44]

They washed the body. They strewed it with unguents and spices.[f] They dressed it in the new ash-coloured habit. Over it, as he had ordered, they sewed a piece of sackcloth, symbol of the poverty and humility that always accompanied him on earth and would follow even beyond the earth.[45]

When everything was finished and he lay, arms crossed, on the rough table that had served him as a bed, Giacoma brought the seigneurial cushion and put it under his beloved head.[g] She spread

---

f. The phrase is from *1 Cel.*, 127. As Father Harkins has pointed out to this translator, this phrase seems to have in it more than immediately meets the eye. Were the usual spices used on Francis or were they not? Why should Thomas say this at all unless there was something peculiar about it?

According to Angelo Clareno, *Expositio Regulae*, p. 5 (he continues), Giovanni della Cappella, one of Francis's first companions, cast in the role of Judas in some early works, stole the balsam that had been prepared for the burial of Francis's body and then went away and hanged himself. (Angelo wrote in 1321–23.) Did Thomas mean that the friars had no spices or an insufficient quantity of them? Also, one must take note of the fact that women bring spices to anoint the body of Jesus (Mark 16:1; Luke 24:1) but do not get the opportunity to do so. Is Thomas drawing a parallel here? A fascinating subject for future investigators.—Trans.

g. "The little pillow for his head" is mentioned in *3 Cel.*, 38. The Cortona cushion bears this inscription: *Confessor Domini Franciscus ad ethera migrans hoc capitale tenuit subter caput almum. Valete in Domino et orate pro me.* ("The Confessor of Christ Francis, while his spirit was soaring to heaven, had this cushion under his venerable head. Be happy in the Lord and pray for me.") We believe that the word *migrans* must have been meant to refer to the time immediately after his death, because all the authors agree that Francis wanted to die in completely impoverished circumstances in homage of Poverty.

the veil over the waxy thin face. It was her trousseau veil, and now more than ever those three letters continued to pulsate in her heart: *Ama. Ama. Ama.*

Those Who Saw the Stigmata

Outside, in the autumn night, people were flowing in from all directions, coming from the city, the villages, the fields. A great throng wanted to see and venerate the Man of the Stigmata. After some discussion about what to do, the opinion of the lady from Rome prevailed. She said that the gift of God should not be concealed but made plain to all, so that no one would be able to doubt it in the future. And so the door was opened.[46]

All the candles that Giacoma had brought were lit. Splendid clouds of incense arose. The funeral vigil began, and, according to Thomas of Celano, "it seemed to be a wake of the angels."[47]

Great was the exultation of the city people in seeing their desires finally satisfied. Exclamations of joy, attestations of faith, prayers, thanksgivings, rose in a confused clamour that increased as the crowd grew.

"Praised and blessed be you, our Lord God, who have entrusted so precious a treasure to us who are unworthy!

"Praise and glory be to you, ineffable Trinity!"[48]

They came. They knelt beside the saint's body for which they had yearned. They kissed the stigmata of Christ. They burst out in marvelling exclamations.[49]

In the records we see them again; their names convey to us the excitement that in that holy vigil moved their violent hearts, now finally subdued in the immense outpouring of love. And, indeed, as has been observed, "Whose heart is so much like stone that it would not be broken to compunction, that it would not be fired to love of God, that it would not be strengthened to good will?"[50]

Giovanni di Simone, the *signore* of Rocca Pàida, was there.

Also Bonaccorso di Ugone, the nobleman of the *contrada* of Santa Maria Maggiore, who had been present at the proclamation of the Pardon.

Giovanni di Guarnerio, who had property next to San Damiano and was a councillor of the commune at the time of Brother Elias's arbitration in regard to the lands on Mount Subasio.

Offreduccio di Negro. Scalla di Alberico. Giovanni di Guitolo.

A man-at-arms, Matteo di Andrea del Prete. The notary Alberico. A magistrate, Tommaso di Rainerio, *camerario* of the commune. A rich bourgeois, Bartolo di Donna Fantina. A canon of the cathedral, Giovanni di Magnolo. Giovanni di Guittolo. Baliero. An inhabitant of Nocera, Giacomo di Pellipario di Margherita.

Giovanni, Francis's Greccio friend who had helped him with the Christmas crèche, had come in haste to be there.[51]

There was also the Assisi knight whom Saint Bonaventure describes as "an educated and prudent man," Girolamo by name, "a very well-known person." The commune records permit us to recognize the kind of person he was in both his actions and in his life, which was marked by the kind of shrewdness that Giotto expressed so well in his painting of him in scarlet toga, ermine mantle, and a cap of vair. He kneels [in Giotto's painting in the Basilica di San Francesco] beside the body of Saint Francis in an attitude of adoration, his posture a singular contrast to the audacity of the eyes, the high brow, the forceful, aquiline profile. The Assisi records identify him as not only an astute doctor of laws but also as an imperious leader, a shrewd magistrate, a *condottiero* experienced in cavalcades and combat.

Son of the Giovanni di Gualterio who in 1216 attended the promulgation of the Indulgence of Porziuncola, he was in the year 1223 consul of the commune in the arbitration of the war between Assisi and Bettona. In the summer of 1228 he led the armed forces of the city to Spello to fight against Frederick II, and in December he handed down a ruling in a question that had arisen between the commune and the podestà. As *camerario* of the commune in 1229, he worked out agreements with the owners of the houses that were affected in the enlargement of the Piazza del Comune. In 1231, he betook himself to the new podestà, Milancio of Bologna, as the commune's ambassador. In 1235, by now an old man, he again led the cavaliers who fought against the imperial forces. In 1230 it will be he, then podestà of the city, who will plot with Brother Elias to have the armed companies of the various quarters of the city seize Francis's body from the friars as it was being carried triumphantly through the Assisi streets and conceal it in the rock under the altar of the new Basilica di San Francesco. By doing so, he drew down upon himself the rage of Pope Gregory IX, who called him "an insolent and sacrilegious man, arrogant and rebellious" and compared him to Uzzah, who was punished for having put his hand on the Ark of God.[h]

---

h. The body of Saint Francis was taken from its temporary resting place in the little church of San Giorgio to the new Basilica di San Francesco on May 25, 1230. As the elaborate procession was nearing its destination, armed men of the commune, acting in collaboration with Brother Elias, seized the coffin, carried it into the church, barred the doors, and buried it in an excavation made in solid rock. Pope Gregory IX, who had proclaimed the canonization of Saint

It can be understood why such a powerful citizen, one consumed by feverish, jealous anxiety for Francis's body, would be among the first to rush to Porziuncola at the moment that the city people's suspicious greediness was at its height.

A little of this temerity, which did not diminish in the face of great scandal in order to make sure of the precious treasure, is in the pious irreverence with which [in Giotto's painting] he, prostrated before the body, dares to touch the holy hands, slide the nails back and forth in the wounds, palpitate the pierced feet, measure the wound in the side.[i]

Giotto, inimitable craftsman, brings to life marvellously and faithfully the accounts of the ancient biographers. For an instant, the adoration is interrupted. The people (intent faces of nobles and merchants) press around this sensible man, who demonstrates and testifies to the miracle. For the rest of his life, he will bear witness to it and be a tireless champion of it.

Candles are burning in the candlesticks. Shields of all kinds in the hands of armed men glitter among the habits and surplices. A captain,

---

Francis on July 16, 1228, did not attend the ceremonies because of urgent political problems. He issued the Bull *Speravimus Hactenus* on June 16, 1230, in which he denounced Brother Elias and the Assisi authorities and laid down heavy sanctions against the city and the basilica itself. However, Brother Elias succeeded in placating the papal wrath a short time later.

One reason for the bizarre event undoubtedly arose from the extraordinary veneration for the relics of saints that was characteristic of the Middle Ages. The body may have been kidnapped to insure the city of its custody and to prevent its being snatched or mutilated by eager relic hunters.

Another explanation that has been suggested is that four years had elapsed since Francis had died; in that time the body had undoubtedly deteriorated. A great many in the enormous crowd thronging the city surely were there to see the stigmata, which were very likely no longer visible. With the body safely hidden from view, the danger of disillusionment vanished.

Still a third explanation that has been put forth is that the enormous crowd of visitors, city people, and friars had, in the emotional circumstances, gotten out of control and that the authorities moved in to restore public order. See Fortini, *Assisi nel medioevo,* pp. 111–19; Dallari, *Frate Elia,* pp. 31–33; Marinangeli, "La Tomba di S. Francesco," *San Francesco Patrono d'Italia* 50:219–26.—Trans.

i. *Leg. Maior,* XV, 4. For a detailed discussion of Girolamo di Giovanni and his family, see NV 2:441–45. Bihl ("De Domino Hieronymo Iohannis") believes that Girolamo was still alive to tell Saint Bonaventure about the event. But this hypothesis is very unlikely, since after 1235 there is no trace of him in city records. It is more likely that one of his descendants or an elder of the city talked about him to Giotto, who was working on the murals in the basilica toward the end of the thirteenth century. The inscription on the mural depicting Girolamo's visit to the bier of Saint Francis, which was reconstructed by Marinangeli ("Serie di affreschi giottesche," *Misc. Fran.* 13:97–112) calls Girolamo *dominus Hieronymus doctor et litteratur celeber.* The title of "doctor," not given by Bonaventure, confirms the hypothesis that an Assisi citizen or a Franciscan friar passed on to the artist the memories of those of the preceding generation.

The other details of this painting, which shows people of the city around the body of Saint Francis—magistrates, notables, men-at-arms—are fully confirmed by historians. Giotto surely obtained information not only from the first biographers, and especially from Saint Bonaventure, but also from an oral tradition very much alive in the city and in the Sacro Convento. For this reason, we have used his paintings as an important historical source for the reconstruction of these last events in the life of Saint Francis.

wearing steel gauntlets and jambs that sprout under the rich tunic and holding a bared sword, stands near the head of Saint Francis, who lies on his funeral pillow.

Nova Vita

As night came on, the number of people grew, the lights multiplied, the chants grew louder. Every sign of grief had disappeared. Jubilation reigned supreme.

Improvised songs burst forth from that tumultuous overflowing of joy. Certainly in the soaring spirits of Francis's faithful company at that time lies the origin of the compelling song in praise of the stigmata and of Francis's great holiness, the song extolling Francis's *nova vita,* his new, first of its kind, life.

> *Sanctitas nova signa . . .*
>
> New signs of highest sanctity,
> Deserving praise exceedingly,
> Wondrous and beautiful to see,
> In Francis we behold.
> Unto the newly gathered band,
> Directed by his guiding hand,
> Francis receives the King's command,
> The new law to unfold.[j]

What glory had been won by the man who "in these last times" re-established the law of the Gospels!

> *Novus ordo, nova vita . . .*
>
> Before the world's astonished view,
> Arise the life and order new,
> Whose sacred laws again renew
> The Evangelic state.

---

j. Wadding *(Scrip. Ord. Min.)* attributes this song to Thomas of Celano. We have seen that Friar Thomas wrote about this night, "Everyone sang a canticle of joy, as their heartfelt gladness prompted them." He was undoubtedly among those who were present when Francis died and who saw the stigmata. In fact, after having told about the rejoicing of the friars and the city people and having minutely described the wounds in the hands, feet, and side, he added: "We who tell about these things have seen them (the stigmata) with our own eyes, have touched them with the hands with which we write; we have bathed with our tears what we testify to with our lips and shall continue forever to affirm, as long as we shall live, what we have already sworn to on the most sacred Gospels. Many friars with us have had, as we have had, the good fortune to verify what we tell here while the Saint was still alive; and another fifty of them, together with many lay persons, had the opportunity of seeing him and venerating him on the occasion of his death." *(3 Cel., 5.)* [Trans., Franciscan Liturgy Projects, *Roman-Franciscan Lectionary.*]

The rule monastic he reforms,
Unto the law of Christ conforms,
And all the Apostolic forms
    He holds inviolate.

What had been the life of The Friar Minor? A poor cord, a coarse untrimmed habit. To live on a little bread, to walk on bare feet.

In raiment coarse and rough endued,
A cord his only cincture rude,
Scanty the measure of his food,
    His feet withal unshod.
For poverty alone he yearns,
From earthly things he loathing turns,
The noble Francis money spurns,
    Despising all for God. . . .

But this poverty of earthly things was changed into the highest triumph the day that Christ placed his seal upon him:

Then Seraph-like in heaven's height
The King of kings appears in sight,
The patriarch, in sore affright,
    Beholds the vision dread.
It bears the wounds of Christ, and lo,
While gazing on in speechless woe,
It marks him, and the stigmata show
    Upon his flesh, blood-red.

The song filled the great forest, where the resin torches crackled. There were more lights burning along the side of the mountain. They were multiplied in all the castles and villages as news of the miracle was proclaimed: the dead saint bore the marks of the crucifixion. He had wounds in his hands and his feet, his side was pierced. And in these five wounds the blood was still continuing to flow.

His body, like the Crucified,
Is signed on hands and feet; his side
Transfixed from right to left, and dyed
    With crimson streams of blood.
Unto his mind words secret sound,

> Things future all in light abound,
> Inspired from on high, the saint has found
> Their sense, and understood. . . .

The city had acquired an inestimable treasure, and steps had to be taken at once to guard it from the rapacity of envious and powerful neighbours.

The companies of the guilds came. The *connestabile* put sentinels at all the roads leading out. The podestà, Berlingerio di Iacopo of Florence, and the *camerario* thought, with Brother Elias, that it would be best to hurry along arrangements to carry the body to Assisi.

It was now already dawn. White light touched the flowers, now stretched to the morning dew. The little creatures of forest and mountain kept watch for the sun.

The coffin appeared on the doorstep of the hut. All the standard-bearers at once unfurled their resplendent flags. The prophecy of the brother who, in the bishop's house in Assisi, had seen many silken cloths unfurled and waving over Francis's sackcloth-clad body had come true.

The trumpets gave the signal. The procession got underway: the clerics in their surplices, the friars, the armed companies, the workmen, the knights, the magistrates, the great crowd of people waving olive branches.[52] The silvery leaves glistened, fluttered, moved like a forest in the air, above the multicoloured mantles, the white ermines. Stronger than the trumpets rose the glorious hymn sung by rank upon rank of friars, dominating all else:

> O father holy, father sweet,
> Devoutly we thine aid entreat,
> May we and all thy brethren meet,
>   Victorious in the strife.
> In virtue's way our footsteps train,
> And bring us with the saints to reign,
> So may thy flock of children gain
>   The joys of endless life.

The priests responded with their song: "Arise, Jerusalem, rise clothed in light; your light has come and the glory of the Lord shines over you." Assisi, "the new Jerusalem," took light from the growing light.

The sun's first ray broke over the summit of Mount Subasio. And at once, as if touched by a magic wand, the city lying along the hill sparkled and shimmered against its light. O *novissimo Oriente!*[53]

When the procession had reached the Ospedale di San Salvatore, it turned along the Strada Francesca and climbed the road of San Damiano. Francis's promise to Clare had to be kept.

And in this way the repairer of the house of Christ went for a last time to the little church where he had heard an anguished plea from a cross.

The little window through which the sisters took communion was opened and the open coffin was placed before it.[54] Alas, that he was returning "being borne by a few who was accustomed to bear many."[55] Alas, that lifeless lay the man who had drawn all the world to him!

The description of the grief of Clare and her sisters is perhaps the finest page written by Thomas of Celano. With moving fidelity, he records what he saw and heard, faithfully repeating their laments and their prayers and their outbursts of weeping.

"Father, Father, what shall we do?

"Why do you forsake us in our misery, or to whom do you leave us who are so desolate?

"Why did you not send us rejoicing ahead of you to the place where you are going, us whom you leave here in sorrow?

"What do you bid us do, enclosed in our cells, us whom you will never again visit as you used to?

"All our consolation departs with you and no solace like it remains to us, buried to the world.

"Who will comfort us in our great poverty no less of merit than of goods?

"O Father of the poor, lover of poverty!

"Who will strengthen us in temptation, O you who experienced innumerable temptations and who knew how to overcome them?

"Who will console us in our trials, O you who were our helper in troubles?"[56]

Faced with that inconceivable separation, even the happiness of their life was forgotten in sorrow over the coming loneliness. Those who kissed his cold hand felt how cold is the reality of death. He had come back and he had gone away forever. In his invisible journey, would they ever be able to catch up with him?

"O most bitter separation!

"O cruel farewell!

"O most dreadful death! It also slays thousands of sons and

daughters bereft of so great a father! It is taking away beyond recall the one upon whom we depended for the success of our own efforts!"[57]

This inconsolable weeping remains the real and bitter grief expressed at the bier of Saint Francis. Even the city people now wept, overcome by the lamentations rising into the Sunday sky.

Then the procession got underway again, to climb upward amid the olive trees on its way to the city. It reached the top of the Assisi hill. In exultation it marched through the part of the city called the *borgo folignate.* It then went in a jubilation of trumpets and songs and festive bells to San Giorgio, the church chosen as Francis's temporary burial place. There the cathedral canons of San Rufino were filing outside, carrying burning torches, to receive the precious body.[58]

On high burned the triumphant sun, flooding sky and earth with exultant splendour.

Notes

Chapter 1

THE WORLD OF SAINT FRANCIS: LORDS AND SERFS

1. "Liber Historiarum," p. 78. 1339. About this work: see Sbaralea, *Supplementum ad Scriptores,* "Trium Ordinum S. Francisci," p. 57; Ehrle, "Notizie sui manoscritti," *Misc. Franc.* 2:21–26; Alessandri and Mazzatinti, *Inventario dei manoscritti;* Alessandri, *Inventario dell'antica biblioteca di S. Francesco,* pp. 184–90; Golubovich, *Biblioteca,* 2:116–37.

A study of Assisi records leads us to believe that Fra (Brother) Elemosina, who is thought to be the author, was the son of Giacomo "di porta Sancti Iacobi de Asisio." He was also a neighbour and probably a relative of the Fra Nicola mentioned in *Liber exemplorum,* 116, *Antonianum* 2:262–63. Elemosina had a brother, Pietruccio, who was also a friar. Both entered the order after 1311, since a record of a sale of property of that date, found in the archives of the Sacro Convento, bears their names and also that of their father. For further details about his family: *NV* 2:70–72.

2. *PL* 77: col. 769.

3. For details of this conquest and for stories of the Carolingians in Assisi territory: Cristofani, *Storie di Assisi,* pp. 41–43; Catalano, *Il romanzo,* pp. 16 ff.; Fortini, *Assisi nel medioevo,* pp. 11–12.

4. On the historical foundation of the belief that the world would come to an end at the end of the tenth century, see Fortini, *Assisi nel medioevo,* pp. 2–5.

5. Arch. Cath., fasc. 1, no. 6; *NV* 3:240. For a lengthy further description and minute analysis of this document, Fortini, *Assisi nel medioevo,* pp. 1–27; idem. "Nuovi documenti," *Atti del 1° congresso internazionale di studi longobardi,* pp. 317 ff.

6. It is certain that in Assisi territory, which was a part of the powerful duchy of Spoleto, a large Lombardian population survived for a long time, alongside the Roman element. It was authentically maintained by tradition and by law. Fortini, *Assisi nel medioevo,* p. 25, n. 24; p. 26, nn. 30, 31, 32; Volpe, *Lombardi e romani (Studi Storici,* vols. 13 and 14).

7. For a complete description of the *castelli* and the *contado* of Assisi, *NV* 3:67–147.

8. Assisi is located on a spur of Mount Subasio. For a description of the mountain, the administrative units into which it was divided, its history, and a discussion of the present reforestation project being carried out on it, *NV* 3:147–71.

9. For additional information about Arce, *NV* 2:306, 311–14; the Ospedale dell'Arce (also known as San Lazzaro and, in a later century, Santa Maria Maddalena), *NV* 2:257–66; Bassiano, *NV* 2:110, 151; and the tower or fortress of San Savino, *NV* 2:147, 153, 155.

10. Arch. Cath., fasc. 1, no. 2; *NV* 3:239. Ermenaldo, whose name appears on a document of the year 963 A.D., is the first count mentioned in the records.

11. Arch. Cath., fasc. 2, no. 9; *NV* 3:269.

12. Arch. Cath., fasc. 2, nos. 55, 56; *NV* 3:278.

13. About Baldovino d'Armoiaffo, *NV* 2:188–89; Tancredi di Ugone di Tebalduccio, *NV* 2:290–92; Tancredi di Alberico, *NV* 2:295–96, Tancredi di Pietro Girardone, *NV* 2:323–24; Tancredi di Limigiano, *NV* 2:387.

14. Solmi, *Sulla storia economica;* Leicht, *La "curtis";* Pivano, *Sistema curtense.*

15. Arch. Cath., fasc. 2, nos. 13 and 51; *NV* 3:269, 277.

16. Gautier, *La Chevalerie;* Parducci, *Costumi ornati.*

17. *Fioretti,* 37.

18. *Per.,* 72; *Spec. Perf.,* 4.

19. *Spec. Perf.,* 72; *Per.,* 71.

20. *Liber Historiarum,* c. 67 r.–75.

21. Loccatelli Paolucci, *Illustrazione dell'antica Badìa,* p. 14.

22. *NV* 3:166.

23. For the history of this monastery, *NV* 2:267–69.

24. Arch. Cath., fasc. 1, no. 83; *NV* 3:254.

25. About this question, see *NV* 2:266–72.

26. Saint Victorinus, reported in some accounts to be a native of Assisi and in others of Assyria, was martyred in Assisi by the Romans in the third century. For more information about him, Fortini, *Assisi nel medioevo,* pp. 47–48.

27. Ancajani, *Del Martire S. Vittorino,* pp. 23, 24, 26.

28. For a description of the company that re-enacted the martyrdom of Saint Victorinus, see chap. 4 of this volume and *NV* 2:119–21.

29. For San Donato di Flebulle, *NV* 3:137–38; San Paolo delle Abbadesse, *NV* 2:388–96; Saint'Apollinare, *NV* 2:392–94; Santa Maria degli Episcopi, *NV* 3:138; Sant'Annessa, *NV* 3:137; Santa Croce del Ponte dei Galli, *NV* 3:135; Sant'Angelo di Panzo, *NV* 2:396–402; San Bartolomeo di Correggiano, *NV* 2:337–39; San Giovanni di Beviglie, *NV* 3:118, 166.

30. Giorgi and Balzani, eds., *Regesto di Farfa.*

31. Arch. Cath., fasc. 1, no. 114; *NV* 3:262.

32. For the very important church of San Giacomo of Assisi, *NV* 3:60–63.

33. For San Masseo: *NV* 3:83–84.

34. For San Nicolò di Campolungo, *NV* 3:130–31; San Benedetto of Satriano, *NV* 2:468–69.

35. For detailed information about the *vescovado* and church: *NV* 2:233–37; 3:24–26.

36. *Chronicon Marcellini Comitis (MGH, Auctores antiquissimi,* vol. 11).

37. In the Council of 649 Aquilino signed himself *Aquilinus Sanctae Asisinatis ecclesiae* (Mansi, *Sacrorum Conciliorum,* 10: col. 1166). For Bishop Magione, cf. *MGH, Leges,* section 3, *Concilia Aevi Carolini,* 2.

38. Arch. Cath., fasc. 1, no. 2; *NV* 3:240.

39. Di Costanzo, *Disamina,* p. 233.
40. Arch. Cath., fasc. 1, no. 4; *NV* 3:239–40.
41. Mochi-Onory, *Ricerche sui poteri.*
42. Arch. Cath., fasc. 7, no. 8; *NV* 3:334–35.
43. Arch. Cath., fasc. 7, no. 1; *NV* 3:333.
44. Arch. Com., B 1-P. A 1; *NV* 3:543–45.
45. Arch. Cath., fasc. 2, no. 10; *NV* 3:269. For the church of Sant'Ansuino, see *NV* 3:27, 28, 30.
46. Arch. Cath., fasc. 2, no. 47; *NV* 3:276–77.
47. Schupfer, *Il diritto privato;* Caggese, *Classi e comuni;* Mayer, *Italienische Verfassungesgeschichte:* Vaccari, *L'emancipazione.*
48. Arch. Cath., fasc. 1, no. 24; *NV* 3:243–44. On manumission *in ecclesia:* de Francisci, "Intorno alle origini," *Rendiconti Istituto lombardo* 44:619 ff.; Mor, *La manumissio in ecclesia.*
49. Arch. Cath., fasc. 8, nos. 1, 3, 5, 14; *NV* 3:337–38, 340–44, 346–47; cf. *NV* 2:132–36.
50. See above.
51. Arch. Com., M 1, fol. 7; *NV* 3:409–10; 2:132–36.
52. *Sermo de S. Rufino martyre (Petri Damiani . . . opera omnia,* ed. Cajetan, 2:178–84).
53. Arch. Cath., fasc. 1, no. 83; *NV* 3:254.
54. *NV* 3:47–48.
55. *NV* 3:104.
56. *NV* 3:36.
57. *NV* 3:38.
58. *1 Cel.* 55.
59. Arch. Cath., fasc. 1, no. 22; *NV* 3:242–43.
60. Arch. Com., M 1; reprinted in full, *NV* 3:556–59.
61. Arch. Cath., fasc. 1, no. 68; *NV* 3:251.
62. On the fairs of Champagne, Roon-Bassermann, *Die Champagnermessen;* Alengry, *Les foires de Champagne;* Bourquelet, *Études sur les foires;* Carabellese, "Un nuovo libro," *Archiv. Stor. Ital.,* 13:357–63; Huvelin, *Essai historique;* Schaube, *Storia del commercio;* Franchini, *Gli Italiani alle fiere;* Davidsohn, *Geschichte von Florenz,* 4:391 ff.; Doren, *Storia economica,* pp. 355 ff.
63. On these "French cloths" *(panni franceschi),* see Davidsohn, *Geschichte von Florenz,* 4:391 ff. He writes that the Italian merchants joined together to go in caravans to the Champagne fairs, and there "sought cloths of the most diverse qualities, to which the major time of the fair *(foire de draps)* was devoted. The types sought were French cloths, those of Champagne itself and of other regions in the south and central part of France; but the cloths prized above all were those of Flanders and of northern France."

The division of the cloth merchants into *tagliaroli* and *franciaroli* is to be found in regulations governing the sale of cloth in Rome. See Gatti, *Statuti dei mercanti;* Stevenson, *Statuti delle arti;* and Doren, *Storia economica,* pp. 248 ff.

Even before the year 1000 the people of Lucca were reproved for wearing "clothes made with foreign wools and according to the French style." See Conte di Valdagno (Marzotto), *Il centenario di un lanificio,* p. 172. This volume contains much valuable information about Italian merchants.

64. In the rare edition of *Fioretti* discovered in 1495 in Milan by Ulderico Zeinzenzeler, the compiler writes (in the second "little flower," "How Saint Francis was

born and baptized") that Francis's father was *messer Pietro de li più nobili de la città da Sisi et de li più ricchi merchandanti di Thoscana* ("Messire Pietro, one of the noblest of the city of Assisi and one of the richest merchants of Tuscany").

65. See the bibliography in n. 60; also Boutiot, *Histoire de Troyes*.

66. Henri d'Avranches, *Leg. Vers. (AF* 10:408). Of Francis's parents, he writes:

> *Mater honesta fuit pueri; pater institor; illa*
> *Simplex et clemens, hic subdolus et violentus.*

The boy's mother was virtuous; his father, a huckster. She was upright and kind; he, deceitful and violent.

And he continues, in a description of the trade that Pietro wished to teach his son (p. 409):

> *Iamque rudimento patris corruptus avari*
> *Iam lucri momenta sequens; iam fallere doctus*
> *Merces multiplicat, multos circumvenit, alte*
> *Se gerit, illecebris intendit, tempora perdit.*

Already corrupted by the training of his avaricious father, already following the money-changers, already having been taught to deceive, he makes a great deal of money. Surrounded by companions, he adopts a lofty manner, seeks diversions, and wastes his time.

In *3 Soc.,* 2, we read that Pietro Bernardone was "absorbed in making money."

67. Saint Gregory of Tours, *Liber in gloria Martyrum (MGH, Scriptores,* vol. 1).

68. The Codex of the Museo dell'opera del Duomo of Perugia and the Codex of the Chiesa Collegiata di San Lorenzo of Spello. On these, cf. Faloci-Pulignani, *La "passio Sancti Feliciani";* Brunacci, "Leggende e culto di S. Rufino," *DPSU* 45:5–91.

Only a fragment of the Spello codex survives, but descriptions of the complete codex from earlier centuries are in existence. The passages summarized or quoted in the text are from the Perugia codex, which is reprinted in full in the article by Brunacci, pp. 81–88.—Trans.

69. Cf. Fortini, *Assisi nel medioevo,* pp. 29–77.

Chapter 2

THE WORLD OF SAINT FRANCIS: WARRIORS AND MERCHANTS

1. Arch. Cath., fasc. 1, nos. 30, 36, 44–46; fasc. 7, no. 5; *NV* 3:244–57, 333–34.

2. Edict of Astolfo of 750 A.D. (*MGH, Leges,* vol. 4).

3. *RIS,* vol. 3. Also see Mabillon, *Acta Sanctorum O.S.B.,* vol. 2, in which the author, in a note to the life of this pope, points out that the passage *Hugonis scilicet de Cisa Urbe Italorum* should read *de Asisa urbe,* since no diocese of Cisa exists in Italy.

4. Over the years a number of persons have given lengthy explanations of the figures on the sarcophagus; among them, Spader, *Assisiensis ecclesiae,* pp. 32–33; Elisei, "Illustrazione di un sarcofago," *Atti dell'Accademia Properziana,* 1:33–49; Paoletti, *Materiali archeologi nelle chiesa . . . San Rufino.* See also Fortini, "Storia di un'Arca," *Lettura,* May 1942, p. 370; idem., *Assisi nel Medioevo,* pp. 52–57.

Professor Paoletti sets forth in detail the chronological, technical, and artistic aspects of the sarcophagus and compares it to others decorated with the myth of Selene and Endymion, a widely used theme in the imperial funerary art of the third century. She puts the date of the San Rufino sarcophagus at 206 A.D.

5. As to what happened to the sarcophagus after Ugone: Bishop Spader (*Assisiensis ecclesiae,* pp. 33, 38) attested (in 1715) that the sarcophagus about which Saint Pier Damiani wrote is the same one that stands today in the crypt of the cathedral. In his time, it was, however, in the high altar. The identity of Saint Pier Damiani's *labrum lapideum* and the pagan sarcophagus in the altar were then well-known; and, in fact, it was during this period that the figure of Saint Rufinus, lying as in death, was painted on the back of the sarcophagus, as one sees it today.

Cesare Orlandi (*Delle città d'Italia,* 2:36) says that the sarcophagus was first found in the ancient Foro Sessoriano, today Piazza Nuova (at the rear of the cathedral). It is an assertion difficult to understand, since he wrote fifty-seven years after Spader, when Saint Pier Damiani's account was common knowledge, while his own version was quite unknown. In fact, the account of Saint Pier Damiani was common knowledge in 1585, when the cathedral was substantially altered by Galeazzo Alessi. For five and one-half centuries earlier than that, the sarcophagus had never left the Assisi cathedral.

Di Costanzo (*Disamina*), accepted Saint Pier Damiani's identification of the sarcophagus without discussion in 1797, twenty-five years after Orlandi's work appeared. He said, "This sarcophagus, which is to be seen even today under the high altar of the cathedral, is pagan, and on the lower part is a relief of the fable of the sleeping Endymion surprised by Luna. It seemed to us, when we saw it the first time, an indecent thing that a fable so obscene should be placed before the eyes of the faithful in that holy place; but, then, remembering the ancient use of the sarcophagus for the ashes of Saint Rufinus and the history of the miracles worked by God through it, we put aside scruples about it." It should be noted that Di Costanzo was particularly well-versed in the study of the Roman antiquities of Assisi, so much so that in this same book he included a chapter on "Ancient Roman Inscriptions" (pp. 443–528).

It should be noted that not one of the many scholars who have studied the Roman antiquities of Assisi from the sixteenth century to today have given us Orlandi's version of the finding of the sarcophagus, which must have been derived from the fact that on Piazza Nuova an ancient Roman sepulchre still stands, popularly called the *torrione.*

From Elisei (p. 35) we know that the sarcophagus was moved from the place where Spader and Di Costanzo saw it. "From persons of greater age than I," he writes, "I have ascertained that it was earlier set into the wall of the chapter house, over the main entrance, the capitulars about that time having had the façade set back and altered. Not long afterward it was taken to the foot of the passageway that leads to the large sacristy, near the door toward the little stairways. Later, with wiser counsel, it was placed under the table of the altar of the aforesaid sacristy. Finally, on September 24, 1895, through the efforts of this writer, with due permission of the chapter, it was taken again to the surviving subterranean portion of the Ugonian church, never to be taken away again, it is to be hoped."

6. For a description of the cistern, which may be visited today, *NV* 3:35. Also cf. Fortini, *Il più ardente poetà,* p. 66.

7. Pellini, *Historia di Perugia,* 1:161.

8. *Purgatorio,* Canto 5, lines 85–131. Buonconte, son of Guido da Montefeltro,

was a leader of the Ghibellines at the battle of Campaldino, in which Florence led a Guelph Tuscan league against Ghibelline cities. The Ghibellines were utterly defeated. Dante is thought to have seen military service in this battle.—Trans.

9. *Inferno,* Canto 33, line 79.

10. Bonaini, Fabretti, Polidori, "Bonifacii Veronensis," *Arch. Stor. Ital.* 16:1–52.

11. For the details and the historical sources of this war, see Fortini, *Assisi nel medioevo,* p. 199.

12. *Paradiso,* Canto 11, lines 43–44. The "holy bishop" is Saint Ubaldo of Gubbio (1084–1160 A.D.); the hill is Monte Ingino.

13. "Diario del Graziano," ed. Bonaini, Fabretti, Polidori, "Cronache inedite," *Arch. Stor. Ital.* 16, pt. 1:165.

14. Ibid., pp. 110–13.

15. Fortini, *Assisi nel medioevo,* p. 299.

16. Carattoli, Guardabassi, Rossi-Scotti, "Descrizione del Santuario," *DPSU* 28:126, 247.

17. *Paradiso,* Canto 11, lines 46–48.

18. Fortini, *Assisi nel medioevo,* p. 279.

19. *Arch. Stor. Ital.,* 16, pt. 1:520, 521–22.

20. Fortini, *Assisi nel medioevo,* pp. 263–87.

21. Ibid., pp. 451–79.

22. Ibid., pp. 521–84.

23. Arch. S. Conv., Istromenti, vol. 2, no. 33; reprinted in full, *NV* 3:474–76.

24. Arch. Cath., fasc. 1, nos. 63, 70; fasc. 7, no. 7; *NV* 3:250, 270, 334.

25. Arch. Cath., fasc. 7, no. 8; *NV* 3:334–35.

26. Arch. Cath., fasc. 7, no. 9; fasc. 1, no. 83; *NV* 3:335, 254.

27. Necrology of Fonte Avellana.

28. Arch. Com., M 1, fol. 2; reprint of text in full, *NV* 3:535–36.

29. Arch. Cath., fasc. 2, no. 85; *NV* 3:284.

30. For further information about the members of this consortium, *NV* 2:317–24.

31. For detailed information about this family, *NV* 2:157–59.

32. This is within the *contrada* of Perlici, known in medieval times as Parlascio. Overlooking the beautiful Tescio valley, it includes some of the most ancient structures, including Roman remains, in the city. For history and description, *NV* 3:47–53.

33. *NV* 3:34–52; 54–60.

34. *NV* 3:54, 60–65.

35. *NV* 2:42.

36. Arch. Cath., fasc. 7, no. 10; *NV* 3:533–34.

37. About these ancient consortiums, see Arch. Cath. from 1052–1101 A.D.: fasc. 1, nos. 46, 52, 79, 85, 100, 105, 108, 115, 130; fasc. 2, nos. 1, 20, 41; *NV* 3:247, 248, 253, 254–55, 258, 259, 262, 265, 271, 275; for general information, *NV* 3:44.

38. Arch. Cath., fasc. 8, no. 49; *NV* 3:357.

39. Arch. Cath., fasc. 2, no. 98; *NV* 3:534–35.

40. For information about the family, *NV* 2:317–18.

41. *NV* 2:318–20.

42. *NV* 2:317, 324–29, 349.

43. *NV* 2:320–22.

44. Fortini, *Il piu ardente poetà d'amore,* p. 97. Cf. also *NV* 3:45–46.

45. Arch. Cath., fasc. 2, no. 104; *NV* 3:44–45, 288.

46. Otto of Freising, *Gesta Friderici Imperatoris,* bk. 2, chap. 13 (*MGH, Scriptores,* vol. 20).

47. See note 28 of this chapter.

48. For information about these ancient boundaries of the *Comitatus Asisinatum, NV* 3:67–70; 535–36. The limits of the territory in that time appear to have been marked with stones; the "Pietra scritta" (stone with inscription) was apparently one of these. The area where it stood is called Pietra scritta even today by the country people.

49. Three documents of Pavia of the years 914, 989, and 1014 A.D. record lands located *in campania papiensis urbis* (Muratori, *Antiquitates italicae,* Dissertatione VIII). A Piacenza record of 1085 A.D. mentions a council in *campanea civitatis (Cronaca piacentina).* In Brescia some years earlier the same term of *Campanea* appears in the records. In Verona the *campanea comunis Veronae* extended to Sommacampagna and to Villafranca, and its public character is made clear in the records, where the *communem campaniam Veronae* is distinct from *ab allodiis* (Ughelli, *Italia sacra,* 5: col. 712, 1178 A.D. On the *vocabolo* Campagna in the *comitato* of Assisi: see *NV* 2:102–3.

50. Arch. Cath., fasc. 2, no. 114; *NV* 3:537. This will have a special importance in understanding an episode in the life of Saint Francis.

51. Ferrari, *Storia delle rivoluzioni,* 2:103.

52. *Cafari et continuarium* (*RIS,* vol. 6).

53. Romualdo, archbishop of Salerno, *Annales* (*RIS,* vol. 7).

54. Arch. Cath., fasc. 8, no. 14; *NV* 3:346–47.

55. Arch. Cath., fasc. 8, nos. 1, 14; *NV* 3:337–38, 346–47.

56. Salvioli, *Annali bolognesi,* 2:28.

57. *Buncompagni Liber de Obsidione Anconae* (*RIS,* vol. 6).

58. Albert of Stade, *Annales,* 1173 A.D. (MGH, *Scriptores,* vol. 16). Cf. Varrentrapp, *Erzbischof Christian I von Mainz.*

59. For the exact description of the first Rocca Maggiore, *NV* 3:53–54.

60. Vollmers-Schulte, *Summa magistri Rufini;* Singer, *Einige Bemerkungen;* idem., *Die Summa decretorum.* Rufinus was at the Lateran Council of 1179, where he signed himself *Rufinus Asisinas.* Mansi, *Sacrorum Conciliorum,* 2: col. 69.

61. Arch. Cath., fasc. 1, no. 129 (1177 A.D.), no. 131 (1179), no. 135 (1182), no. 136 (1182); *NV* 3:292, 293, 294.

62. Arch. Cath., fasc. 2, nos. 129, 130, 131; *NV* 3:292–93.

63. *Annales Casinenses, MGH, Scriptores,* vol. 19.

64. Arch. Cath., fasc. 8, no. 44; *NV* 3:356.

65. See note 64.

66. Arch. Cath., fasc. 2, no. 136; *NV* 3:294.

67. Arch. Cath., fasc. 8, no. 32; *NV* 3:352.

Chapter 3

THE YOUNG YEARS

1. Salverte, *Essai historique;* Trauzzi, *Attraverso l'onomastica.*

2. Propertius, *Elegiarum,* 4. 1. 125–26. Trans. Highet, *Poets in a Landscape,* p. 76. For a lengthy description of these ancient city walls, see Fortini, *Il più ardente poeta d'amore,* pp. 7 ff.

3. Orza, *Gualtieri III;* Bourgeois, *Histoire des comtes de Brienne;* de Sassenay, *Les*

Briennes; Arbois de Jubainville, "Catalogue d'actes," *Bibliothèque de l'École des Chartres* 33:141–86.

4. *NV* 3:10, 32.

5. For records identifying Giovanni di Sasso: *NV* 2:43, 157, 396.

6. For Guido: *NV* 3:58, 236, 368; cf. Fortini, *Assisi nel medioevo,* p. 66.

7. *NV* 3:29–30.

8. Jacobus de Varagine, *Legenda aurea.*

9. For these details, all authentic: *NV* 3:32–33.

10. *NV* 2:80.

11. *Decret. Gregorii IX,* bk. 3, title 1, chap. 12, in *Corpus iuris canonici: Ludi theatrales etiam praetextu consuetudinis in ecclesiis vel per clericos fieri non debent* ("Theatrical games must not be performed in churches or by priests, even under the pretext of custom"). Sicard, bishop of Cremona, after having written about the December liberties, adds that they were forbidden: "Mockers changed a praiseworthy institution into wantonness and devoted themselves to obscene songs, dances, and fornication." *Mitrale (PL* 213: col. 214).

12. S. Bonifatii, *Epist.* 49, 742 A.D. *(PL* 89: col. 74).

13. De Bartholomaeis, *Origini della poesia,* pp. 184–86, 496–99. Fra Salimbene recites some of the verses in his *Cronica,* in expressing disapproval of the founder of a religious sect in Parma, Gerardo Segalleli.

14. *Ordinarium* of Padua, chaps. 38 a, 51 a, 51 b, 52 b. See de Bartholomaeis, as above, pp. 181–82.

15. Seneca, *Ad Lucilium,* VI, 8, 1.

16. *1 Cel.* 1 and 2.

17. *NV* 2:43–52.

18. Caggese, *Dal concordato di Worms,* pp. 66–67; Weiland, *Constitutiones (MGH, Constitutiones,* 1:293–95, 408–20); Manresi, *Atti del Comune di Milano.*

19. Arch. Cath., fasc. 8, no. 39; reprinted in full, *NV* 3:539–40; see also *NV* 2:466.

20. Arch. Cath., fasc. 2, nos. 149, 153, 154; *NV* 3:297–98.

21. Pardi, "Dal Comune alla signoria," *DPSU* 13:397–454; Fumi, "L'assedio di Enrico VI," *DPSU* 22:205–16; Riccardo di San Germano, *Chronica (RIS* 7:276).

22. Arch. Cath., fasc. 2, no. 143; *NV* 3:296.

23. Caggese, *Dal concordato di Worms,* pp. 72–74; *Annales Casinense (MGH, Scriptores,* vol. 19); *Continuatio Acquicinesina (MGH, Scriptores,* vol. 7).

24. *An. Min.,* "Apparatus," chap. III, 3.

25. Michaud, *Histoire des croisades;* Wilken, *Geschichte der Kreuzzuge;* Brehier, *L'Église et l'Orient;* Cognasso, *Le genesi delle Crociate.*

26. This psalm was among the prayers said in Assisi in the time of Saint Francis for the liberation of Jerusalem. Cf. Fortini, *Celebrazione della difesa,* pp. 46 ff.; idem., *Gli ultimi crociati,* pp. 11 ff.

27. Fischer, *Geschichte des Kreuzzugs.*

28. Caggese, *Dal concordato di Worms,* p. 80.

29. Arch. Cath., fasc. 8, no. 4; *NV* 3:341–42.

30. *NV* 3:36–37.

31. *NV* 2:133–34.

32. Arch. Cath., fasc. 2, no. 149; *NV* 3:296. In this 1193 record, one of the witnesses is called *Petrus Johannis Muscacervelli.*

33. Arch. Cath., fasc. 8, no. 39; *NV* 3:539–40.

34. *3 Soc.,* 1. See also *Leg. Maior,* I, 1.

35. From the fourteenth century articles of association of the Arte di Calimala (Guild of Wool Finishers) of Florence.

36. For a description of this ceremony, Fortini, *Assisi nel Medioevo,* pp. 68–69.

37. *Leg. Maior,* I, 1.

38. *1 Cel.,* 2; *3 Soc.,* 1.

39. Giordano, *Chronica,* 10.

40. *3 Soc.,* 1; *2 Cel.,* 3.

41. *Leg. Maior,* I, 1; *1 Cel.,* 17.

42. Arch. Cath., fasc. 2, no. 139; *NV* 3:295.

43. Arch. Cath., fasc. 3, no. 4; *NV* 3:301.

44. *3 Soc.,* 2 and 3.

45. There is a reference to this episode in almost all of the earliest biographies. See *1 Cel.,* 17; *Leg. Maior,* I, 1; *3 Soc.,* 3; *Anon. Per.,* 4.

46. *1 Cel.,* 2.

47. See *3 Soc.,* 21, in which it is said that the San Damiano priest procured special food for Francis because "he knew how delicately he had been brought up, and how in his father's house he had eaten on what was excellent. Francis himself confessed that he would not touch anything that he did not like."

48. Cf. *NV* 2:112.

49. For a discussion of the family wealth, a description of Pietro Bernadone's land and the documents relating to it: *NV* 2:101–12.

50. Arch. Cath., fasc. 2, no. 80; *NV* 3:283.

51. Arch. Cath., fasc. 2, no. 72; *NV* 3:281.

52. *1 Cel.,* 3.

53. Schaube, *Storia del commercio,* Ital. trans. Bonfante; Huvelin, *Essai historique;* Birnie, *Storia economica.*

54. Statutes, Com. Assisi, L. V, r. 85.

55. *NV* 2:147–50, 153–55.

56. *NV* 2:112.

57. Gregorovius, *Storia di Roma,* 2:598.

58. Muratori, *Annali d'Italia,* 1197 A.D.

Chapter 4

WAR WITH PERUGIA

1. Baluze, *Vita Innocentii papae III (RIS* 3:492).

2. Ibid.

3. Arch. Com., Pergama no. 1, B1-A1. Cf. *NV* 3:543–45, where a copy of the Bull is given in full.

4. The pope reconsecrated the high altar of San Lorenzo in Perugia during this month. According to the brief: "Influenced by your entreaties, we accept the state under our protection and that of Saint Peter and we make this secure through this present writing." Bonazzi calls this brief "very famous, as far as we're concerned, since it marks the beginning of the papal era of Perugia." *Storia di Perugia,* 1:254.

5. This is from a letter of Innocent III to the bishop of Assisi in 1199, in which he warns: "unless those excommunicated by you have brought back our letter to you about their absolution or in some legitimate way have established for you the fact of their absolution, you may not believe in their absolution (and) you will, as before,

consider them excommunicated and see that they are shunned." Potthast, *Regesta Pontificum,* 1:77.

6. Arch. Cath., fasc. 2, no. 156; document reprinted in full: *NV* 3:546. About Bernardo di Grasso, *NV* 3:203.

7. Arch. S. Conv., Istr. 1, no. 20; *NV* 3:443. For additional information about Brother Elias: Fortini, *Assisi nel medioevo,* pp. 79–155.

8. Cristofani (*Storie di Assisi,* p. 164) and Bracaloni ("Assisi Medioevale," *AFH* 7:10) also cite this inscription. Their wording of it, however, is incomplete and inexact.

Some years ago the tablet was removed and placed in the city museum; an ugly cement mould was substituted for it. The author, who was mayor of Assisi at the time, was responsible for its being restored to its old place over the ancient city gate in September 1924.

9. About these men: *NV* 2:36, 187, 190.

10. Carducci, "Dello svolgimento della letteratura nazionale" (*Prose,* p. 269).

11. See *NV* 2:136–37.

12. For detailed information about this powerful family and the castle of Sassorosso; *NV* 2:137–46. The castle was rebuilt in 1210, but torn down again in 1244 on orders from the Holy See, because the lords who were living there were judged to be *infideles et inimicii Ecclesiae.*

13. *1 Cel.,* 4.

14. "Brother Leonard of Assisi" is mentioned in *2 Cel.,* 31. Leonardo di Gislerio is the only Leonardo appearing in the records of this period whose rank, social class, and prominence fit the descriptions of the friar in all the reports of the episode: *Per,* 30; *Leg. Maior,* XI, 8; *Leg. Monacensis* (*AF* 10:713). In this last work he is described as a *virum nobilem de Assisio.* See *NV* 2:144–45.

15. For the *signori* of Montemoro: *NV* 2:146–50.

16. For Morico and his sons: *NV* 2:155–56, 282.

17. For the family of Celino del Poggio: *NV* 2:156–57.

18. For these sons of Davino: *NV* 2:146–50.

19. Despite Carsedonio's quarrel with the new commune, he played a large role in city affairs at a later time and was podestà in 1210 and again in 1223. For further information about him, Adinolfo, and Monaldo di Armanno: *NV* 2:153–55.

20. For this rich and valiant family, *NV* 2:151–53. The marble from the palazzo in San Giacomo di Murorotto was given by the sons of Offreduccio, Sanguigno and Tommaso, to Brother Elias for the construction of the Basilica di San Francesco.

21. Ibid.

22. *3 Soc.,* 2.

23. Ibid.

24. Ibid., 3.

25. For detailed discussion and documentation of the existence of the groups and the customs described in this chapter: *NV* 2:113–29. On the *societatis* or companies of the kind to which Saint Francis belonged and the origins of the still-existing Accademia Properziana del Subasio in them, cf. G. Fortini, *La città di poeti,* pp. 7–15.

26. For a history and description of many of these dances: de Bartholomaeis, *Origini della poesia drammatici,* pp. 49–61.

27. *1 Cel.,* 73. See also chap. 12, n. f.

28. *Paradiso,* Canto 10, lines 79–81.

29. *2 Cel.,* 7. Thomas's description of the social banquets, Francis's being chosen leader because he would pay the expenses for all, and the kind of food and drink

served, fit exactly the descriptions of the *compagnia* mentioned in a number of Assisi records. *NV* 2:115–16.

30. *1 Cel.*, 83.

31. *2 Cel.*, 127.

32. The lyrics of the songs in this section are all from Cavaliere, *Cento liriche provenzali.* On the subject of the poetry of Provence, cf. Anglade, *Les troubadours;* Bertoni, *I trovatori d'Italia;* De Bartholomaeis, *Poesie provenzali.* [These songs are those likely to have been sung by Francis and his group; they were widely known. One or two are attributed to troubadours who lived later in the century but surely based on those of still earlier troubadors—so similar are many of them that attribution is often difficult or impossible.—Trans.]

33. Raimbaut de Vaqueiras, *Truan, mala guerra* (Cavaliere, p. 239).

34. Lafranc Cigala, *Un avinen ris vi l'autrier* (Ibid., p. 431).

35. Pistoleta, *Ar agues eu mil marcs de fin* (Ibid., p. 323).

36. Gaucelm Faidet, *Ar hai dreg de chantar* (Ibid., p. 198).

37. Bernart de Ventadorn, *Can vei la leuzeta mover* (Ibid., p. 45). Trans. Smythe, *Trobador Poets,* pp. 34–35.

38. Bertran de Lamanon, *Us cavaliers si iazia* (Cavalier, p. 419).

39. Sordel, *Aitant se plus viu hom quam viu iauzens* (Ibid., p. 404).

40. Folquet (or Falquet) de Romans, *Vers Dieus, el vostre nom e de sancta Maria* (Ibid., p. 312).

41. Perceval Doria, *Felon cor ai et enic* (Ibid., p. 443).

42. Bertran de Born, *Be · m platz lo gais temps de pascor* (Ibid., pp. 115–17). Translation by Taylor, *Minnesingers,* p. 233.

43. Bull fights are mentioned in records of a similar group in Perugia; also, in the seventeenth century the Bollandist fathers Henschenius and Papebrochius, while in Assisi, noted that young men were running through the piazza after a bull. See Battistini, "I Padri Bollandisti," *Studi Francescani* 27:164–65; *NV* 2:126.

44. Orza, *Gualtieri III,* p. 35; Collenuccio, *Compendio,* p. 891.

45. Giannettasio, *Historiae Neapolitanae,* 1:329–30.

46. de Sassenay, *Les Briennes,* pp. 31–32; Krass, *Storia de Lecce,* p. 153.

47. Krass, *Storia di Lecce,* p. 153.

48. Michaud, *Storia delle crociate,* 11:79.

49. Ibid., 12:110.

50. Carducci, *Jaufre Rudel (Opere,* 10:245); Jeanroy, *Chansons de Jaufre Rudel.* In the song *Lanquan li iorn,* the line *Amor de lonh* is repeated after each stanza.

51. Jacopus de Varagine, *Vita S. Francisci* (AF 10:681).

52. For the archival records that concern this war and information about the noble families affected, *NV* 2:137–61.

53. For this *contrada:* NV 2:146, 147, 149, 151, 152, 155, 160.

54. Brizi, "Mura pelasgiche," *Atti Accademia Properziana,* 2:269–74.

55. Arch. Cath., fasc. 8, no. 18; *NV* 3:348–49.

56. Leccisotti and Tabarelli, *Le carte,* For the counts of Collemezzo (or Coldimezzo): *NV* 2:406–15.

57. For details of this submission: *NV* 2:139–41.

58. For a description of similar tactics practiced by Perugia against other cities, and especially Gubbio, and a discussion of the archival records reflecting the use of the tactic against Assisi: *NV* 2:161–65.

59. *NV* 2:165.

60. These lines are the *explicit* of Bonifazio's *Eulistea* (*Arch. stor. ital.* 16:52).

61. Perugia Cod. delle Sottomissioni, c. 29 r. See also *NV* 2:166.

62. For descriptions and genealogies of these families: *NV* 2:146–60.

63. *NV* 2:167. The cities are named in the *Eulistea*.

64. The names of these knights are in quittances given in 1213 and 1215 to the commune of Assisi for money due them for services rendered or horses lost in the war. It was then hard times in Assisi, in which the treasury of the commune was so exhausted that these mounted soldiers could not be immediately paid, despite the fact that most of the city's revenues were devoted to that purpose and an extraordinary tax of two *soldi* per hearth levied to satisfy the obligations. Nevertheless, three years passed before everyone got what was due. In that period, a number of the knights resorted to the right of pillage at the expense of the men of the commune. For information about the knights mentioned here and the others whose names are in the paragraphs that follow: *NV* 2:167–69.

65. For a description of the armed units of the Assisi army, each commanded by a leader called the *vexillifer* or *vessillifero,* and of the armour worn and arms carried, see chap. 2, n. n of this book and *NV* 3:183–87.

66. A document in the Perugia archives of 1203 encouraging Assisani to move to Perugia (Cod. Sottomissioni, 41 r) mentions the names Leonardo, Fortebraccio, and Arlotto di Pilucco, but not Girardo, whose name appeared prominently in earlier records. Nor does he appear again. For this document, *NV* 2:139; for others concerning the castellans and Perugia, p. 140.

67. *2 Cel.,* 37.

68. Ibid.

69. *Per.,* 35; *Spec. Perf.,* 105. This large gathering of the people was undoubtedly for one of the major festivals in which, as has been documented, the knights jousted in the piazza. *NV* 2:121–24.

70. *Per.,* 35; *Spec. Perf.,* 105. Also in *2 Cel.,* 37, there is a note that the knights were executing their usual military games.

71. *Per.,* 35; *Spec. Perf.,* 105.

72. The sentence in *Spec. Perf.* is *Hoc autem dixit quia antiquum odium erat et est inter Perusios et Assisinatos;* in *Per., Hoc autem dixit Beatus Franciscus quia magnum odium fuit inter homines Asisinatos et Perusinos.* The difference in the verbs is important in establishing which of these two texts is the earlier. After the war in which Saint Francis participated, there was not another major conflict between Assisi and Perugia until 1320. In *Per.,* unquestionably the earlier, the hatred is mentioned as something past. In *Spec. Perf.,* however, it is spoken about as a continuing thing, undoubtedly indicative of this source having been written at a later time, when the cities were at odds again. Cf. *NV* 2:13.

73. *2 Cel.,* 37.

74. For a history of the war in Perugia between the nobles and the people that fulfilled the prophecy of Saint Francis: *NV* 2:199–200; 212–14.

75. *2 Cel.,* 37.

76. Cristofani, *Storie di Assisi,* pp. 79–80; Facchinetti, *San Francesco d'Assisi nella storia,* p. 24.

77. Ferrari, *Storia delle rivoluzioni,* 1:546.

78. Doren, *Storia economica,* p. 175, writes: "This is the beginning of the separations of cities and city-states in the struggle for space that is characteristic of Italy in the late Middle Ages. It is a struggle of the large communes against the small, of the large communes among themselves, to take over as much rural territory as possible, to the end not only of enlarging their own power and their status in the world but

also to achieve an economically closed state, at least from the point of view of supplying to the capital all the provisions most necessary. Thus, in the last centuries of the Middle Ages, the Italian city states were at the same time the theatre of the fiercest struggles for power and public wealth and of an intense and splendid cultural life."

79. "The historical records of the epoch give no light at all, limiting themselves to merely recording the various wars between the cities; they are barely able to trace the reasons for some of the battles. One can see that they were fought for fields, villages, *castelli;* and also, as their chroniclers usually put it, they were fought *because of limits.*" Ferrari, *Storia delle rivoluzioni,* 1:511.

80. We can deduce this from the Perugia podestà's ordinance of August 31, 1205, in which he orders that "the Perugia men shall likewise observe a good peace with all Perugini and those of its surrounding land (*comitato*)." Cod. Sottomissioni, c. 18 r.

81. Ferrari, *Storia delle rivoluzioni,* 1:516.

82. Caggese, *Dal concordato di Worms,* p. 88–89.

83. *3 Cel.,* 88–94; *Leg. Maior,* pt. 2, chap. 5.

84. For the sources and documention of Francis's imprisonment: *NV* 2:169–71, 178–79. Bonazzi writes in *Storia di Perugia* (p. 261), "According to tradition, Francis was placed in the prisons of the Campo di Battaglia, under the site on which today stands the Palazzo del Capitano del Popolo."

85. Pagano, *Istoria del Regno,* 2:28.

86. On this battle, cf. *Annales Casinenses (MGH, Scriptores,* vol. 19); Collenuccio, *Compendio dell'Istoria,* 4:90; Riccardo da San Germano, *Chronica (RIS* vol. 7).

87. Orza, *Gualtieri III,* pp. 10, 110.

88. Ibid., p. 126.

89. References to Francis's plan to go to Apulia are to be found in most of the oldest biographies; among them, *1 Cel.,* 4, 7; *2 Cel.,* 6; *3 Soc.,* 5, 6; *Leg. Maior,* I, 3; *Anon. Per.,* 5 and 6. His dream of winning glory and knighthood in Apulia surely indicates a considerable experience and skill in fighting and a mastery of arms. Cf. *NV* 2:183.

90. For the history of this area, and for the noble family that held Rocca Pàida: *NV* 2:430–36, 464–70; see also, in this book, chap. 8, pp. 319–21.

Chapter 5

NOBLE DREAMS

1. Cod. Sottomissioni. See *Arch. Stor. Ital.* 8:138, n. 2.

2. Ibid., c. 22 r. The document is reprinted in its entirety in *NV* 3:554–55.

3. This powerful family first appears in the records in 1110. Marescotto's father, Bernardo, is called "Count" in the record of a sale of land to the Assisi cathedral. *NV* 3:44–46.

4. Arch. Cath., fasc. 8, no. 57; *NV* 3:555–56, for the document bearing their names (a ruling over a local controversy) in its entirety.

5. Arch. Com., M. 1, fol. 1; reprinted in its entirety, *NV* 3:556–59.

6. *1 Cel.,* 3.

7. Cod. Sottomissioni, c. 39 t.; reprinted in its entirety: *NV* 3:559–60.

8. Arch. Com., M. 1, fol. 1; *NV* 3:553.

9. Bonaventure (*Leg. Maior,* I, 2) speaks of a "prolonged illness."

10. *1 Cel.,* 3. In *Leg. Vers. (AF* 10:411) we find a poetic version of this passage, in which we are told that Francis went out to pay a visit to the paternal properties. (For a description of these lands, *NV* 2:111–12.) The land his father owned that was closest to the city, and therefore the easiest for the convalescent to reach, would be that in San Martino d'Argentana.

11. *Leg. Vers. (AF* 10:411).

12. Arch. Cath., fasc. 7, no. 13; *NV* 3:336; also 2:182.

13. Arch. Cath., fasc. 3, no. 9; *NV* 3:552–53.

14. *NV* 2:104.

15. Biniolo di Guiberto is a witness in an 1147 paper in which Guiduccio di Letone makes a pledge to the church of San Giacomo (Arch., Cath., fasc. 2, no. 96; *NV* 3:286). *Gibertus Binioli filius* on May 14, 1193, made a donation of his goods to the church of San Giacomo (fasc. 2, no. 148; *NV* 3:541–42), stipulating, however, a partial revocation in case his son should return. *Philippus Guiberti Binioli filius* became an oblate of the same church in March 1201 (fasc. 3, no. 1; *NV* 3:548).

16. Orza, *Gualtieri III,* pp. 123–74.

17. Krass, *Storia di Lecce,* pp. 156–58, 160. This author writes, "Thus began an extraordinary historical period for the *contea* of Lecce that lasted several centuries and was filled with episodes and personages that seemed straight out of a romantic play." Cf. Foscarini, *Il patriziato Brindisino,* p. 15; de Sassenay, *Les Briennes,* p. 67.

18. Monaci, *Crestomazia italiana,* 1:69.

19. This detail is in *Leg. Vers. (AF* 10:413).

20. Andreas lived in the latter part of the twelfth century and the early part of the thirteenth. His work, entitled *De Amore,* is derived from the lyric poetry of chivalry. It is divided into three books; the second tells of the courts held by the princesses mentioned here. Cf. Rajna, "Tre Studi," *Studi di Filologia Romanza* 5:193–265; *De Amore libri tres,* ed. Trojel; Crescini, "Nuove postille," *Atti del Reale Istituto Veneto* 69:1–99, 473–504. It is impossible that Francis, who knew French lyric poetry inside out, did not know this book.

21. "After love of God, love of the lady was the most sacred ideal of the knight, one that ennobled man, exalted him above himself and made him a hero. . . . The courts of love, the tourneys, the homage that each knight rendered to his lady whose colours he jealously bore, the praises of the lady that are placed above all else in the romantic literature of chivalry—all served to create a feminine ideal, to encompass the lady in a real aureole of gentle graciousness, kindness, and purity, which up to that time she had not had." Salvioli in *Digesto Italiano,* s.v. "Cavalleria."

"Bravura in arms, courage, and love of adventure are essential ingredients of the platonic, romantic, and formalistic cult of being consciously a warrior of Christ and of his Church. Thus, the lady leaves her isolation and becomes an inspiration; the relationship between the sexes tends to acquire a teaching dimension, above all else for the man, the sentiment of feminine gentleness and of the joy of serving the lady disciplining and gentling his warrior roughness and ferocity. Without this attitude—which Ulrico di Liechlenstein said he had learned as a child—none could achieve valour." Calò, in Treccani, s.v. "Cavalleria."

"Love was the highest sentiment of chivalry and the most productive of that enthusiasm that ravished noble souls into high thoughts and good deeds." Carducci, in *Opere,* vol. 10.

22. "One of the first requisites of the courtier was elegant and magnificent dress." *Treccani,* s.v. "Corte." And Salvioli in *Digesto Italiano:* "For its adherents chivalry prescribed shining armour, gold-plated in war, and in the castle silken clothes and furs."

23. *3 Soc., 6; 2 Cel.,* 5; and *Leg. Maior,* I, 3.

24. *NV* 2:104–106.

25. Reports of this vision, a subject also of one of Giotto's frescoes in the Basilica di San Francesco, are in *1 Cel.,* 5; *2 Cel.,* 6; *Leg. Maior,* I, 3; *3 Soc.,* 5; *Anon. Per.* 5. The arms mentioned in the text are specifically named in *Leg. Vers. (AF* 10:413). For a discussion of all these texts: *NV* 2:183–86.

26. This remark of Francis's is reported in *Anon. Per.,* 5. See also *NV* 2:185.

27. The story of Francis's trip is told in *2 Cel.,* 6; *Leg. Maior,* I, 3; *3 Soc.,* 5, 6; and *Anon. Per.* 6. See also *NV* 2:185–86.

28. For additional information about this area: *NV* 2:284–85.

29. On this *passio Sancti Savini,* cf. Fortini, *Assisi nel medioevo,* pp. 35–41.

30. Sabatier, for example, thought that Francis must have, on the way, ascended the peak of Monteluco—a most unlikely route. *Spec. Perf.,* CED, 1:27.

31. Paul the Deacon, *Historia gentis Langobardorum,* bk. 4, chap. 17 (*MGH, Scriptores rerum langobardicarum*).

32. Sources of the entire episode, through Francis's return to Assisi, are *2 Cel.,* 6; *Leg. Maior,* I, 3; *3 Soc.,* 6; *Anon. Per.,* 6, 7. See also *NV* 2:185–86.

33. Galatians 5:14.

34. Acts 9:6.

35. Galatians 5:25–26. Thomas of Celano borrowed the Latin words of this Biblical text to talk about Francis's "worldly glory and vanity" (*1 Cel.,* 4).

36. Orza, *Gualtieri III,* pp. 187 ff.

37. Giovanni de Ceccano, *Chronicon Fossae Novae (RIS,* vol. 1).

38. Sayers, trans., *Song of Roland,* pp. 140–41.

39. Orza, *Gualtieri III,* pp. 211 ff.

40. Descriptions of this gathering are in *2 Cel.,* 7; *3 Soc.,* 7. For a discussion of the sources: *NV* 2:115.

41. One of the earliest albas, the dawn-songs of lovers, author unknown. Cavalier, *Cento liriche provenzale,* pp. 497–98. *Trans. Pound, *Alba Innominata,* in *An Anthology of World Poetry,* ed. Van Doren, p. 660.

42. *3 Soc.,* 7; *2 Cel.,* 7.

Chapter 6

THE HERALD OF THE GREAT KING

1. For further discussion of these events and detailed information about the Assisi exiles who are now returning to their home city: *NV* 2:186–90.

2. *NV* 2:187.

3. *NV* 2:187–88.

4. *1 Cel.,* 6.

5. *Sacrum Commercium,* 5.

6. *1 Cel.,* 7.

7. Ibid.

8. Ibid., 6; *3 Soc.,* 8.

9. Arch. Cath., fasc. 8, nos. 1, 3, 5, 14; *NV* 3:337–38, 340–41, 342–43, 346–47.

10. *3 Soc.,* 8.

11. *2 Cel.,* 8; *3 Soc.,* 10.

12. *2 Cel.,* 8; *3 Soc.,* 10; *Leg. Maior,* I, 6. Many records in Assisi, especially in Arch. Sac. Conv., attest that the custom of making pilgrimages to Rome was practiced widely in Assisi. *NV* 2:221–23.

13. Leo M., *Serm.* 11, no. 2 (*PL* 54: col. 168).
14. John Chrysostom, *De eleemosyna, hom.*, 3, n. 2 (*PG* 49:294).
15. *3 Soc.,* 11; *2 Cel.,* 9.
16. *2 Cel.,* 9; *3 Soc.,* 12.
17. Bédier, *Le Roman de Tristan.*
18. For the lands that Pietro Bernardone owned in this area, *NV* 2:106–11.
19. *2 Cel.,* 9; also *Leg. Maior,* I, 5.
20. Isaiah 53:3–4. [The early biographers all describe the incident in dramatic terms, as if to signify that it marked a major change in Francis.—Trans.]
21. For additional information about this area and the legends associated with it: *NV* 3:85–86.
22. *2 Cel.,* 10; *Leg. Maior,* II, 1; *3 Soc.,* 13. The scarlet is mentioned in *1 Cel.,* 8.
23. *Anon. Per.,* 7.
24. *1 Cel.,* 9; *Leg. Maior,* II, 1; *3 Soc.,* 16.
25. *3 Soc.,* 16; *1 Cel.,* 10. About the families: *NV* 2:46–47, 50–52, 536–42.
26. *Leg. Vers.* (*AF* 10:416).
27. Ibid., p. 420.
28. *1 Cel.,* 11.
29. *1 Cel.,* 11; *Leg. Maior,* II, 2; *3 Soc.,* 17.
30. For information about these families: *NV* 2:43–52.
31. *1 Cel.,* 12; *Leg. Maior,* II, 2; *3 Soc.,* 17.
32. *NV* 2:230–231; *1 Cel.,* 13; *Leg. Maior,* II, 3; *3 Soc.,* 17.
33. *1 Cel.,* 13; *Leg. Maior,* II, 3; *3 Soc.,* 18.
34. *1 Cel.,* 13; *Leg. Maior,* II, 3; *3 Soc.,* 18.
35. *1 Cel.,* 13; *Leg. Maior,* II, 3.
36. Epis. 52, n. 5 (*PL* 22:531). Saint Bonaventure was surely following this same thought when he wrote, "And so the servant of the most high King was left stripped of all that belonged to him, that he might follow the Lord whom he loved, who hung naked on the cross." *Leg. Maior,* II, 4.
37. Sources for the story of the trial in the bishop's court are *1 Cel.,* 14, 15; *Leg. Maior,* II, 4; *3 Soc.,* 19, 20. The procedures followed, the physical setting, and the personages of the court are documented in *NV* 2:232–37. That Francis married Lady Poverty in front of his father in this court is a theme celebrated by (among others) Dante (*Paradiso,* 11, 61–63).
38. The story of Francis's trip to Gubbio and his stay there is told in *1 Cel.,* 16; *Leg. Maior,* II, 5, 6; *Leg. Vers.,* (*AF* 10:428). For additional discussion: *NV* 2:237–56.
39. *Leg. Maior,* II, 5.
40. *1 Cel.,* 15.
41. Cavaliere, *Cento liriche,* p. 315.
42. Arnaut de Maruelh, in Cavalier, *Cento liriche,* p. 129.
43. Cavaliere, *Cento liriche,* pp. 130–31.
44. Thomas of Celano and Bonaventure tell us that Francis went through the woods joyfully singing in French. The passionate prayer given here was included in *Arbor vitae crucifixae* by Ugolino da Casale and was once thought to have been written by Francis himself (Ubaldo d'Alençon, *Les Opuscules,* pp. 267–70). Today, however, it is usually attributed to the author of *Sacrum Commercium,* who was probably Thomas of Celano.
45. For the history of the many battles between Assisi and Perugia in this period, *NV* 2:131–219.
46. *Leg. Maior,* II, 6; *1 Cel.,* 17.

47. *3 Soc.,* 21; *1 Cel.,* 18; *Leg. Maior,* II, 7.
48. *2 Cel.,* 14; *3 Soc.,* 22.
49. *2 Cel.,* 13; *3 Soc.,* 24.
50. *2 Cel.,* 12; *3 Soc.,* 23; *Liber exemplorum (Antonianum* 2:219–20).
51. *2 Cel.,* 12; *3 Soc.,* 23. In *Anon. Per.,* 9, we are given the name of the name of the beggar.
52. *Leg. Maior,* II, 8.
53. *1 Cel.,* 21; *3 Soc.,* 25.
54. Matthew 10:7–14. Thomas of Celano, in his report of the Mass, combines the instructions given in this passage with those of Mark 6:7–12; Luke 9:1–5 and 10:4.

Chapter 7

THE MEN OF PENITENCE OF THE CITY OF ASSISI

1. *Leg. Maior,* III, 5; *Leg. Vers. (AF* 10:502). The dream of the cross of gold but without mention of the dragon is also in *2 Cel.,* 109; *3 Soc.,* 31.
2. Daniel 14:23.
3. *3 Soc.,* 30; *2 Cel.,* 109.
4. *1 Cel.,* 36. Brother Thomas uses the Latin word *regio* in this passage in the medieval sense of *terra*—the core territory of the city, as does Bonaventure in the passage cited in n. 1.
5. For a picture of the abuses in the church of that time, see Sabatier, *Vie,* chap. 3.
6. Arch. Com., A, 1; *NV* 3:543–45.
7. Pressuti, *Regesta Honorii III,* 2:242, no. 4958.
8. This argument and the settlement *post multas altercationes* are recorded in a bull of Gregory IX, the most important part of which is reprinted in Edouard D'Alençon, *L'abbaye de Saint-Benoit,* p. 21. Cf. *NV* 3:165.
9. Bull of January 17, 1222 (Pressuti, *Regesta Honorii III,* 2:33, no. 3739).
10. This detail is in the letter of Innocent III cited in n. 6.
11. Details of the quarrel are to be found in the ruling of the arbiters, Arch. Cath., fasc. 9, no. 1; *NV* 3:592–93. See also the bull issued by Honorius III on March 8, 1217, in which he sanctions and confirms the decisions reached by the two cardinals, *NV* 3:594–95.
12. Arch., Monastery of Sassovivo in Foligno, 1208 A.D.
13. Ibid., 1116 A.D.
14. Arch. Cath., fasc. 2, no. 122, 1170 A.D.; *NV* 3:538.
15. This very ancient custom is mentioned in a cathedral record of May 1074, in which those who have gifts and cannot find any of the canons are instructed to put them on top of the altar of San Rufino. Gifts had to be made to proprietors by those holding properties in emphyteusis. Arch. Cath., fasc. 1, no. 86.
16. See ruling of the consuls on June 13, 1203, Arch. Cath., fasc. 8, no. 57; *NV* 3:555–56.
17. *NV* 2:280.
18. Ibid.
19. Pact of 1203, Arch. Com., M. 1, fol. 1; *NV* 3:556–59.
20. See above. These rules were then common: "When the citizen of a place had been offended in his person or in his things by a citizen of another place or when

he had not been able to achieve from him the fulfillment of whatever obligation, the responsibility fell to the commune. If it did not obtain reparation, it granted the right of retaliation to the petitioner, in virtue of which all that he or others of his town could extort from the debtor, his commune, or his fellow citizen by looting goods and holding persons prisoner was awarded to him in satisfaction of his claims.

"The aforesaid evils, grave enough in themselves, were, moreover, redoubled by the counter reprisals that were often accorded to those who had suffered harm from the first reprisals." Pertile, *Storia del diritto italiano,* 1:256.

21. Ferrari, *Histoire des revolutions d'Italie,* 1:545.
22. Ibid.
23. *Digesto Italiano,* s.v. "Cavalleria."
24. *1 Cel.,* 53; *NV* 2:196–97.
25. Pact between the *maggiori* and the *minori,* Arch. Com., M. 1, fol. 7; *NV* 3:574–78.
26. *NV* 2:192.
27. Ferrari, *Storia delle rivoluzioni,* 2:130.
28. Ibid., p. 131.
29. For a thorough description of the crimes, penalties, and judgements to which the text alludes, see *NV* 3:209–21.
30. *NV* 3:427.
31. Arch. Com., N. 1, fol. 40; *NV* 3:613.
32. Arch. Com., N. 1, fol. 39; *NV* 3:610.
33. *1 Cel.,* 52.
34. Arch. Com., N. 1, fol. 39; *NV* 3:610.
35. Cathedral Lectionary.
36. *Spec. Perf.,* 61; *1 Cel.,* 52.
37. Arch. Com., M. 1, fol. 8; *NV* 3:602–4.
38. These men were witnesses to Bettona's act of submission. See *NV* 3:603.
39. *3 Soc.,* 34.
40. Cathedral Lectionary.
41. This unknown first companion is mentioned in *1 Cel.,* 24. For all the references, documents, and sources specifically referring to Francis's first eleven companions and Silvestro, see *NV* 2:273–306.
42. For Rinaldo: *NV* 3:35, 237. He was a canon of the cathedral from 1211 to 1219 and in 1215 was prior.
43. Cavaliere, *Cento liriche,* p. 6. This is one of the oldest Provençal lyrics, composed by William, count of Poitiers (1071–1127). Eng. trans., Pound, *Personae,* ed. Mauberley, p. 173.
44. *Anon. Per.,* 15.
45. See *NV* 2:191; 3:569. As soon as the emperor renounced his claims to the Papal States, Perugia took up the war again by destroying Valfabbrica, as is revealed in the document in which those living there swear to Perugia that they will never again rebuild the *castello.*
46. For the complete texts of these two documents: *NV* 3:570–73.
47. *Anon. Per.,* 17.
48. *3 Soc.,* 33.
49. See chap. 2, n. n; *NV* 3:185, 186–87.
50. Polidori, *Tavola rotonda,* 2:260–64; Rajna, "Dante e i romanzi," *Nuova Antologia,* June 1, 1920; Zingarelli, "Le reminiscenze del 'Lancelot' " (*Studi Danteschi* 1:65–90); Crescini, "Il bacio di Ginevra" (*Studi Danteschi* 3:5–58).

51. Cf. Fortini, *Il più ardente poeta d'amore,* p. 66.

52. *NV* 2:292.

53. For the documentation of this location and a discussion of the past mistakes made in trying to pinpoint the site, see *NV* 2:306–14.

54. *Leg. Maior,* IV, 3; *1 Cel.,* 42.

55. *Spec. Perf.* 27; *Per.,* 1; *2 Cel.,* 22.

56. *3 Soc.,* 42.

57. Ibid., 44.

58. *1 Cel.,* 32; *Leg. Maior,* III, 8. For this first rule, consult Mandìc, *De protoregula.*

59. *1 Cel.,* 33; *Leg. Maior,* III, 8; *3 Soc.,* 53.

60. *3 Soc.,* 46.

61. *1 Cel.,* 32; *3 Soc.,* 47.

62. *1 Cel.,* 33; *3 Soc.,* 48; *Leg. Maior,* III, 9. On Cardinal John of Saint Paul's, cf. Wenck, "Die römischen Papste," in *Pappstum und Kaisertum,* ed. Kehr, pp. 415–74.

63. On Innocent III, see Luchaire, *Innocent III;* Hurter, *Geschichte des Papstes Innocenz III.*

64. Mariotti, *Saggio di memorie istoriche,* 3:242.

65. *De Contemptu mundi* (PL 217: cols. 702–46).

66. Luchaire, *Innocent III;* Warner, *The Albigensian Heresy.*

67. *3 Soc.,* 49; *Leg. Maior,* III, 9; *2 Cel.,* 16.

68. On the Basilica of St. John Lateran and the Lateran Palace at the time of Innocent III, cf. Oliger, "S. Francesco e il Laterano," *Nel XVI centenario . . . del ss. Salvatore,* 43–46; Lauer, *Le palais de Latran,* p. 193; Huelsen, *Le chiese di Roma.*

69. *Leg. Maior,* III, 9.

70. On this heresy, see Tocco, *L'eresia nel medioevo.*

71. *Leg. Maior,* III, 9.

72. Oliger, "San Francesco e il Laterano."

73. *2 Cel.,* 16, 17; *3 Soc.,* 50; *Leg. Maior,* III, 10.

74. *2 Cel.,* 17; *Leg. Maior,* III, 10; *3 Soc.,* 51.

Chapter 8

"LET THEM BE LESSER BROTHERS"

1. *3 Soc.,* 51; *2 Cel.,* 17; *Leg. Maior,* III, 10.

2. *1 Cel.,* 35.

3. Ibid., 41.

4. Ibid., 23: "He first began to preach where as a child he had first learned to read and where for a time he was buried amid great honour." This author places Saint Francis's preaching at San Giorgio before the conversion of Bernardo di Quintavalle.

5. We limit ourselves to citing the documents reprinted in *NV* 3:546 (1198 A.D.), 560 (1204 A.D.), and 582 (1213 A.D.).

6. *NV* 3:436 (1203 A.D.).

7. *1 Cel.,* 23.

8. *Fioretti,* 27.

9. *Leg. Maior,* IV, 4.

10. Ibid.

11. *1 Cel.,* 83.

12. Ibid., 36.

13. Ibid., 44; *3 Soc.,* 55.

14. *Per.,* 8; *Spec. Perf.,* 55. Records of the time demonstrate that the canons of the cathedral as well as the bishop had a great many churches under their jurisdiction. *NV* 3:97. For the names of the canons, *NV* 3:34–35.

15. *Per.,* 8; *Spec. Perf.,* 55.

16. Francis's words, quoted in *Spec. Perf.,* 55.

17. For more detailed discussion of this period, *NV* 2:192–99.

18. See Cod. Sottomissioni, *Arch. Stor. Ital.* 6:322, n. 2.

19. Caggese, *Dal concordato,* p. 117.

20. This information is taken from a contemporary document from the Archives of the Monastery of Sassovivo, quoted by Jacobilli, *Cronica,* p. 62. Cf. *NV* 2:192.

21. For a more detailed discussion of this subject, *NV* 2:194–99.

22. *1 Cel.,* 38.

23. Ibid.

24. *2 Cel.,* 148; *Leg. Maior,* VI, 5.

25. *Spec. Perf.,* 26.

26. *Fioretti,* 37.

27. *Actus,* 60; *Fioretti,* "Additional Chapters," 12.

28. For description of this area and records of persons living in it, *NV* 2:430–37.

29. *Spec. Perf.,* 85.

30. *1 Cel.,* 23; *Leg. Maior,* III, 2; *Per.,* 67; *3 Soc.,* 26.

31. *1 Cel.,* 83.

32. Ibid.

Chapter 9

SAINT CLARE, LADY OF LIGHT

1. Ortolana's pilgrimage to the Holy Land must have been made in 1192, for only in that year did Saladin, with the end of the Third Crusade, begin to allow Christians to enter Jerusalem. See *NV* 2:343. For more about the passional mentioned, see *NV* 3:234–37; also chap. 10, n. 4, of this book.

2. Cf. *Relazione di Fr. Angelo da Spoleto;* Antonio de' Reboldi, *Itinerarium;* Nicolò di Poggibonsi, *Libro d'oltremare* (Golubovich, *Biblioteca,* 3:60–72, 326–42; 5:1–24).

3. The monastery of Santa Caterina is not mentioned in city records until the thirteenth century, when, in one of several bequests, it is called Sancta Caterine de Picario. Picario (or Picaia) is the hill just beyond Porta Nuova, which is not far from Clare's family house. Like all monasteries for women in Assisi, it must have been established outside the city walls and in troubled times moved inside. *NV* 3:52.

4. *Processo,* ed. Lazzari (*AFH* 13:458, 466). In Thomas of Celano's *Leg. S. Clarae,* ed. Pennacchi, p. 5, we find *Ne paveas, mulier, quia quoddam lumen salva parturies, quod ipsum lumen clarius illustrabit;* other manuscripts have *quod ipsum mundum clarius illustrabit.* [The author puts Clare's birth in 1193 A.D., basing his calculations on the testimony in the *Processo.* See *NV* 2:344.—Trans.]

5. *Leg. Maior,* IV, 6: "(Clare) was the first flower in Francis's garden, and she shone like a radiant star, fragrant as a flower blossoming white and pure in springtime."

6. Testimony of Bona di Guelfuccio, *Processo* (*AFH* 13:489): "At the time she entered religious life, she was a prudent young woman about eighteen years old, who always stayed in the house, remaining hidden and not wishing to be seen; and she did this so that she could not be looked at by those passing in front of her house."

7. Ibid., p. 492. Bona di Guelfuccio also testified that Clare "sent the food she was given to eat to the poor." She added, "This witness testifies that she herself many times carried it to them."

Also, in *Leg. S. Clarae*, 3, we read, "She gladly 'stretched out her hand to the poor' (Prov. 31:20) and from the 'abundance' of her house 'supplied the wants' of many (2 Cor. 8:14)."

8. *Leg. S. Clarae*, 10. The image of the dove is derived from either (or both) Song of Songs 2:14 (Fortini) or Psalms 68:14 (Brady).—Trans.

9. *2 Cel.*, 155; *3 Soc.*, 43; *Spec. Perf.*, 51; *Leg. Maior.* VIII, 3.

10. *Actus*, 32; *Fioretti*, 30; *24 Generals* (AF 3:47).

11. *24 Generals* (AF 3:46).

12. Ibid.; *Fioretti*, 31.

13. *Leg. S. Clarae*, 4.

14. Ibid., 5; *Processo* (AFH 13:489). Giovanni di Ventura added in his testimony (p. 493) that "the aforesaid madonna Clare, when she heard that Saint Francis had elected the way of poverty, proposed in her heart to do the same."

15. *Processo* (AFH 13:489).

16. *Leg. S. Clarae*, 7.

17. Ibid.

18. *Processo* (AFH 13:443). Sister Pacifica testified that she entered the religious life together with Clare. Also in *Leg. S. Clarae*, 7, it is reported that Clare undertook her flight "in good companionship."

19. *Leg. S. Clarae*, 8. Cf. the depositions of Beatrice, Clare's sister, in the *Processo* (AFH 13:480), also Ugolino di Pietro Girardone (p. 488) and Bona di Guelfuccio (p. 489).

20. For further information about the monastery of San Paolo delle Abbadesse: *NV* 2:388–96.

21. Details of this episode are in the *Leg. S. Clarae*, 9. Clare's sister Beatrice also described these events in the *Processo* (AFH 13:480). So did her relative Ranieri di Bernardo and the *famiglio* (man-at-arms) of the house, Giovanni di Ventura. Ibid., pp. 490–91, 493.

22. *Leg. S. Clarae*, 10. Cf. the testimony of her sister Beatrice in the *Processo* (AFH 13:480): "Then Sancto Francesco, frate Phylippo and frate Bernardo escorted her to the church of Sancto Angelo de Panço."

23. *Song of Songs* 2:10–12. These are still sung on the feast of Saint Clare.

24. *Leg. S. Clarae*, 25, 26. This episode was not mentioned in the *Processo*.

25. *NV* 2:101.

26. *Leg. S. Clarae*, 10. Her sister Beatrice also testified that the stay at Panzo lasted but a short time: *Processo* (AFH 13:480). Agnes's name before entering the order is known from a codex of the sixteenth century by Ugolino Verino; see Lazzari, "Un nuovo codice," AFH 13:275. See also Casolini, "La triplice corona," *Chiara d'Assisi* 2:6–12; *NV* 2:344–45.

27. *Seraphice Legislationis*, p. 276. Cf. the fine study by Lazzari, "La forma vitae," *Santa Chiara d'Assisi, VII centenario*, pp. 79–121.

28. For information about these sisters of San Damiano: *NV* 2:402–24.

29. Deposition of Sister Cecilia, *Processo* (AFH 13:467). For records pertaining to Gasdia and her family: *NV* 2:417.

30. Depositions of Sister Filippa and Sister Francesca, *Processo* (AFH 13:455, 471); see also *NV* 2:426.

31. *Processo* (AFH 13:487). For Assisi records pertaining to these witnesses, see *NV* 2:425–26.

32. On this episode, cf. *Leg. S. Clarae,* 37, and *Processo* (*AFH* 13:475–76).

33. John 10:1.

34. John 10:5.

35. Matthew 11:28.

36. Testament of Saint Clare, *Leg. S. Clarae,* 11.

37. Testimony of Sister Filippa, *Processo* (*AFH* 13:458); trans. Brady, *Legend and Writings,* p. 174, n. 1.

38. Cavaliere, *Cento liriche,* p. 299.

39. Ibid., p. 335.

40. Ibid., p. 341.

41. Accounts of this episode are found in some codices of *Leg. S. Clarae; Actus,* 15; *Fioretti,* 15; in Bartolomoeo da Pisa, *De conformitate* (*AF* 4:355). For a discussion of its historical reality, see Cuthbert, "A Disputed Story," *AFH* 6:670–80.

42. *2 Cel.,* 207.

43. *Leg. S. Clarae,* 14.

44. Lazzari, "Il Privilegium Paupertatis," *AFH* 11:275.

45. *Leg. S. Clarae,* 14.

46. Ibid., 37.

47. Ibid., 23.

48. For text of document in full: *NV* 3:429–34.

49. Cf. the depositions of Sister Pacifica in the *Processo* (*AFH* 13:446) and of Sister Angeluccia (p. 484).

50. Cf. the depositions of Sister Pacifica (ibid., p. 444), Sister Benvenuta (p. 449), and Sister Cecilia (p. 466).

51. See Oliger, "De origine regularum," *AFH* 5:428.

52. For identification of Iacopo di Stefano di Presbitero and his family, see *NV* 2:189–90; for text of his will: *NV* 3:462–64. There is no doubt that the war that is mentioned in the will is the one with Foligno in March 1246; the only other wars fought by Assisi during this period were battles against invading Saracens of Frederick II in 1241 and 1242. Iacopo's remarks about looting and other excesses committed by the communal army would not be applicable to these. For details about the war of 1246 and the historical sources from which information about it is drawn, cf. Fortini, *Assisi nel medioevo,* pp. 184–85.

53. *Processo* (*AFH* 13:459).

54. Ibid., pp. 478–79; *Leg. S. Clarae,* 46.

55. Deposition of Sister Filippa, *Processo* (*AFH* 13:459).

56. Ibid. For a detailed account of the last days of Saint Clare, her death, funeral ceremonies, the miracles attributed to her, the translation of her body, and the construction and consecration of the church in Assisi dedicated to her, cf. Fortini, *Assisi nel medioevo,* pp. 106, 198, 199, 217, 222.

Chapter 10

TIME OF RECONCILIATION

1. *NV* 3:32–33. The present structure, now being used as a public wash house, was built in 1316, on the site of the earlier one.

2. Arch. Com., M 1, fol. 2; for complete text, *NV* 3:579–80.

3. For description of the records containing the sentences given on this site, and for a history of the communal buildings on the Piazza della Minerva: *NV* 3:17–22.

4. All the details about the finding and translation of the bones of Saint Rufinus are included in a 248 page passional of the cathedral, dating from the early part of the fourteenth century but using material brought forward from an earlier time. Although considerable doubt has been expressed by some historians as to the authenticity of the material, Fortini has found the names listed in the passional in other Assisi records and believes there is no doubt that it rests on an historical basis. See *NV* 3:234–37 and 2:367–70.—Trans.

5. For a complete description of the façade: *NV* 3:37–41.

6. *Spec. Perf.*, 26; *Per.*, 67.

7. *1 Cel.*, 37.

8. Cf. Edouard d'Alençon, *Frère Jacqueline;* Oliger, "S. Francesco a Roma" (*Italia francescana nel settimo centenario della morte di San Francesco,* p. 80). Mariano da Firenze (*Compendium, AFH* 1:106; 2:92) recorded the fact that it was in this trip to Rome that Saint Francis met Giacoma dei Settesoli. Cf. *NV* 2:453–56.

9. *1 Cel.*, 62.

10. Ibid., 56; *Leg. Maior,* IX, 6. Both men say that despite his infirmities, Francis was so eager that he used to leave his companion behind and hurry on ahead. For this trip to Spain, see also Lopez, "Viaje de San Francisco," *Archivio Ibero-Americano* 1:13–45; 2:257–89; 3:433–69, and the accompanying bibliography.

11. Sevesi, "Le origini della provincia," *Studi Francescani* 13:49–64.

12. *1 Cel.*, 56, 57.

13. *2 Cel.*, 108; *Leg. Maior,* VI, 9.

14. *Fioretti,* 16; *Leg. Maior,* XII, 2.

15. *Fioretti,* 25; *Spec. Vitae,* 56.

16. For laws and regulations concerning lepers, *NV* 2:260–66.

17. *Spec. Perf.*, 58. At the end of the chapter is the note, "The writer saw these things himself, and testifies to them." [The same episode is related in *Per.*, 22, with a similar notation.]

18. *Fioretti,* 26. Monte Casale is a mile or so from Borgo Sansepolcro, which is near Arezzo.

19. *Spec. Perf.*, 32; *2 Cel.*, 89.

20. *1 Cel.*, 62.

21. Angelo Clareno. In *Archiv für Literatur-und Kirchengeschichte des Mittelalters* 1:559 (Ehrle, "Die Spiritualen").

22. Lettre I, October 1216 (*Omnibus,* pp. 1608–1609).

23. For documentation about these persons: *NV* 2:429–45. Tiberio's fresco, painted in 1518, is in the Cappella del Roseto of the Basilica di Santa Maria degli Angeli.

24. *Leg. Maior,* XV, 4.

25. Testimony of Michele di Berarduccio, in Francisci Bartoli, *Tractatus.* For the testimony of Pietro di Zalfano, see *NV* 2:439.

26. *Spec. Perf.*, 84.

27. *Spec. Perf.*, 83.

28. *Spec. Perf.*, 84. This laud, attributed by some to Thomas of Celano, has been shown to go back to the year 1216. See Sabatier, "La plus ancienne mention de l'Indulgence," *Oriente Serafico,* 1916–17, pp. 97–106: "It was evidently made to be sung, to keep alive in the heart of the friars dispersed throughout the world the memory of the sanctuary that was as humble as it was glorious, and until such time as

they left the distant provinces to return to Porziuncola, taking with them new recruits converted to the gospel of Poverty, to be for them the earlier *Psalmi graduum* of the Israelites as they climbed toward Zion." (An English translation of the entire hymn may be found in Englebert, *Saint Francis,* p. 470.)

29. Golubovich, *Biblioteca,* 1:87.

30. Saint Francis possibly had in mind the strong Eucharistic cult flourishing in France and Liege, in part due to the influence of Blessed Marie d'Oignies, a friend of Jacques de Vitry. He may also have been impressed by the fact that about 1215 the bishop of Paris decreed that priests must elevate the Host after the consecration in the Mass. See Brown in Englebert, *Saint Francis,* p. 477, n. 9.—Trans.

31. *3 Soc.,* 62.

32. Giordano, *Chronica,* 5.

33. *2 Cel.,* 201.

34. *Spec. Perf.,* 65; *Per.,* 80.

35. *Spec. Perf.,* 65. *Per.,* 82. Callebaut has demonstrated in an irrefutable manner that this meeting took place in the summer of 1217. "Autour de la rencontre à Florence," *AFH* 19:530–35.

36. About Brother Pacifico, see Cosmo, *Con Madonna Povertà,* pp. 59–81; Padre Ciro da Pesaro, "Fra Pacifico re dei versi," *Picenum seraphicum* 4:121–69.

37. Bertoni, *Poesie, leggende, costumanze,* p. 85.

38. *2 Cel.,* 106.

39. Carducci, *Cantilene e ballate,* p. 7. Cf. de Bartholomaeis, *Le origini della poesia,* p. 71.

40. *Per.,* 23, 43; *Spec. Perf.,* 59, 100.

41. *2 Cel.,* 106.

42. Ibid. The name of the city of San Severino is given us by Bonaventure (*Leg. Minor,* II, 9). For the monastery of San Salvatore: Oliger, "De origine regularum," *AFH* 5:199–200.

The identification of the King of Verses as Guglielmo Divini of Lisciano, near Ascoli, has no historical basis. This meeting is generally put in 1215.

43. *2 Cel.,* 106.

44. Ibid.

45. *Per.,* 23; *2 Cel.,* 122, 123; *Spec. Perf.,* 59–60; *Leg. Maior,* VI, 6. For the history of Trevi in this period and information about the church of San Pietro di Bovara: Bonaca, "Le memorie francescane," *Studi Francescani* 24:26–34.

46. *2 Cel.,* 106.

47. Jordan, "Les premiers franciscains," *Études Italiennes* 8:69–70.

48. About Brother Elias: *NV* 2:299–303; see also chap. 4, pp. 121–22 of this book.

49. Giordano, *Chronica,* 9. Brother Elias and his companions, whose names are not known to us, embarked on the fleet that set sail for the Holy Land in June 1217 from Brindisi, the usual port of embarkation for Crusaders from central Italy.

50. *2 Cel.,* 208; *Spec. Perf.,* 77; *24 Generals* (AF 3:224).

51. *Passio sanctorum martyrum* (AF 3:579–96).

Chapter 11

DAMIETTA

1. The author has drawn material from these sources for this chapter; still others will be listed on succeeding pages:

Recueil des historiens des croisades, the major collection of source materials for the crusades.

Especially for the Fifth Crusade, our present concern: Runciman, *A History of the Crusades,* which has a valuable bibliography; Setton, ed., *History of the Crusades,* a collaboration by several writers; Rosanthal, *A History of Muslim Historiography;* Lewis, "Sources for the history of the Syrian Assassin," *Speculum* 27:475–89; Cahen, *La Syrie du Nord,* which includes a detailed study of the Arab historians of the Crusades, pp. 33–93; Gibb, "Notes on Arabic materials," *Bulletin of the School of Oriental Studies* 7:739–54; Grousset, *Histoire des Croisades;* idem., *L'épopée des Croisades;* Cognasso, *Le genesi delle Crociate;* Ruville, *Die Kreuzzüge;* Stevenson, *The Crusader in the East;* Bréhier, *L-Église et l'Orient;* Prutz, *Kulturgeschichte der Kreuzzüge;* Kugler, *Geschichte der Kreuzzüge;* Michaud, *Histoire des Croisades,* 1st and 2nd eds.; Wilken, *Geschichte der Kreuzzüge.*

See also the extensive bibliography in *Cambridge Medieval History,* vols. 4–6.

2. *Passio sanctorum martyrum* (AF 3:581–82). Mariano da Firenze also lists the names.

3. For Leonardo di Gislerio and his family: *NV* 2:137–46, and in this book, chap. 4, pp. 124–26.

4. These deeds are the famous *Gesta obsidionis Damiatae* written by Alberto Milioli, who was born at Reggio Emilia probably about 1220 and died about 1286. He was a friend, confessor, and teacher of Fra Salimbene. There are four well-known compilations of this material: the *Liber duelli christiani in obsidione Damiatae exacti,* written in the thirteenth century by a Swedish or German writer who was present at the siege; the *Gesta obsidionis Damiatae,* by a priest, Ionnes de Tulbio, more or less in the same period; the *Gesta obsidionis Damiaetae,* attributed to the notary of Piacenza, Giovanni Codagnello, who also wrote the *Chronicon Placentinum ab an. 1012 usque ad ad. 1235;* and finally, the work composed by Milioli and later inserted into chapters 219–220 of his *Liber de Temporibus.* All these compilations are derived from an original text by an unknown author, compiled day by day by someone who undoubtedly participated in the siege. For all four, ed. Holder-Egger, *MGH, Scriptores,* vol. 31.

These *Gesta* were edited for the first time by Muratori, *RIS,* vol. 8. See also Golubovich, *Biblioteca,* 1:313–16.

5. Milioli, *Gesta* (*RIS,* 8:1085). All subsequent references will be from this source and will be cited: Milioli.

6. Ibid.

7. Milioli (p. 1095) tells us of an assault of July 10, 1219, made by the Saracens on a trench of the crusaders, which was in the keeping of *Ianuenses, Spolitani et Romani* ("men of Genoa, Spoleto, and Rome").

We know of the presence of men from Lucca and Bologna through two documents: one, dated June 19, 1220, was drawn up *in civitate Damiate, in ecclesia beati Pauli,* and was concerned with the allotment of a quarter of the city to crusaders from these two cities; the other, dated August 27, is a record of the investing of a Doctor Roberto from Lucca with a portion of the property allotted to them. See Salvioli, *Annali Bolognese,* 2:431–32, n. 487; 442–43, n. 493.

8. *RIS,* 8:947.

9. Milioli, p. 1084.

10. *Vir egregius, nobilis, prudens, magnae fidei et discretionis* ("an outstanding, noble, prudent man, of great faith and discretion"). Ibid., p. 1085.

11. *Chronica* (*MGH,* vol. 32).

12. Ibid.

13. Milioli, p. 1103. Milioli gives us an extremely telling and detailed description of the defense of Damietta.

For other particulars: *Liber de Acquisitione Terrae Sanctae (RIS,* vol. 7), hereafter cited as Pipino. This work is attributed to Bernard the Treasurer, with the Latin text by the epitomist Pipino, a Dominican friar. It is, however, but a compendium of the *Chronique* written by Ernoul, a warrior and a squire of Ibelino, who in 1187 took part in the capture of Jerusalem. See *Recueil, Historiens occidentaux,* 2:346–50; also Golubovich, *Biblioteca,* 1:10–13.

Other sources for the siege and capture of Damietta are the numerous accounts written by Arab historians, especially the contemporary witnesses Ibn al-Atìr and Sibt ibn al-Gawzì, also the later writers Ibn al-Furat Abulfeda, al-Maqrìzì, etc. Translations are in *Recueil, Historiens orientaux* (vols. 1, 2, 5); Michaud, *Bibliothèque* (see vol. 4, which contains Reinaud's *Chroniques arabes,* pp. 386–426); Blochet, trans., *Histoire d'Egypte de Makrìzì,* pp. 314–41; Reinaud, *Extraits de l'histoire des Patriarches;* Röhricht, *Geschichte des Königreiches;* Bongars, *Gesta Dei;* [Oliver of Paderborn, *The Capture of Damietta,* trans. Gavigan]; and others.

Ibn al-Atìr was an eyewitness of the events that he narrates. About this siege of Damietta he writes: "Between the French and Damietta there was the Nile, one branch of which flowed into the sea near this city; and there a large and strong tower had been built [by the Egyptians], with massive iron chains stretched in the river all the way to the walls of Damietta, so as to impede the ships that came by the sea from following the Nile upstream, in Egyptian territory. And if it had not been for this tower and these chains, no one could have stopped the enemy ships from reaching the most remote parts of Egypt." Gabrieli, *Storici arabi,* p. 242.

14. Gabrieli, *Storici arabi,* p. 242. Ibn al-Atìr further writes about this attack on the Tower of the Chain: "The French, despite the fact that they had continually attacked the tower, had not won any success, and they had shattered their machines and instruments of war; with all that, they persevered in opposing that fortress, and did so for four months without succeeding in taking it. At the end of this time, they succeeded in gaining possession of it, and then they cut the chains so that their ships could enter the Nile from the sea and obtain a solid foothold on the mainland."

15. Milioli, p. 1086; also Pipino, p. 828, who says that it was the tears of the Christians that put out the flames burning the towers.

16. Milioli, pp. 1088–90.

17. Ibid., pp. 1086–87; Pipino, p. 829. [Oliver of Paderborn says five hundred were killed, as was learned from deserters (p. 71).—Trans.]

18. Michaud, *Histoire des Croisades,* bk. 12.

19. Milioli, p. 1089; Pipino, p. 830. [Gavigan, trans. Oliver of Paderborn's account, suggests that the disease was scurvy (p. 72, n. 1).—Trans.]

20. Milioli, p. 1092.

21. Pipino, p. 833.

22. Ibid., p. 828.

23. Ibid., p. 834 [Biblical quotation: 1 Maccabees 5:62].

24. Milioli, p. 1093.

25. [For the prophecies: *Quinti Belli Sacri Scriptores Minores,* ed. Röhricht, vol. 2. They are entitled *Le Prophètie de Hannan* (pp. 206–13) and *Prophetia Filii Agap* (pp. 214–28). See also Gavigan in Oliver, *Capture of Damietta,* p. 90, n. 1.—Trans.] The reference to the Assassins is taken from Pipino, p. 839.

26. This episode faithfully follows the account given by Milioli, pp. 1095–97.

27. Ibid., p. 1097.

28. Ibid.

29. Ibid. Also, Pipino, p. 835. Many men of the people came enthusiastically to fight as Crusaders, some for the hope of acquiring knighthood, but their presence aroused no little discontent among the feudal lords and nobles. See Michaud, *Histoire*, bk. 12.

30. *2 Cel.,* 30. Almost the same words are used in *Leg. Maior,* XI, 3. Illuminato is named in the latter source and also by Elemosina in *Chronicon* (Golubovich, *Biblioteca,* 2:121), written about 1335.

31. *2 Cel.,* 30: "The holy man therefore arose and approached the Christians with salutary warnings, forbidding the war, denouncing the reason for it." Cf. *Leg. Maior,* XI, 3; Elemosina, *Chronicon* (Golubovich, *Biblioteca,* 2:121).

32. *2 Cel.,* 30: "But the truth was turned to ridicule, and they hardened their hearts and refused to be guided." Cf. *Leg. Maior,* XI, 3.

Elemosina adds some details: "When they heard these things (from Francis), they were stupified; and, so it is said, the head of the army and some of the leaders agreed that they should call for a truce with the Saracens and avoid an outpouring of human blood and a great slaughter of men. But because of all the shouting to go ahead and fight the Saracens and pay no attention to a despicable and unknown friar, the irrational mob, which rightly should have been punished, grew ever greater. The wiser were not strong enough to restrain the great number of the foolish, so they engaged in battle with the Saracens." *Chronicon* (Golubovich, *Biblioteca,* 2:121).

33. See note 29.

34. Pipino, p. 835.

35. Ibid. The same author adds that the Christians had been trapped in a place between the sea and the river where they could get no good water to drink.

36. Milioli, p. 1098.

37. Pipino, p. 835.

38. Jacques de Vitry, *Historia Orientalis,* chap. 32.

39. This episode was told by Tolosano da Faenza. See *Documenti di storia patria,* 6:704; also Golubovich, *Biblioteca,* 1:179.

40. Pipino, p. 835.

41. *2 Cel.,* 30: "And behold, the whole Christian army was turned to flight and the battle ended in shame, not triumph."

42. Ibid.

43. Ibid.; *Leg. Maior,* XI, 3; Milioli, p. 1098; Pipino, p. 835; Jacques de Vitry, *Historia Orientalis,* chap. 32.

44. Milioli, p. 1098. For the story of the death of John the Baptist: Mt. 14:3–12; Mk. 6:14–29. For Saint Francis's special devotion to John, *2 Cel.,* 3: "He considered the feast of John the Baptist to be more illustrious than the feasts of all the other saints, for the dignity of his name left a mark of mystic virtue upon him."

45. *Leg. Maior,* XI, 3, taken from Sirach 37:18.

46. Milioli, p. 1098.

47. Ibid. (Biblical quotation: Rev. 7:14).

48. Milioli, p. 1098.

49. Ibid.

50. Michaud, *Histoire,* bk. 12.

51. Milioli, p. 1099.

52. From *Cronaca di Ogerio Pane* (*Annali Genovesi,* trans. Monleone, 3:111).

53. Milioli, pp. 1099–1100.

54. Ibid., p. 1100.

55. Ibid.

56. Michaud, *Histoire,* bk. 12.

57. Pipino, p. 825: "Jean, king of Jerusalem, and the patriarch [of Jerusalem], with the bishops of Nicosia, Bethlehem, and Acre, left Acre in May 1218 for Damietta."

58. This letter, "De captione Damiatae," was written in Damietta in February 1220 and directed to "the religious, relatives, and acquaintances who are living in Lotharingia, on the capture of Damietta." (Bongars, *Gesta Dei,* 1:1146–49.)

See also *Historia Orientalis,* chap. 32: "We have seen the founder and master of this Order, the one whom all the others obey as their superior general; he was a simple unlettered man, loved by God and men; he was called Brother Francis." (*Omnibus,* p. 1609.)

59. Isaiah 60:8.

60. Milioli, p. 1101.

61. Ibid., p. 1102.

62. Ricordano Malispini, *Istoria fiorentina* (*RIS,* 8:947–48).

63. Milioli, pp. 1102–3.

64. Ibid., p. 1103; Pipino, p. 837.

65. "De captione Damiatae" (see n. 58); also Pipino, p. 838, says much the same.

66. Michaud, *Histoire,* bk. 12. Ibn al-Atìr, in turn, writes: "After lengthy fighting, the defenders were reduced to the end of their tether, short of supplies, exhausted in the assiduous battle, inasmuch as the French, numerous as they were, alternated in fighting, while there were not in Damietta enough people to permit such rotation. With all this, they made an unparalleled resistance, suffering great losses in the dead and wounded and ill. They endured the siege until the twenty-seventh of shacbàn of 616 (November 8, 1218), when the survivors were powerless to defend the city longer because of their small number and the difficulty of procuring supplies." Gabrieli, *Storici arabi,* p. 245.

67. Milioli, p. 1103; Pipino, p. 838. [The supplies of food in a city of starving people is not explained.—Trans.]

68. Michaud, bk. 12.

69. Pipino, p. 838.

70. Milioli, p. 1103.

71. Pipino, p. 838.

72. Jacques de Vitry, *Historia Orientalis,* chap. 32 (*Omnibus,* p. 1613).

73. In the document cited in n. k, the doctor, Roberto di Lucca, promises all the services due from the crusaders of Bologna to the king.

74. Milioli, p. 1103.

75. "De captione Damiatae" (*Gesta Dei,* ed. Bongars).

76. Pipino, p. 838.

77. We cite the Arab chronicler Ibn al-Atìr: "Once Damietta was conquered, the French settled there and scattered their armed bands through all the surrounding lands, looting and killing, so that the people left the area. The French at once set about arranging and carefully fortifying the piazza to make it impregnable. Malik al-Kāmil, on his part, encamped near the enemy, on the borders of his own territory, intent on defending it. When the French in their own lands learned that their fellow countrymen had taken over Damietta, they began to flock in from everywhere, so that it became their emigration center. The entire Moslem world, men and lands, now found themselves on the point of being submerged, in the east and west alike." Gabrieli, *Storici arabi,* p. 246.

78. Michaud, *Histoire,* bk. 12.

79. *Fioretti,* 24; *Actus,* 27. The same episode is related by Bartholomew of Pisa, *De conformitate* (*AF* 4:482), and by Mariano da Firenze.

80. Michaud, *Histoire,* bk. 12.

81. Fidenzio da Padova, *Liber recuperationis* (Golubovich, *Biblioteca,* 2:19).

82. Gabrieli, *Storici arabi,* p. 192.

83. Marin Sanuto, *Secreta fidelium Crucis* (Bongars, *Gesta Dei,* 2: chaps. 7, 8).

84. "De captione Damiatae" (*Omnibus,* p. 1609).

85. Cf. Fortini, *Assisi nel medioevo,* pp. 141–46; Bartholomew of Pisa, *De conformitate: Hic sepultus est Assisij, etsi super sepulturam in habitu regali sit sculptus* (*AF* 4:347).

See also Gerola, "Chi è il sovrano?" *Dedalo* 8 (1927); "Giovanni e Gualtieri di Brienne," *AFH* 24:338.

86. Jacques de Vitry, "De captione Damiatae" (*Historia Orientalis,* chap. 32).

87. Iacopozzi, "Dove sia avvenuta la visita?" *Frate Francesco* 2:389–93. Also, according to Ibn al Atìr, "The French with all their forces left Damietta to confront Malik-al-Kāmil, making camp in front of him and separated from him by an arm of the Nile called Bahr Ashmun." Gabrieli, *Storici arabi,* p. 247.

88. Pipino, p. 840

89. Michaud, bk. 12.

90. Ibid. Also Maqrìzì, *Description topographique,* Mémoires publiées par les membres de la Mission Archéologique Française du Caire, tome 17:643.

91. *Leg. Maior,* IX, 7.

92. Cf. the letter written by this cardinal to the podestà of Genoa on November 5, 1219, in the *Annali* of Marchisio Scriba (*Annali Genovesi di Caffaro,* trans. Monleone, 3:118–20).

93. Michaud, bk. 12.

94. Fidenzio da Padova, *Liber recuperationis* (Golubovich, *Biblioteca,* 2:19).

95. Romans 1:32.

96. Fidenzio da Padova, *Liber recuperationis* (Golubovich, *Biblioteca,* 2:21).

97. *Leg. Maior,* IX, 7.

98. Ibid., IX, 8.

99. *Novellino,* Novella 73.

100. Jacques de Vitry says that the sultan "kept him with him for a few days and with a great deal of attention listened to him preach the Faith of Christ to him and his followers." *Historia Orientalis,* chap. 32 (*Omnibus,* p. 1612).

101. In August 1934 a large group of Assisi pilgrims, headed by the podestà of the commune, went to Cairo and then into the desert to recall and celebrate this episode in the life of Saint Francis. (The podestà at the time was Arnaldo Fortini.—Trans.)

102. *Verba fratris Illuminati* (Golubovich, *Biblioteca,* 1:36–37; *Omnibus,* pp. 1614–15); see also *NV* 2:303.

103. *Novellino,* Proemio.

104. *Leg. Maior,* I, 5.

105. Ernoul, *Chronique* (Golubovich, *Biblioteca,* 1:12).

106. *Actus,* 27; *Fioretti,* 24.

107. For a description of this relic: Marinangeli, "La trombetta di San Francesco," *San Francesco Patrono d'Italia* 3:67.

108. Pipino, p. 841.

109. Oliver of Paderborn, *Relatio de expeditione Damiantina* (Eckhart, *Corpus* *historicum medii aevi,* vol. 2). [Eng. trans.: Gavigan, *The Capture of Damietta,* in Peters, *Christian Society and the Crusades: 1198–1229,* pp. 108–110.]

110. *24 Generals (AF* 3:281); Mariano da Firenze also tells of the visit.

111. Giordano, *Chronica,* 13.

Also, Fra Salimbene tells in his *Chronica* that he learned from his father, who had taken part in the preceding Crusade of 1204, that "other Lombardians in those overseas districts asked fortunetellers about the condition of their families, but he never wished to consult them; and when he returned, he found his house in such a state that it was a consolation, and the others all found sadness, as the fortunetellers had foretold."

112. Giordano, *Chronica,* 15.

113. Angelo Clareno, *Septem Tribulationum,* "Prima trib.," chap. 11.

114. Cf. the Bull *Sacrosancta* of December 9, 1219, and those of September 19, 1222 (Potthast, *Regesta Pontificum,* 6179, 6879, a, b, c). On the relationship between Ugolino and the monasteries of the Poor Clares, cf. Oliger, *De Origine Regularum (AFH* 5:181–209, 412–47).

115. Giordano, *Chronica,* 12.

116. Richerio, a monk of Sens, in his *Gesta Senonensis ecclesiae (MGH,* vol. 25), made a note of the departure of Saint Francis with a few of his companions. The names of the friars who accompanied Francis on his return voyage are given in Giordano, *Chronica,* 14: Elias, Pietro di Catanio, Caesar of Speyer, and "some other brothers."

117. For information about this return trip, consult Barban's fine publication, *San Francesco del deserto,* p. 33. The sources there cited, in addition to *Leg. Maior,* VIII, 9, are as follows: *An. Min.* (1220), p. 333, no. 4; Beato da Valdagno, *Annali Miss. della Provincia* (1220); Marin Sanudo, *Cronaca Veneziana (RIS,* 22:547); Andrea Dandolo, *Chronicon (RIS,* 12:343).

118. *Leg. Maior,* VIII, 9.

Chapter 12

PERFECT JOY

1. Pietro Antonio da Venetia, *Historia Serafica,* p. 123.

2. Ibid., p. 122; Bartholomew of Pisa, *De conformitate (AF* 5:210–11).

3. For a description of the University of Bologna in this epoch, see Savigny, *Geschichte des römischen Rechts,* vol. 3; Denifle, *Die Universitäten des Mittelalters;* Malagola, *Monografie storiche;* Rashdall, *Universities of Europe.*

4. L. I, rub. 252.

5. Arch. S. Conv., Str., I, 43; *NV* 3:450.

6. *Actus,* 4; *Fioretti,* 5; *24 Generals (AF* 3:36–37). Wadding (*An. Min.,* 1211, 29), on the authority of Mariano da Firenze and other chroniclers, puts the date as 1211, and this is the date generally accepted by historians.

7. *An. Min.,* 1220, 29; Giusta, *Memorie storiche,* p. 3. This first house of the friars was outside Porta Galliere, *in loco S. Mariae de Puliolis,* which is today called San Bernardino.

8. *Fioretti,* "Fifth Consideration."

9. *2 Cel.,* 58; *Spec. Perf.,* 6; *Actus,* 61; *Fioretti,* "Add. Chapters," 12.

10. Golubovich, *Biblioteca,* 1:98.

11. *Fioretti,* 27.

12. Ibid.

13. According to *Leg. Vers.* (AF 10:450), Brother Riccieri feared that Saint Francis would read in his heart the record of his youthful transgressions and cease to love him.

For a fine and detailed reference to this early Franciscan writer, whose venerated body lies in his native town of Muccia (between Foligno and Camerino), see Faloci-Pulignano, ed., "Vita di San Francesco e dei Suoi Compagni," *Misc. Fran.* 8:81–119. Brother Riccieri died in 1236.

14. *Actus,* 36; *Fioretti,* 27. For Brother Pellegrino: Gentili, *Sopra l'Ordine Serafico,* pp. 27 ff.

15. On the goliards and their poetry: Bertoni, *Poesie, leggende. costumanze;* Rozhdestvenskaia, *Les poésies des goliards;* Schmeller, *Carmina burana;* Novati, *Carmina medii aevi.*

16. "Salutatorium." From works collected by Bono da Lucca.

17. Golias, "In romanam curiam."

18. Archpoet of Cologne, "Confesio Golias."

19. "Veris Dulcis," trans. Zeydel, *Vagabond Verse,* p. 116.

20. "Phyllis and Flora," a very long poem about two maidens of noble birth who dispute as to whether knights or clerics make better lovers, is one of the most famous of the goliard poems. The names Phyllis and Flora were also used in many medieval poems to disguise the real identities of the women whom the poet had in mind.

21. Morando da Padova, "Contentio Aquae et Vini."

22. "Hospes laudatur." All listed above are in the *Carmina burana* collection.

23. "After youth's pleasures and old age's cares, the earth will claim us."

24. *Actus,* 36; *Fioretti,* 27; *1 Cel.,* 49; *2 Cel.,* 44a; Julian of Speyer, *Vita* 31 (AF 10:349–50); *Leg. Maior,* XI, 9; *Leg. Monacensis,* 72 (AF 10:713).

25. Faloci-Pulignano, ed., "Vita di San Francesco e dei Suoi Compagne," *Misc. Fran.* 8:113.

26. Ibid., p. 115.

27. As translated by Ciardi, lines 1–9 from Canto 11 of *Paradiso:*

> O senseless strivings of the mortal round!
> how worthless is that exercise of reason
> that makes you beat your wings into the ground!
>
> One man was giving himself to law, and one
> to aphorisms; one sought sinecures,
> and one to rule by force or sly persuasion;
>
> one planned his business, one his robberies;
> one, tangled in the pleasure of the flesh,
> wore himself out, and one lounged at his ease. . . .

28. *2 Cel.,* 189.

29. Zöckler, in *Realenzyklopädie für Protestantische Theologie und Kirche* (3rd ed.), 6:208; Müller, *Die Anfänge des Minoritenordens,* p. 104; Sabatier, *Vie,* chap. 17.

30. *2 Cel.,* 102; *Leg. Maior,* XI, 2.

31. *2 Cel.,* 102.

32. Ibid., 103.

33. Ibid., 163.
34. Ibid., 102.
35. Ibid., 194.
36. *Leg. Maior*, XI, 1.
37. *2 Cel.*, 192.
38. Levi, *Registri de' Cardinali*, No. 84.
39. Walterus de Gysburne, Chronica (*MGH, Scriptores*, vol. 28).
40. *2 Cel.*, 195.
41. Rule of the Second Order of August 9, 1253, chap. 6 (*Speculum Minorum* per Morin, Tract. III, 226 b).
42. *1 Cel.*, 99.
43. Ibid., 100; Giordano, *Chronica*, 14.
44. Giordano, *Chronica*, 14.
45. *2 Cel.*, 145.
46. Ibid; *Spec. Perf.*, 64; *Per.*, 83.
47. Bullarium, 1:6.
48. *2 Cel.*, 143; *Spec. Perf.*, 39; *Per.*, 105.
49. *Spec. Perf.*, 71; *Per.*, 76.
50. *2 Cel.*, 151; *Spec. Perf.*, 46; *Per.*, 106; *Leg. Maior*, VI. 4.
51. *2 Cel.*, 140.
52. *1 Cel.*, 83.
53. *Fioretti*, 10; *Actus*, 10.
54. *Fioretti*, 12; *Actus*, 12.
55. *2 Cel.*, 141; *Spec. Perf.*, 45.
56. *2 Cel.*, 132; *Spec. Perf.*, 63; *Per.*, 41.
57. *2 Cel.*, 139.
58. *Actus*, 59; *Fioretti*, 36. The latter text, a translation of the first, begins thus: "At a certain time when Saint Francis was seriously ill, Brother Leo was taking care of him with great devotion and skill."
59. *2 Cel.*, 130; *Per.*, 40; *Spec. Perf.*, 62.
60. On the episode in the piazza, cf. *1 Cel.*, 52; *Leg. Maior*, VI, 2; *Spec. Perf.*, 61; *Per.*, 39. Each of these sources gives different details; all together they permit an exact reconstruction of what happened. All the aforesaid sources, with the exception of *1 Cel.*, note that the episode took place in the main piazza (Piazza del Comune or della Minerva), where Francis had called the people together.
61. *Tunc erat magnum frigus et tempus hymenale* ("It was winter, it was very cold"), according to *Per.* Similar words are used in *Spec. Perf.* and *Leg. Maior: acerbi frigoris tempore* ("It was bitterly cold").
62. Only in *Per.* and *Spec. Perf.* do we read that Pietro di Catanio was with Francis. Both note that Pietro was the first minister-general, and the latter also calls him a canon of the cathedral. (But see chap. 7, n. f, of this book.) According to *Per.*, they went into the confession or crypt of the church, the place where Saint Rufinus was buried.
63. About the sarcophagus of Saint Rufinus, see chap. 2, pp. 47–49.
64. *2 Cel.*, 129. A similar passage is found in *1 Cel.*, 97: "For so great was the harmony of his body toward his spirit, so great its obedience, that while his spirit tried to lay hold of all sanctity, his body nevertheless did not only not resist, but tried even to outrun his spirit, according to what was written: 'For thee my soul hath thirsted; for thee my flesh, O how many ways' (Psalms 62:2)."
65. *Leg. Maior*, VI, 2.

66. *Spec. Perf.,* 3; *Per.,* 69.
67. Boehmer, *Opuscola;* Lemmens, "Die Anfänge," *Wissenschaftliche Beilage,* 1909.
68. Giordano, *Chronica,* 15.
69. Golubovich, *Biblioteca,* 1:40.
70. *2 Cel.,* 55.
71. *Rule of 1221,* chap. 1.
72. *Spec. Perf.,* 4; *2 Cel.,* 195; *Per.,* 72–74.
73. *Spec. Perf.,* 8; *Per.,* 12.
74. *Spec. Perf.,* 3; *Per.,* 69.
75. *Spec. Perf.,* 13; *Per.,* 112.
76. *Spec. Perf.,* 41; *2 Cel.,* 188.
77. *Rule of 1221,* chap. 2.
78. *2 Cel.,* 81; *Leg. Maior,* VII, 3.
79. *Rule of 1221,* chap. 2.
80. *2 Cel.,* 65; *Spec. Perf.,* 14.
81. *2 Cel.,* 66.
82. Ibid., 68; *Leg. Maior,* VII, 5.
83. *Rule of 1221,* chap. 8.
84. Ibid.
85. Ibid., chap. 9.
86. *2 Cel.,* 74.
87. Ibid., 71.
88. Ibid., 76.
89. Ibid., 70.
90. Ibid.
91. Ibid., 72.
92. Ibid., 73. In *Liber exemplorum* (*Antonianum* 2:239), Brother Masseo tells about Francis's love of poverty, saying that he used to tell the brothers that poverty had been brought to us by Jesus Christ, that it shone more brightly than the sun and therefore the eyes of the flesh cannot see it or function in its light.
93. *Leg. Maior,* IV, 7.
94. *Fioretti,* 13; *Actus,* 13.
95. *2 Cel.,* 60.
96. Ibid., 63.
97. Ibid., 56.
98. Ibid., 62.
99. Ibid., 84.
100. Ibid., 85.
101. Luzzatti, L., "La scoperta di un nuovo 'Fioretti,' " *Apostolato francescano* 4:127–29.
102. *2 Cel.,* 86.
103. Ibid., 88. [the biographer does not explain with what they bought it back!]
104. Ibid., 91.
105. Ibid., 87.
106. *Rule of 1221,* chap. 9.
107. Ibid., chap. 22 (Matthew 5:44).
108. Ibid.
109. Facchinetti, *San Francesco d'Assisi,* p. 350.
110. *Sacrum Commercium,* 50.
111. Appearances of the devil at the Carceri hermitage and his subsequent plung-

ing into the ravine are told in *Fioretti*, 29; *Actus*, 31; *24 Generals* (*AF* 3:48). This hermitage is not named specifically in these sources, but the physical description of the place fits so well that no mistake in identification is possible. See *NV* 3:159.

112. Saint Gregory, quoted by Iacopo Passavanti, *Lo Specchio della Vera Penitenza*, in the chapter entitled "Dove si dimostra che cosa è contrizione."

113. *Sacrum Commercium*, 20.

114. Ibid., 15.

115. Ibid., 31.

116. *Rule of 1221*, chap. 23.

117. *Spec. Perf.*, 7; *2 Cel.*, 57; *Per.*, 11.

118. Eccleston, 6.

119. Ibid.; *Spec. Perf.*, 68; *Leg. Maior*, IV, 10; *Per.*, 114. Giordano (*Chronica* 16) says that three thousand friars were present.

120. *Fioretti*, 18; *Spec. Perf.*, 68; *Per.*, 114.

121. Giordano, *Chronica*, 17. Brother Giordano says that Elias would bend down to listen to Francis, then straighten up and say, "Brothers, thus says *The Brother*," a term used for him by the other friars.

122. *Fioretti*, 18.

123. Giordano, *Chronica*, 17.

124. Ibid., 19.

125. Klüber, *Das Ritterwesen*, 1:417.

126. Cavaliere, *Cento liriche*, pp. 178–80. Trans., Creekmore, *Lyrics of the Middle Ages*, pp. 54–57.

127. The ballad (*ballatetta*) of Guido Cavalcanti comes to mind (Engl. trans., Pound, *Translations*, p. 121):

> *Perch'io non spero di tornar giammai,*
> *Ballatetta, in Toscana,*
> *Va tu leggiera e piana*
> *Dritta a la donna mia . . .*

> Because no hope is left me, Ballatetta,
> Of return to Tuscany,
> Light-foot go thou some fleet way
> Unto my Lady straightway . . .

The poet clearly says that he composed the song just before his death:

> *Tu senti, Ballatetta, che la morte*
> *Mi stringe sì che vita m'abbandona . . .*

> Thou knowest, Ballatetta, that Death layeth
> His hand upon me whom hath Life forsaken . . .

128. Cavaliere, *Cento liriche*, p. 7; see also chap. 7, n. 43, of this book. Engl. trans., Wilhelm, *Seven Troubadours*, pp. 56–57.

129. *2 Cel.*, 125.

130. *1 Cel.*, 23; *Leg. Min.* III, 3.

131. *2 Cel.*, 127.

132. Ibid., 128; *Spec. Perf.*, 96; *Per.*, 97.

133. *Rule of 1221*, chap. 7.

134. Giordano, *Chronica*, 16.

135. Ezekiel 24.
136. *2 Cel.*, 125.
137. *Admonitions*, 27.
138. *An. Min.*, 1221, chap. XXXI. Story from *Fioretti*, 8; *Actus*, 7 (trans. Brown).
139. *Rule of 1221*, chap. 47.
140. *Fioretti*, 41; see also *Spec. Perf.*, ed. Sabatier, and the rich bibliography included in it. Papini wrote an unpublished biography of his life, which is among the manuscripts in the Sacro Convento in Assisi.
141. *Fioretti*, 29.
142. *Fioretti*, 28.
143. *Leg. Maior*, XI, 4.
144. *Fioretti*, 6.
145. *Dicta*, 13, "On Contemplation."

Chapter 13

THE MYSTIC KNIGHT AND CHRIST'S FOOL

1. *24 Generals* (AF 3:109).
2. Ibid., p. 92.
3. Ibid., p. 110; *Fioretti*, 28; *Actus*, 30.
4. *24 Generals* (AF 3:86).
5. Ibid., p. 82.
6. Ibid.
7. The author of this biography in *24 Generals* (AF: 3:74) says that he wishes to tell about the life of Brother Giles "as I learned about it from his companions and also through my own experience, from the holy man himself, who was very close to me." According to Fra Salimbene (*Chronica*, 1284 A.D.), this man is Brother Leo.
8. *Dicta*, 10, "On Resisting Temptations." All translations from Brown, *Little Flowers*, when selections of material are the same. The chapter numbers and titles are those used by Brown. [The *Dicta* were gathered from several early manuscripts and there are varying versions. For a discussion of these, see Vian, trans. and ed., *I Detti*, pp. 187–91.—Trans.]
9. Ibid., 18, "On Persevering in Good."
10. Ibid., 2, "On Faith."
11. Ibid., 10, "On Resisting Temptations."
12. Ibid., 12, "On Prayer and Its Effects."
13. Ibid., 20, "On Obedience and Its Usefulness."
14. Ibid., 10, "On Resisting Temptations."
15. Ibid.
16. *24 Generals* (AF 3:78).
17. *Dicta*, 10, "On Resisting Temptations."
18. Ibid., 12, "On Prayer and Its Effects."
19. Ibid.
20. Ibid., 20, "On Obedience and Its Usefulness."
21. Ibid., 19, "On the Religious Life and Its Security."
22. Ibid.
23. *24 Generals* (AF 3:77).
24. *Dicta*, 18, "On Persevering in Good."

25. Golubovich, *Biblioteca*, 1:105; *24 Generals* (AF 3:77); *An. Min.*, 1215 A.D., chap. XXXV; 1219 A.D., chap. XXXIV; *AA. SS.*, April 23; Lemmens, *Documenta antiqua franciscana*, 1:42, n. 5; 1:67, n. 4; Fortini, *Gli ultimi crociati.*

26. *24 Generals* (AF 3:78).

27. Ibid., pp. 76–77.

28. Ibid., p. 78.

29. Ibid., pp. 76–77.

30. Ibid., p. 84.

31. Cavalca, "Come Cristo sta in croce come uomo inamorato e come cavalier armato," *Lo specchio della croce.*

32. *24 Generals* (AF 3:101).

33. Ibid. In this episode it is said that Brother Giles went to spend time in reflection in the garden, in the part facing the city.

34. For these details, see *24 Generals* (AF 3:94–103).

35. Ibid., p. 110.

36. *Dicta*, 15, "On the Continuous Practice of Spiritual Caution."

37. Giordano da Pisa, "Le nozze spirituali," in *Prediche.*

38. Idem., "Il verace amore," in *Prediche.*

39. *Dicta*, 1, "On Virtues . . . and Vices."

40. *24 Generals* (AF 3:101).

41. Ibid., p. 102.

42. *Dicta*, 4, "On Holy Humility."

43. Ibid.

44. *24 Generals* (AF 3:90, 94).

45. Ibid., p. 112–13.

46. Ibid., p. 113.

47. Ibid.

48. Ibid., pp. 113–14.

49. Wadding, following the chronicler Mariano, puts the conversion of Brother Juniper in 1210. In *24 Generals* (AF 3:54) we read that he was "one of the favourite first disciples and companions of Saint Francis." For further discussion, see *NV* 2:298.

50. *24 Generals* (AF 3:54); *Fioretti, Vita*, 1. *Vita Juniperi*, the life of Brother Juniper as told in *24 Generals* plus some added material, is to be found in many manuscripts and editions of *Fioretti*. All citations of *Vita* refer to the *Fioretti* biography. All Eng. trans from *Life*, trans. Brown, in *Little Flowers.*

51. *24 Generals* (AF 3:59); *La Franceschina*, 2:201; *Vita*, 6.

52. *La Franceschina*, 2: 201; *Vita*, 6.

53. *24 Generals* (AF 3:56); *Vita*, 1.

54. *24 Generals* (AF 3:62); *Vita*, 10.

55. *24 Generals* (AF 3:58); *Vita*, 4.

56. *24 Generals* (AF 3:58–59); *Vita*, 4.

57. *24 Generals* (AF 3:61); *Vita*, 8.

58. *24 Generals* (AF 3:63); *Vita*, 11.

59. *24 Generals* (AF 3:60).

60. Ibid., p. 56; *Vita* 3. According to Brown (*Little Flowers*, p. 347), the tyrant Nicolò di Giovanni Cocco was a ruthless leader in Viterbo's bitter civil conflicts in 1224–27 and was "hacked to pieces" by a sword in 1227 after betraying the city to the Romans.—Trans.

61. *24 Generals* (AF 3:64); *Vita*, 13. [The name varies from one source to another: Accientialbene, Tientialbene, etc. Brown gives it as Brother Tendalbene ("Strive-

for-Good") and identifies him as Giovanni Atti of Todi, who joined the order about 1230. See *Little Flowers,* trans. Brown, p. 348.—Trans.]

62. *24 Generals* (AF 3:64); *Vita,* 14.

63. *Chronica Majora,* 1226 A.D. (*MGH,* vol. 28).

64. *Vita di Innocenzo IV* (*RIS* 3:592).

65. *Leg. S. Clarae,* 44.

66. *24 Generals* (AF 3:61); *Vita,* 9.

67. Oliger, "San Francesco a Roma," *Italia francescana nel settimo centenario,* pp. 80 ff.; Terzi, *S. Francesco a Roma,* pp. 76–79.

68. *De Conformitate* (AF 4:515).

69. Mark of Lisbon, *Chroniche,* p. 470; Mazzara, *Leggendario Francescano,* p. 40; *La Franceschina,* 2:208.

70. *24 Generals* (AF 3:265). This date is found in *An. Min.,* 1258 A.D., n. 10. For the place of burial, see also Bernardo da Bessa, *Liber de Laudibus,* (AF 3:668); *De Conformitate* (AF 4:248, 515); *An. Min.,* 1258 A.D., n. 10. Mazzara, in *Leggendario Francescano,* p. 44, attests: "His relics are in the left column of the High Altar, where the Pulpit stands in which on the most solemn feasts the Epistle is sung; and in 1621 the lead casket in which they are kept was seen, as has been noted. On the outside these words were written on a jasper memorial tablet: *Ossa fratris Iuniperi Socii Sancti Francisci.*" In 1621 the elegant sepulcral monument of Alessandro Camerino was constructed against the right pilaster of the largest arch, and until a short time ago the memorial tablet was over it. See Casimiro da Roma, *Memorie istoriche,* p. 262; Forcella, *Iscrizioni,* 1:226, n. 872. For present location of the relics, see n. e of this chapter.

Chapter 14

LOVE OF ALL CREATURES

1. *Actus,* 16; *Fioretti,* 16. In *1 Cel.,* 58, the episode is said to have taken place *prope Mevanium* or "near Bevagna" and in *3 Cel.,* 20, similarly, *prope Bevanium.* Julian of Speyer, in *Vita* (AF 10:353), says *non longe a castello cui nomen Mevanium;* and in *Leg. Maior,* XII, 3, we read *cum igitur (Sanctus) appropinquaret Bevanio*—"when he was near Bevagna."

By tradition the sermon to the birds was preached in an area called Pian dell'Arca, located along the ancient road between Bevagna and Cannara, a half-hour's walk from the latter.

In *Liber exemplorum,* 69, (*Antonianum* 2:239) we also read that Brother Masseo confirmed that it really happened: "Brother Masseo also spoke of the sermon to the birds because he was present."

2. *Fioretti,* 16.

3. *3 Cel.,* 22; *Leg. Maior,* XII, 5.

4. For the story of Lucchesio and Buonadonna: *AA. SS, Aprilis,* 3:594–610; *An. Min.,* 2:7–8.

5. For Dante as a tertiary, cf. Fortini, *Assisi nel medioevo,* pp. 250–53.

6. *Paradiso,* Canto 11, line 82; trans. Ciardi.

7. "Letter to a Minister" (*Omnibus,* p. 110).

8. Jörgensen, *Saint Francis,* bk. 3, chap. 110. Sabatier also held this opinion.

9. *Leg. Maior,* IV, 11.

10. In *Spec. Perf.*, 67, this place is called *eremitorium de Fonte Columbarum juxta Reate* ("the hermitage of Fonte Colombo, near Rieti"). It is also called Monte di Ranieri and Fonte Palombo in some ancient records (Spila, *Memorie storiche,* pp. 52–62). There is a legend that Francis, wishing absolute quiet for the redaction of the rule, ordered the birds to hush, and from then on their song has not been heard on this mountain.

11. *Spec. Perf.*, 1.

12. Ibid.; *Leg. Maior,* IV, 11.

13. *3 Cel.*, 49.

14. See chap. 10, n. c of this book.

15. Ovid, *Metamorphoses,* Bk. 2, 27–30.

16. *3 Cel.*, 37.

17. *Spec. Perf.*, 112; *Per.*, 101.

18. *Leg. Maior,* VIII, 7.

19. Luke 6:27–28.

20. *Spec. Perf.*, 112.

21. *Per.*, 92; *Spec. Perf.*, 67.

22. *2 Cel.*, 119, 120; *Per.*, 92; *Spec. Perf.*, 67.

23. *2 Cel.*, 200.

24. Sabatier, *Études,* p. 300.

25. The account of the Christmas in Greccio is taken from *1 Cel.*, 84–86. *Leg. Maior,* X, 7.

26. *2 Cel.*, 35.

27. Ibid.; *Leg. Maior,* VIII, 11.

28. *1 Cel.*, 81.

29. Ibid.; *Leg. Maior,* VIII, 8.

30. *1 Cel.*, 61; *Leg. Maior,* VIII, 8.

31. *2 Cel.*, 167; *Leg. Maior,* VIII, 8. These two authors also tell that a Siena noble gave Francis a pheasant who never wanted to leave him: *2 Cel.*, 170; *Leg. Maior,* VIII, 10. There is also a story about a rabbit caught on an island in the lake of Perugia who behaved like the Greccio rabbit: *1 Cel.*, 60.

32. *2 Cel.*, 36.

33. Ozanam, *I poeti francescani,* p. 48.

34. *Actus,* 23; *Fioretti,* 21, trans. Brown.

35. Many "peace pacts" between private citizens and factions are to be found in Assisi archives. For a comparison of these and the peace pact between Saint Francis and the wolf, see *NV* 3:210–11.

36. *1 Cel.*, 79.

37. *Fioretti,* 22.

38. *1 Cel.*, 80.

39. *2 Cel.*, 111; *Leg. Maior,* VIII, 6.

40. *2 Cel.*, 47.

41. *1 Cel.*, 77, 78. Saint Bonaventure also tells of a sheep brought up by Saint Francis at Porziuncola who attended divine services and participated in the worship. He reports that on another occasion when Saint Francis was travelling near Siena, a large flock of sheep in a field left off grazing to run to him. *Leg. Maior,* VIII, 7.

42. *1 Cel.*, 80.

43. *24 Generals* (*AF* 3: 196–97). According to Papini, fifty-six years after the death of Saint Francis, the skeleton of this crow was found on his tomb. *La storia di San Francesco,* Bk. 2, p. 27.

44. *2 Cel.,* 171; *Leg. Maior,* VIII, 9.
45. *The Praises of the Virtues (Omnibus,* p. 132).
46. For the story of the nightingale, see Minocchi's *Leggenda antica,* pp. 116–17.
47. Sabatier, *Études,* p. 300.
48. *3 Socii.,* 14.
49. This is the opening sentence of the Foreword.
50. Psalm 88.
51. *2 Cel.,* 61; *Spec. Perf.* 20.

Chapter 15

THE SERAPH

1. For these songs, see Carducci, *Cantilene e ballate,* pp. 58, 70, 78.
2. These details are from *Actus,* 9, and from *Fioretti,* "First Consideration."
3. These verses have an erotic significance, as two writers have pointed out: Cosmo, "Di un antichissimo frammento di canzone" *Giornale storico della letteratura italiana* 38:37–40; Torraca, "La Scuola poetica siciliana," in *Studi su la lirica italiana del Duecento,* pp. 150–51.
4. John 16:20.
5. *Paradiso,* Canto 11, line 106, trans. Ciardi.
6. *Fioretti,* "Second Consideration." The Gospel passage referred to is Matthew 27:52.
7. *Actus,* 9; *Fioretti,* "First Consideration." On the site where the oak stood, a chapel was built in 1602, called "Chapel of the Birds." For a rich bibliography on La Verna, see the special issue of *La Verna* of 1913 *(Studi Francescani* 11:478–554).
8. *2 Cel.,* 142; *Fioretti,* "First Consideration."
9. *2 Cel.,* 46; *Leg. Maior,* VII, 12; *Fioretti,* "First Consideration."
10. *2 Cel.,* 168; *Leg. Maior,* VIII, 10.
11. *2 Cel.,* 168.
12. *Fioretti,* "Third Consideration"; *Actus,* 39.
13. See note above.
14. *Fioretti,* "Fourth Consideration."
15. *1 Cel.,* 103.
16. Ibid., 104.
17. Ibid.
18. Ibid., 103.
19. Ibid.
20. Ibid.
21. Ibid.
22. *Leg. Maior,* XIV, 1.
23. *1 Cel.,* 103.
24. Ibid.
25. *Per.,* 43.
26. Ibid.; *Spec. Perf.,* 100.
27. *1 Cel.,* 80.
28. In *Per.,* 43, we read of his special love for the sun: "The most beautiful of all the creatures, the one which, better than all the others, could be compared to God."

29. Ibid.; *Spec. Perf.,* 119.

30. *Per.,* 49; *Spec. Perf.,* 116.

31. See note above; also *2 Cel.,* 165.

32. *Spec. Perf.,* 118. This source says that Francis especially loved water "because it symbolizes holy penitence and tribulation, and at Baptism the soul is cleansed from its stains and receives its first purification."

33. Ibid.; *Per.,* 51; *2 Cel.,* 165.

34. *1 Cel.,* 81.

35. *Spec. Perf.,* 118; *Per.,* 51; *2 Cel.,* 165.

36. *1 Cel.,* 81.

37. Ibid.

38. *Spec. Perf.,* 118; Song of Songs 2:1.

39. Job 14:7.

40. *2 Cel.,* 165; *Per.,* 51; *Spec. Perf.,* 118.

41. *Spec. Perf.,* 118.

42. 1 Corinthians 10:4.

43. *2 Cel.,* 165.

44. *24 Generals* (AF 3:67).

45. *Per.,* 43; *Spec. Perf.,* 100.

46. *Per.,* 51; *Spec. Perf.,* 118.

47. *Per.,* 43; *Spec. Perf.,* 100.

48. *Fioretti,* "Third Consideration."

49. *1 Cel.,* 81.

50. *Spec. Perf.,* 119; *Per.,* 43.

51. Isaiah 13:11.

52. For further information about Oportolo di Bernardo: *NV* 2:529–32.

53. The name of the town crier of this time is taken from records concerning the *exbanditi* of this year. *NV* 3:610.

54. For the list of these *exbanditi: NV* 3:608–11.

55. *Per.,* 44.

56. *2 Cel.,* 212.

57. Matthew 5:44.

58. *2 Cel.,* 212.

59. Matthew 5:9.

60. *Per.,* 44.

61. Cf. Fortini, *Assisi nel medioevo,* pp. 29–77.

62. These names recur frequently in three records of this period: the alliance between the commune of Assisi and the *militi* of Perugia (Arch. Com., M. 1, f. 5; *NV* 3:604–6); the decision of the podestà of Assisi in the arbitration of the war between Assisi and Bettona (M. 1, f. 8; *NV* 3:602–4); and the confirmation of the alliance between the commune of Assisi and the *militi* of Perugia (M. 1, f. 5; *NV* 3:611–12).

63. *Per.,* 44; *Spec. Perf.,* 101.

64. For these details, described in the testimony of Sister Agnese, see *Processo* (*AFH* 13:474).

65. *Spec. Perf.,* 101; see also *NV* 2:532.

66. *Per.,* 44; *Spec. Perf.,* 101.

67. See n. above.

68. Ibid.

69. Ibid.

Chapter 16

THE ROUGH WAYS

1. *Per.,* 25; *Spec. Perf.,* 104; *Actus,* 21; *Fioretti,* 19. For *soma,* see chap. 1, n. n.

2. *Per.,* 47; *Spec. Perf.,* 89.

3. *2 Cel.,* 166; *Per.,* 48; *Spec. Perf.,* 115.

4. See n. above.

5. Francis's stay in the bishop's house in Rieti is mentioned in *2 Cel.,* 92; *Per.,* 24. The latter also mentions Teobaldo di Saraceno.

6. *Per.,* 48; *Spec. Perf.,* 115.

7. *2 Cel.,* 92; *Per.,* 52; *Spec. Perf.,* 33.

8. *Per.,* 24. The same rule existed in the statutes of the commune of Assisi; see *NV* 3:215–16.

9. *1 Cel.,* 101.

10. *2 Cel.,* 93; *Leg. Maior,* VII, 6.

11. *1 Cel.,* 105.

12. *Spec. Perf.,* 87.

13. *1 Cel.,* 105; *Per.,* 59.

14. *2 Cel.,* 77; *Leg. Maior,* VII, 10; *Spec. Perf.,* 22. See also *NV* 2:464.

15. *1 Cel.,* 106.

16. *2 Cel.,* 77.

17. *Per.,* 59; *Spec. Perf.,* 22.

18. *2 Cel.,* 77.

19. Fortini, *Il ritorno di San Francesco,* 165–82.

20. Ibid., pp. 175–79. [In 1926 the author was responsible for a ceremonial re-enactment of the journey from Satriano to Assisi. A reliquary and one of Saint Francis's ragged habits was carried in the mounted procession. Such a storm took place as the riders carrying these objects re-entered Assisi. (See Fortini, *Il patrono d'Italia: La patria al suo santo,* pp. 155–61.) The storm mentioned here is likely an imaginative melding of the two events: Francis's return and the re-enactment seven hundred years later. It is quite possible that there was also a storm in 1226; but so far as the translator knows, it is not mentioned in the early sources.—Trans.]

21. *1 Cel.,* 105.

22. *Per.,* 64; *Spec. Perf.,* 121.

23. *Per.,* 28; *Spec. Perf.,* 103; *2 Cel.,* 40.

The first two of these sources report that Francis was ill and living in the palace of the bishop of Assisi. The fact that the young man, when he heard horses, looked out the window shows that the façade faced the piazza.

24. Thomas of Celano, after having told of this exchange, continues: "O martyr and martyr, who smiling and rejoicing most willingly put up with what was most bitter and most difficult to bear!" *1 Cel.,* 107.

25. *Per.,* 64; *Spec. Perf.,* 121; *2 Cel.,* 217.

26. *1 Cel.,* 107; *Leg. Maior,* XIV, 2.

27. *2 Cel.,* 51.

28. *Per.,* 29; *Spec. Perf.,* 111.

29. *Per.,* 98; *Spec. Perf.,* 109.

30. *2 Cel.,* 50.

31. *Spec. Perf.,* 122; *Per.,* 65.

32. *Spec. Perf.,* 123; *Per.,* 100.

33. Cf. chap. 12, pp. 480–82.

34. *1 Cel.,* 106; *Spec. Perf.,* 83. For Francis's praises of Porziuncola, *Spec. Perf.,* 55, 83, 84.

35. Cf. *Leg. Maior,* Preface.

Chapter 17

SISTER DEATH

1. There are references to the *Testament* in *1 Cel.,* 17; *Per.,* 77; *Spec. Perf.,* 65. It is also mentioned several times in Angelo Clareno's *Sept. trib.,* and in Ubertino da Casale, *Arbor Vitae* (1, 8). Pope Gregory IX's Bull *Quo elongati* (Sept. 28, 1230) specifically concerns it—and states that it is not binding on the friars. (*Bull. Franc.,* 1:68–70.) Today no one doubts the authenticity of the *Testament.*

Boehmer (*Analekten,* p. XLI), wrote that Francis must have dictated the *Testament* in the bishop's house between May and September. But, as we have seen, it was only in this last month that he lay ill there.

For the Latin text of the *Testament,* see *Spec. Perf.,* ed. Sabatier, CED, pp. 309–13; also *Opuscula,* pp. 77–82. [It may be found in English translation in a number of works; see especially *Omnibus,* pp. 67–70.]

2. *Spec. Perf.,* 108; *Per.,* 109.

3. *1 Cel.,* 18.

4. *Spec. Perf.,* 108. *Per.,* 109.

5. The text of the letter Saint Francis dictated for Giacoma dei Settesoli is given in *Actus,* 18; from that it was carried over into *Fioretti,* "Fourth Consideration"; *Spec. Vitae;* and *An. Min.* According to some, this text is an arbitrary reconstruction based on elements supplied by *Per.,* 101; *Spec. Perf.,* 112; and *3 Cel.,* 37–39. Cf. Edouard D'Alençon, *Frère Jacqueline,* p. 30, n. 1. But we must remember that in *Liber exemplorum* (*Antonianum* 2:238) Brother Leo is said to have reported the text of the letter in his writings: "Brother Leo, the companion of our blessed father Francis, told you that while he was suffering from that illness that was the cause of his going from this world to the Lord, he called his companions and said to them: 'Send without delay a message to Madonna Giacoma Romana (she was a very religious woman) and write, saying, "Brother Francis begs you to come at once, and bring with you a little ash-coloured cloth (for the habit) and also everything needed to make that special farina dish for the sick that she used to prepare, and even more, candles (for the funeral) . . . '"

6. *3 Cel.,* 37; *Spec. Perf.,* 112; *Per.,* 101.

7. See note above; also *Liber exemplorum* (*Antonianum* 2:238–39); *NV* 2:453–56.

8. *Spec. Perf.,* 112.

9. Ibid.

10. *3 Cel.,* 38. This cushion is preserved in the church of San Francesco in Cortona. Cf. Edouard D'Alençon, *Frère Jacqueline,* p. 56.

11. *Spec. Perf.,* ed. Lemmens, has the detail about the cloth's having been made by Cistercians in overseas countries: *Doc. Ant.,* 2:35. See also *Per.,* 101.

12. 3 Cel., 38. Cf. Edouard D'Alençon, *Frère Jacqueline,* p. 58. This veil is preserved in the Sacro Convento of Assisi.

13. *Spec. Perf.,* 112; *Per.,* 101.

14. *3 Cel.*, 38.
15. *Spec. Perf.*, 112; *Per.*, 101.
16. *2 Cel.*, 217.
17. *3 Cel.*, 38.
18. There is a reference to guards in *3 Cel.*, 32.
19. *3 Cel.*, 38. Giacoma's stay at Porziuncola was for only a few days, because Saint Francis died the same week that she arrived. *Spec. Perf.*, 112; *Per.*, 101.
20. *2 Cel.*, 217; *Leg. Maior*, XIV, 3.
21. *2 Cel.*, 215; *Leg. Maior*, XIV, 3, 4.
22. *2 Cel.*, 215.
23. *Leg. Maior*, XIV, 4; *2 Cel.*, 215.
24. *2 Cel.*, 217; *Leg. Maior*, XIV, 4.
25. *Spec. Perf.*, 88; *2 Cel.*, 216; *Leg. Maior*, XIV, 5; *Per.*, 117.
26. *2 Cel.*, 217; *Spec. Perf.*, 88; *Per.*, 117.
27. *1 Cel.*, 109.
28. Ibid.
29. John 13:1; *1 Cel.*, 110; *Leg. Maior*, XIV, 5.
30. Psalm 142; *Leg. Maior*, XIV, 5; *1 Cel.*, 109. Thomas also says, "He accepted death singing." *2 Cel.*, 214.
31. *1 Cel.*, 112; *Leg. Maior*, IV, 2.
32. *1 Cel.*, 112; *Leg. Maior*, XV, 3.
33. *3 Cel.*, 39.
34. Ibid.
35. *Spec. Perf.*, 112; *Per.*, 101.
36. *1 Cel.*, 114.
37. *3 Cel.*, 39.
38. *1 Cel.*, 112.
39. Ibid., 114.
40. Ibid., 111.
41. *Chronica (MGH, Scriptores,* vol. 32).
42. *1 Cel.*, 112.
43. Ibid., 113.
44. *Leg. Maior*, XV, 2.
45. *Spec. Perf.*, 112. ·
46. *3 Cel.*, 39.
47. *1 Cel.*, 116.
48. Ibid., 112.
49. *Leg. Maior*, XV, 4.
50. *1 Cel.*, 113.
51. For a lengthy documentation of all who saw the stigmata after the death of Saint Francis, see *NV* 2:448–51.
52. *1 Cel.*, 116; *Leg. Maior*, XV, 5.
53. A recall of the lines from Dante's *Paradiso* (Canto II): *Non dica Ascesi . . . ma Oriente*—i.e., the place of the rising sun (Saint Francis). See chap. 3, n. 1 of this book.

Fortini here also recalls his Dante-based description of Assisi in chapter 3.— Trans.
54. *1 Cel.*, 116.
55. Ibid.

56. *1 Cel.,* 117. See also, about this episode, *Leg. Maior,* XV, 5; *Spec. Perf.,* 108; *Per.,* 109.

Sabatier (*Spec. Perf.,* CED, p. 297) is puzzled that the events of the cortège in which the body of Saint Francis was carried to Assisi are not memorialized in the procession through the streets of Assisi every Good Friday morning, during which the sisters in the cloistered convents take part in the kiss of the dead Christ. This author says that he had raised the question with a number of learned clergymen but had never had a satisfactory answer. But the explanation is very simple. The Good Friday procession originated in the *laudi* of the Disciplinati, which they went about reciting all through the city on Good Friday. Substantial traces of the early practice can be found in the *laudarî* (books of lauds recited each day by the confraternities) and in the constitutions of the confraternities. These came only at the end of the thirteenth century and were unrelated to a commemoration of Francis's death. See Fortini, "Il Mistero del Venerdì Santo in Assisi," *Lettura* 24:281–88.

57. *1 Cel.,* 117.

58. *Leg. Maior,* XV, 5; *1 Cel.,* 118.

For information about the temporary placement of the body of Saint Francis in San Giorgio, see Bracaloni, "La Chiesa di San Giorgio in Assisi," *Collectana Francescana* 8:493–511. For the miracles reported to have taken place around the tomb, the canonization of Saint Francis, and the translation of the body, see Fortini, *Assisi nel medioevo,* pp. 85–119.

Bibliography

The asterisk (*) preceding an entry denotes a work added by the translator. Listings conform to those of the National Union Catalogue of the Library of Congress.

I. Fortini, Arnaldo. *Nova Vita di San Francesco.* Assisi, 1959. (*NV*)

The first Italian edition of this work consists of four volumes bound in five. This biography is a translation of the two separate books of volume 1, together with the bibliography and relevant portions of the index, which make up volume 4.

Volume 2 is devoted to a discussion of the primary sources for the life of Saint Francis and to comprehensive collections of historical materials about all the persons, events, and places closely identified with him. It also includes the same detailed information about Saint Clare. Other topics that are treated in depth are the Porziuncola indulgence, the stigmata, the founding of the Franciscan Secular Order (formerly known as the lay Third Order), and the writing of the *Canticle of the Sun.*

Volume 3 provides materials on the city of Assisi and includes historical information about structures in and near the city; the villages, places, and governmental units of the Assisi *contado;* the government, officials, laws, military units, and weapons in the time of Saint Francis; and the dress, houses and their furnishings, daily routines, and customs in that period. Included also are summaries of material in the various Assisi archives. The full texts of records and documents relevant to Franciscan history are given.

Within the limits of feasibility, some portions of this rich collection of materials have been introduced by the translator into notes and footnotes in this book. It is hoped that all the *NV* citations will direct the attention of the researcher to the vast amount of historical material to be found in the complete Italian edition.

Nova Vita is a greatly revised and vastly expanded version of an earlier biography of Saint Francis by Arnaldo Fortini published under the same title in 1926. The 1959 edition, is, however, the *only* one to which citations in the text refer.

II. Source Materials

A. *Writings of Saint Francis*

Those generally recognized include: Rule of 1221 and Rule of 1223, Testament, Religious Life in Hermitages, Form of Life and Last Will for Saint Clare, Admonitions, Praises of God (on the same parchment is the blessing given Brother Leo),

Canticle of Brother Sun, Praises before the Office (often placed with a paraphrase of Our Father; see below), Office of the Passion, Praise of the Virtues, Salutation of the Virgin Mary.

A group of letters (not all of which are accepted as authentic by all historians). These include Letters to All the Faithful, to All Clerics, to a General Chapter, to a Minister, to all Superiors of the Friars Minor, to the Rulers of the People, and to Brother Leo.

Paraphrase of the Our Father, the prayer Absorbeat, and the Letter to Saint Anthony, all considered doubtful by some historians.

Two newly discovered or newly identified works by Saint Francis have been added by the translator:

*Message of Saint Francis to the Poor Clares of San Damiano. Edited by Giovanni Boccali. English translation by Raphael Brown, in Esser, *Rule and Testament,* pp. 217–18. Chicago, 1977.

* Letter of Saint Francis to the Brothers and Sisters of Penance. Edited by Cajetan Esser, *Lettre de Rome* 1 (1977):27–29. English translation by Marion Habig, in Esser, *Rule and Testament,* pp. 221–26. Chicago, 1977.

Collections of these works listed by the author (except for the last two) include:
Boehmer, Heinrich. *Analekten zur Geschichte des Franziskus von Assisi.* Tübingen, 1904. 2nd, edited by F. Wiegand, 1930.
Facchinetti, Vittorino. *Gli scritti di S. Francesco con introduzione e note critiche.* 3rd ed. Milan, 1944.
Opuscula Sancti Patris Francisci Assisiensis. Quaracchi, 1st ed., 1904; 2nd ed., 1941.
Vicinelli, Augusto. *Gli scritti di San Francesco e i Fioretti.* 3rd ed. Milan, 1955.
Wadding, Luke. *B. P. Francisci Assisiatis Opuscula.* Antwerp, 1623.

* English translations of these writings have been taken (with occasional slight variations) from those by Benen Fahy, in *Omnibus,* pp. 1–75.

B. Early Franciscan Source Materials
A comprehensive discussion of the documents, biographies, chronicles, and other works that are primary sources for the life of Saint Francis would require a book in itself, so lengthy is the list, so complex, in some cases, are the questions of authorship and relationship to other works. A description of the major ones can be found in *NV* 2:7–17. There are also extensive treatments of the subject in English by several authors, especially by Raphael Brown, both in special sections devoted to them in his bibliographies in *Omnibus* and in Englebert, *Saint Francis of Assisi* (see below), together with his notes in the latter book, pp. 509–25.

All the major source materials are included in the following sections, however, listed alphabetically to facilitate the location of materials mentioned in the notes and footnotes.

C. Archival Material
Historical information about the city is taken from the rich collection of material in the various Assisi archives. These include the Archivio della Cattedrale di San Rufino, Archivio del Comune (in which is located the earliest surviving copy of the four books of city statutes, dating from the fifteenth century), Archivio del Sacro Convento, Archivio del Monastero di Sant'Apollinare, Archivio del Monastero di

Santa Chiara, Archivio Notarile, and Archivio del Convento della Porziuncola. Most of these are now housed in the Biblioteca di Assisi, the municipal library. Among the many famous and very rare items is Ms. 338, dating from the early thirteenth century, which contains many of the major sources for the life of Saint Francis and Saint Clare and also the oldest known copy of the *Canticle of Brother Sun.*

Also included among the archival materials on which this book is based are various records from the Archivio del Comune di Perugia and the ancient historical poem of Bonifacio da Verona, *L'Eulistea,* which gives the details of the war in which Francis fought as a youth (see also Bonaini, Fabretti, e Polidori).

III. Bibliographies

* Brown, Raphael. A *Francis of Assisi Research Bibliography.* In Englebert, *Saint Francis of Assisi,* 2nd rev. ed., pp. 495–607, and *Omnibus,* pp. 1669–1760.
* Facchinetti, Vittorino. *Guide bibliografiche, San Francesco d'Assisi.* Rome, 1928.
* Frascadore, Ermenegildo and Ooms, Herwig. *Bibliografia delle bibliografie francescane.* Florence, 1965.
* Herscher, Irenaeus. *Franciscan Literature, A Checklist.* St. Bonaventure, N.Y., 1958.

IV. Periodicals

Among the many periodicals mentioned by the author in individual citations, he included these in his bibliography as major sources:

Analecta Bollandiana. Société des Bollandistes. Brussels, 1882—. Periodical forming a supplement to *Acta Sanctorum.*

Annales Franciscaines. Monthly periodical of Capuchins of Paris. 1861—.

Antonianum. Quarterly of the Friars Minor of the Collegio di S. Antonio di Roma. Rome, 1926—.

Archivum Franciscanum Historicum. Quarterly of the Friars Minor of Collegio di S. Bonaventura. Grottaferrata, 1908—.

Archivio Ibero-Americano. Periodical of Franciscans of Spain. Madrid, 1914–35, 1941—.

* *Bolletino della Deputazione di Storia Patria per l'Umbria.* Perugia, 1895—.

Collectanea Franciscana. Quarterly of the Capuchins of Collegio di San Lorenzo da Brindisi in Rome. 1931—. Includes extensive Franciscan bibliographies.

Études Franciscaines. Monthly periodical of Capuchins in France. Paris, 1899–1938, n.s. 1950—.

Italia Franciscana. Bi-monthly journal of the Capuchins. Rome, 1926—.

Miscellanea Franciscana. Bi-monthly journal of the Conventuals. Rome, 1886—.

* *San Francesco, Patrono d'Italia* (formerly *San Francesco d'Assisi*). Monthly periodical of the Basilica di San Francesco. Assisi, 1920—.

Studi Francescani (formerly *La Verna*). Florence, 1903—.

A Special Note

Biblical quotations in English have been taken from *The New American Bible,* New York and London, 1970. Translations of the Psalms in this Bible are from the Hebrew text, in which the numbering system is somewhat different from that in the Vulgate text, which was used by the author. Citations of the Psalms, therefore, have been altered when necessary.

V. Unpublished Manuscripts

Assisi, Biblioteca di. Cod memb. s. XIV, no. 341. "Liber Historiarum S. Romane" [by (Giovanni) Elemosina di Giacomo]. Extract in Golubovich, *Biblioteca*, 2:103–15. See also section IIC.

Florence. Biblioteca Nazionale di Firenze. Ms. cart. Magliabechiana 38, codex 99. "Libro delle vite dei Sancti Frati Minori" [by Mariano da Firenze]. Extract in Golubovich, *Biblioteca*, 1:77–80.

———. MS. II, II, 449, f. 10. "Vita di San Francesco" [by Mariano da Firenze].

Paris. Bibliothèque National Parisien. Cod. Parigino lat. 5006. "Chronicon seu liber ystoria plurime" [by Johanne Elemosine]. Extract in Golubovich, *Biblioteca*, 2:116–37.

Santa Maria degli Angeli. Archivio del Convento della Porziuncola. Ms. of 1804 A.D. "Dissertazione sull'antica chiesa che circondava Porziuncola" [by Angelo Grimaldi].

VI. Books and Articles

Abate, Giuseppe. *La casa dove nacque San Francesco nella sua nuova documentazione storia.* Gubbio, 1941.

———. "La casa paterna di S. Chiara e falsificazioni storiche dei secoli XVI e XVII intorno alla medesima Santa e a S. Francesco d'Assisi." *DPSU* 41 (1944):34–160.

———. *La Leggenda Napoletana di S. Francesco e l'Ufficio rimato di Giuliano da Spira secondo un codice Umbro.* Assisi, 1930.

———. "La nascita del Cantico di Frate Sole nel Palazzo Vescovile di Assisi." *Misc. Fran.* 56 (1956):333–415.

———. "Nuovi studi sulla Leggenda di S. Francesco detta dei Tre Compagni." *Misc. Fran.* 39 (1939):1–55.

———. *Nuovi studi sull'ubicazione della casa paterna di S. Chiara d'Assisi.* Assisi, 1954.

———. "Storia e leggenda intorno alla nascita di S. Francesco d'Assisi." *Misc Fran.* 48 (1948):515–49; 49 (1949):123–53, 350–74.

Acta Sanctorum. Société des Bollandistes. Antwerp, 1643 A.D. ff. See also *Analecta Bollandiana.*

Acta sanctorum ordinis benedictini Edited by J. Mabillon and T. Ruinart. 9 vols. Paris, 1668–1701.

Actus Beati Francisci et sociorum eius. Edited by Paul Sabatier. In Collection d'Études et Documents, vol. 4. Paris, 1902.

Actus S. Francisci in Valle Reatina. Legend taken from Codex 679 of the Biblioteca Comunale di Assisi. Edited by Francesco Pennachi. Foligno, 1911.

Agostino da Stroncone. "Umbria Serafica." *Misc. Fran.* 2 (1887); 3 (1888); 4 (1889); 5 (1890); 6 (1895); 7 (1898).

Albert of Stade. *Annales.* In *MGH, Scriptores,* vol. 16.

Alberti, Leandro. *Descrittione di tutta Italia.* Venice, 1553.

Alengry, Charles. *Les foires de Champagne: Étude d'histoire économique.* Paris, 1915.

Alessandri, Leto. *Inventario dell'antica biblioteca del Sacro Convento di San Francesco in Assisi compilato nel 1381.* Assisi, 1906.

Alessandri, Leto e Mazzatinti, Giuseppe. *Inventario dei manoscritti della biblioteca del convento di S. Francesco di Assisi.* Forlì, 1894.

Alessandri, Leto e Pennacchi, Francesco. *Bullarium Pontificium quod exstat in Archivio Sacri Conventus S. Francisci Assisiensis.* Quaracchi, 1920.

Alighieri, Dante. See Dante.

Amadeo da Solero. *Glorie della Sacra Porziuncola.* Perugia, 1858.

Amaduzzi, Giovanni Cristoforo. *Anecdota litteraria ex mss. codicibus eruta.* Rome, 1773.

Analecta Franciscana, sive Chronica aliaque varia documenta ad historiam fratrum minorum spectantia, edita a Patribus Collegii San Bonaventurae, adiuvantibus aliis eruditis viris. 10 vols. Quaracchi, 1885–1941.

Ancajani, Lodovico. *Del Martire S Vittorino.* Assisi, 1872.

Andrea Cappellano. *De Amore libri tres.* Edited by E. Trojel. Copenhagen, 1892.

* Andreozzi, Gabriele. "L'ubicazione della 'Platea nova' di Assisi (1228–1229)." *Pace e Bene* 24 (April–June 1975):41–43.

Angeli, Franciscus Maria. *Collis Paradisi amoenitas seu sacri conventus assisiensis historiae.* Montefiascone, 1704.

Angelillis, Ciro. *Un punto inesplorato nella vita del Poverello.* Liri, 1928.

Angelini, Nicola. *Brevi notizie intorno a San Rufino Vescovo e Martire, protettore della città di Assisi.* Frascati, 1885.

Angelo Clareno. *Chronicon seu Historia septem tribulationum ordinis minorum.* Shortened version, edited by I. von Döllinger, in *Beiträge zur Sektengeschichte des Mittelalters,* 2:417–526. Munich, 1890. For the first two books in full, edited by Felice Tocco, *Le Due Prime Tribulazioni dell'Ordine Francescano.* Rome, 1908. The remainder of the work, edited by Franz Ehrle, in *Archiv für Litteratur und Kirchengeschichte des Mittelalters,* vol. 2. Berlin, 1886.

———. *Expositio Regulae Fratrum Minorum.* Edited by Livario Oliger. Quaracchi, 1912.

Angelo da Spoleto, *Relazione trasmessa da fr. Elemosina di Assisi.* In Golubovich, *Biblioteca,* 3:60–72.

Anglade, Joseph. *Les troubadours: Leur vie, leurs oeuvres, leur influence.* Paris, 1908.

Annales Bergomates. In *MGH, Scriptores,* vol. 18.

Annales Brixienses. In *MGH, Scriptores,* vol. 18.

Annales Casinenses seu Anonymi Casinensis Chronicon. In *MGH, Scriptores,* vol. 19.

Annales Cremonenses. In *MGH, Scriptores,* vol. 18.

Annali Bolognesi. See Salvioli, L.

Annali di Santa Giustina di Padova. In *MGH, Scriptores,* vol. 19.

Annali Genovesi dopo Caffaro e i suoi continuatori. Edited by Giovanni Monleone. Genoa, 1941. Also: *Annales Genuenses.* In *MGH, Scriptores,* vol. 18, and in *RIS* vol. 3. Contains chronicles of Caffaro, Ogerio Pane, and Marchisio Scriba.

Annibali, De Latera Flaminio. "Della recente chiesa di Rivotorto." In *Supplementum ad Bullarium Franciscanum.* Rome, 1780.

———. *Manuale de' Frati Minori.* Rome, 1786.

———. See also *Bullarium Franciscanum.*

Anonimo Cortenese. *Vita di frate Elia.* Livorno, 1755.

Anonyma Bruxellensis. See Fierens, Alphonse.

Anonymus Perusinus (Anonymous Perugian). Edited by Francesco Van Ortroy. In *Misc. Fran.* 9 (1902):33–48. *Also in *Fonti Francescane,* 1:1121–53.

Ansidei, Vincenzo, ed. *Regestum reformationum Comunis Perusii ab anno MCCLVI ad annum MCCC.* Fonti per la Storia dell'Umbria, no. 1. Perugia, 1935.

Ansidei, Vincenzo, and Giannantoni, L. *I codici delle Sommissioni al Comune di Perugia.* In *DPSU* 6 (1900):317–28; 8 (1902):135–58.

Antolini, Giovanni Antonio. *Del tempio d'Ercole in Cori e di Minerva in Assisi.* 2nd ed. Milan, 1828.

Antonelli, Giovanni Antonio. "Le più antiche carte (sec. XI) del monastero di Sassovivo." *Benedictina* 2 (1948):95–158.

Antonio d'Orvieto. *Cronologia della provincia serafica riformata dell'Umbria.* Perugia, 1717.

Antonio de' Reboldi. *Itinerarium ad montem Sinai.* In Golubovich, *Biblioteca,* 3:326–42.

Arbois de Jubainville. *Catalogue d'actes des comptes de Brienne.* In *Bibliothèque de l'École des Chartres* 33 (1872):141–86.

Archiv für Literatur und Kirchengeschichte des Mittelalters. Edited by Heinrich Denifle and Franz Ehrle. Berlin and Freiburg im Breisgau, 1885–1900; reprinted, Graz, 1955–56.

Arthur du Moustier. *Martirologium franciscanum.* Recognitum et auctum a PP. Ignatio Beschin et Juliano Palazzolo. Rome, 1938.

Assisi, Archives. See section IIC in this bibliography, also Brizi and Pardi.

Assisi Statutes. See *Libri magnifice . . .*

Attal, Salvatore. *Frate Elia, compagno di San Francesco.* Rome, 1936.

———. *La casa dove nacque San Francesco. Studio critico.* Rome, 1942.

———. *San Francesco d'Assisi.* 2nd ed. Padua, 1947.

Auvray, Lucien, ed. *Les registres de Grégoire IX.* Paris, 1896–99.

Azzi Vitelleschi, Giustiniano. *Statuti di Perugia dell'anno MCCXLII.* Rome, 1956.

Bacheca, M. "La cripta triastila di S. Benedetto al Subasio." In *Atti dell'Accademia Properziana del Subasio,* serie V, no. 4 (June 1956).

Baluze, Etienne. *Vita Innocentii papae III.* In *RIS,* vol. 3.

Barban, Bernardino. *L'isoletta di "S. Francesco del Deserto" nelle lagune di Venezia.* Vicenza, 1927.

Bargellini, Piero. *San Francesco d'Assisi.* Turin, 1941.

Barnabé d'Alsace. See Meistermann, Barnabé.

Baronio, Cesare. *Annales ecclesiastici.* Bar-le-Duc, 1864–83.

Bartholi, Franciscus. See Francesco di Bartolo.

Bartholomaeis, Vincenzo de. *Le origini della poesia drammatica italiana.* 2nd ed. Turin, 1952.

———. *Poesie provenzali storiche relative all'Italia.* Rome, 1931.

Bartholomaeo de Pisa. *De Conformitate vitae Beati Francisci ad vitam Domini Iesu.* In *AF* 4 and 5 (1906–12).

Bartoli, A. "I documenti per la storia del Settizonio Severiano." *Bollettino d'Arte del Ministero della Pubblica Istruzione,* 1909.

Bartoli, Francesco. *Storia di Perugia.* Perugia, 1843–46.

Bartolomasi, P. "Il lupo di Gubbio." *Misc. Fran.* 10 (1906):32–56.

Bartolomeo, Tridentino. *Epilogus in S. Franciscum.* In *AF* 10 (1926–40):540–43.

Bassermann, E. See Roon-Bassermann, Elisabeth von.

Bastianini, Giovanni. "L'elegia del Pontano a San Francesco." *Misc. Fran.* 47 (1947):571–78.

Battistini, Mario. "I Padri Bollandisti Henschenius e Papebrochius ad Assisi nel 1660." *Studi Francescani* 27 (1930):161–65.

Beato da Valdagno. *Annali Miss. della Provincia di S. Antonio di Venezia* (1220).

Beauvillé, Victor de. *Recueil de documents inédits concernant la Picardie.* Paris, 1860–82.

Bédier, Joseph, ed. *Le Roman de Tristan par Thomas.* Paris, 1902–05.

———. "Les chansons de geste et les routes d'Italie." In his *Les légendes épiques,* 2:145–293. 2nd ed. Paris, 1917.

Belelli, Giovanni. *L'Istituto del Podestà di Perugia nel secolo XIII.* Bologna, 1936.

Benedetto, Luigi Foscolo. *Il Cantico di Frate Sole.* Florence, 1941.

Bensi, Gaetano. *Il castello di Casacastalda.* Milan, 1957.

Benvenuto dei Rambaldis da Imola. *Comentum super Dantis Aldigherij Comoediam.* 5 vols. Florence, 1887.

Berger, Élie. *Les registres d'Innocent IV.* Paris, 1884–1919.

Bernardus de Bessa. *Catalogus Generalium Ministrorum Ordinis Fratrum Minorum.* In *AF* 3 (1897):693–712.

――――. *Liber de Laudibus B. Francisci.* In *AF* 3 (1897):666–92.

Bernardi Thesaurarii. *Liber de Acquisitione Terrae Sanctae ab an. 1095 ad an. circiter 1230, gallice scriptus, tum in latinam linguam conversus circ. an. 1320 a fr. Francisco Pipino bononiensi Ord. Praed.* In *RIS,* vol. 7.

Berson, Léon Louis (Ubald d'Alençon). "De l'origine française de Saint François d'Assisi." *Études Franciscaines* 10 (1903):449–4⁵ʷ.

――――. *Les Opuscules de Saint François d'Assisi.* Paris, 1905.

Bertoni, Giulio. *I trovatori d'Italia.* Modena, 1915.

――――. *Poesie, leggende, costumanze del medio evo.* Modena, 1917.

Besta, Ernesto. *Storia del diritto italiano.* Milan, 1941–45.

* Bianco, Alfredo. *Asti Medioevale.* Asti, 1960.

Bihl, Michael. "De Domino Hieronymo Iohannis, qui S. Francisci defuncti stigmata palpavit." *AFH* 33 (1940):219–20.

――――. "Documenta inedita Archivi Protomonasterii S. Clarae Assisii." *AFH* 5 (1912):291–98; 6 (1913):144–55.

Bini, Pompeo. *La verità scoperta ne' tre Santuari della città di Assisi: la Basilica di S. Francesco, la Porziuncola, e Rivotorto.* Florence, 1721.

Birnie, Arthur. *Storia economica dell'Europa occidentale.* Italian translation by A. Levi. Milan, 1933.

Boehmer, Heinrich. *Analekten.* See Writings of Saint Francis.

――――. See Giordano da Giano.

Boehmer, Johann Friedrich. See *Regesta Imperii.*

Bonaca, Aurelio. "Le memorie francescane di Trevi." *Studi francescani* 24 (1927):12–35, 113–48.

Bonaini, Francesco; Fabretti, Ariodante; e Polidori, Filippo-Luigi. *Cronache e storie inedite della città di Perugia.* In *Arch. Stor. Ital.,* vol. 16, pt. 1 (1850). Includes *Bonifacii Veronensis, De rebus a Perusinis gestis an. MCL-MCCXCII, historia metrica quae vocatur Eulistea,* pp. 1–52. *Annali attribuiti ad uno di Casa Oddi,* pp. 53–68. *Cronaca detta Diario del Graziani,* pp. 69–750.

Bonaventure, Saint (Giovanni di Fidanza). *Legendae duae de vita S. Francisci Seraphici.* In *AF* 10. *Leg. Maior,* pp. 555–662; *Leg. Minor,* pp. 653–78. Italian translation by A. Battelli. San Casciano, 1926. * English translation by Benen Fahy in *Omnibus. Major Life,* pp. 613–787; *Minor Life,* pp. 789–83.

Bonazzi, Luigi. *Storia di Perugia dalle origini al 1860.* 2 vols. Perugia, 1875–79.

Boncompagno da Signa. *Liber de obsidione Anconae.* In *RIS,* vol. 6.

Bongars, Jacques, ed. *Gesta Dei per Francos.* Hanover, 1611.

Boniface VIII. See Digard, Faucon, Thomas, and Fawtier.

Bonifacio da Verona. *Eulistea.* See Bonaini, Fabretti, and Polidori.

Bormann, Eugen, ed. *Corpus Inscriptionum Latinarum,* 11:783–809. Vienna, 1888.

Bourgeois. *Histoire des comtes di Brienne.* Troyes, 1848.

Bournet, Albert. *S. François d'Assise, étude sociale et médicale.* Paris and Lyon, 1893.

Bourquelet, Louis Félix. *Études sur les foires de la Champagne.* Mémoires de l'Acadèmie des Inscriptions et belles lettres. 2nd Series, vols. 1 and 2. Paris, 1865.

Boutiot, Théophile. *Histoire de la ville de Troyes et de la Champagne meriodionale.* 5 vols. Paris, 1870–80.

* Boyd, Catherine E. *Tithes and Parishes in Medieval Italy: The Historical Roots of a Modern Problem.* Ithaca, N.Y., 1952.

Bracaloni, Leone. "Assisi Medioevale: Studio Storico Topografico." *AFH* 7 (1914):3–19.

——. *Casa, casato e stemma di S. Francesco.* Assisi, 1893.

——. *Il Cantico di Frate Sole composto da San Francesco.* Milan, 1927.

——. "Il prodigioso Crocifisso che parlò a San Francesco." *Studi Francescani* 36 (1939):185–212.

——. "La Chiesa di S. Giorgio in Assisi." *Collectanea Franciscana* 8 (1938):493–511.

——. *La Chiesa Nuova di San Francesco converso, casa paterna del Santo di Assisi.* Todi, 1943.

——. *Storia di San Damiano in Assisi.* 2nd ed. Todi, 1926.

* Brady, Ignatius. See *Legenda Sanctae Clarae.*

Branca, Vittore. "Il Cantico di Frate Sole." *AFH* 41 (1948):3–87.

Bréhier, Louis. *L'Église et l'Orient au Moyen-âge. Les Croisades.* Paris, 1907.

* Brentano, Robert. *Rome before Avignon: A Social History of Thirteenth Century Rome.* New York, 1974.

* ——. *Two Churches: England and Italy in the Thirteenth Century.* Princeton, 1968.

Briganti, Antonio. *Le corporazioni delle Arti nel Comune di Perugia.* Perugia, 1910.

Briganti, Francesco. *Città dominanti e Comuni Minori nel Medio Evo, con speciale riguardo alla repubblica Perugina.* Perugia, 1906.

——. *L'Umbria nella storia del notariato italiano. Archivi notarili nelle provincie di Perugia e Terni.* Perugia, 1958.

Brizi, Alfonso. *Catalogo delle pergamene e degli antichi autografi dell'Archivio comunale di Assisi.* Assisi, 1903.

——. *Della Rôcca di Assisi.* Assisi, 1898.

——. "La facciata del duomo di Assisi non è opera di Giovanni da Gubbio." *Atti dell'Accademia Properziana del Subasio in Assisi* 3 (1910), no. 8:177–93.

——. "Mura pelasgiche in Assisi." *Atti dell'Accademia Properziana del Subasio in Assisi* 2 (1907), no. 16:269–74.

——. *Studi storico-artistici sul duomo d'Assisi.* Assisi, 1881.

——. "Tracce umbro-romane in Assisi." *Atti dell'Accademia Properziana del Subasio in Assisi* 2 (1908), no. 23:405–34.

* Brown, Raphael. *Franciscan Mystic. The Life of Blessed Brother Giles of Assisi, Companion of Saint Francis.* Garden City, N.Y., 1962.

* ——. *True Joy from Assisi.* Chicago, 1978.

* ——. See also *Fioretti,* "Vitae Beati Aegidii," "Vita Juniperi."

* Brunacci, Aldo. "Il messale consultato da San Francesco." *San Francesco Patrono d'Italia* 58 (March, 1978):80–88.

——. "Leggende e culto di S. Rufino in Assisi." *DPSU* 45 (1948):5–91.

Bruni, A. *Specchio di Perfezione tradotto in toscano.* Florence, 1503.

Bruschelli, Domenico. *Assisi città serafica e santuarj che la decorano ad istruzione e guida dei forestieri che vi concorrono.* Rome, 1821.

Bughetti, Benvenuto. "Codices duo Florentini Archivi Nationalis Ordinem Clarissarum spectantes," *AFH* 5 (1912):573–80.

——. "Per la casa paterna di San Francesco in Assisi." *AFH* 34 (1941):243–60, 449–55.

————. "San Leo nel Montefeltro, dove avenne la donazione della Verna." Special issue of *La Verna* (*Studi Francescani 11* (1913):6–86).

Bulgarini, Domenico. *Santo Francesco*. Turin, 1940.

Bullarium Franciscanum. Vols. 1–4. Edited by Johanne Hyacinthe Sbaralea. Rome, 1759–68. *Ad Bullarium Supplementum*. Edited by Annibaldi da Latera. Rome, 1780. Vols. 5–7. Edited by Conrad Eubel. Rome, 1898–1904. *New Series*. Edited by Ulrich Hüntemann and J. M. Pou y Marti. Quaracchi, 1929. *Bullarii Franciscani Epitome*. Edited by Conrad Eubel. Quaracchi, 1908. *Supplement to Epitome*. Edited by Conrad Eubel. Quaracchi, 1908.

Caffaro. See *Annales Genuenses*.

Caggese, Romolo. *Classi e comuni rurali nel medio evo italiano. Saggio di storia economica e giuridica*. 2 vols. Florence, 1907–08.

————. *Dal concordato di Worms alla fine della prigionia di Avignone (1122–1377)*. Turin, 1939.

Cahen, Claude. *La Syrie du Nord à l'époque des Croisades et la principauté franque d'Antioche*. Paris, 1940.

Cajetan, Constantine. See Pier Damiani.

Calamita, Francesco. *La persona di San Francesco d'Assisi, Note d'Antropologia*. Bitonto, 1912.

Calasso, Francesco. *Gli ordinamenti giuridici del rinascimento medievale*. Milan, 1949.

Calimala, Statuti di. See Filippi.

Callebaut, André. "Autour de la rencontre à Florence de S. François de du Cardinal Hugolin (en été 1217)." *AFH* 19 (1926):530–58.

Calò, Giovanni. *Enciclopedia Italiana*, s.v. "Cavalleria e Cavalieri."

Cambridge Medieval History, vols. 4–6. Edited by H. M. Gwatkin, J. P. Whitney, J. R. Tanner, C. W. Previté-Orton, Z. N. Brooke. Cambridge, England, 1927–29.

Camilli, Alessandro. *Memorie francescane in Orte*. Subiaco, 1927.

Campano, Johanne Antonio. *De vita et gestis Brachii perusini*. In *RIS*, vol. 19.

Carabellese, Francesco. "La Puglia e la Terrasanta." *Rassegna Pugliese* 17 (1890), no. 10.

————. "Un nuovo libro di mercanti alle fiere di Sciampagna." *Arch. Stor. Ital.* 13 (1894):357–63.

Carattoli, Luigi; Guardabassi, Mariano; Rossi-Scotti, Giovan Batista. "Descrizione del Santuario di S. Francesco d'Assisi (1863)." *DPSU* 28:88–227.

Cardella, Lorenzo. *Memorie storiche dei Cardinali della Sa. Roma*. 8 vols. Rome, 1792–97.

Cardelli, Enrico. *Studio costruttivo sulla chiesa di San Rufino in Assisi*. Rome, 1929.

Carducci, Giosuè; *Cantilene e ballate, strombotti e madrigali nei secoli XIII e XIV*. Pisa, 1871.

————. *Jaufre Rudel*. In *Opere*, 10:245. Bologna, 1888.

————. *Prose*. Bologna, 1909.

Casella, Mario. "Il Cantico delle Creature." *Studi medievali* 16(1943–50):102–34.

Casimiro da Roma. *Memorie istoriche della chiesa e convento di Santa Maria in Aracoeli*. Rome, 1736.

Casolini, Fausta. *Il Protomonastero di S. Chiara in Assisi. Storia e cronaca (1253–1950)*. Milan, 1950.

————. "La triplice corona. Problemi della vita di S. Agnese di Favarone." *Chiara d'Assisi* 2 (1954):6–12.

————. See *Legenda Sanctae Clarae Virginis*.

————. See Thomas of Celano.

Catalano, Michele. *Il romanzo di Perugia e di Corciano.* Perugia, 1925.

————. "Inventario della Biblioteca di San Benedetto di Monte Subasio." *Atti dell'Accademia Properziana del Subasio in Assisi* 4 (1925):7.

Cattani, Niccolò Antonio. *Breve ragguaglio della natura e qualità dell'acqua nomata dal volgo in Assisi di Mojano.* Assisi, 1737.

Cavalca, Domenico. *Lo Specchio della croce.* Venice, 1515.

Cavaliere, Alfredo. *Cento liriche provenzali.* Bologna, 1938.

Cecchini, Giovanni. *Archivio storico del Comune di Perugia. Inventario.* Rome, 1956.

Ceci, Getulio. *Alla ricerca di fra Iacopone.* Todi, 1932.

* Cencetti, Giorgio, ed. *Le Carte dell'Abbazia di S. Croce di Sassovivo.* 7 vols. Florence, 1973.

Chanson de Roland. * English translation by Dorothy Sayers. *The Song of Roland.* Baltimore, 1960.

Chavin de Malan, François Emile. *Histoire de Saint François d'Assise.* Paris, 1841. Italian translation: *Storia di S. Francesco d'Assisi (1182–1226).* Prato, 1846.

Chiappelli, Luigi. "La formazione storica del comune cittadino in Italia." *Arch. Stor. Ital.* 6 (1926):3–59; 7(1927):177–229; 10(1928):3–89; 13(1930):3–59; 14 (1930):3–56.

* Chioccioni, Pietro. *Assisi Romana e la Romanità di San Francesco.* Rome, 1962.

Chronica XXIV Generalium Ordinis Minorum (1209–1374). Attributed to Arnaud de Sarrant or Samatan. In *AF* 3 (1897):1–575.

Ciatti, Felice. *Delle memorie annali et istoriche delle Cose di Perugia, divisa in quattro parti, cioè: Perugia Etrusca, Roma, Augusta e Pontificia.* Perugia, 1638.

* Cicioni, G. C. "Le rose di San Francesco in Santa Maria degli Angeli." *Misc. Fran.* 18 (1917):3–7.

Ciofi, Giuseppe. *Santuari della serafica Città d'Asisi, con la notitia de' corpi santi, reliquie insigni, e memorie, ch'ivi si conservano.* Ancona, 1664.

Cionacci, Francesco. *Storia della beata Umiliana de' Cerchi, vedova fiorentina del Terz' Ordine di San Francesco.* Florence, 1682.

Ciro da Pesaro. See Ortolani, Ciro.

Clareno. See Angelo Clareno.

Codagnello, Giovanni. *Chronicon Placentium ab an. 1012 usque ad an. 1235.* Edited by L. A. Huillard-Brèholles. Paris, 1856.

————. *Gesta obsidionis Damiaetae. MGH, Scriptores,* vol. 31. See also Golubovich, *Biblioteca,* 1:315.

Cognasso, Francesco. *Le genesi delle Crociate.* Turin, 1934.

Collenuccio, Pandolfo. *Dal compendio dell'istoria del regno di Napoli.* Venice, 1613.

Conte di Valdagno. See Marzotto, Gaetano.

Continuatio Aquicinetina. In *MGH, Scriptores,* vol. 6.

Coronelli, Vincenzo. *Sacro Pellegrinaggio alli celebri e divoti Santuari di Loreto, Assisi.* Venice, 1700.

Corpus iuris canonici. Edited by Emil Albert Friedberg. 2 vols. Leipzig, 1879–81.

Cosmo, Umberto. *Con Madonna Povertà.* Bari, 1940.

————. "Di un antichissimo frammento di canzone conservatoci dagli scrittori francescani." *Giornale storico della letteratura italiana* 38 (1901):1–40.

Cotton, Charles. *The Grey Friars of Canterbury, 1224 to 1538.* Manchester, 1924.

* Creekmore, Hubert. *Lyrics of the Middle Ages.* New York, 1959.

Crescini, Vincenzo. "Il bacio di Ginevra e il bacio di Paolo." *Studi Danteschi* 3 (1971):5–58.

———. "Nuove postille al trattato amoroso d'Andrea Cappellano." *Atti del Reale Istituto Veneto* 69 (1909–10):1–99, 473–504.
Cresi, Angelo. "La benedizione di Fra Leone." Special issue of *La Verna* (*Studi Francescani* 11 (1913):110–22).
Cresi, Domenico. "Chronologia di S. Chiara." *Studi Francescani* 25 (50):260–67.
Cristofani, Antonio. *Delle storie di Assisi, libri sei.* Assisi, 3rd ed., 1902, * 4th ed., 1959. (Page citations from 4th edition.)
———. *Il più antico poema della vita di S. Francesco.* See *Legenda versificata.*
———. *Storia della chiesa e del chiostro di San Damiano.* Assisi, 1882.
Cronaca piacentina. Parma, 1862.
Cronache e storie inedite della città di Perugia. See Bonaini, Fabretti, and Polidori.
Cuthbert of Brighton. "A Disputed Story Concerning St. Clare." *AFH* 6 (1913):670–80.
* Dallari, Primo. *Frate Elia.* Milan, 1970.
Dandolo, Andrea. *Chronicon.* In *RIS,* vol. 12.
Dante Alighieri. *La Divina Commedia.* *English translation by John Ciardi. Reprint editions, 3 vols. Mentor Classics, New York: *Inferno,* 1954; *Purgatorio,* 1961; *Paradiso,* 1970.
Davidsohn, Robert. *Geschichte von Florenz.* 4 vols. Berlin, 1896–1927.
De Angelis, Ferdinando. "Vita di fra Ginepro compagno di S. Francesco d'Assisi." *Ara-Coeli,* June 1958.
De Bartholomaeis, Vincenzo. See Bartholomaeis, Vincenzo de.
De Beauvillé, Victor. See Beauvillé, Victor de.
De Francisci, Pietro. "Intorno alle origini della *manumissio in ecclesia.*" *Rendiconti Reale Istituto Lombardo* 44 (1911):619–42.
Degli Azzi Vitelleschi, Giustiniano. *Statuti di Perugia dell'anno MCCXLII.* Rome, 1913–16.
Delorme, Ferdinand M. See *Legenda Antiqua of Perugia.*
Del Vecchio, A. and Casanova, E. *Le rappresaglie nei comuni mediovali e specialmente in Firenze.* Bologna, 1894.
Demore, François. *Vie de Sainte Claire d'Assise.* Marseilles, 1848. Italian translation by G. Giusti. Rome, 1884.
Denifle, Heinrich. *Die Universitäten des mittelalters bis 1400.* Berlin, 1885.
De Robertis, Giuseppe. "Il Cantico di Frate Sole." *Civiltà* 3 (1942):17–24.
*Devoto, Giacomo. *Le Tavole di Gubbio.* Manuali di Filologia e Storia. Serie III-1. Florence, 1967.
Di Costanzo, Giuseppe. *Disamina degli scrittori e dei monumenti riguardanti S. Rufino.* Assisi, 1797.
Dicta Beati Aegidii Assisiensis. Quaracchi, 1905. *English translation by Raphael Brown. *Sayings of Brother Giles,* in *Little Flowers.* Reprint edition, pp. 261–89. New York, 1958. *Italian translation by Nello Vian. *I Detti.* Milan, 1964.
Diego dalle Grotte di Castro. *Meraviglie di S. Francesco in Gubbio.* Gubbio, 1886.
Dietzel, H. "Ueber Wesen und Bedeutung des Theilbaus in Italien." *Zeitschrift für die gesamte Staatswissenschaften* 41 (1885):29–86.
Digard, Georges; Faucon, Maurice; Thomas, Antoine; Fawtier, Robert, eds. *Les Registres de Boniface VIII.* Paris, 1884–1939.
Digesto Italiano. Milan, Rome, Naples, 1887–1896.
Documenta antiqua franciscana. See Lemmens, Leonardus.
Dobiache, O-Rojdesvensky. See Rozhdestvenskaîa, Olga.
Dombart, Theodor. *Das Palatinische Septizonium zu Rom.* Munich, 1922.

Doren, Alfred Jakob. *Storia economica dell'Italia nel medio evo.* Italian translation by G. Luzzatto. Padua, 1942.

Dramard, Eugène. *Bibliographie géographique et historique de la Picardie.* Paris, 1869–81.

Duchesne, Louis M. *Histoire ancienne de l'Eglise.* 3 vols. Paris, 1910–28.

*Durant, Will. *The Age of Faith.* New York, 1950.

Édouard d'Alençon. *Frère Iacqueline.* 2nd edition. Paris, 1927.

———. *L'abbaye de Saint-Benoit au mont Soubase prés d'Assise.* Couvin, 1909.

———. "La bénédiction de Saint François mourant à frère Elie." *Études Franciscaines* 9 (1903):204–7.

———. *Sacrum Commercium Beati Francisci cum domina Paupertate.* Rome, 1900.

———. *Sancti Francisci assisiensis vita et miracula, additis opuscolis liturgicis.* Rome, 1906.

Ehrle, Franz. *Die Frangipani und der Untergang des Archivs und der Bibliothek der Päpste am Anfang oes 13.* Paris, 1910.

———. "Die Spiritualen ihr Verhältniss zum Franziskanerorden, und zu den Fraticellen." In *Archiv für Litteratur und Kirschenschichte* 1–4 (1885–88).

———. "Notizie sui manoscritti della biblioteca di S. Francesco d'Assisi." *Misc. Fran.* 2 (1887):8–30.

———. See also Angelo Clareno.

Elias (Bombarone), Brother. *Epistola encyclica de transitu S. Francisci.* In *AF* 10:523–28. English translation by Auspicius Van Corstanje, in *The Covenant with God's Poor,* pp. 123–28. Chicago, 1966.

Elisei, Giuseppe. "Illustrazione di un sarcofago gentilesco ora esistente nel sotteranea della antica chiesa ugoniana sotto la presente cattedrale di S. Rufino vescovo e martire in Assisi." *Atti dell'Accademia Properziana in Assisi* 1 (1895), no. 3:33–49.

———. "Il sotterraneo della chiesa Ugoniana del 1028 esistente sotto la cattedrale di S. Rufino vescovo e martire di Assisi." *Atti dell'Accademia Properziana in Assisi* 1 (1897), no. 8:125–135.

———. *Studio sulla chiesa cattedrale di San Rufino Vescovo e Martire in Assisi.* Assisi, 1893.

Elisei, Raffaele. *Della città natale di Sesto Properzio.* 3rd edition. Rome, 1916.

Enciclopedia Italiano. Pubblicata dall'Istituto fondato da G. Treccani. 36 vols. and 3 appendices in 5 vols. Edited by Domenico Bartolini. Rome, 1949.

* *Encyclopaedia Britannica.* 1949 edition. 26 vols. Edited by Walter Yust. Chicago, London, and Toronto, 1954.

* Englebert, Omer. *Saint Francis of Assisi.* Translated by Eve Marie Cooper. 2nd English ed., rev. and aug. by Ignatius Brady and Raphael Brown. Chicago, 1965.

Ernoul. *Chronique.* In *Recueil des Historiens des Croisades—Historiens occidentaux,* 2:346–50. See also Golubovich, *Biblioteca,* 1:10–13.

Esser, Cajetan. "Die älteste Handschrift der Opuscole des Hl. Franciskus (cod. 338 von Assisi)." *Franziskanische Studien* 26 (1939):120–42.

* ———. *The Rule and Testament of St. Francis.* Chicago, 1977.

Etienne de Lusignan. *Chorograffia, et breve historia universale dell'Isola de Cipro principiando al tempo di Noè per in sino al 1572.* Bologna, 1573. See also Golubovich, *Biblioteca,* 1:394–99.

Eubel, Conrad. *Hierarchia Catholica Medii Aevi.* Münster, 1913–1952.

———. See also *Bullarium Franciscanum.*

Eulistea. See Bonaini, Fabretti, and Polidori.

* Fabbi, Ansano. *Antichità Umbre (Natura, Storia, Arte)*. Assisi, 1971.

Fabre, Paul, and Duchesne, Louis M., eds. *Le liber censuum de d'église romaine.* 3 vols. Bibliothèque des écoles Françaises d'Athènes et de Rome, Serie 2. Paris, 1889–1952.

Fabretti, Ariodante. *Statutorum comunis Perusii anno MCCLXXIX.* To incomplete rubric 86, n. p., n. d.

Facchinetti, Vittorino. *San Francesco d'Assisi nella storia, nella leggenda, nell'arte.* Milan, 1926.

————. See also Writings of Saint Francis.

Faloci Pulignani, Michele, ed. "Diploma del Vescovo Corrado, 1335." *Misc. Fran.* 10:86–93.

————. *I libri delle Sottomissioni del Comune di Perugia.* In *Archivio storico per le Marche e per l'Umbria* 1:449–73. Foligno, 1884.

————. *La passio Sancti Feliciani e il suo valore storico.* In *Archivio per la storia ecclesiastica dell'Umbria* 4:137–274. Foligno, 1917.

————. "L'ultima benedizione di San Francesco." *Misc. Fran.* 9 (1902):107.

————. "San Francesco e il monastero di S. Verecondo." *Misc. Fran.* 10 (1906):3–8.

————, ed. "Vita di San Francesco e dei Suoi Compagni, testo inedito di volgare umbro di XIV secolo." *Misc. Fran.* 8 (1901):81–119.

Farfa, Regesto di. See Giorgi and Balzano.

Fatteschi, Giovanni Colombino. *Memorie istorico-diplomatiche riguardanti la serie de' duchi, e la topografia de' tempi di mezzo del ducato di Spoleto.* Camerino, 1801.

Fedele, Pietro. *Il leopardo e l'agnello di casa Frangipane.* In *Archivio della reale Società romana di storia patria* 28:207–17. Rome, 1905.

Felder, Ilarino. *L'ideale di S. Francesco.* Italian translation, 3rd edition. Florence, 1946.

————. *Storia degli studi scientifici nell'Ordine francescano dalla sua fondazione.* Translated by Ignazio da Seggiano. Siena, 1911.

Ferrari, Giuseppe. *Histoire des révolutions d'Italie; ou, Guelfes et Gibelins.* 4 volumes. Paris, 1856–58. 1st Italian ed., rev. and augm. by the author. *Storia delle rivoluzioni d'Italia.* 3 vols. Treves, 1870–72.

Ficker, Julius von. *Forschungen zur Reichs- und Rechtsgeschichte Italiens.* 4 volumes. Innsbruck, 1868–74.

————. See also *Regesta Imperii.*

Fidenzio da Padova. *Liber recuperationis Terrae Sanctae.* In Golubovich, *Biblioteca,* 2:19.

Fierens, Alphonse. "La Question Franciscaine. Vita Sancti Francisci anonyma Bruxellensis d'après le manuscrit II.2326 de la Bibliothèque Royale de Belgique." *Revue d'Histoire Ecclèsiastique* (Louvain) 8 (1907):286–304, 498–513; 9 (1908):38–47, 703–27; 10 (1909); 42–65, 303–7.

————. *Les origines du Speculum Perfectionis.* Louvain, 1907.

* Filippi, Giovanni. *L'arte dei mercanti di Calimala in Firenze ed il suo più antico statuto.* Turin, 1889.

Fioretti (I) di San Francesco. Edited by Giacinto Pagnani. Preface by Arnaldo Fortini. Rome, 1959. * English translation by Raphael Brown: *The Little Flowers of St. Francis. First Complete Edition, with 20 Additional Chapters. Also The Considerations of the Holy Stigmata, The Life and Sayings of Brother Giles, The Life of Brother Juniper.* Garden City, N.Y., 1958. See also Sabatier.

Fischer, Karl. *Geschichte des Kreuzzügs Kaiser Friederichs I.* Leipzig, 1870.

* *Fonti Francescane. Scritti e biografie di San Francesco d'Assisi. Cronache e altre tes-*

timonianze del primo secolo francescano. Scritti e biografie di Santa Chiara d'Assisi. 2 vols. Assisi, 1977.

Forcella, Vincenzo. *Iscrizioni delle chiese e d'altri edifici di Roma.* 14 vols. Rome, 1869–84.

Fortini, Arnaldo. *Altre ipotesi sul luogo dove fu composto il Cantico del Sole.* Santa Maria degli Angeli, 1956.

———. *Assisi nel medioevo. Leggende, avventure, battaglie.* Rome, 1940.

———. "Attualità del francescanesimo." In *Universitalità del francescanismo,* pp. 23–97. Assisi-Rome, 1950.

———. "Calendimaggio in Assisi." *Italia* 8 (1942):51 ff.

———. *Celebrazione della difesa francescana del Santo Sepolcro.* Assisi, 1938.

———. *Cronache dell'anno di Santa Chiara.* Perugia, 1953.

———. "Della casa paterna di Santa Chiara." *AFH* 48 (1955):166–94.

———. "Di alcune questioni riguardanti la composizione del Cantico del Sole." In *Santa Chiara di Assisi, Studi e cronaca del VII centenario,* pp. 275–98. Perugia, 1954.

———. "Frate Elia architetto della Basilica di S. Francesco in Assisi." *Misc. Fran.* 37 (1937):529–45.

———. *Gli ultimi crociati. Cronaca del VI centenario della custodia di Terra Santa, celebrato in Assisi nell'anno giubilare.* Milan, 1935.

———. "I documenti degli archivi assisani e alcuni punti controversi della vita di San Francesco." *AFH* 43 (1950):3–44.

———. *I Fioretti delle Carcerelle.* Venice, 1956.

———. "Il cilizio di Vanna da Coldimezzo." *Chiara d'Assisi* 4 (1956):113–26.

———. "Il culto eroico dei genovesi per il Poverello di Cristo." *Genova* 14 (1934): 13 ff.

———. "Il Mistero del Venerdì Santo in Assisi." *La Lettura* 24 (1924):281–88.

———. "Il nome che Agnese ebbe nel secolo." *Chiara d'Assisi* 3 (1955):16–22.

———. *La patria al suo santo.* Vol. 2 of *Il Patrono d'Italia* (3 vols.). Rome, 1955.

———. *Il più ardente poeta d'amore.* Foligno, 1931.

———. *Il ritorno di San Francesco.* Milan, 1937.

———. *Infondatezza di una recente critica che vorebbe contestare al luogo di San Damiano la gloria del Cantico del Sole.* Assisi, 1955.

* ———. *La lauda in Assisi e le origini del teatro italiano.* Assisi, 1961.

———. "La patria e la famiglia di frate Angelo di Tancredi." *Frate Francesco* 21 (Jan. 1954):37–39.

———. "La sposa di Iacopone." *Dramma sacro* 1 (1950):12.

* ———. *Le corporazioni artigiani medioevali nella città di San Francesco.* Rome, 1962.

———. "Leggende, avventure, battaglie nella rocca di Assisi." *Atti dell'Accademia Properziana del Subasio,* series 4, no. 1, 1920.

———. "Le leggende di San Rufino." *Chiara d'Assisi* 3 (1955):37–43.

———. *L'elemento spirituale della danza in un episodio della vita di San Francesco.* Rome, 1956.

———. "L'ultimo viaggio di San Francesco." *Frate Francesco* 2 (1925):276–80.

———. *Motivi francescani in San Ginesio.* Rome, 1956.

———. *Nella luce di Assisi.* Milan, 1934.

———. *Nel settimo centenario della morte di frate Ginepro da Assisi (1258–1958): Cronaca delle celebrazioni di Roma e di Assisi.* Venice, 1958.

———. *Nel 750° anniversario della fondazione dell'Ordine dei Frati Minori. Storia, cronaca, discussioni.* Santa Maria degli Angeli, 1959.

————. *Nova Vita di San Francesco.* Milan, 1926.

————. "Nuove notizie intorno a Santa Chiara d'Assisi." *AFH* 46 (1953):3–43.

————. "Nuove documenti del diritto e del costume longobardo nell'Archivio della Cattedrale di Assisi." In *Atti del I° congresso internazionale di studi longobardi, Spoleto, 27–30 settembre, 1951,* pp. 317 ff.

————. "San Bonaventura e Assisi." *Doctor Seraphicus* 3 (June, 1956):21–33.

————. "San Francesco e il diritto." *Ius* 8 (January, 1957):104–11.

————. "San Francesco fideiussore di pace." *Rassegna giuridica umbra* 2 (1956):209–13.

————. "Santa Chiara." *La Lettura* 24 (1926):327–35.

————. *Settimana Santa di Assisi.* Venice, 1957.

————. "Storia di un'arca." *La Lettura* 42 (May 1942):370–73.

————. "Sull'epoca in cui fu costruita la primitiva chiesa di San Rufino in Assisi." *Italia Francescana* 30 (1955):352–58.

————. "Terziarie Francescane di Majorca nel primo centenario di fondazione della loro generosa Congregazione." *Chiara d'Assisi* 5 (1957):23–30.

————. "Un monastero sacro al ricordo di Santa Chiara." *Vie d'Italia,* September, 1954.

* Fortini, Gemma. "Calendimaggio in Assisi." *San Francesco Patrono d'Italia* 50 (June, 1970):236–40.

————. *Il santo della patria.* Vol. 1 of *Il Patrono d'Italia* (3 vols.). Rome, 1955.

————. *La città di poeti.* Assisi, 1954.

Foscarini, Amilcare. *Il patriziato brindisino nei secoli XII–XV.* Lecce, 1924.

Franceschina (La). Testo volgare umbro del sec. XV, scritto dal P. Giacomo Oddi di Perugia. 2 vols. Edited by Nicola Cavanna. Florence, 1931.

Franceschini, E. "Biografie di Santa Chiara." In *Santa Chiara d'Assisi, studi e cronaca del VII centenario,* pp. 263–74. Assisi, 1954.

Francesco di Bartolo di Assisi. *Tractatus de Indulgentia S. Mariae de Portiuncola.* Edited by Paul Sabatier. CED, vol. 2. Paris, 1900.

Franchini, Vittorio. *Gli Italiani alle fiere della Sciampagna.* Rome, 1926.

————. *Saggio di ricerche su l'instituto del Podestà nei Comuni medioevali.* Bologna, 1912.

* Franciscan Liturgy Projects. *The Roman-Franciscan Lectionary.* New York, 1975.

Fratini, Giuseppe. *Il Santo Poverello d'Assisi e la città di Gubbio.* Foligno, 1893.

————. *I tempi eroici del povero tugurio di Rivotorto e della cara Porziuncola.* Foligno, 1890.

————. *Storia della basilica e convento di San Francesco d'Assisi.* Prato, 1882.

Fredegand (Callaey) d'Anvers. "L'allegra giovinezza di San Francesco di Assisi." *Italia Francescana* 1 (1926):273–92.

Friedberg, Emil Albert. See *Corpus iuris canonici.*

Fumi, Luigi. "L'assedio di Enrico VI de Svevia re dei Romani contro la città d'Orvieto." *DPSU* 22 (1916):203–16.

Gabrieli, Francesco. *Storici arabi della crociate.* Turin, 1957.

Gabrieli, Gabriele. "San Francesco e il Soldano d'Egitto." *Oriente Moderno* 6 (1926):633–43.

Garampi, Giuseppe. *Memorie ecclesiastiche appartenenti all'istoria e al culto della Beata Chiara di Rimini.* Rome, 1755.

Gatti, Giuseppe. *Statuti dei mercanti di Roma.* Rome, 1885.

Gautier, Léon. *La Chevalerie.* Paris, 1884.

Gemelli, Agostino. *San Francesco d'Assisi e la sua gente poverella*. Milan, 1945. * English translation by Paul J. Oligny: *The Message of St. Francis*, Chicago, 1963.

Gentili, Giovanni Carlo. *Sopra l'Ordine Serafico in San Severino, e sopra la vita di Ser Pacifico Divini, minore riformato. Saggio storico*. Macerata, 1839.

Gerard de Frachet. *Vitae fratrum ordinis Praedicatorum nec non cronica ordinis ab anno 1223 usque 1254*. Louvain, 1896.

Gerola, Giuseppe. "Chi è il sovrano sepolto in San Francesco d'Assisi?" *Dedalo* 8 (1927).

———. "Giovanni e Gualtieri di Brienne in S. Francesco di Assisi." *AFH* 24 (1931):330–40.

Getto, Giovanni. *San Francesco d'Assisi e il Cantico di frate Sole*. Turin, 1956.

Giacomo Oddi da Perugia. See *(La) Franceschina*.

Giannettasio, Nicola. *Historiae Neapolitanea*. Naples, 1713.

Giardina, Camillo. "I boni homines in Italia, contributo alla storia delle persone e della procedura civile e al problema dell'origine del consolato." *Rivista di Storia del diritto italiano* 5 (1932):28–98, 313–94.

Gibb, H. A. R. "Notes on the Arabic Materials for the History of the Early Crusades." *Bulletin of the School of Oriental Studies* 7 (1935):739–54.

Giles, Brother. See *Dicta Beati Aegidii Assisiensis*.

Giordano da Giano. *Chronica*. In *AF* 1 (1885):1–19. Also, *Chronica Fratris Jordani*. Edited by H. Boehmer. CED, vol. 6. Paris, 1908. * English translation by Placid Hermann, in *XIIIth Century Chronicles*, pp. 1–77. Chicago, 1961.

Giorgi, Ignazio e Balzani, Ugo, eds. *Il Regesto di Farfa*. Compilato da Gregorio di Catino e pubblicato della R. Società Romana di Storia Patria. 5 vols. Rome, 1879–92.

Giovanni da Ceccano. *Chronicon Fossae Novae, ab anno primo nostrae salutis usque ad annum MCCXVII*. In *RIS*, vol. 7.

Giuseppe di Madrid. *Vita mirabile della serafica madre Santa Chiara d'Assisi fondatrice del suo amplissimo ordine*. Lucca, 1727.

Giusta, F. *Memorie storiche della Provincia dei Minori Osservanti detta di Bologna*. Bologna, 1717.

Giusto, Egidio Maria. *Archivum Portiunculae id est Patriarchae Pauperum Seraph. Franc. Portiuncula monumentis novis et veteribus adornata per Fratrem Octavium . . .* Assisi, 1916.

———. "L'architetto della Basilica di Santa Maria degli Angeli presso Assisi." *Oriente Serafico* 27–28 (1916–1917):274–83.

———. "La Topografia dell'antica chiesa e dell'antico convento della Porziuncola." *Oriente Serafico* 27–28 (1916–1917):284–350.

Giusto, Egidio e Polticchia, Raimondo. *Storia documentata della Porziuncola*. Santa Maria degli Angeli, 1926.

Glassberger. See Nicholas Glassberger.

Gnoli, Umberto. "L'antica Basilica Ugoniana e il duomo di Giovanni da Gubbio." *Augusta Perusia* 1 (1906):173–81.

———. "L'arte romanica dell'Umbria." *Augusta Perusia* 1 (1906):22–25, 41–43.

Goetz, Walter. "Die regel des Terziarerordens." *Zeitschrift für Kirchengeschichte* 23 (1902):97–107.

Golubovich, Girolamo. *Biblioteca bio-bibliografica della Terra Santa e dell'Oriente Francescano*. 5 vols. Quaracchi, 1906–27.

———. *La storicità e autenticità della casa paterna di San Francesco di Assisi, oggi Chiesa Nuova, e la popolare leggenda della stalletta*. Florence, 1940.

————. *San Francesco e i Francescani in Damiata.* Florence, 1927.

Graf, Arturo. *Roma nella memoria e nelle immaginazioni del Medio Evo.* Turin, 1923.

Gratien de Paris. *Histoire de la Fondation et de l'Evolution de l'Ordre des Frères Mineurs au XIII siècle.* Paris, 1928.

Gregorovius, Ferdinand. *Storia della città di Roma nel medioevo.* Turin, 1925–26. Italian translation of *Geschichte d. Stadt Rom in Mittelalter.* Stuttgart, 1859–72.

Gregory of Tours, St. *Liber in gloriam martyrdom.* In *MGH, Scriptores,* vol. 1.

Grenier, Pierre Nicolas. *Introduction à l'histoire genérale de la province de Picardie.* Amiens, 1856.

Grisar, Hartmann. *Roma alla fine del mondo antico.* Italian translation by Angelo Mercati. Rome, 1930.

Grousset, René. *L'épopée des Croisades.* Paris, 1939.

————. *Histoire des Croisades et du royaume franc de Jérusalem.* 3 vols. Paris, 1934–36.

Guardabassi, Francesco (the Younger). *Storia di Perugia.* Perugia, 1933–35.

Guasti, Cesare. *La Basilica di S. Maria degli Angeli presso la città d'Assisi.* Florence, 1882.

Hartmann, L. M. *Untersuchungen zur Geschichte der byzantinischen Verwallung in Italien (540–750).* 8 vols. Leipzig, 1889.

* Heer, Friedrich. *The Medieval World: Europe 1100–1350.* Translated by Janet Sondheimer. New York, 1962.

Hegel, Karl. *Geschichte der Städteverfassung von Italien.* Leipzig, 1847.

Henrion, Albina. *Sorella Chiara, la Primogenita del Poverello.* Milan, 1921.

Henri d'Avranches. See *Legenda versificata.*

Hofmann, Albert von. *Das Land Italien und seine Geschichte.* Stuttgart, 1921.

Honorius III (Cencio Savelli). *Opera Omnia.* Edited by C. A. Horoy. In *Medii Aevi Bibliotheca Patristica.* 5 vols. Paris, 1879–83.

————. *Regesta.* See Pressuti, Pietro.

Honorius IV (Giacomo Savelli). *Régistres.* See Prou, Maurice.

* Huber, Raphael. *A Documented History of the Franciscan Order 1182–1517.* Milwaukee, 1944.

* Hughes, Philip. *A History of the Church.* 2 vols. Rev. ed., New York, 1949.

Hülsen, Christian Carl Friedrich. *Le chiese di Roma nel medioevo.* Florence, 1927.

Hüntemann, Ulrich, and Pou y Marti, J. M. See *Bullarium Franciscanum.*

Hurter, Friedrich E. von. *Geschichte des Papstes Innocens III und seiner Zeitgenossen.* 4 vols. Hamburg, 1834–42.

Huvelin, Paul. *Essai historique sur le droit des marchés et des foires.* Paris, 1897.

Iacopozzi, Nazareno. "Dove sia avvenuta la visita di San Francesco d'Assisi al Sultano Malek il Kamel." *Frate Francesco* 2 (1925):379–93.

Jacobilli, Luigi. *Bibliotheca Umbriae, sive de scriptoribus provinciae Umbriae alphabetico ordine digesta.* Foligno, 1658.

————. *Cronica della chiesa e monastero di S. Croce di Sassovivo nel territorio di Foligno.* Foligno, 1653.

————. *Vita dei Santi e Beati dell'Umbria e di quelli corpi che riposano in essa provincia.* Foligno, 1647–61.

Jacobi a Voragine. *Legenda aurea. Vulgo Historia lombardica dicta.* Breslau, 1890.

————. *Vita S. Francisci.* In *AF* 10:681–93.

* Jacques de Vitry. *Lettres de Jacques de Vitry (1160/1170–1240), évêque de Saint-Jean-d'Acre.* Ed. crit. par R. B. C. Huygens. Leyden, 1960.

————. *Libro duo, quorum prior Orientalis alter Orientalis, historiae nomine inscribitur.*

Douai, 1597. * Also, edited by J. F. Hinnebusch. *The Historia Occidentalis of Jacques de Vitry.* Fribourg, 1972.
Both letters (see above) and the chapter about Saint Francis are reprinted in Golubovich, *Biblioteca,* 1:2–10. * English translation by Damien Vorreux of these and of extract of sermon about Saint Francis in *Omnibus,* pp. 1608–14.

Jeanroy, A. *Les chansons de Jaufre Rudel.* Paris, 1924.

Joannes de Tulbio. *Gesta Obsidionis Damiatae.* In *MGH,* vol. 31.

Jordan, Edouard. "Les premiers franciscains en France." *Études Italiennes* 8 (1926):65–84, 129–39.

Jörgensen, Johannes. *San Francesco d'Assisi.* Italian translation from the Danish. Rome, 1919. * English translation by T. O'Conor Sloane: *Saint Francis of Assisi.* Reprint edition, New York, 1965.

Julian of Speyer. *Officium Rhythmicum S. Francisci.* In *AF* 10:372–88.

———. *Vita S. Francisci.* In *AF* 10:333–71; preface, xlii-1.

Kleinschmidt, Beda. *Die Basilika San Francesco in Assisi.* Berlin, 1915.

Klüber, Johann Ludwig. *Das Ritterwesen des Mittelalters nach seiner politischen und militarischen Verfassung.* From the French, De La Curne De Sainte Palaye, with notes and preface by Klüber. Nuernberg, 1789.

Krass, Hebert. *Storia di Lecce.* Translated by Gregorio Caruggio. Bari, 1936.

Kugler, Bernhard von. *Geschichte der Kreuzzüge.* Leipzig, 1880.

Lanzoni, Francesco. *Le diocesi d'Italia dalle origini al principio del sec. VII.* Faenza, 1927.

———. "Le origini del cristianesimo e dell'episcopato nell'Umbria Romana." *Rivista storico-critica sulle scienze, teologiche* 3 (1907):739–56, 821–37.

Lauer, Philippe. *Le palais du Latran.* Paris, 1911.

Lazzeri, Zefferino. "Il 'Privilegium Paupertatis' concesso da Innocenzo III e che cosa fosse in origine." *AFH* 11 (1918):270–76.

———. *Il processo di canonizzazione di S. Chiara di Assisi,* In *AFH* 13 (1920):403–507.

———. "La *forma vita* di Santa Chiara e le Regole sue e del suo Ordine." In *Santa Chiara d'Assisi, Studi e cronaca del VII Centenario (1253–1953),* pp. 79–122. Assisi, 1954.

———. *L'antico monastero de Vallegloria a Spello.* Arezzo, 1911.

———. "L'atto di conferma della donazione della Verna." Special issue of *La Verna (Studi Francescani* 11 (1913):87–109).

———. "Un nuovo codice della 'Vita di S. Chiara' di Ugolino Verino." *AFH* 13 (1920):273–86.

Leccisotti, Tommaso, and Tabarelli, Costanzo. 2 vols. *Le carte dell'Archivio di S. Pietro di Perugia.* Milan, 1956.

Leggenda Antica. See Salvatore Minocchi.

Legenda Antiqua S. Francisci. Texte du Ms. 1046 (M. 69) de Pérouse. Edited by Ferdinand M. DeLorme. In *AFH* 15 (1922):23–70, 278–332; also in *La France Franciscaine* 2 (1926). * English translation by Paul Oligny. *Legend of Perugia.* In *Omnibus,* pp. 959–1101.* Also by Salvatore Butler. *We Were With St. Francis.* Chicago, 1976.

Leggenda dei Tre Compagni (Legenda S. Francisci Assisiensis a bb. Leone, Rufino, Angelo eius sociis scripta, quae dicitur Legenda trium sociorum). Edited by Leopold Amoni. Rome, 1880. * English translation by Nesta de Robeck. *Legend of the Three Companions.* In *Omnibus,* pp. 855–955.

Legenda monacensis S. Francisci. In *AF* 10:694–719.

Legenda Sanctae Clarae Virginis. Attributed to Thomas of Celano. Edited by

Francesco Pennacchi. Assisi, 1910. Italian translation by Guido Battelli, with introduction and notes by Arnaldo Fortini. Rome, 1910. Also by Fausta Casolini. Assisi, 1953. * English translation by Ignatius Brady and Sister M. Frances. *Legend and Writings of Saint Clare of Assisi*. St. Bonaventure, N.Y., 1953.

Legenda versificata S. Clarae assisiensis. Edited by Benvenuto Bughetti. In *AFH* 5 (1912):621–31.

Legenda versificata S. Francisci. By Henri d'Avranches. In *AF* 10:405–521. Italian translation by Antonio Cristofani. *Il più antico poema della vita di S Francesco*. Prato, 1882. (This long poem was once attributed to several other authors, especially to Enrico da Pisa and John of Kent. The author was identified by A. G. Little from the Cambridge Codex.)

Leicht, Pier Silverio. *La "curtis" e il feudo nell'Italia superiore fino al sec. XIII*. Verona, 1903.

Lemmens, Leonardus. *Die Anfänge de Franziskaenerordens in Germania*. Berlin, 1909.

———. "Die Schriften des Br. Leo von Assisi." In *Miscellanea Franciscana Ehrle*, 3:25–48. Rome, 1924.

———. ed. *Documenta Antiqua Franciscana*. 3 vols. Quaracchi, 1901–02.

———. ed. *Testimonia minora saeculi XIII de S. Francisco Assisiensi*. Quaracchi, 1926.

Lempp, Edward. *Frère Elie de Cortone. Étude biographique*. Paris, 1901.

Levi, Guido. "Documenti ad illustrazione del Registro del Cardinale Ugolino d'Ostia." *Archivio della R. Società Romana*, 12 (1889):241–326.

———. *Registri dei Cardinali Ugolino d'Ostia e Ottaviano degli Ubaldini*. Fonti per la Storia d'Italia, 8. Rome, 1890.

Lewis, Bernard. "The sources for the history of the Syrian Assassin." *Speculum* 27 (1952):475–89.

Liber duelli christiani in obsidione Damiatae exacti. In *MGH, Scriptores*, vol. 31.

Liber exemplorum Fratrum Minorum saeculi XIII. Edited by Livarius Oliger. In *Antonianum* 2 (1927):203–76.

Libri magnifice civitatis Assisj statutorum. Per Hiernymum Francisci Baldasarris de Carthularijs. Perugia, 1534–43.

Lipsin, Lodovicus. *Compendiosa Historia Vitae S. Francisci*. Assisi, 1st ed., 1557; 2nd ed., 1756.

Little, Andrew George. "Un nouveau texte du témoignage de Michel Bernardi." *Oriente Serafico*, October-August 1916–17, pp. 107–14.

Little Flowers of Saint Francis. See *Fioretti*.

Loccatelli, Vincenzo. *Vita di S. Chiara*. Assisi, 1854.

Loccatelli Paolucci, Tommasso. *Il duomo d'Assisi*. Perugia, 1864.

———. *Illustrazione della casa di S. Francesco di Assisi detta volgarmente la Chiesa Nuova*. Perugia, 1865.

———. *Illustrazione dell'antica badìa di San Benedetto al monte Subasio*. Assisi, 1880.

———. *Suor Diomira Bini di Assisi*. Assisi, 1887.

———. *Vita Breve di S. Chiara*. Assisi, 1882.

López, Atanasio. "El Viaje di San Francisco a Espana." *Archivio Ibero-Americano* 1 (1914):13–45; 257–89, 433–69.

Lorenzo di Fonzo. "Nuova interpretazione del Cantico di frate Sole." *Misc. Fran.* 43 (1943):305–14.

Lucarelli, Oderigi. *Memorie e Guida storica di Gubbio*. Città di Castello, 1888.

Luchaire, Achille. *Innocent III*. 6 vols. Paris, 1904–1908.

Ludovico da Pietralunga. *Descrizione della Basilica di S. Francesco in Assisi*. In *DPSU* 28 (1926). * Republished, ed. Pietro Scarpellini. Treviso, 1977.

Lugano, P. "Le chiese dipendenti dall'abbazia di Sassovivo presso Foligno." *Rivista Storica Benedettina* 7 (1912):47–94.

Luzzatto, Gino. *Storia economica d'Italia: L'antichità e il medioevo.* Rome, 1949.

Luzzatto, Luigi. "La scoperta di un nuovo Fioretti di San Francesco." *Apostolato francescano* 4 (1915):127–29.

Malagola, Carlo. *Monografie storiche sullo studio bolognese.* Bologna, 1888.

Malispini, Ricordano. *Istoria fiorentina.* In *RIS,* vol. 8.

Manacorda, Giuseppe. *Storia della scuola in Italia.* Vol. 1: *Il medioevo.* Palermo, 1913.

Manaresi, Cesare. *Gli atti del Comune di Milano fino all'anno MCCXVI.* Milan, 1919.

Mandelli, Vittorio. *Il Comune di Vercelli nel medio evo; studi storici.* (3 vols. in 4 pts.) Vercelli, 1857–1861.

Mandic, Dominicus. *De legislatione antiqua Fratrum Minorum.* Mostar, 1924.

———. *De protoregula Ordinis Fratrum Minorum.* Mostar, 1923.

Mandonnet, Pierre Felix. *Les Régles et le gouvernement de l'Ordo de Poenitentia au siècle XIII.* Paris, 1902.

Mansi, Johannes Dominicus. *Sacrorum Conciliorum nova et amplissima collectio.* 31 vols. Florence and Venice, 1759–1798.

al-Maqrisi, Ahmad ihn 'Ali. *Description topographique et historique de l'Egypte.* Traduite en francais par U. Bouriant. 4 pts. in 3 vols. Paris, 1900 (i.e., 1895–1900)–1920.

———. *Histoire d'Egypte.* Translated by E. Blochet. Paris, 1908.

Marcellini Comites. *Chronicon.* In *MGH, Auctores antiquissimi,* vol. 11.

Marchisio Scriba. See *Annali Genovesi.*

Marco da Lisbona. Italian translation. *Chroniche degli Ordini istituiti dal Padre San Francesco.* Naples, 1677.

Mariano da Firenze. *Compendium chronicarum Fratrum Minorum.* AFH 1 (1908):98–107; 2 (1909):92–107, 305–18, 626–41; 3 (1910):294–309, 700–15; 4 (1911):122–37, 318–39, 559–87.

———. See also Unpublished Manuscripts, sec. V.

Marinangeli, Bonaventura. "La Tomba di S. Francesco attraverso i secoli." *San Francesco Patrono d'Italia* 50 (1970):219–26.

———. "La trombetta di San Francesco." *San Francesco d'Assisi,* 3 (1922–23):67–69.

———. "Serie di affreschi giottesche." *Misc. Fran.* 13 (1911):97–112.

———. "Sull'orme di San Francesco." *San Francesco d'Assisi* 1 (1920–21):159–62.

Mariotti, Annibale. *Saggio di memorie istoriche civili ed ecclesiastiche della citta di Perugia e suo contado.* Perugia, 1806.

Marzotto, Gaetano (Conte di Valdagno). *Il centenario di un lanificio. Un episodio e una storia.* Milan, 1937.

Masi, G. "Il sindacato delle magistrature communali nel secolo XIV." *Rivista Italiana per le scienze giuridiche,* 1930.

Matthew of Paris. *Chronica Maiora.* In *MGH, Scriptores,* vol. 28; also *Rerum Britannicarum medi aevi scriptores,* vol. 57.

Mayer, Ernest. *Italienische Verfassungesgeschichte,* Leipzig, 1909.

Mazzara, Benedetto. *Leggendario Francescano.* 3rd ed. Edited by Pietro Antonio da Venezia. 12 vols. Venice, 1721–22.

Mazzara, Bonaventure Marino. "La Basilica della Porziuncola e Galeazzo Alessi." *Oriente Serafica* 27–28 (1916–17):254–59.

* Meersseman, G. G. *Dossier de l'Ordre de la Penitence au XIIIe siècle.* Fribourg, 1961.

Meistermann, Barnabé (Barnabé d'Alsace). *Porziuncola, ossia storia di Santa Maria degli Angeli, e dell'origine francescana.* Foligno, 1884.

Mencherini, Saturnino. *Guida illustrata della Verna.* Quaracchi, 1907.

Mengozzi, Guido. *La città italiana nell'alto medioevo.* 2nd ed. Florence, 1931.

Michaud, Joseph François. *Bibliothéque des Croisades.* 4 vols. Paris, 1829.

――――. *Histoire des Croisades.* 7 vols. Paris, 1st ed., 1812–17; 2nd ed., 1824–29. Italian translation: *Storia delle Crociate.* 4 vols. Naples, 1931.

Migne, Jacques Paul. *Patrologia cursus completus.* Paris, 1844–66. Includes *Patrologia Latina,* 221 vols. (1844–55). *Patrologia Graeca,* 165 vols. (1857–66).

Milan, City of. See Manaresi, Cesare.

Milioli, Alberto. *Gesta obsidionis Damiatae, mai 1218–1219, nov. 5.* In *RIS,* vol. 8. (All citations are from this source.) Also in *MGH, Scriptores,* vol. 31.

Minocchi, Salvatore, ed. *La Leggenda antica.* Florence, 1905.

Mirror of Perfection. See *Speculum Perfectionis.*

Mittarelli, G. B. e Costadoni, A. *Annales Camaldulenses.* 9 vols. Venice, 1755–73.

Mochi-Onory, Sergio. *Ricerche sui poteri civili dei Vescovi nelle città umbre durante l'alto medioevo.* Bologna, 1932.

Monaci, Ernesto. *Crestomazia italiana dei primi secoli.* 3 vols. Città di Castello, 1899–1912.

Monleone, Giovanni. See *Annali Genovesi.*

Montagnani, Gaetano. *Storia dell'augusta badìa di S. Silvestro di Nonantola, compendiata e continuata sino al presente.* Modena, 1838.

Monti, Gennaro Maria. *Le confraternite mediovali dell'Alta e Media Italia.* Venice, 1927.

Monumenta Germaniae Historica. Edited successively by George Henrich Pertz, Georg Waitz, Wilhelm Wattenbach, Ernst Ludwig Dümmler, Oswald Holder-Egger, Paul Fridolin Kehr. Hanover-Leipzig, from 1826.

* Moorman, John. *A History of the Franciscan Order from its Origins to the Year 1517.* London, 1968.

Mor, Carlo Guido. *La "manumissio in ecclesia."* Rome, 1928.

Müller, Karl. *Die Anfänge des Minoriteordens und der Bussbruder-Schaften.* Freiburg, 1885.

Muratori, Lodovico Antonio. *Annali d'Italia.* 12 vols. Milan, 1744–49.

――――. *Antiquitates italicae medii aevi.* 6 vols. Milan, 1738–42.

――――. See also *Rerum Italicarum Scriptores.*

Niccola da Vitorchiano. *Memorie antiche e breve descrizione del Santuario di Santa Maria delle Carceri d'Assisi.* Perugia, 1774.

Nicholas Glassberger. *Analecta ad Fratrum Min. Historiam. Narratio de origine et propagatione ordinis ex codicibus mss.* In *AF* 2 (1887).

Nicola da Calvi (or di Curdio). *Vita Innocentii IV, Papa.* In *RIS,* vol. 3.

Nicolò da Poggibonsi, Fra. *Il libro d'oltremare (1346–1350).* In Golubovich, *Biblioteca,* 5:1–24.

* Niermeyer, J. F. *Mediae Latinitatis Lexicon Minus.* Edited by C. van de Kieft. Leiden, 1976.

Novati, Francesco. *Carmina medii aevi.* Florence, 1883.

Novellino. A collection of stories compiled in the thirteenth century by an unknown writer of Florence. 1st ed., edited by C. Gualteruzzi, Bologna, 1525. Gualteruzzi edition, edited by L. Di Francia, in Collezione di Classici italiani. Turin, 1930.

Octave d'Angiers. "Du frère cithariste qui, à Rieti, se récusa." *Études Franciscaines* 44 (1932):549–56.

Oddi, Giacomo da Perugia. See *(La) Franceschina.*

Odoardi, Giovanni. "Un geniale figlio di San Francesco: frate Elia da Assisi, nel settimo centenario della sua morte." *Misc. Fran.* 54 (1954):90–139.

Ogerio, Pane. See *Annali Genovesi.*

Oliger, Livarius. "De origine regularum ordinis S. Clarae." *AFH* 5 (1912):181–209, 412–47.

———. "Descriptio Codicis Sancti Antonii de Urbe unacum appendice textuum de S. Francisco." *AFH* 12 (1919):321–401.

———. "San Francesco a Roma." In *Italia francescana nel settimo centenario della morte di S. Francesco,* pp. 65–112. Santa Maria degli Angeli, 1927.

———. "S. Francesco e il Laterno." In *Nel XVI centenario della dedicazione della arcibasilica Lateranense del SS. Salvatore,* pp. 43–46. Rome, 1925.

———. See also Angelo Clareno and *Liber exemplorum.*

Oliver of Paderborn. *Historia Damiatina.* In *Corpus historicum medii aevi,* edited by Johann Georg von Eckhart. Leipzig, 1723. * English translation by John J. Gavigan. *The Capture of Damietta.* In *Christian Society and the Crusades,* edited by Edward Peters. Sources of Medieval History. Philadelphia, 1971.

Orlandi, Cesare. *Delle città d'Italia.* vol. 2. Perugia, 1772.

Ortolani, Ciro (Ciro da Pesaro). "Fra Pacifico re dei versi." *Picenum Seraphicum* 4 (1918):121–69.

———. *La Beata Ortolana d'Assisi.* Rome, 1904.

Orza, Mariano. *Gualtieri III di Brienne.* Naples, 1940.

Otto of Freising. *Gesta Friderici Imperatoris.* In *MGH, Scriptores,* vol. 20.

Ottokar, Nicola. *La città francesci nel Medioevo.* Florence, 1927.

* *(The) Oxford Dictionary of the Christian Church.* Edited by F. L. Cross. London, 1958.

Ozanam. Antoine Frédéric. *I poeti francescani in Italia.* Italian translation by Pietro Fanfani. Prato, 1854.

Pagano, Filippo Mario. *Istoria del regno di Napoli.* 3 vols. Naples and Palermo, 1832–1839.

Pagliaro, Antonio. "Il cantico di frate Sole." *Idea* 7 (1955):1–2.

———. "Il Cantico di frate Sole." *Quaderni di Roma* 1 (1947):218–35.

Palomes, Luigi. *Storia di S. Francesco.* Palermo, 1873.

Pantoni, D. Angelo. "San Benedetto al Subasio." *Benedictina* 2 (1948):47–74.

Paoletti, Anna. *Materiali archeologi nelle chiese dell'Umbria. San Rufino, Assisi.* Perugia, 1958.

(Fra) Paolino da Venezia. "Chronologia Magna." Extract in Golubovich, *Biblioteca,* 2:83–89. (From Cod. Perugino lat. 4939.)

———. "Satyrica gestarum rerum." Extract in Golubovich, *Biblioteca,* 2:81–83. (From Cod. vaticano lat. 1960).

Papini, Niccola. *La Storia di San Francesco di Assisi.* 2 vols. Foligno. 1825–27.

———. *Notizie sicure della morte, sepoltura, canonizzazione, e translazione di S. Francesco d'Assisi.* 2nd ed. Foligno, 1824.

Pardi, Giuseppe. *Archivi communali umbri.* Fasc. 1, *Archivio comunale di Assisi.* Perugia, 1895.

———. "Dal Comune alla signoria in Orvieto." *DPSU* 13 (1907):397–454.

Parducci, Amos. *Costumi ornati.* Bologna, 1928.

Passavanti, Iacopo. *Lo Specchio della Vera Penitenza.* 1st ed., Florence, 1495. Edited by F. L. Polidori. Florence, 1856.

Passio sanctorum martyrum, fratrum Beraldi, Petri, Adiuti, Acursii, Othonis in Marochio martyrizatorum. In *AF* 3 (1897):579–96.

Patrem, L. M. "Appunti critici sulla cronologia della vita di San Francesco." *Misc. Fran.* 9 (1902):76–101.

Paulus Diaconus (Paul the Deacon). *Historia gentis Langobardorum.* In *MGH, Scriptores rerum Langobardicarum.* Hanover, 1878.

* Pazzelli, Raffaele. *Lineamenti di storia e spiritualità del movimento penitenziale francescano.* Rome, 1979.

Pellini, Pompeo. *Dell'historia di Perugia.* 3 vols. Venice, 1664.

Pennacchi, Francesco. *L'Anno della prigionia di S. Francesco in Perugia.* Perugia, 1915.

———. "Frate Elia." *Frate Francesco,* 1924, pp. 393–410.

———. See also *Actus S. Francisci in Valle Reatina, Legenda S. Clarae Virginis, Speculum Perfectionis.*

Perali, Pericle. "Lettera intorno alla casa paterna e natale di San Francisco, intorno ad un documento perentorio, ma superfluo, e intorno ad una casa dei nepoti del Santo prospiciente sulla *platea nova Comunis.*" *Misc. Fran.* 41 (1941):297–325.

———. "Ottavio Ringhieri, Vescovo di Assisi, e la Casa dove nacque San Francesco." *Misc. Fran.* 42 (1942):237–312.

Pertile, Antonio. *Storia del diritto italiano dalla caduta dell'Impero Romano alla codificazione.* 6 vols. 2nd ed. rev. Turin, 1892–1903.

Perugia. Archives and Statutes. See Ansidei; Ansidei e Giannantoni; Bonaini, Fabretti, e Polidori; Ceccini; Degli Azzi Vitelleschi, Faloci Pulignano; Fabretti.

Perugia. Archivio di San Pietro. See Leccisotti e Tabarelli.

Petersen, Eugen von. "Septizonium." *Römische Mitteilungen,* 1910, pp. 56 ff.

Pier Damiani. *Sermones.* In *Petri Damiani . . . opera omnia . . . studio ac labore domni Costantini Cajetani,* 2:178–84. Bassano, 1783.

Pietro Antonio da Venetia. *Historia Serafica, ovvero Cronica della Provincia di S. Antonio, detta anco di Venetia, dei Minori Osservanti Riformati,* Venice, 1688.

Pipino. See Bernardo il Tesoriere.

* Pirenne, Henri. *Economic and Social History of Medieval Europe.* Translated by I. E. Clegg. Reprint edition. New York, 1937.

———. *Histoire de l'Europe des invasions au XVIe siècle.* Paris-Brussels, 1936.

Pivano, Silvio. *Sistema curtense.* Rome, 1909.

Platzech, Erhard Wolfram. *Das Sonnenlied des heilingen Franciskus von Assisi.* Munich, 1957.

Polidori, Filippi Luigi. *La Tavola rotonda.* Bologna, 1864.

Pompei, Alfonso. "Frate Elia d'Assisi nel giudizio dei contemporanei e dei posteri." *Misc. Fran.* 54 (1954):539–635.

Possevino, Giovanni Battista. *Vite dei Santi e Beati della Città di Todi.* Perugia, 1597.

Potthast, August. *Regesta Pontificum Romanorum inde ab a. post Christum natum MCXCVIII ad a. MCCCCIV.* 2 vols. Berlin, 1874–75.

Pou y Marti, J. M. See *Bullarium Franciscanum.*

* Pound, Ezra. *Collected Early Poems.* New York, 1926.

* ———. *Personae.* Edited by H. S. Mauberly. New York, 1926.

* ———. *Translations.* Edited by Hugh Kenner. New York, 1963.

Pratesi, Plinio. *Sul vero luogo della battaglia detta di Gubbio o di Tagina.* Turin, 1897.

Pressuti, Pietro. *Regesta Honorii pape III.* 2 vols. Rome, 1888–1895.

Processo di canonizzazione di Santa Chiara. See Lazzari, Zefferino.

Procopius of Caesarea. *De bello gothico.* In *Biblioteca Teubneriana,* vols. 1 and 2. Edited by Jacobus Haury. Leipzig, 1905.

Propertius. *Elegiarum,* 4, 1, 125–6. * Translation by Gilbert Highet in *Poets in a Landscape,* p. 76. New York, 1965.

* Prosperi, F. *La facciata della cattedrale di Assisi. La mistica gioachimita pre-francescana nella simbologia delle sculture.* Perugia, 1968.

Prou, Maurice. *Les règistres d'Honorius IV.* Paris, 1888.

Prutz, Hans. *Kulturgeschichte der Kreuzzüge.* Berlin, 1883.

Pucci, Benedetto. *Genealogia degl'Illustrissimi Signori Frangipani.* Venice, 1621.

Quaglia, Armando. *Origine e sviluppo della Regola Francescana.* Naples, 1948.

Quétif, Jacques and Echard, Jacques. *Scriptores Ordinis Praedicatorum.* 2 vols. Paris, 1719-23.

Rajna, Pio. "Dante e i romanzi della Tavola Rotonda." In *Nuova Antologia,* June 1, 1920.

————. "Tre studi per la storia del libro di Andrea Cappellano." *Studi di Filologia Romanza* 5 (1890):193-265.

Rashdall, Hastings. *The Universities of Europe in the Middle Ages.* Oxford, 1895.

* Raymond, Ernest. *In the Steps of St. Francis.* Reprint edition. Chicago, 1975.

Re, Camillo. "Le regioni di Roma nel Medioevo." *Studi e documenti di storia e di diritto* 10 (1889):349-81.

Recueil des historiens des croisades. Publié par les Soins de l'Académie Royale des Inscriptions et Belles-Lettres. 16 vols bound in 18. Paris, 1841-1906.

Regesto di Farfa. See Giorgio, Ignazio e Balzani, Ugo.

Regesta Imperii. Edited by Johann F. Boehmer, Julius von Ficker, and others. 5 vols. Innsbruck, 1881-1901.

Reinaud, Joseph Toussaint (M. Reinaud). *Chroniques arabes.* In Michaud, *Bibliothéque des Croisades,* vol. 4. Paris, 1829.

————. *Extraits de l'histoire des Patriarches d'Alexandrie relatifs au siége de Damiette.* Paris, 1829.

Renan, Ernst. "François d'Assise." In *Nouvelles études d'histoire religieuse.* 3rd ed. Paris, 1907.

Rerum Italicarum Scriptores. Edited by Ludovico Antonio Muratori. 25 vols. Milan, 1723-51.

Riccardo di San Germano. *Chronica.* In *RIS,* vol. 7.

Ricci, Amico. *Storia dell'Architettura in Italia dal secolo IV al XVIII.* Modena, 1857-59.

Ricci, Ettore. *La basilica di S. Maria degli Angeli e i suoi architetti.* Perugia, 1911.

Richerius, monaco di Sens. *Gesta Senonensis ecclesiae.* In *MGH, Scriptores,* vol. 25.

Rinaldi, Odorico. *Annales ecclesiastici, ex tomis octo ad unum pluribus auctum redacti.* Rome, 1667.

Roberti, Melchiorre. "Le cerimonia dell'Episcopello a Padova." *Arch. Stor. Ital.* 31 (1903):172-75.

Robinson, Paschal. "Inventarium omnium documentorum quae in Archivio Protomonasterii S. Clarae Assisiensis nunc asservantur." *AFH* 1 (1908):413-32.

Rodolfo, Pietro, da Tossignano. *Historiarum Seraphice religionis libri tres seriem temporum continentes.* Venice, 1586.

Roger of Wendover. *Chronica sive Flores Historiarum.* In *MGH, Scriptores,* vol. 28. Also in *Rerum Britannicarum Medii Aevi Scriptores,* vol. 84.

Rohault de Fleury, Georges. *Le Latran au Moyen Age.* Paris, 1877.

Röhricht, Reinold. *Geschichte des Königreichs Jerusalem, 1100-1291.* Innsbruck, 1898.

Rolandino da Padova. *Cronica.* In *RIS,* vol. 8.

Rome. Statutes of Guilds. See Gatti and Stevenson.

Romualdo, Archbishop of Salerno. *Annales, 893-1178.* In *RIS,* vol. 7.

Roncaglia, Martiniano. "Fonte arabo-musulmana su S. Francesco in Oriente?" *Studi Francescani* 50 (1953):258–59.

———. "San Francesco in Oriente." *Studi Francescani* 50 (1953):98–106.

Roon-Bassermann, Elisabeth von. *Die Champagnermessen.* Tübingen, 1911.

Rosenthal, Franz. *A History of Muslim Historiography.* Leyden, 1952.

Rozhdestvenskaìa, Olga Antonovaa. *Les poésies des Goliards.* Paris, 1931.

Rughi, L. *Memorie su l'Abbadia di S. Verecondo in Valligegno.* Gubbio, 1935.

Runciman, Steven. *A History of the Crusades.* 3 vols. Cambridge, 1951–54.

Ruville, Albert von. *Die Kreuzzüge.* Bonn, 1920.

Saba, Agostino. *Storia della chiesa.* Turin, 1938–43.

Sabatelli, Giacomo. "Studi recenti sul cantico di Frate Sole." *AFH* 51 (1958):3–24.

Sabatier, Paul. *Description du Speculum Vitae B. Francisci et sociorum eius, edition de 1504.* Paris, 1903.

———. *Études inédites sur S. François d'Assise.* Paris, 1932.

———. *Examen critique des recits concernant la visite de laqueline de Settesoli a Saint François.* Paris, 1910.

———. *Floretum Sancti Francisci Assiensis, liber aureus qui italice dicitur "I Fioretti di San Francesco."* CED, vol. 4. Paris, 1902.

———. "La plus ancienne mention de l'Indulgence de la Portioncule," *Oriente Serafico* 27 and 28 (1916–17):97–106.

———. *Le Privilège de la très haute poverté.* Paris, 1924.

———. *Regola antiqua Fratrum et Sororum de Poenitentia seu Tertii Ordinis S. Francisci.* Opuscules de critique historique, vol. 1, fasc. 1. Paris, 1901.

———. *Speculum Perfectionis, ou Mèmoire de Frère Léon.* Publié avec une Introduction par A. G. Little. Manchester, 1928–31. Also, CED, vol. 1, Paris, 1898.

———. *Vie de Saint François d'Assise.* Paris, 1931. (1st ed., 1894.) Italian translation by C. Ghidaglia and C. Pontani. *Vita di San Francesco d'Assisi.* Rome, 1926. * English translation by Louise Seymour Houghton. *Life of St. Francis of Assisi.* New York, 1911.

———. See also *Actus Beati Francisci et Sociorum eius,* Francesco di Bartolo, *Speculum Perfectionis.*

Sacchetti-Sassetti, Angelo. *Ancora due parole sul convento della Foresta.* Rieti, 1949.

———. *Anecdota Franciscana Reatina.* Potenza, 1926.

———. *Per la storia del convento della Foresta.* Rieti, 1948.

———. *Replica a mons. Terzi sul convento della Foresta.* Rieti, 1956.

———. *S. Fabiano della Foresta o S. Maria della Foresta?* Rieti, 1955.

Sacrum commercium Sancti Francisci cum Domina Paupertate. Quaracchi, 1929. Italian translation by Ermenegildo Pistelli. *Le Sacre Nozze del Beato Francesco con Madonna Povertà.* Foligno, 1926. * English translation by Placid Hermann. *Sacrum Commercium or Francis and His Lady Poverty.* In *Omnibus,* pp. 1531–1596.

* *Saint Francis of Assisi. Omnibus of Sources.* Edited by Marion A. Habig. Chicago, 1973.

(Fra) Salimbene degli Adami da Parma. *Cronica.* Edited by Oswald Holder-Egger. In *MGH, Scriptores,* vol. 32.

* Salmi, Mario. "La cosidetta 'Porta del Morto.'" *Lares* 21 (1955):1–8.

Salvemini, Gaetano. *Magnati e Popolani in Firenze dal 1280 al 1295.* Florence, 1899.

Salverte, Eusèbe. *Essai historique et philosophique sur les noms.* Paris, 1824.

Salvi, Iacomo. *Guida de' Pellegrini che bramano visitare i Santi luoghi della Serafica Città d'Assisi.* Assisi, 1618.

Salvioli, Giuseppe. *Il Digesto Italiano.* s.v. "Cavalleria."

———. *L'iztruzione in Italia prima del mille.* Florence, 1912.

———. *Storia del diritto italiano.* Turin, 1921.

Salvioli, Lodovico Vittorio. *Annali Bolognesi.* 6 vols. Bassano, 1784–85.

Sanctitatis nova signa. Thomas of Celano (?). In *AF* 10:402–3. *Translation by Franciscan Liturgy Projects. *Roman–Franciscan Lectionary.* Washington, 1975.

Sandberg-Vavalà, Evelyn. *La Croce dipinta italiana et l'Iconografia della Passione.* Verona, 1929.

Sansi, Achille. *Documenti storici inediti in sussidio delle Memorie Umbre.* Foligno, 1879.

———. *Storia del Comune di Spoleto dal sec. XII al XVII.* Foligno, 1879–86.

Santa Chiara d'Assisi. Studi e cronaca del VII centenario (1253–1953). Assisi, 1954.

Sanudo, Marin, il Giovane. *Cronaca Veneziana.* In *RIS,* vol. 22.

Sanudo, Marin, il Vecchio. See Torsello.

Sassenay, Fernand de. *Les Briennes de Lecce et d'Athènes.* Paris, 1870.

Sassi, Pio. *Il beato Villano cittadino e vescovo di Gubbio.* Assisi, 1872.

Sassi, Romualdo. "Due nobili di Borgo S. Sepolcro Podestà di Fabriano." *Atti e Memorie della Deputazione Storia Patria per le Marche,* ser. 8, vol. 10 (1955).

———. *"Incarcerati" e "incarcerate" a Fabriano nei secoli XIII e XIV.* Fano, 1957.

Sassovivo, Abbazia di Santa Croce di. See Cencetti and Antonelli.

Savigny, Friedrich Karl von. *Geschichte des römischen Rechts im Mittelalter.* 6 vols. Heidelberg, 1834.

Sbaralea (Sbaraglia), Johannes Hyacinthus. See *Bullarium Franciscanum.*

———. *Supplementum et Castigatio ad Scriptores trium ordinum S. Francisci a Waddingo aliisque descriptos, opus posthumum.* Rome, 1806.

Schaube, Adolf. *Handelsgeschichte der Romanischen Völker des Mittelmeergebiets, bis zum ende der Kreuzzüge.* Munich and Berlin, 1907. Italian translation by Pietro Bonfante. *Storia del commercio dei popoli latini del Mediterraneo sino alla fine delle Crociate.* Turin, 1915.

Schmeller, Johann Andreas, ed. *Carmina burana.* Stuttgart, 1843.

Schupfer, Francesco. *Il diritto privato dei popoli germani.* 4 vols. 2nd ed. Rome, 1909–15.

———. *La società milanese all'epoca del risorgimento del Comune.* Bologna, 1869–70.

Sderci, Bernardino da Gaiole. "L'apostolato di San Francesco e dei Francescani." *Studi Storici* 1 (1909).

Sella, Pietro. *Rationes decimarum Italiae nei secoli XIII e XIV.* Città del Vaticano, 1952.

Seraphice Legislationis textus originalis. Quaracchi, 1897.

Setton, Kenneth Mayer, ed. *A History of the Crusades.* Philadelphia, 1955.

Sevesi, Paul Maria. "Le origini della provincia dei Frati Minori in Milano." *Studi Francescani* 13 (1915–16):49–64.

Singer, A. *Die Summa decretorum des magister Rufinus.* Paderborn, 1902.

———. *Einige Bemerkungen Zu Schultes Rufin-Ausgabe.* Innsbruck, 1892.

* Smythe, Barbara. *Trobador Poets.* London, 1929.

Solmi, Arrigo. *Il Comune nella storia del diritto.* Milan, 1922.

———. *Storia del diritto italiano.* 3rd ed., rev. Milan, 1930.

———. *Sulla storia economica d'Italia nell'alto medioevo.* Rome, 1905.

Spader, Ottaviano. *Assisiensis ecclesiae prima quatuor luminaria.* Foligno, 1715.

Sparacio, Domenico. *Vita di S. Francesco d'Assisi.* Assisi, 1928.

Speculum Minorum, per Martinum Morin. Rouen, 1509.

Speculum perfectionis seu S. Francisci Assisiensis legenda antiquissima, auctore fratre

Leone. Nunc primum edidit Paul Sabatier. CED, vol. 1. Paris 1898. Italian translation by F. Pennachi, *Lo Specchio di Perfezione.* Assisi, 1899, and Rome, 1950. * English translation by Leo Sherley-Price, *Mirror of Perfection.* In *Omnibus,* pp. 1103–1265. See also Sabatier.

Speculum Vitae beati Francisci et sociorum eius. Venice, 1504. See also Sabatier.

Spila, Benedetto. *Memorie storiche della provincia riformata romana.* Milan, 1896.

* Stanislao da Campagnola. *L'Angelo del Sesto Sigillo e L'"Alter Christus."* Rome, 1971.

Stevenson, Enrico, ed. *Statuti delle arti dei merciai e della lana di Roma.* Rome, 1893.

Stevenson, W. B. *The Crusaders in the East.* Cambridge, 1907.

Stumpf, Karl Friedrich. *Die Reichskanzler vornehmlich des X, XI und XII Jahrhunderts.* Innsbruck, 1865–83.

Supino, Igino Benvenuto. *La Basilica di San Francesco in Assisi.* Bologna, 1924.

Tarulli Brunamonte, Luigi. "Documenti per la storia della medicina in Perugia." *DPSU* 25 (1922):159–221.

* Taylor, Edgar. *Lays of the Minnesingers.* London, 1825.

Terzi, Arduino. *Memorie francescane della Valle Reatina.* Rome, 1955.

———. *S. Fabiano de "La Foresta" ascoltò per primo il Cantico di Frate Sole.* Rome, 1957.

———. *S. Francesco d'Assisi a Roma.* Rome, 1956.

Theiner, Augustin. *Codex Diplomaticus Dominii Temporalis S. Sedis.* Rome, 1861–62.

Thode, Henry. *Franz von Assisi und die Anfänge der Kunst der Renaissance in Italien.* Berlin, 1904.

Thomas, Archdeacon of Spalato. *Historia Pontificium Salonitarorum et Spalatensium.* In *MGH, Scriptores,* vol. 20. * Excerpt translated into English by Paul Oligny. "A Sermon by St. Francis at Bologna." In *Omnibus,* pp. 1601–2.

Thomas of Celano. *Vita Prima S. Francisci.* In *AF* 10:1–117. Italian translations by L. Amoni (Rome, 1880), Fausta Casolini (Santa Maria degli Angeli, 1952), L. Macali (Rome, 1954). * English translation by Placid Hermann. *First Life of Saint Francis.* In *Omnibus,* pp. 177–355.

———. *Legenda ad usum chori.* In *AF* 10:118–26.

———. *Vita Secunda S. Francisci.* In *AF* 10:127–268. Italian translations by L. Amoni (Rome, 1880), Fausta Casolini (Santa Maria degli Angeli, 1952), L. Macali (Rome, 1954). * English translation by Placid Hermann. *Second Life of Saint Francis.* In *Omnibus,* pp. 357–543.

———. *Tractatus de Miraculis S. Francisci.* In *AF* 10:269–330. Italian translations by Fausta Casolini (Santa Maria degli Angeli, 1952), L. Macali (Rome, 1954). * Selections translated into English by Placid Hermann. *Treatise on the Miracles of Blessed Francis.* In *Omnibus,* pp. 545–611.

———. See also *Legenda Sanctae Clarae Virginis* and *Sanctitatis nova signa.*

Thomas of Eccleston. *De Adventu Fratrum Minorum in Anglia.* In *AF* 1 (1885):215–56. * Translated by Placid Hermann. In *XIIIth Century Chronicles,* pp. 78–191. Chicago, 1961.

Tini, Andrea. *Della stalletta in cui nacque S. Francesco d'Assisi.* Assisi, 1896.

Tiraboschi, Girolamo. *Storia dell'augusta Badia di S. Silvestro Nonantola.* Modena, 1784–85.

Tocco, Felice. *L'eresia nel medio evo.* Florence, 1884.

———. *Studi francescani.* Naples, 1909.

———. See also Angelo Clareno.

Toesca, Pietro. *Storia dell'arte italiana. Il Medioevo.* Turin, 1927.

Tolosano da Faenza. *Chronicon.* Excerpt in Golubovich, *Biblioteca,* 1:178–81.

Torraca, Francesco. "La scuola poetica siciliana." In his *Studi su la lirica italiana del Duecento,* pp. 89–234. Bologna, 1902.

Torsello (Marin Sanudo il Vecchio). *Liber Secretorum fidelium Crucis super Terrae Sanctae recuperatione et conservatione . . .* Hanover, 1611. See also Golubovich, *Biblioteca,* 1:57–60.

Trauzzi, Alberto. *Attraverso l'onomastica del Medioevo in Italia.* 2 vols. Rocca San Casciano, 1911–15.

Trojel, E. See Andrea Cappellano.

Troya, Carlo. *Storia d'Italia nel Medioevo.* Naples, 1839–59.

Ubald d'Alençon. See Léon Louis Berson.

* Ubertino da Casale. *Arbor vitae crucifixae Jesu.* Venice, 1485. Italian translation by Fausta Casolini. Lanciano. 1937. Also by Feliciano Olgiati. In *Fonti Francescane,* pp. 1683–1722.

Ughelli, Ferdinando. *Italia sacra.* 10 vols. bound in 9. Venice, 1717–22.

Ugolini, F. *Storia dei conti e duchi di Urbino.* Florence, 1859.

Ugolino of Paris. *S. Francesco, i Francescani e la città di Gubbio.* Florence, 1928.

Vaccari, Pietro. *L'emancipazione dei servi della gleba.* Bologna, 1925.

Valentini, Roberto. "Liriche religiose di Gian Antonio Campano." *DPSU* 34 (1937):41–56.

* Van Corstanje, Auspicius. *The Covenant with God's Poor.* Chicago, 1966.

Van Ortroy, Francesco. See *Anonymous Perugian.*

Varrentrapp, Conrad. *Erzbischof Christian I von Mainz.* Berlin, 1867.

Venturi, Adolfo. *La Basilica d'Assisi.* Rome, 1908.

——. *Storia dell'arte italiana,* vol. 5. Milan, 1907.

Verba fratris Illuminati socii b. Francisci ad partes Orientis et in conspectu Soldani Aegypti. Ms. Vat. Ottob. lat. 552. Translation in Golubovich, *Biblioteca,* 1:36–37. * English translation by Paul Oligny in *Omnibus,* pp. 1614–15.

Vicinelli, Augusto. See Writings of Saint Francis.

Villari, Pasquale. *I primi due secoli della storia di Firenze.* 3rd ed. Florence, 1905.

Vincent of Beauvais. *Speculum Historiale.* Edited by Koberger. 2nd ed. Nuremberg, 1483–86.

Vitali, Salvatore. *Paradisus Seraphicus.* Milan, 1645.

"Vita Aegidii." In *24 Generals. AF* 3:74–115.

Vita Beati Aegidii Assisiastis. Attributed to Brother Leo. Edited by Leonardus Lemmens. In *Documenta Antiqua Franciscana,* pp. 37–63. * English translation by Raphael Brown. *The Life of Brother Giles.* In *Little Flowers of St. Francis,* pp. 239–58.

"Vita Juniperi." In *24 Generals. AF* 3:54–64. * English translation by Raphael Brown. *The Life of Brother Juniper.* In *Little Flowers of St. Francis,* pp. 217–37. (Includes excerpt from *La Franceschina,* 2:201.)

Vito da Clusone. *Cultura e pensiero di S. Francesco d'Assisi.* Modena, 1952.

Vollmers-Schulte, Franz. *Die Summa magistri Rufini zum Decretum Gratiani.* Giessen, 1892.

Volpe, Gioacchino. *Il Medioevo.* Florence, 1928.

——. "Lombardi e romani nelle campagne e nella citta." *Studi storici* 13 and 14 (1904 and 1905).

——. *Studi sulle istituzioni comunali a Pisa.* Pisa, 1902.

* Von Galli, Mario. *Living Our Future: Francis of Assisi and the Church Tomorrow.* Translated by Maureen Sullivan and John Drury. Chicago, 1972.

Wadding, Luke. *Annales Minorum seu Trium Ordinum a S. Francisco institutorum.* 3rd ed. Vols. 1–30, Quaracchi, 1931–51. Vols. 31—, Rome, 1956—. Index generalis.

———. *Scriptores Ordinis Minorum.* 1st ed. Rome, 1650. 2nd ed., Rome, 1806. Editio novissima. Rome, 1906.

———. See also Writings of Saint Francis.

* Waley, Daniel. "Le Istituzioni Comunali di Assisi nel passaggio dal XII al XIII secolo." In *Assisi al tempo di San Francesco.* Atti del V Convegno Internazionale della Società Internazionale di Studi Francescani (Assisi 13–16 ottobre 1977), pp. 53–70. Assisi, 1978.

* ———. *The Papal State in the Thirteenth Century.* London and New York, 1961.

Walter of Gisburn. *Chronica de gestis rerum Angliae.* In *MGH, Scriptores,* vol. 28.

Warner, H. J. *The Albigensian Heresy.* 2 vols. London, 1922–28.

Weiland, L. *Constitutiones et acta publica imperatorum et regum.* In *MGH, Constitutiones,* vols. 1 and 2.

Wenck, K. "Die römischen Päpste zwischen Alexander III und Innocenz III." In *Papsttum und Kaisertum.* Edited by Paul Kehr, pp. 415–74. Munich, 1926.

* Wilhelm, James J. *Seven Troubadours: The Creators of Modern Verse.* University Park and London, 1970.

Wilken, Friedrich. *Geschichte der Kreuzzüge.* 7 vols. Leipzig, 1807–32.

* Zeydel, Edwin. *Vagabond Verse.* Detroit, 1966.

Zingarelli, N. "Le reminiscenze del 'Lancelot.' *Studi Danteschi* 1 (1920):65–90.

Zöckler, Englehardt. "Franz von Assisi." In *Realenzyklopädie für Protestantische Theologie und Kirche.* 3rd edition. Edited by Albert Haucke, 6:197–22. Leipzig, 1896–1913.

Index